International Economics

Addison-Wesley Series in Economics

Abel/Bernanke
Macroeconomics

Berndt
The Practice of Econometrics

Bierman/Fernandez
Game Theory with Economic Applications

Binger/Hoffman
Microeconomics with Calculus

Boyer
Principles of Transportation Economics

Branson
Macroeconomic Theory and Policy

Browning/Zupan
Microeconomic Theory and Applications

Bruce
Public Finance and the American Economy

Burgess
The Economics of Regulation and Antitrust

Byrns/Stone
Economics

Carlton/Perloff
Modern Industrial Organization

Caves/Frankel/Jones
World Trade and Payments: An Introduction

Cooter/Ulen
Law and Economics

Eaton/Mishkin
Readings to Accompany The Economics of Money, Banking, and Financial Markets

Ehrenberg/Smith
Modern Labor Economics

Ekelund/Tollison
Economics: Private Markets and Public Choice

Filer/Hamermesh/Rees
The Economics of Work and Pay

Fusfeld
The Age of the Economist

Gerber
International Economics

Ghiara
Learning Economics: A Practical Workbook

Gordon
Macroeconomics

Gregory
Essentials of Economics

Gregory/Ruffin
Economics

Gregory/Stuart
Russian and Soviet Economic Structure and Performance

Griffiths/Wall
Intermediate Microeconomics

Gros/Steinherr
Winds of Change: Economic Transition in Central and Eastern Europe

Hartwick/Olewiler
The Economics of Natural Resource Use

Hogendorn
Economic Development

Hoy/Livernois/McKenna/Rees/Stengos
Mathematics for Economics

Hubbard
Money, the Financial System, and the Economy

Hughes/Cain
American Economic History

Husted/Melvin
International Economics

Jehle/Reny
Advanced Microeconomic Theory

Klein
Mathematical Methods for Economics

Krugman/Obstfeld
International Economics: Theory and Policy

Laidler
The Demand for Money: Theories, Evidence, and Problems

Lesser/Dodds/Zerbe
Environmental Economics and Policy

Lipsey/Courant/Ragan
Economics

McCarty
Dollars and Sense

Melvin
International Money and Finance

Miller
Economics Today

Miller/Benjamin/North
The Economics of Public Issues

Miller/VanHoose
Essentials of Money, Banking, and Financial Markets

Mills/Hamilton
Urban Economics

Mishkin
The Economics of Money, Banking, and Financial Markets

Parkin
Economics

Parkin/Bade
Economics in Action Software

Perloff
Microeconomics

Phelps
Health Economics

Riddell/Shackelford/Stamos
Economics: A Tool for Critically Understanding Society

Ritter/Silber/Udell
Principles of Money, Banking, and Financial Markets

Rohlf
Introduction to Economic Reasoning

Ruffin/Gregory
Principles of Economics

Salvatore
Microeconomics

Sargent
Rational Expectations and Inflation

Scherer
Industry Structure, Strategy, and Public Policy

Schotter
Microeconomics

Sherman/Kolk
Business Cycles and Forecasting

Smith
Case Studies in Economic Development

Studenmund
Using Econometrics

Su
Economic Fluctuations and Forecasting

Tietenberg
Environmental and Natural Resource Economics

Tietenberg
Environmental Economics and Policy

Thomas
Modern Econometrics

Todaro
Economic Development

Waldman/Jensen
Industrial Organization: Theory and Practice

Zerbe/Dively/Lesser
Benefit-Cost Analysis

International Economics

JAMES GERBER
San Diego State University

 **ADDISON-WESLEY**

An imprint of Addison Wesley Longman, Inc.

Reading, Massachusetts • Menlo Park, California • Harlow, England
Don Mills, Ontario • Sydney • Mexico City • Madrid • Amsterdam

Executive Editor: Denise Clinton
Senior Administrative Assistant: Jennifer Vito
Production Supervisor: Louis C. Bruno, Jr.
Marketing Manager: Amy Cronin
Cover Designer: Hannas Design Associates
Cartographer: Chris Lukinbeal
Composition and Prepress Services: Pre-Press Company, Inc.
Printer and Binder: Maple Vail
Cover Printer: Coral Graphics
Print Buyer: Sheila Spinney

Library of Congress Cataloging-in-Publication Data

Gerber, James.
    International economics / James Gerber.
    p. cm.—(Addison-Wesley series in economics)
Includes bibliographical references and index.
ISBN 0-321-01434-0 (hardcover)
1. International economic relations. 2. International economic integration. 3. International trade. 4. Commercial policy.
5. United States—Foreign economic relations. I. Title. II. Series.
HF1359 .G474 1998
337—ddc21

                                                            98-45110
                                                            CIP

3 4 5 6 7 8 9 10—MV—02 01 00 99

CONTENTS

PART TWO: THE INTERNATIONAL ECONOMY/THEORY

PREFACE

This text is an outgrowth of ten years experience teaching a one-semester course in international economics. The course was originally designed to accommodate the needs of non-economics majors, but as student interest in the international economy grew, half or more of my students were economics majors. Student demand for the course also increased by the university's addition of several new internationally focused majors, including international business and international security, and by the growth of area studies programs.

The book was written with the needs of this heterogeneous group of students in mind. It provides a principles-level introduction to the micro and macro sides of the international economy. In addition, it offers an in-depth treatment of several institutional, historical, and policy issues that are usually downplayed in the standard two-course sequence in international economics. These include:

▲ Globalization in historical perspective (Chapter 1)
▲ The roles of international economic institutions (Chapter 2)
▲ Industrial policies (Chapter 7)
▲ International economic integration (Chapter 10)
▲ The U.S.-Japan trade conflict (Chapter 11)
▲ NAFTA and the European Union (Chapters 12 and 13)
▲ The international aspects of changes in Latin America, East Asia, and the transition economies (Chapters 14, 15, and 16).

My primary goal in this book is to make economic reasoning about the international economy accessible to a diverse group of upper-division students who are unlikely to take more than one course in international economics. Theory necessary to this task is presented, but the focus of the text is not on the theoretical apparatus that economists use. Nor is the focus exclusively on policy. Instead, I have tried to use theory, history, and institutional analysis to shed light on events, trends, and policy in the international sphere.

In-depth discussions of these issues provide a setting for theoretical concepts, and they offer an opportunity to develop students' appreciation for the interplay of the separate theoretical strands that run though the field of international economics. It is my experience that this approach provides an opportunity for students from disparate academic disciplines to gain insights into the contributions of economic thought and to see the economic aspects of a problem in a natural setting that involves history, politics, and society.

Chapters have been classroom tested, some of them several times, during the book's development assuring the text's value as a teaching and learning tool. In addition, it has undergone extensive review by colleagues from around the country and suggestions for improvement have been incorporated into the text.

Course level

The presentation assumes that students have taken at least one introductory course in economics. Economic theory is held entirely within a principles level, but concepts such as the production possibilities frontier, supply-and-demand analysis, and national income accounting are not formally developed. Mathematics use is held to simple algebra; technical terms are defined in the text. Each chapter ends with a list of key words and concepts, which are also defined in the glossary. Also at the end of each chapter are a set of study questions and a set of suggested readings.

Addresses for a handful of high quality Web sites are included in most chapters. While many of the sources for the Web sites provide identical information in hard-copy format, there is usually a long lag before the print version is available, and libraries that are not Depositories for government documents may never obtain them. These Web-site listings are designed to reduce noise in the information provided over the Web and to give students a starting point for their own explorations. Students will find these sections useful for the following kind of information:

▲ Web sites of international organizations (Chapter 2 and throughout the text)
▲ Trade data and the trade classification systems (Chapter 3)
▲ Trade practices and the trade policies of various countries (Chapter 5)
▲ American industrial policies (Chapter 7)
▲ Balance of payments data (Chapter 8)
▲ Exchange rate data (Chapter 9)
▲ World regions (throughout the text)

Instructor's manual

The instructor's manual contains materials to assist in teaching the course. Each chapter in the manual begins with an outline of the chapter and a brief discussion of the chapter goals. More than half of the chapters have an additional set of Web addresses along with suggestions for creating research and writing assignments around them. These vary in level of difficulty and sophistication, but each one requires students to apply the ideas and concepts introduced in the chapter to information or data they obtain from the WWW.

The instructor's manual also has answers to the end-of-chapter questions and twenty multiple choice questions for each chapter.

Acknowledgements

Although this book bears my name, its creation was more a group effort than sole authorship conveys. In particular, I could not have written this text without the loving support of my wife, Joan, and my two daughters, Monica and Elizabeth.

I would also like to acknowledge John Greenman, first at Harper Collins and then at Addison Wesley Longman, who provided the insight and expertise neccessary to realize this book. I am also grateful to Louis Bruno, Amy Cronin, Jennifer Vito, and Denise Clinton at Addison Wesley Longman, Mary Ansaldo at Pre-Press Company, and cartographer Chris Lukinbeal at San Diego State University, for their dedication and professionalism.

I must also acknowledge the students who inspired me and gave me valuable feedback as they were subjects in tryouts of chapters of the book in their classroom. Their questions and comments helped make the text a more valuable teaching tool. Finally, I would like to thank my colleagues from around the country who offered valuable suggestions and ideas for improving the text. Each of the following individuals reviewed the manuscript, many of them several times, and provided useful commentary for the development of *International Economics*.

Mary Acker
Iona College
Lee Bour
Florida State University
Tom Carter
Oklahoma City University
Don Clark
University of Tennessee
Al Culver
California State University, Chico
John Devereaux
University of Miami
Lewis R. Gale, IV
University of Southwest Louisiana
Ira Gang
Rutgers University
Joanne Gowa
Princeton University
Corrine Krupp
Michigan State University
Mary Lesser
Iona College
Thomas Lowinger
Washington State University
Mary McGlasson
Arizona State University
Joseph McKinney
Baylor University

Howard McNier
San Francisco State University
Stephan Norrbin
Florida State University
Jeffery Rosensweig
Emory University
Raj Roy
University of Toledo
George Samuels
Sam Houston State University
Craig Shulman
University of Arkansas
David Spiro
Columbia University
Richard Sprinkle
University of Texas, El Paso
Ann Sternlicht
Virginia Commonwealth University
Henry Thompson
Auburn University
Jose Ventura
Sacred Heart University
Jerry Wheat
Indiana State University
Chong K. Yip
Georgia State University

PART ONE

THE INTERNATIONAL ECONOMY

An Historical Perspective

CHAPTER 1

THE UNITED STATES IN A GLOBAL ECONOMY

Introduction

During the summer of 1997, an economic crisis hit East Asia, beginning first in Thailand and then spreading to Indonesia, Malaysia, the Philippines, and South Korea. Currency values fell, stock markets crashed, and credit dried up. Several countries appealed to the International Monetary Fund (IMF) for emergency loans, and by the fall of 1997 the IMF was spelling out the terms and conditions for its assistance. Since the crisis was spreading globally, there was a sense of urgency in addressing the problem. Japanese and European banks were heavily exposed due to a large number of bad loans to the region. North and South American stock markets felt pressures from nervous investors, and American firms prepared for a wave of cheap imports, brought on by the depreciated Asian currencies. While the crisis posed a threat to global economic stability, it was in fact only the latest in a series of episodes over the last decades. The Mexican peso collapse in 1994, speculation against the European Monetary System in 1992, the overvalued U.S. dollar in the mid-1980s, and the onset of the third-world debt crisis in 1982, all posed equally serious challenges to global financial stability.

Each of these events is a dramatic reminder that national economies are linked together through extensive networks of financial and commercial relations. During the last decade, terms like *globalization* and *integration* came into common usage as shorthand references to the strengthening of these networks and the deepening of interdependencies among national economies. While global financial crisis is one reminder of these links, several long-term trends have also fostered a growing American awareness of the international economy and international economic interdependence. Japanese penetration of U.S. automobile and consumer electronics markets in the 1970s and 1980s, growing U.S.–Mexico trade ties and the start of the North American Free Trade Agreement in 1994, and the recent increase in international stock funds have all sparked Americans' interest in the international economy.

Increased awareness of the international economy has been accompanied by two kinds of extreme views. On the one hand, many Americans feel left out by the global changes in technology and economic relations. They see a dark future in which our national economy is ruled by anonymous forces in a world market that is beyond American control. Other Americans see a new global economy that is entirely without precedent. They believe that this new economy requires completely new modes of analysis in order to understand the issues and opportunities it presents. Both views are wrong. The global economy is new, but it is also old. Technology has shortened communication and transportation times, but so did technological developments in the second half of the 1800s. At the margin, the latter may have had a greater effect. The world today is far more integrated economically than in the recent past, but the changes are not without precedent. Americans are affected by prices and products from around the world, but so were the Midwestern wheat farmers, the Chicago meatpackers, and the California fruit growers of the 1890s. Over a century ago, a period of international economic integration occurred which was very simillar to today's. Although the earlier episode was reversed by two world wars and a decade-long world depression, its occurrence tells us that our own period is perhaps not as unique as we might believe it to be.

A brief historical comparison is a useful and sobering exercise for making sense of the extraordinary changes that have taken place in the international economy over the last several decades. The advantage of a long-term perspective is that it can protect us from unrealistic enthusiasm (or fear) about recent changes in international economic relations. We begin with a closer look at a very basic issue: How important is the international economy in relation to our domestic economy?

Globalization in Perspective

There is no doubt that the economy of the United States is more integrated with other national economies than at any time in the last sixty or seventy years. It is tempting to say that global economic integration is greater than at any time in history, yet that is less certain than it may seem. In the age of the Internet, e-mail, and fax machines, it is easy to lose sight of the fact that most of what we buy and sell never makes it out of our local or national markets. We are aware of the fact that the parts in our cars are made in a dozen or more countries, but we should not forget that the vast majority of goods and services we consume are made at home. Haircuts, restaurant meals, gardens, health care, education, financial services, utilities, and most of our entertainment, to name a few, are domestic products. In fact, about of 87 percent of what we consume is made in the United States, since imports are equal to about 13 percent of our gross domestic product (GDP).

> ***Gross domestic product (GDP).*** *Gross domestic product is the market value of all final goods and services produced in a year inside a nation.*

Imports and exports are not the only criteria by which we can judge the importance of the international economy. Integrated economies are linked by more than the goods and services they produce; they are also connected by the movement of capital and labor. Consider, for example, the fifty United States. No one could claim that they are interdependent if workers and investment flows were not free to move across state lines. This is also true of national economies where the degree of freedom in the movement of capital and labor is a key indicator of the depth of their integration. The third marker of economic integration is the movement of prices in different markets. When economies become linked to each other, price differences across markets should shrink as goods and services are allowed to move freely across international boundaries. Each of these indicators, (1) trade flows, (2) factor movements, and (3) similarity of prices, are measures of the degree of international economic integration.

The Growth of World Trade

Since the end of World War II, world trade has grown much faster than world output. World output, which is equivalent to world income, has risen about sixfold over the last fifty years, while world trade has grown about twelvefold. (The reasons for the growth of world trade are examined in Chapter 10.) As a result, trade has become a larger share of most national economies. One measure of the importance of international trade in a nation's economy is the sum of exports plus imports, divided by the gross domestic product (GDP). This ratio is called **openness**.

$$\text{Openness} = (\text{Exports} + \text{Imports}) / \text{GDP}$$

It should be stressed that the openness measure does not tell us about a country's trade policies; that is, countries with higher openness measures do not necessarily have lower barriers to trade, although that is one possibility. In general, large countries are less dependent on international trade because many of their firms can reach an optimal production size without having to sell to foreign markets. As a consequence, small countries tend to have higher measures of openness than do big ones.

Openness measures for the United States are shown in Fig. 1.1. One factor that stands out is the decline in the importance of U.S. international trade between 1890 and 1950. In 1890, the openness indicator was over 15 percent. Openness was relatively high at the end of the nineteenth century due to the increase in world trade brought on, in part, by technological innovations in communications and transportation. For example, the trans-Atlantic telegraph cable (1866) increased the flow of in-

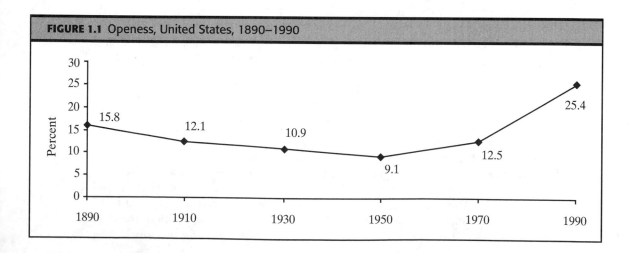

FIGURE 1.1 Openess, United States, 1890–1990

formation between markets, ocean-going steamships and better navigation charts cut travel times, and many nations built national railroad networks. The British navy, which suppressed piracy and provided security on the high seas, also contributed to an increase in international commerce. By 1890, American products like grain, beef, and timber were sensitive to commodity price movements around the world.

From the start of World War I until the end of World War II, many of the gains in market integration were eroded. The two world wars and the Great Depression of the 1930s caused nations to cut their trade ties, partly for strategic military reasons and partly to protect their home industries from import competition during the Depression. Steep tariffs (import taxes) and quotas were enacted throughout the world, and whatever market share was gained at home by some industries was lost abroad by others as export markets collapsed. Total world trade declined dramatically during the interwar period, and, in effect, a significant share of the growth of trade in recent decades has simply brought our economy back to where it was at the end of the nineteenth century.

Fig. 1.1 shows that the relative importance of international trade has increased by about 50 percent since 1890, but an important trend is obscured within this data. In 1890, most U.S. trade was in agricultural products and raw materials, while today most American exports and imports are manufactured goods. More specifically, the importance of capital goods (machinery and equipment) has increased dramatically. As a consequence, producers of manufactured items are far more exposed to international competition than they were at the beginning of the twentieth century.

Fig. 1.2 illustrates the increase in merchandise goods exports only; it does not include imports and service exports. (Services as a share of total exports are about 25 percent.) Relative to the size of our economy (GDP), goods exports increased from their low point of 3.6 percent in 1950 to 7.0 percent by 1990. Over the same period, however, merchandise exports grew from 8.9 percent of goods production to 31.4 percent. In other words, judging by the criteria of international competition,

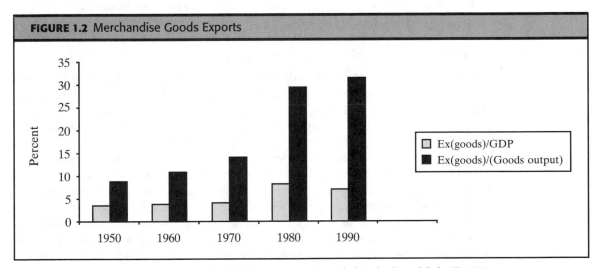

FIGURE 1.2 Merchandise Goods Exports

Ex(goods)/GDP
Ex(goods)/(Goods output)

Source: Irwin, Douglas, "The United States in a New Global Economy? A Century's Perspective." *American Economic Review,* May 1996.

American manufacturers are now far more integrated into the world economy than they were in 1950 (or, for that matter, in 1890).

Capital and Labor Mobility

In addition to exports and imports, factor movements are also an indicator of economic integration. As national economies become more interdependent, labor and capital should move more easily across international boundaries. At the close of the twentieth century, for example, labor is much less mobile internationally than it was at the start of the century. As one indicator of this trend, in 1890 approximately 14.5 percent of the U.S. population was foreign born, while the figure for the 1990s is less than 8 percent. At the start of the twentieth century, many nations had open-door immigration policies; and passport controls, immigration visas, and work permits were the exception rather than the rule. In the 1920s, the United States sharply restricted immigration, and international labor mobility declined. These restrictions lasted until the 1960s, when changes in immigration laws once again encouraged foreigners to migrate to the United States, albeit in numbers far lower than in the 1800s.

On the capital side, measurement is more difficult, since there are several ways to measure capital flows. The most basic distinction is between flows of financial capital representing paper assets (stocks, bonds, currencies, bank accounts, etc.) and flows of capital that represent physical assets (real estate, factories, businesses, etc.). The latter type of capital flow is called **foreign direct investment,** or **FDI.** To some extent, the distinction between the two is immaterial, because both types of capital flows represent shifts in wealth across national boundaries, and both make one nation's savings available to another. Nevertheless, since FDI represents cross-border capital flows related to the purchase of land and businesses, it is longer term and less likely to reverse itself and flow out of a country on short notice.

> *Foreign direct investment. Foreign direct investment, or FDI, is the purchase of physical assets such as real estate or businesses by a foreign company or individual. It can be outward (citizens or businesses in the home country purchase assets in a foreign country) or inward (foreigners purchase assets in the home country).*

When we compare today's trends to those of a century ago, we should keep two points in mind. First, if there was a single world capital market, then the investment rates (i.e., Investment / GDP) of any particular country would not need to be correlated with its savings rates. Capital would flow to the countries that offered the highest (risk-adjusted) rates of return and, since capital is abundant in high-income countries and relatively scarce in developing countries, we should expect to see higher risk-adjusted returns in developing countries and enormous flows into them. While capital flows to developing countries have grown significantly over the last decades, it is, however, still true that the level of investment in any country is highly correlated with its level of savings. Low-savings countries have low investment levels, and high-savings countries have high investment levels. In other words, national savings rates are a far more important determinant of a nation's investment than is the global capital market.

The second point to bear in mind is that, at the end of the 19th century, what was true for trade flows was also true for capital flows. Late-19th-century capital was mobile, due in part to the same technological improvements that increased trade flows. For example, in 1866 the first trans-Atlantic cable linked New York to the world's largest financial market in London, decreasing the time required to obtain market information and conclude a transaction from about three weeks to just one day. One effect was that the gap in interest rates and asset prices between New York and London shrank significantly.

Capital flows at the end of the nineteenth century also increased from the enormous demand for capital by regions such as North America that were undergoing industrial revolutions, and by Britain and other European powers that were investing in mining and other activities in their colonies. At the same time, the development of financial market institutions such as Wall Street and stock, bond, and commodity exchanges aided the growth of capital markets and capital flows. In the late nineteenth and early twentieth centuries Great Britan was the greatest supplier of capital to the world . Britain annually supplied 5 to 10 percent of their GDP to world capital markets and at its peak invested as much abroad as it did domestically. Today, countries with large flows of foreign investment (all kinds) rarely supply more than 2 to 3 percent (net) of their GDP to world capital markets. As was the case for labor mobility and trade flows, capital mobility was also reduced by the two world wars and the Great Depression. Industrial countries began to restrict capital flows during the 1920s, and in most cases, capital mobility did not begin to recover until the 1970s and 1980s.

Four main differences distinguish capital flows at the end of the twentieth century from those at the end of the nineteenth century. First, there are many more financial instruments available now than there were a century ago. Derivatives, ADRs, mutual funds, currency swaps, and so forth represent a wide variety of instruments tailored to nearly every level of income and risk tolerance. Many of these new financial instruments are complex, specialized tools designed to meet very narrow objectives; they are the result of constant financial innovation to meet new demands in the more open global economy. By contrast, at the turn of the century, there were only a few hundred stocks listed on the New York Stock Exchange, and most international financial transactions involved the buying and selling of bonds. Second, and related to the first point, while overall flows of capital are probably smaller today (relative to the size of our economies), international flows of financial capital are much larger. According to the Bank for International Settlements (BIS), in Geneva, *daily* foreign exchange transactions in 1995 were equal to $1.2 *trillion,* whereas in 1973 they were just $15 billion. In addition to foreign exchange transactions, cross-border sales and purchases of stocks and bonds by mutual funds, pension funds, and individual investors have increased enormously. The increase in financial transactions involving currency exchanges is related to a third factor: that the world operated on a fixed exchange rate standard in 1900. This means that there was little or no risk of losing money on a foreign investment due to a decrease in value of the foreign currency. By comparison, protecting against exchange-rate risk is a key component in today's international financial markets and accounts for a significant share of the day-to-day international transactions of financial institutions.

A fourth major change is that the costs of foreign financial transactions have fallen significantly. Economists refer to the costs of obtaining market information, negotiating an agreement, and enforcing the agreement (if necessary) as **transaction costs**. They are an important part of any business's costs, whether it is a purely domestic enterprise or involved in foreign markets. Due to sheer distance, as well as to differences in culture, laws, and languages, transaction costs are often higher in international markets than they are in domestic ones. Today's lower transaction costs for foreign investment means that it is less expensive to move capital across international boundaries. Along with the deregulation of capital controls in the 1970s and 1980s, lower transaction costs have significantly increased capital flows.

> ***Transaction costs.*** *Transaction costs are the costs associated with obtaining market information, negotiating a transaction (exchange), and enforcing the terms of the agreement.*

The sometimes extremely volatile movement of financial capital into and out of national markets is often regarded as a new feature of the international economy—a shortsighted view. Speculative excesses and overinvestment, followed by capital flight and bankruptcies, have occurred throughout the modern era, going back at least as far as the 1600s, and probably farther. U.S. history has number of cases. During the fifty years after 1890, at least four episodes of overspeculation and crisis hit the U.S. economy: 1890 to 1893 (speculation in silver stocks), 1907 (coffee futures and trust companies), 1920 to 1921 (agricultural land), and 1929 (U.S. stocks). As long as people cling to the get-rich-quick dream, and as long as domestic policymakers are subject to human error, the world will probably continue to experience episodes of volatile capital and speculative excess. One of the challenges of economic policymaking is to tame this type of excess without making things worse and without destroying more beneficial types of capital flows.

Trade, Investment, and Global Integration in Historical Perspective

The idea that the United States faces an unprecedented era of globalization is only partially true. Trade, as measured by openness, is about 50 percent more important to the U.S. economy. Labor is less mobile than earlier in our history, but capital is somewhat more mobile. Prices in many U.S. and foreign markets tend to be similar, although there are still significant differences (a pair of denim jeans in the United States and Europe, for example), and they tend to move together (particularly asset prices). The period of most rapid convergence, however, appears to have been during the late nineteenth and early twentieth centuries. Given these patterns, is anything fundamentally different about today's economy other than the size of capital flows and the increased amount of trade? The answer is "Yes."

New Issues in International Trade and Investment

Most high-income, industrial countries have few barriers to imports of manufactured goods. There are exceptions (e.g., processed foodstuffs, textiles, and apparel), but as a general rule, import tariffs are low, and other forms of protection are un-common. Low trade barriers are the result of a process that began at the end of World War II and that has had a slow, cumulative effect in rolling back the high levels of protection that were implemented in the 1920s and 1930s. As countries gradually eliminated their formal restrictions on imports, various domestic policies have become barriers to further increases in trade flows. These policies include sensitive issues such as labor conditions, environmental policy, the rules of fair economic competition, limits on investment, and government support for specific industries. As long as formal restrictions on imports kept out many goods, differences between nations in their domestic policies were unimportant. As formal barriers came down, however, purely domestic policies became hindrances to the further growth of trade flows.

Negotiations between nations can be difficult in these areas both because the rules and laws are complex and because they represent fundamental elements of domestic policy. Reducing a tax on imports is simple by comparison, particularly if other nations agree to similar cuts. When nations open their markets symmetrically, through simultaneous reductions in import taxes, it is easily understood by the electorate and appeals to their sense of fairness. A similar symmetry in changing labor standards, or investment rules, is more difficult to define. When restrictive investment rules are eliminated, for example, it may seem that there is no commensurate action elsewhere and that foreign influence has undermined national sovereignty.

Economists refer to the elimination of **tariffs** (taxes on imports) and **quotas** (quantitative restrictions on imports) as **shallow integration**, or integration at the border. By contrast, the elimination or reduction of trade barriers that stems from domestic policies is referred to as **deep integration**. Deep integration raises numerous questions about national sovereignty.

> ***Tariffs and quotas.*** *Tariffs are taxes on imports. Quotas are quantitative restrictions (i.e., physical limits) on imports.*

> ***Shallow and deep integration.*** *Shallow integration is the elimination or reduction of tariffs, quotas, and other border-related barriers, such as customs procedures that restrict the flow of goods across borders. Deep integration is the elimination, reduction, or alteration of domestic policies when they have the unintended consequence of acting as trade barriers. Major examples include labor and environmental standards, investment regulations, the rules of fair competition between firms, and allowable forms of government support for private industry.*

The issues of deep integration take up a sizable part of the dialogue between nations over matters related to foreign trade and investment. Economically, it is not necessary and is often undesirable that nations should adopt the same or similar policies. Nevertheless, small countries fear that they will be forced to adopt the standards of the United States or some other industrial economy, and large countries like the United States worry that their domestic policies will be determined by the collective action of small countries. An international dialogue on these issues is a relatively new experience.

The Role of International Organizations

At the end of World War II, the United States, Britain, and our allies created a number of international organizations that were given active roles in helping to maintain international economic and political stability. Although the architects of these organizations could not envision the challenges and issues that would confront the international economy over the next fifty years, they gave their institutions the flexibility to survive major changes in the international economy. These institutions play an important and growing role, in part as a forum for addressing the issues of deep integration.

The International Monetary Fund (IMF), the World Bank, the General Agreement on Tariffs and Trade (GATT), the United Nations (UN), the World Trade Organization (WTO began operation in 1995 but grew out of the GATT), and a host of smaller organizations have broad international participation. They serve as forums for discussing and establishing rules, as mediators of disputes, and as organizers of actions to resolve problems. The IMF, for example, is the leading agency for mobilizing resources to counter the crisis in East Asia. While its actions are not without a good deal of controversy, it has taken a leadership role in helping nations to regain stability and avoid the further spread of crisis. (In the nineteenth century, during the period of British economic and military supremacy, some of the functions of the IMF and other organizations were filled by the Bank of England. The most obvious difference between then and now is that the Bank of England was limited in the scope of its actions and was entirely controlled by one government.)

All of today's organizations have their own governance structure involving varying degrees of control by the United States and other leading powers. Many nations argue that they are left out of decision making, and many complain that the United States has too much say. In the United States, some people make an opposite criticism: that these organizations represent foreign entanglements that tie our hands and severely limit our policy options. (Chapter 2 examines this issue in detail.) For better or worse, these organizations represent a series of attempts at creating internationally acceptable rules for trade and commerce and at dealing with potential disputes before they spill across international borders and escalate into deeper problems. They are an entirely new element in the international economy.

Regional Trade Alliances

Agreements among nations are not new. Free-trade agreements and other forms of preferential trade have existed throughout history. What is new is the significant increase in the number of preferential trade agreements that have been formed in the past twenty years, especially in the 1990s. It is still too early to say if this is a new trend or simply a phenomenon that will soon disappear.

Regional trade alliance (RTA) or trade bloc. RTAs are agreements between two or more countries, each offering the others preferential access to their markets. RTAs provide varying degrees of access and variable amounts of deep integration. Examples include the European Union (EU), a highly integrated bloc, and the North American Free Trade Agreement (NAFTA) among the United States, Canada, and Mexico. The NAFTA countries are not deeply integrated.

The formation of preferential trade agreements is controversial. Trade opponents dislike the provisions, which expose more of the national economy to international competition, whereas some trade proponents dislike the preferential nature of these agreements, which invariably favor regions included in the agreement at the expense of regions outside the agreement. The North American Free Trade Agreement (NAFTA), the European Union (EU), the Mercado Común del Sur (Mercosur), and Asia Pacific Economic Cooperation (APEC) are the largest alliances, but they are only the tip of the iceberg of regional economic agreements.

Nine Issues in the International Economy

The chapters that follow will examine new elements of the international economy, and they will also address older, more traditional issues that are still relevant. Each of the following nine themes raises a number of important issues for the international economy. In some cases, international economics provides a relatively straightforward method of analysis for understanding the issues. In other cases, the themes are overlapping, many sided, and interdisciplinary. International economics cannot claim the final word on these issues, yet in the chapters that follow you will find that it provides an analytically powerful and logically consistent approach. It would be a huge mistake to think unclearly about the economics of these issues.

The Gains from Trade

Why is international trade desirable? This is both an old and a new question, one that confronts each new generation. Many people today have doubts about international trade, whereas others are confident of its benefits. Economic analysis clearly demonstrates that the benefits of international trade outweigh the costs; therein lies the reason that virtually all economists support open markets and increased trade. (Recent polls of economists put the level of agreement on this issue at around 98 percent, when a general question is asked about the desirability of closed versus open markets.) The benefits were first analyzed in the late 1700s, and they are perhaps the oldest, strongest findings in all of economics. Given the certainty of the benefits from trade, why do many noneconomists oppose it?

Wages, Jobs, and Protection

Whereas international trade benefits the majority of people in a national economy, it does not usually benefit every member of society. Workers in firms that cannot compete may be forced to find new jobs or to take pay cuts. The fact that consumers pay less for the goods they buy, or that exporters hire more workers, may not help them.

Increased awareness of the international economy has heightened the fears of people who feel vulnerable to changes in the international economy. They fear that wages in the United States must fall in order to compete with workers in low-wage countries or that their jobs may be moved overseas. The solution, according to some, is to keep out foreign goods—particularly goods produced by laborers who are paid less than American workers.

Economic analysis is very clear on this issue. Economists agree that net job and wage effects are not the main reasons for favoring trade. Rather, it is the improvement in the overall allocation of resources that makes international trade a net benefit to an economy. Trade enhances our productivity by insuring that resources are put to their highest valued use. Furthermore, protection from trade is usually one of the most expensive ways imaginable to protect the livelihood of workers whose jobs are disappearing overseas. One of the key issues challenging policymakers is to find the right mix of domestic policies so that the nation benefits from trade while not creating a backlash from those individuals and industries that are hurt.

Regional Trade Agreements

As the world economy becomes more integrated, some regions are running ahead of the general trend. Western Europeans, for example, have eliminated many of the economic barriers separating their nations and are on the verge of a much broader political and economic union. With implementation of the North American Free Trade Agreement (NAFTA) in 1994, the United States, Canada, and Mexico are moving toward a free-trade area. The largest states in the Pacific Basin—including China, Japan, and the United States—have agreed to turn the Pacific region into a free-trade area by the year 2020. The United States is conducting a series of on-again, off-again talks with other nations in the Western Hemisphere, with the objective to create a hemispheric free-trade area. Country by country, Eastern Europe has applied for membership in the European Union, and the Association of South East Asian Nations (ASEAN) has moved toward creating a free-trade zone among its member states.

The issues involved in these agreements are significant. Countries with very different legal systems, product standards, and income levels find that even when there is widespread support for closer commercial ties, the differences in their economies, societies, and political systems place stress on national governments. Furthermore, there is a legitimate concern that if nations group themselves into trade areas, there will be less momentum toward reducing trade barriers globally.

The Resolution of Trade Conflicts

Conflicts between nations over commerce cover a wide variety of issues and complaints. In one sense, these conflicts are routine, because the World Trade Organization (WTO) provides a formal dispute-resolution procedure that has the assent of most of the world's nations. The WTO process does not cover all goods and services, however; nor does it say much about a large number of practices that some nations find objectionable. The ability of nations to resolve conflicts without resorting to protectionist measures is one key to maintaining a healthy international economic environment. Disputes can become acrimonious, so it is imperative that differences of opinion not be permitted to escalate into a wider disagreement. Trade wars are not real wars, but they are harmful enough.

The Role of International Institutions

The organization with the greatest responsibility for resolving trade disagreements is the World Trade Organization (WTO). The WTO came into existence in 1995 and was an adaptation of the General Agreement on Tariffs and Trade (GATT), which was created shortly after World War II. Resolving trade disputes is only one of the new roles played by international organizations. Various bodies also offer organized development assistance, technical economic advice, emergency loans in a crisis situation, and other services and assistance.

As we said earlier, these bodies are unique to our time. They perform services that no one did before World War II (development assistance) or services that were done by a single country (lending in a crisis)—usually the world's greatest military power. These bodies exist today only through the mutual consent and cooperation of participating nations, and without that cooperation, they would dissolve. Their abilities, however, are limited. They cannot prevent crises, and they cannot make poor countries rich. Once a crisis begins, they are not always successful in containing it; when they do succeed, the costs are sometimes large. They are also controversial, sometimes viewed as tools of the United States or as a threat to national independence. They are very likely to grow in function, however, as concerns increase over problems that lack a purely national solution; for example, global warming.

The International Transmission of Local Instabilities

As trade and investment barriers have crumbled, and as fax, e-mail, and satellite communication systems have grown, it is easier to move capital across international borders. This trend is bolstered by lowered transaction costs for foreign investment and increased availability of different types of financial assets. The increase in international capital flows has created an impression that the global economy is more unstable today than in the past. As discussed earlier, financial crisis is an old story, and no one can say for certain if it is more or less common today. Nevertheless, for many countries and investors, the history of world finance is not a familiar subject, and the specter of financial crisis is new.

This fact has led to discussions about techniques for reducing volatile capital flows across international borders. The problem is to determine how to limit some kinds of capital flows without limiting others. In particular, how do countries tame the capital flows that add to instability, without stopping those that create valuable new investment. Some capital flows are highly desirable because they bring surplus savings to regions in need of investment and enable capital-scarce countries such as Mexico and Brazil to obtain higher levels of investment and faster rates of economic growth. Given that the volatility of international capital flows are not likely to disappear on their own, this issue will probably continue to be a topic of discussion among governments and international organizations, as well as in the press.

Crisis and Reform in Latin America

Beginning in the early 1980s, many of the nations of Latin America entered into a crisis brought on by high levels of debt owed to banks and governments outside the region. The crisis was characterized by deep recessions, high interest rates, bankruptcies, falling wages, and increasing poverty. Throughout the region, the 1980s came to be called the Lost Decade, a name that symbolized the absolute inability to meet the area's economic development needs. Beginning in the mid-1980s, a series of policy reforms emerged out of the debt crisis and spread across Latin America. Economies that had been sheltered from international competition were opened, and the region gave up its traditional, inward-looking policies that dated from the 1930s.

The story of this shift in national policies—from inward- to outward-looking perspectives, is one of the most interesting and significant stories in the international economy of the late twentieth century. Will the reforms last? Can they bring real economic improvements to more people than just the ones at the top of the income distribution? Or, as some fear, will volatile capital flows and bad macroeconomic policies become a disastrous mix that leads to financial instability, hyperinflation, and capital flight?

Export-Led Growth in East Asia

Throughout the late 1980s and into the 1990s, it has been hard to ignore the East Asian "miracle." While some economists have pointed out that it is not really a miracle—just a lot of hard work and sound economic policies—the growth rates of the "high-performance Asian economies" are unique in human history. Rates of growth of real GDP *per person* commonly reached 4 to 5 percent per year, with 6 to 8 percent not unusual. South Korea, for example, averaged growth of 8 percent per year in real GDP per capita during the 1980s. At that pace, income per person doubles in under nine years.

The crisis in East Asia, beginning in 1997, has recently tarnished the image of the region, but it would be a mistake to lose sight of the long run. If the region can avoid the ethnic and social conflicts that threaten, it is likely to return to high growth rates in the next few years. Recovery from the crisis will be uneven across the region, but in several East Asian countries, the basic foundation for economic growth will continue to be an object of envy throughout the developing world. Primary and secondary education has raised literacy rates to high levels; public and private investment has built a solid infrastructure; and savings rates are among the highest in the world.

One of the dominant traits of the countries in East Asia is the extent to which they are outward looking and dependent on the growth of their manufactured exports. Can this experience be duplicated elsewhere? To what extent did these countries benefit from policies that targeted the development of specific export-oriented industries? More fundamentally, is there a unique East Asian model?

The Integration of Ex-Socialist Countries into the World Trading System

The collapse of communism and resultant implications for the international economy is a final theme in this book. Eleven years before the fall of the Berlin Wall in 1989, China had begun in 1978 to move slowly toward a more market-based economy. The process there has been a more gradual one than in Central Europe, and the country's enormous size has enabled it to rely more on its domestic market and less on foreign markets. Nevertheless, it has already made a significant impact on both the goods markets and financial markets of the world. China is anxious to join the World Trade Organization, the international body that provides the framework for the rules of international trade; but in order to do so, it must make even deeper changes to its economy than those already accomplished. Whether it succeeds or fails, a nation of 1.2 billion that tries to strengthen its economic ties to the rest of the world will have effects that reach far beyond its borders.

Before the start of their transition to capitalism, the economies of Central and Eastern Europe and the former Soviet Union were integrated by administrative planning and the threat of military force. Markets played little or no role in determining trade patterns. Once the threat of military coercion was withdrawn, trade ties between the former East Bloc nations collapsed. Eastern Europe turned west and immediately began to develop trade ties, preparing to gain entrance to the European Union (EU), where the necessary accommodation to the changing geopolitical landscape poses a serious challenge.

As capitalist financial and goods markets in the formerly communist countries of Central and Eastern Europe, the former Soviet Union, and China grow, the impact on the world economy will be profound. The demand for capital to build modern economies will grow significantly as business practices and legal institutions develop further and encourage greater confidence among outside investors. In several countries, education levels are high, and advanced goods and services such as software and electronics are likely to make major impacts on world markets. To be sure, many of the countries will need a long period of transition before they begin to resemble market economies.

Vocabulary

deep integration

foreign direct investment (FDI)

gross domestic product (GDP)

openness

quotas

regional trade agreement (RTA)

shallow integration

tariffs

transaction costs

Study Questions

1. How can globalization and international economic integration be measured?

2. In what sense is today's U.S. economy more integrated with the world that it was a century ago? In what ways is it less integrated?

3. What is "openness"? How is it measured? Does a low openness indicator convey that a country is closed to trade with the outside world?

4. Describe the pattern shown over the last century by the U.S.'s openness indicator.

5. Throughtout Chapter 1, trade and capital flows were described and measured in relative terms rather than absolute. Explain the difference. Which seems more valid, relative or absolute? Why?

6. The size of international capital flows may not be much greater today than they were 100 years ago, although they are certainly greater than they were 50 years ago. Qualitively, however, capital flows *are* different today. Explain.

7. What are the new issues in international trade and investment? In what sense do they expose national economies to outside influences?

Suggested Reading

Irwin, Douglas. "The United States in a New Global Economy? A Century's Perspective." *The American Economic Review*. May 1996.

Kindleberger, Charles. *Manias, Panics, and Crashes*. New York: Wiley, 1996.

Krugman, Paul. "The Localization of the World Economy." *Pop Internationalism*. Cambridge, MA: MIT Press, 1997.

Maddison, Angus. *The World Economy in the 20th Century*. Paris: OECD, 1989.

———. *Monitoring the World Economy, 1820–1992*. Paris: OECD, 1995.

Williamson, Jeffrey. "Globalization, Convergence, and History," *Journal of Economic History*. June 1996.

INTERNATIONAL ECONOMIC INSTITUTIONS SINCE WORLD WAR II

Introduction

As World War II was drawing to a close, representatives from the United States, Great Britain, and other Allied nations met in the small New Hampshire town of Bretton Woods. The outcome of these meetings was a series of agreements that created an exchange rate system (which lasted until 1971), the International Bank for Reconstruction and Development (IBRD), also known as the World Bank, and the International Monetary Fund (IMF). In 1946, two years after Bretton Woods, twenty-three nations including the United States and Britain began talks on reducing their trade barriers, leading to the General Agreement on Tariffs and Trade (GATT), which began operation in 1948.

Chapter 2 focuses on these global economic institutions, their history, their role in the world economy, and several controversies surrounding their activities. Institutions that do not have a primary economic role, such as the General Assembly of the United Nations or the North Atlantic Treaty Organization (NATO), are not included.

International Institutions

International economic institutions are an important feature of the world economy. When economists and political scientists try to explain the increasing integration of national economies after World War II, the stability and reduced uncertainty created by international institutions is one of the key explanations. Before looking at their impact, we should define what we mean by an institution.

What Is an "Institution"?

Most people probably think of a formal organization when they hear the word *institution*. Economists tend to define institutions more broadly, however. For example, the "New Institutionalists," led by economist Douglas North, have argued that organizations are not institutions in themselves, although they may embody one. In this view, an institution is a set of rules that govern behavior. It tells us what is permissible and what is not; it is a constraint that limits us.

> ***Institution.*** *An institution is a set of rules of behavior. It sets limits, or constraints, on so-cial, political, and economic interaction, and in so doing plays a determining role. It may be informal (e.g., a manner, taboo, custom) or formal (e.g., a constitution or law).*

Institutions can be formal or informal. A formal institution is a written set of rules that explicitly states what is and is not allowed. The rules may be embodied in a club, an association, or a legal system. An informal institution is a custom or tradition that tells people how to act in exactly the same way that a law does, but without the legal enforcement. For example, informal institutions include the rules of socializing, gift exchange, table manners, e-mail etiquette ("netiquette"), and so forth. In this chapter, the term *institution* refers to both rules and organizations.

A Taxonomy of International Economic Institutions

International economic institutions come in many sizes and shapes. They can be lobbying groups for a particular commodity or an international producer's association; the joint management by several nations of a common resource; trade agreements or development funds for a select group of nations; or even global associations. Although this chapter's focus is on global economic institutions, it is useful to look at a taxonomy of international economic institutions from the most limited and specific to the most general. Table 2.1 shows five main types.

The IMF, the World Bank, and the WTO

Three global organizations play a major role in international economic relations and are central to this book: the International Monetary Fund (IMF), the World Bank, and the World Trade Organization (WTO). Two of them, the IMF and the World Bank, date from the end of World War II. The WTO came into being in 1995 as a result of trade negotiations that ended in 1993. The WTO grew out of the General Agreement on Tariffs and Trade (GATT), which it deepens and broadens. Accordingly, it is useful to know the history and function of the GATT as well as the WTO.

The records of each of these organizations are controversial because they give a greater voice to the world's rich countries and because they are seen by some as a threat to national independence and sovereignty. In addition, some economists and noneconomists view these organizations as large bureaucratic structures that soak up resources while dispensing useless or even harmful advice. The effectiveness of these organizations and their role in supporting the growth of world trade are the subjects of some controversy. Those who believe in the inherent stability of capitalist economies tend to see less need for these types of organizations, while those who fear

TABLE 2.1 International Economic Institutions

Type	Example
Commodity or industry specific organizations These range from trade associations to international standards-setting bodies to powerful cartels.	Oil Producing and Exporting Countries (OPEC) International Telecommunications Union (ITU) International Sugar Organization International Lead and Zinc Study Group
Commissions and agencies for managing shared resources	International Boundary and Water Commission (IBWC) Lake Chad Basin Commission Mekong River Commission
Development funds and banks	Inter-American Development Bank (IDB) North American Development Bank (NADBank) Asian Development Bank Islamic Development Bank
International trade agreements involving a few nations (regional trade alliances or trade blocs)	North American Free Trade Agreement (NAFTA) US-Israel Free Trade Agreement Mercado Común del Sur (Mercosur) Asia-Pacific Economic Cooperation (APEC) Enterprise for the Americas Initiative (EAI)
Global organizations for trade, development, and macroeconomic stability	International Monetary Fund (IMF) World Bank World Trade Organization (WTO)

the possibility of international instability uphold the importance of organizations and rules for addressing it. The supporters of the IMF, World Bank, and WTO argue that they are remarkable because (1) they are inclusive, (2) they have created a set of rules governing many international economic relations, and (3) they have provided a forum for discussion and amendment of those rules. Without these organizations, the proponents argue, global economic instability would have been much greater.

The IMF and the World Bank

During World War II, the United States and Great Britain (and a few other Allies) held regular discussions about the shape of the postwar international economic order. They wanted to avoid the mistakes of the 1920s and 1930s, when a lack of international cooperation led to the complete collapse of economic relations. The culmination of these talks was the Bretton Woods meetings in July 1944, where the Allies created the outlines of the International Monetary Fund (IMF) and the International Bank for Reconstruction and Development (World Bank).

The IMF began operation on December 27, 1945 with a membership of twenty-nine countries. Its success is indicated by the fact that in January 1996, there were 181 members. The IMF provides loans to its members under different programs for the short, medium, and long term. Each member is charged a fee, or quota, as the price of membership, the size of the quota varying with the size of the nation's economy and the importance of its currency in world trade and payments. Currently, the IMF has about $218 billion in quotas. Important decisions within the IMF are made by vote, with the weight of each nation's vote proportional to its quota. This gives the high-income countries of the world a voting power that is disproportionate to their population. For example, the United States alone controls almost 18 percent of the total votes, and the G-7 (the seven largest industrial economies—Canada, Italy, France, Germany, Japan, the United Kingdom, and the United States) control almost 45 percent. Some votes on IMF policy require a "supermajority" of as high as 85 percent, giving the United States a veto power on those particular issues. The size of the quota also determines a country's access to loans.

The most visible role for the IMF is to intercede, by invitation, whenever a nation experiences a crisis in its international payments. For example, if a country imports more than it exports, then it may run out of its reserves of foreign exchange that are used to pay for foreign goods. Foreign exchange reserves are dollars, yen, pounds, German marks, or another currency (or gold) that is accepted internationally. If a country lacks reserves, it cannot pay for its imports, nor can it pay the interest and principal it owes on any international borrowings. This is one scenario that warrants a call to the IMF. The IMF makes loans to its members, but it usually extracts a price above and beyond the interest it charges. The price is an agreement by the borrower to reform its finances so that the problem cannot recur. If simple financial reform is insufficient to permanently solve the problem, then the IMF usually requires a borrower to make fundamental changes in the relationship between government and markets in order to qualify for IMF funds. These requirements are known as IMF conditionality, and we will examine them later in this chapter.

The IMF also performs several related functions. In the current world economy, it has been an important source of both technical expertise and capital for the transitional economies of Central and Eastern Europe. These economies lack experience with open markets and large private sectors. They have had to create tax systems, social programs, and business codes from scratch, and the IMF has been a major source of information and financing. This role, too, is not without controversy. The IMF has also been the main provider of funds and advice to the crisis-gripped economies of East Asia. This role has required it to take on a great deal of controversy.

The World Bank was founded in 1944, the same time as IMF. Currently, there are more than 175 members. Members buy shares in the Bank and, similar to the quotas that determine voting rights in the IMF, shareholding determines the weight of each member in setting the Bank's policies and practices. Originally, the World Bank was known as the International Bank for Reconstruction and Development, or IBRD. The name reflected the fact that it was primarily created to assist in the reconstruction of the war-torn areas. As the capital requirements for reconstruction grew, however, it soon became apparent that the IBRD lacked sufficient funds to do the job, and in 1948, the United States created the parallel program known as the Marshall Plan to assist Europe.

By the 1950s, the field of development economics had begun to take off. Several leading economists were able to make credible arguments that the world's less economically developed regions could grow much faster if they could get around the constraints imposed by a lack of investment capital, and the IBRD was encouraged to fill this role as a supplier of capital to developing economies. Today, the IBRD is one of five separate subgroups that make up the World Bank. The role of the IBRD is to lend for specific development projects, such as dams, highways, and schools, and to support major adjustments in government policies that change the way they manage the economy. Other subgroups in the World Bank are focused on the very poor, private sector development, and loan guarantee programs. Only developing countries can borrow from the World Bank.

The GATT, the Uruguay Round, and the WTO

At the end of World War II, a third global economic organization was proposed, to be named the International Trade Organization (ITO). If it had been implemented, the ITO's job would have been to establish rules relating to world trade, business practices, and international investment. U.S. opposition killed the idea of the ITO, however, and no such organization was created until 1995. Nevertheless, in 1946, while they were still considering the idea of the ITO, twenty-three countries opened negotiations over tariff reductions. These negotiations led to some 45,000 tariff concessions affecting $10 billion, or one-fifth of world trade. In addition, a number of agreements were made on rules for trade (ultimately in the expectation that the rules would become part of the ITO). Both the tariff reductions and the rules were implemented in 1948; when the possibility of an ITO died in 1950, the agreements on tariffs and trade rules remained in force as a separate agreement known as the **General Agreement on Tariffs and Trade**, or **GATT**. The GATT has been very successful in gradually bringing down trade barriers. One indicator is that international trade grew at the rate of about 8 percent per year in the 1950s and 1960s, much faster than before the war and faster than growth in the world's total output.

The GATT functions through a series of "trade rounds," in which countries periodically negotiate a set of incremental tariff reductions. Gradually, through the Kennedy Round in the mid-1960s and the Tokyo Round of the 1970s, trade rules other than tariffs began to be addressed, including the problems of dumping (selling in a foreign market below cost or below a fair price), subsidies to industry, and nontariff barriers to trade. As tariffs came down, these nontariff issues became more prominent.

The GATT intentionally ignored the extremely contentious sectors of agriculture, textiles, and apparel. In addition, trade in services was ignored because it was not important. The accumulation of unresolved issues in these sectors, however, along with the increased importance of nontariff trade barriers, led to the demand for a new, more extensive set of negotiations. These demands culminated in the Uruguay Round of trade negotiations that began in 1986 and concluded in 1993. In 1994 the new agreement was signed by 125 countries.

> *Tariffs and Nontariff barriers. Tariffs are taxes imposed on imports. They raise the price to the domestic consumer and reduce the quantity demanded. Nontariff barriers to trade include any trade barrier that is not a tariff. Most important are quotas, which are physical limits on the quantity of permitted imports. In addition, nontariff barriers, or NTBs, include red tape and regulations, rules requiring governments to purchase from domestic producers, and a large number of other practices that indirectly limit imports.*

Every two years, trade ministers from around the world meet to set the broad policy objectives of the WTO. Day-to-day work, however, is done by the WTO's staff (General Council), under the leadership of the director-general. By mid-1997, the WTO had 131 full members and thirty more observer governments who were negotiating to join. Legally, it consists of twenty-nine separate legal texts, plus more than twenty-five declarations, memoranda of understanding, and joint statements. The key concepts of all WTO agreements, however, were carried over directly from the GATT: nondiscrimination and national treatment. More broadly, these concepts are realized in the general mission of the WTO, which includes insurance of market access, promotion of fair competition, and encouragement of economic development and economic reform.

> *Nondiscrimination and National treatment. The concept of nondiscrimination is embodied in the idea of Most Favored Nation status, or MFN. MFN is the idea that every member of the WTO is required to treat each of its trading partners as well as it treats its most favored trading partner. In effect, it prohibits one country from discriminating against another. The main exception to MFN is that it permits trade agreements like the NAFTA (North American Free Trade Agreement) and does not require a country to extend the same treatment to countries outside the agreement. In other words, the United States is under no obligation to treat all countries the same as it treats its NAFTA partners, Mexico and Canada. National treatment says that imports that are allowed in may not be treated any differently from domestically produced goods. In other words, it violates the spirit of the GATT and the WTO to permit imports but not allow them the same market access as domestic goods. Once inside a nation, imports should be treated the same as nonimported versions of the same good.*

The Uruguay Round and the establishment of the WTO were genuine reforms in the rules of world trade. The WTO preserves the GATT while reaching into new areas, including agriculture, textiles, and services; it replaces the GATT's dispute resolution procedure with a much faster and more effective mechanism; and it monitors national trade practices more closely.

CASE STUDY

The GATT Rounds

Agreements in the GATT forum to reduce trade barriers take place in "rounds" of negotiations. Counting the first round, there have been eight rounds of negotiations, the most recent being the Uruguay Round, which ended in 1993. Originally, the GATT was an international agreement and not an organization. The failure to create the International Trade Organization in 1950, however, resulted in the gradual conversion of the GATT into a de facto organization by 1960, with a permanent secretariat to manage it from Geneva. Table 2.2 lists the various rounds of negotiations.

TABLE 2.2 The GATT Rounds

Round	Year	Number of Participants
Geneva I	1947	23
Annecy	1949	13
Torquay	1951	38
Geneva II	1956	26
Dillon	1960–1961	26
Kennedy	1964–1967	62
Tokyo	1973–1979	102
Uruguay	1986–1993	105

The first five rounds were organized around product-by-product negotiations. Beginning with the Kennedy Round, negotiations were simplified. Countries negotiated an across-the-board percentage reduction in all their tariffs for a range of industrial products. One effect is that tariffs have never been uniform across countries. The goal has been to reduce all tariffs, but not necessarily make them the same for all countries.

The Tokyo Round is notable because it was the first round to begin to establish rules regarding subsidies. Subsidies give an industry a competitive advantage, since the national government pays part of the cost of production, either through direct payment or indirectly through subsidized interest rates, artificially cheap access to foreign currency, or in some other way. Obviously, an industry that does not receive subsidies but that must compete against one that does will be disadvantaged. The Tokyo Round began the laborious process of creating rules in this area, one of the most important of which was the agreement to prohibit subsidies for exports of industrial goods (but not agricultural goods or textiles and apparel).

Case Study continues

The subsidy issue of the Tokyo Round was carried forward into the Uruguay Round, where subsidies were defined in greater detail. The Uruguay Round accomplished many other things as well, not the least of which was the creation of the World Trade Organization as a formal organization to oversee and administer the GATT. Additional accomplishments are described in Chapter 6, which explores trade policy and trade barriers in more detail.

The Role of International Economic Institutions

In general, humans rely on institutions to create order and to reduce uncertainty. By defining the constraints or limits on economic, political, and social interactions, institutions define the incentive system of a society and help to create stability. The provision of order and the reduction of uncertainty are so important that when they are absent, economies cannot develop. Within a single nation, the formal rules of behavior are defined by the various levels of government. In the United States, for example, this includes cities, counties, special districts, states, and the federal government. In the international sphere, however, there are no corresponding sets of government. The establishment of rules for international trade and international macroeconomic relations are dependent on the voluntary associations of nations in international economic organizations.

The primary difference between international economic organizations and the government of a single nation is that the former have limited enforcement power. National and local governments have police powers that they can use to enforce their rules; international organizations have no police power, but they do have more subtle powers for encouraging cooperation. For example, the IMF and World Bank can withdraw lines of credit to developing countries. The withdrawal of IMF credit and its "stamp of approval" raises a red flag for private lenders and makes it more costly for uncooperative nations to gain access to capital in private markets. Like-wise, the WTO can legitimize retaliatory sanctions against nations that fail to honor their trade obligations. At bottom, however, international organizations rely on moral suasion and the commitments of individual nations to remain effective. If nations choose to withdraw their support from an international organization, it dies.

The provision of order and the reduction of uncertainty are services that everyone values. This is why we pay police officers, judges, and legislators. Although public order and the lessening of uncertainty are intangibles, they are desired and valued in the same sense that more tangible material objects are. Their economic characteristics are different from most goods and services, however, and they fall into the category known as **public goods.**

The Definition of Public Goods

By definition, public goods are (1) nonexcludable and (2) nonrival or nondiminishable. Nonexcludability means that the normal price mechanism does not work as a means of regulating access. For example, when a signal is broadcast on the airwaves by a television station, anyone with a TV set who lives within its range can pick it up. (Of course, this is not the case with cable stations, which are granted permission to scramble their signals. Signal scrambling by cable companies is actually a clever technological solution to the problem of nonexcludability.)

> **Public goods.** *Public goods share two characteristics: nonexcludability and nonrivalry or nondiminishability. If they are excludable but nondiminishable goods, they are sometimes called collective goods.*

The second characteristic of public goods is that they are nonrival, or nondiminishable. This refers to the attribute of not being diminished by consumption. For example, if I tune in to the broadcast signal of a local TV station, all my neighbors will have the same amount available to them. Most goods get smaller, or diminish, when they are consumed, but public goods do not.

Private markets often fail to supply optimal levels of public goods because of the problem of **free riding.** Free riding means that there is no incentive to pay for public goods because people cannot be excluded from consumption. Given this characteristic, public goods will not be produced optimally by free markets unless institutional arrangements can somehow overcome the free riding. In most cases, governments step in as providers and use their powers to tax as a means to force people to pay for the good.

> **Free riding.** *Free riding occurs when a person lets others pay for a good or service, or lets them do the work, when they know they cannot be excluded from consumption of the good or from the benefits of the work.*

Maintaining Order and Reducing Uncertainty

Two of the most important functions of international economic institutions are to maintain order in international economic relations and to reduce uncertainty. Taken together, these two functions are often instrumental in the avoidance of a global economic crisis. Furthermore, if a national crisis threatens to become global, international institutions often help to bring it to a less costly end and to prevent nations from shifting the cost of national problems to other countries.

The maintenance of order and the reduction of uncertainty are general tasks that require specific rules in a number of areas of international economic interaction. Economists do not completely agree on the specific rules or the specific types of cooperation that should be provided. Nevertheless, the proponents of international institutions, such as economist Charles Kindleberger, have noted several areas where institutions are needed in order to strengthen cooperation and prevent free riding in the provision of international public goods. Among the items he lists are the four public goods in Table 2.3.

Kindleberger and others have argued that the absence of a set of rules for providing one or more of these public goods has usually been a key part of the explanation of historical crises such as the worldwide Great Depression of the 1930s. The specific items in Table 2.3 may be debatable, but the basic point is sound. If no international institutions are available to help nations overcome the tendency to free

TABLE 2.3 Examples of International Public Goods

Public Good	Purpose
1. Open markets in a recession	To prevent a fall in exports from magnifying the effects of a recession
2. Capital flows to less-developed countries (LDCs)	To assist with economic development in economies with capital shortages
3. International money—that is, money for settlement of international debts	To maintain a globally accepted system for paying debts
4. Coordination of last resort lending	To prevent a financial crisis caused by a shortage of liquidity from deepening and spreading to other countries

ride, then international economic stability grows more fragile. As an illustration, consider the first item listed. During recessions, politicians begin to feel enormous pressure to close markets in order to protect jobs at home. During the 1930s, for example, most nations enacted high tariffs and restrictive quotas on imports. This set in motion waves of retaliation as the nations that lost their foreign markets followed suit and imposed their own tariffs and quotas. In the end, no one benefited, and international trade collapsed.

In essence, each nation was free riding. That is, everyone prefers a situation in which all markets are open over one in which all markets are closed. Each nation tries to let other countries be the ones to stay open and to pay the price of a loss of some jobs in import-competing industries. Free riders want to close markets in a recession to reduce imports and create more jobs. At the same time, however, they want all other nations to stay open so that they do not lose any export markets. These desires are inconsistent, however, and the effect of free riding behavior is that all countries retaliate by closing their markets, international trade collapses, and everyone is worse off than before. Kindleberger shows that the shift in trade policies toward high tariffs and restrictive quotas helped intensify and spread the Great Depression of the 1930s.

Kindleberger also argues that the sudden decline in capital flows to developing countries in the 1930s and the complete absence of a lender of last resort deepened the Depression and provided further historical evidence for the importance of international institutions. The lack of a lender of last resort was particularly critical because a number of countries with temporary financial problems soon passed into full-blown financial collapse. As it became impossible for them to pay their foreign debts, the crisis spread from the indebted nations to the lending nations.

> **Lender of last resort.** *In international economics, a lender of last resort is a place where nations can borrow after all sources of commercial lending have dried up. In the world today, the IMF fills this role.*

No one has tried to measure the frequency of potentially disastrous international economic events. Their occurrence is not infrequent, however, and it is relatively easy to list a number of recent events that had the potential, if improperly handled, to turn into major global problems. For example, the debt crisis of the 1980s, in which many Latin American, African, and some Asian countries teetered on the brink of financial collapse, was a potentially global disaster. Countries accumulated debt far in excess of their ability to pay; if they had defaulted, it would have spread to the United States and Europe, since a number of banks counted their loans to developing countries as part of their asset base. Similarly, the collapse of the Mexican peso in December 1994 had the potential to affect many more countries than it actually did. The ongoing adjustment to capitalism of the formerly socialist countries of Central and Eastern Europe could turn into a global nightmare of historical dimensions without the capital flows they are receiving along with their access to markets in the West.

The crisis in East Asia which began in 1997 is the most recent example of a regional event that threatens to leave a lasting, negative impact on the world economy. Like the events of the 1980s and early 1990s, the IMF is deeply involved in trying to contain the crisis with large loans and conditions for receiving them. Meanwhile, in academia, business, and government, there are serious debates about the best course of action to pursue in order to end the crisis and to avoid deeper problems in the future. As of this writing, no one knows which way events will turn.

In each crisis or potential crisis, international institutions play an important role by preventing free riding. Lacking much in the way of formal enforcement mechanisms, international institutions overcome the free rider problem by changing each nation's expectations about every other nation. For example, if all countries are committed to open markets, in good times and bad, then during a worldwide recession no country expects its trading partners to close their markets. As another example, if each country pays a share of the IMF's operating funds, then it overcomes the problems that arise when each country waits for everyone else to make risky loans during a crisis.

The effectiveness of international institutions depends on the credible commitment of the world's nations. If a country agrees to a set of rules but has a reputation for breaking its agreements, then its commitment is not credible. Institutions cannot overcome the free rider problem under those circumstances.

International Institutions and National Sovereignty

National sovereignty refers to the right of each nation to be free from outside interference. International institutions complicate the issue of sovereignty by limiting the range of permissible actions that a national government may take and by imposing conditions for membership. For example, developing countries that have

CASE STUDY

Bretton Woods Conference

After World War I, the United States retreated into relative isolationism under the mistaken belief that noninvolvement in European affairs would protect the country from entanglement in disastrous European conflicts such as the First World War. The rise of Hitler, Japanese aggression in the Pacific, and the start of the World War II showed that this policy would not work.

The United States began to realize its mistake in the 1930s as it watched Hitler take over a large part of the European continent. U.S. and British cooperation and planning for the postwar era began before the United States even entered the war in December 1941, and long before the outcome was known. President Roosevelt and the prime minister of Great Britain, Winston Churchill, met on a battleship off the coast of Newfoundland in August 1941. Soon after, they announced the Atlantic Charter, a program for postwar reconstruction that committed both nations to working for the fullest possible economic collaboration between all nations after the war. Concurrent with the Atlantic Charter, the two nations began high-level discussions about the kind and function of any international institutions that might be proposed.

All parties agreed that in any postwar order, the United States would have to be the political, military, and economic leader. Its wealth and size had surpassed that of Britain several decades earlier, and its leadership during the war gave it prestige and credibility around the world. In addition, the United States' physical infrastructure was not damaged by the war, and it was the only industrial nation set to provide the financial capital and much of the physical material needed to repair the damage caused by the war.

Looking back to the 1920s and 1930s, the postwar planners recognized four serious problems that they should guard against: (1) the worldwide depression; (2) the collapse of international trade; (3) the collapse of the international monetary system; and (4) the collapse of international lending. Discussions during the Second World War were devoted to mainly rules, agreements, and organizations that could be created to avoid these problems. Three international institutions were viewed as central for the achievement of these goals:

1. An international organization to help keep exchange rates stable and to assist nations that were unable to pay their international debts
2. Agreements to reduce trade barriers
3. An international organization to provide relief to the war-damaged nations and to assist with reconstruction

Plans for the postwar period were finalized at a conference held in July 1944 in Bretton Woods, New Hampshire. The Bretton Woods institutions include the International Monetary Fund, the World Bank, and the Bretton Woods exchange rate system. Although it was conceived separately, the General Agreement on Tariffs and Trade is sometimes included because it embodies the goals and ideas of the Bretton Woods planners with respect to international trade. Taken together, these four represent a remarkable constellation of international economic institutions, and each, in its own area, has played a key role in the history of the international economy since 1945.

The founding principles of the Bretton Woods institutions are relatively simple. First, trade should open in *all* countries, not just the United States alone or the United States and the United Kingdom together. In economic terms, this was a call for multilateral opening as opposed to unilateralism (one-sided opening) or bilateralism (two-sided opening). Second, nations should not discriminate against other nations. Whatever tariffs and quotas the United Kingdom or the United States might levy against another country, they should be the same ones imposed on everyone. Third, in order to insure the ability of importers to purchase goods abroad, countries should not limit the buying and selling of currency when its purpose is to pay for imports. Fourth, exchange rates should be fixed but with the possibility for periodic adjustment. These four principles formed the cornerstones of the institutions.

borrowed from the IMF sometimes complain bitterly about the changes they are required to make in their domestic policies. In many advanced industrial economies, such as the United States, some politicians have argued that entanglement in international institutions such as the WTO reduce U.S. sovereignty by giving outsiders power to make rules that limit U.S. policies.

IMF Conditionality

As a lender of last resort, the IMF is often asked to intervene when countries reach a crisis point in their finances and cannot make payment on their international loans. The loans they receive from the IMF may be short, medium, or long term, depending on whether the crisis is a simple, short-run cash flow problem or a longer-run problem caused by inefficient or incompetent government policies.

The IMF's lending practices, such as these it currently exercises in East Asia, Russia, and elsewhere, usually impose conditions on the borrower and require changes in national policies. For example, a country may have originally accumulated foreign debts to support a set of inefficient, state-owned industries, and the IMF may require the borrower to put in place a privatization plan. Another example is the case in which the national government's budget is in persistent deficit as a result of the subsidies it provides consumers or businesses. If the source of the problem is the national budget, the IMF usually requires a reform of government fiscal policies as a condition for receiving loans.

> *IMF conditionality. IMF conditionality refers to the changes in economic policy that borrowing nations are required to make in order to receive IMF loans. The changes usually involve policies that will reduce or eliminate a severe trade deficit and/or a central government budget deficit. In practical terms, they involve reduced expenditures by the government and by the private sector (to reduce imports) and increased taxes.*

In many cases, the required reforms affect social programs. They often lower the living standard of urban residents in particular, and they can lead to greater inequality in the distribution of income. In many Latin American nations, where income inequality is among the highest in the world, IMF policies have intensified inequality and, in a few instances, have led to outright rebellion.

National governments often find it convenient to shift the blame for their belt tightening to someone else, and the IMF (and the rich industrial nations, since they control the IMF's policies) are a convenient target. In addition, until the early 1990s, IMF policies focused almost exclusively on financial issues and ignored the society-wide consequences of their conditionality. More recently, the IMF has begun to take a look at the impacts of its policies on the more vulnerable elements of the borrowing nations, and it has begun to make adjustments.

It is easy to dismiss the concerns of debtor nations by pointing out that they created their own problems: incompetent macroeconomic policies, bloated state bureaucracies, and state-owned industries that are inefficient and corrupt are often at the root of international debt problems. One response to their complaints is that if countries do not like the IMF's conditions, then they should not get themselves into a position where they must borrow in order to stay afloat. The problems with this argument are that it does not address the issues that nations face during a crisis and it increases the risk of the crisis spreading.

Another complication occurs in cases where the government incurring the debt is a military dictatorship or, in some other way, unrepresentative of its citizens. In these cases, the debt may have been realized while the government plundered the nation for the economic gain of a small group of elites. It hardly seems fair that the citizens should have to pay for both a corrupt government and for the international assistance that rescues them. Nevertheless, the right of nations to be self-determining requires the IMF and other outsiders to refrain from judging the moral rightness of borrowing governments. As long as the government in power is recognized by the world's nations, it has the same rights and responsibilities as democratic nations.

Opposition to International Institutions in the United States

IMF conditionality affects developing nations more than it does advanced industrial economies because rich nations almost always continue to enjoy access to private capital markets and rarely need lenders of last resort. Nevertheless, in some rich nations, such as the United States, there is a similar debate over the impact of international agreements on national sovereignty. Specifically, some people worry that entanglement in international agreements limits the range of policy options available and may force changes in domestic policies in order to be in compliance with international agreements.

While it is undoubtedly true that that international agreements cause changes in national domestic policies, the relevant consideration is whether or not the United States and other nations derive benefits that exceed their costs. Some of the benefits are easy to identify: world markets are much more open today than they would have been without a GATT; the debt crisis of the 1980s was contained and did not spread beyond the indebted countries, thanks to the IMF; and the transition economies of Central and Eastern Europe are far more stable than they would have been without the technical assistance and loans of the IMF and World Bank. There is no way to prove what would have happened if the international institutions did not exist today. Nevertheless, they are one of the primary reasons for the fact that world trade has grown faster than world output since the end of World War II and that nations enjoy far greater benefits from economic integration than at any time in the twentieth century.

International Institutions and the End of the Cold War

In the fall of 1989, the Berlin Wall was pulled down. Quickly thereafter, the Federal Republic of Germany (West Germany) moved toward integration with its eastern counterpart. And on December 24, 1991, the Soviet Union ended its existence and was replaced by fifteen independent republics. The end of the Cold War is probably the most important event in world affairs since the end of World War II. Its impact on global economic institutions cannot be overestimated.

While less sudden than the dismantling of the Soviet Union, a second set of events is also shaping future international economic relations. Prosperity in Japan and Europe, rapid economic growth in several countries of East Asia, and the emergence of China as a world economic colossus are generating several geographical centers of economic power. In spite of the deep crisis that began in 1997, the long run outlook continues to be positive for a number of Asian nations. It seems likely that the first fifty years of the twenty-first century will not be dominated by the economic, political, and military leadership of the United States to the extent of the last fifty years of the twentieth century.

A key question is whether or not the international economic institutions that emerged under U.S. leadership after World War II can survive a shift in global power to several geographic centers. Some fear that these institutions depend so greatly on U.S. leadership that they cannot survive the relative growth of economic and political power in Asia and Europe.

Why International Institutions Have Succeeded

Before discussing the post-Cold War viability of the IMF, World Bank, and WTO, it is useful to clarify why these institutions succeeded in the first place. One line of reasoning lists three key reasons for their success. First, the design of the institutions involved a very small number of countries. For example, the Bretton Woods agreements were signed by twenty-nine nations, and most of the work was done by the United States and Great Britain before the conference. By 1996, the IMF had 181 members. Similarly, the original GATT agreement was signed by 23 members, but by mid-1996, the WTO included 123 members plus another 37 official observer nations. Obviously, negotiations are much easier when they need only accommodate the interests of 23 nations instead of 123.

Not only did the small number of countries make negotiations easier, it also made it easier for the United States to bear the costs of leadership. In the first decades after the end of World War II, there was a consistent willingness by the United States to share its gains from economic stability. This was a major inducement to countries to move toward a more integrated and open world economic system. For example, rather than impose punitive conditions on Germany and Japan after World War II (as happened after the First World War), the United States created the Marshall Plan for Europe and the Dodge Plan for Japan to assist with the economic and political reconstruction of each region. Furthermore, the United States did not demand that foreign markets open in a way that was symmetric to its own opening, choosing instead to serve as a model for other countries. A good example of this is the way in which the United States made room for surging Japanese imports in the 1960s and beyond. Finally, the United States has borne the lion's share of the cost of the collective defense of the noncommunist world.

Some economists argue that a second factor in the success of the post-World War II institutions is that Keynesian, demand-management economic policies of the governments of the industrial economies held together a domestic consensus in each country, which permitted greater international openness. National governments put full employment among their highest priorities. Consequently, when imports caused job losses, there was little fear that the displaced workers would stay unemployed for long. In addition, when taxes went to support foreign aid programs, it was easier to accept as long as employment was high and the national economies were growing.

The third factor is that all nations began the postwar period with highly closed markets. This enabled progress to be maintained for some years because they could focus on general tariff reductions and did not have to deal with more contentious issues such as market structures, labor and environmental policies, and so forth.

After the Cold War

Beginning in the 1970s, the world began to change. First, the economic successes of Germany and Japan lessened the United States' willingness to bear the burden of providing international public goods. Japanese and European successes in U.S. markets started to seem objectionable, particularly when highly visible U.S. industries such as automobiles, steel, and consumer electronics were shrinking against a wave of imports. The rapid export expansion of East Asian nations has exacerbated this problem and led domestic U.S. interests to call for greater reciprocity in trade relations. In addition, prosperity in Europe and elsewhere began to call into question the large U.S. military expenditures for the defense of other nations. As long as the Soviets were a threat, the pressure to maintain these expenditures remained great. Once the Cold War ended, however, it became difficult to argue that the United States should pay part of the cost of defending other nations.

The problem of maintaining open markets in the face of imports was compounded by inflation in the 1970s, which began to erode the domestic consensus that fighting unemployment was the number-one priority. As growth slowed throughout the industrial world after the early 1970s, it was no longer certain that all groups within the United States would share in economic prosperity. Even though only a small share of the U.S. federal government's budget went to assist other nations directly, Americans resented any assistance if stability and prosperity elsewhere did nothing to alleviate American problems.

Finally, the successes of the IMF, the World Bank, and the GATT have made future progress more difficult. First, negotiations have gotten bogged down as more nations have joined. For example, the Uruguay Round of negotiations was originally scheduled to last three years, but it dragged on for seven instead. Obtaining the commitment of more than a hundred nations is much more difficult than finding common ground for ten or twenty. Second, negotiations to extend the reach of institutions and to maintain progress toward greater international order now require agreements on very contentious issues. Instead of tariff reductions, progress must now be made on improvements in labor policies, environmental policies, and a host of other sensitive issues.

To return to the important question of the survivability of these institutions in the post-Cold War period, we need to define two opposing points of view. The first is that of a group of political scientists who can be called "Realists." Realists argue that cooperation was the result of U.S. leadership (or, in their terminology, *hegemony*). As long as the United States was willing and able to bear the lion's share of the burden of providing order and reducing uncertainty in the world economy, the international institutions designed by the United States and its allies could survive. In their view, these institutions are extensions of U.S. power and help to maintain it. Once the United States steps back from a dominating world leadership role, the institutions it supported will begin to decay. The alternative view is that of the "Institutionalists." Institutionalists argue that leaders (or hegemons) such as the United States emerge periodically on the world stage and often set in motion a set of institutions that become more or less self perpetuating. That is, the rules of the game, as defined by the leader's organizations can continue to function effectively in spite of the decline in power, prestige, and economic importance of the leading nation.

Clearly, time will tell if the WTO and the other important institutions will begin to decline in importance. It is interesting to note, however, that the WTO itself, and the important extension of the GATT agreement known as the Uruguay Round of trade negotiations, were wrapped up in 1993, ratified by the member nations in 1994, and implemented in 1995. In other words, the lessening of U.S. global leadership has not yet diminished the ability of nations to reach agreement. Nevertheless, only time will tell if the WTO and the Uruguay Round will become effective institutions for maintaining order in world trade relations.

Toward a New World Order?

It is a cliché to talk about the New World Order. In most cases it simply refers to the post–Cold War era of international relations, which we have just entered. Still, there are a number of important issues related to the increasing internationalization of national economies. One issue is whether world leaders can maintain support for the principles of the international institutions created in the second half of the twentieth century. Public support for international institutions cannot be taken for granted now that the Cold War has ended. This is illustrated by America's reluctance to increase its quota at the IMF, opposition to loans to indebted countries such as Mexico, and resistance to expanded trade agreements. Domestic political support for the principles of the international institutions depends in part on the ability of national governments to manage the society-wide effects stemming from the internationalization of their national economies. Increased trade, greater flows of capital across international boundaries, and rising numbers of humans crossing the same boundaries are disrupting traditional patterns of work and culture. Movement of goods, services, capital, and people, are contributing to a worldwide perception of increasing insecurity, and national governments must manage the effects of these flows or watch the erosion of their national consensus of support for international institutions.

To some extent, since the problems of increasing internationalization are global, the solutions will have to be above the national level as well. Along these lines, it has been suggested that a possible direction for the evolution of international economic relations is toward the creation of several new global institutions. New institutions would define a common set of principles for addressing the more serious problems that are developing as a result of increasing internationalization. There are currently four leading candidates for new global institutions: institutions for dealing with environmental problems; for supervising capital markets and the extremely volatile flow of international financial capital; for migration; and for international investment issues. It is an open question whether any of these areas will generate enough international interest and national support to formally establish an organization and some "rules of the game." In some cases, such as the environment, there are already a number of ad hoc international agreements that have been signed by large numbers of nations (such as the use of chlorofluorocarbons, or CFCs). Nevertheless, it is a long way from an ad hoc agreement aimed at a specific problem to a formal set of procedures and rules aimed at a wide variety of problems.

Conclusion

Institutions are the "rules of the game." They can be formal, as in a nation's constitution, or informal, as in a custom or tradition. In either case, humans depend on institutions as a mechanism for creating order and reducing uncertainty.

Perhaps the primary reason for the growth of international trade and investment during the last fifty years has been the stable political environment that existed in the noncommunist world of economically advanced market economies. To a large degree, relations between these nations were stable and relatively orderly as a result of the formal rules laid down in the international institutions.

Chapter 2 has summarized the history of three of the most important international economic institutions. It has examined the economic reasons for creating them and briefly looked at some of the controversies that surround them.

▲ International economic institutions are an attempt to overcome the problem of free riding by individual nations in the sphere of providing international public goods. The most important public goods are order and a reduction in uncertainty. Some economists believe that these goods are best provided when there are agreements that help keep markets open in recessions and in boom periods; when there is an international lender of last resort; when there are sufficient lenders of capital to developing nations; and when there is an adequate supply of money for international payment.

▲ The "Big 3" of international economic organizations are the International Monetary Fund, the World Bank, and the General Agreement on Tariffs and Trade. The latter has been incorporated into a newly created fourth organization, called the World Trade Organization. The IMF, World Bank, and GATT were created at the end of World War II with the purpose of avoiding a return to the destructive economic conditions of the interwar years (between World War I and World War II).

▲ The most controversial aspect of international economic institutions is their ability to impact the domestic policies of sovereign nations. IMF conditionality on loans to developing countries is the primary example of this. Even in advanced industrial economies, however, individuals who fear the extension of the market to international levels view international economic organizations as a Trojan Horse that will lead to a loss of local control over their economic environment.

▲ There is uncertainty as to the ability of the current group of international economic organizations to survive in an environment of declining U.S. leadership. One group, the Realists, believes that these organizations (and the rules they embody) will disappear or greatly diminish in importance if the United States evolves into a co-equal world leader along with Japan and the European Union. Another group, the Institutionalists, sees the extension of the GATT into a broader set of rules under the WTO as evidence that the rules are to a large degree self-perpetuating and not dependent on U.S. leadership.

Vocabulary

Bretton Woods Conference

free riding

General Agreement on Tariffs and Trade (GATT)

IMF conditionality

institution

International Monetary Fund (IMF)

World Trade Organization

lender of last resort

national treatment

nondiscrimination

public goods

tariffs and nontariff barriers

World Bank

Study Questions

1. What is an institution? Give examples of formal and informal institutions. Explain how they differ from organizations.

2. What are the arguments in favor of international organizations? What are the arguments against? Which do you think are stronger?

3. What are public goods, and how do they differ from private goods? Give examples of each type.

4. What are the main tasks or functions of (1) the International Monetary Fund, (2) The World Bank, (3) the General Agreement on Tariffs and Trade, and (4) the World Trade Organization?

5. When nations sign the GATT agreement, they bind their tariffs at their current level or lower. Tariff binding means that the nations agree not to raise the tariffs except under unusual circumstances. Explain how tariff binding in the GATT prevents free riding during a global slowdown.

6. Kindleberger's study of the Great Depression of the 1930s led him to believe that market economies are sometimes unstable and that nations can get locked into prolonged downturns. Other economists are not convinced. Suppose that you disagree with Kindleberger and believe that market-based economies are inherently stable. How would you view the need for international institutions to address the provision of each public good in Table 2.3?

7. Why might the international institutions of the Cold War era disappear? Why might they persist?

Suggested Reading

Kindleberger, Charles. *The International Economic Order: Essays on Financial Crisis and International Public Goods.* Hertfordshire, England: Harvester-Wheatsheaf, 1988.

Kenen, Peter B., ed. *Managing the World Economy: Fifty Years after Bretton Woods.* Washington, DC: Institute for International Economics, 1994.

Schott, Jeffrey. *The Uruguay Round: An Assessment.* Washington, DC: Institute for International Economics, 1994.

Web Sites

All the organizations discussed in this chapter have Web sites that contain information on their histories, structures, and functions. A central node for connecting to a great number of international organizations is the United Nations International Computing Center, UNICC. The URL is *http://www.unsystem.org*. From there, you can select the World Bank, the IMF, the WTO, or a large number of other organizations. Alternatively, you can go directly to the World Bank's site at *http://www.worldbank.org*. The IMF is at *http://www.imf.org*, and the World Trade Organization is *http://www.wto.org*.

PART TWO

THE INTERNATIONAL ECONOMY

THEORY

CHAPTER 3

COMPARATIVE ADVANTAGE AND THE GAINS FROM TRADE

Introduction

This chapter introduces the theory of comparative advantage. A simple model is used to show how nations maximize their material welfare by specializing in goods and services that have the lowest relative costs of production. The improvement in national welfare is known as the **gains from trade**. The concepts of comparative advantage and the gains from trade are two of the oldest and most widely held ideas in all of economics, yet they are often misunderstood and misinterpreted. Therefore it is worth the effort to develop a clear understanding of both.

Adam Smith and the Attack on Economic Nationalism

The development of modern economic theory is intimately linked to the birth of international economics. In 1776, Adam Smith published *An Inquiry into the Nature and Causes of the Wealth of Nations,* a work that became the first modern statement of economic theory. In the process of laying out the basic ground rules for the efficient allocation of resources, Smith initiated a general attack on **mercantilism,** the system of nationalistic economics that dominated economic thought in the 1700s. Although Smith successfully established modern economics, he did not end mercantilist thinking; in the present day, mercantilism is usually labeled economic nationalism.

> *Mercantilism. Mercantilism is the name given to the economic system that arose in Western Europe in the 1500s during the period in which modern nation states were emerging from feudal monarchies. It has been called the politics and economics of nation building because it stressed the need for nations to run trade surpluses to obtain revenues for armies and national construction projects. Mercantilists favored the granting of monopoly rights to individuals and companies, they shunned competition, and they viewed exports as positive and imports as negative. In the contemporary world, the term* mercantilism *is sometimes used to describe the policies of nations that promote their exports while keeping their markets relatively closed to imports.*

The key mistake in mercantilist thinking was the belief that trade was a **zero sum** activity. In the eighteenth century the term *zero sum* did not exist, but it is a convenient expression for the concept that one nation's gain is another nation's loss. A moment's reflection should be enough to see the mistake in this belief, at least as it applies to voluntary exchange. When you buy a gallon of milk, do you lose and the store wins? Why would you buy the milk if that were true? If the store loses, why would they sell it? In fact, voluntary exchange is positive sum. Both sides must gain, or else one or both sides would withdraw from the exchange. In trade, the most accurate metaphor is not football or some other competitive game but aerobics or dance.

> ***Zero sum.*** *Zero sum means that the gains and losses add to zero. Football, baseball, and other competitive sports are zero sum: When one side wins, by definition the other loses. Aerobics and dance are physical activities that are positive sum—all participants win. In the economic realm, voluntary exchange (domestic and foreign trade) are positive sum. While it is true that individual businesses may engage in fierce competition, from the perspective of national economies, trade is more like dance than it is like football.*

No one in the 1770s thought they were living in the midst of an industrial revolution, but Smith was observant enough to perceive that many improvements in the standard of living had occurred during his lifetime as a result of increasing specialization in production. Therefore, he analyzed specialization in order to determine its characteristics and requirements. In the process, he made one of his most important contributions to economics, the discovery that specialization depends on the size of the market.

A contemporary example may be helpful. If the giant automobile manufacturer General Motors was only permitted to sell its cars and trucks in, say, Michigan, they would have much less revenue and would sell many fewer vehicles. They would hire fewer employees, and each person would be less specialized. As it is, GM's market is so large (essentially, it is the world) that it can hire engineers who are completely specialized in small, even minuscule, parts of a car—door locks, for example. Your door lock engineer will know everything there is to know about the design, production, and assembly of door locks and will be able to help GM put them into its cars in the most efficient manner possible. A firm that was limited to the Michigan market could never afford to hire such specialized skills in every area of vehicle manufacture.

One of the keys to Smith's story of wealth creation is access to foreign markets. If no one is willing to import, then every company is limited by the size of the national market. In some cases, that may be large enough (the United States or China), but in most cases it is not. Small- and medium-sized countries cannot efficiently produce every item they consume. Holland, for example, has always imported a large share of its goods and has depended on access to foreign markets in order to earn money to pay for imports.

Smith was highly critical of trade barriers because they decreased specialization, technological progress, and wealth creation. The modern view of trade shares Smith's dislike of trade barriers for mostly the same reasons. Although international economists recognize that there are limitations to the application of theory, the vast majority of economists share a strongly held preference for free and open markets. In Chapters 5 and 6 we will examine trade barriers in greater detail, but at this point we need to develop a deeper understanding of the gains from trade, and to do that we must introduce a simple algebraic and graphical model.

A Simple Model of Production and Trade

We will now construct a model of production and trade to examine the nuts and bolts of trade theory and to understand why economists overwhelmingly favor open markets. We will construct a simple model of an economy and use it to analyze the costs and benefits of trade. Extraneous details are omitted, and only the most important features are included in our model. As with a road map, which is a kind of model of geographical relations, the goal of economics is to provide enough detail to keep the destination in sight but not so much as to make the model unreadable.

Basic Assumptions of Standard Trade Models

We begin with one of the simplest models in economics. The conclusion of this analysis is that if the assumptions hold, then a policy of free trade maximizes a nation's material well-being. Later we will examine some of the cases where real-world conditions do not conform to the assumptions of this simple model and where the policy conclusion that free trade is optimal may be questioned.

The basic model is often referred to as a Ricardian model, since it first took form in the analysis of David Ricardo. The model begins by assuming that there are only two countries, producing two goods, using one input (labor). More complex models can be built with n countries producing m goods and using k inputs, but other than adding a layer of mathematical sophistication, the final outcome is almost the same. The Ricardian model assumes that firms are price takers, or, in other words, markets are competitive, and no firm has market power. The model is static in the sense that it is assumed that technology is constant and there are no learning effects of production that might make firms and industries more productive over time. We will relax both of these assumptions in the coming chapters. Ricardo assumed that labor is perfectly mobile and can easily move back and forth between industries, another simplifying assumption that will be dropped in Chapter 4. In this chapter, we assume that labor is mobile between industries but not across national boundaries.

Measures of Productivity in the Ricardian Model

Before proceeding we must define *productivity* in the Ricardian model. Productivity is the amount of output obtained from a unit of input. Since labor is the only input, we can define **labor productivity** as

$$\text{(units of output)} / \text{(hours worked)}$$

If, for example, two loaves of bread can be produced in 1 hour, then productivity is

$$(2 \text{ loaves}) / (1 \text{ hour})$$

or 2 loaves per hour. If 4 loaves are produced in 2 hours, then productivity is

$$(4 \text{ loaves}) / (2 \text{ hours}) = 2 \text{ loaves per hour}$$

It may scem redundant to keep repeating the units of measurement (loaves for bread and hours for labor), but you will see why it is important to keep track of the units of measurement.

> **Labor productivity.** *The amount of output per unit of labor input.*

Absolute Productivity Advantage and the Gains from Trade

Suppose there are two goods, bread and steel, and two countries, the United States and Canada. Suppose also that each produces according to the productivities given in Table 3.1.

The values in Table 3.1 show that Canada's productivity is greater than the United States' in bread production, and the United States' is greater in steel. Canada has an **absolute productivity advantage** in bread because they produce more loaves per hour worked (3 versus 2 in the United States). At the same time, the United States has an absolute productivity advantage in steel production.

> **Absolute productivity advantage.** *A country has an absolute productivity advantage in a good if its labor productivity is higher. That is, it is able to produce more output with an hour of labor than its trading partner.*

The basis of Adam Smith's support for free trade was the belief that every country would have an absolute advantage in something. Smith thought it did not really matter where the source of the advantage came from. Whether it was due to special skills in the labor force, climate and soil characteristics of the country, or the mental temperament of its people, there would be goods that each country could manufacture, or grow, or dig out of the ground more efficiently than its trading partner. Consequently, every country could benefit from trade.

In the numerical example outlined in Table 3.1, each loaf of bread costs the United States 1.5 tons of steel. Put another way, the **opportunity cost** of bread is 1.5 tons of steel, since each unit of bread produced requires the economy to move labor out of steel production, forfeiting 1.5 tons of steel that it could have produced instead. This follows from the fact that each hour of labor can produce either 2 loaves of bread or 3 tons of steel. We can write this ratio as the barter price of bread:

$$P_{us}^b = \frac{3 \text{ tons}}{2 \text{ loaves}} = 1.5\left(\frac{\text{tons}}{\text{loaves}}\right)$$

TABLE 3.1 Output per Hour Worked		
	U.S.	*Canada*
Bread	2 loaves	3 loaves
Steel	3 tons	1 ton

where *b* is for bread and *us* is the country. Similarly, we can write the U.S. price of steel as the inverse:

$$P^s_{us} = \frac{2 \text{ loaves}}{3 \text{ tons}} = 0.67\left(\frac{\text{loaves}}{\text{tons}}\right)$$

You should be able to verify that the Canadian price of bread will be 0.33 (tons/loaf) and that steel will cost 3 (loaves/ton).

> ***Opportunity cost.*** *Opportunity cost is the value of the best forgone alternative to the activity actually chosen. For example, if the United States chooses to produce another loaf of bread, the best forgone alternative is steel production, and the amount or value of steel given up in order to produce another loaf of bread is 1.5 tons.*

If the United States can sell a ton of steel for more than 0.67 loaves of bread, it is better off. Similarly, if Canadians can obtain a ton of steel for fewer than 3 loaves of bread, they are better off. Obviously, there is an opportunity for each country to gain from trade. All the United States needs to do is to offer to sell steel for fewer than 3 loaves of bread but more than 0.67 loaves; anywhere in that range, both Canadians and Americans will benefit. In the end, trade will occur at a price somewhere between these two limits:

$$3.0\left(\frac{\text{loaves}}{\text{ton}}\right) > P^s_w > 0.67\left(\frac{\text{loaves}}{\text{ton}}\right)$$

where P^s_w = the world price of steel (i.e., the trade price). Without knowing more details about the demand side of the market, it is impossible to say whether the price will settle closer to 3.0 (loaves/ton) or 0.67 (loaves/ton). The closer the price is to 0.67, the more Canada benefits from trade, and the closer it is to 3.0, the more the United States benefits. Nevertheless, as long as it is between these two limits, both countries benefit from trade.

Comparative Productivity Advantage and the Gains from Trade

The obvious question to ask at this point is what happens if a country does not have an absolute productivity advantage in a good. It is not hard to imagine an extremely poor, resource-deficient nation with low literacy and scarce capital . What can these countries produce more efficiently than the United States or Germany? Why would a rich country want to trade with them when they are relatively lacking in everything? The answer is that even if a country lacks a single good in which it has an absolute productivity advantage, it can still benefit from trade. Furthermore, and perhaps even more surprising, is that rich, high-productivity countries that are well endowed with resources also benefit from trade with poor countries. In other words, the idea that nations benefit from trade has nothing to do with whether they have an absolute advantage in producing particular goods. In order to see this, we must first develop a few more basic concepts.

The Production Possibilities Curve

The **production possibilities curve (PPC)** shows the tradeoff a country faces when it chooses its combination of bread and steel output. Figure 3.1 illustrates a hypothetical PPC for the United States. Point B on the PPC is an efficient point of production because it utilizes existing resources to obtain the maximum possible level of output. The assumption of full employment is equivalent to assuming that the United States is operating at a point like B that lies on its PPC. At point A, the economy is inside its production curve and is operating at an inefficient level of output because it is not obtaining the maximum possible output from its available inputs. At point A, there is waste in the economy, since a greater quantity of bread and steel could be produced with the existing labor supply. Point C is infeasible. Existing resources do not permit the production of bread and steel in the combination indicated.

> ***Production possibilities curve.*** *The production possibilities curve shows the maximum amount of output possible given the available supply of inputs. It also shows the tradeoff that a country must make if it wishes to increase the output of one of its goods. In other words, it shows how much of one good must be given up in order to increase output of the alternative good.*

The PPC in Figure 3.1 is a straight line because it is assumed that the tradeoff between bread and steel does not change. If the economy operates near the bread axis, where it is producing mostly bread, the tradeoff is the same as it would be if the economy produced mostly steel: ⅔ of a loaf of bread for every ton of steel. The tradeoff between bread and steel is another way to refer to the opportunity cost of steel. This follows from the definition of opportunity cost as the best forgone alternative: in order to produce a ton of steel, the United States gives up ⅔ a loaf of bread. In Figure 3.2, the slope of the PPC is −0.67, the number of loaves of bread forgone (Δbread) divided by the quantity of steel obtained (Δsteel):

Slope of the PPC = (Δbread output) / (Δsteel output) = opportunity cost of steel

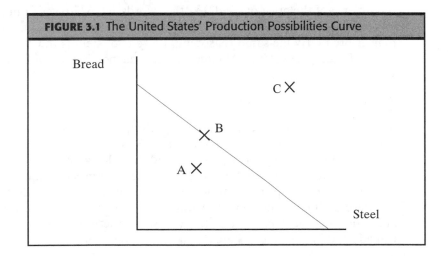

FIGURE 3.1 The United States' Production Possibilities Curve

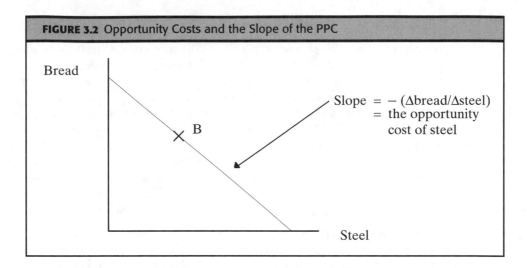

FIGURE 3.2 Opportunity Costs and the Slope of the PPC

Bread

× B

Slope = − (Δbread/Δsteel)
       = the opportunity
         cost of steel

Steel

Relative Prices

Suppose that the slope of the PPC is −0.67, as in Figure 3.2. If the United States does not trade, it gives up 0.67 loaves of bread for an additional ton of steel. This tradeoff is called either the **relative price** of steel or the opportunity cost of steel. The term *relative price* follows from the fact that it is not in monetary units but instead in units of the other good. If no trade takes place, then the relative price of a good must be equal to its opportunity cost in production.

> **Relative price.** *The price of one good in terms of another good. It is similar to a money price, but rather than express the price in terms of dollars and cents, relative prices are in terms of the quantity of the first good that must be given up in order to buy a second good.*

It is easy to convert the relative price of steel into the bread price: simply take the inverse of the price of steel. In other words, if 0.67 loaves of bread is the price of one ton of steel in the United States, then 1.5 tons of steel is the price of one loaf of bread. By the same reasoning, 1.5 tons of steel is the opportunity cost of a loaf of bread in the United States when production is at point B in Figure 3.2.

The Price Line, or Trade Line

Suppose that in the absence of trade, the opportunity cost of steel in Canada is 3 loaves of bread per ton, and in the United States it is 0.67 loaves per ton (as given in Table 3.1). The complete absence of trade is called **autarky** by economists. In this situation, both the United States and Canada are limited in their consumption to the goods that they produce at home. It was implied, however, that both countries can raise their consumption levels if they trade. In particular, for trade to be desirable, the price of steel must settle somewhere between the opportunity costs in Canada and in the United States. That is, countries benefit if

$$3.0 \text{ (loaves/ton)} > P_w^s > 0.67 \text{ (loaves/ton)}$$

Autarky. *The complete absence of foreign trade; total self sufficiency of a national economy.*

Suppose that the price settles at 2 loaves per ton. In the United States, the pre-trade price was 0.67 loaves per ton. This is illustrated in Figure 3.3 where the United States' PPC is shown with the production point at A. The trading possibilities for the United States are illustrated by line TT, the price line or trade line. TT has a slope of −2 and passes through point A, the United States' production point on its PPC. If the United States chooses to trade, it could move up TT, trading each ton of steel for two loaves of bread. This is a better tradeoff than it gets if it tries to make more bread, since along its PPC each ton brings only ⅔ more loaves of bread. While it always impossible to produce outside the PPC, in effect, the United States can consume outside it by trading steel for bread.

Price line or Trade line. *Like the PPC, the price line (TT) shows the cost of one good in terms of another. Unlike the PPC, however, the price line is the price in trade rather than the production tradeoff. It is also called the trade line.*

The Gains from Trade

You should wonder why the United States would choose to make bread at all, since each time a ton of steel is given up for more bread production, it brings in only ⅔ loaf of bread. If the United States were to specialize in steel production and trade for bread, it could do much better, since it would get 2 loaves for each ton. This possibility is illustrated in Figure 3.4. Here the United States' pretrade production point is at A. This is also its consumption point, since in the absence of trade, consumption must equal production. Point B in Figure 3.4 represents production that is completely specialized in steel. With the opening of trade, production could occur

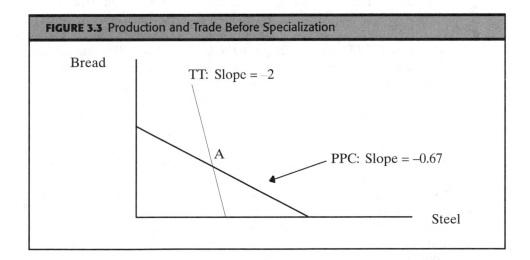

FIGURE 3.3 Production and Trade Before Specialization

Bread

TT: Slope = −2

A

PPC: Slope = −0.67

Steel

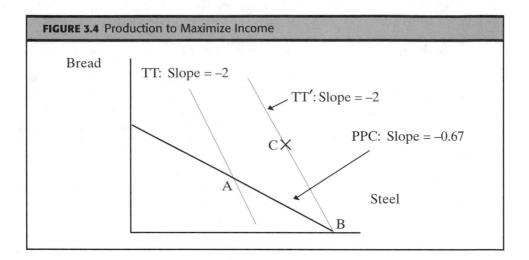

FIGURE 3.4 Production to Maximize Income

at B, and the United States could trade up along TT′, which has a slope of −2, the same as TT. If the United States produces at B and moves up TT′, it can reach a point like C, which is unambiguously superior to the consumption bundle available when production is at point A. C is superior is because it represents more of both bread and steel than is available at A. Similarly, for any combination of bread and steel that is available along the PPC, or along TT if the United States produces at A and trades, there is a consumption bundle on TT′,which represents more of both goods.

Gains from trade. *The increase in consumption made possible by specialization and trade.*

The most important thing to note about production point B is that it maximizes U.S. income. This follows from the fact that it makes available the greatest combinations of bread and steel. To see this, consider that no other point of production puts the United States on a price line that lies farther out from the origin. Every other production point on the United States' PPC lies below TT′, and every trade line with a slope of −2 that passes through the PPC at a point other than B also lies below TT′. In other words, given the United States' PPC and a trade price for steel of 2, the largest bundle of consumption goods is obtained when the United States specializes in steel and trades for its bread.

The United States benefits from trade, but does Canada? Unequivocally, the answer is yes. Consider Figure 3.5 where point A is Canada's pretrade production point on its PPC. Along Canada's PPC, the opportunity cost of steel is 3 loaves of bread per ton. After trade, the price settles between 0.67 and 3.00, at 2 loaves per ton. With a trade price of 2 (price line TT), Canada maximizes its income by moving along its PPC to where it is completely specialized in bread production. It can then trade bread for steel at a trade price that is more favorable than its domestic trade-off of 3 loaves per ton. Canada too, can consume at a point on TT that is outside its PPC and above and to the right of its pretrade equilibrium at point A. Canada, like the United States, is better off, because with trade it gets a larger combination of both goods than it can produce for itself.

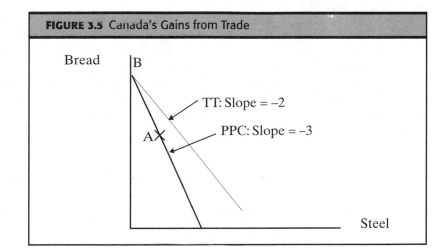

FIGURE 3.5 Canada's Gains from Trade

Domestic Prices and the Trade Price

Now we know that as long as the trade price is between the pretrade domestic prices in Canada and the United States, both countries can gain from trade. What ensures that the trade price actually settles within this range, 3.0 (loaves/ton) > P_w^s > 0.67 (loaves/ton)? What would happen if, for example, P_w^s was equal to 4, or 0.5?

Consider the first case when the trade price is 4 loaves per ton of steel. At $P_w^s = 4$, the trade price of steel is greater than the production cost in each country. Clearly, the United States would want to continue to specialize in steel and trade it for bread. Nothing has changed with regard to the U.S. strategy for maximizing its consumption bundle, or income. The only difference now is that the United States gets 4 units of bread for each unit of steel, instead of 2 as before. In Canada's case, the higher price of steel now makes it profitable for Canadian producers to switch to steel production. This follows from the facts that the production opportunity cost of steel is 3 loaves of bread, but each ton produced can trade for 4 loaves. By specializing in steel production and trading for bread, Canada maximizes its consumption bundle.

Finally, it should be obvious that both countries are specialized in steel production and that no one is producing bread. Both Canada and the United States will bring their excess steel to market looking to trade it for bread, but neither country has any to trade. There is a bread shortage and a glut of steel. Consequently, bread prices rise, and steel prices fall. This goes on at least until the trade price of steel falls below the opportunity cost of production in Canada, the higher-cost country. Once P_w^s is less than 3, Canadian producers switch back to bread, steel production goes down, bread is up, and trade can resume.

In the second case, where P_w^s is less than 0.67, Canada continues to specialize in bread, and the United States switches. Bread is the surplus good, steel is in short supply, and a similar dynamic occurs that causes the price to move in order to ensure both goods are produced. The equilibrium trade price, then, has to be within the range we specified earlier, between the opportunity costs in the two countries. In our case, this is between 0.67 and 3.0 loaves per ton.

Without more information we cannot say much more about the trade price. Will it be close to 0.67 or to 3.0? The answer depends on the strength of demand for each good in both countries, but we have not explicitly included demand in our model, so we cannot say. We do know that if the price is closer to 0.67, the gains from trade are larger for Canada, and if it is closer to 3.0, the United States benefits more. Nevertheless, both countries gain as long as it is between the two opportunity costs, and economic forces determine that the price must be in that range.

Absolute and Comparative Productivity Advantage Contrasted

Absolute productivity advantage is defined as having higher labor productivity. We saw that if each country has an absolute productivity advantage in one of the goods, they can both benefit by specializing in that good and trading it for the other good. Note, however, that the gains from trade we saw did not depend in any way on each country having an absolute advantage. In fact, what mattered was the pretrade tradeoffs, or opportunity costs, of bread for steel in each country. The opportunity costs were derived from the productivities, but since they are a ratio, vastly different levels of productivity can lead to the same tradeoff. For example, we assumed that Canada could produce either 3 loaves of bread, or 1 ton of steel with 1 hour of labor. If the numbers were 6 and 2, or 1 and ⅓, however, the result would have been the same: Each ton of steel costs 3 loaves of bread.

The concept of comparative advantage is based on the idea that nations maximize their material well-being when they use their resources where they have their highest value. In order to know the highest-valued usage for any resource, we must compare alternative uses. If, by comparison to the United States, labor in Canada is *relatively* more productive in bread than in steel, then Canada should produce more bread and trade for steel.

> *Comparative productivity advantage. A country has a comparative productivity advantage in a good, or simply a comparative advantage, if its opportunity costs of producing a good are lower than those of its trading partners.*

The distinction between absolute and comparative productivity advantages is one of the most important in economics. It is also one of the least well understood, in spite of the fact that it is relatively simple. Noneconomists, even very sophisticated commentators on the international scene, often sound as if they do not grasp the basic differences between the two concepts. For example, it is common to read or hear comments about American competitiveness that assume that if the United States does not have absolute advantage, it will not be able to sell its products abroad. Our model explains why this logic is erroneous. Furthermore, even the least productive of nations exports some goods. To reiterate the point, comparative advantage allows nations to benefit from trade, whether they lack an absolute productivity advantage in anything or have an absolute productivity advantage in everything.

Comparative Advantage and "Competitiveness"

The rhetoric of "competitiveness" is so common in our public discourse that it is useful to consider its relationship to comparative advantage. In the analysis so far, comparative advantage resulted from productivity differences between nations in autarky. In our simple model of a barter economy, wages, prices, and exchange rates were omitted. Real businesses do not barter steel for bread, however, and they cannot pay their workers by dividing up the firm's output.

In general, by ignoring money wages, money prices, and exchange rates, we assumed that all goods and labor were correctly priced. In other words, it is assumed that the prices of both outputs and inputs are an accurate indication of their relative scarcity. In this case, there is no difference between a nation's comparative advantage in a good and the ability of its firms to sell the good at a price that is competitive. That is, if all markets correctly value the price of inputs and outputs, then a nation's commercial advantage in a good will be determined by its comparative advantage.

Unfortunately, markets sometimes fail to produce optimal outcomes. This means that at times, outputs and inputs can be incorrectly priced. Sometimes, under- or overvaluation of a good stems from inherent difficulties in measuring the true value of a good or in measuring its true cost of production. For example, we may ignore air pollution and its costs when we measure the value of owning a car. Other times, under- or overvaluation may result from government policies, as when prices are maintained at an artificially high or low level. In either case, the fact that a market price may not accurately reflect the economic value of an input or an output means that a wedge is driven between commercial or competitive advantage and comparative advantage.

It is often (incorrectly) argued that nations should pursue commercial advantages for their firms even if it means a misallocation of resources. In effect, this means a country follows policies that lower living standards by failing to maximize the value of national output. In terms of Figures 3.5 and 3.6, this is equivalent to asserting that the United States and Canada should each remain at point A, where the United States overestimates the value of producing its own bread and Canada overestimates the value of steel. Both countries end up with consumption bundles that are suboptimal from the standpoint of national welfare.

Consider a real-world example. Indonesia has tried to develop an aircraft industry in spite of the fact that it lacks a comparative advantage in aircraft production. Nevertheless, through a combination of government policies (some of which have paid foreigners to buy the planes!) the price to foreigners has been competitive at times. Obviously, from the perspective of Indonesian national welfare and the optimal use of scarce Indonesian resources, this is a mistake. From the perspective of a business, however, Indonesian policies have made it profitable to make airplanes, even though it means using resources in ways that are suboptimal from the national perspective.

> ***Competitive advantage.*** *The ability to sell a good at the lowest price. Competitive advantage may be the result of high productivity and a comparative advantage. Alternatively, it may be the result of government subsides for inefficient industries.*

This case illustrates the common mistake of equating nations with business enterprises. Indonesian plane manufacturers care about their subsidies and any other policy that makes them profitable. The national interest, however, is to achieve the most efficient allocation of resources possible within the framework of the nation's laws and values. It is possible to make individual firms highly profitable through subsidies or protection from international competition, while at the same time and through the same policies cause the nation's overall standard of living to be lower than it would be otherwise. While most American businesses do not receive subsidies, they are not in business to insure that resources are efficiently allocated at the national level. If they can legally tip the playing field in their direction, many would not hesitate.

Another important distinction between nations and business enterprises is that nations do not compete with each other in any normal sense of the word. Economic relations between the United States and Canada, or any pair of nations, are not equivalent to the commercial competition that exists between companies such as Coke and Pepsi. If Canada grows, the United States does not go out of business or suffer in any identifiable way. In fact, Canadian growth would be a stimulus to U.S. growth and would create spillover benefits for Americans. Cola companies fight over a relatively static market size, but nations can all simultaneously increase their incomes.

Economic Restructuring

Economic restructuring refers to changes in the economy that may require some industries to grow and others to shrink or even disappear altogether. For example, the United States has seen a dramatic decrease in the size of its steel industry and, some years later, a rebirth of a new industry based around smaller, more specialized steel mills. In any dynamic economy, some types of economic activity will be growing, and others will be scaling back or dying. In some cases, these changes are a direct consequence of increased openness to foreign competition. For example, the influx of Japanese cars has played a major role in the reorganization and restructuring of the U.S. auto industry.

Economic restructuring. *A movement from one point to another along a country's PPC.*

In our simple Ricardian model, after the opening of trade the United States was able to maximize its well-being by shifting workers out of bread production and into steel production. Even though this restructuring of the U.S. economy improved overall economic welfare, it does not mean that it benefited every individual— a nation's gains from trade may be divided in different ways, and it is usually the case that some individuals benefit while others are hurt by trade. If there are net gains from opening trade (which are measured by an increase in the consumption bundle), then it means that the economic gains of the winners are greater than the economic losses of the losers, and therefore the nation as a whole is better off. Nevertheless, opening an economy to increased foreign competition is rarely painless and usually generates a number of new problems. In the model used in this

CASE STUDY

The U.S. and Mexican Auto Industries

When the United States and Canada began negotiations with Mexico to include Mexico in an expanded North American free-trade zone, American and Canadian autoworkers expressed fears that they could not compete with Mexican workers, who were paid much lower wages. Union representatives of the autoworkers argued in front of Congress that Mexican autoworkers earning between $4 and $5 per hour would overwhelm U.S. workers, who earn more than $35 per hour in wages and benefits in the Big Three (GM, Ford, Chrysler) auto plants. The result, they argued, would be a loss of jobs and a migration of the industry to Mexico.

As it turns out, the autoworkers and their union representatives were wrong. Since signing NAFTA, U.S. and Canadian exports of autos to Mexico have actually increased. What happened? How are the United States and Canada able to overcome such enormous disadvantages in wages (between seven to one and eight to one) and actually increase exports of cars to Mexico? The answer is a simple lesson in comparative advantage.

Mexican workers earn a lot less than U.S. and Canadian workers simply because they are a lot less productive. The primary reasons for this are because they have fewer machines at work, and the machines they do have are older and less efficient. In addition, the surrounding economy outside Mexican auto factories does not function as smoothly because the transportation, water, power, and communication systems are less developed. In economic terms, Mexican workers have less capital, both at work and in the supporting economy outside their plants.

Table 3.2 shows the costs for vehicle assembly based on "good" practices (but not the "best") of each country. A plant in the United States requires about twenty hours per vehicle for assembly, and in Mexico it takes around thirty hours. In spite of the faster assembly times, U.S. labor costs are much

TABLE 3.2 Cost Structure for Auto Assembly in the United States and Mexico, Around 1990

	U.S.	*Mexico*
Labor	$ 700	$ 140
Parts, components, subassemblies	7,750	8,000
Component shipping costs	75	600
Finished vehicle shipping	225	400
Inventory costs	20	40
Total cost	$8,770	$9,180

Source: Congress of the United States, Office of Technology Assessment, *U.S.-Mexico Trade: Pulling Together or Pulling Apart?* (1992), p. 145.

Case Study continues

higher ($700 versus $140) due to the higher wages paid. However, the advantage of Mexican producers in the area of labor costs is completely lost elsewhere in the assembly process. The biggest offsetting factors are component and final vehicle shipping costs, where the United States has a $700 cost advantage (($400 + $600) – ($225 + $75)). The $700 cost advantage more than compensates for the $560 ($700 – $140) labor cost disadvantage. The net result is that the application of labor and capital to automobile assembly in the United States is more productive than using capital and labor in Mexico to assemble cars. From the perspective of economic policy, Mexico should seek to raise the productivity of its capital and labor used in automobile production, or else use its capital and labor resources in some other activity.

The key to this outcome is overall productivity, or the amount of output per unit of input. In the simple Ricardian model of trade introduced earlier, labor was the only input, and money prices did not come into the picture. In the real world, however, labor is but one input along with capital and natural resources such as energy. Also, inputs and outputs are priced in dollar terms rather than in terms of the relative prices of output. Under these more realistic conditions, it is the combination of labor, capital, and natural resources that determines overall productivity and which country can make each good with the lowest opportunity cost.

This example illustrates an important principle of international trade theory. A country can have higher wages and still produce at a lower cost as long as its productivity is higher than its trading partner's. In this example, U.S. productivity overcomes higher U.S. wages so that the opportunity cost of car production is actually lower in the United States than in Mexico.

Should Mexico abandon car production, then, and completely specialize in something else? Not quite. Another difference between our model and the actual world we live in is that countries do not completely specialize. There are many reasons for this, including the facts that some goods are never traded (haircuts and restaurant meals, for example) and that most industries probably have increasing costs rather than the constant costs portrayed in our straight-line PPCs. The latter fact makes the PPC a bowed-out curve rather than a straight line and leads to incomplete specialization as opposed to the total specialization of our simple Ricardian model. To understand this, however, we need to introduce some additional concepts in Chapter 4.

chapter, it is likely that bread producers may not know much about steel production. They may not know where to go to find work, and they may leave behind a community that is dying as its most mobile and economically active citizens find work elsewhere.

When the U.S. auto industry was in its least-competitive position against the Japanese in the early 1980s, our overly simplified model of comparative advantage would have counseled laid-off autoworkers to leave Michigan and move to California where they could find jobs in the booming computer and defense industries. Obviously, this is not realistic advice for most autoworkers. The fact that the U.S. economy was open to Japanese auto manufacturers certainly helped U.S. consumers and U.S. firms that bought cars . It increased our selection of automobiles and enabled us to buy better-quality cars at lower prices. It is another matter, however, for the U.S. autoworkers who lost their jobs.

Most economists would agree that this tradeoff is worth it because the availability of Japanese cars, or foreign-made goods in general, increases our choices as consumers, lowers the cost of inputs, increases competition and innovation, and enables us to obtain a greater bundle of goods with our incomes. The availability of imports puts pressure on domestic producers to improve their product quality and to hold down their costs of production. Finally, it leads to the diffusion of technological change, which benefits us all. No one would argue, for example, that if a German drug company invented a cure for AIDS or cancer that we should prohibit its importation because it may hurt the income of a lot of doctors and perhaps lead to the closing of some hospitals. The gain to the nation would vastly outweigh the losses to those adversely affected by the changes in medicine.

While it is easy to show that trade barriers are a suboptimal solution to the social problems of economic change that are caused by trade, it is uncertain what the optimal policies are. To a large extent, political assumptions about the way the world works will color the solutions offered by economists, political scientists, and other social scientists. For example, some ardent believers in less government intervention into the economy would argue that government should not have any policies for handling unemployment or the economic collapse of communities that is caused by the rapid growth of imports. They maintain that unemployment is a self-correcting problem; laid-off workers will look for new jobs and will, if necessary, accept lower wages. The argument is also frequently heard that government cannot efficiently deal with these sorts of problems; it creates inefficient, bureaucratic programs that live on long after they become unnecessary. Others make a value judgment that this sort of social problem should not be a governmental concern, that it should be left up to the private economy and individual initiative.

One alternative to this purely laissez faire approach to economic restructuring caused by trade is for the government to look for ways to get the winners to compensate the losers. The proponents of this view justify it on several grounds. First, the nation as a whole benefits from trade, so there are newly added resources to the economy that make compensation possible. In addition, compensation reduces the incentives for those that oppose trade to organize against imports. If industries or workers think they are unable to compete, they may organize to restrict trade. Promises of financial assistance and help in finding another job may weaken this urge. In this view, compensation is a useful tool for undermining the antitrade position.

The practice of offering **trade adjustment assistance** is common in many countries, including the United States. These programs usually take the form of extended unemployment benefits and worker retraining, along with a temporary imposition of a tax on imports in order to create some breathing room for an industry suffering from a sudden surge in imports. For example, the U.S. government created a special program of benefits for workers who are hurt by trade with Mexico due to the signing of the North American Free Trade Agreement (NAFTA). In 1994, the first year of NAFTA, 17,000 workers qualified for TAA under the NAFTA provision. Generally, in order to qualify for the benefits, workers must demonstrate that they were laid off as a result of imports from Mexico or because their firm relocated to Mexico. Needless to say, it is sometimes difficult to establish a direct link between imports and a job loss; a poorly managed firm may have been on its way out of business with or without imports.

> *Trade adjustment assistance. Government programs that offer temporary assistance to workers that lose jobs because of foreign trade or their firms moving abroad.*

The important point is that trade creates change, and it may be difficult for some people, industries, or communities to deal with change. When a nation moves along its PPC toward a different mix of industries, there is a period of transition that is painful for some. Economic restructuring does not happen overnight, and although it is desirable for the higher living standard it brings, change and transformation cost time and money.

Conclusion

While the basic idea of comparative advantage is simple, it is often confused with the notion of absolute advantage. Intuitively, most people understand the idea in their everyday lives. I do not make my own clothes because I have more valuable uses for my time. If I use my talents appropriately, I get more clothes and more of other goods. (I do not even think about the fact that I run a trade deficit with the department store that sells me clothes.)

Many people have a harder time accepting this concept on a national scale, but it is equally true. The United States does not need to grow bananas, for example, in order to consume them. In fact, by using our capital, labor, and land for more appropriate uses, we get both more bananas and more of other goods.

The reasons for the confusion are often political. We rightly worry about unemployment and people who lose their jobs because of cheaper imports, yet, as we will see, keeping people at work in industries where the country no longer has a comparative advantage is far from the best way to handle the problem. We also worry that imports may cause us to lose technologies that are critical to our commercial future or our military might. Both issues are taken up in Chapters 5 and 6.

▲ The single most important determinant of trade patterns is the opportunity cost of producing traded goods. Countries that sacrifice the least amount of alternative production when producing a particular good have the lowest opportunity cost, or a comparative advantage. The idea of comparative advantage has been one of the most enduring concepts of economic thought and has been a central theme in international economic policy since the mid-1800s.

▲ Nations that produce according to their comparative advantage are maximizing the benefits they receive from trade and, consequently, their national welfare. This is the same as maximizing their gains from trade.

▲ Comparative advantage is often confused with absolute advantage. The latter refers to the advantage a nation has if its absolute productivity in a particular product is greater than its trading partners. It is not necessary to have an absolute advantage in order to have a comparative advantage.

▲ One common fallacious argument against following comparative advantage is that workers in other countries are paid less than American workers. This argument neglects the issue of productivity. Developing-country wages are lower because the value of output from one hour of labor is less. Labor productivity is less because workers are generally less skilled, they have less capital on the job, and they have less capital in the surrounding economy to support their on-the-job productivity.

▲ Businesspeople and economists look at the issue of trade differently because they have different objectives in mind. Businesspeople are often concerned about their ability to compete— that is, to sell a particular item in a given market at the lowest price. Their perspective is that of the firm. Economists focus on the efficient use of resources at the national or global level. The perspective is that of all firms taken together.

Vocabulary

absolute productivity advantage

autarky

comparative productivity advantage

competitive advantage

economic restructuring

gains from trade

labor productivity

mercantilism

opportunity cost

price line

production possibilities curve (PPC)

relative price

trade adjustment assistance

trade line

zero sum

Study Questions

1. Use the information in the following table on labor productivities in France and Germany to answer the questions.

Output per hour worked		
	France	*Germany*
Cheese	2 kilograms	1 kilogram
Cars	0.25	0.5

    a) Which country has an absolute advantage in cheese? In cars?

    b) What is the relative price of cheese in France if it does not trade? In Germany if it does not trade?

    c) What is opportunity cost of cheese in France? In Germany?

    d) Which country has a comparative advantage in cheese? In cars? Show how you know.

    e) What is the upper and lower bound for the trade price of cheese?

    f) Draw a hypothetical PPC for France, and label its slope. Suppose that France follows its comparative advantage in deciding where to produce on its PPC. Label its production point. If the trade price of cars is 5 kilos of cheese per car, draw a trade line showing how France can gain form trade.

2. Explain how a nation can gain from trade even though not everyone is made better off. Isn't this a contradiction?

3. Economic nationalists in America worry that international trade is destroying out economy. A common complaint is that agreements like NAFTA (North American Free Trade Agreement) open our economy to increased trade with countries such as Mexico, where workers are paid a fraction of what they earn in the United States. Explain the faulty logic of this argument.

4. Many people believe that the goal of international trade should be to create jobs. Consequently, when they see workers laid off due to a firm's inability to compete against cheaper and better imports, they assume that trade must be bad for the economy. Is this assumption correct? Why, or why not?

5. Suppose that the Untied States decides to become self sufficient in bananas and even to export them. In order to accomplish these goals, large tax incentives are granted companies that will invest in banana production. Soon, the American industry is competitive and able to sell bananas at the lowest price anywhere. Does the U.S. have a comparative advantage? Why, or why not? What are the consequences for the overall economy?

Suggested Reading

Blaug, Mark. "Adam Smith," and "David Ricardo," *Economic Theory in Retrospect*. Cambridge, MA: Cambridge University Press, 1978.

Dertouzos, Michael, Richard Lester, and Robert Solow. *Made in America: Regaining the Productive Edge*. Cambridge, MA: MIT Press, 1989.

Greenaway, David, ed. *Current Issues in International Trade*. New York: St. Martin Press, 1996.

King, Philip, ed. *International Economics and International Economic Policy: A Reader*. New York: McGraw Hill, 1995.

Krugman, Paul. "Competitiveness: A Dangerous Obsession," *Pop Internationalism*. Cambridge, MA: MIT Press, 1996.

———, "What Do Undergrads Need to Know about Trade?," *op. cit.*

CHAPTER 4

MODERN TRADE THEORY

Introduction

The theory presented in Chapter 3 did not consider the determinants of comparative advantage. It was assumed that countries had different levels of productivity, but the reasons why one country might be more productive than another in a particular line of production was never analyzed. In this chapter, the idea of comparative advantage is examined in more detail, beginning with the factors that determine it. We will also examine the impact of trade on income distribution. In the simple model in Chapter 3, it was assumed that everyone that wanted a job could find one and that after trade began, anyone laid off from the shrinking industry found employment in the expanding one. There is often significant opposition to expanded trade, however, because some people fear that increased trade will downsize their industry, and they do not view themselves as having options for employment in the expanding sectors. We also saw that trade causes the price of the export good to rise and the price of the import good to fall, making the nation as a whole better off. In reality, we consume both export and imports goods, and the fact that the nation is better off may not reflect your individual circumstances if your consumption is heavily weighted toward the export good.

We will also discuss the idea that not all trade is motivated by comparative advantage. For example, a majority of the trade between the United States and Canada (the world's largest bilateral trade relationship) is cars and car parts. In other words, we export the same thing we import. Furthermore, some of the United States' trade with developing countries appears at first to be based on something other than comparative advantage because in many cases we import relatively high-tech goods, such as semiconductors and VCRs. We will look at these cases where, at first glance, comparative advantage appears not to play a role.

Modern Trade Theory

In Chapter 3, comparative advantage depended on each country's relative productivity, and those were given by assumption at the start of the exercise. Smith and Ricardo thought that each country would have its own technology, its own climate, and its own resources, and that differences between nations would give rise to productivity differences. In the twentieth century, several economists have developed a more detailed explanation of trade in which the productivity differences of each country depend on the country's endowments of the inputs (called factors of production or, simply, factors) that are used to produce each good. The theory has various names: the Heckscher-Ohlin theory (HO), the Heckscher-Ohlin-Samuelson theory, or the Factor Proportions theory. They all refer to the same set of ideas.

The Heckscher-Ohlin (HO) Trade Model

The HO trade model begins with the observation that nations are endowed with different levels of each input (factors). Furthermore, each output has a different "recipe" for its production and requires different combinations and levels of the various inputs. Steel production, for example, requires a lot of iron ore, coking material, semiskilled labor, and some expensive capital equipment. Clothing production requires unskilled and semiskilled workers with rudimentary capital equipment in the form of sewing machines.

In order to analyze how the availability of inputs creates productivity differences, we must first define **factor abundance** and **factor scarcity**. The hypothetical example in Table 4.1 illustrates these concepts. The United States' capital-labor ratio (K_{us}/L_{us}) is $^{50}/_{150}$ or $\frac{1}{3}$. In Canada, K_{can}/L_{can} is $^{5}/_{10}$ or $\frac{1}{2}$. Since Canada's capital-labor ratio is higher ($K_{can}/L_{can} > K_{us}/L_{us}$, or $\frac{1}{2} > \frac{1}{3}$), we call Canada the capital-abundant country. With just two inputs, Canada is also the labor-scarce country. Note that Canada is capital abundant relative to the United States even though it has only $\frac{1}{10}$ the absolute quantity of capital. However, each Canadian worker is better equipped with capital than each American worker, and this makes Canada *relatively* better endowed with capital.

Relative abundance of a factor implies that its relative cost is less than in counties where it is relatively scarce. Conversely, relatively scarce resources are more expensive. Consequently, capital is relatively cheap in Canada and labor is relatively expensive. It follows that economies have relatively lower costs in the production of goods where the "recipe" calls for greater quantities of the abundant factor and smaller quantities of the scarce factor. In this example, the United States will have a lower opportunity cost in production that uses relatively more labor and relatively less capital, while Canada's opportunity cost will be lower in production that uses relatively more capital and less labor.

The Heckscher-Ohlin trade theory makes exactly this point. It asserts that a country's comparative advantage lies in the production of goods that use relatively

TABLE 4.1 An Example of Factor Abundance		
	United States	*Canada*
Capital	50 machines	5 machines
Labor	150 workers	10 workers

abundant factors. In other words, comparative advantage is determined by a nation's factor endowment, and once this is determined, it should be possible to predict exported goods. (It is also possible to predict imported goods because the model is symmetric.)

> **Heckscher-Ohlin Theory.** *Countries have a comparative advantage in goods with production requirements that intensively use the relatively abundant factors of production. Conversely, countries will not have a comparative advantage in goods with production requirements that intensively use the relatively scarce factors of production.*

To clarify this idea, let's consider the United States: What are its abundant factors, and what are the characteristics of the goods the United States is likely to export? The United States is richly endowed with a wide variety of factors. It has natural resources in the form of rich farmland and extensive forests. It has highly skilled labor, such as scientists, engineers, and managers. Although savings rates are not very high, the wealth of the nation has enabled it to create an abundance of physical capital, both public and private. Its exports, therefore, should include agricultural products, particularly those requiring skilled labor and physical capital, and all sorts of machinery and industrial goods that require intensive input of physical capital and scientific and engineering skills.

One leading U.S. export is commercial jet aircraft—a product that requires a vast array of physical capital and scientific, engineering, and managerial talent. The United States is also a major exporter of grains and grain products, such as vegetable oils. These are produced with relatively small labor inputs, very large capital inputs (combines, tractors, etc.), farmland, and a great deal of scientific research and development that has produced hybrid seeds, pesticides, herbicides, and so forth.

Gains from Trade in the HO Model

In the Ricardian model we assumed that each country faced a constant set of trade-offs: 2 loaves of bread for 3 tons of steel (United States) or 3 loaves of bread for 1 ton of steel (Canada). The constant costs of the Ricardian model stemmed from the fact that there was one homogeneous input: labor. Labor could be used to make bread or steel. Workers did not vary in their skills, and since there was no capital input, each worker was as productive as the next. Consequently, when labor was reallocated from bread to steel, or vice versa, the tradeoff was always at a constant rate.

In the HO model, we have a multiplicity of inputs—labor, capital, farmland, and so forth—so each worker may be equipped with a different quantity of supporting inputs, such as capital. Obviously, at the end of the day, a worker with a $5 shovel will have dug a smaller hole than one equipped with a $150,000 earth-moving machine. Furthermore, the quality of labor and capital can vary in addition to its quantity. Some labor is skilled, and some is unskilled. Certain jobs require scientific or other technical training, while others require only basic literacy or even less. Similarly, capital can be low or high tech, and resources like farmland have different fertility and climate characteristics. In effect, each important qualitative difference can be treated as a key characteristic of a separate input, so unskilled and skilled labor can be considered different factors.

If we have multiple inputs with various suitabilities for different tasks, we can no longer assume a PPC with constant costs. Rather, the economy is assumed to have increasing costs, implying that each country has a rising opportunity cost for each type of production. Consequently, as the United States or Canada moves labor, capital, and land into bread production, each additional unit of bread leads to a greater loss of steel output than the one before. The reason is straightforward: If we want more bread, we take resources out of steel. In doing so, the optimal strategy is to move resources that are relatively good at bread production but poor at steel production. This leads to the greatest gain in bread with the smallest loss of steel. The next shift in production, toward more bread, cuts deeper into the stock of resources used for steel production, and in all likelihood there will not be resources to move that are as good at bread and as poor at steel as the previous production shift. Consequently, in order to get the same increase in bread, we give up more steel than before. This result is symmetric, so shifts going the other way, toward more steel, cause the opportunity cost of steel to rise with each shift. Figure 4.1 illustrates a PPC with increasing costs.

As with constant costs, the tradeoff between bread and steel is equal to the slope of the PPC. Since the PPC is curved, its slope changes at every point, and we must measure the tradeoff at the point of production. For example, in Figure 4.2, if the United States is producing at point A, then the opportunity cost of an additional ton of steel is equivalent to the slope of the PPC at point A. Since the PPC is a curve rather than a straight line, the slope is measured by drawing a tangent line at the point of production and measuring its slope.

Most of the analysis of the gains from trade in Chapter 3 carry over into the HO model. In order to demonstrate this, assume that point A is the U.S. production point in autarky and that at point A the opportunity cost of steel is 0.67 loaves of bread. This means that the slope of the tangent at A is −0.67. Also assume that Canada's opportunity cost of steel is above the United States' at 3 loaves of bread per ton, the same as before. Within the framework of the HO model, we can now

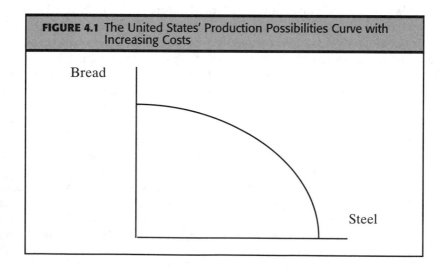

FIGURE 4.1 The United States' Production Possibilities Curve with Increasing Costs

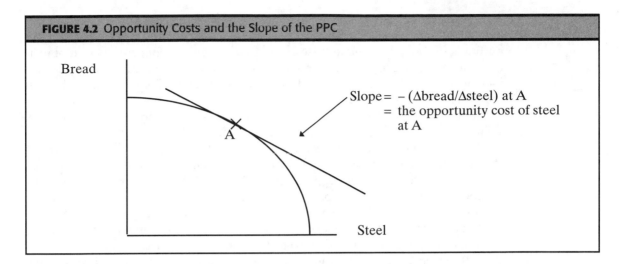

FIGURE 4.2 Opportunity Costs and the Slope of the PPC

describe the source of these productivity differences. The United States is relatively well endowed with inputs used to make steel, while Canada is relatively well endowed with bread-making inputs.

Also assume that after trade begins, the world price, or trade price, for steel is 2 loaves of bread per ton of steel, the same as the example in Chapter 3. As before, this would follow if Canada's autarky price was greater than 2. After trade opens, the United States can continue to produce at A and not trade, or it can produce at A and trade. Figure 4.3 illustrates the possibilities if the United States stays at point A on its PPC.

TT is the price line with slope -2 passing through A and showing the combinations of bread and steel that are available when production is at A and trade is possible. In Figure 4.3, TT′ is a trade line that is tangent to the PPC at point B, an alternative production point to the right of A and closer to the steel axis. If the United States

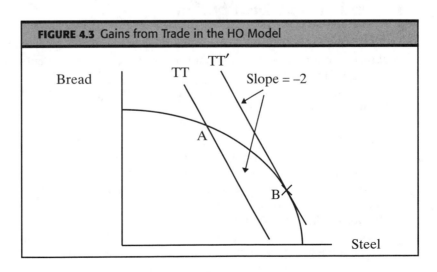

FIGURE 4.3 Gains from Trade in the HO Model

exploits its comparative advantage and shifts toward increased steel production, higher costs come into play. This is the same as saying that the marginal cost of steel output is rising. As production rises, the gap between the opportunity cost of production and the trade price narrows until finally, at point B, they are equal. Further increases in steel production would push the cost above its value in trade and, therefore, are not warranted.

At point B, the opportunity cost of steel equals its trade price. Since the model is symmetric and the opportunity cost and trade price of bread is the inverse of the steel, the same equivalency holds for bread. To the left of B, the opportunity cost of steel (bread) is less (greater) than the trade price, so more (less) production is warranted. To the right of B, the opportunity cost of steel (bread) is greater (less) than the trade price, so less (more) production is warranted. Only at point B does the opportunity cost equal the trade price. Since no other changes can make the United States better off, point B is the production combination that maximizes U.S. income.

Graphically, the superiority of point B can be seen by first comparing B to A. Point B is clearly superior to A in terms of the consumption possibilities because for every point along TT there is another point on TT′ that offers more of both goods. That is, TT′ lies above and to the right of TT. Since a greater combination of both goods is available if the United States produces at B and trades, B is superior to A. Furthermore, when the trade price is 2, every other production point along the PPC leads to smaller consumption bundles. That is, at any other production point, a trade line with a slope of -2 that passes through the point will lie below and to the left of TT′, representing smaller combinations of steel and bread. Consequently, point B maximizes U.S. income by creating the largest possible consumption bundle.

The notion of gains from trade in the HO model is nearly the same as the Ricardian model. The only significant difference is that in the HO model, specialization is not complete. The United States continues to make some bread, and Canada makes some steel.

Trade and Income Distribution

Recall that in the Ricardian model of comparative advantage, the nation as a whole gained from trade, and, by assumption, we ruled out the potentially harmful effects of trade on some members of society. When trade began, the economy shifted from one point on its production frontier to a different point. Workers that were affected by the production shift simply moved out of the declining industry and into the expanding one. Everyone had the same skills, and each type of production required only labor, so everyone had access to a job, and everyone benefited from both the fall in the price of the imported good and the rise in the price of the exported one.

The Heckscher-Ohlin trade model is a more sophisticated way to analyze the gains and losses from trade because it drops these unrealistic assumptions. Labor can be divided into two or more skill categories, other types of inputs can be included, and industries can require different mixes of the various inputs. Under these more realistic assumptions, it can be shown that while trade benefits the nation as a whole, some groups within the nation benefit more than others, and some will actually be harmed. Furthermore, it can be shown that there is a systematic relationship between the factor endowments of a country and the winners and losers from trade. Opening the discussion to an analysis of winners and losers adds an important and necessary element of realism. We are all aware that not everyone favors increased trade, and without an analysis of trade's income distribution effects, we have no basis for understanding the opposition to increased trade.

The Stolper-Samuelson Theorem

The analysis begins by recognizing that everyone's income depends on the inputs he or she supplies to the economy. Labor earns wages that may be high or low depending on the skill level; owners of capital earn profits; landowners earn rents. The amount of income earned per unit of input depends on the demand for the inputs as well as their supply. The demand for a particular input is sometimes referred to as a **derived demand**, since it is derived indirectly from the demand for the output it is used to produce. If the output is in high demand, and consequently its price is high, then the inputs that are used to produce it will benefit by receiving higher returns.

In general, any change in the economy that alters the price of outputs will have a direct impact on incomes. We have seen that trade causes output prices to change. Specifically, the price of the export good rises, while the price of the import falls. The movement of prices causes a change in the demand for each factor and leads to a change in the returns paid to each factor. Hence, trade impacts income distribution.

When trade begins and output prices change, resources leave the sector that produces imported goods and move into the sector that produces exports. In the HO model, unlike the simple Ricardian model, different goods are produced with different combinations of inputs, so the movement along the production possibilities frontier causes a change in the demand for each input. Factors that are used intensively in the imported goods sector will find that the demand for their services has shrunk—and so has their income. Conversely, factors used intensively in the export sector will experience an increase in the demand for their services and in their incomes. In sum, when trade begins, incomes of the factors used intensively in the import sector fall, and incomes of the factors used intensively in the export sector rise.

These effects are summarized in the Stolper-Samuelson theorem, which is derived from the HO theory. The Stolper-Samuelson theorem says that an increase in the price of a good raises the income earned by factors that are used intensively in its production. Conversely, a fall in the price of a good lowers the income of the factors it uses intensively.

> *The Stolper-Samuelson theorem. The Stolper-Samuelson theorem is derived from the Heckscher-Ohlin trade model. It says that if the price of a good rises, then the income of factors used intensively in its production rises also. Conversely, if the price of a good falls, then the income of factors used intensively in its production falls.*

Figure 4.4 illustrates these tendencies. Suppose that the United States and Canada can make bread or computers, using capital and labor. Suppose also that bread is the labor-intensive product,

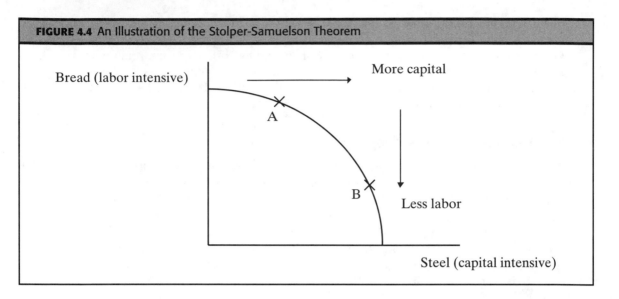

FIGURE 4.4 An Illustration of the Stolper-Samuelson Theorem

$$K^b/L^b < K^s/L^s$$

and the United States is relatively well endowed with capital, compared to Canada.

$$K_{can}/L_{can} < K_{us}/L_{us}$$

According to the HO theory, the United States will have a comparative advantage in steel, which it will export in return for Canadian bread. In Figure 4.4, after trade begins, the United States moves along its PPC toward the steel axis from point A to point B.

As the United States shifts along its PPC, the change in the mix of goods produced leads to lower demands for labor and higher demands for capital. The steel industry will pick up some of the labor laid off in the bread industry, but since it is not as labor intensive as bread, its increase in demand for labor is less than the fall in demand in the bread industry. The net result is that labor in both industries experiences a fall in demand, leading to a fall in wages and income earned. Note that Stolper-Samuelson does not state that all the factors used in the export industries are better off, nor that all the factors used in the import-competing industry get hurt. Rather, the abundant factor that is used to determine comparative advantage and exports is favored, and the scarce factor sees a decline in its income, regardless of industry.

The Stolper-Samuelson theorem is a starting point for understanding the income distribution effects of trade, but it only tells part of the story. An extension of the theorem, called the **magnification effect**, shows that the change in output prices has a magnified effect on factor incomes. For example, if after opening trade, bread prices declined by 75 percent, then the fall in labor income will be greater than 75 percent. Similarly, if the price of an export good (steel) rises by, say, 50 percent, incomes earned by the intensively used factors in the export sector (capital) rise more than 50 percent.

The magnification effect.   *Changes in goods prices have a magnified effect on the incomes of factors used intensively in their production. If an output price rises (falls), the percentage change in the income of the intensively used factor will rise (fall) by a larger percentage.*

The ultimate effects on income of an opening of trade depend on the flexibility of the affected factors. If labor is stuck in bread production and unable to move to the steel sector, it could be hurt much worse than if it were completely flexible to move. Another example illustrates this point: within the debate over U.S.-Mexico free trade, there is a small but intense controversy surrounding avocado production. Mexico has a comparative advantage in avocados because it is well endowed with the necessary inputs (a particular quality of land and climate, together with unskilled labor and a little capital). If free trade were to open in the avocado market, the owners of avocado orchards in California would find their investments in land, equipment, and avocado trees worthless. Why would anyone pay $1 or more per avocado when Mexican ones sell for 25¢ or less? However, many of the California avocado groves are located in the suburbs of sprawling metropolitan regions, and presumably, if the land were worthless for avocado production, it could be put to valuable use in another line of production—for example, as housing developments. Consequently, the income of the landowners may not decline in the long run, although in the short run, they may be unable to put their land to an alternative use. In order to build these considerations into a trade model, we must turn now to a short-run version of the HO model.

The Specific Factors Model

In the short run, the ability of factors to move between different output sectors is more limited. For example, suppose stiffer competition in the world steel industry causes American steelworkers to take pay cuts, and perhaps some lose their jobs. In the long run, most of the laid-off steelworkers will find jobs outside the steel sector, but in the short run, they are stuck with cuts in pay and layoffs. Similarly, physical capital is usually dedicated to a particular use and cannot be converted into producing a different product, and, as we have seen, land is usually tied up in a particular kind of use and cannot be switched to something else instantaneously. In the long run, however, plants and equipment can be redirected to a different line of production, land can be put to different uses, and workers find jobs doing something else.

In order to highlight the ability of labor and other factors to find alternative employment in the long run but not in the short run, economists sometimes add conditions to the HO model. Suppose there are three factors—land, labor, and capital—and two goods—steel and bread. Assume that the production of steel takes capital and labor, while bread takes land and labor. In this version of the HO model, labor is called the variable factor because its use varies between both goods. Land and capital are called the specific factors because their use is specific to bread and steel, respectively.

The model just described is an example of the **specific factors model,** a special case of the HO model. The difference is that the HO model assumes that factors mi-

TABLE 4.2 A Specific Factors Model		
	Outputs	
Inputs	**Bread**	**Steel**
Specific factors	Land	Capital
Variable factors	Labor	Labor

grate easily from one sector to another, from steel to bread, for example. In the specific factors model, each good is produced with a specific factor, whose only use is in the production of that good, and a variable factor, which is used to produce both goods. The specific factors (land and capital) are immobile and cannot move between bread and steel, while the variable factor (labor) is completely mobile between industries.

The determinants of comparative advantage with a specific factors model is similar to the analysis with a HO model. As with HO, comparative advantage depends on factor endowments. The main difference in the two models is that the specific factor plays a critical role. Suppose that Canada is relatively well endowed with land and the United States is relatively well endowed with capital. Then Canada exports bread, and the United States exports steel. The reasoning is the same as with the HO model. Since Canada is well endowed with the specific factor used to make bread, its opportunity cost of bread production is lower than it is in the United States, where land is relatively less abundant. Similarly, steel uses capital, which is abundant in the United States and relatively scarce in Canada.

The analysis of the income distribution effects of trade is straightforward. When trade opens, each country follows its comparative advantage and moves toward greater specialization. The shift in production alters the demand for the specific factor that is used in the industry that shrinks. In each country, the specific factor in the declining industry experiences a fall in income. For example, Canada cuts back on steel production in order to concentrate on bread, which it exports for steel. Canadian owners of capital are hurt, since the structure of the economy changes away from the production of capital-intensive steel, while Canadian landowners experience precisely the opposite effect. Their incomes rise as the demand for land to produce bread exports rises. In the United States, landowners lose and capital owners win.

In this example, the income distribution effects of trade on labor, the variable factor, are indeterminate. Since labor is mobile, workers laid off in the declining sector find employment in the expanding sector. Canadian workers find that steel is cheaper, so they are better off to the extent they consume products that embody steel. On the other hand, the fact that the world price of bread is above the price Canadians paid in autarky means that they are worse off to the extent that their income goes to buy bread. The net effect on Canadian labor depends on which effect is strongest, rising bread prices or falling steel prices. U.S. workers face rising steel prices and falling bread prices, and, again, the net effect is ambiguous and depends on their consumption patterns.

CASE STUDY

Forecasts of Winners and Losers Under NAFTA

When the United States, Mexico, and Canada began negotiations over the North American Free Trade Agreement, one of the major issues in the United States was the effect of free trade on the livelihood of various groups. The Heckscher-Ohlin trade model, the Stolper-Samuelson theorem, and the specific factors model were each used to analyze this effect.

Since the United States and Canada are similarly endowed with labor, capital, and land, and since they began a free-trade arrangement in 1989 (the Canadian-United States Trade Agreement, or CUSTA), NAFTA was not expected to significantly affect U.S.–Canadian trade. Mexico, however, was a different case. Where the United States and Canada have relatively abundant supplies of skilled labor, including scientists, engineers, managers, technicians, and professionals, Mexico has shortages of skilled labor and an abundant supply of unskilled and semiskilled labor. In addition, capital is relatively abundant in the United States and Canada and relatively scarce in Mexico. Finally, Mexico's climate and soils make it a good location to produce many kinds of fruits and vegetables, but it is a poor location for grains.

Given these simple observations, it was relatively straightforward to estimate the winners and losers in a U.S.-Mexico trade agreement. Mexican industries that were expected to pose the greatest challenge to the United States were the ones that combined the experience of Mexico's relatively scarce entrepreneurs and managers with its abundant supply of unskilled and semiskilled labor. To the extent that these industries could avoid large inputs of capital, they were likely to be even more competitive.

One of the first industries that was expected to gain was Mexico's small, but significant, apparel industry. Clothing manufacture requires little capital, some managerial expertise to obtain orders for clothing and insure their timely delivery to purchasers, and an abundant supply of relatively less-skilled labor. (The fashion design industry is another matter. The focus here is on basic, standardized apparel, such as undershirts or socks.) In the United States, large sections of this industry exist only as a result of U.S. quotas on imports. Consequently, many long-run forecasts of the impacts of NAFTA on U.S. garment workers were negative. Unions in the apparel industry were cognizant of this fact, and they formed one of the strongest bases of opposition to NAFTA. In effect, labor in the apparel industry viewed itself as a specific factor that, given their skills and location, was unable to shift to another line of employment.

Industries that are similar to clothing manufacturing are leather goods, furniture, and building materials (stone, clay, and glass manufacturers). Each requires some material inputs (wood, cloth, leather, stone, and so on), less capital than in more advanced manufacturing processes, and a lot of basic labor.

In the area of agriculture, it was forecast that some labor-intensive fruit and vegetable crops would expand into Mexico and contract in the United States.

Case Study continues

Case Study continued

These included frozen vegetables such as broccoli and cauliflower, and citrus crops such as oranges for frozen juice. Not surprisingly, Florida citrus growers and California avocado growers both opposed the agreement. As owners of specific factors (citrus and avocado groves), they had no alternative uses for their land.

On the other hand, U.S. crops that were capital rather than labor intensive were expected to benefit. Notable examples are cereals, both for human and animal consumption, and oilseeds. These crops use enormous quantities of agricultural machinery, together with extensive land inputs and a favorable climate to produce grains and legumes at prices that are competitive with the best in the world. In Mexico, producers of corn opposed the agreement.

A second type of industry that feared more open competition with Mexico was basic manufacturing. Industries included in this category are automobiles, some kinds of industrial machinery (e.g., pumps, diesel engines, electrical motors), and fabricated metal products, such as screws and fasteners. The capital requirements for production are much higher in these areas, but the products are so well established that there is little input of skilled labor in scientific research or product development. The labor used in the manufacturing process is more skilled than agricultural labor but can be trained on the job as long as it is literate.

An example of the opposition to NAFTA in the area of basic manufacturing is the autoworkers' union. Automobile manufacturing requires more capital than clothing or furniture, but many autoworkers feared that under the terms of a more open North American market, U.S. automakers would relocate their capital in Mexico where unskilled and semiskilled labor are relatively abundant and inexpensive. Autoworkers viewed alternatives to their current employment as dismal, and for that reason they formed one of the strongest blocs against NAFTA. Although they were not able to stop the agreement, they were instrumental in the creation of an expanded federal program for assisting workers whose livelihoods were harmed by the agreement.

In reality, the net effect of trade opening in basic manufacturing is ambiguous. Mexico's ability to compete depends on a number of additional factors in the wider economy. For example, auto assembly requires delivery to the factory of thousands of parts. If they must come all the way from Detroit or Windsor, Ontario, it may be uneconomical to assemble cars in Mexico. (Forecasts are that the Mexican car industry will grow over time, but there is a debate as to whether this will be at the expense of U.S. and Canadian producers or at the expense of European and Japanese firms.) In addition to parts suppliers, these more capital-intensive manufacturing processes depend on the reliable, low-cost transportation and communication systems, along with overall infrastructure, such as power systems, water delivery, and waste disposal.

In the United States and Canada, the industries that were expected to benefit included the very capital-intensive grain and oilseeds industries. In addition, it was expected that a wide variety of more advanced manufacturing industries, including telecommunications, computing, aircraft, measuring and control devices, chemicals, and so on, would see growing markets. Furthermore, a number

Case Study continues

of skilled, high-wage service industries were also expected to expand, including banking, insurance, business services, engineering services, and others. Like advanced manufacturing, each of these service industries requires highly skilled, well-educated labor.

Forecasts of NAFTA's effects on income distribution depend on a number of other assumptions. In the simplest model, the prices of goods produced with abundant unskilled labor should rise in Mexico and fall in the United States, while goods produced with abundant skilled labor and capital should do the opposite. Consequently, in the short to medium run, unskilled labor is the beneficiary in Mexico, and skilled labor and capital benefit in the United States. The losers in Mexico are owners of Mexican capital that cannot move to alternative uses and skilled Mexican labor that likewise has no alternative use. In the United States, unskilled, immobile labor loses.

Two good summaries of these issues are *North American Free Trade: Issues and Recommendations* (1992), by Jeffrey Schott and Gary Clyde Hufbauer, and *North American Free Trade: Assessing the Impact* (1992), edited by Nora Lustig, Barry P. Bosworth, and Robert Z. Lawrence. See also *U.S.-Mexico Trade: Pulling Together or Pulling Apart?* (1992), Congress of the United States, Office of Technology Assessment.

Empirical Tests of the Theory of Comparative Advantage

All the popular theories of trade are variations on the idea of comparative advantage. In addition, each theory makes predictions about the goods that a country will export and import. Therefore, it should be relatively straightforward to test each theory by holding its predictions up to actual trade flows and seeing if the two match. Unfortunately, empirical tests of trade theories are more difficult to conduct than they are to describe. Part of the problem is that it is difficult to measure variables such as factor endowments and prices in autarky.

The trade theories presented in this chapter and in Chapter 3 are the two most popular theories: the Ricardian theory of trade, based on relative productivities, and the Heckscher-Ohlin theory, based on factor endowments. In the Ricardian theory of Chapter 3, comparative advantage depended on relative productivity. This model is easier to test because it is easier to measure labor productivity than factor endowments. Therefore, it is not surprising that statistical tests of the Ricardian theory have been more successful. In general, they have confirmed the hypothesis that trade patterns between pairs of countries are determined to a significant degree by the relative differences in their labor productivities. More specifically, as labor productivity in a particular industry increases, the greater the likelihood the country becomes a net exporter of the good.

Tests of the Heckscher-Ohlin theory of trade have been mixed. One of the problems for any researcher in this area is that it is difficult to obtain a uniform set of measurements of factor endowments. In the presentation of the model in this chapter, only two inputs were considered, although we expanded that to three when we covered the specific factors model. In reality, there are many more than three factors. There are different kinds of labor (unskilled, semiskilled, managerial, technical, and so forth), and there are many varieties of natural resources and capital. None of these categories have standardized definitions, and consequently each type of labor, capital, and natural resource is measured differently in each country. As a result, formal statistical analyses of tests of the HO theory have concluded that measurement errors in the data are a major problem.

Nevertheless, the consensus among economists seems to be that endowments matter, although they are far from the whole story. Even if it were possible to accurately measure factor endowments, technological differences between countries would not be captured, and these can be a significant source of productivity differences. In addition to technology, other important determinants of trade patterns not considered by the factor endowment theory are economies of scale, corporate structure, and economic policy.

While the theory of trade based on factor endowments receives only mixed empirical support, it nevertheless remains the foundation of most economists' thinking about trade. This may seem curious, but there is actually a good reason for it. While factor endowments cannot explain all of the world's trade patterns, they do explain a significant part of it. Therefore it is useful to begin with factor endowments and to supplement this view with other ideas. Perhaps most importantly, the factor endowment schema is a useful way to categorize the income distribution effects of trade. For both these reasons, the HO model and its variations remain at the core of international economics.

Alternative Trade Models

Several alternative trade models are popular in the literature. Each of the three models presented below focuses on an attribute of production in an industry or group of industries that makes them unlike the simple models assumed by the Ricardian and HO models. Two of the three (product cycle and intra-firm trade) are elaborations of the theory of comparative advantage. The third model, trade based on economies of scale and product differentiation, builds on a model that is genuinely different from the factor endowment theory.

The Product Cycle

The product cycle model of trade was developed by Raymond Vernon. The model is an insightful analysis that incorporates ideas about the evolution of manufactured goods and technology. One of its greatest strengths is that it can explain exports of sophisticated manufactured goods from countries that have shortages of skilled labor and capital.

Vernon pointed out that many manufactured products, such as automobiles, VCRs, and semiconductors, go through a product cycle in which the inputs change over time. Initially, when these goods are brand new, there is a great deal of experimentation in both the characteristics of the final product and its manufacturing process. For example, when video machines were first developed for the home market, there was a wide variety of different forms to choose from. There were laser discs, betamax, and VHS, each of which had different sets of options, often even within the same technology. That is, while betamax differed from VHS, the features on a VHS machine were not standardized either.

In this early stage of production, manufacturers need to be near a high-income market, where consumer feedback is greatest. Experimentation with basic design features requires information about the market's reaction. Consequently, there must be both a consumer base with substantial income and skilled marketing to advertise information about the product. In addition, on the input side, experimentation and improvement in design and manufacturing require scientific and engineering inputs, along with capital that is willing to risk failure and an initial period of little or no profits. Both the consumption side and the production side necessitate that product research, development, and initial production take place in industrial countries.

Over time, however, the product begins to leave the early phase of its development and production and enters the middle phase (Figures 4.5 and 4.6). The product itself begins to be standardized in size, features, and manufacturing process. Experimentation with fundamentally new designs begins to wane as product development shifts toward incremental improvements in a basic design. In the middle phase, production begins to shift to countries with low labor costs. Standardized manufacturing routines are increasingly common, using low-skilled and semiskilled labor in assembly-type operations.

Countries reach the late phase of the product cycle when consumption in high-income nations begins to exceed production. At this point, an increasing share of the world's output is moving to developing countries where abundant unskilled and

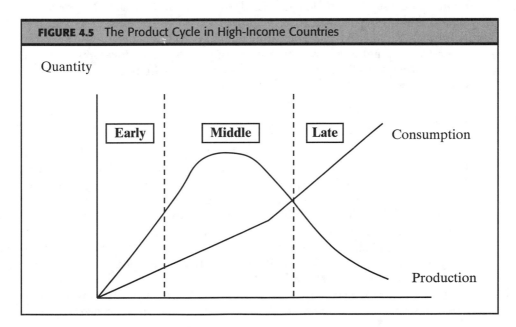

FIGURE 4.5　The Product Cycle in High-Income Countries

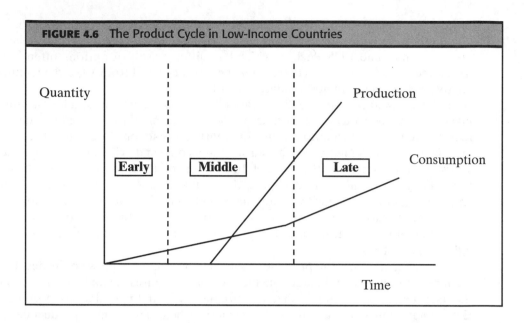

FIGURE 4.6 The Product Cycle in Low-Income Countries

semiskilled labor keep labor costs low. The pressure on high-income countries in the late phase is to turn toward innovation of new products, which starts the cycle over again.

The product cycle is a more elaborate story about technology than either the Ricardian or HO models. It may seem to differ fundamentally from those models, but in fact it is very similar. At its core is a story about opportunity costs. As manufacturing processes become standardized, they can be performed by relatively unskilled labor. In effect, the blend of inputs changes over time, from highly skilled scientific, engineering, and marketing elements to basic unskilled and semiskilled labor. Consequently, the opportunity cost of production in developing countries becomes lower than the cost in high-income countries. In essence, it's the Ricardian story once again.

Intra-firm Trade

Advances in transportation and communications have played an important part in the development of a product cycle. Jet aircraft, container ships, fax machines, satellite systems, and e-mail have enabled firms in Japan, Taiwan, or the United States to relocate part of their production far from their home base of operations. Goods produced in Guangdong province in China or along the U.S.-Mexican border in Ciudad Juarez, can be monitored from a home base in Chicago or Osaka. As a result, a significant share of world trade is international trade between a parent company and a foreign-owned affiliate, called **intra-firm trade**. An example is U.S. exports of Toyota Camrys from Toyota of America to Toyota in Japan.

Intra-firm trade occurs for several reasons. When a firm spreads its production across international boundaries, it can take advantage of differences in the price of

CASE STUDY

U.S.-China Trade

China is the world's most populous nation, with more than 1.2 billion people in mid-1995, according to the World Bank. It is also one of the world's poorest nations. The World Bank puts it GNP per capita at the equivalent of $620 (at market exchange rates, 1995). About 20 percent of China's adults are estimated to be illiterate.

China's economy was substantially closed to the outside until 1978, when it began significant economic reforms. Initially, the reforms were limited to agriculture, but they quickly incorporated a number of special economic zones in the coastal regions (see Chapter 16). China's proximity to Hong Kong, along with large populations of Chinese in Taiwan, Hong Kong, Singapore, and other regions of East Asia, enabled it to attract huge amounts of foreign investment once it became receptive to capital inflows. The net result is that its economy and, especially, its exports have grown rapidly over the last two decades.

China's resource endowment includes a huge population of unskilled and semiskilled labor and a relative scarcity of scientific and engineering talent. It is not surprising, therefore, that its exports are heavily weighted toward labor-intensive manufactured goods. Table 4.2 lists the top ten Chinese exports to the United States in 1996. The major items are simple manufactured goods that use China's abundant labor together with a little capital: toys, shoes, apparel, and so forth. In the top ten, items 1, 2, 3, 5, 6, and 8 fall into this category.

TABLE 4.2 Top Ten Chinese Exports to the United States, 1996

Item	Dollar Value (Millions of $)
1. Baby carriages, toys, games, sporting goods	8,015
2. Footwear	6,392
3. Women's/girls' coats, capes, etc.	2,099
4. Telecommunications equipment	1,951
5. Trunks, suitcases, etc.	1,670
6. Articles of plastic	1,591
7. Radio broadcast receivers	1,571
8. Miscellaneous articles of apparel	1,555
9. Parts for office machines and data processing machines	1,439
10. Data processing machines	1,431

Source: Department of Commerce, *United States Foreign Trade Highlights, 1997.* http://www.ita.doc.gov/otea/, August 1997.

Case Study continues

Case Study continued

Item 7 might also be categorized as producing a relatively unsophisticated product with labor-intensive manufacturing.

Items 4, 9, and 10, however, appear to be different. These are high-tech items related to telecommunications and computing (data processing), and they also illustrate the product cycle. These Chinese exports originate in assembly operations, many of which have been set up with capital from outside China. A telephone manufacturer, for example, decides to take advantage of low wages by producing a standardized product in China. Once the assembly plant is built, only a handful of skilled workers are required to keep it running. Most workers can be quickly trained to fasten together pieces and to perform simple diagnostic tests on the product. The result is that China exports telecommunications equipment and appears to have a developing high-technology sector. No design, research, or industrial engineering takes place there, however.

Similarly, several decades ago, plastics and radio receivers (items 6 and 7) were exclusively products of industrial countries. They became standardized, along with the methods for producing them, and production migrated to places where unskilled labor was relatively more abundant. In sum, China's successful export drive has utilized two forces: a shift toward its comparative advantage and the product cycle.

inputs. Unskilled labor is abundant in China, for example, so by locating assembly processes there, manufacturers are able to significantly reduce their direct labor costs. A second reason for intra-firm trade is to reduce the costs of intermediate inputs that are obtained in foreign markets. For example, an American manufacturer may find that it can reduce the price and secure a more continuous flow of quality inputs if it goes through a foreign subsidiary rather than buying the inputs from wholly independent foreign firms. And finally, intra-firm trade is also a means to reduce distribution costs. A manufacturer may find it cheaper to work with distributors that it owns than with independent firms.

Recent estimates indicate that in 1994 about one-third of U.S. merchandise exports and about two-fifths of U.S. merchandise imports take place in the context of intra-firm trade. The proportions vary significantly by country, however. For example, U.S. intra-firm trade with Mexico is about 26 percent of U.S. merchandise exports to Mexico (1992) and 35 percent of imports. U.S. intra-firm trade with Germany (exports, 40 percent; imports, 60.5 percent) and Canada (exports, 41 percent; imports, 47 percent) are slightly higher and with Japan (exports, 70 percent; imports, 71 percent) are significantly higher.

In many respects, intra-firm trade may be another elaboration of the idea of comparative advantage through the product cycle. For example, Sony and Sanyo decide to assemble televisions in Tijuana, Mexico, where labor costs are low and they are close to the large U.S. market. They keep their research and design labs at home in Japan (or in San Diego, across the border from the assembly operations), however, where engineering and scientific talent are relatively abundant. In this example,

Sony and Sanyo are sharing their production globally in order to take advantage of factor price differences across international boundaries.

However, there are also reasons to believe that a significant share (no one knows how much) of intra-firm trade is not determined by comparative advantage. Firms may locate in a foreign market to deter entry by competitors; to use low production costs for one product line to subsidize production of another product line (cross-subsidization); to subsidize one region's customers by another's; or to escape taxation. In addition, firms may view multiple locations as "insurance" against unforeseen events, such as political upheavals, radical exchange rate fluctuations, and so forth.

There is little consensus among economists about the meaning of all this. On the one hand, it is simply another form of trade, and no special considerations are necessary. On the other hand, the market power and strategic behavior of multinational corporations (MNCs) cause some to argue that this type of trade is significantly different. They argue that since this trade is (partly) unrelated to resource endowments or input costs, it should be viewed through the lens of national industrial regulation and antitrust, or else markets will become less open to competition.

There is one area of agreement, however. As firms spread around the globe, developing affiliates in foreign markets, it becomes increasingly difficult for them to keep their technology proprietary. This is especially true as firms expand the amount of R&D (research and development) that they do abroad. In this regard, there is no doubt that the expansion of MNCs has helped diffuse technology across national boundaries and has undermined the efforts of countries to keep their technology within their own borders.

Intra-industry Trade

In the examples given so far, trade is the export of one good in exchange for the import of a different good. The fact is, however, that much of the world's trade is the export and import of the same good, or **intra-industry trade** (i.e., trade within the same industry). Intra-industry trade may also be intra-firm trade, or alternatively, it may involve products from entirely unrelated firms. For example, the United States' largest export category to Canada is cars and car parts, the same as its largest import category. Often, this trade takes place within a single firm such as Chrysler or General Motors.

Empirical measures of the importance of intra-industry trade vary widely because the definition of any given industry varies. For example, if computers are defined as office machinery, then computers and pencil sharpeners are in the same industry. By this definition, relatively more U.S. trade appears to be intra-industry. Conversely, if very detailed definitions are used, then auto transmissions and auto engines might be defined as different industries, and less U.S. trade appears as intra-industry. Estimates of the share of U.S.-manufactured goods trade that is intra-industry are between one-third and two-thirds. The available evidence suggests that it is probably higher in volatile, high-technology industries, where rapid generation of new products and constant variations of old products lead to greater product differentiation. Intra-industry trade also grows in importance as a nation's income rises.

Intra-industry trade cannot be based on comparative advantage in the Heckscher-Ohlin sense (i.e., due to differences in factor endowments), although parts of it may be due to productivity differences from variations in R&D or technology. This follows from the fact that intra-industry trade is the exchange of similar items, implying similar relative factor endowments. Furthermore, intra-industry trade is greatest between advanced industrial economies, where differences in factor endowments are least.

One of the chief characteristics of intra-industry trade is differentiated products. That is, export and import products are similar in function and are usually close substitutes, but they have individual characteristics that make them distinct. For example, a Canadian minivan may serve many of the same purposes as a U.S.-made sedan, but they are not the same vehicle. Each appeals to different consumer tastes and preferences, and each has its own market niche. Therefore, one of the main benefits of intra-industry trade is that it permits individual firms within an industry to differentiate their products and increase the variety of options and choices available to consumers.

Another characteristic of goods that are traded intra-industry is that they are subject to economies of scale in their production. In other words, as production increases, the cost per unit falls. Consequently, when trade expands the market to include foreign consumers, firms can produce in larger batches and lower the cost per unit, which lowers the price to consumers. This is particularly true for complex machinery such as cars, jet airplanes, and semiconductors, which require huge initial investments in order to get started. In these cases, the greater the volume of output, the lower the average cost.

Intra-industry trade is usually (but not always) less contentious than inter-industry trade, based on differing factor endowments. With intra-industry trade, both countries' industries have opportunities to expand their exports, although the total number of firms may ultimately decline. In the factor-endowment-based trade examples, each country's economy underwent structural changes after trade opened, and some industries shrank while others grew. Politically, this is a more stressful kind of change and often results in greater opposition by sectors of society that expect to lose from the opening of trade.

Trade, Wages, and Jobs in Industrial Countries

Since the 1960s, manufacturing in North America and Europe has become a smaller part of the economy when measured as a share of GDP and as a share of overall employment. In Europe, the assumption that a shrinking manufacturing sector is a significant problem has been emphasized by high rates of overall unemployment and very slow growth in the total number of new jobs created in the economy. At the same time, wage inequality has increased, rather slowly at first, then more rapidly in the 1980s. Wage inequality has been particularly severe in the United States and has primarily affected younger workers and workers with less schooling or fewer skills.

CASE STUDY

U.S.-Canada Trade

In 1965, the United States and Canada implemented a free-trade policy that covered autos and auto parts. The results were dramatic, particularly on the Canadian side of the border. Prior to the Auto Pact, Canada required most cars sold domestically to be made inside the country. The relatively small market in Canada meant that only a few different car models were produced, each in small batches that cost more to make, since automakers could not take full advantage of economies of scale in production. After the Auto Pact, automakers refocused production on a smaller number of models, which were produced for the combined Canadian and U.S. market. Canadian productivity in the automobile industry rose dramatically as the scale of production increased. In addition, as imports from the United States increased, Canadian consumers had many more models to choose from.

Overall, the automobile industry began to completely integrate production in the United States and Canada. Trade between the two countries rose dramatically, and it eventually grew into the largest bilateral trade relationship of any two countries in the world. Table 4.3 illustrates the importance of intra-industry trade.

TABLE 4.3 U.S.–Canadian Merchandise Trade, 1996 (Billions of U.S. Dollars)

Top 7 U.S. Exports	Value	Top 7 U.S. Imports	Value
Motor vehicle parts*	13.6	Cars and other motor vehicles*	25.5
Cars and other motor vehicles*	8.1	Crude oil	7.4
Thermionic, cold cathode, photocathode valves	5.3	Paper and paperboard	7.3
Data processing machinery	5.1	Motor vehicle parts*	6.9
Internal combustion engines*	4.8	Wood	6.5
Trucks, special purpose vehicles*	3.2	Misc. unclassified commodities	6.4
Telecommunications equipment	2.9	Trucks, special purpose vehicles*	6.3

*Represent products related to motor vehicle manufacturing.

Source: Department of Commerce, *United States Foreign Trade Highlights, 1997.* http://www.ita.doc.gov/otea/, August 1997.

Case Study continues

Case Study continued

Four of the top seven U.S. exports to Canada are motor vehicles or related products. Similarly, three of the top seven imports, and an overwhelming share of the value of the top seven imports, are car related. Clearly, intra-industry trade is fundamental to the U.S.-Canadian trade pattern.

It is also interesting to note that the top seven U.S. import products include a number of Canadian exports that take advantage of Canada's rich endowment of forests (paper and wood) and oil. This part of the trade relationship illustrates a traditional pattern based on differing factor endowments.

Many observers question whether the rise in manufactured imports from low-wage, developing economies has something to do with these trends. Could it be that the high-wage, industrialized nations are losing jobs to developing economies and, at the same time, are having their wages forced down in order to remain competitive?

Let's take each trend separately. The first issue is whether trade has a negative impact on the number of jobs available to workers in high-wage countries. Economic theory offers some evidence on this issue. In the medium run and long run, the absolute number of jobs depends mainly on factors such as the age and size of the population, rules governing the hiring and firing of employees (labor market policies), the generosity of the social safety system (incentives to work), and macroeconomic factors such as the level of demand in the economy. In the short run, trade may cause specific firms and industries to decline if they cannot compete; however, as workers are laid off, they are available for hire elsewhere in the economy. In most industrial countries, including the United States, rising unemployment usually causes the central bank to cut interest rates and loosen credit. Consequently, macroeconomic policy is much more likely to determine employment levels than are changes in trade flows that affect one or two manufacturing industries and a relatively small share of our GDP.

The problem of persistently high unemployment in some European countries, such as Spain and France, cannot be caused by trade. While it is possible that some of the lost manufacturing jobs throughout the industrial world have resulted from increased trade flows, the inability of laid-off workers to find new jobs must be attributed to labor market policies that restrict job creation or macroeconomic policies that restrict overall economic growth. Ten or fifteen years of high unemployment, which has been the norm in many European countries, is a long enough time period for even the most radical restructuring to occur. The fact that unemployment remains high means that new jobs are not created elsewhere in the economy.

Furthermore, a majority of the reductions in manufacturing employment in all industrial countries appears to have resulted from productivity gains, not trade. Manufacturing is easier to automate than services (e.g., automating gardening, house cleaning, or health care is very difficult, if not impossible) and as a consequence has much faster rates of productivity growth than services. In essence, because productivity grows so fast in manufacturing, it takes fewer and fewer people to produce the tangible, manufactured products we consume. Many services, on the other hand, have stagnant or very slow rates of productivity growth. Often the same number of workers is required today as it was centuries ago; one haircut, for example, still takes only one barber (who may or may not be faster), and modern musicians are no more "productive" at playing Bach's Brandenburg Concertos than they were in the 1700s. When incomes rise, we consume more services and more manufactured goods, but because the services require more or less the same number of workers per unit made, and manufactured goods can be made with fewer workers per good, a growing share of our total employment ends up in services.

The second issue concerns the impact of trade with less-developed countries (LDCs) on the wages of workers in the advanced industrial economies. This question has been studied by many economists, and the general consensus is that trade may have caused some of the decline in wages for the less skilled (and, hence, some of the increase in wage inequality), but it is responsible for only a small share of the overall changes. The primary culprit seems to be technological changes that have reduced the role of unskilled and semiskilled labor in manufacturing.

The Stolper-Samuelson theorem predicts that if the United States and other industrial countries have relatively scarce supplies of unskilled labor (by comparison to less-developed countries), then trade will cause the wages of unskilled workers to fall. Over the years, however, firms can alter their use of inputs to take advantage of cheaper ones and to conserve on more expensive ones. The key is that the time frame must be sufficiently long so that firms can alter their capital and other inputs. In the case of skilled and unskilled labor the reverse has happened. As skilled labor has become more expensive, firms have used relatively more, and as unskilled labor has become cheaper, they have used less. This trend has gone on for over two decades, so firms have had plenty of time to alter their production technologies, if they can. The only logical explanation is that technology has created larger roles for skilled labor and smaller ones for the unskilled.

While it seems the consensus of professional economic opinion is that technological change and not trade is responsible for the lion's share of both the decline in manufactured jobs and the growth of wage inequality, there is also a widespread recognition that economists really aren't sure. A small number of economists have produced controversial calculations showing that trade has played a far larger role in the growth of wage inequality than is generally recognized. At any rate, the policy conclusions are likely to be the same. Regardless of the causes, there seems to be a greater need for education and training programs targeted at the less skilled. Professional opinion is completely opposed to the idea that society as a whole should give up the gains from trade in order to protect the wages of a subgroup of society.

Conclusion

The theory of comparative advantage based on underlying productivity differences remains one of the most robust ideas in all of economics. Many of the alternatives to Ricardo's simple idea of comparative advantage are, in effect, elaborations and extensions of his model. These elaborations allow economists to incorporate recent phenomena such as the product cycle and intra-firm trade.

The main elaboration of the theory of comparative advantage in the twentieth century was the creation of the Heckscher-Ohlin model. The model provides a powerful analytical approach for determining a nation's comparative advantage. Economists are divided, however, over its empirical relevance. Tests of the Heckscher-Ohlin model are difficult to construct and have a mixed record at successfully predicting trade patterns. Some economists favor the abandonment of the HO model except as a means for analyzing the income distribution effects of trade. Others continue to view it as a part of the foundation of trade theory.

In either case, national differences in productivity or factor endowments cannot account for all trade. The combination of economies of scale and product differentiation have led to tremendous growth in intra-industry trade, particularly between high-income, industrial economies. While subtle differences in technological capability may explain some of this trade, it also depends on the ability of firms to differentiate their product enough so that their competitor's product is not a perfect substitute.

▲ The Heckscher-Ohlin model hypothesizes that comparative advantage is based on national differences in factor endowments. Countries export goods that have production requirements that are intensive in the nation's relatively abundant factors. They import goods that require intensive input from the nation's relatively scarce factors.

▲ The Heckscher-Ohlin model has implications for the income distribution effects of trade. The opening of trade favors the abundant factor and reduces the use of the scarce factor. Consequently, the income or returns earned by the abundant factor rises, while it falls for the scarce factor.

▲ The specific factors model is similar to the HO model. In the specific factors model, some factors of production are assumed to be relatively immobile between different outputs. Consequently, when trade opening expands the production of the export good, the specific factor used to produce the export good experiences a rise in the demand for its services, and its income increases. The specific factor used to produce the import good experiences a fall in demand for its services, and its income declines. The specific factors model can be viewed as a short- to medium-run version of the HO model.

▲ Empirical tests of the theory of comparative advantage give mixed results. While underlying productivity differences explain a significant share of trade, national differences in factor endowments are less successful at explaining trade patterns.

▲ Several alternative trade models have been hypothesized. Most are elaborations of the theory of comparative advantage. Three of the most popular alternative trade theories are the theory of the product cycle, the theory of intra-firm trade, and the theory of intra-industry trade. The product cycle focuses on the speed of technological change and the life history of many manufactured items through periods of innovation, stabilization, and standardization. The theory of intra-firm trade allows a role for comparative advantage but also has industrial organization elements. It is impossible to state a general rule about the determinants of intra-firm trade. The theory of intra-industry trade incorporates the concepts of economies of scale and product differentiation to explain trade patterns. Of the three (product cycle, intra-firm trade, and intra-industry trade) it is the most distinct from the theory of comparative advantage.

▲ In the medium to long run, trade has little or no effect on the number of jobs in a country. The abundance or scarcity of jobs is a function of labor market policies, incentives to work, and the macroeconomic policies of the central bank and government. In the short run, trade may reduce jobs in an industry that suffers a loss in its competitiveness, just as it may increase jobs in an industry with growing competitiveness.

▲ The consensus among economists is that trade between developing and high-income countries may have contributed slightly to the decline in real wages for unskilled workers in the industrial economies. The main culprit, however, is thought to be technological changes that have reduced the demand for unskilled labor and increased it for skilled, highly educated labor. This point is not settled, however, and continues to receive a significant amount of empirical investigation.

Vocabulary

derived demand	intra-industry trade
factor abundance	magnification effect
factor scarcity	product cycle
Heckscher-Ohlin (HO) theory	specific factors model
intra-firm trade	Stolper-Samuelson theorem

Study Questions

1. According to the following table, which country is relatively more labor abundant? Explain how you know. Which country is relatively capital abundant?

	United States	*Canada*
Capital	40 machines	10 machines
Labor	200 workers	60 workers

2. Suppose that the U.S. and Canada have the factor endowments in the preceding table. Suppose further that the production requirements for a unit of steel is two machines and eight workers, and the requirement for a unit of bread is one machine and eight workers.

    a) Which good, bread or steel, is relatively capital intensive? Labor intensive? Explain how you know.
    b) Which country would export bread? Why?

3. Suppose that, before trade takes place, the U.S. is at a point on its PPC where it produces 20 bread and 20 steel. Once trade becomes possible, the price of a unit of steel is two units of bread. In response, the U.S. moves along its PPC to a new point where it produces 30 steel and 10 bread. Is the country better off? How do you know?

4. Given the information in questions 1 and 2, explain what happens to the returns to capital and labor after trade begins.

5. Suppose that there are three factors: capital, labor, and land. Bread requires inputs of land and labor, and steel requires capital and labor.

    a) Which factors are variable, and which are specific?
    b) Suppose Canada's endowments are 10 capital and 100 land and the U.S.'s are 50 capital and 100 land. Which good does each country export?
    c) How does trade affect the returns to land, labor, and capital in the U.S. and in Canada?

6. Describe the changes in production requirements and the location of production that take place over the three phases of the product cycle.

7. Does intra-firm trade contradict the theory of comparitive advantage? Why, or why not?

8. What are the main requirements for intra-industry trade? Is intra-industry trade consistent with the predictions of the Heckscher-Ohlin trade model?

Suggested Reading

Baldwin, Robert. "The Effects of Trade and Foreign Direct Investment on Employment and Relative Wages," *OECD Economic Studies,* No. 23, Winter 1994.

Deardorff, Alan. "Testing Trade Theories and Predicting Trade Flows," *Handbook of International Economics*, edited by R. Jones and P. Kenen. New York: North Holland, 1984.

Freeman, Richard. "Are Your Wages Set in Beijing?," *Journal of Economic Perspectives.* Summer 1995.

Grant, Richard, Maria Papadakis, and J. David Richardson, "Global Trade Flows: Old Structures, New Issues, and Empirical Evidence," *Pacific Dynamism and the International Economic System*, edited by C. Fred Bergsten and Marcus Noland. Institute for International Economics, Washington, D.C., 1993.

Stolper, Wolfgang, and Paul Samuelson. "Protection and Real Wages," *Review of Economic Studies.* November 1941.

Appendix: Finding Trade Data

U.S. Data

Data on U.S. trade in individual commodities are easy to find. The problem for the first-time user of U.S. data is to make sense of the classifications used to categorize goods and services. Export and import statistics are initially collected and compiled into 8000 and 14,000 commodity classifications, respectively. These classifications conform to a standard for classifying goods known as the Harmonized Commodity Description and Coding System, or the Harmonized System (HS). The HS was developed by the Customs Cooperation Council in Brussels, Belgium, and included participants from the United States, Canada, Western Europe, and Japan. The United States and most other developed countries use this system. A source of confusion is that the description of U.S. data in HS format bears the names TSUSA (Tariff Schedule for the United States, Annotated) for imports and Schedule B for exports.

A second system of classifying goods is also used by the United States, the United Nations, and many other nations. This is the Standard International Trade Classification (SITC). The SITC is on its third revision, so it is sometimes called the SITC-Rev. 3. The Harmonized System and the SITC are interrelated, and in effect the SITC scheme is an aggregation of the HS. For example, the United States takes its 8000 HS categories of exports and summarizes them into 3000 SITC categories, which it calls Schedule E. The HS categories for imports are rearranged in SITC codes and called Schedule A. The SITC system is useful for international comparisons and is the form in which the most commonly available U.S. publications present their data.

Table 4.A lists the names used by U.S. publications to label imports and exports, classified according to the HS or SITC system. For example, reading across the row labeled *Exports*, we see that HS export data is called Schedule B and that Schedule E is the rearrangement of the data into SITC format.

Two other commodity classifications are in use, and although they are of lesser importance worldwide, they are relevant for research on the United States. One is another summarization of the HS into what is called the End Use Commodity Category. It consists of 6 principal categories and 140 broad category definitions. Several of the more commonly found U.S. publications use these commodity definitions to summarize reported data. The final classification scheme is the Standard Industrial Classification (SIC) code, which is used to classify industries. SIC code trade data are useful because this is the primary basis on which the United States reports industrial information. Having the trade data on the same basis allows comparisons to be made between industries and for the trade data to be linked up with the characteristics of particular industries.

There are numerous U.S. publications with trade data. They appear in various media, including hardcopy, CD-ROM, computer tape, and online. A complete description can be found in the U.S. Department of Commerce publication, *Guide to Foreign Trade Statistics*. The *Guide* describes the classification systems in use, the publications available, and how to obtain them. The government documents department of any federal depository library should have it. It is also available online through the federal government's subscription data archive, STAT-USA.

	Harmonized System (HS)	Standard International Trade Classification (SITC)
Exports	Schedule B	Schedule E
Imports	Tariff Schedule of the United States, Annotated (TSUSA)	Schedule A

TABLE 4.A U.S. Names for Trade Data Classifications Schemes

Perhaps the easiest source of free online data is located on the Web Server for the International Trade Administration (*http://www.ita.doc.gov*). The ITA servers offer access to annual publications, such as *United States Foreign Trade Highlights*, and several databases. You can find trade by region, by commodity (under the HS, SITC, and SIC classification schemes), and by country. In addition, the ITA site shows exports by state and city.

The hardcopy (and/or microfiche) publications listed below are relatively easy to find sources.

1. FT900 *U.S. Merchandise Trade* and *Supplement*
    This monthly report contains the data that the Bureau of the Census uses to issue its press releases. It summarizes the data in "end-use" form but also reports by principal SITC categories. The *Supplement* appears a few days after the FT900 report and includes data on exports by state and on the basis of SITC and SIC categories.

2. FT925 *Exports, General Imports, and Imports for Consumption*, SITC-Rev. 3, *Commodity by Country*
    This publication is issued monthly and in an annual edition that summarizes the year. Data are in SITC format.

3. FT947 *Exports and General Imports, Six-Digit HS Commodity by Country*
    This annual publication presents the data in HS code format.

4. *National Trade Data Bank (NTDB)*
    The NTDB is available in CD-ROM format and online through STAT-USA (*http://domino.stat-usa.gov/hometest.nsf*). The CD is available by subscription at a moderate price ($59 for one issue, or $575 per year, in 1998). It is updated monthly. Most depository libraries seem to be receiving it. It holds the equivalent of approximately 200,000 pages of information, including HS-classified trade data. When using the HS data ("Exports/Imports by Commodity" and "Exports/Imports by Country" in the NTDB program files), there are descriptions of the classification codes in separate files at the end of the program. These are worth looking at. Another program in the NTDB contains data on annual exports by state. The data are presented in Standard Industrial Classification (SIC) codes and can be compared with various kinds of state-level industrial data, such as the Department of Commerce's *Economic Censuses*, or *County Business Patterns*. The name of the program on the NTDB is the "State of Origin of Exports". It is developed by the Massachusetts Institute for Social and Economic Research (MISER) at the University of Massachusetts, Amherst.

International Data

Most international data are presented in the SITC-Rev. 3 format. The main sources are:

1. *International Trade Statistics Yearbook*
    The *Yearbook* is published by the United Nations, along with the more general *Statistical Yearbook*. The *Yearbook* of trade statistics is more

detailed in its treatment of commodity flows. Goods are classified on the basis of SITC-Rev. 3 codes.

2. *Direction of Trade Statistics (DOTS)*

   DOTS is one of several sister publications of the IMF volumes. The publication schedule is similar, with a different group of countries covered in quarterly installments and an annual *Yearbook* that combines the data on all countries. DOTS is probably the easiest to use, clearly presenting information on how much individual countries trade with other nations. For example, if you want to know how much Mexico trades with Canada and what share of total Mexican trade it represents, the information is there. Annual data for the most recent seven or eight years are presented, along with the percentage changes over the time period. DOTS does not disaggregate the data by commodity.

3. International trade information can also be obtained over the World Wide Web. One of the best sources is at the International Trade Center, a partnership between the WTO and the United Nations Committee on Trade and Development (UNCTAD) to provide trade information. The ITC can be reached through its gopher site at *gopher://iccuc2.unicc.org/ 11/itc/dir3*. Alternatively, it can be reached in hypertext format at *http://www.intracen.org/itc*. After opening the http address, click on infobases, then click on ITC infobases. This links up to the COMTRADE Databank which is maintained by the United Nations Statistical Division. It contains exports and imports by commodity and country for more than 100 countries and is more current than the *International Trade Statistics Yearbook*. It also provides various other sources of trade related information, including charts for each nation showing relative export performance by commodity.

THE THEORY OF TARIFFS
AND QUOTAS

Introduction

Chapters 5 and 6 are an introduction to the theory and policy of tariffs and quotas. In the economics literature, this analysis is called commercial policy. Chapter 5 is an introduction to tariff theory, and Chapter 6 focuses on an empirical estimate of the direct costs of protectionism and the arguments used by proponents of restricted trade. The inefficiency and expense of tariffs and quotas as a means to protect industries and jobs will be apparent after measuring their direct costs.

In general, tariffs have been negotiated down to very low levels in the industrial world, with the partial exception of agriculture, textiles, and apparel. These sectors were excluded from the GATT until the Uruguay Round and continue to have relatively high barriers to trade in many industrial countries. This is an unfortunate situation for many developing countries, which often have a comparative advantage in precisely those areas. Developing countries also differ from the industrial world in that they tend to have much higher levels of protection, but, again, there are numerous exceptions.

Analysis of a Tariff

Barriers to trade come in all shapes and sizes. Some are obvious, or "transparent," whereas others are hidden. Some barriers directly limit the quantity of imports, but others indirectly limit imports by causing the price to rise. Tariffs limit imports by imposing a tax on them. This causes consumers who do not want to pay both the price and the tax to switch to relatively cheaper domestic goods or to drop out of the market altogether. Tariffs also encourage domestic producers to increase their output because demand switches from foreign to domestic goods.

In the analysis that follows, we will be looking at only the effects of tariffs and quotas on the industry in which they are imposed. For example, the economy-wide effect of a tariff in, say, the steel industry will not be analyzed. In the language of economics, the analysis in Chapter 5 is known as partial equilibrium analysis because it considers the effects of tariffs and quotas on only a part of the economy—the market in which the trade barrier is erected. Before we turn to tariff analysis, however, we must first introduce two important concepts, consumer and producer surplus.

Consumer and Producer Surplus

What is the maximum price you would be willing to pay for a gallon of milk? The answer is likely to be different for each consumer, depending on income, how much they like milk, whether they have kids that need it, whether they can tolerate lactose or not, and a number of other factors, many of which are subjective. In fact, all information on the subjective value that consumers place on milk is contained in the market demand curve for milk. Remember that a demand curve describes the total quantity of a good that consumers are willing and able to buy at each and every price. As the market price falls, a greater quantity is purchased because more consumers will feel that the lower price is equal or below the value they place on the good.

Suppose, for example, that you would be willing to pay $3.50 for a gallon of milk, but the price is actually only $3.20. In essence, each gallon of milk you buy provides you with $0.30 of value that is "free" in the sense that it is over and above what you must pay. This excess value is called **consumer surplus**. It is the value received by consumers that is in excess of the price they pay. It occurs because not everyone values each good the same, yet for most goods, there is only one price. Consumer surplus can be measured if the demand curve is known. Since the demand curve is a summary of the value that each consumer places on a particular good, the area between the demand curve and the price line is a measurement of consumer surplus.

Figure 5.1 shows hypothetical market demand and supply curves for milk. At the market equilibrium price of $3.20 per gallon, 10,000 gallons will be supplied and demanded. Many people value milk at a higher price, however, and the value they

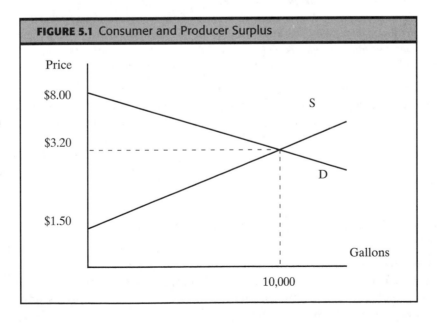

FIGURE 5.1 Consumer and Producer Surplus

receive in consuming milk is greater than the price they pay. If the price were to rise to $8.00 per gallon, no milk would be purchased. In Figure 5.1, consumer surplus is the area below the demand curve and above the price line of $3.20. The size or value of consumer surplus is the area of the triangle given by the formula ($\frac{1}{2}$) × (height) × (width), or ($\frac{1}{2}$) × ($4.80) × (10,000), which is equal to $24,000. This equals the difference between the value of the milk consumed and the total amount consumers spent for it.

Consumer surplus is a real savings to consumers. If firms had a way to determine the maximum price that each consumer was willing to pay, then theoretically they could charge every individual a different price and thus reduce consumer surplus to zero. Luckily for us all, firms usually cannot get this information without going through a long and costly interview procedure. As a result, it is usually impractical (and in some cases, illegal) for firms to charge different customers different prices. Nevertheless, some firms such as car dealers manage to charge different prices for the same goods. The easiest strategy for most firms is simply to charge everyone the same price, so consumer surplus is a real savings for most consumers in most markets.

On the production side, there is a concept analogous to consumer surplus called **producer surplus**. In our hypothetical milk example, if you owned a dairy farm and were willing and able to produce milk at $3.00 per gallon, you would be receiving producer surplus of $0.20 per gallon if you sold milk at $3.20. Recall that the supply curve for a market is the sum of supply curves for the firms in the market and that it reflects the minimum price firms will accept and still produce a given amount. In Fig. 5.1, some firms are willing to produce at $2.00 per gallon, and at every price above $1.50 at least some firms will have output to sell. Every firm that is willing to sell for less than the equilibrium price of $3.20 earns revenue that is above the minimum they need. This excess or surplus revenue is their producer surplus.

> *Consumer and producer surplus.* *Consumer surplus is the difference between the value of a good to consumers and the price they have to pay. Graphically it is the area under the demand curve and above the price line. Producer Surplus is the difference between the minimum price a producer would accept to produce a given quantity and the price they actually receive. Graphically it is the area under the price line and above the supply curve.*

As in the case of consumer surplus, we can measure producer surplus. Measurement in this case depends on knowing the parameters of the supply curve (where it crosses the price axis and its slope) because producer surplus is the area above the supply curve and below the price line. In our example, it is equal in value to the triangle given by the formula ($\frac{1}{2}$) × ($1.70) × (10,000), which equals $8500. This is the revenue received by producers that is in excess of the minimum amount of revenue that would be required to get them to produce 10,000 gallons of milk.

The Effect of a Tariff on Prices, Output, and Consumption

We will use the concepts of producer and consumer surplus when we discuss the income distribution effects of tariffs and quotas. Before we analyze those effects, however, we must begin with a description of the effects of tariffs on prices, domestic output, and domestic consumption.

Figure 5.2 shows the domestic or national supply and demand for a good that is imported. We are assuming that there is one price for the good, which we will call the world price, or P_w, and that foreign producers are willing to supply us with all of the units of the good that we want at that price. This is equivalent to assuming that foreign supply is perfectly elastic, or that the United States does not consume a large enough quantity to affect the price. We will drop this assumption below when we discuss the case of a large country. Note that the world price is below the domestic equilibrium price. This means that domestic producers are not able to satisfy all of domestic demand at the market price of P_w and that consumers depend on foreign producers for some of their consumption. Specifically, at price P_w, consumers demand Q_2 but domestic producers supply only Q_1. The difference, $Q_2 - Q_1$, or line segment Q_1Q_2, is made up by imports.

Now suppose that the government imposes a tariff of amount "t." Importers will still be able to buy the good from foreign producers for amount P_w, but they will have to pay the import tax of "t," which they tack onto the price to domestic consumers. In other words, the price to consumers rises to $P_w + t = P_t$, as shown in Figure 5.3. The price increase in the domestic market has effects on domestic consumption, domestic production, and imports. First, the price increase squeezes some people out of the market, and domestic consumption falls from Q_2 to Q_2^*. Next, on the production side, the higher price encourages domestic production to increase from Q_1 to Q_1^*. The increase in domestic production occurs because domestic firms are able to charge a slightly higher price ($P_w + t$) in order to cover their increasing costs while remaining competitive with foreign firms. Finally, imports decrease from Q_1Q_2 to $Q_1^*Q_2^*$. To summarize, tariffs cause the domestic price to rise by the amount of the tariff, domestic consumption falls, domestic production rises, and imports fall.

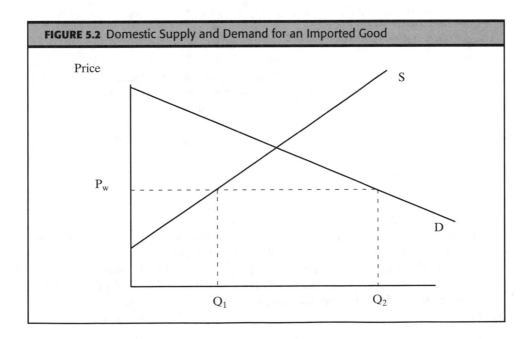

FIGURE 5.2 Domestic Supply and Demand for an Imported Good

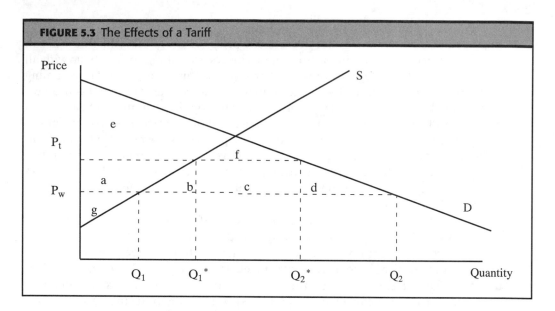

FIGURE 5.3 The Effects of a Tariff

The Effect of a Tariff on Resource Allocation and Income Distribution

Tariffs have more subtle effects than just a rise in prices and a fall in imports. The increase in domestic production requires additional resources of land, labor, and capital to be reallocated from their prior uses into the industry receiving the protection under the tariff. Also, when the price changes, so do consumer and producer surplus.

Let's consider the effect on consumer surplus first. Figure 5.3 shows both the pre- and post-tariff price and output levels. Remember that consumer surplus is the entire area above the price line and below the demand curve. When consumers pay price P_w, this is areas a + b + c + d + e + f. After the tariff is imposed and the price rises to P_t, consumer surplus shrinks to e + f. The difference, area a + b + c + d, represents a loss to consumers. Some of the extra value or consumer surplus they received before the tariff has disappeared because after the tariff they are paying more for each good.

Unlike consumer surplus, producer surplus grows. Pre-tariff producer surplus is area g, and post-tariff is g + a. The difference, or the amount of increase, is area a. This is the additional revenue that is above the minimum necessary to encourage domestic firms to increase their output from Q_1 to Q_1^*. On net, producers are better off. What about consumers and the nation as a whole?

If we consider the whole loss to consumers, areas a + b + c + d, we see that it can be subdivided into several different areas. Part of the loss, area a, is a transfer from consumer surplus to producer surplus. Although the loss makes consumers worse off, it makes producers better off by the same amount. Therefore, the nation as a whole is neither better nor worse off unless it can be established that giving the resources to producers somehow benefits or harms national welfare. This part of the lost consumer surplus is an income distribution effect of the tariff, since it re-arranges national income by transferring resources from one group (consumers) to another group (producers).

Another income distribution effect of the tariff is represented by area c. Note that the height of this area is equal to the tariff, and the width is the amount of imports after the tariff is imposed. Therefore, this part of lost consumer surplus is equal to (tariff) × (imports), which is the amount of revenue collected by the government when it enacts the tariff. In this case, the income distribution effect is a transfer from consumers to the government. Again, it is assumed that there is no net effect on national welfare since the loss by consumers is exactly matched by the gain of government. As long as this transfer does not reduce or raise national welfare, there is no net effect.

The two remaining areas of lost consumer surplus are b and d. Both represent net national losses, and both involve a misallocation of resources. Consider area d first. Along the demand curve between Q_2^* and Q_2, there are consumers that value the good above the cost of purchasing it at the world price. As a result of the tariff, however, they have been squeezed out of the market and are not willing or able to pay price P_t. The fact that consumers value the good above the cost of obtaining it in the world market but cannot purchase it is a net loss to the nation. Economists refer to the destruction of value that is not compensated by a gain somewhere else as a **deadweight loss**. Area d is this type of loss.

The final area to consider is b. Along the domestic supply curve between Q_1 and Q_1^*, output is increased at existing plants. Given that the supply curve slopes upward, firms can only increase their output if the price is allowed to rise. In other words, in order to obtain the additional output, domestic producers must be able to charge a higher price that will cover their rising costs for each additional unit. At the pre-tariff price of P_w, the total cost of imports $Q_1Q_1^*$ would have been the price times the quantity, or $(P_w) \times (Q_1Q_1^*)$. The cost of producing the same goods at home is equal to the cost of the imports plus area b. In other words, the triangle b is the additional cost to the nation when it tries to make the extra output $Q_1Q_1^*$ instead of buying it in the world market at price P_w. Area b is a resource misallocation and a net loss to the nation because the same goods ($Q_1Q_1^*$) could have been acquired without giving up this amount. Area b is another deadweight loss, sometimes referred to as an **efficiency loss** because it occurs on the production side.

> ***Deadweight loss and efficiency loss.*** *Deadweight loss and efficiency loss are pure economic losses with no corresponding gains elsewhere in the economy. Efficiency loss in this example refers to the loss of income or output that occurs when a nation produces a good at a cost higher than the purchase price.*

We can summarize the net effect of the tariff on the nation's welfare by subtracting the gains of producers and government from the losses of consumers: (a + b + c + d − a − c) = b + d. The two triangular areas are losses for which there are no compensating gains and, therefore, represent real losses to the nation as a whole. Table 5.1 summarizes all the effects of the tariff that we have noted.

TABLE 5.1 Economic Effects of the Tariff in Figure 5.3

	Pre-tariff	Post-tariff
Price to consumers	P_w	P_t
Domestic consumption	Q_2	$Q_2{}^*$
Domestic production	Q_1	$Q_1{}^*$
Imports	$Q_1 Q_2$	$Q_1{}^* Q_2{}^*$
Consumer surplus	$a + b + c + d + e + f$	$e + f$
Producer surplus	g	$g + a$
Government revenue	0	c
Deadweight consumption loss	0	d
Deadweight production (efficiency) loss	0	b

Other Potential Costs

These effects of tariffs are the ones that are most predictable and quantifiable. In the next chapter, there are some actual estimates of the production and income distribution effects of tariffs and quotas for a number of industries in the United States and Japan. These are not the only effects of tariffs, however, and three others should be noted. These are the effects if trading partners retaliate, the impact of protection on domestic innovation and productivity, and the incentive for firms to engage in rent-seeking behavior. Each of these effects broadens our focus to a consideration of more than the directly affected industry.

Retaliation   Retaliation can add to the net loss of a tariff by hurting the export markets of other industries. For example, the United States imposed a tariff on European (mainly Italian) pasta a few years ago due to a number of trade practices that the United States felt discriminated against U.S. pasta manufacturers. In return, the European Community retaliated by imposing tariffs on U.S. manufacturers of vegetable oils—corn, soybean, safflower, and other cooking oils. The cost of the U.S.-imposed tariff affected not just U.S. consumers of Italian pasta, who were forced to pay higher prices, but workers and owners of capital in the U.S. vegetable oil industry. In essence, in addition to the deadweight losses brought on by the tariff were losses suffered by the vegetable oil industry, which lost export markets. A further problem is that retaliation can quickly escalate. For example, in the 1930s, many nations were in depression and sought to reduce imports through tariffs. The net result was that these nations imposed high tariffs, and these nations gained jobs in industries that competed with imports but lost jobs in industries that produced exports. In the end, no jobs were gained, and everyone had a lower standard of living because production decisions were no longer optimal.

Innovation   A long-run and more costly effect of tariffs is that they often reduce the incentive to innovate new products or to upgrade the quality and features of existing ones. When domestic firms are isolated from foreign competition, there is less incentive to improve their products and processes. As a result, the nation misses many of the benefits of competition. It is admittedly difficult to measure this effect. Nevertheless, there is a fairly substantial body of research accumulated over the years that shows that outward-looking policies lead to higher rates of economic growth than do inward-looking policies.

Rent seeking   Hypothetically, tariffs could stimulate product improvement if domestic producers know they are temporary and if they believe they will be removed. The reason this is often only a hypothetical effect is that while firms have tariff protection, they often hire the best lobbyists available and work to keep the protection in place. In other words, the protected firms engage in **rent-seeking** behavior.

> ***Rent seeking.*** *Rent seeking is any activity by firms, individuals, or special interests that is designed to alter the distribution of income to their favor. Political lobbying, legal challenges, and bribery are common forms of rent-seeking behavior. These activities use resources (labor and capital) but do not add to national output. For this reason, rent seeking is a net loss to the nation. Rent seekers are successful only to the extent that they are able to take income from some other group, usually consumers or the losers in a legal battle. The more a society rewards rent seeking, the greater the quantity of resources that will be devoted to it, and the less efficient the nation's economic system will become.*

From a cost-benefit point of view, the question a firm might ask is whether it is more profitable to hire lobbyists to work for protection or to hire scientists, engineers, and skilled managers to make the business more efficient. New products have an uncertain acceptance by consumers, and new capital equipment is expensive. In other words, the increased productivity route has costs and risks. If protection is easy to obtain, then it may be a less risky strategy to hire lobbyists instead of scientists and engineers. If protection is uncertain, then the hiring of lobbyists (who can also be expensive) will be a risky strategy as well. For this reason, political systems that do not easily provide protective tariffs are much more likely to avoid one source of wasted resources.

The Large Country Case

Economists distinguish between large and small countries when it comes to tariff analysis. As a practical matter there may not be much difference between the two, but in theory it is possible for large countries to actually improve their national welfare with a tariff so long as their trading partners do not retaliate. In economic terms, a large country is one that imports enough of a particular product so that if it imposes a tariff, the exporting country will reduce its price in order to keep some of the market it might otherwise lose.

The large country case is illustrated in Figure 5.4. Suppose that the United States, a large country, imposes a tariff of size t on its imports of oil. The imposition of a tariff causes P_w, the world price, to fall to P_w^*, offsetting some or all of the deadweight loss from the tariff.

Looking more closely at Figure 5.4, we can compare the large and small country cases. The situation before the tariff is the same as in Fig. 5.3. After the tariff, the

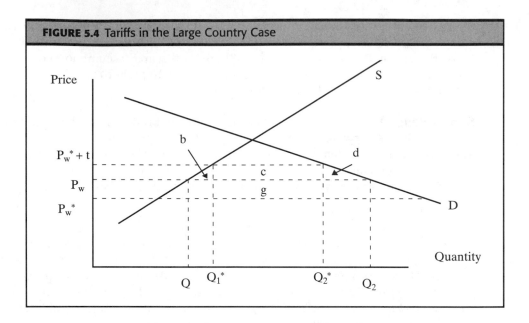

FIGURE 5.4 Tariffs in the Large Country Case

main difference between the two cases stems from the fact that foreign suppliers cut the price to P_w^* after the tarrif is levied. Consequently, less additional domestic production occurs, and fewer consumers are squeezed out of the market. In other words, areas b and d in Figure 5.4 are smaller than they would be in the small country case where there is no price drop. A smaller deadweight loss is not the only effect, however. In Figure 5.4, area g represents tariff revenue, which together with area c is the total tariff revenue collected. However, compared to the pre-tariff situation, area g is a net gain to the importing nation. Pre-tariff, area g was money paid for imports. After the tariff, and due to the price decline, it is part of the revenue collected by the government and, hence, stays within the nation.

As long as g > b + d, a large country can improve its welfare by imposing a tariff. This outcome, however, assumes that there are no retaliations. That is, if the nations against whom the tariff is levied decide to retaliate with tariffs of their own, then the gains can quickly turn into net losses.

Effective Versus Nominal Rates of Protection

One of the ironies of tariff protection is that often it is not what it seems. In fact, the amount of protection given to any one product depends not only on the tariff rate but also on whether there are tariffs on the inputs used to produce it. Suppose, for example, that the United States decided to tariff the importation of laptop computers. If American-made laptops have foreign parts in them, then the amount of protection they receive from a tariff depends also on whether there are tariffs on their imported inputs. It is conceivable, in other words, that the protection given by a tariff on laptops could be completely undone by forcing laptop manufacturers to pay tariffs on their imported inputs.

Economists distinguish between the **effective rate of protection** and the **nominal rate of protection**. The nominal rate is what we have discussed so far in this chapter—the rate that is levied on a given product. The effective rate of protection takes into account both the nominal rate and any tariffs on intermediate inputs. Consequently, it gives a clearer picture of the overall amount of protection that any given product receives. The nominal rate is defined as

$$(VA^* - VA) / VA$$

where VA is the amount of domestic **value added** under free trade, and VA* is the amount of domestic value added after taking into account all tariffs, both on final goods and intermediate inputs.

> ***Nominal and effective rates of protection.*** *Nominal rates are measured as the amount of a tariff (or the tariff equivalent of a quota) expressed as a percentage of the good's price. Effective rates take into account levels of protection on intermediate inputs as well as the nominal tariff levied on the protected good. Effective rates are measured as the percentage change in the domestic value added after tariffs on the intermediate and final goods are levied.*

> ***Value added.*** *Value added is the price of a good minus the value of intermediate inputs used to produce it. It measures the contribution of capital and labor at a given stage of production.*

Consider the example in Table 5.2. Suppose that laptop computers sell for $1000, and foreign producers are willing to sell the United States all it wants at that price. In order to make a laptop, American manufacturers must import $600 worth of parts, so that a domestic laptop actually has $400 of value added in the United States ($1000-$600 = $400). Then the United States decides to impose a 20 percent tariff. After the 20 percent tariff is levied, the price rises to $1200. Value added in the United States is now $600 ($1200 – $600), and the effective rate of protection is 50 percent (($600-$400) / $400). That is, a 20 percent tariff provides 50 percent protection! This happens because a large share of the value of the final product is produced elsewhere, so all of the domestic protection falls on the share produced in the United States. And as we

TABLE 5.2 Nominal and Effective Rates of Protection			
	No Tariff	A 20% Tariff on the Final Product	A 20% Tariff Plus a 50% Tariff on Imported Inputs
Price of a laptop computer	$1000	$1200	$1200
Value of foreign inputs	$600	$600	$900
Domestic value added	$400	$600	$300
Effective rate of protection	0	50%	–25%

have seen, the tariff raised the proportion of the total value added that was made in the United States by 50 percent, even though it was only a 20 percent tariff.

Now consider what happens if the United States decides to also protect domestic component manufacturers and levies a large tariff on intermediate inputs. If the tariff on foreign parts is 50 percent, the cost of intermediate inputs rises from $600 to $900. With a 20 percent tariff on the value of the final product, the price of imports stays at $1200. This is the price American laptop makers must meet. Value added after the imposition of the tariff on intermediate inputs is $300 ($1200 - $900), and the effective rate of protection is now –25 percent (($300-$400) / $400). That is, even with a 20 percent tariff on foreign laptops, American laptop makers receive *negative* protection. The tariff on the final product is more than offset by the tariffs on the intermediate products, so that the overall situation leaves producers more exposed to foreign competition than if there were never any tariffs levied at all.

Negative rates of effective protection are not uncommon. Part of the reason stems from the fact that tariffs are enacted in a piecemeal fashion over long periods and are not constructed in a planned and coherent way. Pressures from domestic lobbyists, considerations of strategic interests, and numerous other forces go into the shaping of national tariff systems. Consequently, it should not be too surprising to find contradictory tariffs policies that completely undo the effects created by a previous policy.

This discussion should add a note of caution to attempts to determine exactly which industries are protected. Clearly, the notion of effective rates of protection is more relevant than nominal rates. With tariff rates, what you see may not always be what you get.

Analysis of a Quota

The economic analysis of quotas is nearly identical to that of tariffs. **Quotas** are quantitative restrictions that specify a limit on the quantity of imports rather than a tax. The net result is much the same: both tariffs and quotas lead to a reduction in imports, a fall in total domestic consumption, and an increase in domestic production. The main difference between quotas and tariffs is that quotas that are not followed up with additional policy actions do not generate tariff revenue for the government. The lost tariff revenue can end up in the hands of foreign producers as they raise their prices to match demand to supply. Hence, the net loss from quotas can exceed that from tariffs.

In terms of Fig. 5.3, consumers still lose area a + b + c + d, but government does not collect area c as a tax. (We will examine what happens to area c, but you might see if you can reason it out for yourself.)

Types of Quotas

The most transparent type of quota is an outright limitation on the quantity of imports. Limitations are sometimes specified in terms of the quantity of a product coming from a particular country, and at other times there is an overall limit set without regard to which country supplies the product. For example, under the international agreement between the United States and a number of textile- and garment-producing countries known as the Multi-Fiber Arrangement, the United States sets limits on imports of each type of garment (men's suits, boys shirts, socks, etc.). The total allowable quantity of imports of each good was further divided by country, so, for example, Hong Kong and Haiti would each have different limits on each type of apparel that they could export to the United States.

Another type of quota is an import licensing requirement. The United States uses this form infrequently, but a number of other nations have relied on these quotas for the bulk of their protection. For example, until 1989 they were the main form of protection in Mexico. As the name implies, import licensing requirements force importers to obtain government licenses for their imports. By regulating the number of licenses granted and the quantity permitted under each license, import licenses are essentially the same as quotas. They are less transparent than a quota, however, because governments usually do not publish information on the total allowable quantity of imports, and foreign firms are left in the dark about the specific limits to their exports.

A third form of quota, and the one that has been common in U.S. commercial policy, is the **voluntary export restraint** (**VER**), also known as the voluntary restraint agreement (VRA). Under a VER, the exporting country "voluntarily" agrees to limit its exports for some period of time. The agreement usually occurs after a series of negotiations in which the exporter may be threatened with much more severe restrictions if they do not agree to limit exports in a specific market. Given that there is usually more than a hint of coercion, it may be a misnomer to call these restrictions "voluntary."

VERs are much like any other quota in their economic effect, but they are a stroke of genius from the perspective of a politician wishing to placate both sides on a trade issue. On the one hand, they allow elected officials to proclaim their support for free trade and opposition to outright quotas or tariffs. This satisfies the proponents of free markets. At the same time, the official can claim that through skilled negotiations, they have persuaded the exporting country to voluntarily restrict their shipments. This appeals to the domestic industries that face competition from the imports and to constituents that believe in protection for domestic industries.

Because of their political expediency, and because they are the culmination of a series of negotiations between the importing and exporting countries and therefore appear to be voluntary, VERs became popular over the last three decades. Another factor contributing to their use is the limitation placed on the use of tariffs by industrial countries. Every industrial nation has signed the international agreement known as the General Agreement on Tariffs and Trade (GATT, see Chapter 2). Under the obligations agreed to in the GATT, countries have bound their tariffs at current levels and have agreed not to raise them except under various extraordinary conditions, and even then only as a temporary emergency measure after consultation with GATT authorities. Until recently there was no limitation on the use of VERs, but recent negotiations included a ban on the use of VERs to protect industries from sudden import surges.

The Effect on the Profits of Foreign Producers

The main difference between tariffs and quotas is that there is no government revenue from nontariff barriers. In place of tariff revenue, there are greater profits for foreign producers. These are usually called **quota rents**.

> *Quota rents. Quota rents are the excess profits earned by foreign producers (and sometimes domestic distributors of foreign products) in an export market. The extra profits occur whenever a quota causes a price increase in the market receiving the exports.*

In Figure 5.5, The world price is set at P_w, domestic production is Q_1, and imports are Q_1Q_2. Suppose that the government decides to set a quota on imports of quantity $Q_1Q_2{}^*$. At price P_w, demand exceeds supply, which is equal to Q_1 domestic plus $Q_1Q_2{}^*$ imports. Consequently, the price will rise until supply equals demand, and that happens when the gap between the domestic supply curve and the domestic demand curve is equal to $Q_1Q_2{}^*$. This is illustrated in Fig. 5.6, where domestic supply is shown as having grown to $Q_1{}^*$, and the domestic price is P_q, which is above P_w.

Figure 5.6 looks the same as Figure 5.3 which was used to illustrate a tariff in a small country case. That is because they have nearly identical effects on production, consumption, and prices paid by consumers. Indeed, for any given quota there is some tariff that will accomplish the identical import restriction. One difference stands out, however. In the tariff case, the government earned revenue from imports, area c in Figures 5.3 and 5.6. In the quota case, no revenue is earned. Instead, area c represents the extra profits of foreign producers due to the higher prices.

Two circumstances can mitigate or limit the ability of foreign suppliers to earn extra profits. First, if there are a large number of foreign suppliers, then competitive conditions may prevent them from raising their prices. And second, a clever government

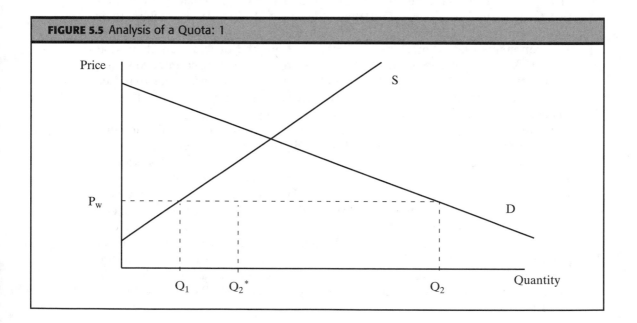

FIGURE 5.5 Analysis of a Quota: 1

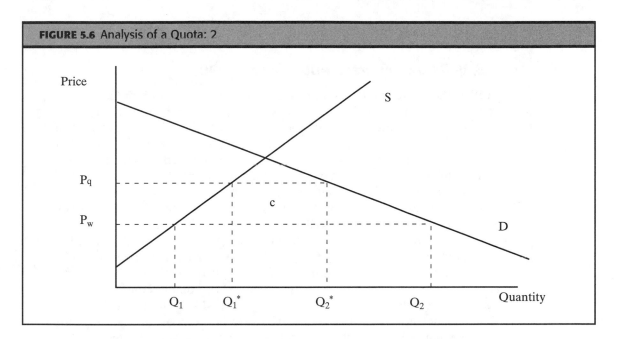

FIGURE 5.6 Analysis of a Quota: 2

can extract the extra profits from foreign producers through the implementation of an auction for import licenses.

Suppose that the country imposing the quota decides to auction off the right to import. How much would a foreign supplier be willing to pay? In Figures 5.5 and 5.6, they were willing to sell the amount of the quota ($Q_1Q_2^*$ in Figure 5.5, or $Q_1^*Q_2^*$ in Fig. 5.6) at price P_w. A rational supplier, therefore, should be willing to pay amount P_q minus P_w for the right to sell in the market with the quota. This would leave them exactly as well off as they were before the price increase, albeit selling fewer units. In equilibrium, an auction market should lead to bids for the right to sell that are exactly equal to the projected price increase. With an auction market, then, the government can potentially collect the same revenue with a quota that it would with a tariff. Of course, administrative costs of a quota may be higher, since the government must implement its auction market.

Hidden Forms of Protection

While outright quantitative restrictions, import licensing requirements, and VERs are each a form of quota, there are numerous other forms of protection that function the same as quotas. Any kind of trade barrier that reduces imports without imposing a tax functions more or less like a quota. For this reason, economists divide the different forms of protection into two main categories: tariffs and **nontariff barriers**. Nontariff barriers can be subdivided into quotas and nontariff measures. Nontariff measures are often nontransparent, or hidden, in that they are not presented as trade barriers or forms of protection even though they serve that purpose. They include government purchasing practices that discriminate against

CASE STUDY

U.S. VERs on Japanese Autos in the 1980s

In 1980, the United States experienced a short recession. For automakers, the economic slowdown came at a bad time, since they were struggling to meet new safety and emissions regulations and ever-increasing pressure from Japanese car makers. Imports of Japanese cars jumped from 15.2 percent of the market in 1979 to 22.2 percent in 1980. The combined effects of the new auto regulations, the strength of imports, and the economic slowdown caused U.S. automakers to lose $4.7 billion in 1980—the most they had ever lost.

In June of 1980, the autoworkers' union, the United Auto Workers (UAW), appealed to the U.S. International Trade Commission (USITC) for temporary protection. The UAW was soon joined in its appeal by the Ford Motor Company. It is the job of the USITC to conduct investigations to determine if a sudden surge of imports is hurting American industries. In November of 1980, at the conclusion of their investigation, the USITC commissioners voted 3-2 against the UAW and the Ford Motor Co. The USITC found that the recession and the shift in the U.S. car market away from large, gas-guzzling cars were the main sources of problems, not imports. President Carter resisted further entreaties from the car industry, but legislation in Congress to restrict Japanese cars to 1.6 million vehicles per year for 1981–1983 moved forward. President Reagan took office in January 1981, and in May he announced a voluntary export restraint agreement that his administration had reached with Japan. The VER agreement limited the Japanese to exports of 1.82 million vehicles for 1981 and was subsequently lowered to 1.68 million when it was renewed for 1982 and 1983. The restraints were continued after 1983 but at the higher level of 1.85 million for 1984 and 1985.

The quotas pushed up the price of both domestic and imported cars. The average price increase for Japanese cars was estimated at between $725 and $960, holding constant the quality and option features, while U.S. cars went up between $360 and $425 per car. The price increase for Japanese cars is estimated to have put an extra $2 billion per year in the pockets of Japanese and European manufacturers (who also benefited from the price increase) by 1984. The total cost to consumers was estimated at around $5.8 billion in 1984. Around $2.6 billion of the loss in consumer surplus was a gain in producer surplus. An estimated 55,000 U.S. jobs were saved by the VERs, at a cost to consumers of $105,000 *per job saved* ($5.8 billion divided by 55,000 jobs).

The critics of this agreement point out that the U.S. auto industry was already adjusting to the difficulties it faced and that most of these had stemmed from poor management, not Japanese imports. Detroit lost a big share of the market when it delayed competing for the small-car market after the two periods of oil shortages and gas price hikes in 1973–1974 and 1979. By 1981, the average domestic car was more than 25 percent more fuel efficient than cars of the same weight in 1972–1973, and the car weighed 30 percent less, giving it an even greater increase in fuel efficiency.

Critics also point out that before the VERs, most Japanese car manufacturers had targeted the subcompact and entry-level car markets, but the revenue from the increase in car prices and the limits on the numbers of cars they could sell gave Japanese car companies strong incentives to enter the midsized and luxury car markets where profits per car are greater.

One final effect of the VERs and the threat of U.S. protection is that it probably strengthened the incentive for Japanese manufacturers to begin production in the United States. Between 1982 and 1991, six Japanese companies and two joint ventures between U.S. and Japanese firms invested $7.9 billion in U.S. automobile assembly plants, with a capacity to produce 2.5 million cars and employ 31,000 workers. By contrast, between 1979 and 1984, U.S. firms closed ten assembly plants and reduced their workforce by more than 170,000.

Sources: Hufbauer, Berliner, and Elliott. *Trade Protection in the United States: 31 Case Studies*, Institute for International Economics, Washington, DC: 1986; and Robert Crandall. "Import Quotas and the Automobile Industry," *The Brookings Review*, Summer 1984.

foreign producers, local content requirements, product and safety standards, and excessive regulation.

> **Transparency and nontransparency.** *Transparency refers to any trade barrier that is clearly defined as a barrier. Tariffs are the most transparent type of trade barrier because they are usually clearly specified and published in each country's tariff code. Nontransparency refers to a disguised or hidden trade barrier. An example is a government regulation that requires foreign imports to meet a poorly defined safety requirement. In addition, it may require testing of the imports in special laboratories that have a limited capacity and that charge extremely high prices for testing. The net result is the same as a tariff—a reduction in imports—but producers of the foreign imports are never quite certain what the added costs will be or how many units they will ultimately be able to get into the country.*

It may seem fair to allow national governments to favor their own nation's suppliers. The problem occurs when major sectors of an economy (health care, transportation, communications, power generation, and so on) are wholly or partially state owned. Foreign firms are shut out of a significant share of economic activity if they cannot sell to governments. Furthermore, if one country's health care is private and another's is public, then there is an asymmetry in market access: firms in one country can supply the other but not vice versa. The asymmetry appears unfair and easily leads to trade friction, which can spill over into other markets. For this reason, nations have attempted to use international negotiations with the framework of the General Agreement on Tariffs and Trade (GATT) to open public procurement to trade. This effort has met with some success.

Other common forms of protection that act like quotas are esoteric or unclear safety standards, special product certification that only domestic firms seem to know how to comply with, and excessive bureaucratic regulation and red tape. It should be noted that safety standards are not trade barriers and that they are a vital part of the regulatory apparatus of a nation. In spite of this, they are often used by

CASE STUDY

Japanese Snow, U.S. Meat, and Mexican Tuna

Nontariff barriers provide some of the most unusual examples of economic reasoning in all of policy making. Nearly every country has stories about the economic excuses for trade barriers it has encountered from its trading partners. Three of them are given here. The problem with anecdotes such as these is that however interesting they may be, you can never know if they are exceptional cases of trade policy or if they represent the general tendency. Yet, while they may or may not be representative, they often give insight into how difficult it can be to get to the bottom of some trade disputes.

The first case involves Japanese snow, a weak Japanese ski equipment industry, and a strong European competitor. Japan felt that it would eventually have a comparative advantage in the manufacture of ski equipment because they excel in the high-technology area of materials science, and snow skis are put together with advanced synthetic materials. The problem was that it is a young industry in Japan, and at current prices and levels of productivity it could not compete with the far more experienced European producers. Furthermore, under its obligations as a signatory to the GATT, placing tariffs on European equipment was not an option. Consequently, in the mid-1980s, Japanese trade officials announced that they were banning the importation of foreign snow skis as a safety precaution. Japanese snow, they claimed, is different, and foreign equipment is unsafe. Their announcement was greeted around the world with derision and legal challenges through the GATT, and Japan never went through with its planned import ban.

In the case of Japanese skis, it was clear that the safety standards were phony and that they were an attempt to protect a domestic industry without appearing to do so. In the next example, the technical legitimacy of the safety standard is beyond the ability of consumers (or economists) to unravel.

In January of 1988, the European Community (now called the European Union) banned the use of all growth hormones in livestock production. The ban eliminated U.S. beef and pork from the EC market. Growth hormones are used in most U.S. meat production to speed up the animals' weight gain in feedlots. Faster growth means a more rapid turnover and lower costs to U.S. meat producers. The U.S. Food and Drug Administration has certified growth hormones as safe, but the EC disputed these scientific findings. The United States claims that the ban was a subterfuge to provide protection to less efficient EC meat producers under the guise of health and safety standards. The United States says the science is clear and indisputable, but the EC disagrees. Who is right?

In the first case, the safety standards were phony, while in the second, they are at least questionable. The third case involves safety standards for nonhumans, and it reflects a difference in the environmental tradeoffs nations are willing to make. The case involves tuna caught by Mexican fishermen and sold in the United States. Fishermen plying the waters of the eastern tropical Pacific catch yellowfin tuna by following dolphins. No one knows why, but the yellowfin tuna often swim below dolphins. Because of their swimming habits, when the yellowfin tuna are netted, dolphins tend to be trapped as well. This causes many to drown or, in the past, to be killed when the fishermen brought in their nets. In 1988, the United States passed the U.S. Marine Mammal Protection Act, which banned imports of tuna from countries that could not certify that their harvesting of tuna minimized the harm to dolphins. In 1990, all Mexican tuna was banned from the U.S. market due to the failure of Mexico to certify its catch. Mexico claims that the mortality of dolphins in its tuna-fishing operations is below the levels set by the international agency that monitors tuna fishing (the Interamerican Tropical Tuna Commission) and wants the United States to end its ban, which has hurt several west coast ports, such as Ensenada. The United States refuses to change its certification process even though a GATT decision ruled against the U.S. ban irrespective of the impact of tuna fishing on dolphin mortality. The International Dolphin Conservation Program, a multilateral agreement to protect dolphins and other marine species in the eastern Pacific Ocean, was signed by eight counties including the United States and Mexico on May 21, 1998. The agreement should provide the basis for removing the U.S. prohibition of Mexican imports.

The Japanese snow case is a blatant attempt by a country to protect an uncompetitive domestic industry while trying to appear as if it is protecting the safety of its people. The U.S. meat case raises a more serious question about consumer safety, but it illustrates the way in which protection can potentially hide behind serious scientific disputes. The Mexican tuna case reflects a fundamental difference in the strength of environmental values in countries at very different levels of economic development. In the growth hormone and yellowfin tuna cases, both sides make strong cases for their point of view, and the ability of negotiators to resolve the dispute on objective grounds seems limited. Both of these cases illustrate how difficult dispute resolution can be when protection hides behind safety or other standards and how protection often becomes intertwined with noneconomic values.

governments that want to limit imports and are unable to do so outright. Still other barriers require foreign firms to do something specific in order to have access to the market. For example, local content requirements force foreign manufacturers to buy or produce locally a percentage of the value of the goods they sell. This forces foreign producers to invest inside the country they are exporting to or to buy inputs from domestic firms.

Conclusion

The reduction of trade barriers through international negotiations is one of the brightest successes of the post–World War II international economy. Tariff rates throughout most of the industrial world average around 2 to 4 percent, and many developing countries have substantially opened their economies to world trade. Still, nations continue to protect selected industries in spite of the costs imposed on consumers and domestic resource allocation. The direct costs of these policies, and the major reasons given for maintaining them, are subjects for Chapter 6.

▲ Tariffs increase domestic production and employment at the cost of greater inefficiency and higher prices. The production and distribution effects are measured by estimating the changes in producer surplus and consumer surplus.

▲ In addition to short-run welfare and efficiency effects, tariffs have long-run costs of increased rent seeking, slower innovation, and the loss of export markets through the retaliation of trading partners.

▲ In theory, a large country can improve its welfare with a tariff. In general, welfare-improving tariffs tend to be small, and they only improve welfare if there is no retaliation by supplying nations and no external costs such as increased rent seeking.

▲ Economists distinguish between nominal and effective rates of protection. The effective rate is the difference in domestic value added with and without tariffs, expressed in percentage terms.

▲ Quotas have similar effects as tariffs, although the overall national losses are greater due to the transfer of quota rents to foreign producers. Auction markets, in which governments auction the right to import an item under a quota, can reduce the amount of quota rents and, in the limit, provide the same revenue as an equivalent tariff.

▲ Administratively, quotas take many forms. They can be well-specified quantitative restrictions on imports, negotiated limits on a trading partner's exports, or requirements to obtain a license to import.

Vocabulary

consumer surplus

deadweight loss

effective rate of protection

efficiency loss

government procurement

large country case

nominal tariff

nontariff barrier

producer surplus

transparency

quota

quota rents

rent seeking

tariff

value added

voluntary export restraint (VER)

Study Questions

1. Graph the supply and demand of a good which is produced domestically and imported. Assume that the country is not large enough to affect the world price. Illustrate the effects that a tariff on imports has. Discuss:

a. the income distribution effects;
b. the resource allocation effects;
c. the effects on domestic production and consumption;
d. the effects on government revenue;
e. the effect on the price of the good.

2. Suppose the world price for a good is 40 and the domestic demand-and-supply curves are given by the following equations:

Demand: $P = 80 - 2Q$
Supply: $P = 5 + 3Q$

a. How much is consumed?
b. How much is produced at home?
c. What are the values of consumer and producer surplus?
d. If a tariff of 10 percent is imposed, by how much do consumption and domestic production change?
e. What is the change in consumer and producer surplus?
f. How much revenue does the government earn from the tariff?
g. What is the net national cost of the tariff?

3. Under what conditions may a tariff actually make a country better off?

4. In addition to the production and consumption side deadweight losses, what are some of the other potential costs of tariffs?

5. The Uruguay Round of the GATT began a process of phasing out the use of voluntary export restraints. Why did they come into widespread use in the 1980s? For example, given that VERs are a form of quota, and that they create quota rents and a larger reduction in national welfare than a tariff, why did nations use them instead of tariffs?

6. The GATT strongly favors tariffs as a protective measure over quotas or other nontariff measure. One of the first things it encourages new members to do is to convert quotas to their tariff equivalents. One of the main reasons tariffs are preferred is because they are more transparent, particularly by comparison to nontariff measures. Explain the idea of transparency, and how nontariff measures may be nontransparent.

7. Suppose that bicycles are made in the United States out of a combination of domestic and foreign parts.

a) If a bike sells for $500 but requires $300 of imported parts, what is the domestic value added.
b) If a 20 percent tariff is levied on bikes of the same quality and with the same features, how do the price and the domestic value added change? (Assume the U.S. cannot cause the world price to change.)
c) What is the effective rate of protection?
d) If in addition to the 20 percent tariff on the final good, a 20 percent tariff on imported parts is also levied, what is the effective rate of protection for American bicycle manufactures?

Suggested Reading

Baldwin, Robert E., "Trade Policies in Developing Countries," in Ronald Jones and Peter Kenen (eds), *Handbook of International Economics*. Amsterdam: North Holland. 1984.
Corden, W. M. *Trade Policy and Economic Welfare*. Oxford: Oxford University Press, 1997.

Crandall, Robert, *Regulating the Automobile*. Washington, DC: Brookings Institution Press. 1986.

Hufbauer, Gary Clyde, Diane T. Berliner, and Kimberly Ann Elliott, *Trade Protection in the United States: 31 Case Studies*. Washington, DC: Institute for International Economics. 1986.

—— and Howard R. Rosen, *Trade Policy for Troubled Industries*. Washington, D.C.: Institute for International Economics. 1986

Appendix: Finding Information on Foreign Trade Practices

The tariff and quota policies, along with other relevant information on the commercial polices of nations, can be found in three different government documents.

1. *Country Commercial Guides*, published by the International Trade Administration of the Department of Commerce. This is an annual document containing general business and economic information about foreign countries as it effects U.S. businesses. A brief overview of each country's commercial guide is available online for a free at *http://www.ita.doc.gov/uscs/ccglist.html*. The complete guide is available from the State Department at *http://www.state.gov/www/about_state/business/com_guides/indes.html*.

2. *Country Reports on Economic Policy and Trade Practices*, published by the State Department. This annual publication covers more than 100 nations and contains general economic background as well as specific information about exchange rate policies, barriers to U.S. exports and investment, protection of intellectual property rights, and workers' rights. *Country Reports On Economic Policy and Trade Practices* are available online from the State Department at *http://www.state.gov/www/issues/economic/trade_reports/index.html*

3. *National Trade Estimate Report on Foreign Trade Barriers*, by the Office of the United States Trade Representative (OUSTR). Also an annual report, the report contains detailed information about tariffs and other barriers that affect goods, services, investment, and intellectual property rights. The report is available online from the Office of the United States Trade Representative, at *http://www.ustr.gov/reports/index.html*

All three are available in hard-copy versions, as programs on the National Trade Data Bank (NTDB) CD ROM and internet site (http://domino.stat-usa.gov), and at the above Web sites. Although each source is written by a U.S. government agency and, consequently, reflects a U.S. bias, each contains a wealth of information about the trade practices of other nations.

CHAPTER 6

TARIFF POLICY

Introduction

An argument was made in Chapter 5 that tariffs and quotas lower national welfare by creating deadweight losses. In this chapter, we will look at some empirical measures. In the United States, these costs are not nearly as high as they are in some countries, but they still add up to about $64 billion, or around $250 per year for every man, woman, and child. One of the main reasons for looking at the costs is to ask the question that economists must always ask: Are tariffs and quotas the cheapest and most efficient way to accomplish the goals they are set up to achieve? As you will see, the answer is a resounding "No!" We will examine the most common goals that nations set for tariffs and quotas, and alternative policies that may be used to reach them at a lower cost.

The Costs of Protection in the United States and Japan

Between 1947 and 1992, the average U.S. tariff fell from 20 percent to 5 percent. The United States was not unusual in this regard, and tariff rates throughout the industrialized world fell to comparable levels. A few industries have bucked this trend, however. In the United States, the most notable exceptions are textiles and apparel; in Japan, the biggest exceptions are agricultural goods and a few manufacturing industries such as textiles.

With the overall decline in the use of tariffs, the United States has increasingly relied on VERs and other nontariff barriers. In the 1980s, these were applied to steel, autos, and machine tools, among others. Japan has also used quantitative restrictions such as import bans (e.g., rice) or VERs (e.g., Korean clothes and textiles). In addition, Japan has provided generous subsidies to industries such as dairy and vegetables.

It is interesting to note that in both countries (the United States and Japan) the sectors most likely to receive special protection are not high technology or cutting edge manufacturing. Instead, they tend to be labor-intensive remnants of earlier economic eras. Agriculture, textiles, and clothing are by far the most protected. They are also the most in need of protection in order to survive, since both Japan and the United States have lost their comparative advantages in many parts of those sectors as they developed into high-wage, capital-intensive, industrial economies.

Total Costs and Costs per Job Saved in Both Countries

In the United States, twenty-one industries account for one-half of the total cost to consumers of formal protection. Textiles and apparel are by far the most highly protected sector, costing each man, woman, and child an average of about $100 per year. For the year 1990, the total cost to consumers of all tariffs and quotas in the United States is estimated to have been around $64 billion, or roughly 1.3 percent of the U.S. GDP.

Estimates of the cost to Japanese consumers of their nation's trade protection are more difficult. This is due to the fact that tariffs and quotas are fairly low, and most observers argue that nontransparent barriers (administrative regulations, product certification requirements, and so forth) make up the bulk of Japanese protectionism. These arguments will be discussed later when the U.S.-Japan trade conflict is examined in greater detail. The conflict is interesting partly because it is not about tariffs and quotas, but over more complex issues, such as nontransparent barriers, industrial structure, and macroeconomic policies. One recent study has estimated that in 1989, Japanese trade barriers, both formal and nontransparent, cost Japanese consumers between $75 and $110 billion, or between 2.6 and 3.8 percent of their GDP. Forty-seven industries accounted for all of this cost.

Table 6.1 itemizes the impact of Japanese and U.S. tariffs and quotas. Forty-seven Japanese industries and twenty-one U.S. industries making up the bulk of each country's protection are grouped together into six categories. The number in parentheses after each category is the specific number of industries with high levels of protection included in the category data. Column A is an estimate of the share of consumer surplus transferred to producers as an increase in producer surplus; column B is tariff revenue; column C is the quota rent; column D is the production side efficiency loss plus the consumption side deadweight loss; and the last column $(C + D)$ is the net national welfare loss. Since each category of goods includes many separate items, some protected by tariffs and others by nontariff restrictions, most categories generate both tariff revenues and quota rents.

The values for the totals for each country are also presented in Figure 6.1 (page 110), with the Japanese number first, followed by the U.S. value in italics.

Table 6.2 (page 111), carries the analysis one step farther. The total cost to consumers is shown in the first column. This is the sum of columns A, B, C, and D in Table 6.1. The second column shows the number of jobs saved as a result of the higher U.S. or Japanese production level. The third column is the cost to consumers per job saved (column 1 divided by column 2). First note the general pattern of Table 6.2. In Japan, more than one-half of the total cost to Japanese consumers of their nation's protection is in the food and beverages sector (despite the fact that Japan is the world's largest importer of agricultural products); in the United States, the bulk of the cost is in the light manufacturing sector—clothing manufacturing and textiles, to be specific. Neither the United States nor Japan concentrates its protective barrier in high technology or other cutting edge industries of the future. Instead, older, labor-intensive industries receive the bulk of the protection in each country. Other industrial nations would undoubtedly exhibit a similar pattern (e.g., agriculture in Europe is highly protected).

TABLE 6.1 Japanese and American Protection (Millions of Dollars)

	Producer Surplus Gained	Tariff Revenue	Quota Rents	Efficiency and Consumption Deadweight Losses	National Welfare Loss
Japan (1989)	**A**	**B**	**C**	**D**	**(C+D)**
Food and beverages (17)	43,210	1,086	6,909	7,189	14,098
Textiles and light industry (6)	3,341	812	3,059	1,767	4,826
Metals (7)	2,546	77	2,185	354	2,539
Chemical products (11)	8,466	135	3,866	3,033	6,899
Machinery (6)	12,286	25	4,233	5,043	9,276
Total, Japan	69,849	2,135	20,252	17,386	37,638
United States (1990)					
Food and beverages (5)	1,775	176	646	350	996
Textiles and light industry (9)	12,242	5,403	6,124	2,574	8,698
Chemical products (2)	222	232	0	30	30
Machinery (1)	157	0	350	35	385
Miscellaneous (2)	1,288	50	0	557	557
Total, United States	15,684	5,861	7,120	3,546	10,666

Notes: The numbers in parentheses are the number of industries with high levels of protection included in each category. The Japanese totals make up the majority of total protection in Japan, while the U.S. figures include the twenty-one industries comprising about one-half the total protection in the United States. The sources are Sazanami, Urata, and Kawai, *Measuring the Costs of Protection in Japan;* and Hufbauer and Elliott, *Measuring the Costs of Protection in the United States.*

The failure of industrial nations to open wide their markets in agriculture, foodstuffs, textiles, and apparel is particularly unfortunate for developing nations, as these are often the leading industries in economic development. Textiles, apparel, and food processing are often less capital intensive and more labor intensive than other branches of industry. This makes them likely areas of comparative advantage for many developing countries that tend to be labor abundant and capital scarce. Historically, these are often the industries that develop first in an industrializing nation, in part because of the relatively simple technology and low investment requirements. Restrictions on market access in the high-income countries inevitably hurts many developing countries by limiting the size of the market over which they can exercise their comparative advantage.

The total number of jobs saved in column 2 may seem like a lot, but relative to the size of the U.S. economy, it is not. Over the long run, the average number of jobs added to the U.S. economy *each month* is more than 200,000. Therefore, U.S. trade barriers in the most highly protected industries save the equivalent of one or two months' worth of new jobs at a cost to U.S. consumers of over $32 billion per year.

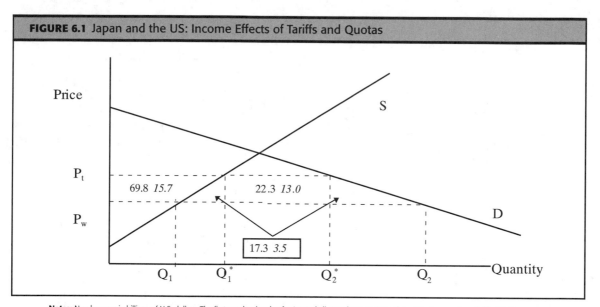

FIGURE 6.1 Japan and the US: Income Effects of Tariffs and Quotas

Notes: Numbers are in billions of U.S. dollars. The first number is value for Japan; italic numbers are U.S. values. All values are from Table 6.1. Coverage for the United States is only about one-half the value of U.S. tariffs and quotas in 1990.

The cost per job saved is in column 3: $169,000 per job each year in the United States and a whopping $602,000 per job per year in Japan.

In many respects, the last column of Table 6.2 is the point of this exercise. While everyone agrees that job creation is a good thing, it is important to ask how much we pay for the jobs we create. If a government agency were to implement a job-creation program at a similar cost (or even one-quarter this cost), citizens would be outraged. Because we pay for this grossly inefficient jobs program through higher prices, however, we do not associate the policy with its cost. When we pay $35 for a pair of denim jeans, we do not consider that a part of the price is because of our trade policy. The lesson we derive from Tables 6.1 and 6.2 is that trade policy is a grossly inefficient way to create jobs because it relies on too many intervening variables and does not go straight to the heart of the problem. If job creation is the issue, then tariffs and quotas are very expensive substitutes for good macroeconomic policy and flexible labor markets.

The Logic of Collective Action

Given that the costs to consumers are so high for each job saved, why do people tolerate tariffs and quotas? Ignorance is certainly the case for some goods, but for some tariffs and quotas, the costs have been relatively well publicized. For example, many people are aware of the fact that quotas on sugar imports cost each man, woman, and child in the United States between $5 and $10 per year. The costs are in the form of higher prices on candy bars, soft drinks, and other products containing sugar. Few of us work in the sugar industry, or any industry for that matter, that benefits from protection, so the argument that our jobs depend on it is weak at best.

In a surprising way, however, we probably permit our tariffs and quotas because of a version of the jobs argument. The economist Mancur Olson studied this prob-

TABLE 6.2 Jobs Saved by Japanese and American Protection

	Total Cost to Consumers (Millions of U.S. $)	Jobs Saved	Cost to Consumers per Job Saved (U.S. $)
Japan (1989)			
Food and Beverages (17)	58,394	76,600	762,000
Textiles and Light Industry (6)	8,979	18,500	485,000
Metals (7)	5,162	5,300	974,000
Chemical products (11)	15,500	6,500	2,385,000
Machinery (6)	21,587	75,200	287,000
Total, Japan	109,622	182,100	602,000
United States (1990)			
Food and Beverages (5)	2,947	6,035	488,000
Textiles and Light Industry (9)	26,443	179,102	148,000
Chemical Products (2)	484	514	942,000
Machinery (1)	542	1,556	348,000
Miscellaneous (2)	1,895	4,457	425,000
Total, United States	32,311	191,664	169,000

Source: See Table 6.1

lem and similar ones and noticed two important points about tariffs and quotas. First, the costs of the policy are spread over a great many people. Second, the benefits are concentrated. For example, we all pay a little more for candy bars and soft drinks, but a few sugar producers reap large benefits from our restrictions on sugar imports. In cases such as this, Olson found, there is an asymmetry in the incentives to support and oppose the policy. (Olson's famous study of this issue was contained in his book, *The Logic of Collective Action*.) With trade protection, the benefits are concentrated in a single industry. The tariff may help a few owners of capital and the workers in the industry. Consequently, it pays for the industry to commit resources to obtaining or maintaining its protection. The industry will hire lobbyists and perhaps participate directly in the political process through running candidates or supporting friendly candidates. If people in the industry think their entire livelihood depends on their ability to limit foreign competition, they have a very large incentive to become involved in setting policy.

The costs of protection are spread over all consumers of a product. The $5 to $10 per year that it costs each of us because of sugar quotas is hardly worth hiring a lobbyist or protesting in Washington. Few people think to ask a political candidate where he or she stands on the issue. (Do you?) Thus, one side pushes hard to obtain or keep protection, and the other side is silent on the matter. Given this imbalance, the interesting question might be why there are not more trade barriers.

CASE STUDY

The Uruguay Round of the GATT Negotiations

The Uruguay Round of the General Agreement on Tariffs and Trade (GATT) concluded in 1993 after nearly seven years of hard negotiations. Originally, it was scheduled to be completed within four years, but because it was the most ambitious round of multilateral trade negotiations ever undertaken, it was more contentious than anticipated and took longer to complete. Most of the 123 nations that participated ratified the agreement in 1994, and it went into effect at the start of 1995. (The tariff costs in Table 6.1 are before the Uruguay Round changes.)

There are four main categories of effects created by the Uruguay Round, as summarized in Table 6.3. Trade barriers are reduced to open markets wider; trade rules were reformed in several areas but most notably in the area of subsidies; several new issues were addressed; and the institutional structure of the GATT was made stronger and placed on a more permanent footing. In addition to each of these items, the agreement also committed the members to open negotiations in a number of new areas according to a timetable specified in the agreement. For example, negotiations over opening a $500 billion world telecommunications market were begun shortly after the agreement was signed, and in 1997, a telecommunications agreement was completed.

The Uruguay Round was significant in several ways. One of its biggest accomplishments was the inclusion of agriculture and textiles. While the provisions regarding these two sectors are relatively mild, a precedent has been set for future negotiations. In addition, the Uruguay Round developed separate agreements (i.e., outside of the GATT) on trade in services (GATS), intellectual property protection (TRIPS), and foreign investment (TRIMS).

Another major breakthrough was the reorganization of the institutional structure of GATT. Recall from Chapter 2 that in its original form, GATT was an agreement but not an organization. The original framers of the GATT hoped to create an International Trade Organization (ITO) that would coordinate trade agreements and oversee the implementation of the GATT. The ITO was never created, however, and the GATT established its own secretariat to administer the agreement. In the meantime, subsets of GATT members have negotiated several global agreements covering areas such as government procurement, civil aviation, meat, and dairy products. The creation of GATS, TRIPS, and TRIMS adds to this process of creating agreements that are separate from the GATT.

The Uruguay Round creates a superstructure called the World Trade Organization (WTO) to administer all of the agreements, including the GATT. The WTO also oversees the new, more efficient dispute settlement process and the Trade Policy Review Mechanism (TPRM). The TPRM conducts periodic reviews of the trade policies of each of the WTO members and publishes the results. The TPRMs are a good source of information about trade policies of specific countries

The WTO's Web site provides a wealth of history and background information. It also provides access to the TPRMs it has conducted, results of dispute settlement process, news releases, and lots of other information. It is located at: http://www.wto.org.

TABLE 6.3 The Uruguay Round of the GATT Negotiations

Category	Examples
Trade barriers reduced	• Across-the-board cut of 40 percent in tariffs on most industrial products • Agriculture reduces export subsidies and some domestic production subsidies; NTBs are converted to tariffs. • Phaseout of textile quotas over ten year period; cut tariffs.
Trade rules	• Clarification of the definition of subsidies • Classification of allowable and nonallowable subsidies
New issues	• General Agreement on Trade in Services (GATS) • Agreement on Trade Related Aspects of Intellectual Property Rights (TRIPS) • Agreement on Trade Related Investment Measures (TRIMS)
Institutional reform	• Creation of the World Trade Organization (WTO) • Reorganization of the dispute settlement procedure • Creation of the Trade Policy Review Mechanism

Why Nations Protect Their Industries

Historically, developing countries have used tariffs for a variety of reasons; foremost among their reasons has been the revenue tariffs generate. In a developing country's economy, a large percentage of economic activity lies outside of formal markets in which there is record keeping. Subsistence farmers sell their surplus in the town market, and repairmen and craftsmen take on jobs without leaving a paper trail of work orders or receipts. In this environment, income taxes and sales taxes are difficult if not impossible to impose. Tariffs, on the other hand, can be relatively easily collected by inspectors at the ports and border crossings. They simply have to observe the goods coming in and their value and then levy a fee (i.e., the tariff) on the person transporting the goods. The United States is a case in point. Although the GATT has limited tariffs by industrial countries, tariff revenues were the greatest source of income for the U.S. government until well into the twentieth century. In addition to the need for revenue, there are four broad categories of reasons that nations give for imposing trade barriers.

The Pauper Labor Argument

The pauper labor argument is a perennial U.S. justification for trade barriers. It was used throughout the nineteenth century and, most recently, has been resurrected by the opponents of the North American Free Trade Agreement. The argument states that nations must protect their markets against imports from countries where wages are much lower because, otherwise, the advantage of lower wages will either wreck the domestic industry or force it to match the lower ("pauper") wages. In the debate leading up the ratification of the North American Free Trade Agreement by Congress, opponents argued that Mexico would have an unfair advantage in trade with the United States because Mexican firms pay their workers a fraction (on average, about one-eighth) of the wages paid to American workers.

The pauper labor argument is an unsophisticated argument for protection. Its fundamental flaw is that it fails to consider productivity differences. Mexican workers, for example, earn about one-eighth of the salary of U.S. workers because their productivity, on average, is about one-eighth of the level of U.S. workers. Mexico has lower productivity because the education and skill levels of its workforce are less than in the United States, Mexican workers have less capital at work than U.S. workers, and the infrastructure of the Mexican economy is not as developed as the infrastructure of the United States. As Mexican workers gain more skills and education, and as the capital available on the job and in the surrounding economy increases, their productivity will rise, and so will their wages.

The Infant Industry Argument

A much more sophisticated argument for protection is the infant industry argument. The argument is mainly associated with the tariff policies of developing nations that protect their "infant" industries against the competition of more mature firms in industrial countries. Although the concept is closely associated with developing nations, developed ones use this argument on occasion to justify protection in some high-technology cases. (Japanese skis are an example.) Two beliefs lie at the root of the infant industry argument. The first is that market forces will not support the development of a particular industry, usually because foreign competition is too well established, but also possibly because the industry is too risky. The second belief is that the industry in question has some spillover benefits—or positive externalities, in economics jargon—that make the industry more valuable to the national economy than simply the wages and profits it might generate (see the appendix to this chapter). Whenever there are spillover benefits, the market may not support the development of an industry to the optimum level. With positive externalities, many of the benefits of production are captured by other firms or individuals outside of the producing firm. Since the producer does not get the full benefit of their own production, they produce less than the amount that is most beneficial for society.

Positive externalities are usually argued to be in the form of linkages to other industries or of a technological nature. As an example of the linkage case, many nations have attempted to start their own steel industries because they assumed it would create a cheaper source of steel for other industries, such as cars. The problem with this argument is that it does not demonstrate that there is some inherent advantage in making something as opposed to buying it, or in other words, that the car industry will have a special advantage if it can buy steel from local producers. If the car industry is forced to buy from local producers who never manage to obtain world levels of efficiency, protection on the domestic steel industry may actually harm the car industry. This is what happened to firms in Brazil when the government tried to start a domestic computer industry by keeping out foreign producers. The policy actually had negative linkage effects on Brazilian businesses because they had to pay higher prices for computers and got lower-quality machines in the bargain. Brazil would have been much better off importing its computers, as it does now.

While it is clearly possible for skills and expertise gained in one industry to carry over and benefit production in a different industry, it is difficult to prove the infant industry argument for protection. Technological externalities can happen when workers change jobs and take the skills they have learned to their new employment, or whenever an industry creates information or technology that is useful somewhere else in the economy. As a practical matter, however, it is difficult to know in advance when there will be technological spillovers, and, accordingly, it is difficult to judge which industries should be protected.

Even if technological externalities are present, it is not enough to establish the validity of the infant industry argument. Two more conditions must hold. First, the protection that is offered must be limited in time, and second, the protected industry must experience falling costs. The time limits on protection insures that the industry does not become a permanent recipient of transfers from consumers, and the presence of falling costs insures that the policy will eventually pay for itself. The goal is an industry that provides a rate of return on capital that is equal to alternative investments. Given that the returns are initially too low to attract private investment, the initial excess costs must decline so that returns can rise.

The National Security Argument

Every nation protects some industries as a way to guard its national security. In trade terms, national security can be interpreted in the narrow sense of military capability or in a broader sense of cultural identity. The most obvious examples of national security in a narrow sense include weapons industries and, somewhat more broadly, strategic technologies. Some nations also include strategic minerals such as the exotic ores used in jet aircraft. Protection for the sake of making available specific minerals or other resources is not an optimal policy. A better policy is to build stockpiles of the mineral by buying large quantities in peacetime when it is cheap.

A broader definition of national security includes the cultural industries—movies, television programming, music, print media, and theater. Many nations worry that if they allow completely free trade in the cultural industries, then the most commercially viable firms will dominate, and the cultural values of the home country will be obscured and forgotten. Since the United States has the strongest presence in the movie and television industry, and throughout much of the rest of the entertainment industry, the goal of protecting national cultural values is usually an argument in favor of protecting a nation's television, movie making, and music against complete domination by its U.S. counterparts. For example, the precursor to the North American Free Trade Agreement, called the Canadian-United States Free Trade Agreement (signed in 1988), established the right of Canada to require its TV and radio stations to broadcast a certain proportion of Canadian-produced programs. There are similar requirements in music, theater, and the print media. U.S. television and movie producers naturally opposed this limitation on free trade and demanded the right to sell an unlimited amount of U.S.-produced entertainment. They lost this argument, however, and they lost again when the Uruguay Round of the GATT was signed. The new multinational trade accord allows all nations to place similar requirements on their movies, television, and other cultural industries.

The issue of free trade in military and cultural industries inevitably involves noneconomic values and issues. How, for example, can we begin to assess the effects on Canadian culture and society of limitations on U.S. television programming? Given that many industries argue that their products are absolutely essential to maintaining military capability, how can we assess the strategic value of particular products or technologies? Economists tend to defer to the judgment of scientific and engineering experts on questions of strategic importance, pointing out that a less costly option is stockpiling the needed materials when possible. In the case of protection for cultural industries, economists are not qualified to make judgments, since the issue is fundamentally not about economics.

The Retaliation Argument

A final category of reasons given by nations to justify trade barriers is retaliation for unfair trade practices. When country A decides that country B's trade practices unfairly discriminate against country A's exports to B, a common response is to impose a trade barrier. The goal is to persuade country B to change its behavior and to give a more favorable treatment to A's exports to B. Retaliatory tariffs and quotas can provide an incentive for negotiations, but they can also lead to escalating trade wars.

Economic analysis is of limited utility in understanding this situation, since the outcome depends on political processes that determine how nations respond to pressure, their willingness to negotiate, and the outcome of negotiations. There are three camps of economists on this issue. One camp argues that free trade is beneficial regardless of the actions of a country's trading partners. If other countries choose to protect their markets, this argument goes, then it lowers their standard of living, and we would be foolish to do the same by imposing trade barriers in retaliation. An other camp argues that since free trade is beneficial, it is in everyone's interest to see it followed as widely a possible. Therefore, if a tariff today will cause other nations to open their markets tomorrow, the world economy will benefit in the long run.

A third group argues that countries that have a closed market or that restrict market access by imposing barriers to trade have an unfair advantage, particularly in high-technology products. They have a domestic market all to themselves, and they can compete freely in other nation's markets that are more open than their own. In cases where the size of the market is important, the ability to sell to a market larger (home plus foreign) than their competitor's may give the firms in the protected market a competitive advantage. If firms in the open market are forced out of business, then the technology, skills, and expertise that go with it will exist only in the firms from the country that adopted the strategy of protecting its market. To ensure that this scenario does not play out, and so that we do not lose critical technologies, some would argue that we should use the threat of retaliation to force open markets that are presently closed.

CASE STUDY

Economic Sanctions

Economic sanctions are a form of trade restriction. Unlike tariffs and quotas, which affect imports alone, sanctions are often on exports as well as imports and may include financial components as well. Access to international credit through privately owned banks or international lending agencies may be limited or blocked, as may investment by domestic firms in the country singled out for sanctions. Examples of export prohibitions included the U.S. rule during the Cold War that prohibited computer sales by domestic firms to the Soviet Union, and current prohibitions on selling goods or services to Iraq and Iran. The world community's boycott of investment in South Africa before the ending of apartheid is an example of an investment sanction as well as a trade sanction.

Economic sanctions go beyond simple trade or investment measures. In most cases they are used as one of several tactics aimed at achieving a broader policy objective—the ending of Soviet expansion or Iranian terrorism or South African apartheid. Another feature of sanctions is that they are often accompanied by additional measures, ranging from diplomatic pressure to military invasion.

The logical question to ask about sanctions is "Do they work?" In an important two-volume study of this question, three economists analyzed 121 episodes of economic sanctions throughout the world since World War I. Table 6.4 summarizes their findings. They found it useful to categorize the goals of sanctions into five separate groups: those designed to create a relatively modest policy change (e.g., to free a political prisoner or to limit nuclear prolifera-

Case Study continues

TABLE 6.4 Economic Sanctions Since World War I		
Goal	*Number of Cases*	*Successes*
Modest policy change	51	17
Destabilize a government	21	11
Disrupt a military adventure	18	6
Impair military potential	10	2
Other	20	2

Source: Gary Clyde, Hufbauer, Schott, and Kimberly Ann Elliott. *Economic Sanctions Reconsidered.* Washington DC: Institute for International Economics. 1986.

tion); those intended to destabilize a government; sanctions aimed at disrupting a military adventure of another nation (e.g., stopping Iraq's invasion of Kuwait); those designed to impair another nation's military potential; and a fifth category of other goals, such as stopping apartheid, or the Arab League's boycott of oil sales to the United States in retaliation for support for Israel.

In order to be classified a success, the policy outcome must have been the one desired by the country imposing the sanctions, and the sanctions must have been a contributor to the policy outcome. Hufbauer, Schott, and Elliott find 38 successes in the 121 cases they examine, but they report a drop in the number of successes after about 1973. Success with sanctions is correlated with the strength of international support and the use of military force. In addition, the weaker and smaller the targeted country, the greater the probability for success.

The Politics of Protection in the United States

Although U.S. trade with the rest of the world has grown, domestic political pressures inside the United States to protect domestic industries have frequently been intense. Part of the reason stems from the fact that internal Congressional changes have removed some of the insulation Congress enjoyed in the 1950s and 1960s from industry lobbyists. Another reason stems from the end of the Cold War and the lessening of U.S. willingness to sacrifice trade issues for the sake of maintaining close geopolitical alliances. A third reason is the rise of the export-oriented East Asian newly industrializing countries (NICs) and the pressure they have put on a number of domestic U.S. industries. Finally, the growth of the U.S. trade deficit and the widespread fear in the 1980s that the United States had lost its competitive edge also contributed to a greater reluctance to open U.S. markets without regard to the behavior of other countries and foreign firms. For each of these reasons, trade conflicts have become more open.

Protection in the United States is usually obtained either through direct action by the president (e.g., the VERs on Japanese autos in the 1980s) or through one of four different legal procedures: (1) countervailing duties; (2) antidumping duties; (3) escape clause relief; and (4) Section 301 retaliation. In each case, a firm, an industry trade association, or a government agency may petition the federal government to initiate an investigation into foreign country or foreign firm practices.

Countervailing Duties and Antidumping Duties

A countervailing duty is a tariff that is granted to a U.S. industry that has been hurt by foreign country subsidies of its national firms. Since subsidies permit a firm to sell its goods at a lower price and still make a profit, an effect of subsidies is to make firms more competitive. The goal of a countervailing duty is to raise the U.S. price of the foreign good to a level high enough to countervail the effect of the subsidy. The idea is to level the playing field between domestic firms that receive no subsidies and foreign ones that do.

The key to countervailing duties is to define what subsidies are. The definition often seems inherently subjective and, as a consequence, is an ongoing source of tension between countries. In the past, the United States had its own definition, but it was often at odds with trading partners over the application of the definition. One of the benefits of the Uruguay Round of the GATT is that, for the first time, it provides a definition of subsidies.

> **Subsidies.**   *The Uruguay Round of the GATT defines a subsidy as (1) a direct loan or transfer, (2) preferential tax treatments, such as tax credits, (3) the supply of goods or services other than general infrastructure, or (4) income and price supports.*

An antidumping duty is a tariff levied on an imported good that is selling at a price that is considered to be less than fair value. Firms sometimes find it advantageous to sell goods in a foreign country at a price that is below their home market price and that may even be below the cost of production. Selling below the cost of production in a foreign market is possible if the home market price is sufficiently high to cover the losses. One advantage of doing so is that it increases market share and enables a firm that is new to a market to establish itself with consumers. The Uruguay Round of the GATT created a common procedure for determining whether a firm is dumping.

> **Dumping.**   *Dumping is the sale of a good in a foreign market at less than fair value.* **Fair value** *is generally the average price in the exporter's home market or the average price in third country markets.*

Both dumping of goods and subsidizing of firms are considered unfair trade practices. The GATT allows nations to impose tariffs on the goods of firms that dump or that sell at a low price because they are subsidized. In the United States, the procedure for firms to obtain protection requires them to first file a petition with the International Trade Administration in the Department of Commerce. The

ITA will investigate, and if they determine that dumping or subsidization is occurring, then they turn over the case to the independent regulatory commission known as the United States International Trade Commission (USITC). The USITC conducts an additional investigation to determine if substantial harm has been done to the domestic industry and if an antidumping or countervailing duty is warranted. Countervailing duties and especially antidumping duties have become the most commonly sought after form of protection in the United States. In particular, the relative success of U.S. firms in proving that foreign companies are dumping has encouraged a large number of antidumping petitions to be filed. Some observers argue that the success of antidumping petitions is largely due to biases in the method used to determine the fair value of foreign goods sold in the United States.

Escape Clause Relief

Escape clause relief is so named because it refers to a clause in the U.S. and GATT trade rules that permits an industry to escape the pressure of imports by temporarily imposing a tariff. Escape clause relief is a temporary tariff on imports in order to provide a period of adjustment to a domestic industry. It is initiated when an industry or firm petitions the USITC directly for relief from a sudden surge of imports. The burden of escape clause relief is on the firm; it must establish that it is been harmed by imports and not by some other factor, such as bad management decisions. In 1980, when the United Auto Workers sought protection for the domestic car industry, it was under the rules of escape clause relief. In practice, it has become so difficult to obtain relief from import competition under this procedure that few cases are filed.

Section 301 and Super 301

Section 301 of the U.S. Trade Act of 1974 requires the president's chief trade negotiator, the United States Trade Representative (USTR), to take action against any nation that persistently engages in unfair trade practices. The action usually begins with a request for negotiations with the targeted country. The goal of the negotiations is to change the policies of countries that restrict U.S. commerce in an unreasonable or unjustifiable way. Note that it is left to the United States to define unreasonable and unjustifiable restrictions on U.S. commerce.

Super 301 was passed in 1988 as part of a larger trade bill. It requires the USTR to name countries that systematically engage in unfair trade, to open negotiations with them over their practices, and to retaliate if the negotiations are not fruitful in producing changes.

Applications of Section 301 and Super 301 are widely regarded as arbitrary, often unfair, and one sided; and they are most often the result of internal U.S. political pressures to take a tough stance against a particular country. The United States usually initiates a Section 301 action by requesting consultations or negotiations with the target nation, and often the discussion does not go through the GATT dispute-resolution process. Many nations feel that this has weakened the GATT and reduced its effectiveness. Whenever the world's largest nation acts outside the GATT process, it reduces the legitimacy of the agreement. Furthermore, it creates a perception that the United States plays by its own rules, rather than by the rules of the international agreement it signed.

For their part, U.S. lawmakers argue that the GATT is too slow and rigid. While waiting for a GATT decision, whole industries could disappear. Furthermore, prior to the Uruguay Round, the GATT had little to say about many new trade issues, such as trade in services, intellectual property protection, and investment restrictions. Therefore, the United States found it more expedient to go straight to the country with which it had a dispute. The new World Trade Organization of the GATT was designed to streamline dispute resolution and to discourage retaliation outside of the GATT forum. It remains to be seen, however, if the United States's use of Section 301 and Super 301 will be curtailed.

Conclusion

Trade barriers are rarely the optimal method to support industrial development, and they are never the optimal policy for creating or protecting jobs. Although there is no doubt that trade barriers encourage domestic production, they impose costs on the economy that are much higher than necessary. This is the basic policy lesson of commercial policy.

If tariffs and quotas are suboptimal as industrial strategies, then how do nations speed up their industrial development? This is the question every country would like to have answered but that, unfortunately, lacks a simple and direct answer from economics and economists. In terms of international trade, the question is really about the ability of nations to create their own comparative advantage. There is no simple answer to this question either, as there are many components to the analysis of comparative advantage and its determinants. We will tackle the idea of trying to create comparative advantage in Chapter 7.

The numbers presented in Chapter 6 indicate that the costs of protection in countries such as the United States and Japan are relatively modest. If the United States were to dismantle all its trade barriers unilaterally, there would not be much of an increase in GDP. It is important to recognize, however, that the costs to many countries may be much higher than our measurement techniques can demonstrate. Protected industries seldom innovate unless there are some other pressures acting on them. Throughout Latin America, for example, and in many other places in the world, the highly protected domestic market of local producers enabled them to earn monopoly profits without having to compete against outside firms. The result was a much slower rate of technological progress and an industrial sector ill prepared for the integrated world economy of the 1990s and the twenty-first century.

▲ Regardless of their cost or their ability to achieve a desired objective, every nation uses trade barriers. In most industrial nations, they are not used to develop comparative advantage in new industries, but rather to protect old industries that can no longer compete or to temporarily protect industries that are under pressure from new competitors. Textiles and apparel, two of the first industries established in the United States, are the most protected sectors of the U.S. economy.

▲ Tariffs and quotas are grossly inefficient mechanisms for creating (or keeping) jobs. Because the costs are hidden in the prices consumers pay for both foreign and domestic goods, few people realize how inefficient they are.

▲ The primary beneficiary of trade barriers are producers who receive protection and government that receives tariff revenue. The losers are consumers. Because the gains are concentrated among a relatively few people, and the losses are dispersed across many, there is usually only a small economic incentive for anyone to oppose trade barriers but a large incentive to seek them.

▲ The valid arguments in favor of protection involve economic returns to society that are undervalued or not counted by markets. That is, it must be the case that the market does not take into consideration the gains that spill over from production. The total value of producing a good, including any spillovers, is extremely difficult to measure, however, and it is often impossible to know the future value of the skills or technological sophistication an industry creates.

▲ In addition to presidential action, there are several forms of protection in the United States.: countervailing duties to counter a foreign subsidy, antidumping duties to counter dumping of foreign goods, escape clause relief to counter an import surge, and 301 actions to retaliate against foreign trade practices that have been labeled as unfair by the U.S. Except for the escape clause relief, each type of tariff requires a demonstration that foreign products are competing unfairly in the U.S. market and that they have harmed domestic producers. The most common form of tariff imposition is an antidumping duty.

▲ The unilateral application of tariffs in the U.S. is a significant source of trade friction between the U.S. and other countries.

Vocabulary

antidumping duties	fair value
countervailing duties	infant industry
dumping	Section 301 and Super 301
escape clause relief	subsidies
externality	

Study Questions

1. Which industries are more heavily protected in the United States and Japan? Are high-income or low-income nations more affected by American and Japanese trade barriers? Explain.

2. What new areas of trade and investment received coverage under the agreement signed after the Uruguay Round of the General Agreement on Tariffs and Trade.

3. Given that tariffs and quotas cost consumers and that they are grossly inefficient means for creating or preserving jobs, why do citizens allow these policies to exist?

4. What four main groups of arguments do nations use to justify protection for particular industries? Which are economic, and which are noneconomic?

5. Evaluate the pauper labor and infant industry arguments for protection.

6. Are tariffs justified as a retaliatory measure against other nations? Justify your answer.

7. What four legal procedures do American firms have at their disposal for seeking protection? What are the conditions that would generate a request for each kind of protection?

Suggested Reading

Bagwati, Jagdish. *Protectionism.* Cambridge, MA: MIT Press, 1989.

Baldwin, Robert. "The Case Against Infant-Industry Tariff Protection," *Journal of Political Economy.* May-June, 1969.

Destler, I. M. *American Trade Politics, Second Edition.* Washington, DC: Institute for International Economics, 1992.

Hufbauer, Gary Clyde, and Kimberly Ann Elliott. *Measuring the Costs of Protection in the United States.* Washington, DC: Institute for International Economics, 1994.

Krugman, Paul. "Free Trade and Protection," in *The Age of Diminished Expectations.* Cambridge, MA: The MIT Press, 1994.

Sazanami, Yoko, Shujiro Urata, and Hiroki Kawai. *Measuring the Costs of Protection in Japan.* Washington, DC: Institute for International Economics, 1995.

Appendix: Externalities

Externalities are costs or benefits that accrue to someone or some group other than the firm or individual that creates them. The classic example of a negative externality is unregulated pollution produced by a firm. An often cited and easily understood example of a positive externality is the pollination of fruit trees that occurs when a beekeeper puts his hives out to produce honey.

In the case of industrial production and industrial policies, the goal of capturing positive externalities is often cited as a justification for direct government intervention. Naturally, this justification is often a thinly veiled excuse for channeling public resources into industries or firms so as to benefit powerful special interests. Nevertheless, there are cases in which industries generate positive externalities, and it would be an exaggeration to say that every instance of direct government intervention to support an industry is wasteful.

Externalities are a case in which markets fail to produce the socially optimal amount of a good or service. The key results of this market failure are summarized in Table 6.A.1.

When there are positive externalities, firms produce too little output, which sells at too high a price. This point is demonstrated graphically in Figure 6.A.1.

TABLE 6.A.1 Price and Quantities in the Presence of Externalities

	Type of Externality	
	Positive	**Negative**
Price	Above optimum	Below optimum
Output	Below optimum	Above optimum

Let S-S and D-D be the normal supply and demand curves for a market in which production of a good generates some kind of positive externality. It is not necessary to define exactly the source of the externality, but it could be enhanced skills, technological innovation, or any other benefit to society that cannot be completely captured by the firms in the market. Under normal competitive conditions, firms will produce Q_1 and sell it at price P_1. The equilibrium at point A is determined in the usual way, as the intersection of market supply and market demand.

The key to understanding the effects of positive externalities is to look more closely at the market supply curve. Market supply curves are the (horizontal) sum of individual firm supply curves and represent the marginal cost of producing each additional unit. If we were to add up the costs of producing each individual unit, it would total an amount equal to the area under the supply curve from 0 to Q_1. This area represents the total cost to the economy of producing the free-market equilibrium quantity of Q_1.

This is not the end of the story, however, when there are positive externalities. In this case, each unit of production generates a benefit that is felt somewhere in the economy, outside the market for the good itself. Since economists are interested in

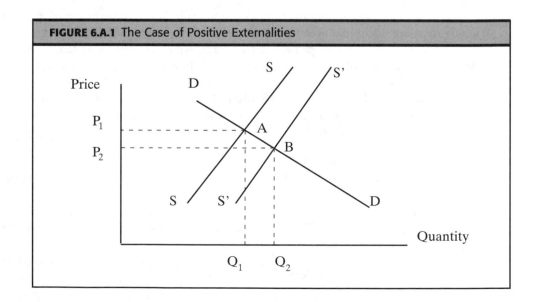

FIGURE 6.A.1 The Case of Positive Externalities

knowing the full impact on society of the production and consumption of a good, these additional benefits must be taken into account. This is precisely what the alternative curve S'-S' does.

For each good, the value of the benefit is subtracted from the cost of production. This is reasonable because the curve S-S illustrates the cost to society in terms of inputs that are no longer available for some alternative production. By subtracting the value of the external benefits, we are accounting for the fact that some of those costs are partially offset by benefits that are outside the market but still inside the economy.

The alternative curve S'-S' is not what firms will produce, but it shows the socially optimal price (P_2) and level of production (Q_2). The vertical difference between S-S and S'-S' is the value of the external benefit created by each unit produced. The difference between the free-market equilibrium at point A and the socially optimal equilibrium at point B is that point B indicates that the free-market price is too high and output is too low. This accords with Table A.

The idea of an industrial policy that is targeted on a specific industry is to offset some of the industry's costs through various direct and indirect subsidies. The goal is to provide enough of an offset so that in effect the curve S'-S' becomes the industry supply curve.

Obviously, in order to carry out an efficient industrial policy of this kind, government planners must be able to precisely measure the size of the benefit. That is, they have to know the vertical distance between S-S and S'-S'. They also have to be able to get the subsidy to the industry without creating some other distortion in the economy, such as raising expectations by other industries that they should receive subsidies as well.

CHAPTER 7

INDUSTRIAL POLICIES AND COMPARATIVE ADVANTAGE

Introduction

The original core idea of comparative advantage was that nations should concentrate their production on goods that have the lowest opportunity costs and trade them for goods they do not produce. If they followed this prescription, national income and welfare would be greater than if they tried for self-sufficiency. In this chapter we will examine the idea of comparative advantage in more detail. One of the key concepts of this chapter is that comparative advantage changes over time. In the case of the United States, for example, our comparative advantage has changed in a number of areas. We used to have the world's lowest costs and greatest efficiency in the production of basic steel, but this is no longer the case. In the 1950s, consumer electronics were another strength, but today there are few U.S.-made electronic products on the market. Meanwhile, U.S. strengths have grown in aircraft, satellites, biotechnology, and software, to name just a few areas.

The fact that comparative advantage changes over time raises a number of questions, including the most basic question of whether or not comparative advantage can be altered by design. If it can, then is it possible to put into place policies that change a nation's comparative advantage in a specific way? Are there limits to how far a country can go with these policies? For example, could nonindustrial economies put into place a set of policies that ultimately lead to a high-technology, advanced industrial economy? Can specific industries or specific products be targeted, or must nations accept the fact that they might gain a comparative advantage in, say, high-technology production without really being able to choose the specific high-technology products? In other words, if policy makers can alter their nation's comparative advantage, can they do so with precision?

Static and Dynamic Conceptions of Comparative Advantage

In each of the trade models discussed so far, the idea of comparative advantage plays a central role. Whether looking at a nation's trade from the standpoint of the simple Ricardian model introduced in Chapter 3 or the Heckscher-Ohlin model of Chapter 4, nations maximize their welfare if they produce the goods with the lowest opportunity costs. This idea may seem to offer little hope for less-developed nations, when their most abundant input is unskilled labor. Nations that primarily produce minerals or agricultural commodities or other natural resources would like to develop high-income economies like everyone else, but their climates and resource endowments, together with their abundant supply of unskilled labor, give them a comparative advantage in primary commodities. If these nations stay with their comparative advantage, it may seem like industrial development is impossible. How can a nation move on into simple manufacturing and then into more and more complex forms if it sticks with its endowment of minerals or agricultural commodities and unskilled labor?

There is no simple answer to this question and, clearly, if industrial development were easy, most countries would probably be relatively high-income nations by now. Nevertheless, one of the reasons that the idea of comparative advantage may mistakenly appear to be of limited use to developing countries is that it is usually presented as a static concept. In this case, the term *static* refers to the fact that there is no time dimension attached to it. Metaphorically speaking, the concept has been treated like a snapshot rather than a video that shows movement over time. One way of looking at industrial development and rising living standards is to see them as shifts in the nation's comparative advantage. In this view, comparative advantage is dynamic, meaning it changes over time. Korea today has a comparative advantage in many types of production that were out of its reach three decades ago (e.g., VCRs and microwave ovens).

Some economists have argued that the dynamic nature of comparative advantage goes beyond economic development. In this view, comparative advantage is "path dependent," meaning that the goods an advanced industrial nation produces today determine its capabilities in the future. For example, several years ago in the United States a debate raged about high-definition television (HDTV). Many people favored a targeted development of this technology because they felt that it would lead to new generations of semiconductors, medical equipment, avionics, and other high-tech spinoffs. If we did not have HDTV today, they argued, we would lack the ability to produce these related products. Semiconductors are another example. Can a nation produce computers if it lacks the ability to produce semiconductors at competitive costs levels? If it does not produce computers, will it write software? No one knows for certain the extent to which these different products are connected to each other, and economists are divided on this issue. One group believes that if one type of production is missing, the others disappear as well. The opposite view maintains that that there is no necessary connection. We can make computers without making semiconductors simply by buying semiconductors in the world market. As Jagdish Bhagwati, a leading trade economist pointed out, England makes the world's best marmalade without producing a single orange.

Simple common sense tells us that national economies change over time. Furthermore, as technology, the labor force, and the public infrastructure change, a nation's comparative advantage must be changing as well, since it is partly determined by those aspects of the national economy. Given that national comparative advantage changes over time, a question that leaders in many countries ask is whether they can determine the precise dimensions of those changes. For example, can a nation pick a specific industry or product and then engineer their economy so that it will have a comparative advantage in its production? Is that too complex a challenge for national governments or planning agencies and something they are better off leaving to market forces? Although there is no agreement on the answers to these questions, it is worth examining their economic implications in some detail. We can begin by clarifying the choices nations face.

General and Specific Policies to Alter a Nation's Comparative Advantage

It is useful to distinguish between two different levels of policies that nations use to alter their comparative advantage. On the one hand, there are policies aimed at improving the overall economic environment. These policies are more general in focus and are not targeted on any specific industry. In effect, they are not much different from the strategies nations might follow in order to encourage general economic development. Every nation has policies of this sort, and they all try to do more or less the same thing: provide educational opportunities, generate savings and mobilize it through the financial system, maintain a stable macroeconomic environment (low inflation, stable exchange rates, and positive real interest rates), and develop a secure and healthy business climate in which entrepreneurs are willing to invest.

On the other hand, nations also pursue more specific policies that target individual industries. These are the policies that many people refer to as **industrial policies**. They differ from the first kind of policies in the same way that creating a steel industry differs from general industrial development.

> *Industrial policy. A policy designed to create new industries or to provide support for existing ones.*

The edges of both kinds of policies begin to blur into each other. For example, if a government supports academic research in the science departments of its universities, is it a specific or more general policy? What if the research is designed to find a specific commercial use for military technology? The point here is not to quibble over the terms *general* and *specific* but rather to recognize that both kinds of policies exist. Building a strong and efficient system of universal public education is very different from providing subsidies to the semiconductor industry, yet both policies may lead to a shift in comparative advantage.

Although most nations practice both kinds of policies, the majority of economists support the more general kind and are very cautious about the more specific kind. In the remainder of this chapter we will look at the justifications for targeting specific industries and the reasons why economists are so wary. Hereafter, these policies will be referred to as industrial policies. A thorough discussion of the more general type of policies can be found in any text on economic development.

Industrial Policy

There is little doubt that nations can successfully target a new industry for development. Most types of economic activity will grow if they have human and financial resources poured into them. As economists, however, we should not be concerned with the question of whether country X can produce good Y; instead, the concern is whether country X can produce good Y at an opportunity cost that is less than the price of buying Y on the world market. That is, could an alternative use of the resources deliver a greater benefit to the nation? Undoubtedly, the United States could become a major producer of bananas if it built enough greenhouses and trained enough experts in indoor banana production. No one argues that this would be a wise use of U.S. capital and labor, however. Simply because a nation has the capability of producing a good, it does not follow that it also has a comparative advantage.

Theoretical Justifications for Industrial Policies

There are two major categories of reasons used to justify interventions by governments to support specific industries. The first justification is fairly common, while the second is rare; both require measurements that are difficult to make.

Market Failure

Market failure is the term used to describe situations where free markets fail to allocate resources optimally, and as a consequence, too much or too little of a particular good is produced. In effect, market failures result whenever there is a difference in the **private returns** and **social returns** to an activity. When social returns are greater than private returns, the socially optimal level of production is greater than the level the private economy will produce. When social returns are less than private, the free market will generate too much production. In effect, a difference between social and private costs means that there are costs and benefits external to the market: **externalities**.

> *Market failure. Market failure occurs whenever free markets fail to produce the socially optimal amount of a good or service. Market failure has numerous causes, including externalities and monopolistic or oligopolistic market structures.*

> *Private and social returns. Private returns are the value of all private benefits minus all private costs, properly adjusted to take into account that some costs and benefits are in the future and must be discounted to arrive at their value in today's dollars. Social returns include private returns, but they also add costs and benefits to the elements of society that are not taken into consideration in the private returns. For example, a firm that generates pollution that it does not have to clean up imposes costs on society, which causes social returns to be lower than private returns. Similarly, a firm that creates labor force skills that can be transferred to other activities creates benefits that raise social returns relative to private ones.*

There are numerous reasons why social returns and private returns may differ, and each of them can, in theory, justify some degree of government intervention. In practice, however, it can be extremely difficult to implement an efficient policy that is free from political pressures.

Learning effects are one of the most often cited reasons for supporting new industries. One type of learning effect occurs through the creation and spread of knowledge as production takes place. Firms other than the one that imparts the new knowledge can benefit from the movement across firms of workers who bring skills and expertise with them. When knowledge created by one firm is applicable to other firms, learning effects will occur if the knowledge spreads. In this case, the social return to the new knowledge is greater than the private return, since the firm generating it finds some of its value accruing to economic agents outside the firm. The end result is likely to be too little investment in this type of knowledge.

An important case of learning effects comes from the first entrant into a particular industry. The first firm in an industry demonstrates that the industry is feasible. This is valuable information for other firms that are potential entrants. The first firm also often leaks marketing and technological information to other firms. In essence, the first firm provides valuable information about technical and economic feasibility that aids the entrance of future firms. Again, under these conditions, the social returns are higher than the private ones.

A related learning effect occurs in the area of research and development. Firms that develop new technologies may create breakthroughs that pay handsome profits. Before long the new product will be taken apart and improved upon by a competitor. In essence, the competitor benefits from the original research and development by being able to copy and improve upon them. Although the original innovator is unable to capture the full monetary benefit of its R&D, the benefits are not lost. Society as a whole is made better off by the original innovation and by the improvements done by the second firm. A variation of the learning effect of R&D is the problem of obtaining existing information. Often, existing technology may provide a solution to a common problem, but information about the technology may lie buried in a government research lab or in a Japanese technical journal. Firms could pay to search these sources of technical information, but once they find the answer to their problem, there is a high probability that all their competitors will be able to copy it because it is difficult to keep information within a single firm.

In addition to learning effects, divergence between private and social returns can occur as a result of imperfections in capital markets. According to this argument, new firms may have difficulty attracting sufficient start-up capital. The same applies to existing firms that need to borrow to develop new products or processes. Capital for borrowing is not provided through normal markets ruled by prices. If capital was provided in this way, then the firms willing to pay the highest interest rate would obtain a loan. Obviously, lenders avoid this situation because those willing to pay the highest interest rate are probably the riskiest investments in most cases. Consequently, new products, which tend to be risky, may receive too little funding, and firms that are on the frontier of new technologies will have to look outside of traditional capital markets for their investment capital.

Imperfect capital markets may also lead to market failure when economies of scale are involved. Proponents of industrial policies cite the fact that many large-scale projects require a set of interdependent investments to be made all at once. For example, a potentially internationally competitive steel industry may require simultaneous investment in port and rail linkages. By itself, each piece may be unprofitable, but taken together the result would be a large, competitive sector.

These ideas are illustrated in Figure 7.1. Supply and demand are plotted for a competitively produced good that generates external benefits when it is produced. The supply curve S_{priv} is a normal market supply curve, embodying all of the private costs encountered by firms that engage in production. It is labeled with the sub-

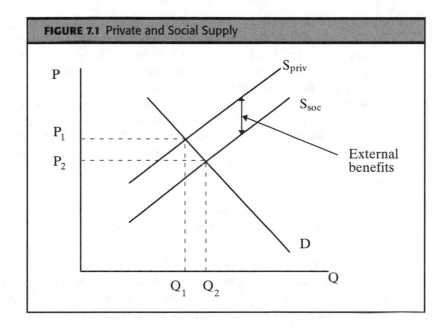

FIGURE 7.1 Private and Social Supply

script "priv" to indicate that only the private costs, the costs paid for by the firms producing the good, are taken into account. Since production entails some external benefits to members of the society (who are not specified in this model), we can off-set some of the costs of production with the external benefits. These are subtracted from the supply curve to derive the social supply curve, S_{soc}, which embodies the private costs minus the external benefits. The supply curve S_{soc} is more comprehensive than S_{priv}, since it takes into consideration all the costs and benefits to society, not simply the private ones.

As can be seen in Figure 7.1, private markets lead to output Q_1 at price P_1. From the standpoint of the social optimum, however, the price is too high and the quantity is too low. The social optimum at P_2 and Q_2 takes into account the costs and benefits that are external to the firms producing, along with their internal costs and benefits. In effect, private agents earn less than the social return, which includes the external benefit that firms cannot capture. As a result, there is less than the socially optimal amount of investment in the activity generating the returns. For advocates of indus-trial policies, the solution is activist government intervention to increase the level of the desirable activity. We will look at the form that the government activism should take, but first we turn to the second major justification for industrial policies.

Strategic Trade

A second justification for industrial policies that target specific industries goes by the name of **strategic trade policy.** The two essential ingredients for strategic trade policy are (1) the industry has strong economies of scale, and (2) firms in the industry have market power that enables them to earn higher than normal profits. Economies of scale implies that if firms produce less, their costs per unit will rise. Consequently, in some cases, it is possible that if new firms capture a share of the market, everyone will produce less and experience higher costs. The net result might be that no firm is profitable any longer. The disappearance of the excess profits whenever another firm tries to enter the market acts like a barrier to entry and keeps new firms out. Yet, as long as they stay out, the firms in the market earn higher than normal profits.

Strategic trade policy is aimed at capturing these excess profits for firms based in the home country. Setting aside for a minute the practical difficulties of enacting strategic trade policy, in theory it is possible to convince foreign firms to leave the industry by starting a well-publicized and credible system of subsidies to new domestic firms. The size of the subsidy should be sufficient to enable the home country firms to earn profits. As long as they gain some share of the market, foreign firms will become less profitable.

> **Strategic trade policy.** *Strategic trade policy is the use of trade barriers, subsidies, or other industrial support policies that are designed to capture the profits of foreign firms for domestic firms.*

Strategic trade policy tries to make foreign firms as unprofitable as possible so that they will leave the market. The probability of this outcome increases as the market share captured by the home country firm increases. If the program of subsidies succeeds in getting foreign firms to leave, then domestic firms can expand their market share further and capture some or all of the excess profits that were previously going to foreign firms. No foreign firms will be tempted to reenter the market as long as they believe that the subsidies will keep the home country firm profitable and thereby keep it in the market.

Here is a hypothetical example. Suppose that a Japanese firm has a highly profitable high-definition television (HDTV) on the market, and an American firm is considering development of a similar product. The problem faced by the American firm is that the capital investment required to enter this market is enormous, in the tens of billions of dollars. This is too much capital to risk in a speculative venture that will immediately encounter stiff competition from an already established and profitable Japanese firm. Still, as the only supplier to the world market, the Japanese firm is earning above normal profits, a very enticing prospect for a potential market entrant.

Suppose the profits earned by the Japanese firm (J-Electronics, Inc.) and the American firm (A-Electronics, Inc.) are as given in Table 7.1, both with and without production. As the American firm surveys its options, it notes that it has a choice of

TABLE 7.1 A Hypothetical Payoff Matrix for HDTV Production		
	A-Electronics	
J-Electronics	**Enter market**	**Stay out of market**
Stay in market	A (–10) J (–10)	A (0) J (25)
Leave market	A (25) J (0)	A (0) J (0)

entering the market and losing (–10) or staying out and losing 0. Obviously, staying out of the market is the better choice. The stable outcome under these circumstances is that J-Electronics stays in the market, and A-Electronics does not enter.

Suppose, however, that the U.S. government decides to offer a subsidy to the American firm. The subsidy should be enough to keep A-Electronics profitable regardless of the behavior of the competitor, J-Electronics. Let's say that the U.S. government offers a subsidy of 15 if A-Electronics enters the market. Under these conditions, the payoffs will be those detailed in Table 7.2.

With the subsidy, the preferred action by the U.S. firm is to enter the market. If it stays out, it earns 0, but if it enters, it earns either 5 or 40, depending on the reaction of the Japanese firm. J-Electronics can be assured that A-Electronics will enter the market. Therefore, its choice is between –10 if it stays in the market or 0 if it leaves. The rational decision for J-Electronics is to leave, ensuring that the U.S. firm captures the above-normal profits that were accruing to the Japanese firm.

Is this scenario feasible? That is a difficult question to answer, and we will reserve analysis until after we have discussed the techniques used for carrying out industrial policies of this sort. At this point, you should be wary on several counts. First, we have assumed that the firms involved and the government have a lot more detailed information about costs and profits than they are likely to have in reality. Second, we assume that the Japanese government does not retaliate in any way. In addition, we have assumed that the U.S. government and A-Electronics have been able to get around the prohibitions on direct subsidies under the GATT rules and that there is no multilateral response through the WTO dispute-resolution process. If any one of these assumptions fails to hold, then the outcome will not follow the story script.

Techniques

There are a variety of techniques that are used to carry out industrial policies, but what they all have in common is that they channel some of the nation's resources to the targeted industry. This can be accomplished in numerous ways, the most obvious of which is to offer direct subsidies to firms in the targeted industry. This has become more difficult in recent years, however, because it is likely to provoke retaliation by foreign governments whose firms are hurt. Under the Uruguay Round of the GATT, there are newly defined limits on this kind of activity.

TABLE 7.2 The Payoff Matrix After A-Electronics Is Offered a Subsidy of 15

	A-Electronics	
J-Electronics	**Enter market**	**Stay out of market**
Stay in market	A (5) J (–10)	A (0) J (25)
Leave market	A (40) J (0)	A (0) J (0)

It is not necessary to provide direct transfers to targeted industries in order to support them. Governments have a wide range of options, including providing information about conditions in foreign markets (most countries do this through their embassies and consulates); helping with negotiating contracts; lobbying foreign governments to adopt the technical standards of firms in the home country; and tying foreign aid to purchases from home country firms.

One common practice in many newly industrializing countries is for the government to sell foreign exchange to the favored firms at below-market prices, which enables them to buy capital goods from abroad at very low cost. A second common technique is for governments to provide loans to private firms at below-market interest rates. Alternatively, the government may guarantee a loan obtained from the private sector, enabling borrowers to obtain much more favorable interest rates. Similarly, governments may provide special tax treatment to targeted industries, which, like loan guarantees, also increases their profitability.

Governments also use their own purchases as a way to develop an industry. For example, they may require that suppliers be based in the home country. This can affect a wide range of activity, including medical equipment for state-owned hospitals, power-generating equipment for state-owned utilities, telecommunications equipment for state-owned phone and broadcast media, military hardware, and so on. In some cases — for example, suppliers of military hardware in the United States — firms are guaranteed a profit on the development of new products. Essentially, this removes all risk from the firm and spreads it across taxpayers.

Governments commonly encourage firms to work together, either through the direct funding of the research done by consortia and/or through the relaxation of antitrust laws. This decreases the probability that competing firms will duplicate each other's research and development efforts, but it increases their market power. Finally, governments may directly own firms, although this is less common in capitalist countries. In countries where they do (France, for example), they are run more or less like private firms. These firms may or may not receive favorable treatment, but their track record indicates that government ownership is not an effective way to insure international competitiveness.

Proponents of industrial policies stress that no matter which technique is used to target an industry, it is critical for governments to refrain from coercion. Firms should be allowed to refuse assistance (and the inevitable strings attached) if that is what they decide, and any action by the government to penalize their noncooperation will only weaken the industry and lower the probability of a successful program.

Problems with Industrial Policies in Practice

While every economist recognizes that markets do not always produce the optimal outcome, most are skeptical about the practicality of using industrial policies to solve the problem of market failure. A major problem is that it is exceedingly difficult to obtain the information necessary to measure the extent of market failure. For example, an efficient industrial policy requires governments to provide just the right amount of additional resources to the targeted industry. This implies that governments should keep adding resources as long as the external benefits are greater than the cost of the resources. The problem is that no one is capable of measuring the benefits precisely, particularly if they are spread throughout the economy and if they are realized only over a long period of time. It is not hard to imagine a situation where some government program spends $100 million to capture $50 million of external benefits. Without hard numbers, this is always a possible outcome. The case of strategic policy is similar. It requires a government to know the costs of production for foreign firms and to correctly anticipate their reaction when they face subsidized competition. While it is conceivable that the production costs may be known, it is impossible to know their reactions. Even if these objections could somehow be resolved, there are three other problems that make industrial policies questionable.

Determining the Industry to Target

Perhaps the most basic question is which industry to target. If everyone acknowledges that a particular industry has a bright future, then entrepreneurs and investors will probably jump on it. The prospect of future profits is all it takes for private markets to channel resources toward a new venture.

On the other hand, we have established that if there are external benefits, markets may underinvest. Consequently, one possibility for choosing industries to target is to pick the ones that have the largest external benefits. The problem with this strategy is that the positive externalities that develop out of new inventions are usually a surprise to everyone involved, and it is impossible to know beforehand that they will occur.

Another strategy is to target high value-added industries. Recall that **value added** is the difference between the cost of materials and the value of the output. In part, value-added is determined by the contribution of labor to production, and high value-added industries are usually ones in which wages are high. Value-added also measures the contribution of capital, and it is really a mixture of the two—labor and capital. Therefore, value-added may be high because the industry uses a lots of capital, because labor is highly skilled, or both. The problem with targeting high value-added industries is that while the strategy sounds good in theory, it often makes no sense in practice. For example, two of the highest value-added industries in the United States are petroleum refining and tobacco products. No one, to my knowledge, has argued that these industries should be targeted for future development. In any case, it is not clear why high value-added industries will not be developed more efficiently through market processes. In other words, there is nothing inherent in their nature that creates more external benefits than in other industries.

Rent Seeking

A second major problem with industrial policies is that they encourage rent seeking. Recall that rent seeking was defined in Chapter 5 as any activity by firms, individuals, or special interests that is designed to alter the distribution of income in their favor. If firms know that government is willing to subsidize R&D or new investment, they will spend resources to obtain some of the subsidies. This may require hiring lobbyists, economists, engineers, and others, whose job is to persuade Congress or the Department of Commerce that their industry should be targeted.

The extent to which industrial policies encourage resources to be wasted in lobbying and other noneconomically productive activities partly depends on the administrative process through which targeted industries are chosen and the political culture of the country enacting the industrial policy. Countries that have a greater degree of corruption in their political system are likely to have a much harder time choosing between industries on the basis of scientific, technological, or economic criteria. Even in relatively corruption-free environments, however, the problem of industrial policies encouraging rent seeking is real.

International Spillovers

A third issue is that it is often impossible to contain the external benefits of R&D spending within national boundaries. New technologies soon spread across the nations that have the technological sophistication to take advantage of them. One set of estimates puts the benefits to foreigners of R&D spending by the home country at around one-fourth of the total benefits. This is not necessarily a problem, but if one of the purposes of the industrial policy is to enhance the competitiveness of home-based industries, it is ironic that in the end they benefit foreign firms.

Government officials often try to prevent foreign firms from benefiting by excluding them from participation in joint ventures, research consortia, and other groups that are formed to carry out industrial policy objectives. For example, Sematech (Semiconductor Manufacturing Technology) is a consortium open to any U.S.-owned semiconductor manufacturer. Half its funding comes from its members, and the other half comes from the U.S. government. Its purpose is to maintain a U.S. lead in the manufacture of semiconductors. The fact that many U.S. firms have separate joint ventures in research and production with European and Japanese firms greatly lessens the probability that a new breakthrough will remain solely a U.S. secret for long. Nor is this a unique situation. GM, Ford, and Chrysler, all of whom stand to benefit from the Motor Vehicle Manufacturing Program, have joint ventures with Toyota, Mazda, Isuzu, Suzuki, and so on.

U.S. Industrial Policies

It is often believed that the United States does not have industrial policies to promote the competitiveness of specific industries, that these are policies more common to Japan, Europe, or the East Asian NICs. Although the United States' comparative advantage and international competitiveness probably have little to do with industrial policies, they have nevertheless become a fairly common part of the nation's overall economic policy.

U.S. Traditions

Until the 1930s, the United States regularly supported the use of tariffs to protect specific industries, but it was relatively infrequent that direct subsidies were provided to specific industries. Not counting the extensive involvement of government, both state and federal, in the development of the Unites States' infrastructure (e.g., support for roads, canals, railroads, and highways), there were two main exceptions to the general rule of avoidance of direct support for specific industries: agriculture and manufacturing industries supplying the military.

In the agricultural sector, the most obvious externality is in the ability of neighboring farms to copy each other's techniques. Consequently, many types of research and development generate benefits that are external to an individual farm. For this reason, a policy that targets agricultural research may be warranted on theoretical grounds.

In the case of agriculture, the United States passed the Morrill Act in 1862, which gave federally owned lands to states for the purpose of establishing agricultural research colleges. This was followed in 1887 by the Hatch Act, which set up stations to conduct agricultural research of use to the locale in which it was located, and in 1914 by the Smith-Lever Act, which established a system of cooperative education for farmers.

It is uncertain whether these programs were an optimal use of resources. The climate, the available land and its fertility, the relatively high level of literacy among American farmers, the ability to overcome labor shortages with new innovations in farm machinery, and the development of a transportation infrastructure all worked to create a comparative advantage in agriculture. The United States would have emerged as a world supplier of grains and other commodities with or without the support of the universities, research stations, and extensions service. The United States' agricultural position was probably enhanced by the support it received, but it is unknown whether the benefits exceeded the costs.

The theoretical justification for industrial policies in the defense industry is fairly clear. Defense is a public good (if one person gets it, everyone does, whether they pay for it or not), and the economic incentive is to let others pay. For this reason, economists and noneconomists alike agree that it is impossible for markets to provide defense and that it must be done by governments. This does not mean, however, that governments have necessarily to be directly involved in the production of war goods.

In the post–World War II era, the weapons and tools of the United States' defense forces have been produced by private firms. The U.S. government has provided very substantial resources in order to keep these firms in business, under the assumption that it would be detrimental to U.S. defense capability if the nation had to rely on foreign producers for major weapon systems.

Few people would disagree with this viewpoint. Nevertheless, some economists have argued that the United States has had a wide variety of industrial policies throughout the second half of the twentieth century, but it has hidden them behind the mantle of defense in order to gain greater support. The research consortium Sematech is a case in point. Sematech was founded in 1987 by the Department of Defense in response to the growing need to use Japanese semiconductors in U.S. jet aircraft. Sematech's goal was to regain technological superiority in the manufacture of semiconductors, and it seems to have largely succeeded. Many people, however, view Sematech as simply a subsidy to IBM, Motorola, Texas Instruments, and other U.S. corporations—that it was given to help restore their international competitiveness but sold to the public with claims of a military need.

Whether the national defense justification is genuine or not, the United States has rarely used the direct subsidies form of industrial polices (military equipment production is the major exception). More often, U.S. policies have sought to create new research and to disseminate existing information that might otherwise have been overlooked. The United States' agricultural development policies are a case in point, as is Sematech.

The Political Debate of the 1980s

The two periods in U.S. history when the debate over commercial (i.e., nonmilitary) industrial policies has heated up were both times when the country felt threatened by outside economic forces. The first period occurred in the 1790s, when the United States feared domination by Great Britain, and the U.S. Secretary of the Treasury Alexander Hamilton published his *Report on Manufactures* which, in the language of the time, called for a national effort to develop greater manufacturing competitiveness.

The second period of debate began in the late 1970s when the United States began to feel vulnerable to fiercely competitive Japanese manufacturing. First steel, then consumer electronics, autos, and semiconductors seemed to either vanish in the United States or be on the verge of collapsing as wave after wave of Japanese imports captured increasing market shares in the United States and abroad.

In the 1990s, as the Japanese economy has temporarily floundered, it is difficult to understand the panic that seemed to strike U.S. corporate executives and policy makers as they watched lower-priced, higher-quality Japanese goods gain ground in a number of industries that the United States had once dominated. By the mid-1980s, the U.S. trade deficit with Japan had jumped enormously, from roughly equality of exports and imports in 1975 to a deficit for the United States of around $60 billion in 1987 (see Chapter 11). At the same time, the overall U.S. trade deficit went from a slight surplus in 1975 to deficits of $150 to $170 billion in the mid-1980s (see Chapter 8).

Several of the U.S. industries that lost ground to imports were major employers. This meant that, in some cases, not only American corporations but millions of American workers were affected by the growth of imports. In addition, whole communities that had been built around steel mills or car assembly plants began to take on the aspect of modern-day ghost towns, with boarded-up downtowns and rows of empty houses.

At the same time that many U.S. industries were getting pounded by imports, technological progress began to favor skilled workers over unskilled. The effect was twofold. First, it reduced the number of workers needed to produce a specific level of output; and second, it widened the wage differences between skilled and unskilled workers and contributed to growing inequality. In the early 1980s, many thoughtful books and papers appeared that argued that the United States was "de-industrializing." On the one hand, some argued that this was a good thing because it was inevitable for societies to pass through stages from agriculture to industry to services, and the United States was further along in its transformation to an information-based society than were most other economies. Consequently, the U.S. was certain to be a world economic leader in the 21st century. On the other hand, many analysts argued that the loss of manufacturing was symptomatic of a much deeper problem in the U.S. economy: an inability to compete with Japan and the new industrializers in East Asia.

From the vantage point of the late 1990s, it seems that both the optimism and the pessimism about the changes in the U.S. economy were overblown. The rise of Japan and the newly industrialized economies of East Asia have caused the United States to lose its comparative advantage in some relatively labor-intensive production, such as shipbuilding and basic steel manufacturing. (This does not mean that the United States does not produce these goods, only that it produces a lot less.) At the same time, the pressures to move away from more labor-intensive production have been reinforced by technological changes that favor more capital-intensive and skilled-labor-intensive production. In the long run, however, the flexibility of the U.S. economy and its ability to adapt to entirely new circumstances in the world economy remain its greatest strengths.

One outcome of the experience with ballooning trade deficits and declining wages for unskilled workers was an opening of the industrial policy debate at the highest levels of U.S. economic policy. The proponents argued that the market economy of the United States was not capable of an optimal response to the challenges from abroad, while many opponents feared that resources would be wasted by another, newer government bureaucracy. Until President Clinton, the opponents of industrial policies won the political debate, and no president openly embraced the idea. Both Presidents Reagan and Bush, however, seemed to hedge their bets by supporting policies that were, in effect, industrial policies called something else.

Under President Clinton, there has been a relatively modest but overt move toward the use of industrial policies to support specific industries. It remains to be seen what will become of these policies after his presidency is over. Both support of and opposition to the use of industrial policies cut across political parties. In other words, if a Republican were elected, the policies could be dismantled or grow or remain the same, depending on the specific person.

Responding to Other Nations' Industrial Policies

There are two questions relevant to formulating a response to other nations' industrial policies. The first concerns the economic impact on domestic firms of foreign industrial policies: Should nations respond, and if so, how? The second concerns what types of responses should be allowable under the GATT framework.

The Costs and Benefits of Doing Nothing

The answer to the first question depends on the impact of the foreign industrial policy on domestic firms. In many cases, foreign subsidies benefit citizens in the home country by making foreign products cheaper and better. On these grounds, foreign industrial policies are beneficial. However, even though foreign industrial policies may

CASE STUDY 1

Examples of Some Current U.S. Industrial Policies

Examples of U.S. industrial policies are easy to find. All one needs to do is to log onto the World Wide Web and connect to the U.S. Department of Commerce home page. The Commerce Department is the most active of U.S. cabinet-level departments, but other branches of the executive have their own policies also.

The following examples are some of the federal government policies that pass for industrial policies. Each has international competitiveness or technological innovation (or both) as key elements of their mission. In many cases, the policies primarily provide access to information that may otherwise be difficult to obtain, but in other cases they engage in direct research and development.

In addition to the following, a large number of state governments have policies that provide direct or indirect subsidies to industries located within their boundaries. The last source cited here provides a partial and unsystematic listing of some of these state-level programs.

Each of the agencies listed has a Web site address that can be accessed by Internet connection. You can find a lot more information about each agency and its mission by connecting to its Web site and browsing through the menus. You should think about the theoretical justification for each of the programs as you read the descriptions.

1. Advanced Technology Program *(http://www.atp.nist.gov/)*
   ATP funds R&D projects that have "strong commercial potential" but are high risk. Projects are selected based on industry suggestions, but awards are granted through "announced competitions." On average, participants pay for more than half the total costs. A list of current programs includes Advanced Vapor Compression Refrigeration Systems; Catalysis & Biocatalysis Technologies; Component-Based Software; Digital Data Storage; Digital Video in Information Networks; Information Infrastructure for Healthcare; Manufacturing Composite Structures; Materials Processing for Heavy Manufacturing; Motor Vehicle Manufacturing Technology; Technology for the Integration of Manufacturing Applications; and Tools for DNA Diagnostics .

2. Manufacturing Extension Partnership *(http://www.mep.nist.gov/)*
   MEP is modeled after the agricultural extension service. It provides technical manufacturing expertise to "assist smaller U.S. manufacturers in increasing their global competitiveness." It also assists with "quality management, workforce training, workplace organization, business systems, marketing, or financial issues."

3. National Technology Transfer Center *(http://iridium.nttc.edu/nttc.html)*
   NTTC is a "hub of a national network linking U.S. companies with federal laboratories to turn government research results into practical, commercially relevant technology."

4. Asia-Pacific Technology Program *(http://www.ta.doc.gov/asiapac)*
   APTP brings Japanese technical literature to U.S. industry. It also provides technical and policy information obtained from China under the U.S.-China Civil Industrial Technology Initiative. Within the context of the regional trade grouping known as Asia Pacific Economic Cooperation, it pursues joint projects "that promote regional economic growth through technology" with member countries.

5. National Institute of Standards and Technology: Technology Services *(http://www.nist.gov/)*
   NIST provides standards, measurements, calibration services, laboratory accreditation services, and information services to U.S. industry and government. It also lobbies for the adoption of U.S. standards and measurement practices around the world. NIST maintains many laboratories, including NIST Electronics and Electrical Engineering Laboratory; NIST Manufacturing Engineering Laboratory; NIST Chemical Science and Technology Laboratory; NIST Physics Laboratory; NIST Materials Science and Engineering Laboratory; NIST Building and Fire Research Laboratory; NIST Computer Systems Laboratory; NIST Computing and Applied Mathematics Laboratory.

6. National Telecommunications and Information Administration *(http://www.ntia.doc.gov/)*
   NTIA advises the president on "telecommunications policy, trade, and technology issues." The Institute for Telecommunication Sciences (ITS) provides the NTIA with "scientific, engineering, and technological competence." The ITS "works to enhance technology innovation and competition in the U.S. communications industry, to expand trade opportunities for U.S. communications firms, and to increase productivity in U.S. industry, government, and academia." The ITS has a number of programs, including the following: Digital Networks Program; Video Quality Program; Objective Audio Quality Research Program; International Standards Program; Data Communications Network Testing Program; Advance Satellite Communications Program; High Frequency Radio Interoperability Program; Radio Testing Program; Integrated Telecommunications Evaluation Facility Program; Radio Spectrum Measurement Program; Spectrum Measurement System Development Program; Modern Propagation Research Program; Personal Communication Services Program; Federal Technology Transfer Program; Telecommunications Analysis Services Program.

7. Office of Air & Space Commercialization *(http://cher.eda.doc.gov/oasc.html)*
   OASC's role is to "assist the secretary of commerce in the formulation and implementation of policies which foster the growth and international competitiveness of the U.S. commercial space sector" and to "promote the commercial use of space by U.S. private industry."

Case Study 1 continues

Case Study 1 continued

8. **USDA Agricultural Research Service** *(http://www.ars.usda.gov/)*
    ARS's mission is to "(1) provide access to agricultural information and develop new knowledge and technology needed to solve technical agricultural problems of broad scope and high national priority; (2) ensure adequate availability of high-quality, safe food and other agricultural products to meet the nutritional needs of the American consumer; (3) sustain a viable and competitive food and agricultural economy; (4) enhance quality of life and economic opportunity for rural citizens and society as a whole; and (5) to maintain a quality environment and natural resource base."

9. **USDA Economic Research Service** *(http://www.econ.ag.gov/)*
    ERS provides "economic and other social science information and analysis for public and private decisions on agriculture, food, natural resources, and rural America."

10. **Cooperative State Research, Education, and Extension Service** *(http://www.reeusda.gov/)*
    The antecedents of this program go back to the Morrill Act of 1862, the Hatch Act of 1887, and the Smith-Lever Act of 1914. Respectively, these acts established (1) the land-grant colleges that were given a mandate to perform agricultural and engineering research; (2) the agricultural experiment stations to perform research and disseminate information; and (3) the Cooperative Extension System, which provides training and education to farmers.

11. **Defense Advanced Research Projects Agency** *(http://www.arpa.mil/)*
    DARPA's primary responsibility is "to help maintain U.S. technological superiority and guard against unforeseen technological advances by potential adversaries." DARPA also looks for new dual-use technologies—that is, those with commercial and military uses.

12. **Semiconductor Manufacturing Technology** *(http://www.sematech.org/public/home.htm)*
    Sematech is probably the best-known program sponsored by DARPA. It is set up as a nonprofit corporation with the objective to "solve the technical challenges required to keep the United States number one in the global semiconductor industry." Its membership is open to all U.S.-owned semiconductor manufacturing firms that collectively supply about half the research funds

13. **Office of Economic Conversion Information Exchange** *(http://netsite.esa.doc.gov/oeci/)*
    OECI provides information about "defense adjustment and defense conversion, economic development, and technology transfer." It acts as a clearinghouse for information about a wide range of projects, from MAGLEV (magnetically levitated trains) to CALSTART (California's advanced transportation technology industrial policy) to THOMAS EDISON (Ohio's advanced technology industrial policy).

CASE STUDY 2

Targeting Motor Vehicle Manufacturing Processes

Descriptions of a number of ongoing research and development programs with federal government sponsorship can be found within the Advanced Technology Program (ATP) of the National Institute of Standards and Technology, in the Department of Commerce. A Web site with a complete list is at *http://www.atp.nist.gov/atp/focusprg.htm#Ongoing.* A specific example, and one that clearly shows the dimensions of U.S. industrial policy and its commercial reach, is the Motor Vehicle Manufacturing Technology Program. The ATP describes the benefits of the Motor Vehicle Manufacturing Technology Program as follows:

Changeovers to new car, van, or truck models are engineering and manufacturing marathons, taking U.S. automakers and their suppliers an average of 42 to 48 months to cross the finish line. With more agile equipment and processes that sharply reduce the time and cost of converting factories to new models, the nation's automotive industry can significantly reduce the span from initial design to consumer-ready vehicle and sprint ahead of the competition. . . .

The ATP focused program on motor vehicle manufacturing technology will foster innovations in manufacturing practices that could slash time-to-market to 24 months, markedly better than even the best times logged to date by foreign or domestic car makers. With the reusable, modular equipment and processes envisioned by the program, the cost of retooling car-manufacturing facilities—now ranging between $1.2 billion and $2.9 billion, depending on the extent of the changeover—could be reduced by as much as tenfold. The savings would reduce the size of break-even production volumes needed to recover investment costs, making it profitable for U.S. automobile companies to compete in small-volume markets at mass-production prices . . . .

The automotive sector, which accounts for about 4 percent of the U.S. gross domestic product and employs more than 2 million people, will be the initial beneficiary of the anticipated technologies . . . . Outside the sector, a variety of other manufacturing industries, from metal furniture to precision instruments, will be able to exploit targeted improvements in machining, grinding, and other widely used processes . . . .

The ATP ends its discussion of its Advanced Motor Vehicle Technology Program by noting:

Domestic auto manufacturers devote the bulk of their R&D to product research. The fraction allocated to process-oriented R&D tends to focus on shorter-term, incremental improvements, in contrast with the major gains in performance and capabilities that the ATP-focused program will foster. Moreover, individual car companies will not independently fund work likely to yield non-appropriable, or widely shared, benefits that competitors can profit from without having to make that same R&D investment.

Case Study 2 continues

Case Study 2 continued

> The total funding for the Motor Vehicle Manufacturing Technology Program is $156 million, with approximately $83 million coming from the federal government and the rest from the private sector.
>
> *Source:* http://www.atp.nist.gov/atp/focus/mvmt.htm

benefit home country consumers, governments and domestic firms worry that they provide an unfair advantage to foreign competitors. For this reason, governments often object to foreign industrial policies and threaten some form of retaliation.

We have already seen the concept of path dependency. This is simply the idea that a nation's capabilities depend on the path it chooses. In other words, the set of goods that a nation will be able to efficiently produce in the future depends on the types of goods it chooses to produce today. This concept is easy to state but difficult to measure because it requires some knowledge about the future evolution of technology and science. Nevertheless, many nations worry about the future consequences of their firms getting squeezed out of certain types of production by foreign firms that are subsidized by their governments. Even if home-country consumers get a bargain, there is the worry that future living standards will be lower than they would be otherwise, because the nation lacks some types of experience and skills.

It may not be the case, however, that foreign industrial policies hurt domestic firms. Indeed, if there are international spillovers, foreign subsidies may generate new ideas and inventions that can easily be appropriated by domestic firms. Ultimately, each case is different and requires a different response.

Permissible Retaliation Within the GATT Framework

One significant improvement in trade rules achieved by the Uruguay Round of the GATT negotiations is a clearer definition of subsidies. Subsidies are defined as financial contributions by a government or other body acting in its behalf. This includes direct transfers (including loans and loan guarantees), tax credits, provision of goods and services, and income and price supports.

Signatories to the GATT are not prohibited from using subsidies, but when they result in harm to another country's domestic industry, either directly or indirectly through limiting market access, then the injured country may impose countervailing duties. Recall from Chapter 6 that countervailing duties are tariffs that are imposed to counteract the effects of subsidies by foreign governments. The GATT agreement also establishes a set of rules for determining if the subsidies have harmed firms in other countries.

It may seem that the rules forbid any industrial policy that successfully alters a nation's comparative advantage. There are two reasons why this is not the case. First, the agreement specifically permits subsidies that are given for research and development activities so long as the R&D is "precompetitive." In other words, it must be given at an early stage of the development process and cannot be used to develop a specific commercial product. As an example, research on the design of automotive suspension systems is permitted, but the design of a new car that will incorporate the research is not. Technological research to develop improved X-ray lithography techniques in order to cram more semiconductors onto a circuit board are permitted, but the development of a commercially available machine that uses the new techniques is not.

The second reason why the new GATT rules do not prohibit industrial policies is that if the policies are successful in altering a nation's comparative advantage, then the new industry should not need further subsidization. What the GATT rules forbid is the continuous subsidization of commercial enterprises. Yet, if the enterprises require continuous subsidization, it is questionable if it has truly been successful.

Conclusion

In principle, once the determinants of a nation's comparative advantage are known, they can be changed. For example, widening and deepening the nation's schools and universities to reach more people will alter the supply of unskilled and skilled labor. Similarly, creating new incentives to save will lower the cost of capital and increase its supply.

For most advanced industrial economies, and some not so advanced, these kinds of general policies are given—highly skilled labor of all kinds and physical capital are abundant. A key question for many of these economies is whether or not there are more policies targeted that might be used to create comparative advantages in very specific industries such as medical equipment, aircraft, measuring and control devices, semiconductors, and so forth.

Given that the factor endowments of many advanced industrial economies are relatively similar, a small shift in technological knowhow can have a relatively profound effect on a nation's comparative advantage. For this reason, most nations pursue industrial policies that are designed to help specific industries to gain a technological advantage over its international competition.

▲ Industrial policies are usually enacted through some kind of direct or indirect government subsidy. The subsidies may focus on accelerating basic research or they may directly finance some part of the development and production of commercial products.

▲ The problem these policies encounter is in choosing which industry or which product should be targeted for development. Since industrial policies ignore market signals, the choice of industries and products requires some clever guesses about the evolution of technology. In essence, it requires government planners, or governments in conjunction with businesses, to see something that markets have overlooked. Market failures are not uncommon, but most economists are skeptical that they can be easily spotted and that the right policies to correct them are easily enacted.

▲ Industrial policies also run into the problem of rent seeking. When firms perceive that governments are giving something of value, they will expend resources trying to obtain it. The prospect of subsidies or some other governmental support easily leads to wasteful expenditures on lobbying and other attempts to influence government decisions.

▲ If industrial policies lead to technological breakthroughs, it is difficult to keep the information within national boundaries.

▲ The United States has cautiously implemented a number of industrial polices in recent years, although broader and more general support has rejected the idea. American history has several examples of industrial policies, most notably in agriculture.

▲ Industrial policies have become more difficult to implement with the Uruguay Round of the GATT. Countries are prohibited from directly subsidizing the development of commercial products but may still support "pre-competitive" research and development.

Vocabulary

externalities	social return
industrial policy	strategic trade policy
market failure	value added
private return	

Study Questions

1. What are the general kinds of policies that nations can implement in order to alter their comparative advantage? Explain how these policies alter comparative advantage within the framework of a Heckscher Ohlin trade mode.

2. Explain the concept of path dependency as it applies to technological development. How does path dependency intersect with the industrial policy debate?

3. Briefly describe the U.S.'s history with industrial policies that target specific industries. Does the United States have these kinds of policies today?

4. What are the theoretical justifications for targeting specific industries?

5. Why are most economists either against the use of specific industrial targets, or very cautious in their support?

6. What techniques are used to implement industrial policies?

7. Are targeted industrial policies allowed under the rules of the Uruguay Round of the GATT? Explain.

8. Suppose a foreign country uses industrial policies to create a competitive advantage for one of its industries. What is the optimal response by the home country?

Suggested Reading

Fallows, James. *Looking at the Sun: The Rise of the New East Asian Economic and Political System*. New York: Pantheon Books, 1994.

Norton, R. D. "Industrial Policy and American Renewal," *Journal of Economic Literature,* V, 24, No. 1, 1986.

Ostroy, Sylvia, and Richard Nelson. *Techno-Nationalism and Techno-Globalism: Conflict and Cooperation*. Washington DC: Brookings Institution, 1995.

Tyson, Laura D'Andrea. *Who's Bashing Whom?: Trade Conflict in High-Technology Industries*. Washington DC: Institute for International Economics, 1992.

CHAPTER 8

TRADE AND THE BALANCE OF PAYMENTS

Introduction to the Current Account

The international transactions of a nation are divided into two main components. One component tracks the flow of goods and services into and out of the country; the second component tracks the flow of financial capital. The account that records the first component is called the current account, and the second is referred to as the capital account. In this chapter, we briefly examine both accounts and the system used to keep track of each country's international transactions. The primary goal is to understand the relationship between savings and investment on the one hand and the trade balance on the other. In addition, we will use the international accounts to examine the meaning of international indebtedness and to discuss its consequences. We begin with an example from the United States.

The Trade Balance

In 1997, the United States purchased $1,047.8 billion in goods and services from foreign producers. The composition of the purchases included a wide array of items, from Japanese Nintendos to Taiwanese computer parts, from Venezuelan oil to Canadian cars, and from luxury vacations in Cancun, Mexico, to Europasses on the European passenger rail system. In the same year, U.S. firms sold to foreigners $937.6 billion in goods and services. The single most important item in the United States' exports was aircraft, but wheat, patent rights, software, and trips to Disneyworld also figured importantly in the total.

The difference between exports and imports of goods (i.e., excluding services) is called the nation's merchandise **trade balance.** In 1997, the United States' merchandise trade balance was $679.3 billion in exports minus $877.3 billion in imports, or –$198.0 billion. Since the balance was negative, the United States had a **trade deficit.** If it had been positive, then the United States would have had a **trade surplus** or, to say the same thing another way, the United States would have been exporting more goods than it was importing.

Note that the merchandise trade balance does not include services, a category in which the United States has a large surplus ($87.7 billion in 1997). This is because the merchandise trade balance is calculated monthly, which is too short a time frame to get an accurate measurement of service exports and imports. Goods are tangible; they pass through ports where they can be tabulated by customs officials, and they require paperwork, such as bills of lading. Services, on the other hand, are intangible and do not pass under the watchful eye of customs inspectors. Hence, they are harder to measure and are reported on a less frequent basis (quarterly).

The Current Account Balance

The merchandise trade balance is the most commonly cited measurement of a nation's transactions with the rest of the world. The widespread dissemination of the monthly trade balance statistics through press releases and news articles makes it the most familiar concept in international economics, as well as the basis of many people's understanding of U.S. international economic relations. It probably also has an unintended effect of causing the public to concentrate too heavily on tangible, manufactured goods, to the detriment of services trade.

A statistic that is reported every three months, or quarterly, is the **current account balance.** The current account balance is not available on a monthly basis because it requires far more work to gather the necessary data. The current account balance measures all current (noncapital) transactions between a nation and the rest of the world. It has three main items: (1) the value of goods and services exported, minus the value of imports; (2) investment income, defined as income received from investments abroad, minus income paid to foreigners on their U.S. investments; and (3) unilateral transfers, defined as any foreign aid or other transfers received from foreigners, minus that given to foreigners. The simplest framework for conceptualizing these three components is in terms of credits and debits, is portrayed in Table 8.1

The current account. *The current account is a record of transactions in goods, services, investment income, and unilateral transfers between the residents of a country and the rest of the world.*

Each of the three items—goods and services, investment income, and unilateral transfers—has credit (positive) and debit (negative) components. If the sum of the credits is greater than the sum of the debits, the nation has a current account surplus; otherwise, it has a deficit. Note also that the investment income items are not movements of investment capital but are the income received or income paid on previous

TABLE 8.1 Components of the Current Account		
	Credit	*Debit*
1. Goods and services	Exports	Imports
2. Investment income	Income received on foreign investments	Income paid to foreigners on their U.S. investments
3. Unilateral transfers	Transfers received from abroad	Transfers made to foreigners

flows of investment capital. For example, financial capital sent to Germany to buy a German bond would not be included, but the interest received on the bond would be. (The capital that leaves the United States is counted in the **capital account**.)

It is useful to think of investment income flows as payments for the use of another nation's capital. In this sense, they are similar to payments either made or received in return for services of capital. If U.S. mutual funds invest in the Mexican stock market, for example, the initial investment will not show up directly in the current account, but the subsequent flow of dividends back to the mutual fund manager in the United States will be counted. Conceptually, it is as if U.S. investors are receiving payment for the rental of U.S. capital to Mexican firms. In this sense, it is similar to a payment for a service. The third item in the current account balance includes payments made that are not in exchange for a good or service; for example, foreign aid or the sending home of the wages of immigrants temporarily residing in another country. In the U.S. case, these payments are usually relatively small, but they can figure very importantly in the current account balances of developing countries receiving either substantial foreign aid or large remittances of wages from their citizens working abroad and sending home their wages.

Table 8.2 gives a picture of the U.S. current account in 1997. The large deficit for 1997 ($155,215 million) was about average by comparison to the previous decade, as can be seen in Figure 8.1, which shows the U.S. current account balance since the end of World War II. Large deficits in the current account began around 1982 and have been a more or less constant feature of the U.S. economy ever since. Between 1982 and 1987, the current account deficit grew from $11.4 to $167.3 billion. Between 1987 and 1991, the current account improved (partly as a result of large unilateral transfers to the United States in 1991 as payment for Operation Desert Storm), but since 1991, it has deteriorated once again.

TABLE 8.2 The U.S. Current Account Balance, 1997 (Millions of Dollars)		
	Credit	*Debit*
1. Goods and services		
Exports of goods	679,325	
Exports of services	258,268	
Imports of goods		–877,279
Imports of services		–170,520
2. Investment income		
Investment income received	241,787	
Investment income paid		–247,105
3. Net unilateral transfers		–39,691
Merchandise trade balance		–197,954
Current account balance		–155,215

Source: Bureau of Economic Analysis, *Survey of Current Business,* Vol. 78, No. 7, July 1998.

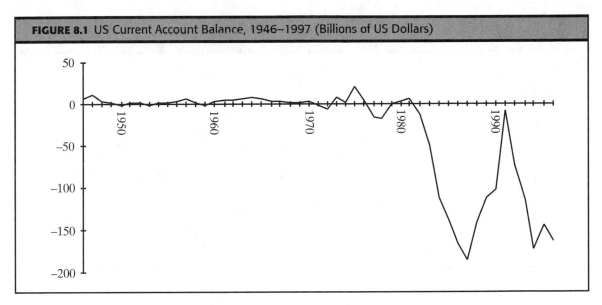

FIGURE 8.1 US Current Account Balance, 1946–1997 (Billions of US Dollars)

For many Americans, the dramatic decline in the current account balance that began in the early 1980s was a shock. Some saw it as indication of declining competitiveness, while others argued that it was a necessary consequence of the large federal government budget deficits that began around the same time.

Trade Deficits and Budget Deficits

In the early 1980s, at the same time that the United States was moving from a position of more or less balanced trade to one of large trade deficits, it began to experience large federal budget deficits (Figure 8.2). Given that the two deficits appeared to be sychronized in the early 1980s, it seemed logical to infer that there was a connection between the trade balance and the federal budget balance. In fact, many students often confuse the two and speak as if they are one and the same. It is important to keep in mind, however, that the trade deficit is completely separate from the federal budget deficit. In the 1980s and early 1990s, some politicians and policy analysts began calling them the "twin deficits," but in a practical sense they are entirely different entities. There is a connection between them, however, enough so that in the second half of the 1980s, some economists maintained that if we reduced the U.S. federal budget deficit, the U.S. trade deficit would decline also. As a result of this kind of assertion, it became popular to believe that a $1 reduction in the budget deficit would create a $1 reduction in the trade deficit. As we will see, this is a gross oversimplification of the relationship between trade and budget deficits, and it is just plain wrong as an empirical fact. As of this writing, in mid-1998, the federal budget is projected to have a tiny surplus, while the current account deficit will most likely be $150 to $200 billion and growing, even as the budget moves further into surplus.

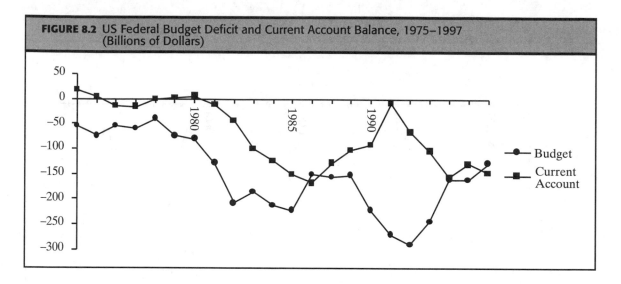

FIGURE 8.2 US Federal Budget Deficit and Current Account Balance, 1975–1997 (Billions of Dollars)

The situation with today's budget and current account balances clearly demonstrates that the two do not have to move together. Any connection between the two is mediated by savings and investment. Given a large enough pool of savings, a nation can run large budget deficits and large trade surpluses. Alternatively, with a small pool of savings, a nation might run a budget surplus and still have a trade deficit, a picture that looks a great deal like the latter part of the 1990s. The robust economy generated larger than expected tax revenues, while the low unemployment rate meant that social expenditures were falling. Nevertheless, weak economies outside the United States, particularly in Japan and East Asia, meant that U.S. exports grew more slowly than imports, leading to an increase in the current account deficit.

Trade Deficits and the National Accounts

Let's examine the relationship between all the variables mentioned so far: current account balances, budget balances, savings, and investment. This will, in turn, allow us to avoid some common mistakes in international economic reasoning, such as blaming a particular country or a group of countries for the U.S. trade deficit.

The National Income Accounts

First, we will define the main macroeconomic aggregates of a national economy. The notation adopted here is the same as that pertaining to national income accounting in principles of economics texts. All the variables and their definitions are listed in Table 8.3.

TABLE 8.3 Variable Definitions	
Variable	*Definition*
Y_D	Gross domestic product, GDP
Y_N	Gross national product, GNP
C	Consumption expenditures
I	Investment expenditures
G	Government expenditures on goods and services
X	Exports of goods and services
M	Imports of goods and services
CA	Current account balance
S_p	Private savings (savings of households and firms)
T	Net taxes, or taxes paid minus transfer payments received

Recall from principles of economics (or Chapter 1 of this book) that a nation's **gross domestic product (GDP)** is defined as the value of all final goods and services produced inside the boundaries of a nation. It is the most common measure of the total output of a nation, region, or any geographical area within which the total value of production can be measured. A key part of the GDP concept is that in order to avoid the problem of double counting, the GDP adds up the value of *final* goods and services. For example, we added up the value of steel sold to a car maker and the value of the cars, we would be counting the steel twice, once as steel and a second time as part of the value of the car. In order to avoid this problem, we only add up the value of goods that have arrived at their final use, either as a consumer good, as a government purchase, or as the purchase of machines and equipment by firms.

> **Gross domestic product and gross national product.** *Gross domestic product (GDP) is the market value of all final goods and services produced inside a nation's boundaries. Gross national product (GNP) is the market value of all final goods and services produced by the residents of a nation, regardless of where the production takes place.*

An alternative concept for measuring a nation's output is **gross national product,** or **GNP.** For most countries, the differences between the two concepts are very small. GNP is equal to GDP plus income received from abroad minus income paid to people living abroad. The difference between GNP and GDP is precisely equal to lines 2 and 3 in Table 8.1: the investment income and unilateral transfers components of the current account balance.

Another way to express GDP is in terms of its components. GDP is equal to the sum of consumer expenditures plus investment expenditures plus government expenditures on goods and services plus exports of goods and services minus imports of goods and services. Algebraically,

$$(1) \qquad Y_D = GDP = C + I + G + X - M$$

Equation 1 is the definition of GDP.

If we add investment income and unilateral transfers to GDP, we have GNP. Doing so, however, turns net exports, the $(X - M)$ component of the national accounts, into CA, the current account balance:

(2)
$$Y_N = GNP = C + I + G + CA$$

We will work with equation 2 because we are interested in the relationships between macroeconomic variables, such as the government budget, and the whole complement of current account variables, including income received from and paid to foreigners.

From the point of view of the people receiving income, there are three choices or obligations for the income they receive. They may consume it, save it, or use it to pay taxes. In reality, they do a combination of all three. Since the aggregate income received is equal to the total of all income in the economy, we can write equation 3 as an alternative definition of GNP:

(3)
$$Y_N = C + S_p + T$$

The Role of Savings in a National Economy

Equations 2 and 3 are different ways of defining GNP. This allows us to write

(4)
$$C + I + G + CA = C + S_p + T$$

or by subtracting consumption from both sides

(4a)
$$I + G + CA = S_p + T$$

Rearranging terms produces

(4b)
$$S_p + (T - G) = I + CA$$

The term in parentheses on the left side is the government budget balance. Since T is government revenue (or income), and G is government expenditure, if $(T - G)$ is positive, the government budget is in surplus and, if negative, in deficit. By placing the government budget balance on the left-hand side, we are emphasizing that there are two sources of savings in an economy: the private sector supplies S_p, and the public or governmental sector supplies $(T - G)$. Another way to think of the two terms is that S_p is private savings, while the quantity $(T - G)$ is public savings. If the government budget is in deficit, then the government is dis-saving and must borrow from the private sector. In essence, government borrowing reduces total national savings.

From equation 4b we see that a nation's savings (private plus public) is divided into two uses. First, it is a source of funds for investment. This role is crucial, since new investments in machinery and equipment are the source of much of our income growth over time. New investment is necessary to upgrade the skills of the labor force, to provide more capital on the job, and to improve the quality of capital by introducing new technology. If the government budget is in deficit, the public component of savings is negative and the left-hand side of equation 4b is smaller. Consequently, the total supply of national savings available for investment will be less.

If, on the other hand, the government budget is in surplus, it augments private savings and increases the funds available for investment.

Second, national savings are a source of funds for foreign investment. If the current account is in surplus (CA positive), national savings finances the purchase of domestic goods by foreign users of those goods. In return, or as payment, the domestic economy acquires foreign financial assets. These financial assets may take many different forms, but for now you can think of them as IOUs that promise to pay for the goods at a later date. Since a positive current account leads to the acquisition of foreign assets, it is equivalent to an investment in a foreign country.

Algebraically, if CA is a negative number, then domestic investment—I— can be greater than it would be otherwise with a given amount of savings. In other words, with a negative current account balance, foreign savings supplements national savings. If a nation runs a current account deficit, it purchases more goods and services than it sells abroad. The difference between foreign sales and foreign purchases is paid for by foreigners who, in return, acquire assets in the deficit country. In effect, the deficit country borrows against its future output, assuming that at some future date, the surplus country may decide to sell its assets in return for goods and services that can be transported home. When that date arrives, the country that initially ran a deficit will have to run a current account surplus in order to provide the goods and services (exports) demanded.

Equation 4b says that a change in the level of private savings must be matched by an offsetting change in public savings (the government budget), changes in investment, changes in the current account, or some combination of all three. If private savings are very high, then the government can run a budget deficit, while the nation still manages to have high levels of investment and a current account surplus. On the other hand, if private savings are low, it will be harder to support a budget deficit while keeping investment up.

The experience of the United States in the 1980s illustrates these points. For reasons not well understood, private savings by households and businesses fell to record lows in the first half of the 1980s. At the same time, public savings reached record lows as well (T-G was negative and large in absolute value). The deep recession of 1981–1982, the 23 percent reduction in federal income tax rates in 1981–1983, and the ongoing buildup in military expenditures led to record high budget deficits. Given that both private and public savings were down, it was not surprising that investment levels fell as well and that the United States began to run large trade deficits with the rest of the world. In the 1990s, as the budget deficit disappeared, we have not witnessed a corresponding fall in the trade deficit. The reason, as should be apparent from the equation, is that there have been movements in private savings and investment.

Table 8.4 shows the value of savings, investment, budget balances, and trade balances for the United States and six other countries in 1993. The sample of countries is the G-7 (Group of Seven) that comprises the seven leading industrial nations. For purposes of comparison, each country's variables are expressed as a percentage of their GNP. This enables us to compare countries of very different sizes without confusing the size differences with behavior differences.

TABLE 8.4 Private Savings, Investment, Government Budgets, and Current Account Balances as a Percent of GNP, 1993

	S_p	$T-G$	I	CA
Canada	20.8	−6.3	18.8	−4.3
France	23.0	−4.7	17.3	1.0
Germany*	20.5	−0.1	19.0	1.4
Italy	25.0	−6.5	17.3	1.2
Japan	26.8	5.9	29.6	3.1
UK	18.8	−6.0	15.1	−2.3
U.S.	19.0	−4.1	16.4	−1.5

*West Germany only.

Source: United Nations, *National Accounts Statistics: Main Aggregates and Detailed Tables, 1993.* New York, 1995.

In Table 8.4, there is a general but imperfect relationship between budget deficits and trade deficits. Countries with budget deficits have current account deficits as well, while budget surpluses (Japan and also Germany, whose budget was almost balanced) are associated with current account surpluses. The relationship is not perfect, however, and Italy, for example, had an enormous government budget deficit but by no means the largest trade deficit. Italy's public dis-saving was partly offset by an unusually high savings rate. Italy pays a price for its large budget deficit, however, in the form of a lower investment rate. Japan's private savings were not much more than Italy's, but because it had a large government surplus to augment its private savings, its investment rate was more than one and a half times Italy's.

The cases of Canada, the United Kingdom, and the United States represent another tendency. The total (private and public) supply of savings that is available for investment was the lowest of the countries sampled. The availability of private savings for financing investment was low to begin with, and then it was stretched further by the need to finance large-budget deficits. Consequently, investment as a share of GNP was the lowest of the countries sampled. Essentially, there simply were not enough funds to provide private savings to the government for its deficit and to the private sector for investment.

The case of Canada represents somewhat of an alternative to the U.S. and UK pattern. Savings rates were essentially the same as the U.S. rates, and the government budget deficit was even larger than the United States'; but Canada invests substantially more. The difference was due to the fact that Canada had a much larger current account deficit. The inflow of foreign goods and services enabled Canadians to raise the share of their GNP that was given over to investment in spite of their mediocre savings and large budget deficit. The price that Canadians pay for their current account deficit is that foreigners gain ownership of a larger piece of the Canadian economy—Canada's real estate, factories, government bonds, and stocks. This worries some Canadians, but in point of fact, there is probably little or no reason to be concerned. We will examine the consequences of this later in the chapter, but for now we need to clarify the long-run consequences of low savings.

In the long run, if low savings rates persist, then investment will be less; and there will be a slower accumulation of new capital equipment and new technology. The end result is that everyone's standard of living rises more slowly. Since the noticeable effects are slow to appear, and since it is often a case of comparing "what is" with "what might have been," stagnating living standards may not be noticed for a long time. When they are finally noted, people are still not likely to connect them with low savings rates and low rates of investment.

At the microeconomic level of individual firms, a low rate of national savings reduces the ability of individual enterprises to remain at the frontier of their industry. The scarcity of funds available for investment increases the rate of interest charged by lenders and, as the cost of borrowing rises, it raises the cost of building new plants and equipping them with new technology. The fact that a firm cannot afford to invest does not necessarily mean that it is unable to compete; it does mean, however, that it will be more difficult to compete with cutting-edge products that command the highest prices. There are many consequences of low savings rates, but reduced investment levels is the direst over the long term.

The U.S. Current Account Deficit in Perspective

We have seen that there is a big difference between a government budget deficit and a current account trade deficit. Nevertheless, because they are both a form of accounting deficit (one in the government's accounts, the other in a nation's accounts with the rest of the world) and because the term *deficit* by itself connotes something negative, there is an instinctive tendency to believe that a current account trade deficit has negative implications for the economy. Is this true?

Is the Current Account Deficit Necessarily Bad?

The current account relationship to total savings and investment is an identity, which means that it does not tell us why the U.S. economy runs a current account deficit. That is, in equation 4b,

$$S_p + (T - G) = I + CA$$

the left and right sides are equal by definition. We cannot say that CA is negative because savings are low any more than we can say it is negative because investment is too high. Consequently, there are a number of ways to interpret a negative current account trade balance, and clearly not all of them are bad.

For example, one interpretation is that the deficit enables the United States to invest more than it could otherwise. Greater investment is beneficial, since investment is correlated with long-term growth. A related interpretation stresses that foreigners are willing to run surpluses with the United States because of the confidence they have in the U.S. economy. In order to obtain the U.S.- dollar-denominated assets that they want, our trading partners must earn dollars by selling goods and services in the U.S. market. This enables them to obtain the dollars they need to purchase factories, real estate, stocks, bonds, and other U.S.-based assets. The fact that foreigners have decided to store a portion of their wealth in the United States is a significant indicator of confidence in the long-term health of the American economy. In addition, it provides the United States with investment funds.

Another interpretation of the U.S. current account deficit is that it reflects a lack of "competitiveness" in the U.S. economy. Clearly, some American industries are more competitive than others, but reference to the overall U.S. economy in terms of its competitiveness has little or no meaning. (See Chapter 3.) No matter how uncompetitive or backward an industry or a firm might be, it can always compete by selling its goods for less. If U.S.-made products were inferior to those made in another country, then the U.S. firms making those goods would simply have to move "down market" and accept a lower price for their outputs. People bought the infamous Yugo automobile, for example, in spite of the fact that it was not a very good car. It was cheap, however, and in some market segments, consumers were looking for a cheap car above all else. The problem with having a large number of industries that become uncompetitive is that the national standard of living rises more slowly, or perhaps not at all. All else equal, selling exports for less reduces a nation's material welfare. In essence, the idea of competitiveness is really about the ability of a country to increase productivity so that it can increase its living standard—and productivity is largely about savings and investment.

Another reason sometimes cited as the cause of the U.S. trade deficit is the trade policies of other nations. This argument is even less valid than the previous argument for two reasons. First, the trade practices of any one nation are not likely to influence the overall current account balance with the rest of the world. Most nations have trade deficits with some of their trading partners, which they balance against trade surpluses with others. Second, the current account deficit of the United States cannot be due to the restrictive trade policies of other nations because foreign markets are more open today than at any time since 1900. Yet, the U.S. current account deficit took off in the 1980s. Consider the bilateral deficit with Japan. In 1994, the U.S. current account deficit with Japan was $65.1 billion, up from $55.4 billion in 1993. To a casual observer, it seems logical to blame it on Japanese trade barriers, especially since there are a lot of stories about Japanese resistance to imports. The problem, however, is that everyone agrees that no matter how closed the Japanese economy may be to outsiders, it is more open today than it has ever been.

One potentially serious problem with a current account deficit is that it increases the dependency of a country on inflows of foreign capital. The deficit must be financed somehow, which is to say that the nation running the deficit has to attract sufficient foreign capital to pay for the excess of imports over exports. In the case of the U.S. this is not a serious problem at current levels of the deficit, but for smaller, developing nations, the ability to attract sufficient foreign capital to finance a large current account deficit is by no means certain. Sudden shifts in investor sentiment can lead to crises when foreign financing dries up. We will take a more detailed look at these capital flows in the second half of the chapter, where the capital account is examined.

Policies to Eliminate a Current Account Deficit

A key question for large current account deficit countries is what kind of policy will eliminate the imbalance. Although the deficit for the U.S. may not be harmful, in the case of Mexico, Thailand, and a number of other countries, large current account deficits have led to crises when foreign investors suddenly lost confidence and refused to risk additional capital flows for financing the deficits. Indeed, most financial analysts look closely at the size of a nation's current account deficit when they consider the economic conditions in a nation. Deficits of a size that is equal to several percentage points of GDP, or higher, are not necessarily harmful, but they raise a flag of caution because they create vulnerabilities to sudden shifts in investor expectations.

The keys to eliminating a current account deficit lie in the macroeconomy. The appropriate policies, which must be used together, are called **expenditure switching policies** and **expenditure reducing policies**. Expenditure switching policies work at the margin to shift national expenditures away from foreign goods and towards domestic ones, while expenditure reducing policies shrink overall expenditures inside an economy. When the IMF is called in to help with a balance of payments crisis, these policies are typically high on the list of prescribed actions.

Expenditure switching can take many forms. Basically they include any policy that reorients domestic spending away from foreign goods (reduces imports). Primary examples of the kinds of policy that are favored are a temporary tariff on imports and an exchange rate depreciation (see Chapter 9). Both actions raise the price of foreign goods and make domestic ones relatively cheaper. A potential side effect is overheating the domestic economy. Switching to domestic goods can lead to bottlenecks and excess demand, both of which encourage inflationary pressures to build. As a consequence, expenditure switching policies are generally accompanied by expenditure reducing policies. The latter includes any policy that reduces overall expenditure in the economy; for example, a tax increase or a cut in government spending.

> *Expenditure switching and expenditure reducing policies. Expenditure switching policies are designed to shift the expenditures of domestic residents. If the problem is a trade deficit, they should shift towards domestically produced goods; if the problem is a trade surplus, they should shift towards foreign goods. Examples of these policies include changes in the exchange rate and changes in tariffs and quotas. Expenditure reducing policies are ones that reduce the overall level of domestic expenditure. These are appropriate for addressing the problem of a trade deficit and include cuts in government expenditures and/or increases in taxes.*

In terms of equation 4b, the goal is to raise private and public savings by reducing private and public expenditures. In addition, it is common for investment to temporarily decline. Since the left-hand side of equation 4b rises and investment (I) may fall, the current account must approve. These policies are not without their own costs, however. For example, the decline in overall expenditures, while necessary during a crisis, can also cause a recession. Consequently, the expenditure switching part of the policy is important because it shifts some of the current aggregate spending from foreign markets to domestic ones.

CASE STUDY

The U.S. Current Account Balance and the Japan Trade Deficit

In 1997, the United States ran a current account deficit with Japan of $64.1 billion. Let us consider what would have happened inside the U.S. economy if, somehow, the deficit with Japan could have been erased overnight. The main question to ponder is whether this would have wiped out a substantial proportion of the United States' overall current account deficit, which in 1997 was $155.2 billion (see Table 8.2). The tendency is to believe that if we could eliminate our trade deficit with Japan, then the overall trade deficit would be substantially reduced. In fact, this is incorrect economic reasoning. The analysis we just developed will help you to see why, if you have not already figured it out.

If the U.S. trade deficit with Japan were to shrink, then either imports fall or exports rise, or some combination of both. In an accounting sense, it does not matter which happens; they both result in an improvement in the current account balance, CA. Recall once again the relationship of the current account to other macroeconomic variables, given in equation 4b:

$$S_p + (T - G) = I + CA.$$

In order for CA to move from a large deficit toward zero or a surplus, something else must happen. Either investment falls, private savings rise, or the government budget moves toward surplus. If none of these happen, then CA cannot change, since the equation is an identity. In other words, unless the United States invests less, saves more, or increases the federal budget surplus, or does some combination of all three, the current account balance cannot change. A reduction in the trade deficit with Japan would simply show up as an increase in the trade deficits with other nations.

The point can be made another way. Equation 4b shows a nation's savings-investment balance, taking into account the flows of savings and investment across national borders. It cannot be broken up into separate balances describing bilateral trade relationships with each trading partner. The United States and every other country in the world have trade deficits with some trading partners and surpluses with others. Equation 4b shows the overall balance, so that any change in a particular trade relationship must be countered elsewhere in a nation's trade accounts.

Introduction to the Capital Account

The capital account records and categorizes the flow of financial capital into and out of a nation. The two primary subcategories of the capital account balance are (1) net changes in U.S.-owned assets abroad and (2) net changes in foreign-owned assets in the United States. The capital account's presentation of assets is "net" rather than "gross." The net change in U.S.-owned assets is the difference between assets sold and assets bought. For example, U.S. residents may purchase shares in the Mexican stock market while simultaneously selling Mexican bonds. The net change in U.S.-owned assets is the difference between the value of the shares purchased and the bonds sold. The gross change in U.S. assets owned abroad is simply the total quantity of assets bought—for example, the value of the purchased stock shares. Obviously, gross changes are less informative because they do not subtract assets sold, but the net change provides a measure of the dollar value of the change in the United States' stake in foreign economies.

> **Capital account.** *The capital account is a record of the transactions in financial assets and liabilities between the residents of a nation and the rest of the world.*

The Capital Account Balance

The capital account balance is a mirror image of the current account balance, so we know that if a nation's current account is in deficit by $20 billion, its capital account balance must be in surplus by the same amount, $20 billion. There are two basic reasons for the relationship between the current and capital account. The first reason is that every current account transaction (e.g., imports or exports) involves a flow of assets that are used to pay for the goods. A specific example will make this point more concrete. Suppose that the current account is in deficit by $100 billion. In order to cover the deficit, the country must sell to foreigners an extra $100 billion in assets over and above what it acquires from foreigners. That is, foreign capital inflows must exceed outflows of domestic capital by the amount of the current account deficit. In the next section, we will examine the types of capital inflows and outflows that are most common, but for the sake of simplicity, consider them currency flows that are used to acquire bank accounts. A net inflow of foreign capital equal to $100 billion would be equivalent to foreigners opening bank accounts with that amount in them. Essentially, the deficit country "pays" for the deficit by providing foreigners with financial assets; in the long run, foreigners will most likely convert the financial assets into real goods and services, since bank accounts and other assets are accepted only if there is an expectation that it may be converted to something real (i.e., nonfinancial) in the future.

If the capital account balance is the current account balance with an opposite sign, what of other financial flows that are not in response to current account transactions? In an accounting sense, their net value must be zero, which is the second reason that the current account and capital account mirror each other. The reason they net out to zero is simple: a purchase of an asset is simultaneously the sale of an asset of equal value. For example, if U.S. citizens buy shares in the Mexican stock market, they must sell dollars or some other U.S. asset. (If they pay for the shares by writing checks drawn on a Mexican bank, then it does not enter the capital account, since it is the change of one foreign asset for another.)

Two final points about the capital balance concern the mechanics of the accounting procedure. First, since capital inflows are used to finance a current account deficit, which is a negative balance, capital inflows are a positive entry. Conversely, capital outflows occur whenever a positive current account balance is maintained, and, therefore, capital outflows are a negative entry in the capital account balance. The easiest way to conceptualize this point is to see capital outflows as imports of assets (negative entry) and inflows as exports of assets (positive entry). Table 8.5 illustrates all the points made so far about the capital account and the balance of payments. Capital inflows are equivalent to foreign purchases of assets in the United States and are entered as positive balances; capital outflows are U.S. purchases of foreign assets and are negative items.

At the very bottom of Table 8.5, the last item entered is in the row labeled "Statistical discrepancy." Previously, it was stated that the sum of the current account plus the capital account must total zero. The statistical discrepancy is the amount by which the two are off. It is calculated as minus one times the sum of the current account plus the capital account, so for 1997 it is

$$\{(-1) \times (-155,215 + 254,939)\} = -99,724$$

The statistical discrepancy exists because our record of all the transactions in the balance of payments is incomplete. Although the errors could be in either the current or capital accounts, it is believed that most of the reason for the statistical discrepancy comes from the capital account, since it is relatively easier to make mistakes in tracking assets than in tracking the flow of goods.

Types of Capital Flows

It is often useful to subdivide the capital flows in Table 8.5 into categories that reference their origin and their purpose. For example, both capital inflows and capital outflows can originate in either the private sector or the public (governmental) sec-

TABLE 8.5 The U.S. Balance of Payments, 1997 (Millions of Dollars)

	Credit	Debit
1. Goods and services		
Exports	937,593	
Imports		−1,047,997
2. Investment income		
Investment income received	241,787	
Investment income paid		−247,105
3. Net unilateral transfers		−39,691
Current account balance (1 + 2 + 3)		−155,215
4. Net change in U.S. assets abroad		−478,502
5. Net change in foreign assets in the U.S.	733,441	
Balance on capital account (4 + 5)	254,939	
Statistical discrepancy		−99,724

Source: Bureau of Economic Analysis, *Survey of Current Business.* Vol. 78, No. 7, July 1998.

tor. The U.S. government can acquire foreign assets, and foreign governments can acquire U.S. assets. In the United States and most industrial countries, however, the bulk of the capital flows are private. In addition to categorizing according to private or public, it is also useful to know the kinds of assets sold or purchased. As we will see, this tells a lot about the pressures on an economy, as well as its strengths. In essence, capital flows can be reserve assets, portfolio assets, or real assets. Each of these is illustrated in Table 8.6, is where the capital account for the United States in 1997 is broken into several of its major subcategories.

Net changes in U.S. **official reserve assets** are primarily the purchase or sale of foreign currencies. When the Federal Reserve tries to prop up a falling U.S. dollar (see Chapter 8), it sells German marks, Japanese yen, or other currencies that are commonly accepted in international transactions. Widely used foreign currencies (including the dollar) are assets that can be used to settle international debts, and they constitute the most important type of official reserve asset. Typically, when nations have trouble repaying their international debts, it is because they have run out of foreign currency, and their creditors will not accept the debtor country's currency. For example, when Mexico ran into trouble in late 1994, it was because the government had dollar-denominated debts and an insufficient supply of dollars to pay them. Ultimately, Mexico was able to get several loans, including one from the International Monetary Fund, which was denominated in Special Drawing Rights, or SDRs. SDRs are an artificial currency created by the IMF and that serves as an official reserve asset. Gold is also used as an official reserve asset.

Official reserve assets. Official reserve assets are assets held by governments that may be used to settle international debts. Primarily they consist of key foreign currencies, such as the dollar, the yen the mark, the Swiss and French francs, and the British pound. In addition, they include gold and SDRs (special drawing rights), the unit of account used by the IMF.

TABLE 8.6 Components of the U.S. Balance of Payments, 1997 (Millions of Dollars)

	Credit	Debit
1. Net change in U.S. assets abroad		–478,502
A. U.S. official reserve assets		–1,010
B. U.S. government assets, other than official reserve assets	174	
C. US private assets		–477,666
2. Net change in foreign assets in the United States	733,441	
A. Foreign official assets in the United States	15,817	
B. Other foreign assets in the United States	717,624	

Source: Bureau of Economic Analysis, *Survey of Current Business.* Vol. 78, No. 7, July 1998.

In Table 8.6, the debit of $1,010 million for the United States in 1997 in the official reserve asset row indicates that the United States bought (imported) official reserve assets. Primarily, these consisted of purchases of German marks and Japanese yen and credits at the IMF. If the United States had made net sales of yen and marks, the balance would be positive, since the sale of an asset is conceptually equivalent to an export.

Row 1.B in Table 8.6 includes other assets acquired (debit) or sold (credit) by the federal government. These mainly represent loans to foreign governments, the rescheduling of past loans made to foreign governments, payments received on outstanding loans, and changes in nonreserve currency holdings, such as Mexican pesos or Israeli shekels.

Row 1.C represents the largest value of any of the flows in the upper part of the table. The most important elements are purchases of foreign securities (stocks and bonds) and direct investment. **Direct investment** is the purchase of real assets as distinguished from financial assets. It includes real estate, manufacturing operations, distribution networks, and other tangible assets. In 1997, direct investment abroad by U.S. residents totaled $121,843 million, while purchases of securities equaled $87,981 million. Together, these two items accounted for nearly $210,000 million, or about 44 percent of the total net acquisition of private assets abroad ($477,666 million).

> ***Direct investment and portfolio investment.*** *Direct investment is the purchase of real assets such as businesses or real estate. Portfolio investment is the purchase of financial assets such as stocks, bonds, bank accounts, or related financial instruments.*

Direct investment and portfolio investment are similar in that they both give their holders a claim on the future output of the foreign economy. The are very different, however, in their time horizons, and this can have dramatic effects on the host country, or the country that sold the assets. Direct investments are difficult to liquidate quickly and therefore represent a longer-term stake in the host country. Factories cannot be sold overnight, nor can other real assets. Firms making these sorts of commitments are usually taking a longer view and are willing to endure the inevitable ups and downs of the host country's economy. Portfolio investments in stocks and bonds tend to be more short term in their nature. While it is true that many investors may decide to hold their foreign securities through all kinds of ups and downs, by their nature, stocks and bonds are much more liquid than real estate or factories. It is common, therefore, for portfolio investors to have a shorter time horizon and to move quickly if they expect a sudden downturn. In late 1994, for example, when Mexico decided to devalue its currency, there was a sudden rush for the exit as a large number of investors in Mexican bonds and stocks did not want to end up holding assets that were denominated in a currency that suddenly became less valuable. The sudden sell-off of Mexican stocks and bonds put enormous pressure on the currency, and the peso all but collapsed as the economy fell into recession.

The growth of stock markets around the world, particularly in the newly industrializing countries of South America and Asia, represents a worldwide expansion of the buying and selling of stocks and related assets. In the capital accounts of the purchasing countries, it shows up as a net increase in private assets owned abroad (line 1.C in Table 8.6). In the countries with the newly opened stock markets, the inflow of foreign capital shows up as a net increase in foreign assets (line 2.B).

Line 2.A of Table 8.6 is symmetric with 1.A. When the federal government needs to borrow money to cover its deficit or to refinance its debt, foreign governments may purchase a share of the bonds sold, and that transactrion will show up in line 2.A. These are equivalent to reserve assets for the foreign government because they are easily liquidated and the dollar is universally accepted as payment for international debt. Private foreign interests may also purchase bonds, however, and they show up in line 2.B, along with other private investments in the U.S. economy. The $717,624 million purchase of U.S. assets by private foreign interests consists of three components: bank assets and purchase of Treasury securities in the United States ($294,769 million), direct investment in the United States ($93,449 million), and privately issued securities and other financial instruments ($329,406 million).

Capital Controls

Until a few years ago, most nations limited the movement of capital across their national borders. More recently, the volatility in capital markets has brought back widespread interest in some form of control to limit the damage that sudden capital flight out of a country can cause. In economic terms, these are called capital controls. Nations have used various stratagems to stem capital flight, such as limiting the quantity of capital that any one transaction could involve, taxing transactions, or requiring advance notice and waiting periods. These limitations are usually aimed at limiting speculation, particularly currency speculation that might force the central bank to alter its monetary policy. If Mexico's financial markets had been less open at the end of 1994, for example, it is unlikely that the sudden decline of the peso would have happened, nor the resulting inflation and recession of 1995. (On the other hand, if Mexican financial markets had been more closed, it is also unlikely that Mexico would have achieved the investment rates it did in 1991 to 1993. Mexico's case will be discussed in more detail .)

During the last decade, financial markets have become more open and less restrictive in the types of capital account transactions they permit. For example, the European Union removed its capital controls as part of the preparation for the Single Market of 1993, and many newly industrializing countries have removed or reduced capital controls in order to attract more international investment. Empirically, capital controls that limit capital outflows (the most destructive kind) also channel investment capital away from the country imposing the controls. Policy uncertainties and the possibility of devaluations cause most foreign investors to feel uncomfortable if they cannot get their money out of a country in a timely manner. The redirecting of investment flows away from countries that impose controls is an undesired side effect that causes many governments to think twice before setting controls. Low-savings countries that depend heavily on foreign capital may find the reduction in foreign investment to be too high a price to pay for reducing the volatility in their capital flows.

Empirical studies show that it is better to impose controls on inflows rather than outflows. Controls on inflows are less likely to redirect foreign investment because,

CASE STUDY

The Mexican Peso Devaluation of 1994

On January 1, 1994, the North American Free Trade Agreement (NAFTA) between Canada, the United States, and Mexico took effect. Throughout 1994, U.S.-Mexican trade expanded by almost one-fourth (23.7 percent), and capital continued to flow into Mexico, much of it from Japan and the European Union. Between 1990 and 1993, Mexico experienced capital inflows of $91 billion, or an average of about $23 billion per year, the most of any developing country. The capital inflows were in the form of private portfolio investments ($61 billion), direct investments ($16.6 billion), and bank loans ($13.4 billion).

The administration of President Salinas (1988–1994) actively encouraged large inflows of foreign capital as a way to maintain investment rates far above the level that domestic Mexican savings could support. Since $S_p + (T–G) = I + CA$, Mexican savings of around 14 percent of GDP in 1994 could not support investment of more than 20 percent of GDP unless there was an inflow of savings from the rest of the world. Mexico ran large current account deficits, equal to 5 percent of GDP in 1991 and 6.5 percent in 1992 and 1993. The enormous inflow of foreign goods and services permitted more investment directly by providing capital goods that Mexico could not make itself, and indirectly by satisfying consumption through foreign goods and thereby allowing domestic factories to produce investment goods. This was the strategy of the Salinas government, and it seemed to be working. NAFTA inspired confidence in Mexico's institutional stability and guaranteed access to the wealthy U.S. market for any goods made in Mexico.

During 1994, the world capital market began to shift toward a more conservative, risk-averse stance. In February 1994, interest rate movements in the United States and exchange rate movements around the world led to large losses for a number of banks and others investors. Portfolio managers began to reassess the investments they had and to look for ways to reduce their exposure to risk. The January insurrection of subsistence farmers in the Mexican state of Chiapas raised the specter of political instability there, and the March assassination of the presidential candidate Luis Donaldo Colosio added fuel to the fire.

Amid the growing perception that the Mexican peso was overvalued, the newly elected president of Mexico, Ernesto Zedillo, announced in early December 1994 that the government would devalue the peso by 15 percent. The peso had been trading at about 3.5 to the dollar, so a 15 percent decline in value would have placed it at slightly more than 4 to the dollar. The news sparked a rush for the exit, however, as everyone tried to sell off assets in portfolios that were denominated in pesos. No one wanted to be caught holding assets that were to lose 15 percent of their value in the next few days, and the huge inflow of portfolio investment during the prior years meant that there was a large volume of peso-denominated assets in the hands of non-Mexicans.

As the supply of pesos jumped, the demand declined, and the value fell through the floor. By the second half of February 1995, the peso had fallen to almost 8 to the dollar. When the dust settled and a US-IMF-Mexican stabilization plan was put into effect, the peso regained some of its lost value; and by June of 1995, it was trading at 6.25 to the dollar.

From Mexico's perspective, the problem is how to maintain high investment rates when savings rates are low. The strategy of relying on large foreign inflows of world savings through a large capital account surplus (current account deficit) proved to be unstable, given that so much of the foreign capital was invested in short-term portfolios rather than longer-term direct investment. The administration of President Zedillo addressed the short-run problem by seeking financial support from the IMF and the United States in order to prop up the value of the peso. The medium-to-long-run issues were addressed with a package of austerity measures that cut government spending, increased taxes (moved (T-G) toward a surplus), and reduced consumption. Electricity prices and gasoline prices were raised (both supplied through government-owned enterprises), and credit was restricted through steep increases in interest rates and new limits on bank lending. These measures reduced consumption and increased savings, provided a greater pool of domestic funds for investment purposes, and reduced dependence on foreign capital inflows. In the short run, however, the fall in consumption and government expenditures caused a recession. The overall decline in Mexico's GDP was around 5 to 6 percent in 1995, and more than 500,000 people lost their jobs in the first few months of the crisis. Nevertheless, the handling of the crisis earned Mexico high marks in international capital markets, and by 1996 foreign capital had returned and the economy began to grow at a healthy rate.

once they are in, investors know they can take their money out. No matter what form of controls are enacted, however, over time they become less effective at accomplishing their intended objective. Financial markets are extremely innovative when it comes to designing new instruments, and they tend to find a way around any given set of rules after a period of time.

Trade Deficits and the International Investment Position

Each year that a nation runs a current account deficit, it borrows from abroad and adds to its indebtedness to foreigners. Each year that a nation runs current account surplus, it lends to foreigners and reduces its overall indebtedness. If the total of all domestic assets owned by foreigners is subtracted from the total of all foreign assets owned by residents of the home country, the resulting measurement is called the **international investment position**. If the international investment position is positive, then the home country could sell off all its foreign assets and have more than enough revenue to purchase all the domestic assets owned by foreigners. If it is negative, then selling off all foreign assets would not provide enough revenue to buy all the domestic assets owned by foreigners.

> ***International investment position.*** *The international investment position of a nation is the value of all foreign assets owned by its residents, businesses, and government, minus the value of all domestic assets owned by foreigners.*

To give an example of the international investment position, consider the United States at the end of 1997. The market value of all assets outside the United States but owned by U.S. citizens, corporations, and governments was $5,007 billion. These included foreign factories, shares of stocks in foreign companies, foreign bonds, foreign currency, and other assets owned by residents of the United States and the U.S. government. Meanwhile, the market value of assets inside the United States that were owned by foreign individuals, businesses, and governments was valued at $6,330 billion. As a result, the international investment position of the United States was ($5,007 − $6,330), or −$1,323 billion. Since the number is negative, foreigners own more assets in the United States than U.S. interests own in the rest of the world. Before the United States began to run large trade deficits, the international investment position of the United States was positive. Although the United States has never stopped accumulating assets abroad, it has done so at a much slower pace than foreigners have accumulated assets inside the United States. Accordingly, the international investment position peaked around 1983 at $288.6 billion and then rapidly declined over the next six years to zero in 1989. Since then, it has been negative and growing in absolute size.

The Benefits and Costs of Foreign Investment

Does it matter that an inflow of foreign capital leads to a rise in foreign ownership? There are clearly benefits from capital inflows, but are there costs as well? Many Americans worry that the large current account deficit is leading to such large claims against the future production of the U.S. economy that Japan or some other country will soon own the U.S. capital stock. This worry is clearly pointless, since the direct investment position of foreigners in the U.S. economy is about 4 percent of the U.S. capital stock in 1996, calculated (*Survey of Current Business,* July 1998) as

$$(\text{Total foreign direct investment in the United States.}) \,/$$
$$(\text{Stock of fixed private capital in the United States.})$$

$$= (667.0 \text{ billion}) \,/ \,(16,503.4 \text{ billion}) = 0.040$$

This is an overestimate because the numerator includes real estate (land), but the denominator does not. The leading purchasers of U.S. businesses and real estate are the United Kingdom (19 percent of total), followed by Japan (18 percent), the Netherlands (12 percent), Germany (10 percent), and Canada (9.4 percent).

We will examine the potential benefits of foreign investment first, and then we will think about the costs, if any. In recent years, each of the NAFTA countries (Canada, United States, and Mexico) has had sizable inflows of foreign capital in response to current account deficits. The relatively low savings rate of each of the three countries has been supplemented by foreign capital so that overall investment rates have been higher than would have been possible otherwise. In each country's case, there have been direct and tangible benefits. For example, between 1980 and 1991, Japan invested more than $25 billion of its trade surplus in U.S. manufacturing. By the start of the 1990s, the Japanese owned 66 steel works, 20 rubber and tire factories, 8 major car assembly plants, and 270 auto parts suppliers, employing more than 100,000 workers in the United States. Furthermore, the investment came at a time when the Big 3 U.S. auto manufacturers (Chrysler, Ford, and GM) were laying off and relocating production abroad. Some of the firms were acquisitions, but many were new plants built from scratch with Japanese savings. The experiences of Mexico and Canada were similar in that investment and employment have been greater as a result of the foreign investment that has occurred.

Still, it must be recognized that foreign investment is not a solution to low savings rates. No matter how integrated we seem to become, or how mobile investment is, the fact remains that the most important determinant of investment in a national economy is the national savings rate, private plus public. In other words, even in today's highly integrated world economy, countries that have low savings rates also have low rates of investment.

Another effect of foreign investment is that it is often the primary mechanism through which technology is transferred and new techniques are spread. Throughout the post–World War II period, one of the main ways in which European and Japanese companies have been able to catch up to their American counterparts is through borrowing and adapting technology that first came to their countries through U.S. investments. As Japanese and European engineers, scientists, and managers gained experience working in more advanced U.S. firms, they were able to take their new skills with them into domestically owned firms. In addition, foreign-owned firms develop networks of supplier relationships that also serve as channels through which new technology can spread. Without foreign investment, it would be much harder to learn about new processes, new production technologies, and new organizational forms. Today, this relationship is particularly important for developing countries, where a significant portion of the capital, technology, and skills that they need will come via foreign investment.

If the benefits are identifiable as greater investment levels and new technology, the costs are harder to pin down. One potential cost is that foreign investment provides a gateway into a nation's inner circles of power. As a city planner who consults with Japanese investors in the United States was heard to declare, each Japanese car plant in the United States comes with two senators. In the United States, as in every nation, money and economic clout provide political access. In the case of a small, poor country, large corporations can wield proportionately greater power than in large or wealthy nations because the playing field is relatively empty and there are few countervailing powers to balance their economic clout. In the case of richer nations, such as the United States, France, or Germany, the national sovereignty issue is much less important because the political clout of a wealthy foreign investor is diluted by the contending interests of numerous powerful domestic enterprises and interest groups.

Even if national sovereignty is not an issue, national security concerns are. Many people wonder if foreign-owned firms might not be a liability in an international conflict. It is at least conceivable that foreign-owned firms may transfer technology or pass along sensitive information about production capabilities, if not engage in outright sabotage, when it is in the interests of their owners to do so. Histories of U.S.-owned operations in Germany and German-owned operations in the United States during World War II paint a picture of minimal danger from this quarter. The main reason is that enemy assets are frozen or nationalized in time of war. During World War II, German chemical companies operating inside the United States were confiscated, as were U.S. assets in Germany. The German branch of the Ford Motor Co. was instructed to produce trucks for the German war effort but failed to achieve high levels of output because it had always depended on parts suppliers elsewhere in Europe. The war cut off these traditional supply linkages, and the German branches were not organized or trained to produce the parts themselves. Essentially, the German operations of the Ford Motor Co. struggled to remain good corporate citizens of their host nation; meanwhile, operations of Ford in the occupied nations of Belgium and the Netherlands were less compliant and occasionally engaged in production slowdowns and sabotage. The story of German chemical facilities inside the United States is similar. They, too, suffered from reduced productivity as a result of having been cut off from their traditional suppliers and sources of technology. Chemical technology was superior in Germany, and the U.S. firms that took over the foreign-owned facilities in the United States lacked the skills and technological understanding to operate them to full capacity.

The astute reader will no doubt have noticed that all the discussion of costs and benefits of foreign investment has focused on foreign direct investment as opposed to portfolio investment. Obviously, with portfolio investment, there can be no transfer of new technologies. Other than that, many of the benefits and costs are the same. Foreigners that invest in a country's stock market, for example, provide financial capital that can be used by domestic firms to bolster their investment. Given the "hands-off" nature of financial or portfolio investment, however, there is less scope for affecting a wartime situation. Finally, one previously mentioned cost to the host country of foreign portfolio investment is the sudden shift of foreign financial capital out of a nation. This can have severe repercussions, as Mexico found out in late 1994.

Conclusion

In this chapter we began by looking at the relationship between several key macroeconomic variables: private savings, public or government savings, investment, and the current account balance. The relationship is important because it directly determines whether a nation runs surpluses or deficits in its trade with the world. It is also probably one of the most important but least understood economic relations in international economics.

▲ Competitiveness and unfair trade practices, while important to particular firms and industries, are not the ultimate causes of trade balances. Many countries that lag technologically, for example, still experience balanced trade or even surpluses.

▲ If theUnited States, or any other nation, wishes to reduce its trade deficit, its options are limited: (1) save more, which means consume less; (2) invest less, and slow the rate of improvement of its standard of living; (3) reduce its public dis-saving by balancing the government's budget; or (4) some combination of all three.

▲ One consequence of the persistent current account deficits in the United States is an inflow of foreign capital in order to finance the excess of consumption over production. A second consequence is the erosion of the international investment position.

▲ Capital flows are reported and tracked in the capital account that, together with the current account, makes up the balance of payments accounts. There are several kinds of capital flows: governmental and private, and short term and long term. The costs and benefits of these flows were characterized in terms of national sovereignty, national security, technology transfers, and investment.

▲ Foreign investment inevitably becomes controversial whenever and wherever it occurs because it seems to many citizens that foreign interests are "taking over." The reality of that fear depends in great part on the size and wealth of the host country and the stability and openness of its political system. Even in the United States, however, where foreigners actually control a very small percentage of the assets of the country, there are fears that they are gaining control over the political process and that they will leave the nation vulnerable to a sudden withdrawal of assets and technology.

Vocabulary

capital account	international investment position
capital controls	investment income
current account	national income accounts
direct investment	official reserve assets
expenditure switching policy	portfolio investment
expenditure reducing policy	special drawing rights (SDR)
foreign direct investment	trade balance
foreign portfolio investment	trade deficit
gross domestic product (GDP)	trade surplus
gross national product (GNP)	unilateral transfers

Study Questions

1. Use the following information to answer the questions a) to c) below.

Net unilateral transfers	-50
Exports of goods and services	500
Net increase in U.S. government's nonreserve foreign assets	30

Net increase in foreign ownership of U.S. based nonreserve assets	400
Net increase in U.S. private assets abroad	250
Invest income received in the U.S.	200
Net increase in U.S. ownership of official reserve assets	20
Imports of goods and services	600
Net increase in foreign ownership of U.S. based reserve assets	100
Investment income paid abroad by the U.S.	300

a) What is the current account balance?

b) Does the capital account equal the current account?

c) What is the statistical discrepancy?

2. Look at each of the cases below from the point of view of the balance of payments for the United States. Determine the subcategory of the current account or capital account in which each transaction would be classified, and state whether it would enter as a credit or debit.

a) The U.S. government sells German marks for dollars.

b) A migrant worker in California sends $500 dollars home to his village in Mexico.

c) An American mutual fund manager uses the deposits of his fund investors to buy Brazilian telecommunication stocks.

d) A mutual fund manager in New York takes the earnings of the fund's Brazilian telecommunications stocks and converts them to dollars to pay out dividends on the fund.

e) A Japanese firm in Tennessee buys car parts from a subsidiary in Malaysia.

f) An Italian importer of American semiconductors deposits 2 billion Italian lira into the semiconductor company's foreign bank account in Milan.

g) An American church donates five tons of rice to help with famine relief in the Sudan.

h) An American retired couple flies from Seattle to Tokyo on Japan airlines.

i) The Mexican government sells pesos to the United States Treasury and buys dollars.

3. Weigh the pros and cons of a large trade deficit.

4. Is the budget deficit of a country linked to its current account balance? How so? Explain how it is possible for the United States' current account deficit to grow while the budget deficit has disappeared.

5. Compare and contrast portfolio capital flows with direct investment capital flows.

6. Why is a current account surplus equivalent to foreign investment?

Suggested Reading

Bhagwati, Jagdish, "The Capital Myth: The Difference between Trade in Widgets and Dollars," *Foreign Affairs*. May/June, 1998.

Bureau of Economic Analysis, "U.S. International Transactions, Fourth Quarter and Year, 1997," *Survey of Current Business*. April, 1998.

———, "The International Investment Position of the United States in 1997," *Survey of Current Business*. July, 1998.

Graham, Edward, and Paul Krugman. *Foreign Direct Investment in the United States*. 3[d] Edition. Washington, DC: Institute for International Economics, 1995.

Krugman, Paul. "The Trade Deficit." and "Global Finance," in *The Age of Diminished Expectations*. 3[d] Edition. Cambridge, MA: MIT Press, 1997.

Appendix 1: Measuring the International Investment Position

It may seem like a straightforward job to add up the value of assets, but nothing could be further from the truth. Consider the following problem: The United States ran trade surpluses in the 1950s and 1960s and accumulated large holdings of foreign assets. In the 1980s and 1990s, the United States ran trade deficits, and foreigners accumulated large holdings inside the United States. In the 1990s, a sizable proportion of U.S.-owned assets were purchased decades ago, when prices were much lower and foreign-owned assets were purchased recently, after the worldwide inflation of the 1970s and the early 1980s. If asset values are tallied up using their historical cost, the price at the time of purchase, then foreign-owned assets appear more valuable, not necessarily because they are but simply because they were acquired more recently when world prices were higher.

It seems logical to expect that the reporting of asset values would be done on current cost basis rather than on historical cost basis, where current cost is the cost of purchasing the asset in the current period. Unfortunately, it does not happen like this. In the United States, firms use historical cost as the basis for valuation of assets in company records, and this is the basis they use in reporting their foreign holdings to the agency that collects the data, the Bureau of Economic Analysis. The difference between current cost and historical cost does not affect the measurement of portfolio investment, which is relatively short term, but it has significant effects on the measurement of direct investment because it is held for longer time periods.

Until 1991, the United States only calculated the historical cost of U.S.-owned foreign assets. As a result, the U.S. international investment position appeared to go negative very rapidly as large trade deficits in the mid-1980s led to a rapid accumulation of new assets in the United States by foreign interests. More recently, in the 1990s, the United States began to report all assets on a current value basis. The primary deficiency in this data as it now stands is that it cannot be broken down into country-specific or industry-specific data. Therefore, we know the overall international investment position for the United States, but we cannot accurately examine the U.S.-Japan bilateral investment position, since we only have U.S. assets in Japan on a historical cost basis.

Appendix 2: Finding Balance of Payments Data

Current account and international investment data are readily available for most nations of the world. Many databases are also available in electronic form, either on CD-ROM or over the Internet. While some data sources tend to be more current than others, each has its own strengths and weaknesses. The hardcopy versions of the following data sources are available in most university libraries and many public libraries. The CD-ROM-based versions are increasingly common in university libraries, often in the government documents section. Data for the United States is readily available free over the Internet in a variety of locations. Electronic data for other countries is more limited. The International Monetary Fund is perhaps the best source of comprehensive data for most of the world's nations. The IMF charges for its data.

United States Data

1. The quickest way to find balance of payments online is to go to the Bureau of Economic Analysis' Website at *http://www.bea.doc.gov/* and point your browser to data under the heading "International." Or, you can go directly to *http://www.bea.doc.gov/bea/di1.htm*

2. Survey of Current Business (*http://www.bea..doc.gov/bea/pubs.htm*)
   For the United States, the most up-to-date and current data on the balance of payments are available in the *Survey of Current Business* (*SCB*). The *SCB* is a monthly publication from the Department of Commerce's Bureau of Economic Analysis. Each month's issue has several articles describing and presenting recent data on the U.S. economy. The *SCB* generally reports the previous year's international transactions in the March issue. Updates are made later in the year.

3. Economic Report of the President (*http://www.access.gpo.gov/eop/*)
   The *Economic Report of the President* is an annual publication that details the economic issues and general approaches that the president's administration will tackle. Appendix B of the *Report* contains historical data going back to World War II on most major macroeconomic and many microeconomic variables.

4. National Trade Data Bank (NTDB) *(http://www.stat-usa.gov/)*
   In 1988, Congress passed legislation requiring the Department of Commerce to make trade data and export promotion information available to the public in electronic form. The result was the creation of the National Trade Data Bank, which is perhaps the most successful effort to date to put government documents on CD. More than one-half of the nation's 1400 federal depository libraries receive the NTDB CD-ROM. In addition to the CD format, the NTDB is available for a small subscription on the World Wide Web through the Web server of STAT-USA. The NTDB combines data from nineteen federal agencies, such as the Federal Reserve, the State Department, and the Department of Agriculture, and others. Most all of the information published by the federal government that relates to the international economy is contained in the NTDB. The total number of documents is estimated to be around 105,000, which is equivalent to 200,000 pages of text.

International Data

1. *International Financial Statistics (IFS)*
   This is a regular publication of the International Monetary Fund. It appears quarterly, with an annual Yearbook at the year's end. Each of the quarterly volumes contains a subset of the world's nations, and the Yearbook collects them all into one volume. As the name implies, *IFS* focuses on financial data, but it also contains information on current accounts and international capital flows. The *IFS* also has the most recent estimates of GDP and its major components along with population. Coverage is of

most of the world's nations, and the most recent *Yearbook* usually contains a decade of data for each country. The IMF publications are used by many international agencies and private enterprises. Nearly all university libraries and many city libraries will have *IFS*.

2. *Balance of Payments Statistics (BOPS)*

   This is a sister publication of the International Monetary Fund that complements the data in *IFS*. Publication format is similar, with quarterly volumes covering a selection of nations and an annual Yearbook that combines all countries into one large volume and a thin supplement. The *BOPS* has the most up-to-date and detailed current and capital account statistics of any international data source.

3. *United Nation's Statistical Yearbook* and related volumes

   The *Statistical Yearbook* is generally somewhat less current than the IMF data listed above. It does contain a much greater variety of data, however. The *Statistical Yearbook* is a combination of data from several more specialized UN sources, including the *United Nation's National Account Statistics, Demographic Yearbook, Industrial Statistics Yearbook, Energy Statistics Yearbook*, and *International Trade Statistics Yearbook*. The *Statistical Yearbook* has the advantage of combining in one place a great quantity of data, usually going back one decade. Its major disadvantage is that it lacks the detail that can be found in the more specialized volumes. The most current data can be located in the United Nation's *Monthly Bulletin of Statistics*. Most university libraries are likely to have one or all of these volumes.

CHAPTER 9

EXCHANGE RATES AND EXCHANGE RATE SYSTEMS

Introduction

The topics of exchange rates and exchange rate systems are less settled than most of the other issues we have examined so far. Many important exchange-rate-related issues have several contending points of view that often lead to mutually contradictory conclusions. For example, should exchange rates be fixed or not? Fixed exchange rates such as a gold standard have some benefits, but there are also significant costs. Another fundamental question is whether the United States, or any other country, can eliminate a trade deficit by depreciating its currency. Can central banks and treasury departments effectively intervene in exchange markets in order to determine their money's value? Should they?

Chapter 9 explores some of these issues, along with a few basic relationships, such as why people hold foreign currencies and how supply and demand determine the international value of a nation's money.

Exchange Rates and Currency Trading

The **exchange rate** is the price of one currency stated in terms of a second currency. For example, 8.75 pesos per dollar is the exchange rate with the Mexican peso, and 1.5 marks per dollar is the rate with the German mark. Exchange rates can also be given as the inverse: dollars per peso or dollars per mark. For example, we usually state the U.S.-UK rate as 1.7 dollars per pound, but we could just as accurately quote the inverse, which is about 0.59 pounds per dollar.

> **Exchange rate.** *The exchange rate is the price of one currency expressed in terms of a second currency.*

Exchange rates are reported on a daily basis in the financial pages of nearly every major newspaper. Table 9.1 shows a selection of exchange rates from the New York Federal Reserve Bank. These rates, like rates reported in the financial press, are equivalent to wholesale prices rather than retail. In other words, tourists planning to vacation in Switzerland cannot purchase Swiss francs at the rate of 1.49 per dollar. On the other hand, banks, currency traders, and corporations that wanted to buy or sell millions of dollars worth of foreign exchange on July 29, 1998, would have found prices fairly close to those listed in the table.

The values in Table 9.1 are in a constant state of change. With flexible exchange rate systems, currencies are, like any other asset, subject to the push and pull of market forces. When a currency gains value, it buys more units of other currencies and is said to have **appreciated**. When it loses value, it is described as having **depreciated**.

> **Currency appreciation and depreciation.** *A currency appreciates when it can buy more units of another currency. It depreciates when it buys fewer units. If the dollar appreciates against the German mark, then the mark has depreciated against the dollar. An appreciation is a rise in the currency's value; a depreciation is a fall in its value.*

Reasons for Holding Foreign Currencies

Economists identify three general reasons why people choose to hold a foreign currency rather than their own. The first reason is for trade and investment. Traders (importers and exporters) and investors routinely transact in foreign currencies, either receiving or making payments in another country's money. Tourists would be included in this category because they hold foreign exchange in order to buy foreign goods and services.

The second reason why people hold foreign exchange is to take advantage of interest rate differentials. This particular use of foreign currencies is referred to as

TABLE 9.1 Exchange Rates for Selected OECD Countries, July 29, 1998

Country	Currency Unit	U.S. Dollars per Unit	Units per U.S. Dollar
Australia	dollar	0.6105	1.6380
Austria	schilling	0.0801	12.4790
Belgium	franc	0.0281	35.5660
Britain	pound	1.6440	0.6083
Canada	dollar	0.6649	1.5039
Denmark	krone	0.1480	6.7585
France	franc	0.1682	5.9465
Germany	mark	0.5639	1.7735
Italy	lira	0.0006	1,749.50
Japan	yen	0.0070	142.46
Netherlands	guilder	0.5000	2.0000
Spain	peseta	0.0066	150.7000
Sweden	krona	0.1264	7.9110
Switzerland	franc	0.6725	1.4870

Source: New York Federal Reserve Bank (Available online at *http://www.ny.frb.org/pihome/mktrates/forex12.shtml*, July 29, 1998.)

interest rate arbitrage. Businesses that purchase financial assets seek the highest return on their money (for a given level of risk) and will increase the value of foreign bonds in their portfolios when foreign interest rates are higher. By moving financial capital out of countries where interest rates are low and into places where they are high, these businesses keep interest rate differentials from moving too far apart, and they link national macroeconomies. For example, when Germany raises its interest rates, it tends to pull up French and other European rates through the movement of savings out of France and into Germany. Ultimately, France and other European countries may have to respond with a similar increase in interest rates.

The third general motive for holding foreign exchange is for purposes of speculation. Speculators are businesses that buy or sell a currency because they expect its price to rise or fall. They have no need for foreign exchange to buy goods or services or financial assets; they simply expect to realize profits or avoid losses through correctly anticipating changes in a currency's market value. Speculators are often reviled in the popular press, but in fact, they help to bring currencies into equilibrium after they have become overvalued or undervalued.

Institutions

There are four main participants in foreign currency markets: retail customers, commercial banks, foreign exchange brokers, and central banks. Of these, the most important are the commercial banks. Retail customers include firms and individuals that hold foreign exchange for any of the three reasons just listed. That is, they may need it for transactions purposes, to adjust their portfolios, or because they want to profit from expected future currency movements. In most cases, they buy and sell through a commercial bank. Commercial banks in many parts of the world hold inventories of foreign currencies as part of the services they offer their customers. Not all banks provide this service, but those that do usually have a relationship with several foreign banks where they hold their balances of foreign currencies. When a surplus accumulates, or a shortage develops, the banks trade with each other to adjust their holdings.

In the United States, foreign exchange brokers also play an important role. It is not very common for U.S. banks to trade currency with foreign banks. Instead, American banks tend to go through foreign exchange brokers, who bring together buyers and sellers. Brokers do not usually hold foreign exchange themselves. Brokers also sometimes serve as agents for central banks. The market, then, works as follows. An individual or firm that needs foreign exchange calls its bank. The bank quotes a price at which it will sell the currency. The price is based on one of two possible sources of supply: (1) the bank may have an account with another bank in the country where the currency is used, or (2) it may have to call a foreign exchange broker. The broker keeps track of buyers and sellers of currencies and acts as a dealmaker by bringing together a seller and bank that is buying for its customer.

In most cases, currency trades take the form of credits and debits to a firm's bank accounts. For example, a local U.S. importer that must make payment in yen can call and tell its bank to transfer yen to the Japanese bank of the firm that supplies the importer with goods. The importer will have a debit to its local bank account that is equivalent to the cost of the yen. If the U.S. bank has a branch or correspondence bank in Japan, it can electronically notify the Japanese bank to debit the yen from the account of the U.S. bank and credit it to the Japanese bank of the supplier. If the U.S. bank goes through a currency trader instead of dealing directly with Japanese banks, then it first buys yen that are in an account with a Japanese bank, and then it requests that some or all of its yen assets be transferred to the bank of the Japanese supplier of the U.S. importer.

Exchange Rate Risk

Firms that do business in more than one country are subject to **exchange rate risks**. These risks stem from the fact that currencies are constantly changing in value and, as a result, expected future payments that will be made or received in a foreign currency may be a different domestic currency amount from when the contract was signed.

> **Exchange rate risk.** *Exchange rate risk occurs when an individual or firm holds assets that are denominated in a foreign currency. The risk is the potential for unexpected losses (or gains) due to unforeseen fluctuations in the value of the foreign currency.*

Suppose, for example, that a U.S. semiconductor manufacturer signs a contract to send a British computer manufacturer a shipment of microprocessors in six months. If the U.S. manufacturer agrees on a price in British pounds, it must know the value of the pound six months from now in order to know the dollar equivalent of its future revenue. If the U.S. manufacturer specifies that the microprocessors be paid for in dollars, then it shifts the exchange rate risk to the British firm. The U.S. company knows the exact dollar amount it will receive in six months, but the British firm is uncertain of the price of the dollar and, therefore, the pound price of microprocessors.

Financial markets recognized this problem long ago, and in the nineteenth century they created mechanisms for dealing with it. The mechanisms are the **forward exchange rate**, and the **forward market**. The forward exchange rate is the price of a currency that will be delivered in the future, while the forward market refers to the market in which the buying and selling of currencies for future delivery take place. Forward markets for currencies are an everyday tool for international traders and investors. They allow an exporter or importer to sign a currency contract on the day they sign an agreement to ship or receive goods. The currency contract guarantees a set price for the foreign currency, usually either 30, 90, or 180 days into the future. By contrast, the market for buying and selling in the present is called a **spot market**. The prices of foreign currencies quoted in Table 9.1 are spot prices, although many newspapers report forward market prices as well.

Suppose a U.S. semiconductor manufacturer signs a contract to deliver the microprocessors to the British firm in six months. Suppose also that the price is stated in British pounds. The manufacturer knows precisely how many pounds it will earn six months from now, but it does not know whether the pound will rise or fall in value, so it does not know for certain what it will earn in dollar terms. The solution is to sign a forward contract to deliver British pounds six months from now in exchange for U.S. dollars at a price agreed upon today. Using the forward market, the U.S. manufacturer avoids the risk that comes from exchange rate fluctuations.

Forward and spot markets. In forward markets for foreign exchange buyers and sellers agree on a quantity and a price for a foreign exchange transaction that takes place in (usually) 30, 90, or 180 days from the time the contract is signed. Spot market transactions are concluded at the same time the price is agreed upon, although there is usually a lag of a day before the currency is actually delivered.

Forward markets are important to financial investors as well as to exporters and importers. We have seen that interest arbitrage is one of the primary reasons why people hold foreign currencies. Recall that interest rate arbitrage is defined as the movement of funds from one financial asset and currency when interest rates are higher abroad. Banks and other financial firms usually hedge against the foreign exchange risk they incur while holding the foreign asset by buying a forward contract to sell foreign currency at the same time the interest-earning asset matures. This is known as **covered interest arbitrage.**

Interest rate arbitrage and covered interest arbitrage. Interest rate arbitrage is the transfer of funds from one financial asset and currency to another to take advantage of higher interest rates. Covered interest arbitrage occurs when the firm transferring funds also signs a forward currency contract to sell its earnings when its foreign assets mature. By doing so, the firm protects itself against unforeseen fluctuations in currency values.

The Supply and Demand for Foreign Exchange

The value of one nation's money, like most things, can be analyzed by looking at its supply and demand. For example, an increase in the demand for the dollar will raise its price (cause an appreciation in its value), while an increase in its supply will lower its price (cause a depreciation). These are only tendencies, however, and depend on other factors remaining constant. Unfortunately, since other factors almost never remain constant, supply and demand analysis is a useful tool for understanding the pressures on a currency, but it does not permit economists or financial analysts to predict currency movements.

Supply and Demand Curves for Foreign Exchange

Figure 9.1 shows the demand for British pounds in the United States. The curve is downward sloping, like all other demand curves, indicating that as the pound becomes cheaper (depreciates relative to the dollar), the quantity of pounds demanded by Americans increases. Note also that we are measuring the exchange rate on the vertical axis. Since it is $ per £, it is the price of a pound in terms of dollars, and an increase in the exchange rate, R, is a decline in the value of the dollar. In other words, movements up the vertical axis represent an increase in the price of foreign currency (which is equivalent to a fall in the price of a dollar).

For Americans, British goods are less expensive when the pound is cheaper and the dollar is stronger. Hence, at depreciated values for the pound, Americans will switch from American or third-party suppliers of goods and services to British suppliers. Be-

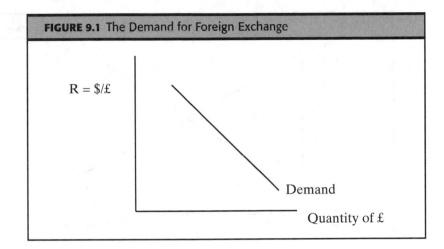

FIGURE 9.1 The Demand for Foreign Exchange

fore they can purchase goods made in Britain, however, they must first exchange U.S. dollars for British pounds. Consequently, the increased demand for British goods is simultaneously an increase in the quantity of British pounds demanded.

Figure 9.2 shows the supply side of the picture. The supply curve slopes up because British firms and consumers are willing to buy a greater quantity of American goods as the dollar becomes cheaper (i.e., as they receive more dollars per pound). Before British customers can buy American goods, however, they must first convert pounds into dollars, so the increase in the quantity of American goods demanded is simultaneously an increase in the quantity of foreign currency supplied to the U.S.

Figure 9.3 combines the supply and demand curves. The intersection determines the market U.S.-UK exchange rate and the quantity of pounds supplied to the

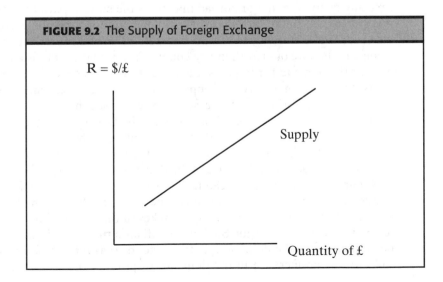

FIGURE 9.2 The Supply of Foreign Exchange

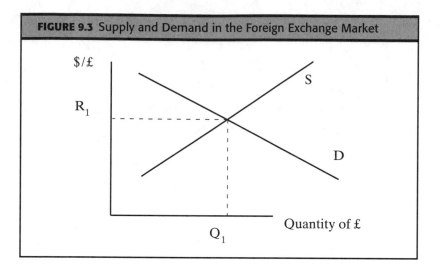

FIGURE 9.3 Supply and Demand in the Foreign Exchange Market

United States. At exchange rate R_1, the demand and supply of British pounds to the United States is Q_1.

So far, we have determined that the supply curve slopes up to the right and the demand curve slopes down. The next step in supply and demand analysis is to consider the factors that determine the position of the curves. These are the forces that cause the curves to shift left or right and that establish a new equilibrium exchange rate.

We identified three major reasons why people hold foreign currency rather than their own: for reasons related to trade and direct investment, to take advantage of interest rate differences, and to speculate. Changes in one or more of these three motives for holding foreign currencies can lead to a shift in the demand and supply curves in Figure 9.3. For example, taking the trade and direct investment motives first, any factor at home or abroad that alters the current pattern of trade and direct investment will shift either the American demand for a foreign currency or the foreign supply of a currency to the U.S. market. A frequently encountered example is a change in the rate of growth in one country. Economic growth is a primary determinant of the demand for imports if the growth is at home, or of the demand for exports if the growth is abroad. Suppose, for example, American growth accelerates relative to Great Britain. In this case, we expect to see the boom cause an increase in the demand for British goods. Consequently, the U.S. needs to buy greater quantities of the British pound, which is reflected in an outward shift in the demand for pounds curve. The effect is to increase the price of the pound, or—to say the same thing another way—to decrease the price of the dollar. This is illustrated in Figure 9.4.

A number of other forces can lead to similar increase in the demand for British goods. As one example, if investors in the U.S. were to become bullish on Britain and seek to increase their investment stakes in the country, the American demand for pounds would shift right. Similarly, if inflation turned up in the U.S., there would be an increase in the demand for British goods that remained less inflation prone, followed by an increase in the demand for pounds and a rise in the price of the

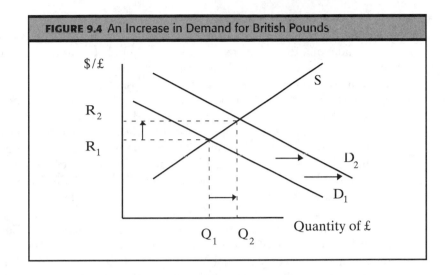

FIGURE 9.4 An Increase in Demand for British Pounds

pound. Until the dollar value of the pound rises, British goods are relatively cheaper in dollar terms than the inflation-prone American ones.

Each of these examples can be presented in a symmetrical way that emphasizes higher British growth or inflation, as well as British confidence about the U.S. economy. The result is a shift in the supply of pounds to the U.S. If Britain's economy booms, then more American goods are bought and our exports go up. This raises our earnings of pounds and is equivalent to an increase in the supply of pounds to the U.S. market. The result is a cheaper pound and a more expensive dollar. This effect is illustrated in Figure 9.5.

Motives for holding foreign currencies—the covered-interest arbitrage motive and the speculative motive—can be analyzed in a similar fashion. Higher interest rates abroad lead to an increase in the demand for the foreign currency, whereas higher

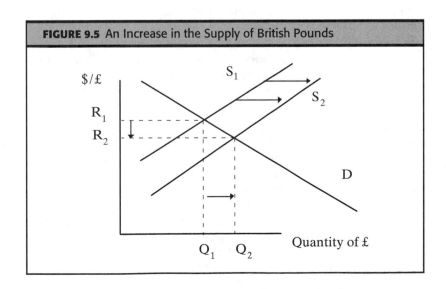

FIGURE 9.5 An Increase in the Supply of British Pounds

rates at home increase the supply. Similarly, expectations of a decline in the value of the dollar lead to a demand for foreign currencies, whereas expectations of a decline in the value of a foreign currency increase its supply to our market. In the case of expectations, we have already seen in Chapter 5 how expectations about the decline in the value of the peso helped to cause a collapse in Mexico's currency in December 1994. No one wanted to hold pesos, everyone wanted dollars, and the supply of pesos rose dramatically—pushing down its value and pushing up the value of the dollar.

Table 9.2 catalogs the major factors that determine shifts in the supply and demand for foreign currencies. Table 9.2 with Figures 9.4 and 9.5, form the basis for a beginning analysis of the impact of economic events on currency values. Unfortunately, they make the analysis look far easier than it really is. The problem they hide is that the real world rarely allows one thing to change at a time. In most instances of economic change, a large number of simultaneous events exist — some of which reinforce each other and some of which counteract each other. Consequently, the utility of a prediction of how a single event might affect currency values is relatively low. Events rarely come in singles.

An example will clarify this problem. Suppose the U.S. economy booms, but the Federal Reserve raises interest rates in order to forestall the development of inflationary pressures. The boom increases the U.S. demand for foreign currency, and the rise in interest rates increases the supply. The shift in the demand curve puts downward pressure on the dollar, but the shift in the supply curve puts upward pressure

---

TABLE 9.2 Major Determinants of the Supply and Demand for Foreign Currency in the United States

	Increases in the U.S. Demand for Foreign Currency	*Increases in the Supply of Foreign Currency*
1. Trade and direct investment factors		
The business cycle	U.S. economic expansion (more U.S. imports)	Foreign economic expansion (more U.S. exports)
Inflation	U.S. inflation (foreign goods relatively cheaper)	Foreign inflation (U.S. goods relatively cheaper)
Expectations of future growth	Increased potential for foreign growth (attracts outward U.S. direct investment)	Increased potential for U.S. growth (attracts foreign investment in the United States)
2. Interest rate changes	An increase in foreign interest rates, or a decline in U.S. rates	An increase in U.S. interest rates, or a decline in foreign rates
3. Speculation	Expectations of a future decline in the value of the dollar, or a future rise in the value of a foreign currency	Expectations of a future decline in the value of a foreign currency, or a future rise in the value of the dollar

CASE STUDY

Speculation Against the Pound, the Franc, and the Lira

From 1979 to 1999 the monetary system of the European Union was known as the European Monetary System, or EMS. Two key features of the EMS were an exchange rate system and an artificial currency known as the European Currency Unit, or ECU. The ECU was a weighted average of the currencies of the countries that belonged to the EU and the EMS. Its function was to serve as an anchor for the various individual currencies by fixing the value of each currency in terms of the ECU and thereby limiting fluctuations of national currencies around each other. Since all currencies were fixed in terms of ECUs, they were also fixed in terms of each other. The goal of the system was to prevent dramatic currency fluctuations that might lead to trade and investment effects that would be harmful to cooperation within the European Union. The EU recognized a need to permit day-to-day minor adjustments in currency values, however, and until late 1992 each country's currency was allowed to fluctuate by ±2.25 percent around its fixed ECU value.

For more than a decade after it began, the EMS performed much better than most economists expected. The EU currencies were relatively stable in relation to each other, and there seemed to be little difficulty in making adjustments when one or more currencies became seriously over- or undervalued. Then in 1989, the Berlin Wall fell. To everyone's surprise, West Germany and East Germany immediately began discussion over the terms and conditions that would permit them to reunify in the near future. A major concern was that East Germany's economy needed huge amounts of investment in order to close the gap in living standards between the two countries. West Germany feared that if they failed to provide the economic resources for rebuilding the East, a flood of immigrants would pour into the West. In the long run, it was better to rebuild the Eastern economy, even if it was expensive in the short run. Consequently, the West began to make large expenditures on roads, telecommunications, power, and other infrastructure. In addition, the East's transition from communism to capitalism created high levels of unemployment, requiring further payments from the West. Besides investment funds and unemployment benefits, the West decided to help the East by converting East German marks into West German marks at a 1:1 rate in spite of the fact that the real value of the East German mark was considerably less. The expenditures to rebuild the East together with the sudden increase in East German purchasing power caused bottlenecks in West Germany's economy. The central bank became concerned that the economy was overheating and that inflation might take off. It responded by raising short-term interest rates.

Germany's economy is the largest in Western Europe, and when Germany raises interest rates, it affects everyone else. One of the first impacts was a surge in the demand for the German mark, as investors sought to take advantage of the higher interest rates by buying assets denominated in marks. The

Case Study continues

Case Study continued

rebuilding of East Germany was partly financed with reconstruction bonds, and there was no shortage of relatively low-risk, West German financial assets for sale.

As expected, the rise in German interest rates increased the demand for marks and decreased the demand for the French franc and other EU currencies (see Figure 9.6). In France, the franc-mark exchange rate started to move toward its new equilibrium at R2, outside the 2.25 percent band. According to the rules of the EMS, the French government was required to intervene in currency markets and to keep the franc within the 2.25 percent margin around the mark. One possible strategy for France would have been to sell its reserves of German marks (increase the supply of marks to French investors). This would shift the supply curve for German marks to the right and bring the exchange rate back down to R1. One problem with this strategy is that the French government's limited reserves of German marks were unlikely to satisfy the increased demand. The second strategy available to the French government was to increase French interest rates in step with German rates. This was the strategy that France hoped to avoid, however. An increase in interest rates causes economic activity to slow down, and France appeared to be on the verge of a recession.

Inside and outside France, currency speculators observed the dilemma of the French government and began to sell large quantities of francs in the expectation that the franc would ultimately fall out of the 2.25 percent band. In effect, they were betting that the franc's future value would be less than its current value. In September of 1992, Italy, Spain, Britain, and a number of other countries faced the same pressures as speculators began to sell Italian lira, British pounds, Spanish pesetas, and so on, as well as the French franc (see Figure 9.7).

The core problem was that the exchange rate policies of the EU countries were inconsistent with their macroeconomic policies. Either the currencies'

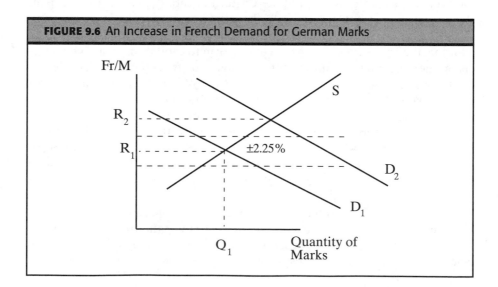

FIGURE 9.6 An Increase in French Demand for German Marks

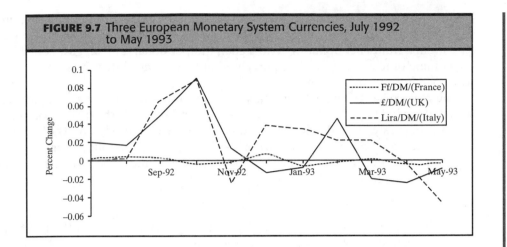

FIGURE 9.7 Three European Monetary System Currencies, July 1992 to May 1993

values had to be realigned with each other at a different set of exchange rates (a higher value for the German mark), or the low interest rates had to be increased. Initially, most countries tried to avoid choosing between a stable exchange rate and a low interest rate. Ultimately, every country had to choose.

France raised its interest rates and kept its currency aligned with the German mark; Italy and Spain devalued their currencies but stayed in the EU exchange rate system; and Britain devalued and dropped out of the exchange rate system, preferring instead to let the value of the pound float up and down in currency markets according to its supply and demand. In 1993, the obligation of the EMS countries to keep their currency fluctuations within ±2.25 percent was relaxed to ±15 percent.

on it. Does the dollar rise or fall in value? It is impossible to say. Unless we know the relative strengths of the two movements, it is not possible to predict the direction of change in the value of the dollar.

Nominal and Real Exchange Rates

The rates in Table 9.1 (page 177) state the price of foreign exchange, but they do not tell what the foreign currency is worth. For example, suppose that the exchange rate with France does not change, but during the year French inflation is 4 percent and U.S. inflation 1 percent. After one year, the five francs that cost one dollar will buy 3 percent less in France than the dollar buys in the United States. The relatively higher inflation in France (3 percent higher than in the United States) causes the value of one dollar's worth of francs to erode more rapidly than the value of the dollar. Consequently, the real purchasing power of a U.S. dollar converted into French francs has fallen.

From the point of view of tourists and businesspeople who use foreign exchange, the key item of interest is the purchasing power they get when they convert their dollars, not the number of units of a foreign currency. An American importer trying to decide between French and Italian textiles does not really care if he or she gets 5.01 French francs per dollar or 1548 Italian lira per dollar. The biggest concern is the volume of textiles that can be purchased in France with 5.01 francs and in Italy with 1548 lira.

The **real exchange rate** is the market exchange rate (or **nominal exchange rate**) adjusted for inflation. Let R_r equal the real rate and R_n equal the market or nominal exchange rate. Both the nominal and real rate are measured in units of domestic currency per unit of foreign currency—for example, 0.2 dollars per franc. In addition, let P equal the home country price level and P^* the foreign country's price level. The formula for the real exchange rate is

$$R_r = R_n(P^*/P)$$

A base year is arbitrarily chosen as a standard for comparison, and P and P* are both set equal to 100. As a result, in the base year,

$$R_r = R_n(100/100) = R_n$$

Over time, if inflation is higher at home than in the foreign country, then P rises more than P^*, and R_r falls, meaning the domestic currency appreciates in real terms. Suppose, for example, that the U.S. dollar-French franc nominal exchange rate is $0.20 per franc and that the United States has 10 percent inflation while France has 0 percent. Then, the real U.S.-France exchange rate (in terms of dollars per franc) would be

$$R_r = 0.2 * (100/110) = 0.1818$$

Tourists, investors, and businesspeople can still trade dollars and francs at the nominal rate of 0.2 dollars per franc (plus whatever commissions they must pay to the seller). After the price increases in the United States, however, the real purchasing power of the U.S. dollar has risen in France compared to what it buys at home. The real exchange rate of 0.1818 tells us that French goods are now 10 percent cheaper than U. S. goods that have risen in price. As long as the nominal exchange rate remains unchanged, French goods remain less expensive to both American and French purchasers. In real terms, the franc has depreciated and the dollar has appreciated.

> ***Real and nominal exchange rates.*** *The nominal exchange rate is the actual exchange rate in currency markets. The real exchange rate is the inflation-adjusted nominal rate. The real rate is useful for examining changes over time in the relative purchasing power of foreign currencies.*

Changes in the value of real exchange rates play an important role in international macroeconomic relations. Many developing countries, for example, control the nominal value of their currency (R_n). If inflation runs higher than their trading partner's ($\Delta P > \Delta P^*$), however, the real value of their currency appreciates. Over a period of time, if uncorrected, this causes an increase in imports and a decline in exports. In a number of cases, the net result is a buildup of large current account deficits, followed by a crisis and the collapse of the nominal exchange rate. (Some examples are Mexico in December 1994 and Thailand in 1997.)

Determinants of Exchange Rates in the Long Run

Few tasks in economics are more difficult and riskier than trying to predict exchange rates. Currency markets are as volatile as stock markets, and no one yet has been able to devise a system to consistently and accurately forecast exchange rates. Nevertheless, there is substantial evidence that over the very long run (periods of a decade or more), exchange rates are determined by two main factors: the law of one price (also known as purchasing power parity) and differences in productivity growth.

The **law of one price,** or **purchasing power parity,** states that a currency should buy the same quantity of goods when converted to another currency as it can buy at home. In other words, the exchange rate should be at a level that keeps the real purchasing power of money constant when it is converted to another currency. If the law of one price does not hold, then a dollar in the United States buys a different (larger or smaller) bundle of goods than it buys in Japan when the dollar is converted into yen. If a dollar buys more in the United States than its yen equivalent buys in Japan, then businesses could make profits by shipping goods from the United States where they are relatively cheap and selling them in Japan where they are relatively more expensive. If a dollar's worth of yen buys more in Japan, goods will flow in the opposite direction, from Japan to the United States.

The law of one price can be thought of as a long-run tendency for the real exchange rate to remain constant. Since the real rate equals the nominal rate times the relative price levels, the law of one price essentially states that if foreign prices rise more than domestic prices ($\Delta P^* > \Delta P$), then the nominal rate should appreciate (R_n falls—it takes fewer dollars to buy a unit of foreign currency) by the same percentage. These forces can take highly variable and sometimes very long periods of time to materialize, however, so the law of one price does not permit anyone to forecast tomorrow's or next year's dollar-yen exchange rate. In addition, even over the long run, there can be substantial deviations in a nation's currency from the law of one price. For example, between 1970 and 1994, the dollar depreciated against the German mark by 3.2 percent per year on average (R_n rose by 3.2 percent per year). At the same time, the price level in the United States rose faster than the German price level ($\Delta P > \Delta P^*$), but the difference was only 1.9 percent per year on average. About 1.3 percent per year was unaccounted for ($3.2 - 1.9$), and that showed up as a real depreciation of the dollar (a rise in R_r). Table 9.3 shows these figures and similar ones for the dollar-yen exchange rate.

Differences in U.S.-Japanese and U.S.-German manufacturing productivity growth rates are given in row two of Table 9.3. Although U.S. productivity levels are higher, rates of growth of Japanese and German productivity were superior in the period from 1980 to 1994. Faster productivity growth is equivalent to a relative decline in prices and leads to a real appreciation in currency values over the long run. As Japanese or German workers increase their output at a faster pace than American workers, Japanese yen and German marks increase their purchasing power at home. Ultimately, the increased buying power becomes a more or less equivalent increase in purchasing power abroad (i.e., in the United States). From the U.S. standpoint, R_r rises, which is a real depreciation of the dollar.

TABLE 9.3 Determinants of Long-Run Changes in Exchange Rates, U.S.-Japan and U.S.-Germany, 1980–1994

	U.S.-Japan	U.S.-Germany
1. $\Delta P - \Delta P^*$, in percents	0.9%	1.9%
2. Differences in productivity growth, foreign minus U.S., in percents	2.1%	1.1%
3. ΔR_n, in percents	+4.9%	+3.2%
4. Unexplained portion	4.9 - 3.0 = 1.9	3.2 - 3.0 = 0.2

Source: Kenneth Kasa, "Understanding Trends in Foreign Exchange Rates," *FRBSF Weekly Letter,* Federal Reserve Bank of San Francisco, June 9, 1995.

Exchange Rate Systems

Exchange rate systems are the rules that nations attach to the movement of their exchange rates. There are a number of different categories of sets or rules that nations may adopt, but they all are modifications of two fundamental categories: fixed and floating exchange rate systems. Historically, fixed exchange rate systems have usually been a gold standard or a modified gold standard and have been far more common than a floating exchange rate system.

Both fixed and floating exchange rate systems have advantages and disadvantages. The weight of economic opinion has probably tended to favor floating exchange rates, although this is by no means unanimous.

The Gold Standard and Fixed Exchange Rates

Gold standards are a form of fixed exchange rates. Under a pure gold standard, nations keep gold as their international reserve. Gold is used to settle most international obligations, and nations must be prepared to trade it for their own currency whenever foreigners attempt to "redeem" the home currency they earned when they sold goods and services. In this sense, the nation's money is backed by gold.

There are essentially three rules that countries need to follow in order to maintain a gold exchange standard. First, they must fix the value of their currency unit (the dollar, the pound, the franc, etc.) in terms of gold. This fixes the exchange rate. For example, under the modified gold standard of the Bretton Woods system (1947–1971) the U.S. dollar was fixed at $35 per ounce, and the British pound was set at £12.5 per ounce. The exchange rate was $35/£12.5, or $2.80 per pound.

The second rule of the gold standard is that nations keep the supply of their domestic money fixed in some constant proportion to their supply of gold. This requirement is an informal one, but it is necessary in order to insure that the domestic money supply does not grow beyond the capacity of the gold supply to support it.

Consider what would happen if a country decided to print large quantities of money for which their was no gold backing. In the short run, purchases of domestically produced goods would rise; in the medium to long run, domestic prices would follow them up. As domestic prices rise, foreign goods become more attractive, since a fixed exchange rate means that they have not increased in price. As imports in the home country increase, foreigners accumulate an unwanted supply of the home country's currency.

This is the point at which the gold standard would begin to become unhinged. Under the rules of the gold standard, nations must be willing to redeem their own currency with payments in gold, and they must freely allow gold to be imported and exported (third rule). If gold supplies are low in relation to the supply of domestic currency, gold reserves will run out when the nation tries to redeem its currency from foreigners. This spells crisis and a possible end to the gold standard.

Under any fixed exchange rate system, whether it is based on gold or not, the national supply and demand for foreign currencies may vary, but the nominal exchange rate does not. It is the responsibility of the monetary authorities (i.e., the central bank or treasury department) to keep the exchange rate fixed.

Figure 9.8 shows an increase in the U.S. demand for British pounds. In the short run, a rise in demand is caused by one of the factors listed in Table 9.2: increased U.S. demand for UK goods, higher UK interest rates, or the expectation that the value of the dollar will fall against the pound. If R_1 is the fixed U.S.-UK exchange rate, then the United States must counter the weakening dollar and prevent the rate from rising to R_2. (Remember, R_2 represents more dollars per pound than R1; therefore, the dollar is worth less.) One option is to sell the United States' reserves of British pounds. This shifts the supply curve out, as in Figure 9.9, and keeps the exchange rate at R_1.

Under a pure gold standard, nations hold gold as a reserve instead of foreign currencies and the United States sells its gold reserves in exchange for dollars. This

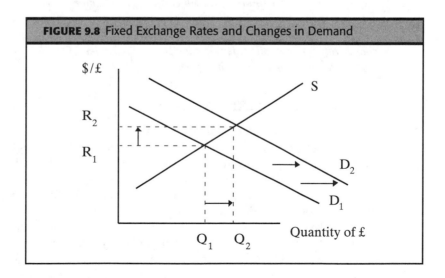

FIGURE 9.8 Fixed Exchange Rates and Changes in Demand

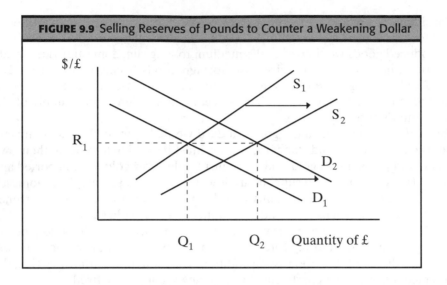

FIGURE 9.9 Selling Reserves of Pounds to Counter a Weakening Dollar

action increases the demand for dollars and offsets the pressure on the dollar to fall in value.

As the United States sells its gold reserves, one of two things can happen. Either the demand for gold by people supplying dollars is satisfied and the pressure on the dollar eases, or the United States begins to run out of gold. If the latter happens, the United States may be forced to devalue the dollar. Under a gold standard, a devaluation is accomplished by changing the gold price of the dollar. If the dollar was set at $35 per ounce of gold, a devaluation would shift the price of gold to something more than $35, and each ounce of gold sold by the United States buys back a greater quantity of dollars.

> ***Devaluation and revaluation.*** *Devaluation and revaluation are equivalent to depreciation and appreciation, except that they refer to changes in a currency's value under a fixed exchange rate system. A devaluation is a decline in the value of a currency under a fixed exchange rate system, while a depreciation is a decline under a flexible system. Revaluation and appreciation have similar interpretations.*

Alternative Exchange Rate Systems

Fixed exchange rates under a gold standard are one extreme in the spectrum of possible exchange rate systems. At the other extreme are **floating (or flexible) exchange rates**. Under a floating exchange rate system, the value of a nation's currency "floats" up and down in response to changes in its supply and demand. When demand exceeds supply, it appreciates in value (R_n falls), and when supply is greater than demand, it depreciates (R_n rises).

Between fixed and floating exchange rates, there are a number of other types of exchange rate systems. The simplest way to categorize these systems is on a scale that measures the amount of flexibility each allows. At one end are freely floating rates, which are the most flexible. One step down the spectrum of flexibility is a

CASE STUDY

The End of Bretton Woods and Pegged Exchange Rates

The Bretton Woods system of exchange rates was put into place at the end of World War II. It included most nations outside the former Soviet Union and its allies. The exchange rate system was a major component of the institutions that were designed to manage international economic conflict and to support international economic cooperation. In addition to the exchange rate system, the other institutions that were created at the same time included the International Monetary Fund (IMF), the International Bank for Reconstruction and Development (IBRD), or World Bank, and the General Agreement on Tariffs and Trade (GATT). (See Chapter 2.)

Each institution had its own role in the management of world economic affairs. The roles of the exchange rate were to provide stability by eliminating excess currency fluctuations, to prevent nations from using exchange rate devaluations as a tactic for gaining markets for their goods, and to insure that there was an adequate supply of internationally accepted reserves so that nations could meet their international obligations.

In the **Bretton Woods exchange rate system,** the dollar was fixed to gold at the rate of $1 equaled $\frac{1}{35}$ ounce of gold, or $35 per ounce. Every other currency within the system was fixed to the dollar and, therefore, indirectly to gold. Unlike a pure gold standard, however, countries could use U.S. dollars as their international reserve and did not have to accumulate gold or tie their money supply to their gold reserves.

The Bretton Woods exchange rate system had one fatal flaw—the dollar. The United States was in a privileged position, since its currency was treated the same as gold. This meant that the United States could simply increase its money supply (the supply of dollars) and gain increased purchasing power over European, Japanese, and other country's goods. Other nations preferred the United States to maintain a relatively robust supply of dollars as well, since this insured that there was an adequate supply of international reserves for the world economy.

Problems with this arrangement began when the U.S. economy expanded at a different rate than the economies of its trading partners. In the mid-to-late 1960s, the United States deepened its involvement in the Vietnam War while simultaneously creating the "War on Poverty" at home. Both policies generated large fiscal expenditures that stimulated the economy. While U.S. expansion raced ahead of expansion elsewhere, Europeans found themselves accumulating dollars more rapidly than they desired. The dollars were a byproduct of U.S. economic expansion and partially reflected the price increases that were accompanying the expansion.

Under a different type of exchange rate system, it would have been appropriate for the United States to devalue its currency. U. S. prices had risen relative to foreign prices; the real exchange rate had appreciated as a

Case Study continues

consequence; and trade deficits were beginning to become a permanent feature of the U.S. economy.

One policy would have been to devalue the nominal dollar exchange rate, but this was not an option. Since every currency was tied to the dollar, there was no way for the United States to selectively devalue against a group of other currencies. An alternative was for the United States to devalue against all currencies by changing the gold value of the dollar. By the late 1960s, is was becoming apparent that this would be necessary.

Persistent U.S. deficits had led to an accumulation of dollars outside the United States that greatly exceeded the United States' supply of gold. In other words, the United States lacked the gold reserves to back all of the dollars that were in circulation. Official recognition of this fact led to the **Smithsonian Agreement** of December 1971, in which the major industrialized countries agreed to devalue the gold content of the dollar by around 8 percent, from $35 per ounce to $38.02. In addition, Japan, Germany, and other trade surplus countries revalued their currencies.

Although the Smithsonian Agreement was hailed by President Nixon as a fundamental reorganization of international monetary affairs, it quickly proved to be of too little and only temporary benefit. The gold value of the dollar was realigned again in early 1973, from $38.02 to $42.22. In addition, further devaluation occurred against other European currencies. The end of the system came in March 1973, when the major currencies began to float against each other. A few currencies, such as the British pound, had begun to float earlier.

In each case, the strategy of allowing the exchange rate to float in response to supply and demand conditions was adopted as a means of coping with speculation. When speculators had perceived that the dollar was overvalued at $38 or $42 per ounce, they sold dollars in anticipation of a future devaluation. The dollar was not the only currency speculated against. Other weak currencies such as the pound and the Italian lira had also been correctly perceived as overvalued and had been sold off by speculators. In the end, the central banks of the weak-currency countries found it impossible to support an unrealistically high value of their currency. The costs of buying up the excess supply of their currencies at overvalued prices proved to be too great. The simplest solution was to let the currencies float.

managed floating rate. The difference between a managed floating rate and a purely floating exchange rate is that the national government occasionally intervenes in international currency markets in an attempt to "manage" the direction of change. Intervention takes the form of buying the home currency in order to increase its demand and prop up its value, or selling the home currency in order to encourage depreciation. Countries with floating exchange rates use these tactics whenever policy makers think there is a need to nudge their currency up or down, or to stop an ongoing change. Nearly all governments try to manage their exchange rate at some point in time. Consequently, most of the nations that have adopted floating exchange rate systems are in fact using a managed floating system.

A **target zone exchange rate system** is similar to a managed floating system. The most prominent example is the European Monetary System of the fifteen-member European Union, prior to the single currency of 1999. With a target zone, exchange rates are allowed to float freely within some well-defined range, or band. The band defines a line of intervention; that is, it is like a managed float except the limits of a currency's flexibility are precisely defined.

A less flexible system than the exchange rate band is an **adjustable peg exchange rate**, such as the Bretton Woods system. An adjustable peg is a fixed exchange rate that is adjusted periodically. Developing nations often use an adjustable peg or something very similar as a way to keep their exchange rate more or less fixed in real terms. Given that

$$R_r = R_n(P^*/P)$$

regular adjustment to R_n keeps the real exchange rate, R_r, from appreciating when domestic inflation is greater than the inflation rate of the country's trading partners.

Fixed Versus Flexible Exchange Rate Systems

The primary distinction between the exchange rate systems described above is whether the value of the nation's currency is determined by the forces of supply and demand, with perhaps some assistance from government intervention, or whether it is fixed, with perhaps some periodic adjustments.

One of the reasons that some economists give for favoring fixed exchange rate systems is that they reduce the uncertainty associated with fluctuating currency values. The value of a nation's currency does not change day to day, and foreign trade and investment decisions are more likely to be based on economic conditions other than currency shifts.

The underlying assumption is that the fixed exchange rate is sustainable. Even fixed rates change, however, as underlying conditions change. For example, we have seen that if a nation experiences higher inflation rates than its trading partner, then its real exchange rate will appreciate, leading to a rise in imports and a fall in exports. We have also seen that these changes in trade flows will increase the demand for foreign currency. This situation is illustrated in Figure 9. 10.

If the fixed rate is R_f, then any increase in the demand for a foreign currency must be met by the monetary authority (i.e., the central bank or the finance/treasury ministry, whichever is charged with stabilizing the exchange rate). In Figure 9.10, the appropriate government agency will have to supply $Q2 - Q1$ quantity of foreign currency from its supply of international reserves. Otherwise, the nominal exchange rate will rise to eliminate the gap between supply and demand for the foreign currency.

Defending the exchange rate can become very expensive, particularly if it fails. If the nominal rate ultimately rises (R_n rises, the home currency depreciates), the government will have sold foreign currency at too low a price; in other words, it paid too much to buy back its own currency.

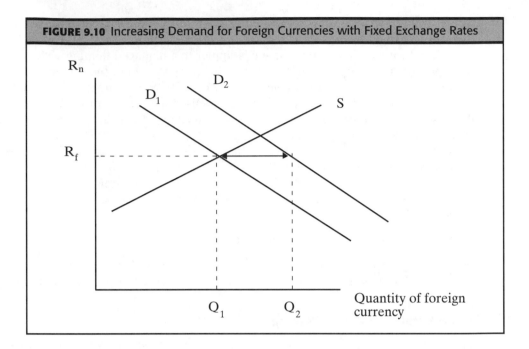

FIGURE 9.10 Increasing Demand for Foreign Currencies with Fixed Exchange Rates

An alternative to supplying $Q_2 - Q_1$ quantity of foreign currency is to raise interest rates. As we have seen, this will reduce the demand for foreign currencies and increase the demand for the home currency.

Both of these strategies for keeping the exchange rate fixed have potential problems. Selling reserves of gold or foreign currency can last only so long. No government has an inexhaustible supply, and once the available reserves are sold, the exchange rate must change. On the other hand, a change in interest rates may solve the problem of the exchange rate, but there is no guarantee that interest rate increases are the right policy from a macroeconomic perspective. If the country is in recession, interest rate increases are the last thing that is needed.

The advantage of a floating exchange rate is that it is much less likely to run into this tension between maintaining the exchange rate and pursuing policies that are good for the domestic economy. Policymakers can carry out monetary policies without regard to the differences between inflation rates or the differences between interest rates. Consequently, governments can ignore the effects on exchange rates of policies designed to fight a recession or to increase the rate of economic growth.

Liberating macroeconomic policies from the constraint of supporting the exchange rate is one of the strongest arguments in favor of floating rates. It is also one of the strongest arguments against them. Some economists argue that the removal of the discipline of maintaining fixed rates is harmful because it leads to greater inflation. Released from the need to keep inflation close to the rate in other countries, policy makers are free to pursue more inflationary policies as they try to increase the rate of economic growth.

CASE STUDY 1

Curing Hyperinflation in Argentina

Argentina's recent history is a good example of the positive benefits of a fixed exchange rate. Through much of the 1980s, the country suffered from extremely high rates of inflation. Between 1985 and 1990, the lowest it reached was 90.1 percent in 1986, but in 1989, it skyrocketed to the astronomical level of 17,236 percent (Table 9.4).

Argentina tried a number of reforms in the mid-1980s. The most famous, the Austral Plan, included a currency reform in which the Argentine peso was replaced with a new currency called the austral. The austral was fixed or pegged, but regular adjustments were made to try and keep the real exchange rate constant. In addition to fixing the exchange rate, the government also fixed the prices of government services, hoping that they would "anchor" prices elsewhere in the economy and prevent them from rising. When economy-wide prices rose, however, the fixed prices for government services resulted in large budget deficits that, in turn, created a need for monetary expansion to finance the government.

Tax collection was both lax and subject to widespread corruption. Consequently, the only way to finance the large government deficits was to print money. The resulting inflation quickly turned into hyperinflation, the condition in which money ceases to have value, and barter becomes common. Traffic fines, for example, were denominated in terms of gallons of gasoline, rather than in australs.

An added problem was that despite the regular adjustments of the nominal exchange rate, the rate of inflation made it impossible to keep up with the

TABLE 9.4 Inflation and Real Exchange Rates in Argentina, 1985–1994

	1985	1986	1987	1988	1989
Inflation	672	90	131	372	17,236
Real exchange rate (1990 = 100)	97	108	119	130	149

	1990	1991	1992	1993	1994
Inflation	1518	62	17	11	4
Real exchange rate (1990 = 100)	100	73	65	59	58

Note: An increase in the index number for the real exchange rate is an appreciation.

Source: Inter-American Development Bank, *Overcoming Volatility*, Economic and Social Progress in Latin America, 1995 Report, p. 25.

Case Study 1 continues

price increases, and the real exchange rate tended to become seriously over-valued. Predictably, the overvalued exchange rate resulted in a growing trade deficit and a looming balance of payments crisis.

In 1991, the new government of Carlos Menem passed Argentina's Convertibility Law. The law fixed the value of a new austral to the U.S. dollar at the rate of 1:1. In order to insure the fixity of the austral, the Convertibility Law requires that no new money may be printed unless the treasury holds a dollar of international reserves to back it up. In order to prevent a spiraling budget deficit, Menem took numerous steps to increase government tax revenues (including the firing of a large number of tax collectors suspected of corruption) and radically cut government expenditures.

One way to look at Argentina's policy is that it is the same as a gold standard, only instead of gold, Argentina backs its currency with U.S. dollars. Like the gold standard, the Convertibility Law has placed Argentina in a very tight monetary straitjacket. The cost of this policy is that the country has abandoned its right to use its money supply as an independent means of stimulating the economy. The benefit is that it has cured itself of hyperinflation.

CASE STUDY 2

The Great Depression and the Gold Standard

The Great Depression of the 1930s was a shattering experience. Coming on the heels of a decade of relative prosperity in which incomes rose and consumers began to equip their homes with major appliances such as cars, washing machines, refrigerators, and radios, it destroyed the faith and optimism of many Americans. People were thrown out of work as unemployment reached 25 percent of the labor force, farms and homes were sold at auction to pay back interest and back taxes, banks collapsed by the thousands, and for a long while, no end was in sight.

Most countries suffered through the Depression, although its timing and severity varied. It seemed to start in the United States in 1929, although Britain's economy was in trouble from the middle of the 1920s. One line of inquiry has been to understand its beginnings and to examine how it spread across the world. What triggered its beginnings in the United States? The stock market crash, while dramatic, is generally dismissed as a causal explanation because it happened after the onset of the Depression, and the market recovered much of its lost value over the subsequent six months.

Since the 1960s, a widely accepted explanation for the severity of the Depression in the United States was the incompetence of the Federal Reserve. At a time when the economy was shrinking, the Fed followed contractionary money supply policies. These served to reinforce the downward spiral in the economy and intensified the Depression. While this explanation has much to

Case Study 2 continues

Case Study 2 continued

recommend it, it also has a few weak spots. For example, why did the Fed suddenly become so incompetent? Also, the Depression was worldwide; how did it spread to other countries?

Recent scholarship has modified the "blame the Fed" explanation, in part by examining the constraints that limited the range of responses available. After World War I, most nations returned to the gold standard, and the primary responsibility of the Fed was preserving the gold value of the dollar. In order to fulfill its responsibility, the Fed was required to use its interest rate and monetary policy as a means to attract gold to the United States whenever reserves began to run low. This usually meant an interest rate increase and the avoidance of open market purchases (the buying of government bonds), which expand the money supply and lead to the outflow of gold reserves.

In 1928, before the Depression's onset, U.S. monetary policy turned contractionary. The Fed was worried about speculation on the stock market and wanted to make it more difficult for brokers to borrow from banks. The Fed raised U.S. interest rates and unintentionally created an inflow of gold to the United States.

U.S. policy put pressure on countries in Europe, which began to lose their gold reserves. Consequently, the contractionary policy in the United States spread to Europe, as nations began to raise their interest rates and slow their rate of money growth in order to stop the outflow of gold. The irony is that each country was acting responsibly according to the dictates of the gold standard, but each was also following polices that would result in the collapse of capitalism.

At several points during the years that followed, U.S. and foreign policies turned even more contractionary. In 1931, it was widely expected that the United Kingdom would leave the gold standard altogether, and speculation turned against the pound. In September, Britain left the gold standard, and speculators immediately shifted their attention to the dollar. The sell-off of dollars resulted in serious gold outflows and, once again, the Fed responded by raising interest rates in September and October of 1931. The U.S. economy continued its downward spiral.

It is no coincidence that the first countries to leave the gold standard (the United Kingdom and the countries that followed it out of the gold standard in September 1931) were the first to experience recovery. Once their policies were freed from the constraint of supporting a fixed rate of exchange, they could turn them toward economic expansion.

In the United States, Franklin Roosevelt took office in March of 1933 and immediately suspended the gold standard. It does not seem likely that he had the foresight of modern macroeconomics or that he understood the relationship of gold to the Depression. Nevertheless, it was a fortuitously good move, as the economy began its long, slow recovery from its worst economic crisis of the twentieth century.

Optimal Currency Areas

Fixed exchange rates reduce much of the uncertainty that comes from fluctuating currency values. They also encourage economic agents to base their international trade and investment decisions on economic efficiency rather than currency fluctuations. Fixed rates, however, tie a nation's monetary policies to supporting the exchange rate, often at the cost of forsaking more urgent domestic problems, such as fighting unemployment or recession. In addition, for a fixed exchange rate to work, it must be credible. That is, world markets must believe that the fixed currency value will continue indefinitely into the future and that it represents an equilibrium value.

The tradeoffs between fixed and flexible rates have led economists to investigate the conditions under which the tradeoffs are less severe. In other words, is it possible to obtain the best of both worlds: to have the certainty and stability of fixed rates without the straitjacket of having to ignore domestic economic issues when they conflict with exchange rate policies? The geographical area in which these conditions are present is known as an **optimal currency area**.

An optimal currency areas is the geographical area within which it makes sense to fix the exchange rates or to use one currency. In general, they require two conditions. First, the business cycles of the nations within the area must be synchronized. Economic expansions and contractions should occur more or less simultaneously throughout the group so that one monetary policy is appropriate for all members. Otherwise, one nation may prefer an expansionary policy to counteract a recession, while others favor a contractionary policy in order to offset inflation.

We have also seen that differences in inflation rates will ultimately cause nominal exchange rates to change. Consequently, if the tolerance or preference for inflation differs among nations, they will eventually be forced to alter their fixed rates.

> ***Optimal currency area.*** *An optimal currency area is a region of fixed exchange rates or a single currency. It is optimal in the sense that it is precisely the right geographical size to capture the benefits of fixed rates without incurring the costs.*

A second criterion for an optimal currency area is that the factor inputs of labor and capital are mobile between the member countries. This allows workers and capital to leave countries or regions where work is scarce and to join the supply of labor and capital in booming regions. In effect, free migration of the factors of production smooths out some of the differences in the business cycle by taking unemployed inputs and moving them to where they are needed.

Perhaps the best-known example of an attempt to create an optimal currency area is the European Monetary System (EMS). The EMS was created in 1979 by the European Community (now known as the European Union) as a target zone fixed exchange rate system. Under the terms of the Maastricht Treaty, the European Union is scheduled to move to a single currency, to be called the "euro," in 1999. There is still some doubt about the consequences of a single currency, however, and the lack of synchronization of business cycles in Europe has caused a number of observers to begin to question its desirability. The Maastricht Treaty and the move to a single currency is discussed in Chapter 13.

Flexible Exchange Rates and Government Intervention in Currency Markets

In March of 1995, the Bank for International Settlements (BIS), a clearinghouse for the world's central banks, reported that the daily flow of currency trades in the world's markets was $1.2 *trillion*. In other words, more than one-sixth of the U.S. GDP is traded every day in the form of currency trades. Given this huge volume of daily trades, it may seem impossible for a central bank to influence the value of its currency through buying and selling in the world's markets. In a sense, it is similar to a consumer expecting that his or her demand for a new car will move the market demand enough to change the price of cars.

All governments are relatively limited in their ability to intervene in foreign exchange markets. When market participants believe that a currency is going to fall in value, they will sell it. A marketwide sell-off overwhelms any central bank and makes it impossible to stabilize the currency above the market-determined equilibrium value. Central banks lack sufficient reserves to counter this kind of currency movement and, when they try, they quickly lose their reserves. Sometimes, however, central banks can effectively influence the value of their currency. When currency traders have different opinions about the exchange rate, or when there are no strong opinions, or when the exchange market is looking to central banks for an indicator of future policy, central bank intervention can be effective.

Two related factors enable central banks to sometimes succeed in influencing the market value of their currencies. The first factor is a portfolio effect that stems from the desire of currency traders to maintain the maximum value of their portfolio of foreign currencies at all times. When central banks buy and sell currency, it changes the relative market supply of the nation's money.

Portfolio-balance theory states that a change in the composition (relative supplies) of assets will alter their expected future return, in part by causing investors to rebalance their portfolios. In other words, when intervention works, central bank purchases of the domestic currency reduce its supply relative to the supply of foreign currencies; this causes currency traders to rebalance their portfolios by increasing their holding of the domestic currency, which is expected to be scarcer (more valuable) in the future.

A second effect is related to the release of new information. A change in central bank policy, for example a switch from a relatively tight policy to a looser one, or vice versa, forces currency traders to reevaluate their positions in each currency. At any given moment, an exchange rate reflects all the available information about a particular currency, and a change in the stock of information causes a reassessment of the currency's value. For example, when banks buy back their own currency, traders incorporate the fact of intervention into their expectations about the future direction of policy. Central bank currency purchases signal a more restrictive monetary policy and higher interest rates in the future, two good reasons to increase the share of the currency in private portfolios. Purchases by foreign currency traders reinforce the central bank intervention and cause the currency to rise in value.

CASE STUDY

The Plaza and Louvre Accords

The Plaza and Louvre Accords are two famous examples of organized interventions by the central banks of several industrial economies. Their goal in each case was to control the value of the dollar.

Between January 1980 and January 1985, the exchange value of the dollar rose from an index of 85.52 (1973 = 100) to 152.83, or 78.7 percent. (An increase in the index is an appreciation.) Several factors were at work, including high U.S. interest rates, a strong U.S. economy after 1982, and a policy of nonintervention in currency markets.

The impact on trade balances was devastating. Imports were drawn into the United States at an extremely fast pace, while exports either could not keep up or, for some industries, declined in absolute terms. A number of important U.S. export industries were severely hurt by the high value of the dollar, including agricultural equipment and commercial aircraft manufacturers.

The first Reagan administration had adopted a policy of nonintervention in currency markets. They repeatedly expressed a commitment to floating rates that were entirely market determined. Currency traders incorporated the U.S. policy of laissez faire into their outlook and formed their expectations about the future value of the U.S. dollar on the assumption that there would be no intervention or attempt to alter the value of the dollar.

In 1985, a new group of policy makers took over in the Treasury Department. Led by James Baker and Richard Darman, the new team was much more pragmatic and less ideologically committed to the laissez faire policy. In addition, by 1985, significant domestic political pressure had built up calling for a change in currency policy.

With the introduction of a new team at the Treasury Department, exchange rate markets seemed to expect a shift in U.S. policies toward the dollar. After peaking in February 1985, the dollar depreciated by 13 percent over the next six months. Then, on September 22, 1985, the finance (Treasury Department) ministers and central bank governors from the Group of 5 (G-5) met at the Plaza Hotel in New York City. (The G-5 includes the United States, Japan, Germany, France, and the United Kingdom. The G-7 includes the G-5 plus Canada and Italy.)

In their communiqué at the end of their meeting, the G-5 announced that "some further orderly appreciation of nondollar currencies is desirable." The dollar immediately fell another 4 percent. The central banks of the United States, Germany, Japan, and other G-5 countries coordinated their interventions in the exchange markets so that each was a net seller of dollars. Over the two years following the Plaza Accord, the dollar continued to trend downward.

Figure 9.11 shows these movements in the overall value of the dollar (the value of the dollar relative to the currencies of U.S. trading partners, measured with an index) and the value of the dollar relative to the yen and the mark. From the time of the G-5's Plaza Agreement in September 1985, until the be-

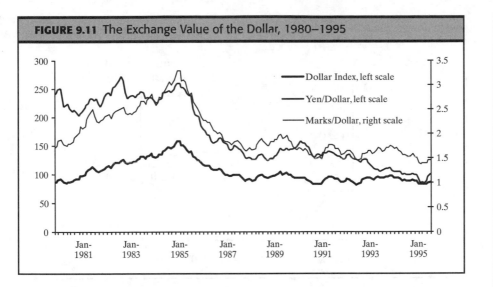

FIGURE 9.11 The Exchange Value of the Dollar, 1980–1995

ginning of 1987, the dollar fell by 28.5 percent. Against the yen and mark, it fell by 34.5 percent and 34.4 percent, respectively.

By 1987, many countries were beginning to feel that the dollar had fallen far enough. On February 21 and 22, at a meeting of the G-7 that took place at the Louvre in Paris, an agreement was reached that the dollar should be stabilized at its current level. Figure 9.11 shows that after the February meeting, the dollar's value wanders around some, but there is no trend up or down over the subsequent few years.

Exchange Rates and the Trade Balance

Recall from Chapter 8 that the appropriate policies for eliminating a trade deficit included expenditure switching and expenditure reducing polices. A key component of most expenditure switching policies is a depreciation in the value of a nation's currency. The process in which the trade balance responds to an increase in the price of foreign exchange is called the adjustment process.

The **adjustment process** is the term used to describe changes in the trade deficit that are caused by a change in the exchange rate. There are two characteristics of the adjustment process that are important to keep in mind. First, trade balances do not respond instantly to a change in the exchange rate. In the United States, for example, there is a median average lag of about nine and a half months between a change in the exchange rate and the response by U. S. exports. The median average lag for import responses is slightly less but still more than seven months. Consequently, it is a mistake to think that exchange rate changes will affect trade flows overnight.

Second, in the short run of one year or less, the trade balance is likely to move in an opposite direction from the anticipated one. In other words, in the first year after a fall in the value of a nation's currency, the trade deficit is likely to grow rather than shrink. This is known as the **J-curve**, and it is illustrated in Figure 9.12.

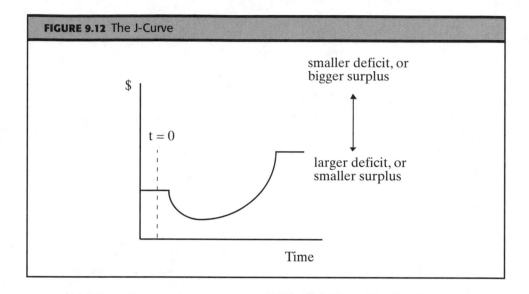

FIGURE 9.12 The J-Curve

$

t = 0

Time

smaller deficit, or
bigger surplus

larger deficit, or
smaller surplus

CASE STUDY

The Adjustment Process in the United States

From the third quarter of 1980 to mid-1987, the U.S. trade deficit widened from 0.48 percent of GDP to over 3.5 percent of GDP. In 1985, the Plaza Accord among the G-5 created a cooperative effort to bring down the value of the dollar. The dollar began to fall in early 1985 with the introduction of a new team of officials at the Treasury Department; from January 1985 to January 1987, it fell from an index of 152.83 to 101.13, or nearly 34 percent.

While the dollar was falling, the trade deficit continued to widen. This proved disconcerting to a number of politicians, economists, and others who had predicted a significant decline in the U.S. trade deficit as a result of the depreciation. Some journalists and politicians began to argue that the trade deficit would never respond to a change in the value of the dollar, that foreign trade barriers would make it impossible for the United States to substantially expand exports, and that our own open market would ensure a growing volume of imports, regardless of the dollar's value.

Nevertheless, after a little more than two years, the trade balance began to respond to the fall in the dollar. Figure 9.13 illustrates the change in the value of the dollar and the current account from 1980 to 1990. It is apparent that there is a striking similarity in their movements but a lag of more than two years between the peak in the dollar and the peak and subsequent decline in the trade deficit.

The question economists have debated since this episode is why it took so long for trade balances to respond to the decline in the value of the dollar. There are several possible explanations to this question. One is that the prior

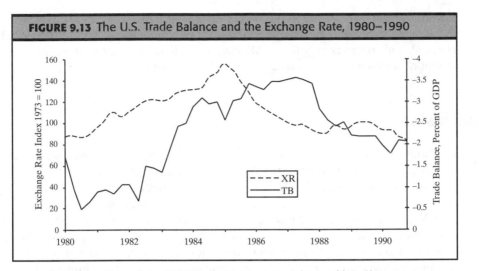

FIGURE 9.13 The U.S. Trade Balance and the Exchange Rate, 1980–1990

Source: Business Cycles Indicators, BCI DataManager, Gary F. Langer; *Economic Report of the President.*

increase in the dollar's value had padded the profit margins of foreign producers. From 1980 to 1985, their exports to the United States rose in terms of their domestic prices, even though they sold in the United States for the same dollar prices. Consequently, when the dollar began to fall, foreign producers were initially able to keep dollar prices constant and absorb the decline in its value by realizing lower profits in terms of their domestic currency.

Another possible reason for the long lag between the dollar's depreciation and improvement on the current account was that the depreciation began from a point at which not all the previous effects of the dollar's rise had been felt. In other words, the effects of earlier appreciations were still working their way through the system.

A third and final reason for the long lag was that exports began to increase from a much lower base than imports and needed to increase much more rapidly in percentage terms in order for the trade deficit to begin to close.

If the domestic currency falls in value at time t = 0, there will be a period of no noticeable effect on the flow of goods and services. When imports and exports begin to shift, the immediate change will be an increase in the value of imports. In other words, the trade balance moves toward deficit or toward an increase in the size of the deficit if one already exists. Only after a year or more will a depreciation show up as an improvement in the trade balance.

The reason for a short- to medium-run deterioration in a trade balance after a depreciation is fairly straightforward. A change in currency values alters the relative prices of domestic and foreign goods—with a depreciation, foreign goods become more expensive and domestic goods cheaper (relative to the price of foreign goods). Ultimately, this will cause households and firms to switch away from foreign goods and toward domestic goods, but in the short run, they lack information about alternatives to foreign goods. New domestic suppliers must be found, the quality of their products checked, and contracts negotiated. Meanwhile, until the alternative domestic suppliers are found, foreign goods continue to be used, even though they cost more.

Conclusion

Exchange rates are one of the main economic linkages between nations. Consequently, it is important to understand how they are determined and what impacts they have on national economies. Economists analyze exchange rates as if they are just another commodity in the economy: a simple supply-and-demand model of exchange rate determination presents most of the basics and leads to a clear understanding of their tendencies to depreciate or appreciate. Regardless of their importance, however, prediction of future exchange rates is impossible. For the most part, this is due to the fact that a great many variables influence exchange rates, and it is impossible to anticipate the effect of each and every one.

Chapter 9 has summarized many of the key issues related to exchange rates and their impacts on national economies.

▲ Exchange rates are unpredictable but, in the long run, national differences in productivity and inflation will show up as changes in the exchange rate. In the short run, national differences in GDP growth and interest rates are critical.

▲ People hold foreign currency in order to buy goods and services, to take advantage of interest rate differentials, and to speculate. The primary institutions in the exchange rate market are commercial banks and foreign exchange brokers.

▲ Firms use forward exchange rate markets to protect against exchange rate risk.

▲ Real exchange rates are equal to nominal or market exchange rates adjusted for inflation. They give a better picture of the purchasing power of a nation's currency.

▲ Fixed exchange rate systems help limit the growth of inflation, but they eliminate the ability of governments to use monetary policies to regulate the marcoeconomy. Flexible exchange rate systems free a nation's macroeconomic polices from the constraints of maintaining a fixed exchange rate, but they create greater volatility between currencies and cannot act as a brake on inflation.

▲ Central bank intervention in exchange rate markets is futile in attempts to counter a strong market movement. Under normal day-to-day conditions, intervention can often be effective.

▲ Currency depreciations are a key element of macroeconomic policies designed to reduce a trade deficit. Depreciation usually worsens the trade deficit in the short run but, after a year or more, it begins to shrink the trade deficit.

Vocabulary

adjustable peg exchange rate system	J-curve
adjustment process	law of one price
appreciation	Louvre Accord
Bretton Woods exchange rate system	managed floating rate
covered interest arbitrage	nominal exchange rate
depreciation	optimum currency areas
devaluation	Plaza Accord
exchange rate	purchasing power parity
exchange rate risk	real exchange rate
floating exchange rate	revaluation
forward exchange rate	Smithsonian Agreement
forward market	spot market
gold standard	target zone exchange rate system
interest rate arbitrage	

Study Questions

1. Draw a graph of the supply of and demand for the Canadian dollar by the American market. Diagram and explain in words the effect of each of the following events.

   a) More rapid growth in Canada than in the U.S.
   b) A rise in U.S. interest rates
   c) An increase in expectations of future rapid growth in Canada
   d) A recession in the U.S.
   e) Expectations of a future depreciation in the Canadian dollar

2. Suppose the dollar-French franc exchange rate is 0.17 dollars per franc, and the dollar German mark rate is 0.58 dollars per mark. What is the franc-mark rate?

3. Suppose the dollar-yen exchange rate is 0.01 dollars per yen. Since the base year, inflation has been 2 percent in Japan and 10 percent in the U.S. What is the real exchange rate? In real terms, has the dollar appreciated or depreciated against the yen?

4. Which of the three motives for holding foreign exchange apply to the following?

   a) A tourist
   b) A bond trader
   c) A portfolio manager
   d) A manufacturer

5. Suppose that German inflation is 1 percent and U.S. inflation is 3 percent while German productivity growth is 2 percent and American is 1 percent. In the long run, should the dollar appreciate or depreciate? How much? Why should we be surprised if the changes you foresee do not materialize?

6. What is the difference between interest arbitrage and covered interest arbitrage?

7. If a U.S. visitor to Mexico can buy more goods in Mexico than he or she can buy in the U.S. when converting dollars to pesos, is the dollar undervalued or overvalued? Explain.

8. In a fixed exchange rate system, how do countries address the problem of currency market pressures which threaten to lower or raise the value of their currency?

9. In the debate on fixed versus floating exchange rates, the strongest argument for a floating rate is that it frees macroeconomic policy from taking care of the exchange rate. This is also the weakest argument. Explain.

10. What is the J-curve, and how is it relevant to expenditure switching policies in the U.S. that are implemented to reduce the current account deficit?

Suggested Reading

Dominguez, Kathryn and Jeffrey Frankel. *Does Foreign Exchange Intervention Work?* Washington, DC: Institute for International Economics, 1993.

Eichengreen, Barry, ed. *The Gold Standard in Theory and History.* New York: Methuen, Inc., 1985.

———. "The Origins and Nature of the Great Slump Revisited," *Economic History Review.* XLV, 2, May 1992.

Feldstein, Martin. "Does One Market Require One Money?," *Policy Implications of Trade and Currency Zones.* A Symposium Sponsored by the Federal Reserve Bank of Kansas City, 1991.

Krugman, Paul. *Has the Adjustment Process Worked?* Washington, DC: Institute for International Economics, 1991.

Melvin, Michael. *International Money and Finance, 4th Edition.* New York: Harper Collins, 1995.

Appendix: Finding Foreign Exchange Rates on the World-Wide Web

Two excellent sources of current and historical exchange rate data are the Federal Reserve Board and the investment banking firm J. P. Morgan. Both have good Web sites with a variety of information which can easily be downloaded.

1. The Federal Reserve Board (*http://bog.frb.us/Releases*)
   The Fed has nominal exchange rates for the U.S. dollar from 1971 to the present. It also has a dollar exchange rate index which is based on the currencies of ten large industrial economies. You can choose daily, monthly, or annual rates. Fed site also provides current (today) rates.

2. J. P. Morgan (*http://www.jpmorgan.com/MarketDataInd/Forex/currIndex.html*)
   The investment bank's Web site offers trade weighted exchange rates (i.e., an index that compares each currency to a basket of other currencies). In addition, they provide both real and nominal exchange rate indices. Included in the real exchange rate indices database are twenty-two OECD countries and twenty-three emerging market countries. The data is monthly, 1970 to the present.

PART THREE

THE INTERNATIONAL ECONOMY:

ISSUES

CHAPTER 10

REGIONALISM AND DEEP INTEGRATION

Introduction to Regional Economic Integration

If you were to conduct a random poll of businesspeople on their opinions about the most significant trend of the last thirty years, one leading response would undoubtedly be the "globalization" of the economy. In this chapter, we will look at the implications of the increasing economic interdependence among nations. We will distinguish between two forms of economic integration, shallow integration and deep integration, and examine the major reasons for each. In addition, we will look at the role of trade agreements and at a number of new areas of conflict that have arisen as deep integration moves forward.

To begin with, it is useful to define economic integration. The primary component of economic integration is an increase in trade and investment flows between countries. Trade and investment may be the full extent of integration in some cases, but usually, as trade grows, pressure builds to remove any remaining trade and investment barriers. This often brings about some reform in trade laws and domestic policies that hinder trade. For example, product standards, patent laws, policies on mergers between firms, environmental protection standards, and a host of other domestic policies may emerge as points of conflict between nations when tariffs are low. The offending domestic policies are often created for reasons entirely unrelated to trade, but in economic environments with low tariffs and no quotas, they become barriers to increased trade.

The term **shallow integration** will be used for changes in the rules "at the border." That is, shallow integration refers to tariffs and quotas, customs procedures, and other border-related issues. **Deep integration** goes beyond border-related matters and refers to the harmonization (making rules similar) or mutual recognition (keeping different but accepting the other country's rules within their jurisdiction) of various national domestic policies, such as environmental standards, product standards, and labor standards, or the rules of fair economic competition.

> ***Harmonization and mutual recognition.*** *Harmonization occurs when two or more countries negotiate a common standard or policy. Harmonization can occur with respect to safety standards, technical standards, environmental standards, legal standards, certification, or with respect to any requirement set forth by national policies.*

Mutual recognition occurs when, instead of the harmonization of standards, countries choose to further their integration by keeping their standards different but at the same time recognizing and accepting each other's standards within their national jurisdictions. Under these circumstances, "competition between standards" will ensue. Individuals and businesses will prefer to adopt the standard that meets their needs most closely or that gives them an economic advantage. It is argued by some that over time the best standard will emerge as the one in greatest use.

Economic integration is a continuum. Some nations and regions have stopped at fairly mild reductions in tariffs, while others have become economic unions. Next we'll look at four broad classifications in the taxonomy of degrees of economic integration.

Degrees of Formal Economic Integration

Economists recognize four general categories of integration beyond the level of simple trading partners. The categories are cumulative in that each one includes the features of the previous one. The four categories are useful for classifying relations between nations, but it should be kept in mind that reality is far messier than any classification scheme. Most formal agreements between nations combine elements from two or more of the categories, as shown in the following examples.

Free-Trade Area

The simplest kind of formal agreement is a free-trade area. An example is the North American Free Trade Agreement (NAFTA). In a free-trade area, goods and services are allowed to trade across international boundaries without paying a tariff or encountering limitations from quotas. In reality, however, most-free trade areas such as NAFTA do not allow completely free trade. Nations usually reserve some restrictions for particularly sensitive items. For example, Canada places limits on the quantity of U.S. television programs that may be shown on Canadian stations, while the United States limits the movement of foreign-owned airlines between American cities. In addition, nations usually keep their own health, safety, and technical standards and may deny entry to products from partners within the free-trade area if they do not meet the national standards. For example, the United States does not permit certain agricultural products from Mexico to enter for fear that they might contain weevils or other pests that could injure U.S. crops (e.g., avocados).

Customs Unions

The next higher level of integration is called a customs union. A customs union is a free-trade area plus a common set of tariffs toward nonmembers. By the mid-1970s, the European Union had evolved from a free-trade area into a customs union. As with a free-trade area, however, many items were left out of the agreement. In the European case, autos are an example, since each nation retained its own tariffs and quotas with respect to Japanese autos.

Common Markets

The third level of integration is termed a common market. A common market is a customs union plus an agreement to allow the free mobility of inputs, that is, labor and capital. The clearest example, again, is the European Union, but the three NAFTA countries have elements of a common market (without the common external tariff), since they allow nearly complete mobility for capital but not for labor. NAFTA also grants relatively free mobility for "professional" labor but not for labor in general.

Economic Union

The final level of economic integration is economic union. An economic union is a common market plus substantial coordination of macroeconomic policies, including a common currency and harmonization of many standards and regulations. The clearest examples are the states of the United States or the provinces of Canada. The BENELUX Union of Belgium, the Netherlands, and Luxembourg is an example of separate nations that have formed a union. The European Union is set to become an economic union, including the proposed introduction of a single currency no later than 1999.

CASE STUDY

How Many Regional Trade Agreements (RTAs) Are There?

Each of the four levels of integration is an example of a regional trade agreement (RTA), or "trade bloc." Determining exactly how many agreements exist is difficult for two main reasons. First, many of the agreements do not fit neatly into any of the four categories; that is, they are not quite free-trade areas, yet they have elements of free-trade, customs unions, and even common markets. In several cases, they can only be described as areas of economic cooperation, less than a free-trade area, but with significant elements of integration and cooperation. Second, many of the agreements are either on paper only (have no real effect) or have yet to be fully negotiated and/or implemented. Until there is substantial implementation, there is always the possibility that one side or the other will give in to special interests or be unable to overcome other barriers that lead to an eventual collapse of the agreement.

With these two caveats in mind, the WTO reports that since the implementation of the GATT in 1948, they have been notified of nearly 150 RTAs. A great many of them have come into existence in the 1990s (approximately 60), and about 80 of the 150 are currently in force. Countries that have signed the GATT are obligated to notify the GATT secretariat when they form an RTA, but the WTO also reports that not all the RTAs currently in force among WTO members have done so. In addition, almost all WTO members belong to at least one RTA. Europe accounts for about 65 percent of the RTAs currently in

Case Study continues

force, and about 78 percent of all RTAs involve either developed countries only (43 percent) or developed and developing countries (35 percent).

Table 10.1 lists many of these RTAs currently in force. They range from tariff agreements on a subset of the nation's output to common markets and economic unions. The dates in parentheses are the dates of implementation of the agreements. In addition to these formal associations, there are a great many more international institutions that foster economic integration, such as regional development banks, regional councils, and other consultative bodies.

TABLE 10.1 Regional Trade Blocs	
Region/Country	*Objective*
Africa	
AEC–African Economic Community (1991)	Economic union
CBI–Cross Border Initiative (1993)	Economic union
CEPGL–Communauté Economique des Pays des Grands Lacs (1976)	Free-trade area
COMESA–Common Market for Eastern and Southern Africa (1993)	Common market
ECCAS–Economic Community of Central African States (1992)	Common market
ECOWAS–Economic Community of West African States (1975)	Common market
IOC–Indian Ocean Commission (1984)	Economic cooperation
Lagos Plan of Action (1980)	Economic union
MRU–Manu River Union (1973)	Economic union
SACU–Southern African Customs Union	Common market
SADC–Southern Africa Development Community (1992)	Economic cooperation
UDEAC–Union Douanière des Etats de l'Afrique Centrale (1966)	Common market
WAEMU–West African Economic and Monetary Union (1994)	Economic union
Asia	
AFTA–ASEAN Free Trade Arrangement (1992)	Free-trade area
ANZCERTA–Australia-New Zealand Closer Economic Relations Trade Agreement (1983)	Free-trade area

Case Study continued

Region/Country	Objective
APEC–Asia-Pacific Economic Cooperation (1989)	Economic cooperation
Bangkok Agreement	Economic cooperation
EAEC–East Asia Economic Caucus (1990)	Economic cooperation
SAARC–South Asian Association for Regional Cooperation (1992)	Economic cooperation
Europe	
Baltic FTA (1993)	Free-trade area
Belarus-Russia Economic Union (1994)	Economic union
BENELUX–Belgium-Netherlands-Luxembourg Economic Union (1948)	Economic union
Baltic (Estonia, Latvia, Lithuania) bilateral FTA's with Switzerland, Finland, Norway, Sweden (1992–1993)	Free-trade areas
CEFTA–Central European Free Trade Arrangement (Visegrad Agreement) (1992)	Free-trade area
CIS (Commonwealth of Independent States) Economic Union (1993)	Economic union
Customs Union Between Czech and Slovak Republics (1993)	Customs union
Customs Union Between Kazakhstan, the Kyrgyz Republic, and Uzbekistan (1994)	Customs union
EEA–European Economic Area (1994)	Common market
EFTA–European Free Trade Association (1960)	Free-trade area
EFTA–Turkey Free Trade Area (1991)	Free-trade area
EU–European Union (1957)	Economic union
EU Association Agreements with Bulgaria, Czech Republic, Hungary, Poland, Romania, Slovak Republic (1991–1993)	Free-trade areas
EU FTA with Baltic countries (Estonia, Latvia, Lithuania) (1994)	Free-trade areas

Case Study continues

Case Study continued

EU Cooperation and Partnership Agreements with FSU (Former Soviet Union countries of Belarus, Kazakhstan, the Kyrgyz Republic, Moldova, Russia, Ukraine) 1994	Free-trade areas
EU–Turkey Association Agreement (1963)	Customs union
Intra-CIS (Commonwealth of Independent States) Bilateral Trade Arrangements (1992–1993)	Economic cooperation
Middle East	
ACM–Arab Common Market (1964)	Customs union
AMU–Arab-Maghreb Union (1989)	Economic union
BSEC–Black Sea Economic Cooperation Project (1992)	Economic cooperation
ECO–Economic Cooperation Organization (1985)	Economic cooperation
GCC–Gulf Cooperation Council (1981)	Common market
Western Hemisphere	
ANCOM (or Andean Pact)— Andean Common Market (1969)	Common market
Argentina-Brazil (1990)	Common market
CACM–Central American Common Market (1961)	Customs union
CARICOM–Caribbean Community (1973)	Common market
CARICOM-Colombia (1991)	Free-trade area
CARICOM-Venezuela (1991)	Free-trade area
Chile-Colombia FTA (1993)	Free-trade area
Chile-Venezuela FTA (1993)	Free-trade area
Colombia-Central America FTA (1993)	Free-trade area
Colombia-Ecuador-Venezuela FTA (1992)	Customs union
Colombia-Venezuela (1992)	Free-trade area
EAI–Enterprise for the Americas Initiative (1990)	Free-trade area
El Salvador-Guatemala FTA (1991)	Free-trade area
Group of 3: Colombia-Venezuela-Mexico FTA (1993)	Free-trade area
LAIA–Latin America Integration Association (1960)	Common market

Case Study continues

Case Study continued

Region/Country	Objective
Mercosur–Southern Cone Common Market (1991)	Common market
Mexico-Chile FTA (1991)	Free-trade area
Mexico-Costa Rica FTA (1994)	Free-trade area
Mexico-Costa Rica-El Salvador-Guatemala-Honduras-Nicaragua FTA (1994)	Free-trade area
NAFTA–North American Free Trade Agreement (1994)	Free-trade area
Nueva Ocotepeque Agreement (1992)	Free-trade area
OECS–Organization of East Caribbean States (1991)	Free-trade area
US-Canada FTA (1989)	Free-trade area
US-Israel FTA (1985)	Free-trade area
Venezuela-Central America FTA (1992)	Free-trade area

Source: Harmsen, Richard, and Michael Leidy, "Regional Trading Arrangements," in *International Trade Policies: The Uruguay Round and Beyond. Volume II: Background Papers.* Prepared by an IMF Staff Team, under the direction of Naheed Kirmani. Washington, DC: International Monetary Fund, 1994.

Factors Creating Economic Integration

Since the end of World War II, world output has grown about sixfold, while world trade has grown about twelvefold. Preferential trade agreements are partly responsible for relatively faster growth of trade, particularly in the last two decades, but even countries that are outside of any formal trade area have experienced significant increases in international trade and investment. The increase in trade after 1950 was a break with trends during the 1914–1950 period, when trade and factor flows were restricted by war, depression, and national policies. By the early 1970s, world trade (as a percentage of world output) had grown to the level it had reached before World War I, and it has continued to grow since then. The growth of world trade and of preferential trade agreements raises several questions. First, why does world trade continue to grow? Second, why are more countries joining trade blocs? It should not be surprising that both questions have many answers, and many of the answers overlap. Some of the same factors that lead to greater trade also encourage countries to sign formal trade agreements. In particular, the formation of a trade bloc can "lock in" the gains from trade and make it more difficult for a trading partner to close its market in the future.

Political Factors

One of the most important reasons for the growth of international trade and investment since World War II is politics. A key political factor was the creation of a set of international institutions at the war's end that serve as a forum for discussion of international economic issues, as mechanisms for intervention in a country's domestic affairs in times of crisis, and as providers of momentum for greater economic openness. The International Monetary Fund, the World Bank, and the General Agreement on Tariffs and Trade have each contributed to the maintenance of a more stable environment than existed during the interwar years of the 1920s and 1930s. Although they are not perfect institutions, they have helped create a credible set of rules for maintaining a perception of relative fairness in international economic relations, while at the same time designing and implementing mechanisms for dealing with international economic crises. The results have been an increase in cooperation and a more open international economic environment. Cooperation, conflict resolution, and stability are critically important to reducing uncertainty and promoting growth.

A second political factor that has increased international trade is the role of the United States. As the world's largest economy and Cold War leader of the noncommunist world, the United States' support for increased economic ties around the globe, along with its willingness to open its own market to foreign products, helped provide a stable economic environment for trade. After World War II, if the United States had returned to the relative isolationism it practiced in the 1920s and early 1930s, the world would have been much worse off. First, without the funds the United States supplied for rebuilding Europe and Japan through the Marshall and Dodge Plans, it would have taken much longer for the war damage to have been repaired. Second, without access to the U.S. market, many industrial and developing nations would have lacked the market they needed to sell their products.

Market Access and Economies of Scale

A key factor in European economic integration and Canada's desire to form a free-trade area with the United States is the recognition that many countries are too small to take advantage of economies of scale. Producers in the Netherlands, Denmark, Sweden, and elsewhere lack the population base necessary to efficiently produce a lot of what they consume; they must depend on trade. Similarly, Canada depends on the United States both as a market for its exports and as a major source of its imports. Even the larger economies of Japan and Germany need to export a substantial share of their output in order to prosper and to have sufficient earnings to buy imports.

In the European case, there was a conscious decision in the mid-1980s to increase the degree of economic integration, essentially from a customs union to a common market, in order to attain greater scale economies through the removal of many of the remaining barriers to the flow of goods and services. In addition, the Europeans sought to remove the barriers to the flow of capital and labor between countries. Meanwhile, in Canada, there were some fears in the 1980s that protectionist sentiment might continue to grow in the United States, reducing Canada's access to its most important market. These fears were an important part of the reason for the Canadian–U.S. Trade Agreement (CUSTA), which was implemented in January 1989.

The desire to maintain market access and achieve greater economies of scale is instrumental in generating greater cooperation in resolving difficult conflicts over domestic policies that function (often unintentionally) as trade and investment barriers. For example, throughout much of Asia and Latin America, there is a greater willingness to harmonize national policies toward investment and service industries. More extensive trade ties between countries often lead to a greater recognition of the subtle ways in which nations are different, particularly with respect to rules governing investment by foreigners or with respect to the regulation of service-sector industries, such as financial services, telecommunications, or health care. In developing countries, growing trade ties and the desire to attract additional foreign capital have led to changes in national policies in order to encourage greater investment by foreigners. In developed countries, where capital is not as scarce, trade ties often lead to some pressure to harmonize investment rules, product standards, and safety standards in order to enlarge the size of the market and to capture greater economies of scale.

Technology and International Sourcing

As telecommunications and transportation technology have improved, intrafirm trade has grown. Firms can locate different parts of their production processes in different countries, where they can take advantage of differences in national endowments. (Recall the discussion of intrafirm trade in Chapter 4.) For example, labor-intensive production can be sent to regions where labor is plentiful and cheap; research and development can be done where scientists and engineers are in plentiful supply; and product testing can be done where consumer markets are large and wealthy. The ability of firms to slice up their production processes in order to relocate different parts to different countries depends on two critical factors. First, firms must be able to coordinate and control the output of smaller units located around the globe. In order to do this, they need cheap transportation and efficient communication. Second, they must be able to move inputs and semifinished goods across international boundaries with a minimum of delay and with as few tariffs and quotas as possible. While the ability to coordinate and control production across international regions depends on technology, political factors such as the effectiveness of GATT and the willingness of nations to open their borders are important to the freedom of movement of inputs and outputs.

The fact that more firms are relocating parts of their production around the globe is seen by many people as a negative feature of closer international economic ties. People in industrial countries fear they will lose their jobs due to the unavoidable cost-cutting pressures on employers to move production to Taiwan, Mexico, or Indonesia. When foreign direct investment involves closing plants in the home country in order to open new ones elsewhere, it is usually workers at the bottom of the pay scale who are adversely affected, raising questions about the income-distribution effects of international trade and investment (see Chapter 4 for a discussion of this issue). At the same time, the ability of firms to relocate some or all of their production outside their home country enables them to stay competitive in international markets. In some cases, the only real choice may be between moving part of the production overseas or going out of business altogether. In these cases, workers as well as consumers benefit from the increased mobility of firms.

Economic Crisis in Developing Countries

A third factor that has created closer economic ties between countries is the debt crisis of the 1980s. The crisis began in 1982 when Mexico announced that it lacked the U.S. dollars it needed to pay interest and principal on the money it had borrowed in the late 1970s and early 1980s. The crisis soon spread to Brazil, Argentina, and a number of other (mostly Latin American) countries. We will look at the debt crisis in more detail in Chapter 14, but at this point it should be noted that when countries lack the ability to make payments on their debt, they usually turn to the International Monetary Fund for help. It is the IMF's responsibility to help countries in this situation, but it usually imposes conditions on the borrowing country. The conditions include cutting their budget deficits, balancing their trade, and opening their economy to market forces, both domestic and foreign. In Mexico's case, the IMF was one factor that led to a long series of reforms in the Mexican economy, which resulted in a dismantling of most of Mexico's trade barriers and, ultimately, in the Mexican request to create a free-trade area with the United States. In Brazil and Argentina, the economic reforms that took place in the wake of their debt crises resulted in a free-trade agreement between the two countries plus Uruguay and Paraguay.

The 1980s were a disastrous period for Latin America and for much of Africa as well. The fallout of the debt crisis caused a number of countries to become stuck in very low or even negative growth. At the same time that these regions were stuck in the debt crisis, a number of East Asian countries experienced accelerated growth. South Korea, Taiwan, Malaysia, Singapore, and Hong Kong began to have an impact on economic thinking in the slow-growth economies outside Asia. Many countries outside East Asia had pursued economic development strategies that were too inward focused and did not provide incentives for firms to become competitive in world markets. The shift in economic philosophy from an inward orientation to a more outward one was a natural outcome of the debt crisis and the lack of growth in the inward-focused countries.

Background Issues in Economic Integration

As formal agreements between countries have proliferated in the 1980s and 1990s, the most talked-about issue has been the effect on nonparticipants. For example, Americans worried about "Fortress Europe" forming behind the walls of the common market that was created by the Single European Act of 1987. Asian and Caribbean producers have worried that NAFTA would lead to eliminating many of their products from the North American market. Closely related to these fears were concerns that the success of the new trade agreements would undermine GATT and prevent further liberalization of trade on a worldwide basis.

Market-Led versus Institutionally Led Integration

Before we delve into each of these issues, we need first to distinguish between economic integration, which is market led, and that which occurs under a formal trade agreement. Trade under the auspices of a formal agreement (free-trade area, common market, etc.) may be termed *institutionally led integration*.

Market-led integration can occur without any explicit agreement between countries. Since it does not establish special trade rules within a geographical region, it cannot pose an alternative to GATT or the WTO but, in fact, market-led integration is usually a result of prior GATT negotiations.

Institutionally led integration is another matter, however, and is viewed by some economists as a threat to the multilateral GATT and WTO. Some economists worry that the political support for multilateral liberalization (opening of world markets) will be diverted toward regional agreements instead and that these regional agreements may actually lower global economic welfare. World welfare could be hurt if trade policy inside the RTAs is captured by protectionist forces that impose restrictive trade relations with nonmembers. In addition to protectionists diverting political support and capturing trade policy, some economists worry that RTAs will form integrated regions that are larger and more powerful than single states. That would lead the firms inside the RTA to gain some market power over world markets.

These fears are mitigated by several factors. First, prior to the recent spate of trade agreements, most formal trade agreements outside of Europe were relatively ineffective and of little consequence. The Asian countries lacked an effective formal trade agreement, although the Association of South East Nations, or ASEAN, took a few timid steps toward reducing trade barriers among its members. Within Latin America and Africa, attempts at creating trade blocs in the 1960s had failed or had resulted in organizations that existed only on paper. Agreements such as the Andean Pact were kept ineffective by rivalries between the member states and their economic philosophy of self-sufficiency, which downplayed the importance of trade.

Second, RTAs involve reciprocal obligations. Since there is a reciprocity involved, it makes the political justification of trade liberalization easier. Economic interests that might be harmed by more open trade cannot claim that the country is getting nothing in return. Third, a formal agreement is a way to lock in a set of policies, either your own or your trading partner's. By converting the lowered trade barriers from a national commercial policy into an international agreement, it becomes much more costly to change the policy. For example, Canada sought the Canadian–U.S. Trade Agreement because it wanted to make certain that rising protectionism inside the United States did not limit Canada's access to the U.S. market. President Salinas of Mexico wanted the North American Free Trade Agreement partly because it would lock his administration's trade policies inside an international agreement and make it very difficult for his successors to switch policies.

Fourth, RTAs could potentially raise global welfare if they serve as a testing ground for new ideas. The WTO, with 132 nations as of December 1997, is relatively cumbersome as a forum for new ideas. Under CUSTA, Canada and the United States developed a new technique for resolving disputes, and under NAFTA, new agreements on environmental and labor standards have been tried. New ideas eventually find their way into WTO agreements; in the meantime, an RTA can serve as a "laboratory" for experiments.

Another important consideration is that RTAs, for the most part, allow countries to trade with their natural partners. Trade blocs are usually regional agreements that include countries with common borders and significant trade relations prior to the agreement. For example, prior to the Canadian–U.S. Trade Agreement, the United States and Canada were each other's most important trading partners. Before NAFTA, Mexico's most important trading partner was the United States, and Mexico was third most important for the United States. The members of the EU share borders and a long history of significant trade relations. In both North America and Europe, the signing of formal trade agreements only hastened a natural outcome by helping to remove barriers to trade within the region.

Finally, RTAs have served some nations, such as the United States, as a way to gain political leverage in wider WTO negotiations. Signaling to the rest of the world that a country can develop alternative agreements outside of the WTO puts pressure on countries that wanted to be certain of successful multilateral negotiations. Obviously, this tactic would not work for a small country, but the size of the United States, Brazil, or the unified European market makes it possible for larger nations to use trade blocs strategically as a means to force agreements that other nations might wish to resist. (This may have negative as well as positive elements.)

Trade Diversion and Trade Creation

Every RTA, whether it is a free-trade area or some other form of economic integration, treats its members differently from the way it treats nonmembers. Members have preferential access to each other's markets and are often free from other restrictions on trade and investment. While the problem of RTAs becoming completely closed to nonmembers has never been serious, there is concern that trade may be shifted in a way that favors insiders over more efficient outside producers. This is perhaps the strongest argument against RTAs. If an agreement causes efficient producers to cut back and relatively less efficient ones to expand, global economic welfare is reduced.

Suppose, for example, that the United States has restrictive tariffs on clothing imports and that, prior to signing the NAFTA agreement, the tariffs were uniformly applied to all countries. In other words, the tariff on imports of clothes from the Dominican Republic was the same as the tariff on Mexican apparel. If the Dominican Republic is a more efficient producer than Mexico and can produce apparel for less, then the world is better off when the United States imports Dominican-made apparel, since there is a more efficient allocation of resources if Dominican production expands (instead of Mexican production) to meet U.S. demands.

Now, suppose that after signing NAFTA, the U.S. tariff on Mexican apparel drops to zero but the tariff on Dominican goods remains as before. Mexican goods become cheaper in the U.S. market. If the tariff is greater than the cost difference between Mexican and Dominican goods, the United States would shift its consumption from the lower-cost Dominican producers to the higher-cost Mexican producers. In trade economics this is called **trade diversion.** Trade diversion is a common problem with preferential trading agreements and, when economists oppose the formation of a specific RTA, it is often because they think that trade diversion will outweigh any other gains the bloc creates.

A numerical example will help to clarify this point. Let the cost of producing a man's shirt be $5 in the Dominican Republic and $5.50 in Mexico. Initially, before the RTA, the U.S. tariffs all imported men's shirts at 20 percent. The price to consumers of Dominican shirts is $6, and the Mexican shirts are $6.60, so U.S. consumers buy their shirts from the Dominican Republic, the lower-cost producer. After the United States signs a free-trade agreement with Mexico, the price of a Mexican shirt in the U.S. markets falls to $5.50, 50 cents less than the $6 Dominican shirt. Consequently, the RTA causes Mexico, the higher-cost producer, to expand production, and the Dominican Republic, the lower cost producer, to reduce production. Note that Mexico is worse off due to the resource misallocation that creates a production inefficiency (it expands a relatively inefficient industry), and the United States is worse off because the $6 it paid for a Dominican shirt included a $1 transfer from consumers to producers that did not affect U.S. national welfare. Now, we are paying a net price that is 50 cents higher for our shirts.

The opposite of trade diversion is **trade creation**. Suppose the United States makes it own apparel because lower-cost producers in Mexico face steep tariffs when they try to sell to the United States. After signing NAFTA, the United States switches from making apparel itself to buying it from lower-cost Mexican producers. In this case, the agreement has created trade and improved the overall allocation of resources within the United States and Mexico.

> ***Trade diversion and trade creation.*** *Trade diversion occurs when trade policies cause a shift in production and imports from a lower cost producer to a higher cost producer. Trade creation is the opposite: trade policies cause a shift in production from a higher cost producer (often a domestic one) to a lower cost producer.*

Most trade agreements such as NAFTA cause both trade diversion and trade creation. One key to understanding whether a trade agreement is positive or negative on balance is calculating whether trade creation or trade diversion will be greater. If trade diversion is larger, then the trade agreement would lead to a less efficient allocation of resources when its effects are considered both inside and outside the bloc. The members of the bloc might still be better off than they would be without the agreement (largely because the costs of trade diversion are imposed on nonmembers), but from the world's standpoint, there is a net loss.

Trade Blocs and GATT

Considering the principles of GATT (Chapter 2), allowance of RTAs seems contradictory. The GATT is built on the idea of Most Favored Nation (MFN) status as one of its core operating principles. Recall that this principle states that nations should offer to all countries the same market access that they provide for their most favored trading partner. This principle is designed to prevent countries from discriminating against another nation by imposing much higher tariffs on them alone. The idea of a preferential trade agreement contradicts MFN status because some countries are included and others are excluded. For example, when the United States signed NAFTA, it did not give Japan the same access to its market that it gave to Mexico and Canada, the other two members. If they are meaningful, preferential trade agreements must violate the GATT principles of MFN and nondiscrimination.

The general interpretation of the GATT charter (Article XXIV) is that RTAs are permitted whenever trade creation outweighs trade diversion. This issue has never been tested in a GATT/WTO hearing, however, as no country has ever complained to the GATT/WTO that a particular trade bloc is discriminating against it. Most countries seem willing to let RTAs continue to develop as long as they have some assurances that they will not face new restrictions on their exports to the bloc members.

Countries at Different Stages of Economic Development

Most trade agreements include nations that are more or less homogeneous in their standard of living. For example, Mercosur is made up of developing countries (Brazil, Argentina, Uruguay, and Paraguay); the Central European Free Trade Area is composed of countries at roughly the same point in their transition from communism to capitalism; and the European Union is mostly high-income industrial nations (with the partial exceptions of Portugal and Greece). NAFTA is unique in its inclusion of a large developing country with two high-income industrial ones. When NAFTA was created, Mexico's average income per capita (at market exchange rates) was between one-seventh and one-eighth that of the United States. By comparison, when Portugal joined the EU, its income level was between one-fourth and one-fifth that of Germany. Furthermore, Portugal is a small country with fewer than 10 million people, whereas Mexico is a large country with a population of nearly 90 million.

The economic integration of advanced industrial economies with developing countries is much more difficult than integration within a homogeneous region. The degree to which capital and labor must be reallocated to different activities is greater, as are migration pressures from the lower-income to the higher-income economy. Differences in environmental, labor, and product safety standards are greater and lead to deeper conflict over the effects of differing standards.

Deep Versus Shallow Integration

Until the late 1980s, most economic integration occurred through changes in tariffs, quotas, customs procedures, and other border-related policies. More recently, international pressures to change policies that are deeply rooted in the domestic economy have grown. These new areas of discussion and negotiation are extremely sensitive because, historically, they were considered to be exclusively national issues of little or no consequence to international economic relations. In today's economy, however, national policies toward labor standards, environmental standards, antitrust, industrial support, and investment have become intertwined with national trade policies.

Between the end of World War II and the late 1980s, cuts in tariffs and quotas offered the greatest chance for opening trade. As tariffs and quotas gradually shrank, other barriers to trade and investment became more apparent. In perhaps the majority of cases, these newly discovered barriers were not erected with the purpose of limiting trade or foreign investment, and they would not be significant barriers as long as trade was below a certain volume. The increases in trade flows, however, caused many countries to become more aware of the domestic national policies of their trading partners and how policies "behind the border" limited market access and the ability of foreign-owned firms to develop an economic presence inside the trading partner's national boundaries. It would be accurate to say that reductions in trade barriers have led to pressures for further reductions and that the newest set of issues involves a variety of national economic policies that limit the market access of foreign firms.

New Issues for Deeper Economic Integration

When an independent nation signs an international agreement, whether in the area of economics or not, the agreement places limits on its ability to act. Tariff treaties limit its ability to tax imports; nuclear arms treaties limit the development and deployment of weapons; and so forth. The specific items on the deep integration agenda are controversial because of their effects on national sovereignty. When nations negotiate these issues, they are discussing the terms by which they will voluntarily limit their control over national policies. As with all international agreements, the recognition of potential benefits is an incentive to engage in discussion and negotiation on issues of deep integration. Nevertheless, the loss of some control over national policies makes these issues far more controversial than simple tariff negotiations.

We will now examine the leading issues of deep integration and their relationship to international economic relations.

Environmental Policies and Standards

Environmental issues are naturally international issues: pollution and environmental degradation have no respect for international boundaries. While these issues have long been a topic for discussion between nations, they have only recently become associated with international trade and investment talks.

Awareness of the relevancy of environmental issues to international trade and investment was sparked by a dispute between the United States and Mexico over methods used to harvest yellowfin tuna. Recall that in Chapter 5 the U.S.–Mexico tuna dispute was cited as an example of a case in which it is difficult to disentangle protectionist motives from a genuine concern about the environment. The U.S. environmental law, called the Marine Mammals Protection Act, requires U.S. tuna boats to minimize the number of dolphins they unintentionally kill when harvesting yellowfin tuna. Tuna fishers had to change their methods and equipment, and canneries were required to certify that the tuna they sent to market was "dolphin safe." The U.S. environmental law protecting dolphins was used as the legal basis for an exclusion of Mexican tuna from the U.S. market, sparking a complaint by Mexico against the United States to be filed with GATT.

The GATT never officially released its findings, since Mexico dropped the complaint during the period leading up to the signing of NAFTA. The world organization did issue a general ruling, however, stating that the process by which products are obtained cannot be used to discriminate against the product. In other words, within the rules of GATT, the United States cannot discriminate against Mexican tuna, no matter how it is caught. For the record, in May of 1998, the United States, Mexico, and six other tuna-harvesting countries signed an agreement to use fishing technology that protects marine mammals. This agreement is expected to form the basis for a reintroduction of tuna imports in the U.S.

The tuna episode raises a basic question about the connection between environmental laws and trade: Are environmental laws simply a new form of trade protection? This is not meant to downplay the importance of the environment but rather to point out that many nations may use environmental standards as a means of disguised protection. Suspicion of motives is not limited to nations. Economists worry that many environmentalists oppose all forms of growth, particularly in the developing world where the problem of pollution and environmental degradation are more visible. For their part, environmentalists worry that economists are insensitive to the finite nature of resources and that they will push developing countries into imitating American (or European, or Canadian, or Japanese, etc.) consumer culture. Similarly, labor unions worry that businesses will use the weaker environmental laws in some developing countries to relocate their operations abroad. The competitive advantage that a firm gains when it relocates to a country with weak environmental standards is called **ecodumping.** Firms that compete against goods that are priced low due to the fact that they are made in regions with weak environmental standards argue that this is another form of dumping, or selling below fair market value, made possible by the lack of environmental standards.

One of the fundamental issues of these disputes is whether international trade should be linked to environmental policies. In other words, should the failure of a country to uphold environmental standards justify imposing trade penalties? Historically, the rules and the spirit of the GATT have avoided linking trade to nontrade issues. The goal is to treat trade by its own rules and not to use it as a weapon to enforce compliance on nontrade issues. The fear was that GATT-legitimized trade penalties to enforce compliance on nontrade issues would lead to a large number of trade sanctions and an overall reduction in trade. This historic stance was undermined, however, by the Uruguay Round. A subagreement of the Round, called the Trade Related Aspects of Intellectual Property Right agreement, or TRIPS, confers the right to impose trade penalties on countries that do not honor rights for intellectual property such as copyrights, patents, and trademarks. Hence, there is now a precedent for linking trade to a nontrade issue.

In the environmental arena, there are few international agreements of substance. Furthermore, many environmental problems are local rather than international. Consequently, the issue of what standards to enforce become a critical issue. The lack of agreement on many key items such as greenhouse gases, deforestation, watershed destruction, topsoil erosion, and fisheries depletion, is complicated by the fact that some of these problems have no immediate impact across national borders. Consequently, the linking of trade to the environment may result in the application of one nation's standards inside the borders of another nation—which all nations find unacceptable, even when the standards are desirable.

Given the growing tension both within and between nations, the WTO has begun to show greater concern for understanding the linkages between trade, trade policy, and the environment. To date, WTO-issued reports have worried environmentalists because they have asserted that no discrimination against one country's goods should happen for environmental reasons. In addition, they pointed out that subsidies and other interventions in the agricultural sector are responsible for much of the world's environmental problems and that as income increases, most developing countries begin to place a higher value on a cleaner environment. Many environmentalists object to this stance, since they view it as invalidating or weakening strong national environmental laws.

The WTO recently created a Committee on Trade and the Environment, and future international agreements on the trade aspects of environmental rules are likely to develop within this body. The Committee has a relatively broad mandate to investigate many different areas of intersection between trade and the environment. Some of its more fundamental concerns are with the impacts of product standards, packaging and labeling requirements, and recycling on the world trading system; the design of a dispute settlement process; how environmental measures affect market access; and the relationship of trade agreements to environmental agreements.

Labor Policies and Standards

The International Labor Office (ILO) is the organization that administers international agreements on labor standards. The ILO is based in Geneva, Switzerland, and is a part of the United Nations. For the most part, it is a research organization that gathers data and information on conditions in the world's nations. It also reports on the compliance of nations with international agreements on the use of prison labor, child labor, and so forth, and it issues voluntary guidelines for workplace conditions and the treatment of labor.

Because the ILO rules are relatively mild, developed nations sought to include a stricter set of labor standards within the Uruguay Round agreement. The United States hoped to expand on current international standards through the creation of a separate agreement that would be lodged within the World Trade Organization (WTO) but that would be distinct from the GATT. The model the United States had in mind was similar to the WTO's Committee on Trade and Development, which stands outside of the GATT, but with the difference that the labor agreement would contain specific commitments to a minimum set of standards. Developing nations were highly suspicious of including labor standards in a WTO agreement, however, and the idea never materialized.

The advanced industrial economies have two reasons for wanting to create a new agreement on labor standards. First, there are humanitarian concerns about the conditions that prevail in some parts of the developing world. There are a wide variety of practices that occur in various locales and that all people find offensive. For example, in some places children as young as five or six are sold by their parents into forced labor; workers find themselves indebted to factory owners and are forced to toil for a lifetime without freedom to leave; prisoners are forced to meet production quotas on penalty of death if they fail; and labor leaders are tortured and killed.

Second, developed countries have economic motivations for wanting stricter agreements on labor standards. They argue that low labor standards give firms in developing countries an unfair economic advantage. If nations permit the use of small children forced to work sixty or seventy hours a week for the equivalent of pennies, it gives their firms (and others that locate there) a competitive advantage. Similarly, nations that prevent workers from organizing unions or bargaining collectively create competitive advantages for their firms. Workers and firms in industrial nations with labor laws that afford more protection to their workforces are put at commercial disadvantage by competition against products made in countries with weak labor standards. The use of weak labor standards to gain a commercial advantage is often referred to as **social dumping.**

There were five main provisions that the high-income, industrialized nations sought to include in the WTO:

▲ Freedom of association for workers
▲ The right to organize and bargain collectively
▲ The freedom from forced or compulsory labor
▲ A minimum age for employment
▲ Minimum standards for working conditions

These provisions may seem relatively mild to a high-income industrial economy, but they were strenuously resisted by developing countries. First, it was pointed out that there was a certain amount of hypocrisy in wanting developing countries to adhere to labor standards that no advanced industrial economy accepted until fairly recently. The United States for example, was a slave society until the 1860s, and the right to bargain collectively was not recognized until the 1930s. Conditions in factories, mines, and on farms were terrible throughout most of world until late into this century, and while the average working conditions in the advanced industrial economies are infinitely better than a century ago, there are still frequent lapses.

Second, developing countries argue that the conditions of workers in advanced industrial economies cannot be applied to them. In many developing countries, families depend on the incomes of ten- and twelve-year-old children; the application of a minimum working age of sixteen, as proposed by the United States, would be disastrous for these families. No country defends the enslavement of children or other such practices, but developing countries point out the difficulties they face in enforcing their laws. Bureaucracies are weak, inspectors are poorly paid, and government resources are limited. Similarly, poor nations argue that they lack the wealth to provide clean and safe working conditions for every worker. Finally, many view the proposals put forward by rich nations as an invasion of their national sovereignty and their right to determine their own national labor policies.

> ***Ecodumping and social dumping.*** *Ecodumping is a term used to describe the pricing of a product below the competition's price when the lower price is partly or wholly possible as a result of production in a country with weak environmental standards. Social dumping is similar to ecodumping, except that the low price occurs as a result of production in a country with weak labor standards.*

Third, developing nations argue that many of the issues raised by developed ones have the appearance of humanitarian concerns but, in fact, are excuses to protect their industries from foreign competition. They argue that although rich nations may not like the conditions in poor nations, their concerns are actually aimed at reducing competition, not at raising living standards of workers. The pressure to engage in meaningful negotiations over a set of standards is likely to continue into the foreseeable future.

Antitrust (Competition) Policy

In the United States, we call it antitrust policy, but trade economists and most of the world refer to it as **competition policy**. Competition policies deal with the organization of industry in a national economy. There are three main areas of competition policies:

▲ *Market structure*: Markets may be competitive, oligopolies, monopolistically competitive, or monopolies.
▲ *Market behavior*: Firms within an industry may compete and price fairly, or they may collude and overcharge customers. They may earn large monopoly profits that are used to finance expansion into new markets.
▲ *Market performance*: Industries may deliver rapid progress with increasing productivity, or they may stagnate and decline in importance.

National policies in each of these areas vary considerably. In the United States, we rarely give firms permission to form cartels in which they can collude to set prices and output quantities. Notable exceptions are professional sports teams and exporters. The latter are often allowed to group themselves together for the purpose of forming a single seller to foreign purchasers. As a single seller, this may give the firms greater market power and some ability to control the export price.

> **Competition policy** *Competition policies are the rules within a nation that govern economic competition. They are primarily concerned with the limits to cooperation between firms, especially mergers, acquisitions, collusion, and joint ventures.*

British practices are similar to those in the United States, but historically, Germany has permitted companies to form cartels that set prices and output levels for the whole industry. Japanese and Korean practices have been more like Germany's, and they have also permitted manufacturers to collude with distributors and retailers so that only the manufacturer's products will be carried. In the United States, this is a gray area of the law: sometimes it is permitted; sometimes it is not.

Historically, most nations have tried to enact policies that will allow them to capture the gains that come from economies of scale. As the Age of Mass Production began in the late 1800s, large-scale industrial enterprises emerged, and national policymakers realized that the average cost of production often continued to fall as output levels climbed higher and higher. Most nations wanted firms to get big in order to capture the productivity gains of size and speed of production. The problem with size, however, is that it leads to market power. Industries that are controlled by one large firm, or by a handful of firms, can influence prices and may be able to prevent new firms from entering the market. These kinds of power over the market usually lead to outcomes that hurt consumers.

To get around this problem, nations permit firms to become large so as to take advantage of the economic benefits of their size, but they regulate the markets in order to ensure that consumers are not harmed by the lack of competition in the market. The kind and degree of regulation vary enormously, however. Nations such as Japan and Korea fear that forcing their large industrial giants to compete will lead to ruinous competition. These giant firms have enormous quantities of capital invested and hire tens or hundreds of thousands of workers. If "competition to the death" were to break out, the social and economic consequences would be enormously disruptive, they argue. Whole communities that grew up around the defeated firm might go under. Furthermore, the surviving firm is likely to be in bad shape after its struggle. If its financial resources are depleted, it is not likely to engage in expensive and risky research, and it may find it hard to withstand the arrival of well-financed foreign firms that are prepared to lose money for some period of time until they gain a large market share.

Nations such as the United States and Britain have generally not feared competition among industrial giants as "ruinous." In their view, competition between firms such as the computer makers IBM, Compaq, and Apple, or the car and truck makers GM, Ford, and Chrysler, have increased the rate of innovation and brought new and better products to consumers at a much faster pace than would have occurred otherwise. Given the differences in national outlooks, it is not surprising that U.S. and British policies are hostile to collusion between firms, while Japanese and Korean firms permit a greater degree of collusion.

Competition policies and international trade interact in several ways. First, if nations permit firms in an industry to collude, it can hurt outsiders (i.e., foreign firms). For example, high-technology firms might agree to share research and development costs, to split markets into each firm's territory, to hold back their best technology for themselves, or to set prices. The ability of firms to collude in their home markets raises their profits on goods sold at home and acts as a source of financing for capturing market share abroad.

Second, if national policy permits individual firms, or groups of firms, to sign exclusive agreements with distributors and retailers, foreign firms will find it much more expensive and difficult to enter the market. The same is true when manufacturers work closely with their buyers and suppliers. For example, Japanese manufacturing firms often form themselves into groups of buyers and suppliers that work closely with each other (see Chapter 11). These firms purchase each other's stock and have corporate boards of directors that overlap. The most common method for any firm to invest in a foreign market is to purchase an existing firm. With the arrangement just described, however, outsiders cannot acquire enough of the stock to gain control. Furthermore, it is likely to be more difficult to sell goods in the market if most buyers are committed to working exclusively with their group of firms.

A third intersection between trade and competition policies is in the area of international mergers, acquisitions, and joint ventures. National competition policies are relatively ineffective at limiting or controlling business agreements made outside their boundaries. Yet, agreements between two or more firms based in different countries can have significant effects on competition and collusion inside each of the nations. For example, if Toyota bought GM (an unlikely scenario!), would the U.S. auto market see significantly less competition? Recently, Boeing, the large commercial aircraft manufacturer, acquired Lockheed, its only real competitor outside of the European Airbus consortium. The European Union threatened retaliation if the merger went through, arguing that it would give Boeing a near monopoly and significantly limit competition. While the EU did not prevent the merger, they did manage to impose a number of conditions on Boeing's business practices.

Competition policies are a reflection of national values, ideas, and history. They are extremely difficult to harmonize, in part because they have become intertwined with the business culture and economic institutions of each country. To simply change to a different set of competition policies would be a bit like setting a business enterprise down on the moon. Yet, competition policies are also a growing source of trade friction, as the Boeing-Lockheed merger makes clear. In Chapter 11, a large part of the trade conflict between the United States and Japan will be characterized as a result of some fundamental differences in economic policies governing competition. As a result of their increasing role in causing trade friction, competition policies will continue to gain attention from policy makers and trade negotiators.

Investment Barriers

Barriers to investing in foreign markets can hurt a company's trade in several ways. First, for many firms, barriers to investing in foreign markets are nearly equivalent to tariffs or quotas that limit their exports. For example, many industrial processes require capital equipment that must be demonstrated, adapted to special needs, and serviced. If the manufacturer is permitted to sell the good in a foreign market but is not allowed to establish a branch or subsidiary that can provide the after-sale services, its products are not competitive.

A second effect of investment barriers shows up mainly in high-technology. In order must stay competitive, many high-technology firms state that they must locate some of their research and development activities in the geographical area where the cutting edge technology is being produced. That is, unless they are in the milieu that is producing the best and most advanced products, they have no chance of keeping up with the latest developments.

Third, investment barriers are often in the form of performance requirements. These are rules that permit foreign firms to set up operations inside the host country only so long as they fulfill a set of requirements. Performance requirements on foreign investors range across a wide variety of activities. For example, they may require that the foreign firm hire a certain proportion of host country managers; locate in a particular region of the country that has been targeted for development; earn a certain quantity of foreign exchange through exports; buy inputs from domestic suppliers; or license or sell their technology to host country firms.

Many of the goals of performance requirements are in the best interests of the host country. They can speed the development of industrial development by providing technology, training, foreign exchange, and a market for host country suppliers.

Needless to say, foreign firms view performance requirements as a competitive disadvantage. They raise the cost of doing business and, sometimes, provide competitors with their best technology.

The Uruguay Round of the GATT broke new ground in the area of international investment. Trade-related investment matters, or TRIMs, were part of the agreement that set limits on new performance requirements and began a discussion of phasing out existing requirements. Given the capital needs of developing countries and the desire of foreign firms to enter new markets, there are strong reasons to believe that discussions in this area will continue for the foreseeable future.

Industrial Support Policies

Industrial support policies, or simply industrial policies, are used in nearly every country of the world. In the advanced industrial economies, their main focus is the development and competitiveness of high-technology industries, but they are used by developing countries as well to build basic industries such as steel and autos. In Chapter 7, we looked at these policies as a means to creating comparative advantage. We saw that it is often thought that high technology has a number of positive externalities associated with it and that these lead to less than the optimal amount of investment.

Industrial policies affect trade through the government support they provide for domestic industries. Foreign firms that receive no government support can legitimately claim to be at a disadvantage if they try to compete with firms that are receiving government subsidies. The issue can become particularly contentious when a firm receiving subsidies tries to enter the home market of firms that are not subsidized. Rightly or wrongly, policy makers often fear that the loss of a high-technology industry will begin to erode a nation's standard of living. The fear is that the loss of one industry will spill over and hurt suppliers and erode skills and technical knowledge in the labor force. Ultimately, a nation may lose its ability to remain on the frontier of a wide variety of new, high-wage, high-skill industries.

Whether this is a realistic scenario or not is almost immaterial. Most nations agree that there is an element of unfairness to competition between subsidized and unsubsidized firms, and they have laws such as Section 301 of the U.S. trade law (see Chapter 6), which provide for investigation of complaints of unfair trade practices and for retaliation if the complaints are borne out. The fact that nations have different definitions of unfair subsidies led to an increasing level of trade tension. For example, Boeing argues that its competitor, Airbus, receives unfair subsidies from its sponsoring countries; Airbus argues that Boeing has been heavily subsidized as well, since many of its planes were developed under military contracts that guaranteed Boeing a profit.

The Uruguay Round began to sort out some of these arguments by establishing a set of rules for subsidization. In general, nations may impose tariffs on foreign imports if the imported good's production is directly subsidized. Nations may not take action in cases where the subsidy is very general and goes to pay for research that is not product specific or pays for basic infrastructure and labor force training. There remains a significant gray area, however, and some practices are likely to be subject to future WTO dispute resolution.

Conclusion

The economic gains from shallow integration are well known: a better resource allocation, greater productivity, and higher living standards. The economic benefits of deep integration are less certain, however. For example, natural environments differ, and a single set of environmental standards may turn out to protect the environment less and generate fewer economic benefits than a multiplicity of standards. Similarly, labor standards may need to be adapted to cultural environments; there is little consensus about the optimal set of competition policies; developing countries may actually benefit from performance requirements; and industrial policies may overcome the problem of externalities and benefit everyone.

The point is not that deep integration is necessarily a bad thing. Rather, it is that many issues of deep integration are new and lack the analysis that has developed around older issues such as tariffs and quotas. In fact, several of the issues of deep integration appear to be beneficial on first glance. Economists have many concerns, however.

First, there remains a basic question about whether nations should harmonize their environmental, labor, competition, and industrial support policies or whether they should simply agree to live with each other's differences. Strong arguments can be made that harmonization lessens the differences between nations and thereby destroys some of the sources of comparative advantage. Harmonization in these cases would have unintended harmful consequences.

Second, much of the actual conflict over deep integration issues may be little more than a smoke screen for imposing trade barriers. The extent to which these issues can be further clarified by the WTO and other international organizations will help to define the boundaries between protectionism and legitimate trade grievances.

▲ Economists recognize four levels of economic integration. These are (1) free-trade areas, which permit freedom of movement of outputs; (2) customs unions, which are free-trade areas that share a common external tariff towards nonmembers; (3) common markets, which are customs unions that also allow inputs to move freely; and (4) economic unions, which are common markets that have substantially harmonized economic policies.

▲ Political factors are among the leading reasons for the creation of economic integration. In addition, the desires for market access and economies of scale, international sourcing, and the debt crisis in developing countries have each played major roles.

▲ Several background issues affect the speed toward economic integration and influence its outcome. Among these are whether integration is market led versus institutionally led and whether countries are at different stages of economic development.

▲ The key issue for judging the desirability of special trade agreements between nations is whether the agreement creates more trade than it diverts.

▲ Until fairly recently, most economic integration agreements could be considered "shallow agreements," or agreements dealing with border issues such as tariffs, quotas, and customs procedures. The reduction in tariffs has exposed a number of domestic policy areas where, often unintentionally, national policies inhibit international trade and investment.

▲ Deep integration issues include environmental policies and standards, labor polices and standards, antitrust (competition) policies, foreign investment policies, and industrial support policies.

Vocabulary

common market	harmonization
competition policy	mutual recognition
customs union	shallow integration
deep integration	social dumping
ecodumping	trade creation
economic union	trade diversion
free trade area	

Study Questions

1. What are the four main types of regional trade agreements, and what are their main characteristics?

2. How have each of the following factors contributed to an intensification of international economic integration?

   a) Politics
   b) Technology
   c) Economies of scale
   d) Economic crisis

3. What are the main differences between market-led and institution-led regional integration schemes? Why do some economists fear the latter but not the former?

4. Explain why the political and economic pressures inside the United States that stem from the U.S.-Canada Free Trade Agreement differ from the pressures that developed in the wake of the North American Free Trade Agreement between the U.S., Canada, and Mexico.

5. How might NAFTA or another regional trade agreement lead to trade diversion?

6. How is deep integration different from shallow integration? Why is deep integration on the agenda of many nations now, when it was not fifty years ago?

7. What are ecodumping and social dumping? How do they relate to the idea of national comparative advantage?

8. Explain how competition policies overlap with trade policies.

9. The Uruguay Round of the GATT implemented a set of rules designed to curb the use of subsidies. What are the rules, why did the GATT countries think it desirable to develop them, and how might countries get around them?

Suggested Reading

Bhagwati, Jagdish, and Anne O. Krueger. *The Dangerous Drift to Preferential Trade Agreements.* Washington, DC: The American Enterprise Institute, 1995.

Federal Reserve Bank of Kansas City. *Policy Implications of Trade and Currency Zones: A Symposium Sponsored by The Federal Reserve Bank of Kansas City.* FRB, Kansas City, 1991.

Haggard, Stephan. *Developing Nations and the Politics of Global Integration,* Washington, DC. Brookings Institution. 1995.

Lawrence, Robert. *Regionalism, Multilateralism, and Deeper Integration,* Brookings Institution 1996.

Albert Bressand, and Takatoshi Ito. *A Vision for the World Economy: Openness, Diversity, and Cohesion.* Brookings Institution, 1996.

Rodrik, Dani. *Has Globalization Gone Too Far?* Institute for International Economics, 1997.

Schott, Jeffrey, Ed., *Free Trade Areas and U.S. Trade Policy.* Institute for International Economics, 1989.

CHAPTER 11

THE UNITED STATES AND JAPAN: DEEPENING TIES BETWEEN TWO SYSTEMS

Is Japan Different?

In 1997, the U.S. trade deficit (goods and services) with the European Union was $16.7 billion, while the trade deficit with Japan was $55.6 billion. The United States imported more from the EU than it did from Japan—$157.5 billion versus $121.3 billion—but it still had a smaller deficit because the United States sold far more to the EU than to Japan—$140.8 billion versus $65.7 billion. Because the European market is so open to American products, trade tensions are not as severe as they are between the U.S. and Japan. This is true in spite of the fact that the U.S. imports more from Europe than from Japan.

The fact that the United States has a deficit with Japan does not by itself tell much about Japanese trade policies. For example, the deficit with Japan could be entirely the result of comparative advantage instead of closed markets. The theory of comparative advantage does not predict that each country's trade will be balanced with every other country nor that it will even be balanced overall. The United States runs deficits with some countries, and we pay for it by running surpluses with others. We saw in Chapter 7 that the determinants of the overall trade balance have more to do with national savings than they do with trade barriers, but the overall trade balance cannot be used to predict balances with individual countries. Japan's surplus with the United States might be due to Japan's comparative advantage in manufactured consumer goods (autos and electronics, for example) and the United States high level of demand for those goods.

Nevertheless, many people suspect that the reason for the trade imbalance with Japan is not due to comparative advantage. Instead, they suspect that the Japanese market is partially closed to outsiders. This is a view that is fueled by the enormous differences between the U.S. and Japanese economies, cultures, and society. Economic differences in competition policies, industrial organization, and industrial support policies are exacerbated by our lack of understanding of Japanese culture and society. Inevitably, this leads to more trade conflict, particularly in this era of deeper integration.

This chapter examines the dimensions of the U.S.-Japan trade conflict. Given that the conflict has political and cultural elements as well as economic ones, it should be no surprise that economists disagree about the causes of the trade imbalance. Two issues are critical. The first is whether or not the Japanese economy is organized in a fundamentally different way than U.S. or Western European economies. If it is different, then it is important to know how the differences can be defined and measured, how important they are to the trade relationship, and whether they confer advantages to Japanese firms. The second issue concerns the most productive way to manage the conflict. Should quiet negotiations be used, or should there be headline-seeking retaliatory measures? Should the problems be addressed all at once or sector by sector? If negotiations lead to a resolution, how do we measure compliance with the settlement?

The U.S.-Japan trade conflict is not about tariffs, quotas, or other visible trade barriers. For example, the average Japanese tariff on imports of manufactured items is only about 2 percent. A comparison of tariffs and quotas in industrial nations, including the United States and Japan, shows that the differences do not tell us very much about trade. After several rounds of tariff and quota reductions through the General Agreement on Tariffs and Trade, virtually all high-income industrial economies have relatively low tariffs and quotas.

In Chapter 10, we saw that the economics of deeper integration have led to the intertwining of a range of domestic and international issues, including (1) environmental policy, (2) competition (antitrust) policy, (3) investment policy, (4) labor standards policy, and (5) industrial support policy. To a large extent, the standards and policies of industrial economies have converged over the last fifty years, but, as we also saw in Chapter 10, there remain substantial areas of disagreement, negotiation, and conflict.

The United States and Japan have significant differences in three of the areas: competition policy, investment policy, and industrial policy. Differences in national policies have created conflict that is difficult to resolve because it involves policies that are embedded in the structure and organization of the each country's economy. Changes in national competition policies, for example, require more than a rewriting of laws or a greater dedication to antimonopoly enforcement. The end result could be a fundamental reorganization of the system of doing business, including a reworking of relationships between businesses and between business and government. A second reason that the U.S.-Japan trade conflict seems to drag on without resolution is that Japan's emergence as an economic superpower has placed the country on a more equal economic footing with the United States and lessened Japan's need to defer to U.S. interests. Japanese residents have grown increasingly impatient with what they perceive as U.S. bullying and unreasonable demands.

The Two Poles of the Debate: Traditionalists and Revisionists

Is Japan's economy different? This is a simple question with a very complex answer. It should be easy to define differences, but in reality it is difficult to be certain whether any distinguishing characteristics are merely superficial or not. Do the numerous cultural differences fundamentally affect the Japanese economy? Is Japan's style of capitalism new and different? Is Japan's economy simply an example of Western-style capitalism with an overlay of Eastern culture?

One school of thought in the United States, which we call the Traditional School, argues that Japan's economy is not very different from the United States', at least not in the way it is put together or the way it functions. They just do some things better. The Japanese spend more hours in school and at work each year, they save and invest a larger share of their GNP, and they concentrate more on the quality of the goods they make. Traditionalists see the United States' pressure on Japan to change its economic practices as sour grapes from an economy that saves and invests too little and, as a result, has lost a number of markets in a fair, head-to-head competition.

In Chapter 8 we compared the United States' and Japan's savings and investment rates (see Table 8.4). The year 1993 was fairly typical in terms of the long-run pattern; gross private savings in the United States was 19.0 percent of GNP, and 26.8 percent in Japan. While the United States invested 16.4 percent of GNP, Japan invested 29.6 percent. Given these huge disparities, it is no wonder that Japan has grown faster and become more competitive in a number of markets.

Traditionalists point out that many U.S. firms have succeeded in Japan and that poor business decisions explain the failure of the rest. For example, unsuccessful firms have entered the market with products unsuited to Japanese conditions and preferences; or they look for short-run profits rather than taking a long-run view of their presence in Japan; or they have failed to offer the type of after-market services that Japanese customers expect. In other words, when U.S. firms fail, it is because they do not do their homework and study the Japanese market. Trade history is filled with examples, from the attempt to sell software that is in English text only, to giant American-sized refrigerators that do not fit in Japan's smaller homes and crowded kitchens, to cars with steering wheels on the wrong (left) side.

Traditionalists stress the United States' low savings rate and high consumption, which create a huge current account deficit. Much of the overall deficit, they argue, shows up in a deficit with Japan because of the comparative advantage Japan has in manufactured goods. Its lack of natural resources, plentiful supply of savings, and highly educated labor force give Japan a comparative advantage in capital-intensive manufacturing. It must export manufactured goods in order to pay for the raw materials, such as oil and food, that it has to import. Given that Japan makes such excellent quality products, for example cars and consumer electronics, and that the United States is a high-income, consumer-oriented society, Japan will probably always run a trade surplus with the United States.

The alternative to the Traditionalist School of thought, which we will call the Revisionist School, argues that Japan's economy differs from standard Western-style capitalism in a number of ways. The differences are hard to measure, but they effectively limit access to the Japanese economy for foreign firms and foreign investors. Revisionists agree with a number of points made by Traditionalists: (1) Japanese savings and investment are keys to its high growth rates and strong export performance; (2) Japan has a comparative advantage in manufactured goods; (3) even if markets in Japan were completely open, the United States would still have a trade deficit with Japan; and (4) many U.S. firms have failed because they have not exercised good business sense when they tried to enter the market.

On the other hand, Revisionists see a number of differences between Japan and the average high-income economy. The most important differences can be grouped into three main areas: (1) the organization of Japan's industrial markets, (2) the distribution system, and (3) business-government relations. Unlike a tariff or quota, these cannot be easily measured since they are largely qualitative differences. Their effects, however, can be observed when foreign trade and foreign investment in Japan are compared with other large industrial economies.

Revisionists tend to have two concerns about the Japanese economy. Their first concern is that the differences between Japan and other industrial countries will generate destructive conflicts and hinder the process of deeper economic integration. In the Revisionist view, it is largely the Japanese economy that must change in order to accommodate the rest of the world because it is their economy that is farthest from the norms of North America and Europe.

Second, Revisionists worry that Japan is using its competition, industrial support, and investment policies to protect its home market in selected high-technology sectors. These policies enable firms to develop within a protected base and to use high prices at home as a means of generating the profits necessary to sell at low prices throughout the rest of the world. In one sense, this is a bargain for the rest of the world (we get cheaper, higher-quality products than would be possible otherwise), but in another sense, it may be harmful. If tomorrow's possibilities depend on today's capabilities, then conceding high-technology markets to Japanese firms may result in the loss of future technological capacity. That is, if the skills and learning experiences gained from today's production will determine society's future ability to produce skill-intensive, high-technology goods, then it is detrimental over the long run to allow Japan to use a protected home base to finance low-cost sales abroad.

From the point of view of academic economists, it is this second concern of the Revisionists that is most controversial. Other than agriculture, Traditionalists refuse to concede that Japan's economy is protected from outside competition in any major way. Also, while it may be theoretically correct to state that a nation's future technological capacity depends on what it produces today, Traditionalists argue that the relationship between the present and the future is too indeterminate and indirect to use it as a guide for setting trade policy.

Revisionists and Traditionalists are not likely to resolve their differences before the United States and Japan resolve theirs. The most important point about their debate is not who is right but the fact that many independent, outside observers think that the Japanese market is less open to foreign goods and foreign investment than any other major industrial economy. Whether this is an accurate picture of reality matters less than the fact that large numbers of people act as if it is. For Japan to overcome this handicap, it will either have to open itself more to the outside, or convince large numbers of people that it already has. In either case, the burden is on Japan to define its role in a more open and integrated world economy.

Objective Indicators

Revisionists use several key statistics to show that the Japanese economy is less open than other high-income, industrial nations. One of them is the greater success of U.S. firms in penetrating European markets: if Germans will buy U.S. products, why not the Japanese? In the Revisionist view, the problem is a lack of Japanese imports of manufactured goods, not only from the United States but from other countries as well.

Table 11.1 compares several indicators of international interaction in the U.S., German, and Japanese economies. The first row is the percentage of total consumption that is made up by imported manufactured goods in 1990, a representative year. The percentage of the typical Japanese consumption bundle that is produced by foreign firms is only about one-third the percentage in the United States or Germany.

Row 2 of Table 11.1 shows the percentage of all domestic sales that are made by foreign-owned domestic firms. In other words, in the United States in 1990, 10 percent of all sales by firms located in the United States were made by firms that were also foreign owned. If the number is larger, foreign direct investment in an economy must be greater, and vice versa. Japan's tiny 1 percent figure is viewed by Revisionists as an indicator of the lack of openness of the Japanese economy to investment by foreign firms. Their assumption is that if it was possible to invest, then firms in the United States, Europe, and other countries would have a larger share of sales in Japan given the size and the wealth of the market.

The last row of Table 11.1 is an index of intra-industry trade. Recall that intra-industry trade is trade that does not occur as a result of comparative advantage. With intra-industry trade, countries export the same thing they import. Nations benefit from this kind of trade because it expands the selection of goods to choose from: Americans do not *have* to choose an American car; they can buy a European or Asian model with different features. Revisionists interpret the low level of intra-industry trade in Japan to mean that Japanese consumers are denied the choices available to consumers in other industrial nations and that, within Japan, Japanese firms are able to reduce competition from foreign firms.

TABLE 11.1 Comparison of the United States, Germany, and Japan

	U.S.	Germany	Japan
Share of imported manufactured goods in total consumption, 1990	15.3%	15.4%	5.9%
Share of domestic sales by foreign-owned firms in total domestic sales, 1990	10%	18%	1%
Index of intra-industry trade, 1991	64.5	64.7	38.9

Source: Robert Z. Lawrence, "Japan's Different Trade Regime," *Journal of Economic Perspectives*, Summer 1993.

If the Revisionist view is correct, then the Japanese economy is less open to imports and to foreign investment than the economies of other industrial nations. The statistics in Table 11.1 suggest this, but they neither prove it nor do they offer an explanation. The Revisionist argument becomes more convincing when the mechanisms used to create a more closed economy are clearly spelled out. For this, we must turn to an examination of some characteristic differences in Japan's style of capitalism.

Japan's Unusual Form of Capitalism

One of the main distinguishing features of Japan is that it is difficult, if not impossible, to determine who owns the capital in Japanese capitalism. In the typical capitalist economy, the owners of capital are relatively easy to spot, and either they or their appointed agents make decisions about the best use of the capital. In Japan, firms often seem to have no single set of owners in the sense that American or Canadian firms are owned by stockholders, partnerships, or individuals. The consequences are significant.

The Limited Role of Stockholders in Japanese Corporations

Japan's large firms commonly have around 75 percent of their stock locked up in the hands of the firms they do business with. In other words, firms such as Toyota and Nissan are mostly owned by their suppliers, their banks, their insurance companies, and a mix of the other firms they work with. This phenomena, in which firms own each other, is called **cross-ownership**. Since the firms involved in cross-ownership do not sell each other's stock, there is only 25 percent of the stock available for purchase by independent stockholders. The significance of this is that independent stockholders are more likely to be focused on dividends and share values, while inside, cross-holding share owners are more likely to be concerned about long-run business relations. As we will see, this helps give large Japanese firms the luxury of concentrating on the longer run without the worry of stockholder revolts or hostile takeovers.

The answer to the question, Who owns the large Japanese firms? is they own each other. This is almost the same, however, as saying they own themselves. Consider a simplified scheme in which three firms—call them Alpha, Beta, and Gamma—each own 25 percent of a fourth firm, Delta. In addition, 75 percent of Beta is owned by Alpha and the two others, and likewise for the ownership of Gamma and Delta. Who owns Alpha? On the one hand, you can say it is owned by the other three, but on the other hand, Alpha owns a part of each of the other three, so it owns itself.

The net result of this ownership scheme is that there is no room for independent stockholders to exercise control. Firms are controlled by their managers, who are appointed by the board of directors of each firm, but the board membership is appointed by the other firms and overlaps (has some of the same members) with the boards of the other firms. In other words, within a group of cross-owning firms, control is exercised by a closed, old-boy network. Management is self-appointed and self -perpetuating. The inability of outsiders to gain control through buying up stock means that there is no possibility for hostile takeovers or terminating the existing management. Outsiders that want to gain control of a firm in order to make it more profitable or to force it to pay out higher dividends have no way to do so. There simply is not enough stock available for purchase in the stock market. Furthermore, given that foreign investment often occurs through outright purchase of an existing firm, foreign direct investment in Japan is less because there are so few opportunities to buy a controlling interest in Japanese firms.

The Objectives of Japanese Enterprises

Independent outside stockholders have no mechanisms such as hostile takeovers to force managers to maximize profits and dividends. Additionally, although boards of directors control firms through their appointment of management, they do not own firms in a personal sense, like stockholders do in the United States. Under these conditions, maximizing profits in order to pay higher dividends is neither a goal of firms nor something they can be forced to do through changes in the board of directors.

This is not to say that Japanese firms do not care about profits. Obviously, every firm needs profits if it is to survive in the long run. The lack of hostile takeovers and the absence of impatient stockholders expecting a fat dividend check make it easier for Japanese firms to take a longer view of their goals and objectives. Profits become a necessary ingredient to long-run prosperity, but they are not an end in themselves. (In an economic sense, profits are a constraint rather than an objective.)

In the United States, a simple explanation of firm behavior is that they attempt to maximize profits. This is in the interests of stockholders, who ultimately are able to exercise control over the firm. What do Japanese firms do? If they downplay short-run (quarterly) profit maximization, and if they are controlled by their managers who are, in turn, appointed by the board of directors, then it is not obvious what their goals are. Profit maximization does not necessarily lead to rewards for those in charge, since they are salaried employees. In particular, profit maximization would be against management's interests if it entailed downsizing (layoffs) or if it hurt the long-run employment prospects of management.

One possibility is that Japan's large firms maximize employee benefits. In other words, since firms are largely owned by each other, they are operated so as to maximize the benefits of the primary stakeholders in the firm, its employees. This is done through maximizing job security (often this is equivalent to lifetime employment) and avoiding layoffs during recessions. It is also done by a demonstrable commitment to sharing productivity gains with all employees and through labor-management consultation and cooperation.

Benefits and Costs

Maximizing employee benefits in the broad sense (not just in monetary terms) has numerous benefits, but it is not without costs as well. One benefit is that technological progress is more easily achieved because workers do not fear losing their jobs due to improvements in the production process. Another benefit is that firms are willing to spend more to train employees because they recognize that the employees will not leave for a job elsewhere and take their training with them. Employee pay is partially based on seniority, and workers that leave a firm start over. As a result, there is much less jumping from job to job than in the United States, and as workers accumulate experience, their flexibility and skills improve.

The costs of this system are not negligible. First, problems arise because not every employee is competent. Yet, if job security is given to all new hires, firms have to carry low productivity workers on their payroll for most of their working life. Second, the system creates frustration for talented people who want to move up but who have to wait their turn as those with more seniority are promoted first.

Two additional costs have social as well as economic impacts. First, in many respects the firm becomes a community with a shared value of long-term success. Employee commitment to the firm is often outstanding because the firm's success will determine the employee's future living standard and because employees accumulate a lifetime of attachments. On the other hand, the firm partly replaces the family. Employees are expected to show extreme dedication and often work long hours of overtime and take few vacations. Finally, the system is essentially closed to women. Women are required to choose between family and career, and unlike many other industrial nations, it is not possible for most women to have both.

Is Lifetime Employment Disappearing?

It is common nowadays to hear people claiming that the system of lifetime employment is breaking down. The recession of the 1990s, the overvalued yen in the first half of the decade, and the deepening financial and economic crisis in the second half have put enormous pressure on Japanese manufacturers. Some major firms, such as Nissan, have closed plants (workers were moved to other plants) for the first time since the end of World War II. Other strains are showing as well. Japanese women are beginning to demand more options, and young people want more freedom to work at a variety of jobs. As a result of these forces, some observers have claimed that the end of lifetime employment is in sight.

Before jumping to conclusions, three points should be carefully considered. One is that the same changes were proclaimed in the late 1960s and early 1970s. That cohort of restless Japanese youth are today's responsible adults. The second point is that the system of cross-ownership, close interfirm relationships, and self-appointed management has not changed. The pressures on firms are perhaps greater today as they try to cope with a deep financial crisis, but if power and control within a firm have not changed, why should the firm's goals and objectives change?

It is also important to recognize that the system described here has never applied to the whole Japanese economy. Only the largest, most modern, and most competitive firms were able to offer lifetime employment. Below that upper tier of employers, there are vast numbers of subcontractors, many of them just barely surviving with long hours of work. In some sectors of the economy, Japan has firms that lead the world in productivity and quality. In other sectors, however, Japanese productivity is way below the United States and other industrial nations. Workers in the food processing sector in Japan, for example, are only about 25 percent as productive as U.S. workers in the same sector. Working conditions correlate directly with productivity, and in the low-productivity sectors, conditions have never included lifetime employment.

Keiretsu

As we have seen, independent, outsider stockholders have little or no say in Japanese corporate governance. Instead, the major firms are primarily owned by the firms they do business with—their suppliers, distributors, bankers, and so forth. This type of industrial organization is called a *keiretsu* in Japan. *Keiretsu* are families of legally separate firms that are tied together through cross-ownership, business relations, and interlocking directorates (shared membership on their board of directors). There are two categories of *keiretsu*; both have attributes that create economic advantages and barriers to trade.

> **Keiretsu.** *Keiretsu are groups of legally separate firms that are tied together into familylike relationships through cross-ownership, business relations, and interlocking directorates. Keiretsu members usually seek another member to do business with before going outside the group.*

Vertical and Horizontal

Keiretsu are categorized in general terms by their type of integration—vertical or horizontal. Horizontally integrated *keiretsu* have family or group members that are spread out across the economy and not concentrated in one type of production. The most important and largest examples of horizontal *keiretsu* are integrated around a major financial institution and usually include life and casualty insurance companies, trading companies, and manufacturing companies. The six largest have names that are relatively well known in the United States: Mitsui, Sumitomo, Sanwa, Mitsubishi, Fuyo, and Daiichi Kangyo. These six conglomerates include approximately one-half of the 200 largest Japanese firms and account for approximately 15 percent of all sales in Japan. In addition to interlocking directorates and cross-ownership, the management of the firms in a *keiretsu* jointly plan their economic strategies and regularly meet to discuss conditions and business practices.

Firms in vertical *keiretsu* are usually organized around a single large industrial corporation and include allied firms, subcontractors, and important consumers. In the automobile industry, Toyota and Nissan are examples; in electrical equipment, Hitachi, Toshiba, and Matsushita; and in steel, Nippon Steel. Although they tend to be concentrated in a single industry (autos, electronics, etc.), they often have ties to distributors and to a financial institution.

One of the problems of measuring the impact of *keiretsu* on the economy is that they are difficult to define once you go beyond the most obvious examples. Relationships are often fluid over time, and it is difficult to specify which firms are in which corporate groups. In addition, firms within a vertical *keiretsu* may rely on firms in a separate, horizontal *keiretsu* for some of their business; Toyota, for example, uses Mitsui for much of its banking. For this reason, many Traditionalists have argued that *keiretsu* are little more than social clubs, a vehicle for managers of different firms to get to know one another so that they will have golf partners and drinking buddies. In spite of the difficulty of measurement, Revisionists counter that Japanese corporate groups have specific economic functions that individual firms would be economically irrational not to utilize.

Reducing the Cost of Information

The primary economic effect of corporate groups is that they lower a type of costs that economists refer to as **transaction costs.** Transaction costs include the costs of acquiring market information; of arranging an economic exchange, such as the purchase of inputs or the distribution of outputs; and of enforcing the contractual agreement under which the economic exchange takes place. Legal costs, marketing costs, insurance costs, and quality checks of purchased inputs are all a part of production, but they do not directly increase output.

> *Transaction costs. Transaction costs are the costs of gathering market information, arranging a market agreement, and enforcing the agreement. It includes legal costs, marketing costs, insurance costs, quality checks, advertising, distribution, and after-sales service costs.*

Transaction costs are unavoidable, and they are often a sizable percentage of a firm's total costs. Japanese corporate groups effectively lower these costs by offering each supplier firm a ready-made market for its output, and each producer of final products the detailed, technical information about inputs that only the supplier firm would have in a more traditional capitalist system.

Firms in a corporate group share information about their technical capabilities and financial situation in the same way that two divisions of a single firm might. Toyota, for example, knows much more about its parts supplier's capital equipment, technical expertise, and finances than General Motors knows about the independent firms that supply it with auto parts. At the same time, Toyota will share information with its suppliers about its new car models. The goal is to use the added expertise of its suppliers to improve the car design and to avoid problems in both the manufacturing process and the final product. The closeness of firms within a *keiretsu* enables technical information to pass back and forth and reduces the uncertainty firms have about the quality of purchased inputs. This lowers costs by eliminating some expensive and time-consuming quality checks and by avoiding design and engineering mistakes that turn out to be impossible to build or to make function properly. The closeness of firms, and the fact that they do not conduct business with rivals outside the group, permits trade secrets and other sensitive information to be passed along whenever there is an advantage to doing so.

In the ways described, firms in a corporate group act almost as if they were part of a single large firm. In other ways, however, they keep an arm's-length relationship. Each firm is legally and financially independent, so that when financial problems occur, they are limited to the affected firm(s). For example, suppose that technological breakthroughs make obsolete certain computer chips that Toshiba buys for its notebook computers. Toshiba's chip supplier must either make the necessary investment to modernize its production or look for something else to do. The impact on Toshiba will be minimal, as the company can turn to alternative suppliers for its new chips. In other words, when it has to, Toshiba can use the flexibility of the market to look for the best deal. If Toshiba had owned the supplier, it would be stuck with obsolete chip-making equipment, and it would have to pay the costs of modernization. Toshiba may decide to help its supplier obtain the financing it needs to modernize, but there is no requirement to do so.

In an industrial economy, firms must decide when to use the market to supply it with goods and services and when to produce them inside the firm. Should the firm own its suppliers, or should it buy its parts in the market? Should it own its own distribution network or rely on outside distribution specialists? What about retail outlets and marketing and advertising? There are advantages and disadvantages to doing tasks in-house and in using outside firms. In many respect, *keiretsu* offer the best of both—the flexibility to seek the latest technology and best suppliers, along with the reliability of in-house production.

Japan's Industrial Organization, Foreign Trade, and Investment

So far we have seen that Japan's system of corporate governance lessens the role of independent stockholders and increases the power of management in the setting of long-run goals and objectives. In addition, we have seen that interlocking directorates and cross-shareholding are associated with the ordering of firms together into corporate groups. The question that remains to be addressed is whether these features of the Japanese economy influence or determine Japanese trade relations with the rest of the world and whether they have effects on the quantity of foreign investment in Japan. In other words, do *keiretsu* reduce Japanese imports and reduce foreign investment in Japan?

Ultimately, this must be an empirical question, not a theoretical one. That is, it must be measured. Trade economists have attempted to gather data on the extent to which *keiretsu* control production in a sector of the economy, say automobiles, and then have tried to see if imports by Japan are less than expected after all other factors that determine imports have been accounted for. Not surprisingly, perhaps, there is support for two opposing views in the work that has been done so far. Some economists have concluded that *keiretsu* do cause imports to be less, while others have shown that they have no effect. In other words, the results of the statistical analysis are inconclusive and will not nail down an answer one way or another. For that reason, economists and political scientists who study Japan have turned to more theoretical work to buttress their views.

From a theoretical perspective—that is, in terms of what we know about economic incentives and the effects they have on firm behavior—it is not difficult to construct an argument that *keiretsu* do indeed lower the quantity and value of imports into Japan, and that they also reduce foreign direct investment. The mechanisms are not hard to imagine; many of them have already been hinted at in the discussion of *keiretsu.*

First, the cross-shareholding of firms within a group prevents foreigners from directly acquiring major Japanese firms. Since direct acquisition of firms is one of the main avenues of foreign direct investment, the overall rate of foreign investment is lower in Japan. Second, members of a *keiretsu* conduct the majority of their business with other members—not with outsiders. As a result, suppliers of intermediate parts, such as automobile parts manufacturers, find it difficult to break into the Japanese economy. Toyota, Nissan, and others have their own parts manufacturers with whom they have long-term relationships and share proprietary information. Their system of production is not set up to seek the lowest bidder nor to switch among a large number of suppliers for any given part, depending on who has the lowest price at any given point in time.

For outsiders, the obvious solution to the problem of not being able to buy Japanese firms is to establish their own production facilities. That is, instead of trying to buy existing Japanese firms, U.S. and European companies must set up their own factories. At this point, however, they run into another feature of *keiretsu*: they often control the existing distribution channels. For example, in the dispute between the U.S. film producer, Kodak, and its Japanese counterpart, Fuji, Kodak complained that Fuji has signed exclusive contracts with the four main distributors of photographic film and effectively denied them access to the normal distribution channel in Japan. In other words, even when foreign firms establish an independent presence in the Japanese market, oftentimes the problem of distribution persists as a major obstacle.

U.S. Views on Japan's Economic Policies

The role of the distribution system in keeping out foreign goods goes beyond the problem of *keiretsu* ties to distributors. The distribution system and related issues are a central element in a set of charges of unfair practices the United States has made against Japan's economic policies. Two other major components of the U.S. critique of the Japanese trading system are the lack of enforcement of antitrust laws (recall from Chapter 10 that antitrust policies, or competition policies, are national policies designed to foster competition and prevent collusion in domestic industries) and the lack of transparency in the setting of standards and certification requirements for specific products.

Enforcement of Competition Policies

According to the Revisionists, one of the greatest obstacles facing foreign firms trying to invest or to sell in Japan is the lack of antitrust enforcement. Not only is collusion permitted, but in many cases it is actively encouraged by powerful government bureaucrats within the Ministry of International Trade and Industry (MITI), the Ministry of Finance (MOF), and other branches of government. On paper, Japanese antitrust laws are very similar to U.S. laws, largely because they were passed at the end of World War II during the period of U.S. occupation. The laws were intended, in part, to break up the enormous concentration of wealth that existed in the handful of families that controlled the predecessor of the *keiretsu*, which were called *zaibatsu*. (The term *zaibatsu* derives from the Chinese ideogram for "financial conglomerate.") Over the course of the 1950s and 1960s, the *keiretsu* developed many of the same anticompetitive features of their predecessors but without the personal, family-centered concentrations of wealth and power that defined the *zaibatsu*.

Japanese antitrust practice often permits collusion between firms as well as legal limitations on competition. Much, but not all, of the collusion takes place in the context of *keiretsu* relationships. For example, it is often legal for Japanese manufacturers to sign exclusive agreements with retailers and distributors specifying that the retailer or distributor may only carry the manufacturer's product line. In other words, if you sell Hitachi's consumer electronics, you cannot sell Sony's products. In technical terms, this is called vertical foreclosure; in the United States, it is a gray area of antimonopoly law. In Japan, where many goods are sold in small, family-run outlets, there is a powerful incentive for retailers to stick with one company's product line and to refuse to carry foreign products, especially if the foreign manufacturer has an unproven track record in the Japanese market. In the U.S.-Japan auto dispute, vertical foreclosure became an issue when the United States complained that Japanese auto dealers would not carry American cars. The same practices form part of the basis for U.S. complaints in electronics, insurance, glass, film, and a number of other products.

Two other practices that have come under U.S. attack are the limitation of sales incentives by retailers and the permission given to firms to establish industrywide codes of "fair competition" (by the Japan Fair Trade Commission, or JFTC). These practices are viewed by the United States as permitting collusion by Japanese firms in the setting of prices and as eliminating the advantage many U.S. firms have in marketing and retailing. By limiting competition in certain markets, Japanese antitrust practices prevent foreign firms from gaining market share through price cutting or other tough competitive practices. Largely in response to U.S. pressure, the JFTC has begun to review its fair competition codes and to increase its antitrust enforcement. The number of staff at the JFTC investigating antitrust complaints has grown, as has the number of investigations into complaints. On the other hand, prosecution for antitrust violations remains uncommon, and the budget of the JFTC is far below its relative size in the United States.

The Distribution System

In addition to permitting anticompetitive practices, the United States has alleged that the distribution system is unfair to foreign producers. Part of the complaint stems from reasons already discussed—exclusive licensing agreements with retailers. A past target of U.S. negotiations was the Large Retail Store Law, which required advanced notice to small retailers before large retail outlets could be constructed. The law was passed in 1975 to protect small shops from large Japanese retailers and originally required simple notification. Gradually, however, the law came to require more formal negotiation over large retail store openings, and it took on an aspect of discriminating against large U.S. discounters such as Toys-R-Us, Wal-Mart, Radio Shack, Home Depot, Blockbuster Video, and so forth. At one point, it was alleged to take as long as thirteen years to complete the negotiation process required to gain approval to open a large retail outlet.

U.S.-Japan bilateral negotiations have removed the Large Retail Store Law as a major obstacle, and U.S. retailers are increasing their presence in Japan. The dollar impact of the entry of these firms is not likely to be great, however, as much of what they sell does not come from the United States. Nevertheless, as price competition increases, it will force Japanese retailers to search out the lowest-priced goods of a given quality, and overall Japanese imports will increase.

A second major impediment in the distribution system is that it is largely made up of small, capital-poor, family-operated retailers. This affects imports in three ways. First, small store sizes reduce the shelf space that is available for foreign goods. Second, Japanese law requires retailers to have licenses for some goods. Small stores are less likely than large, well-capitalized stores to have the time and expertise to obtain retail licenses. Third, small store size increases the probability that the retailer will be "captured" by domestic manufacturers and forced to sell only one company's product line. The problem of vertical foreclosure is an issue of differing antitrust policies (i.e., competition policies) and, in some cases, lack of antitrust enforcement. In general, however, the small size of Japanese retail outlets is not directly a matter of government policy, although various policies (such as the Large Retail Store Law) have prevented the growth of large outlets and discount stores.

Transparency

In many cases, the U.S.-Japan trade problem boils down to a lack of transparency. Recall that a transparent trade barrier is one that is visible and obvious—such as a tariff. Nontransparent barriers are government policies that effectively limit imports but that are disguised as safety regulations, product certification standards, paperwork requirements, national security rules, and so forth. U.S. firms often complain that the procedures for entering the Japanese market are not spelled out clearly and that the requirements change without notice.

The insurance industry, for example, claims that the rules for obtaining a license to sell insurance in Japan are not readily available. The medical equipment industry claims that Japanese health insurance will not cover new procedures that use the latest technology and that it is impossible to discover the procedure for becoming an approved treatment. The construction industry faces the catch-22 of not being able to bid on major projects unless the company has prior Japanese experience, but there is no way to obtain experience. The auto industry complains that the bulk of Japanese auto repairs must be done in government-certified garages, which are largely controlled by Japanese car manufacturers and therefore use only Japanese-manufactured parts.

Perhaps most of the nontransparencies in Japanese trade strategy stem from the close relationship between large firms and the government bureaucracy. Recall that aspects of this relationship were discussed in Chapter 7 under the topic of industrial policy. Economic philosophy in Japan has favored a controlled form of competition in which bureaucrats at the powerful ministries design industrial policies to encourage whole industries. One of the goals of economic policy has been to avoid cut-throat competitive behavior that leads to price wars and bankruptcies. A second goal has been to foster economic development by protecting the home base from foreign competition. In the 1950s and 1960s, this was done through the outright use of tariffs and quotas. As those forms of protection disappeared through successive rounds of GATT negotiations in the 1960s and 1970s, the Japanese system responded partly by opening its economy to the world but also by relying on a greater use of nontransparent barriers to protect industries in which it was not prepared for open international competition—construction, medical equipment, autos, and insurance, to cite just a few.

Unfortunately, the number of anecdotes about trade barriers that masqueraded as silly safety or other types of requirements seems to grow almost daily. It is unfortunate because these accounts, while often humorous, obscure the real issues in the U.S.-Japan trade conflict. They also provide ready-made excuses for U.S. firms that failed in Japan as a result of their own lack of effort or inattention to the distinctive features of the Japanese market. In the end, the question of whether a market is partially closed or not is an empirical question. That is, it must be measured, and the mechanisms used to keep it closed must be identified. Anecdotes are interesting stories, but it is never clear if they are representative of the overall situation or merely aberrations from the norm.

The Japanese View of U.S. Policies

From the Japanese perspective, many of the complaints of U.S. firms and the U.S. government are a combination of sour grapes and unacceptable intrusions into domestic Japanese affairs. They are sour grapes because U.S. firms tend to blame everyone but themselves for their inability to succeed in the quality-conscious Japanese market. They are intrusions into domestic affairs because the United States has no legal right to set Japanese antitrust policy or product-certification standards. If the *keiretsu* system gives Japanese firms a competitive advantage, then why, they ask, should they dismantle it? The United States should instead seek to emulate it and create its own *keiretsu*. If U.S. law prevents this, then the real problem is the competitive *dis*advantage of U.S. institutions.

Japanese officials cite three other problems in the United States: the lack of savings, the short-run attitudes of U.S. management, and the bullying tactics used by the United States to get its way. The United States will continue to run an overall current account deficit until it either (1) saves more, (2) reduces its government deficit (i.e., increase public savings), (3) invests less, or (4) does some combination of all three. In all likelihood, if saving stays the same, then any reduction in the deficit with Japan will simply show up as an increased deficit somewhere else—China, Korea, and Southeast Asia, perhaps. In the Japanese view, the primary cause of the bilateral deficit is Japan's comparative advantage in high-quality manufactured consumer goods. Nearly everyone agrees, whether Traditionalist or Revisionist, that there is no scenario in which the U.S. trade deficit with Japan completely disappears. The composition of supply and demand in the two economies implies that Japan will continue to produce high-quality manufactured consumer goods, which it will sell to the United States and other nations in order to earn the revenues it needs to pay for its imports of raw materials and other goods.

A second point raised by Japan is that U.S. firms take a short-run view of their operations. This hurts their ability to break into the Japanese market because it places time limits on their commitments. It is much harder for U.S. firms to commit to several years of investment without profits, which is what they have to do to become successful in Japan. The strategy for success often involves the creation of a long-term relationship with Japanese firms, in essence becoming a part of a corporate group. Firms that are looking for short-run profits cannot make a commitment of several years to developing a relationship with a Japanese firm. U.S. firms often labor under the watchful eye of independent stockholders who are willing to sell off shares or to engage in hostile takeovers if they think their interests are not sufficiently protected. In addition, U.S. firms are headed by managers who are constantly changing jobs. In some cases, this limits the ability of firms to adopt longer-run strategies; instead, they must focus on quarterly profits and dividends. From the Japanese perspective, this is another competitive disadvantage of the U.S. economic system. If stock markets and the U.S. system of corporate governance prevent firms from thinking long term, whose fault is that? Certainly not Japan's.

Finally, Japan has come increasingly to resent what it perceives as bullying tactics by the United States. In the Japanese view, the United States makes demands that Japan change its domestic policies, and then it threatens some form of retaliation—tariffs or quotas—if it is not satisfied with the changes. Many of the problems that the United States complains about are beyond the scope of Japanese policy, for example, the problems of small retail outlets and legal forms of *keiretsu* collusion. Furthermore, the United States often demands that Japan meet numerical targets for imports (e.g., importing 20 percent of all semiconductors purchased by Japanese firms), which the government has no legal method of enforcing. How would the United States react if the shoe were on the other foot and a much stronger and bigger Japan demanded that the United States change a number of its domestic policies and that private U.S. firms import a certain quantity of their materials?

Japanese Prices Are Different

This chapter began with a description of the Traditionalist and Revisionist views. For a number of years, the issue of Japanese differences hinged on an explanation of the reasons for Japan's low level of manufactured imports. Traditionalists argued that it was a result of Japan's comparative advantage in manufactured goods, while Revisionists countered that although Japan does have a comparative advantage, it does not fully explain the relative lack of manufactured imports. In addition to its comparative advantage, the Revisionists argued, many Japanese markets are relatively closed by nontariff barriers, such as the *keiretsu* system of interfirm relations, government red tape, safety standards, certification requirements, and so forth.

Since manufactured imports could be low as a result of either reason—comparative advantage or closed markets—this line of reasoning has not been able to settle the issue of whether Japan is open or not. Clearly, the United States can point to a number of mechanisms by which specific markets appear to be closed, but this does not solve the issue either. Pointing to such a mechanism, the control of distribution channels within a *keiretsu*, for example, does not tell us the amount by which imports are reduced or what the trade picture would look like if markets were more open. For example, there are many reasons that the United States sells so few cars in Japan, and not all of them have to do with *keiretsu.* If Japanese auto *keiretsu* were to magically disappear, the United States still would not sell a lot of cars for some years—until they have enough cars with the steering wheel on the right side and until quality, size, and service issues are resolved to the satisfaction of Japanese consumers.

An entirely different way of coming at the issue of Japanese differences is to look at the prices of goods. Several studies have been done, nearly all of which paint a picture of higher Japanese prices. In 1991, the U.S. Department of Commerce and the Japanese Ministry of International Trade and Industry (MITI) conducted a joint study in which they surveyed the retail prices of 112 separate items. They compared identical products in Japan and the United States and found that the Japanese products had 37 percent higher prices on average. The question naturally arises as to why U.S. exporters or Japanese importers do not buy in the United States, ship to Japan, and sell there. Over time, arbitrage (buying in the low-priced market and selling in the high-priced one) would bring the two prices together, but the price differences have persisted.

One explanation for the price differences is that they are the result of nontariff trade barriers. In this view, prices for imports are forced up by the trade barriers, and the higher prices for all goods (Japanese and non-Japanese) protect the excess profits of Japanese producers in their home market. These higher prices then become a source of revenue to finance sales outside of Japan at relatively low prices.

The critics of this view point out that the prices in the MITI-U.S. Department of Commerce study covered only 112 items, and they were retail prices. Retail prices in Japan tend to be higher than elsewhere due to the relatively inefficient Japanese distribution system. Inefficient distribution is a problem, but it is not the same thing as a trade barrier as it is a problem for Japanese and non-Japanese goods alike.

A more recent study (but using data from 1989) compared the prices of Japanese imports at the border, before they enter the distribution system, with the prices of similar Japanese goods at the factory gate, before they enter the distribution system. Domestic Japanese prices that are higher than import prices are only possible if they are somehow protected from full-price competition—through government red tape that adds to the cost of the imported good once it enters Japan, product certification costs, or some other nontariff barrier. The data in Table 11.2 represent the forty-seven subcategories of imports that are the most highly protected in Japan and that make up about 20 percent of total Japanese imports. For this 20 percent of imports, the effect of the average nontariff barrier is equivalent to a tariff of an astounding 174 percent. If all the nontariff barriers were to be removed, it is estimated that imports of these items would increase by 101 percent, or about $53 billion in 1989 terms. It should be noted, however, that if the trade barriers were removed, Japan would reallocate resources away from the less efficient sectors, causing another set of changes in exports and imports. As a result, it is unlikely that the trade balance would change by $53 billion.

The study from which the data in Table 11.2 are drawn is not perfect, and critics of the Revisionist point of view do not hesitate to say so. Nevertheless, it is the most recent attempt to measure nontariff barriers in the Japanese economy, and it is consistent with a number of past studies. A growing body of evidence points in more or

TABLE 11.2 Nontariff Barriers for Selected Japanese Goods, 1989

Category	Number of Items	Estimated Tariff Equivalent of Nontariff Barriers
Food and beverages	17	272.5 %
Textiles and light industries	6	91.5%
Metal products	7	58.7%
Chemical products	11	126.9%
Machinery	6	139.9%
Total (20% of Japanese imports)	47	173.5%

Source: Sazanami, Urata, and Kawai, *Measuring the Costs of Protection in Japan*, 1995.

less the same direction: Japanese tariffs and quotas are low, but nontariff barriers are significant. The effects that would result from a complete removal of all trade barriers remain as controversial as ever, but the average effect estimated by seven separate studies conducted between 1980 and 1991 was that Japanese imports of manufactured goods would increase by 41 percent.

Attempts at Reducing Trade Friction

While economists may not agree about the extent of Japanese differences, or the effects that would result from the removal of all trade barriers, one fact is not in dispute: the U.S.-Japan trade dispute is a constant source of friction between the two countries, and it often seems about to blow up into a more serious confrontation that could, potentially, damage the world trading system. For this reason, it is in everyone's interest to see that the dispute is managed in a spirit of cooperation and that its effects are contained within the U.S.-Japan relationship and do not spill over into third-party conflict.

The Opening of the Deficit in the Early 1980s

Prior to the 1980s, there was not much conflict, in large part because there was no systemic trade deficit. In the 1970s, the U.S. consumer electronics industry felt that it was victimized by Japanese dumping, but the U.S. political system was relatively unresponsive to their complaints. Furthermore, it appeared that Japanese firms were willing to accept much lower profit margins than American firms would, and most U.S. manufacturers voluntarily decided to get out of the consumer electronics business. Many, such as Motorola, decided to focus on industrial electronics instead. (Motorola now sees this as a strategic mistake.)

The pattern of U.S.-Japan trade relations changed in the 1980s (see Figure 11.1). First, the U.S. auto industry found itself at an extreme disadvantage against Japanese

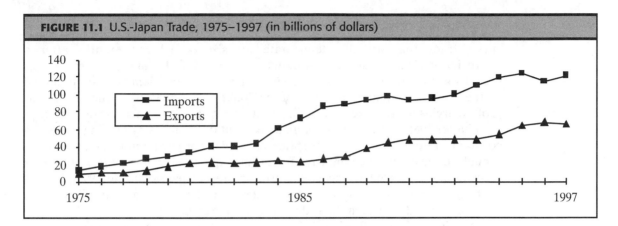

FIGURE 11.1 U.S.-Japan Trade, 1975–1997 (in billions of dollars)

imports: U.S. cars cost more, got worse mileage, and were of a lower quality. Given that the auto industry and related sectors employed millions of Americans, it was impossible to ignore their cries for government intervention. The second change that occurred in the 1980s was the opening of a persistent and large trade deficit with Japan. Between 1980 and 1987, the U.S. merchandise trade deficit with Japan jumped from approximately $12 billion to almost $60 billion. Since 1987, it has varied somewhat but has more or less stayed in the range of $45 to $65 billion.

It is difficult to argue that this increase in the deficit is all Japan's fault. Between 1980 and 1997, U.S. exports to Japan grew by almost $45 billion, or 225 percent. Imports, meanwhile, grew by almost $90 billion, or nearly 300 percent. In other words, U.S. firms had very good success selling in Japan, but our high-consumption economy coupled with Japan's comparative advantage in consumer goods like cars and electronics means that we are likely to run a bilateral deficit into the foreseeable future.

The Plaza and Louvre Agreements

Three factors have put pressure on U.S. and Japanese officials to look for ways to reduce the bilateral trade deficit: (1) the relatively sudden increase in the size of the trade deficit during the first half of the 1980s; (2) its persistence over the 1980s and 1990s; and (3) the loss of U.S. leadership in a number of new technologies.

The first attempts to manage the relationship were through coordinated efforts to bring down the value of the dollar. Between October 1980 and October 1982, the dollar rose in value against the yen by 30 percent, from 209.32 to 271.61 yen per dollar. Thereafter, the yen traded in the 240–260 range until late in 1985. In that year, the Group of Five (G-5) leading industrial countries convened in New York at the Plaza Hotel to discuss, among other things, the problem of the strong dollar. Their agreement, called the **Plaza Accord**, committed the five nations to sell dollars in a coordinated effort to bring down its value. By 1987, the yen had significantly appreciated against the dollar and was trading around 145 yen per dollar. This led to the Louvre Agreement between the G-7, which called for the stabilization of the dollar-yen exchange rate.

Recall from Chapter 9 that a change in a country's currency value does not immediately improve its trade balance. In fact, due to the phenomenon called the J-curve, trade may actually deteriorate for six to eighteen months after a depreciation. This is exactly what happened in the U.S.-Japan case, as the deficit grew from 1985 to 1987 and then began to shrink. The problem was compounded by the previous run-up in the value of the dollar before 1985, which had increased profit margins of Japanese firms selling to the United States. When the dollar began to fall after 1985, Japanese firms were able to cut their profits by holding the prices constant in dollar terms and accepting fewer yen for each good. As a result, although the trade balance improved with the expected lag, it did not improve as much as many people had expected. Furthermore, between 1988 and 1991, the dollar began another episode of strengthening against the yen, and, predictably, in 1991, the trade deficit began to widen once again. See Figure 11.2.

With the election of President Clinton in 1992, U.S. policy encouraged the dollar to fall in international currency markets. Although this policy was not official and was strongly opposed by the Japanese, the United States encouraged the dollar to fall as low as 80 yen for a short period of time. In 1995, it averaged 95 yen; but since then, the dollar has gradually risen in value. Persistent weakness in the Japanese economy led to low interest rates and a lack of investment opportunities. These factors, plus the severe financial crisis that was uncovered in the second half of the 1990s, have all reduced demand for the yen. As a consequence, it has not been possible for the U.S. to maintain its policy of a weak dollar against the yen.

MOSS Talks

The policy of letting the dollar fall in value against the yen is a macroeconomic approach to the U.S.-Japan trade problem. At the same time, the United States initiated a series of microeconomic measures to deal with the trade deficit. These efforts consisted of bilateral (U.S.-Japan), sector-specific negotiations that focused on improving market access for all foreign goods, not just U.S. ones. One group of such

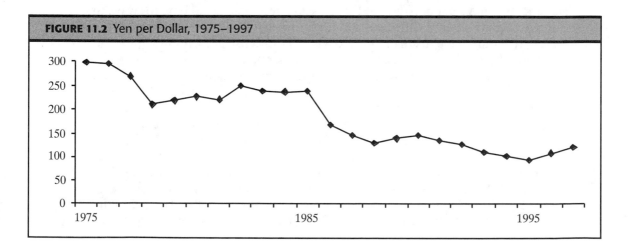

FIGURE 11.2 Yen per Dollar, 1975–1997

negotiations occurred during 1985 to 1987 under the title Market Oriented Sector Specific (MOSS) talks. The sectors chosen for inclusion in the MOSS talks were those in which it was thought that the U.S. products were strongly competitive and in which the main problem in gaining access to the Japanese market was government regulations. These included medical technology and pharmaceuticals, software, supercomputers, wood and paper products, and selected telecommunications equipment. In addition to the MOSS talks, separate talks were also undertaken in a number of other specific sectors, the most notable being semiconductors.

The U.S. goal was to increase market access for *all* foreign firms. To this end, the U.S. strategy was to determine a set of mutually agreeable rules for product certification and product standards, along with methods for making the standards and certification processes well known. The U.S. strategy was designed to overcome the complaints expressed by many firms that Japanese standards and certification processes for introducing new products were both secretive and costly due to their uniqueness. Finding out the steps that must be taken to bring a product into Japan was, in many cases, a major effort in itself.

The MOSS talks were generally viewed as a success from both the U.S. and Japanese points of view. Product standards moved toward convergence although complete harmonization remains a long way off; rules for entering the Japanese market were more clearly spelled out in a number of sectors; agreements were concluded in the sectors mentioned; and, finally, the effects on imports and exports of these agreements were left to the market, with no specific targets laid down. In some cases, U.S. exports to Japan have grown (computers and supercomputers), while in others cases, European exports have grown (pharmaceuticals), and in still others, the United States is investigating alleged noncompliance with the agreement and has left open the possibility of retaliation (wood and paper products).

The MOSS talks are significant not only for the agreements they reached in specific sectors but also because they were the beginning of a systematic focus on bilateral, sector-specific negotiations. This approach to reducing trade friction has remained the primary U.S. tactic since 1985. Outside of the first round of MOSS talks, separate negotiations have taken place in semiconductors, construction, commercial satellites, financial services, cellular phones, apples, glass, insurance, autos and auto parts, air freight services, and photographic film and paper.

The Structural Impediments Initiative

A third set of initiatives took place between 1989 and 1992. Unlike previous initiatives that had focused on macro or micro issues, the Structural Impediments Initiative (SII) added economic structures to the discussion table. These include a number of general regulatory issues (i.e., not sector specific), such as enforcement of antimonopoly laws in the case of the *keiretsu,* improving private company disclosure rules so that the full extent of *keiretsu* ties would be better known, liberalization of foreign direct investment rules and procedures, and the opening of the distribution system. The talks begun under the SII were largely responsible for the reform of the previously mentioned Large Retail Store Law.

In addition, the United States and Japan pushed each other into committing to various policy reforms that underpin economic activity. For example, Japan made commitments to stimulate its consumer economy by encouraging longer vacations and by increasing government expenditures. At the same time—since in the Japanese view much of the problem stems from a lack of U.S. savings—Japan extracted commitments from the United States to reduce its federal budget deficit. Similarly, the United States promised to improve its educational system under the theory that "smarter" workers will produce more competitive products. It is probably accurate to say that the more general and less specific the goals of the SII, the smaller the probability that they will have an effect.

The State of the Debate: Bilateral Managed Trade and Deeper Integration

Bilateral, sector-specific negotiations have successfully resolved disputes in a number of cases; nevertheless, there are significant problems, and not all policy analysts agree that they should be the main U.S. tactic. Many observers, both inside and outside the United States, believe that bilateral negotiations reduce the ability of the GATT and the new World Trade Organization (WTO) to resolve disputes. Bilateral deals easily create an impression around the world that the United States and Japan are colluding and that U.S. access to the Japanese market will come at the expense of third parties, for example, European firms. Furthermore, if the two largest national economies in the world choose not to use the WTO to resolve their disputes, then there is less incentive for other nations to seek multilateral agreements. Finally, the failure to resolve a bilateral dispute puts greater domestic pressure on the United States to retaliate against Japan. Again, this undermines multilateral efforts to resolve disputes by making it appear that some countries (the United States, in this case) will not honor their international obligations under the GATT agreement. Ironically, a multilateral dispute-resolution decision within the WTO would insulate the president and Congress from industrial lobbyists and lessen the pressure on them to retaliate against foreign practices.

> ***Managed trade.*** *Managed trade is an attempt to reduce trade friction by either (1) specifying a set of rules of fair practices in sectors where there has been conflict or (2) specifying an outcome, such as the percent of a country's market that should be held by foreigners. The first type is generally more consistent with the goal of using markets to allocate inputs and outputs. Managed trade can be bilateral or multilateral.*

In spite of these problems, the United States continues to view bilateral negotiations as one of its primary approaches to dispute resolution. In part, this stems from the legal procedure of U.S. trade law (Section 301 in U.S. trade law, see Chapter 6), which requires the president to open negotiations after a U.S. investigation finds evidence of unfair trade practices. The second reason for the United States' use of bilateral negotiations is that they can be carried out much more swiftly and are less cumbersome than multilateral talks—particularly in cases that involve the gray areas of the GATT, such as monopolistic *keiretsu* practices. (It still has not been determined if *keiretsu* style economic behavior can be addressed through the GATT dispute-resolution process or not. If it cannot, then the options are to include it in a future round of GATT talks—which may take a decade or more and may still be rejected as a topic for discussion—or to engage in bilateral talks.)

In general, U.S. strategy has sought to use the bilateral talks to define a common set of rules. The alternative, and one that has been used on occasion, is to define a particular outcome. For example, the U.S.-Japan Semiconductor Trade Agreement, signed in 1986, included an outcome goal of raising the foreign share of the Japanese semiconductor market to 20 percent within five years. In theory, the preference for rules over outcomes is justified because it leaves market mechanisms in place. By contrast, the specification of outcomes replaces market-based decision making with some form of administrative guidance in which market shares are allocated artificially.

Bilateral negotiations in which objective outcomes are specified have been vigorously attacked and consistently resisted by the Japanese since their experience with the Semiconductor Trade Agreement. They have labeled efforts to impose numerically based outcome targets as "managed trade." A recent example of the Japanese distaste for numerical targets occurred in 1995 when the United States announced that it would impose tariffs of 100 percent on imports of Japanese luxury autos. One of the main stumbling blocks for negotiators was over the issue of numerical targets. The United States wanted a guarantee that Japanese auto manufacturers would increase their purchase of U.S.-made parts by $9 billion, while the Japanese preferred to discuss market-access rules. In the end, both sides seemed to get what they wanted, since theUnited States announced a dollar amount by which Japanese purchases would increase, and the Japanese announced that all numbers were outside the agreement. What happens when each side claims the other has failed to honor its commitment is anybody's guess.

Numerical targets, or outcomes-based negotiations, may be necessary in cases where there is no way to effectively monitor compliance with an agreed-upon set of rules, or where a country may comply with the letter of a rule but act contrary to its spirit. It is relatively easy for nations to render rules ineffective through bureaucratic stalling or sudden implementation of previously unknown rules or through a number of other tactics. In the U.S.-Japanese case, rules have been interpreted differently by each side as a result of language and cultural differences. In several cases (wood and paper products, telecommunications, and construction, to name three), the United States has argued that the rules laid forth in negotiations have not been enforced in Japan, while Japan has cited an entirely different interpretation of the rules. As a consequence, U.S. policy has shifted toward greater preference for numerical targets as a means of verifying compliance with rules. To repeat an earlier point, however, a negotiated outcome is not an optimal economic policy, since there is no way to predict what outcomes will occur in an open-trading regime. For example, when changes in Japanese rules governing the introduction of new drugs opened their market to greater foreign competition, U.S. exports did not increase, although European exports to Japan did. In the official (i.e., governmental) U.S. view, however, numerical targets are often necessary to insure compliance with the rules.

A second development in the resolution of the trade conflict was foreshadowed in the SII, which formally recognized the need to discuss issues of deeper integration, such as competition policy. Although the SII was too broad to be effective, it did serve the purpose of opening the door to negotiations on these deeper issues. The current effort, launched in 1993, is called the "Framework for a New Economic Partnership." The Framework talks encompass a wide assortment of issues, including problems related to government procurement, competition policy, buyer-supplier relationships (e.g., vertical foreclosure), restrictions on foreign investment in Japan, and economic harmonization of product standards and certification requirements.

It would be unrealistic to point to these talks as a panacea or solution to the trade conflict. Nevertheless, incremental change in a number of these areas is likely to occur. Over the long run, the slow cumulative effect of individually small changes will move the United States and Japan further toward a resolution of their conflict than any alternative strategy. Sector-specific approaches will also continue to be tried (in part because U.S. law and U.S. sentiment both require it), and while they may or may not work, depending on the sector, they almost certainly will not get rid of the underlying causes of the conflict.

Conclusion

The spectacular rise of Japan and the highly visible presence of Japanese consumer goods in the U.S. economy sometimes encourage a sense of paranoia in America. Although this sentiment and the tensions it creates are absent at the moment, due to the health of the U.S. economy and the weakness of the Japanese, it is certain that they will return in the not distant future. When these tensions are blended with a few anecdotes about *keiretsu* or the efforts of Japanese bureaucrats to keep their markets closed with phony safety standards, it almost seems that U.S.-Japan trade is harmful to the U.S. economy. Two points on this score are essential to keep in mind. First, whatever competitiveness problems U.S. firms experience, they are largely the result of self-inflicted wounds: lack of investment, lack of foresight, complacency, and bad management. Second, U.S.-Japan trade is a mutually advantageous relationship. Americans have benefited from the tough competition in the auto industry (our cars are better, as a result), the high-quality consumer electronics, the cheaper semiconductors, and innovative products like Sony Walkmans.

It is no coincidence that the U.S.-Japan trade conflict intensified in the post–Cold War period. In part, the reason stems from a change in the tactics adopted by the Clinton administration, but it also reflects a bipartisan U.S. view that it is less important for the United States to follow policies that help to maintain Japan's prosperity or that minimize U.S.-Japanese conflict as one part of a strategy for containing communism. Nevertheless, no matter how confrontational trade relations become, it is important to keep the conflict in perspective. Japan and the United States are allies that share a commitment to democratic values. Both nations benefit from their economic relationship, and trade and investment will undoubtedly grow. Trade conflicts, as serious as they might be, are a far cry from more overt forms of conflict, such as military confrontations.

Over the long run, perhaps the core issue in the conflict is how Japan can fit itself into an open-world trading system. Since World War II, the Japanese economy has been more highly regulated than many other industrial economies, and while competition, investment, and industrial support policies have shared features with the policies of other nations, they also contain features unique to Japan. The transition toward greater harmonization between Japanese, U.S., and European policies is difficult and inevitably entails conflict and compromise. In this regard, the lessons of the 1920s, when the United States emerged as the world's leading economic and military power, are instructive. During that period, the failure of the United States to define a role of greater world leadership for itself ultimately proved harmful to all nations. The change in Japan's relative world standing is not quite as dramatic, but the world costs of Japanese failure to fit its policies into a more open and integrated world economy would be substantial. For this reason, it is in the interests of all nations to look for mutually agreeable solutions to the U.S.-Japan trade conflict.

▲ Traditionalists view Japan's economy as essentially the same as the economies of other industrialized nations. Revisionists view it as essentially different, particularly with respect to business-government relations, the lack of antitrust enforcement, and the lack of transparency in policy making.

▲ Japanese *keiretsu* are business groups of independent firms. Firms in a *keiretsu* enjoy close ties, including the sharing of strategic plans, sensitive financial data, and product and market information. *Keiretsu* probably reduce the costs of information and may reduce imports and foreign investment in Japan. In addition, they eliminate the market for corporate governance.

▲ Prices in Japan are consistently higher than prices elsewhere, even for the same items and even for items produced in Japan. Non-Japanese view this as evidence that policies are designed to boost exports and discourage imports by keeping consumption low.

▲ U.S.-Japan trade talks have evolved through several stages, beginning with the Plaza and Louvre exchange rate management agreements in the mid-1980s. The United States began Market Oriented Sector Specific (MOSS) talks to eliminate trade barriers on a case-by-case basis and has continued this approach since the late 1980s. The Structural Impediments Initiative (SII) sought to eliminate structural barriers to trade, but the lack of specific and obtainable objectives made this approach ineffective.

Vocabulary

cross-ownership	Plaza Accord
keiretsu	Structural Impediments Initiative
Louvre Agreement	transaction costs
managed trade	vertical foreclosure
Market Oriented Sector Specific (MOSS) talks	

Study Questions

1. Is Japan's economy organized differently from that of the U.S.? Make two arguments, one taking the *yes* side and the other taking the *no* side.

2. Why cannot objective indicators, such as measures of imports or intraindustry trade, settle the question about the openness of the Japanese economy?

3. What are *keiretsu* and are they important to trade and investment patterns?

4. How does the Japanese distribution system enter the debate over Japanese trade and investment practices?

5. What are the U.S. complaints about Japanese competition policies? If valid, how might they be important in determining Japan's trade pattern?

6. What are the Japanese complaints about U.S. policies? If valid, how might they be important in determining the U.S.-Japan trade pattern?

7. Give specific examples and state the purpose of each of the following approaches to resolving trade tensions between the U.S. and Japan:

   sector specific talks
   structural talks
   managed trade
   exchange rate policy

Suggested Reading

Bergsten, C. Fred, and Marcus Noland. *Reconcilable Differences? United States-Japan Economic Conflict.* Washington, DC: Institute for International Economics, 1993.

Krugman, Paul. "Japan," in *The Age of Diminished Expectations.* Cambridge, MA: The MIT Press, 1994.

Lawrence, Robert Z. "Japan's Different Trade Regime: An Analysis with Particular Reference to *Keiretsu*," *Journal of Economic Perspectives,* Vol. 7, No. 3, Summer 1993.

Saxonhouse, Gary R. "What Does Japanese Trade Structure Tell Us About Japanese Trade Policy?" *Journal of Economic Perspectives,* Vol. 7, No. 3, Summer 1993.

Sazanami, Yoko, Shujiro Urata, and Hiroki Kawai. *Measuring the Costs of Protection in Japan.* Washington, DC: Institute for International Economics, 1995.

Tyson, Laura D'Andrea. *Who's Bashing Whom? Trade Conflict in High-Technology Industries.* Washington, DC: Institute for International Economics, 1992.

van Wolferen, Karel. *The Enigma of Japanese Power.* New York: Vintage Books, 1990.

CHAPTER 12

ECONOMIC INTEGRATION IN NORTH AMERICA

Introduction

After several years of negotiations, the North American Free Trade Agreement (NAFTA) began its official life on January 1, 1994. In Mexico, NAFTA was greeted by a group of armed rebels that seized several towns in the southern state of Chiapas. In the United States, NAFTA was ratified by Congress after a close and bitter debate in which both the proponents and opponents had exaggerated (and misread) the likely impacts. The debate in Canada was not nearly so dramatic, but then Canadians had just gone through a similarly divisive struggle over the Canadian-United States Trade Agreement (CUSTA) that began in 1989, and Canadian commerce with Mexico is relatively small.

For many U.S. economists, it seemed odd that a relatively dry and straightforward agreement should turn into one of the most contentious issues of the 1990s. After all, U.S. barriers to Mexican imports were already low; if Mexico decided to lower its barriers to U.S. and Canadian products, then what could possibly be controversial? Plenty, as it turns out, and as this chapter explores.

Economic and Demographic Characteristics of North America

Before we turn to the history and controversy over NAFTA, it is useful to have an idea of the size of the combined North American market. Table 12.1 shows population and GNP comparisons that are measured in two different ways. By any measure, the combined market is enormous. In 1997, it had approximately 12 million more people than the fifteen members of the European Union, and more than 180 million more than Mercosur, the South American customs union of Brazil, Argentina, Paraguay, and Uruguay.

International income comparisons are more complicated than population comparisons. The third column in the table is one (typical) way to make comparisons. Mexican and Canadian incomes are converted to U.S. dollars, using the average exchange rate over the entire year. This method shows that the average Canadian income is about 68 percent of the United States', and the average Mexican income is around 14 percent. The first problem with this comparison is that regardless of

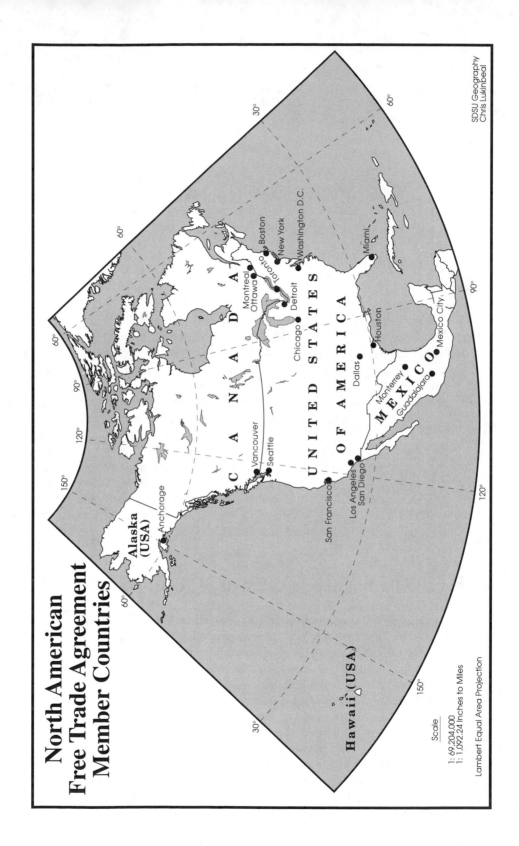

North American
Free Trade Agreement
Member Countries

C A N A D A

UNITED STATES

OF AMERICA

M E X I C O

Alaska
(USA)

Hawaii (USA)

Anchorage

Seattle
Vancouver
San Francisco
Los Angeles
San Diego
Dallas
Houston
Monterrey
Guadalajara
Mexico City
Chicago
Detroit
Toronto
Montreal
Ottawa
Boston
New York
Washington D.C.
Miami

30°
60°
60°
90°
120°
150°
60°
30°
60°
90°
120°
150°

Scale

1: 69,204,000
1: 1,092.24 Inches to Miles

Lambert Equal Area Projection

SDSU Geography
Chris Lukinbeal

changes in either nation's output, fluctuations in the exchange rate can lead to dramatically different values for Mexican or Canadian GNP when measured in dollar terms. A second problem is that real prices vary across countries. Haircuts, restaurant meals, and maid services, to name just a few, cost far less in real terms in Mexico than in the United States. As a consequence, the average annual income in Mexico of $4166 buys more goods and services than a similar income would in the United States.

The fourth column shows income comparisons in **purchasing power parity** terms. Purchasing power parity comparisons make adjustments for differences in prices and exchange rates. It can be interpreted as the U.S. dollar value of the real quantity of goods and services that a typical Mexican income buys. In other words, GNP per person in Mexico is enough income to buy goods and services that would cost $7157 in the United States. However, if a Mexican citizen took that amount of pesos, converted them to dollars, and brought them to the United States, they would only get $4166 worth of goods and services.

Measurements of GNP per capita at market exchange rates and at purchasing power parity prices both convey important information. Market exchange rate comparisons tell what a nation can buy externally (outside the nation), while purchasing power parity prices tell what it can buy internally (inside the nation). As an exporter, I would be more interested in the former, but as someone interested in knowing how Mexico's living standards compare to those of the United States, I would want to know the latter.

Two more points about Table 12.1 are worth considering. First, even though Mexico is a developing country, the NAFTA market is very rich. Few countries have a higher GDP per capita than the weighted average of Canada, Mexico, and the United States, and total GDP at market exchange rates is over $9 *trillion*. Second, NAFTA combines nations that are at very different levels of economic development. Even though Mexico is one of the wealthiest nations in Latin America, the gap between its per capita income and the United States' adds a layer of political pressure to NAFTA due to issues such as immigration, environmental enforcement, and the movement of low-wage industries, among others. On the other hand, the

---

TABLE 12.1 Population and GDP for the NAFTA Countries, 1997

	Population (Millions)	GDP, (Billions of U.S. Dollars)	GDP per person (U.S. Dollars)	GDP per Person, PPP (U.S. Dollars)*
Canada	30.3	617.6	20,383	23,631
Mexico	96.6	402.5	4,166	7,157
United States	267.9	8,083.4	30,173	30,173
Total	394.8	9,147.9		

*Author's calculations.
Sources: IMF, *International Financial Statistics Yearbook, 1997,* Washington, D.C., 1997; INEGI, "Banco de Información Económica INEGI," (Available: http://www.inegi.gob.mx/); Statistics Canada, "Canadian Statistics" (available: http://www.statcan.ca/start.html/).

opportunity for growth in Mexico is enormous. A rapidly growing economy of 96 million people could have a significant long-run effect on U.S. and Canadian markets.

Table 12.2 shows the importance of trade between each pair of countries. With or without NAFTA, the trade between each of the three pairs of countries is an important share of each nation's overall trade, with the exception of Canada-Mexico. Both Canada's and Mexico's trade with the United States is far greater than their trade with any other country; in the United States, Canada is the number one trading partner, and Mexico is number three, after Japan. In fact, the United States and Canada trade more than any other pair of countries in the world.

Mexico and Canada both depend on trade more than the United States does. Recall that one way to measure how much a country depends on trade is to calculate its openness ratio ((Exports + Imports) / GDP). Using this measure, 1996 trade was equal to nearly 74 percent of Canada's GDP, 62 percent of Mexico's GDP, and 24 percent of the United States' GDP. These numbers reflect the general proposition that the smaller a nation is, the more it must trade in order to achieve a given level of prosperity. Small markets are less able to realize the economies of scale that come from producing in large volume, and they cannot produce the variety of products that large markets can. Through trade, they can overcome the limitations of size. The numbers also indicate the importance of trade to Canada and its much smaller role in the U.S. economy. The relative importance of trade is a good indicator of Canada's interest (and also Mexico's) in maintaining unobstructed access to the U.S. market and in negotiating lower trade barriers.

The Canada-U.S. Trade Relationship

The United States and Canada trade more than any other two countries in the world. In 1997, for example, the combined value of U.S. exports to Canada and imports from Canada was $359 *billion* (U.S.). Figure 12.1 illustrates the constant upward trend in US-Canada trade. On average, from 1963 to 1997, Canadian exports to the United States have increased 12 percent per year, while U.S. exports to

TABLE 12.2 Merchandise Trade of the NAFTA Countries, 1996 (Millions of U.S. Dollars)				
		Exports by:		
	Canada	Mexico	United States	World
Imports by:				
Canada	——	4,281	114,626	170,038
Mexico	855	——	56,761	89,464
United States	164,761	74,111	——	817,785
World	200,146	95,991	622,945	——

Source: IMF, *Direction of Trade Statistics Yearbook, 1997,* Washington D.C., 1997.

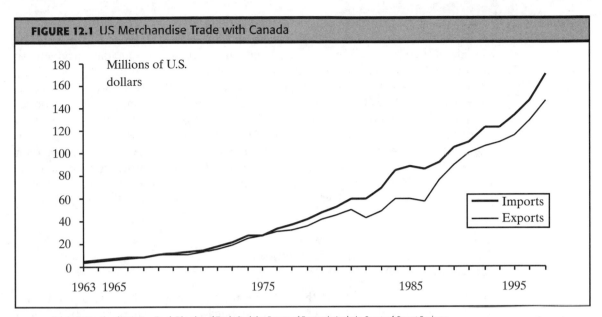

FIGURE 12.1 US Merchandise Trade with Canada

Source: International Monetary Fund, *Direction of Trade Statistics;* Bureau of Economic Analysis, *Survey of Curent Business.*

Canada have grown 11 percent per year. Since 1963, the real values of both annual exports and annual imports have increased more than sixfold, a remarkable achievement considering that real GDP during the same period grew less than threefold. In addition to the world's largest trade relationship, the United States' political and military relationship to Canada is closer than with any other nation. Canadian defense firms, for example, may bid on U.S. defense contracts as if they were U.S. firms.

Given the history of close ties and the importance of trade, it is not surprising that the United States and Canada would join together to form a free-trade area and that they would do so before NAFTA was created. The Canadian-United States Trade Agreement, or CUSTA, began life on January 1, 1989, exactly five years before NAFTA. In many respects, it set the stage for the NAFTA by setting a framework for beginning negotiations. Even CUSTA, however, was not the first important trade agreement between Canada and the United States. Twenty-four years before the implementation of CUSTA, in 1965, Canada and the United States implemented an agreement on trade and investment in automotive products, the single largest component of U.S.-Canadian trade.

The Auto Pact of 1965

Although the Auto Pact agreement was limited to trade in automotive products, it is a very successful example of gains from trade. By removing barriers to trade, the Pact permitted the big three Detroit automakers (General Motors, Ford, and Chrysler) to produce for a single, combined market. Prior to the agreement, Canadian content laws required that cars sold in Canada had to be mostly produced there as well. The relatively small market size caused factories in Canada to lose some of the economies of scale of their American counterparts, and, not surprisingly, Canada's productivity in automotive products was around 30 percent below the U.S. level.

With the coming of free trade in cars and car parts, Detroit automakers (who were also Canadian automakers) were able to consolidate some types of production in Canada and other types in the United States, and both locations began to produce for both markets. The impact on trade was stunning. Between 1963, when firms began to anticipate an opening of Canada-U.S. auto trade, and 1969, Canadian exports to the United States grew 169 percent, while U.S. exports to Canada grew 114 percent. Most of the trade growth was in automotive products, and even today, they remain the single largest component of trade between the United States and Canada.

The Canadian-U.S. Trade Agreement (CUSTA) of 1989

From the Canadian viewpoint, the 1980s brought to the foreground two trends that had to be addressed. First the United States began to be a less reliable trade partner. The problem was the United States' expanded use of countervailing and antidumping duties, and "voluntary" export restrictions that were imposed on a number of U.S. imports. In addition, U.S. rhetoric indicated a greater willingness to use these unilateral measures as a means of gaining political support from declining U.S. industries. Although VERs and antidumping and countervailing duties did not directly affect an important share of U.S.-Canadian trade, the specter of the United States turning increasingly protectionist was a problem for Canada. Their dependence on international trade means that protectionism in the United States is a direct threat to their standard of living.

The second problem facing Canada in the 1980s was the need to restructure many of its firms and industries in order to keep them competitive in a more global environment. Many observers inside Canada felt that Asian manufacturing was beginning to exert strong competitive pressures on Canadian firms. Without significant modernization and rebuilding, Canadian firms were likely to lose markets at home and abroad.

Creating a free trade agreement with the U.S. was one solution to the problem of growing U.S. protectionism and increasing Asian competitiveness in manufacturing industries. This solution locks the United States into an international agreement requiring it to keep its market open and, at the same time, puts pressure on Canadian manufacturers to make the changes necessary to stay competitive. The Canadian-United States Free Trade Agreement was implemented in 1989 after several years of negotiations.

The impacts of CUSTA were more or less as expected. Between 1987 and 1994, Canadian exports to the United States grew 87 percent, while U.S. exports to Canada grew 91 percent. In percentage terms, this growth is not quite as rapid as the period before and after the implementation of the Auto Pact, but given that trade was already at a high level in 1987, a near doubling of the trade flow represents an enormous volume of trade. Canada's exports to the United States grew by $62 billion, and the United States' exports to Canada grew by $75 billion.

The debate over U.S.-Canadian free trade was low key and dispassionate in the United States. In Canada, however, a heated public discussion erupted when it was announced that the United States and Canada were negotiating an agreement. The opponents of the trade agreement feared that (1) Canada might not be able to compete with U.S. firms, which had the advantages of economies of scale; (2) expanded

CASE STUDY

Quebec Secession

Will Quebec secede from Canada and become an independent nation?

This is the question many Canadians are asking themselves. Quebecers have voted twice, each time rejecting the idea of Quebec sovereignty, but they will vote again, and polls indicate the yes and no votes are close. The first vote was in 1980, and separation was rejected 60–40. The second vote was in 1995, and the outcome was the same, but this time the "no" majority won by the narrow margin of 50.6 to 49.4. According to polls that were taken in late 1995, there is a growing feeling among Canadians that a breakup is inevitable.

Canada is made up of ten provinces and two territories (which will split into three territories in 1999). The territories are in the far north and are very sparsely populated, while the two provinces of Quebec and Ontario are the most populous. Conceptually, Canadians are asking themselves if their nation is a confederation of ten equal provinces as the constitution indicates or if in fact it is a union of two nations—French- and English-speaking North Americans. Naturally, most citizens outside Quebec conceptualize the country in the first way, while many Quebecers see it in the second.

Unlike the recent breakups of Czechoslovakia, Yugoslavia, and the Soviet Union, Canada's is happening under democratic conditions. Politicians inside Quebec campaign on the issue, referendums are set, and people vote. To date, the vote has been to stay within the Canadian confederation, but the failure of the two votes to resolve the deeper issues of French Canadian identity within the sea of English-speaking Canada has led to calls for a new referendum. As Jacques Parizeau, the premier (governor) of Quebec, said before the 1995 vote, "A 'yes' vote means 'yes', while a 'no' vote means 'try again.'"

How would Quebec fare as an independent nation? This is the question that many people have been asking as they try to anticipate the economic costs and benefits of independence. Are they economically viable? Would they be allowed to join NAFTA and the WTO?

The issue of viability is fairly certain: the province has seven million people, more than many other small nations, and it is well endowed with natural resources. Many of the leading industries are resource based—for example, aluminum production, dairy and poultry, paper and paper products, and hydroelectric power. Quebec has first-world public infrastructure, and its citizens

Case Study continues

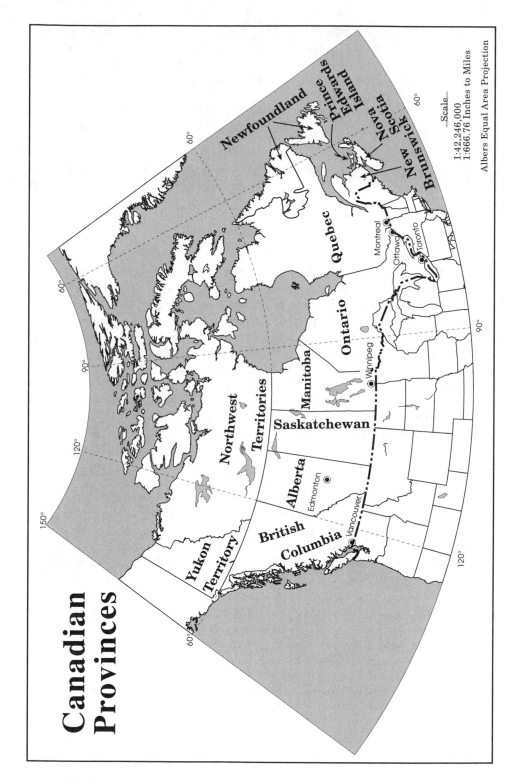

Canadian Provinces

Yukon Territory

British Columbia

Vancouver

Alberta

Edmonton

Northwest Territories

Saskatchewan

Manitoba

Winnipeg

Ontario

Quebec

Newfoundland

Prince Edward Island

Nova Scotia

New Brunswick

Montreal

Ottawa

Toronto

60°

90°

120°

150°

60°

90°

120°

60°

Scale
1:42,246,000
1:666.76 Inches to Miles

Albers Equal Area Projection

are well educated. All the ingredients exist for a high-income nation, and in the long run, there is no question that the province would be an economically viable nation.

The short run is a different matter, however. There is substantial uncertainty about the kinds of investment policies, tax policies, commercial policies, and so forth that a new government would put into place. Uncertainty implies risk, and risk leads to capital flight. Prior to the October 1995 referendum, several leading firms announced that they would leave the province in the event of a yes vote; meanwhile, there is a widespread belief that firms have been quietly shifting the key elements of their operations out of the province. The exodus of firms and people that choose to stay Canadian citizens could radically alter the current economy. No one can say how important these movements might be because, in part, they will depend on the outcome of negotiations that will happen between Canada and Quebec.

Negotiating the terms of a breakup will be complicated, but it is in everyone's interest to negotiate with good will. (The same could be said about the breakup of a marriage, but many divorces still turn out to be very hostile negotiations.) Among the more pressing issues are the division of the federal debt, the division of federal assets, the treatment of individuals and groups that do not want to leave Canada, Canada's access to the Atlantic provinces, and Quebec's accession to international organizations such as the WTO, GATT, NAFTA, and NATO.

The provincial governments of Quebec have repeatedly stated that they will take responsibility for a fair share of the federal debt. The question everyone asks, however, is what is a fair share? Different groups have different estimates, and this will undoubtedly be a major subject of any future negotiations. Quebec has also claimed a right to all federal assets within the province, including military equipment. The federal government is reluctant to agree to this, particularly in the case of advanced military technology such as fighter aircraft.

Before the October 1995 referendum, two of Quebec's aboriginal groups, the Cree and the Inuit, voted nearly unanimously (95 percent) to stay in Canada. While Native Americans are only approximately 2 percent of the province's population, they claim vast stretches of the province's land. The Cree have stated that they will secede from Quebec if the province secedes from Canada, but the provincial governments of Quebec have been adamant that their boundaries will not change in the event that they split from Canada. If any issue has the potential to lead to violence, this is probably it.

A similar issue concerns people who live outside Quebec but work in the province and those who live in Quebec but work in Ontario. Will these people (many of whom are federal government workers) have to move?

If Quebec eventually votes for independence, it will leave the Atlantic provinces (New Brunswick, Nova Scotia, Prince Edward Island, and Newfoundland) geographically isolated from the rest of the country. Quebec will control both sides of the St. Lawrence Seaway, and Canada's railroads and highways run through Quebec. Would there be tariffs on Canadian shipments

Case Study continues

Case Study continued

> to the Atlantic provinces? Would Quebec charge fees for the use of "their" transportation lanes. Again, this issue has an uncertain outcome and would depend on future negotiations.
>
> Until Canada and Quebec have fully agreed on the terms of separation, no country or international organization will be able to negotiate with Quebec. To do so would violate international laws concerning interference with a sovereign nation's internal affairs. Consequently, Quebec's membership in the various international organizations and its trade relations with other nations must wait to be negotiated.
>
> For further reading: *Dividing the House: Planning for a Canada Without Quebec,* by Alan Freeman and Patrick Grady, Toronto: Harper Collins, 1995.; and *Oh Canada! Oh Quebec!,* by Mordecai Richler, New York: Alfred A. Knopf, 1992.

trade might force Canada to jettison many of its social programs; and (3) perhaps the deepest concern, Canadian culture might come to be dominated by U.S. news, information, arts, and entertainment industries.

The issue of Canadian competitiveness is largely an issue of the need to gain economies of scale and to increase productivity through organizational or technological changes within firms. This issue is at the core of the concept of comparative advantage and the changes that must be made in order to capture the gains from trade. For the most part, the real issue for a high-income, industrialized country such as Canada is the length of time over which the changes can be expected to occur, and not whether firms are capable of competing.

The Canadian opponents of CUSTA also argued that it would erode Canada's social programs. For many citizens, universal health care coverage and income maintenance programs are part of the national identity and features that make Canada unlike the United States. The opponents of CUSTA argued that the intensification of competition with the United States would lead to the abandonment of many of these programs until Canada's social policies would be the same as the United States'. The reason given for the predicted cuts in social programs was to reduce business taxes in order to make Canadian firms more competitive. Given that taxes are but one component of business costs and that in some cases there are offsetting reductions in cost elsewhere, it is not at all certain what the final impact of free trade will be on Canadian social programs. In the case of health care, for example, it makes more sense to argue that the United States' system is a competitive disadvantage, since it raises the cost of hiring workers when they must be provided with health care benefits by their employer. In Canada, by contrast, health care is a general societal right and is paid for out of general government revenues and individual taxes. A complicating factor for examining the impact of free trade on social spending is that by the mid-1990s, Canada's federal and provincial deficits had grown to the point where governments were forced to scale back some social programs. The cuts are a result of large and unsustainable deficits at both the provincial and federal levels and are not caused by increased trade.

The final, and most contentious, issue from the Canadian point of view is the possibility of U.S. cultural domination. A very wide spectrum of opinion, including both opponents and proponents of expanded free trade, argue that the combination of Canada's smaller population and its proximity to the United States will destroy its national identity if it allows completely free trade in the cultural industries. These industries include music in all of its venues, radio, television, newspapers, book publishing, magazines, drama, cinema, painting, and so forth. Under the rules of CUSTA, Canada is allowed to protect its national identity by imposing quantitative restrictions on imports of "cultural products." In most cases, the rules allow Canada to impose domestic content requirements on the culture industry; for example, television, radio, and theater. The content requirements make it illegal for a radio station, for example, to program twenty-four hours a day of U.S.-origin music. Cable TV companies give preferences to Canadian-based TV networks, and there are national rules that favor Canadian theater companies, artists, and so on across the cultural spectrum.

Recent Mexican Economic History

While Canada's interests in CUSTA were relatively straightforward, Mexico's interests in signing NAFTA were more complex. Like Canada, Mexico wanted to guarantee its access to the U.S. market; unlike Canada, however, Mexico needed to fundamentally alter its economic strategy. The decision to seek closer economic ties to the United States was one of many major policy changes that Mexico made between the late 1980s and early 1990s. By the time the agreement was ratified in 1993, Mexico had completely abandoned the economic policies it had followed since the end of World War II.

Import Substitution Industrialization (ISI)

Until the mid-1980s, Mexico's economic policy and development strategy was inward rather than outward oriented. Inward orientation meant that Mexico favored self-sufficiency over trade and that domestic production was used to replace imported goods. The name for this policy is **import substitution industrialization**, or **ISI**. ISI was the dominant economic strategy throughout Latin America from World War II until the 1980s (see Chapter 14).

> ***Import substitution industrialization (ISI).*** *Import substitution industrialization is an economic development strategy that emphasizes the domestic production of goods that substitute for imports. ISI policies decrease both imports and exports.*

ISI policies are industrial policies that target the development of manufacturing sectors that rely heavily on imported goods. Supporters of ISI theorized that a country should be able to begin by producing simple consumer nondurables such as toys, clothing, food products (e.g., beverages, canned goods) and simpler consumer durables, such as furniture. Gradually, the focus of industrial targeting would shift to include more complex consumer goods (appliances and autos) and intermediate industrial goods (pumps, generators, basic metals). In the third stage, complex industrial goods would be produced (chemicals, electronic equipment, machine tools).

From 1950 to 1973, Mexico's GDP per capita grew at the rate of 3.1 percent per year when measured in purchasing power parity terms. By comparison, Canadian and American growth rates over the same period, and measured in the same way, were 2.9 percent and 2.2 percent, respectively. Mexico's growth was also favorable when compared to Asia, Europe, and the rest of Latin American. By the criteria of growth in GDP per capita, ISI policies were relatively successful. In addition, the policies helped the structure of the Mexican economy shift toward greater industrial production. Between 1950 and 1980, industry rose from producing 21.5 percent to 29.4 percent of GDP.

Although ISI policies seem to have succeeded in stimulating GDP growth and a shift toward industry, they also created a number of long-term problems in Mexico and elsewhere. Most seriously, ISI policies reduced the flexibility of the economy and hurt its ability to handle changing world conditions. Equally serious was the fact that ISI created conditions that fostered corruption. Consequently, it is an open debate whether these policies were optimal and whether they could have continued indefinitely. We will take up these issues in more detail in Chapter 14, when we look at Latin American reforms.

In the 1980s, the nations of Latin America began to abandon the inward-oriented, antitrade policies of the 1950s, 1960s, and 1970s. In most cases, the shift in economic policy favored stronger markets, more trade, and a reduced role for industrial policies. In many cases, the changes were triggered by the inability of the nations to continue to make payments on the enormous debt that had been accumulated in the 1970s and early 1980s. Mexico's role in the historic shift of Latin American policies was to be a leader, both in the sudden appearance of a severe debt crisis and in the shift of its policies away from ISI.

The Onset of the Debt Crisis of 1982

When Lopez Portillo became president of Mexico in 1976, he entered office with a number of constraints. Mexico was operating under an International Monetary Fund (IMF) stabilization program that began in 1976 during his predecessor's (Luis Echeverría) term in office. In 1976, Mexico was a fairly typical case of a government that had borrowed in world financial markets and then found that it could not keep up with its commitments. In order to receive assistance from the IMF and other lenders, the Mexican government was required to make substantial cuts in expenditures and programs. Consequently, during Portillo's first year in office, he was forced to continue the program of austerity and budget cuts.

By 1978, little more than a year after Portillo's election, Mexico's rich reserves of petroleum were coming into production, and the budget crisis was solved. In 1979, the second world oil shortage began; oil prices rose dramatically, bringing up government revenues as well. (Pemex, or Petroleos Mexicano, is owned by the Mexican government and has a monopoly on oil exploration, development, and sales.)

Economic forecasters around the world were predicting that crude oil prices were headed ever upward and that by the year 2000 they could easily reach $100 per barrel. In 1978, the Portillo administration responded to the high and rising oil prices by pouring money into economic and social programs in an attempt to restart the economy. Portillo declared that the era of scarcity was over and that the problem for Mexico was to "manage the abundance." The ambitious expenditure and investment programs required the government to seek capital from international financial markets because the domestic level of savings was insufficient, despite the high oil revenues. The oil reserves caused Mexico's credit worthiness to be solid, however, as future oil sales were almost a guarantee that debt could be repaid. By 1982, the deficit of the federal government reached 14.1 percent of the GDP, an extraordinarily high level.

It should be noted that people and economies around the world acted as if the oil shortage and high prices were a permanent feature of the world economy. In retrospect, it is easy to understand their mistake: new oil takes time to discover and to come into production, and it takes time for businesses to find new, less oil-intensive equipment and to look for oil substitutes. Most individuals cannot immediately buy more fuel-efficient cars or adjust their demands for heating oil. Over time, however, all these changes will take place in response to an increase in oil prices.

In 1981, the situation for Mexico began to unravel. First, world oil prices started to fall. At the time, few people inside or outside Mexico believed that it was the beginning of a trend. By 1982, however, it was apparent that oil prices were not going to stay high and that Mexico's credit worthiness was under serious pressure. At the same time, a second problem was beginning to bedevil Mexico's finances. The Mexican government's international debt was mostly from commercial banks and was at variable interest rates. In 1979, the U.S. Federal Reserve began to fight inflation in the United States with monetary policies that caused interest rates to reach extraordinarily high levels. Each upward tick of U.S. and world interest rates caused a significant increase in the interest charges on Mexico's debt, so that at precisely the same time that oil revenues were falling, Mexico was required to pay more on its debt.

There was a certain amount of reluctance on the part of the U.S. government and international lenders to acknowledge the severity of the problem as it developed through 1982. By August of 1982, however, it was unavoidable. Mexico's holdings of dollars and other international reserves had fallen below what they needed in order to make repayment possible. On August 12, 1982, the government announced that it was temporarily suspending repayment of the principal it owed. The "debt crisis" had begun.

The Lost Decade: 1980s

The 1980s have become known as the **Lost Decade**, because GDP growth was nearly nonexistent during that time. Foreign capital stopped flowing into the country, credit became scarce, and investment declined. These factors, along with the budget cuts, peso devaluations, and debt repayment, brought on a severe recession. The debt crisis of 1982 was a more severe repeat of the crisis of 1976. At bottom, both crises were the result of macroeconomic mismanagement, and both stemmed from levels of government expenditure that required significant foreign borrowing. When the government's capacity to make payment on its debts declined, the crises began.

In response to the 1982 crisis, Mexico worked out an agreement with the U.S. government, a cartel of U.S. banks, and the International Monetary Fund. In essence, Mexico agreed to significant budget cuts and peso devaluations. The latter were to insure that the country's exports were sufficient to earn the foreign revenue it needed in order to continue to repay what it had borrowed. In return, Mexico's debt repayment was restructured, and a small amount of new loans were made for the purposes of helping with temporary liquidity shortfalls. A downside to the devaluations of the peso was that they caused inflation. Imported goods became more expensive, and Mexican producers that relied on imported parts or capital equipment were forced to raise prices in order to cover their higher costs. In addition, producers that directly competed with imports could raise their prices without losing sales, since the imported goods had gone up in price.

Partly as a result of the inflation, partly due to the budget cuts, the real incomes of the middle class fell dramatically. The wage data are striking: between 1983 and 1988, real wages fell by 40 to 50 percent. Overall, inflation adjusted per capita GDP fell by about 15 percent between 1982 and 1986. (In the United States, a "normal" recession causes a decline in per capita GDP of 1 to 3 percent.) In addition, as the government sought to reduce its expenditures, spending on health care and education was cut. The poor were also hurt by the inflation and budget cuts, but because much of their income is nonwage and in the form of the product of subsistence farms, their incomes probably suffered less in percentage terms.

Structural Reforms in the Mexican Economy

There were three main lessons from the debt crisis of 1982. First, it was clear that Mexico's management of its macroeconomy had to change. Both the 1976 and 1982 crises had resulted in large part from poor handling of the macroeconomy, and the consequences had been disastrous. Second, and related to the first point, the government could no longer use public expenditures as a means for starting economic growth. Third, it was necessary to give markets a much larger role (and state intervention a smaller role) in order to attract the capital needed for investment and growth.

In 1982, President Miguel De la Madrid was elected, and he began the process of reducing the economic role of the state. Conditions were so bad in the aftermath of the 1982 crisis, however, that little progress was made. Nevertheless, trade barriers slowly began to diminish (especially after 1985), and the budget deficit was eventually reduced. By the end of his presidency in late 1988, the policies were in place to bring inflation under control.

President Carlos Salinas entered office in December 1988. Growth had been poor throughout much of the decade, but Salinas understood the impossibility of using government expenditures to stimulate a recovery. The additional problem he faced was that the private sector lacked confidence in the economy and the government, and was hesitant to invest. His key tasks, as he saw it, were to reduce the costs of servicing Mexico's international debt, to create a climate in which Mexicans would bring home the financial capital they had sent abroad during the turmoil of the 1980s, and to attract foreign capital for investment in Mexico.

CASE STUDY

Mexico's Export Processing Industry

A large share of the trade between the United States and Mexico is intrafirm (25 to 35 percent) and occurs in the context of Mexico's special export processing sector. Mexico began its program in 1965, when the government initiated the Border Industrialization Program (BIP) with its Decree for the Development and Operation of the Maquiladora Export Industry. The primary purpose of the plan was to generate employment along its northern border, where large numbers of workers had suddenly become unemployed due to the termination of the agricultural guest worker program (called the *bracero* program) in the United States.

The BIP created an **export processing zone**, or **EPZ**, in which foreign firms could set up an assembly-type operation and escape Mexican tariffs on the parts and materials they imported as long as they exported the assembled goods. In addition, U.S. tariffs on imports from the EPZ were usually limited to the share of the value of the product created in Mexico. In other words, American firms such as General Motors or 3M can set up assembly operations in Mexico and pay no Mexican tariffs on the goods the assemblers bring into Mexico as long as they export the output. When the output is shipped back to the United States, they may qualify for special U.S. tariff treatment, which allows them to avoid tariffs on the share of the value that was created outside Mexico.

The firms that located in the export processing zone became known as *maquila* (mah-kee´-lah), and the industry as a whole is referred to as the *maquiladora* (mah-kee-lah-dor´-ah) industry. Although there are many areas outside the border region that qualify for free-trade status, the greatest concentrations of *maquila* are across the border from El Paso in Ciudad Juarez and across from San Diego in Tijuana.

The *maquiladora* industry grew steadily during the 1970s, and by 1980, there were 620 plants employing 120,000 workers. After the crisis of 1982, a decision was made in Mexico City to diversify exports away from oil, and greater encouragement was given to *maquiladora* operations. In addition, the depreciation of the peso and the proximity to the U.S. market made these operations more attractive to foreign investment. As a result, the period of most rapid growth began after 1983.

In mid-1998, the *maquiladora* industry employed nearly one million Mexican workers in more than 3500 firms. Their output was about one-third of total Mexican manufacturing and the source of about 44 percent of total exports. In addition, the *maquiladora* industry is the second largest earner of foreign exchange for Mexico, after oil exports. In a year in which oil prices are down (1998, for example) maquiladora exports are likely to surpass oil in value.

Non-Mexican firms are motivated to locate a branch of their production in the *maquiladora* industry by several factors in addition to tariffs. Labor costs are a primary consideration. In 1995, total compensation costs averaged $1.51

Case Study continues

versus $17.61 in United States manufacturing. The differences in labor costs indicate that much of the intrafirm trade between American firms and their subsidiaries or affiliates in the *maquiladora* industry is an example of trade based on comparative advantage and factor cost differences.

In many low-wage countries, low labor costs are more than offset by the lack of nearby suppliers and the poor condition of roads, sewer hookups, and other critical pieces of infrastructure. In the case of the *maquiladora,* most firms are close to the U.S. market, where suppliers are also located and poor road conditions are less of an aggravation. In addition, Mexico has built many full-service industrial parks that provide good infrastructure to the firms that locate in them.

For better or worse, the *maquiladora* sector is relatively unaffected by macroeconomic conditions inside Mexico. For example, during the recent recession of 1995, while the national economy was shrinking by 5 to 6 percent, total employment in the *maquiladora* industry grew by 9.4 percent. In effect, the industry responds to macroeconomic conditions inside the United States much more than it does to Mexican conditions.

One negative consequence of the industry's close ties to the United States (and, increasingly, Japan and South Korea) is that it does not stimulate local Mexican production. It is estimated that in 1996, only 2 percent of industry inputs came from Mexico. San Diego, for example, supplies nearly $2 billion worth of inputs to plants located mostly just across the border in Tijuana. The challenge for Mexico in this arrangement is that the industry has not functioned as a market for Mexican producers and consequently has had a minimal impact on Mexico's overall economic development outside of the creation of jobs for unskilled workers and the revenues it earns from its exports.

The North American Free Trade Agreement (NAFTA), signed by the United States, Canada, and Mexico, has provisions that eliminate the special tariff status of the *maquilas* on January 1, 2001. Some have feared the demise of the industry, but that seems unlikely since several spillover effects of NAFTA have provided incentives for continued investment. Most importantly, in order for a product to qualify for free-trade status under NAFTA, a significant share of its value must be produced in the United States, Canada, or Mexico. As a result, garment, electronics, and car parts manufacturers, as well as firms in other industries, have been expanding their supplier base and production facilities.

The growth of the electronics industry and the car parts industries, in particular, has begun to alter the nature of the industry from low-skilled, labor-intensive assembly to higher-skilled production. How far this trend will continue is uncertain, but it bodes well for the possibility that the industry will begin to have stronger positive effects on the Mexican national economy.

Source: United States International Trade Commission, "Production Sharing: Use of U.S. Components and Materials in Foreign Assembly Operations, 1992–1995." USITC Publication No. 3032. April 1997.

The key to Salinas's strategy was capital for investment. Without investment, there could be no growth and no modernization of Mexico's economy. Traditionally, the government had been one of the primary sources of investment capital, but that role was foreclosed by the debt crisis. In the future, Mexico would have to rely on private sources for its investment, both at home and abroad.

In order to attract domestic and foreign investment, Salinas and his advisors argued that they had to strengthen the role of markets. Investors needed to perceive that their economic fortunes would depend on the quality of the products they made and the efficiency with which they were produced and delivered. In the past, economic success or failure often depended on arbitrary government rules that changed prices and limited supplies of key goods throughout the economy.

Salinas carried forward the reforms begun under De la Madrid and added several of his own. Progress continued to be made on bringing the government budget under control. To help with this, and to demonstrate the reality of the change in Mexico's policies, Salinas began to speed up the sell-off of state-owned enterprises. In 1982, the government owned 1155 enterprises, ranging in size from the nation's largest firm, Pemex, all the way down to small retail outlets. By 1992, the number of state-owned enterprises had fallen to 217. Most significantly, Salinas announced in May 1990 that he was reprivatizing the banks.

Salinas needed to tackle the debt problem in order to reduce the outflow of Mexican savings going to pay interest and principal on debts contracted in the 1970s and 1980s. The flow of savings out of the country reduced the pool of funds available for investment inside Mexico and was one of the reasons why growth had been slow. In 1989, when the United States announced the introduction of the Brady Plan for debt relief, Salinas acted quickly to put Mexico first in line. Named after Nicholas Brady, U.S. secretary of the treasury, the goal was to address the international debt crisis throughout the developing world. (See Chapter 14 for more details.) Mexico was the first case and ultimately received a reduction in its debt of about 10 percent. Perhaps more important than the modest amount of debt relief, Mexico's participation in the Brady Plan, along with other policy measures such as the reprivatization of the banks, began to significantly alter international perceptions about the country and its future prospects.

On the trade front, Salinas carried forward De la Madrid's reforms by continuing to reduce tariff levels and by freeing more imports from licensing requirements. These reforms had been slowed under the De la Madrid presidency because the dropping of import restrictions caused the trade deficit to increase, and Mexico's shortage of international reserves made it costly to have a large excess of imports over its exports.

Reprivatizing the banks, reducing trade barriers, curbing inflation, cutting the budget deficit, and renegotiating Mexico's international debt were key components in the reorientation of Mexico's economic strategy. It was still not enough, however, in the eyes of many potential investors inside and outside Mexico. One problem was that the reforms in the Mexican economy were not necessarily permanent. While people might applaud the Salinas administration, what would the next president do? As long as the reforms were the policies of a single presidential administration, they could be reversed.

In order to provide credibility to the permanency of economic reforms and to restore investor confidence in the country, Salinas took the bold step of proposing to negotiate a trade agreement with the United States. His hope was that by signing the trade agreement he would tie up many of the reforms in an international treaty, making it much harder, if not impossible, to reverse them in the future. The proposal for a North American Free Trade Agreement with the United States was a bold break with Mexico's recent past. Although the United States and Mexico had come to agreement on several important issues during the 1980s, U.S.-Mexican relations had been lukewarm at best through most of the twentieth century. The memory of the bitter dispute over Mexico's nationalization of its oil industry in 1938, the historical loss of about one-third of the country to the United States in the nineteenth century, and the different languages and cultures have created misunderstanding and a lack of trust on both sides.

Closer economic ties with the United States seemed to offer Mexico the guarantees that international investors wanted. Not only would it make future policy reversals more difficult, it also offered full access to the wealthy American market for anyone that produced their goods in Mexico. The proposal seemed to accomplish its goals: capital began to pour into Mexico, both from foreign investors and from Mexican nationals who had sent their savings out of the country during the turmoil of the debt crisis. Between 1990 and 1993, Mexico attracted over $90 billion in outside capital, or about one in five of every dollar that went to developing countries from private sources.

The North American Free Trade Agreement (NAFTA)

Trade flows between the United States and its NAFTA partners have significantly increased in the 1990s. Given that trade flows were growing before the implementation of NAFTA, and that they have continued to grow afterward, it is impossible to say how much of the increase in trade is directly due to the trade agreement. Some of the increase before NAFTA's implementation may have been in anticipation of freer trade, while much of the growth since then may have occurred without the agreement. Given that tariffs on about half of the goods traded between the United States and Mexico were eliminated immediately in 1994, it makes sense to think that NAFTA caused at least some of the growth in trade. Nevertheless, U.S.-Canadian trade expanded with little or no change in tariffs, and overall U.S. and world trade increased in the 1990s.

The first important feature of NAFTA is that most forms of trade barriers come down. Since the United States and Canada were relatively open economies with few trade barriers before NAFTA, most of the change has come on the Mexican side. For example, between 1993 and 1996, average U.S. tariffs on Mexican goods fell from 2.07 to 0.65 percent. By contrast, Mexican tariffs on U.S. goods fell from 10 to 2.9 percent. These reductions in tariffs under NAFTA were a continuation of the decline in Mexican tariffs that began in the mid-1980s during the De la Madrid presidency. Between 1982 and 1992, the percentage of Mexico's imports that required import licenses from the government declined from 100 to 11 percent. At the same time, tariffs were falling from an average level of 27 to 13.1 percent. By 1994, at the beginning of the implementation of the agreement, Mexico's economy was substantially open to the world.

The time period over which the remaining tariffs and investment restrictions will be phased out varies from sector to sector. In cases where there is expected to be significant new competition, industries were given a longer grace period to prepare themselves for stiffer competition. Some sectors will not reach zero tariffs or become completely open to foreign investment for as long as ten years. Although each country wants the gains from trade, they also want to avoid a sudden disruption of their economies.

A second feature of NAFTA is that it specifies North American content requirements for goods that are subject to free trade. That is, in order to qualify for free trade or the reduced tariff provisions of the agreement, a specified percentage (usually 50 percent) of the value of the good must be made in North America. The purpose of local content requirements is to prevent non-NAFTA countries from taking advantage of low tariffs in one NAFTA country in order to gain access to all three. Most trade economists dislike these provisions because they increase the likelihood of trade diversion. Production of inputs in lower-cost, nonmember countries could be reduced if firms move their operations to NAFTA countries in order to meet the content requirements. Nevertheless, content requirements were politically necessary in order to pass the agreement in Canada and the United States.

A third feature of the agreement is that it establishes a system of dispute resolution. When a disagreement arises, any country may request an investigation. This will set into motion a process in which a binational panel investigates and issues a finding. Both countries are bound by the results of their finding. It is hoped that this will lead to greater consultation and cooperation between countries before trade disputes develop too far.

In terms of the issues of deeper integration that were discussed in Chapter 10, NAFTA itself does not go very far. The agreement follows the general principle of national treatment with respect to investment in each other's economies, but there is no attempt to harmonize antitrust laws. In addition, each country has specified a handful of sectors and economic activities that are closed or severely restrict foreign investment. In general, however, capital is free to move within the three countries. In the case of environmental and labor laws, there is an expression of support for "upward harmonization," but each country's laws remain unique. Industrial support policies are not discussed, but in this case and several others, the United States, Canada, and Mexico defer to the WTO rules.

The NAFTA Debate in the United States

The proposal for a trade agreement with Mexico reignited the debate over free trade in the United States. In particular, organized industrial labor and environmental groups opposed the agreement, along with a handful of specific industrial and agricultural interests that feared stiffer competition with Mexico. Noneconomic opposition to NAFTA came from a number of politicians and citizens who expressed doubts about signing a trade agreement with a country that lacked strong democratic institutions.

Labor Issues

Blue-collar industrial labor unions were the most vocal opponents of NAFTA. In part, their opposition is a modern-day expression of the same "pauper labor argument" that was used to support high tariffs in the second half of the nineteenth century. Recall that the pauper labor argument rejects free trade because of the fear that competition with low-wage countries will drive down wages at home and cause jobs to migrate overseas. In other words, high-wage U.S. labor will be forced to compete for jobs against impoverished workers from Third-World countries. The core mistake of this view is the failure to take into account the productivity differences between U.S. and Mexican workers. Labor in Mexico earns less for three general reasons: (1) average Mexican education and skill levels are lower than in the United States; (2) the average Mexican worker has less capital on the job, and the capital they do have is less sophisticated; and (3) the public infrastructure of roads, ports, water delivery systems, communication systems, and power and waste disposal systems is less reliable and less developed than in the United States. The net outcome of these three fundamental differences in human and physical capital is that productivity levels are lower in Mexico, and, as a consequence, wages are lower.

In terms of the pauper labor argument, workers in the United States have no reason to worry about negative effects from NAFTA. This is not the whole story, however; the Stolper-Samuelson theorem predicts that workers with skills that are in abundance in Mexico may be hurt by the agreement. Recall from our simple model in Chapter 4 that trade favors the abundant factors in a nation that are used intensively to make the export good and that trade hurts the scarce factors that are used intensively in the production of the import good. Given that Mexico is relatively well endowed with unskilled labor and that the United States is relatively well endowed with skilled labor, trade between the United States and Mexico is likely to exert downward pressure on the wages of unskilled American labor. Garment workers, unskilled and semiskilled auto workers, and unskilled assembly line workers may find their wages held down or their jobs moved out of the country. As always, the key question is how big an effect there will be, particularly in comparison to the macroeconomic policies of the Federal Reserve, which, in the short run, exert far more influence over wages and jobs than trade.

Organized labor in the United States is still a significant political force, even though a smaller and smaller segment of the workforce belongs to industrial unions. During the NAFTA debate, industrial unions formed the core of a pressure group that pushed the Clinton administration to seek a separate agreement that paralleled NAFTA but focused solely on labor issues. The agreement came to be known as the side agreement on labor, or, more formally, the North American Agreement on Labor Cooperation. It was one of two such agreements; the other dealt with environmental issues. The labor side agreement requires both the United States and Mexico to enforce their own labor laws, especially laws pertaining to child labor, minimum wages, and workplace safety. Countries are required to permit investigators to examine alleged infringements of these protections, and fines may be levied. The agreement does not permit investigations into the rights of workers to organize, nor does it cover this aspect of labor law.

In the United States, labor interests sought the side agreement in order to prevent U.S. companies from fleeing to Mexico in order to take advantage of lax enforcement of labor laws. In addition, they wanted to be certain that Mexico did not gain a competitive advantage over U.S. firms and workers by using child labor, by paying less than minimum wage, or by cost cutting that allowed unsafe and unhealthy working conditions. Ironically, the first instance in which the international panel has been called to investigate the nonenforcement of workplace health and safety rules was in the United States. In 1996, Mexican unions protested that a U.S. firm was abusing Hispanic telemarketers in San Francisco and that the U.S. government had failed to enforce U.S. workplace health and safety laws.

In the final analysis, most industrial labor groups expressed complete dissatisfaction with the labor side agreement and continued to oppose ratification of NAFTA. In essence, they remain unconvinced that U.S. workers can compete with Mexico without lowering their own wages. In their view, much, if not all, of U.S. trade with developing countries is unfair to U.S. workers and is responsible for a significant erosion in living standards in the United States.

This, of course, is completely at odds with standard economic analysis. It also contradicts the conclusions of most empirical investigations of the links between trade and living standards. Recall that Chapter 4 covers this issue and that the lion's share of the growth in inequality is attributable to technological changes that have reduced the demand for unskilled workers. This trend has little or nothing to do with NAFTA. However, in a period in which corporate downsizing and rapid technological change make everyone feel less secure, trade agreements such as NAFTA probably add to that uncertainty.

In another sense, the unionists may be right about NAFTA. The labor side agreement (and the environmental one as well) look to be toothless. That is, during the first few years of the agreement they have not required countries to do anything that they would not have done without NAFTA. Cynics argue that this is by design, that the labor side agreement is only for show, and that its real function was to win votes in Congress during the ratification process in 1993. Time will tell whether the labor and environmental institutions have a real purpose or not.

Environmental Issues

The second major side agreement is called the North American Agreement on Environmental Cooperation. This agreement was motivated by two main concerns. One was the desire to prevent U.S. and Canadian firms from relocating to Mexico where they might take advantage of less stringent environmental enforcement. The second concern was the growth of environmental pollution along the U.S.-Mexico border. Like its labor laws, Mexico's environmental laws are quite good in general, but enforcement has often been lacking, due either to a lack of resources or corruption. The high visibility of this issue in North America has required the nation to get tougher in its enforcement, and in this way, NAFTA has helped generate some desirable environmental outcomes.

Some environmental and labor groups remain concerned, however, that U.S. and Canadian firms will go to Mexico in order to escape the more stringent environmental enforcement in those countries. While there is some evidence that electronics firms along the border may have been motivated in part to relocate to Mexico in order to escape environmental costs in the United States, others have argued that these costs are usually not great enough to warrant relocating, nor are they worth the disadvantages of producing in Mexico. This issue is an area of active investigation by researchers on both sides of the border.

The issue of pollution along the U.S.-Mexico border is of considerable importance to the people that live there. Since the 1980s, population growth along the border has caused additional strains on the environment. One of the main contributing factors is the growth of the *maquiladora* industry. The majority of the industry is located in Mexican cities along the border and across from U.S. cities. For example, the largest concentrations of *maquiladoras* are in Tijuana, across from San Diego, and Ciudad Juarez, across from El Paso. Not only does the growth of the *maquiladora* industry increase the level of industrial pollution, but in addition the availability of jobs and their proximity to the United States attract a rapid migration from the interior of Mexico. Tijuana's population, for example, grew above the rate of 5 percent per year in the 1980s. The rapid influx of people and industry puts heavy burdens on the public infrastructure of roads, sewers, water systems, and so forth. Unfortunately, much of this new population and industrial growth occurred during the Lost Decade of the 1980s, at a time when the federal government of Mexico had few resources to spend on urban development. Consequently, sewage and water systems have been strained beyond capacity.

The environmental degradation dilemma raises several interesting issues with respect to NAFTA. First, can wealthy communities such as San Diego realistically expect poorer cities such as Tijuana to have the same set of environmental safeguards and regulations? The same question applies to the U.S.-Mexico relationship as a whole. Given the scarcity of resources in Mexico (relative to the United States), and given the economic history of the United States, Western Europe, and other high-income regions where environmental conditions were ignored until recently, it seems unreasonable to hold developing countries to the same standards that apply in countries where incomes are four or five times greater. It is interesting to note that according to surveys conducted in the early 1990s, Mexican citizens view the importance of the environment in very similar terms as Americans.

Some national environmental groups see the treaty as an excellent opportunity to begin to address the issues of the border and of environmental degradation throughout Mexico generally. First, throwing an international spotlight on the country has created incentives to deal with the worst problems. The Salinas administration, for example, has permanently closed some oil refineries in the heavily polluted Mexico City air basin. Second, and probably more important, the treaty provides a formal, institutional framework in which issues and problems can be discussed and resolved. Without the institutional framework, each problem is addressed on an ad hoc basis in which lines of authority and responsibility are less clearly defined. Specifically, the side agreement on the environment creates a mechanism for investigating environmental disputes, such as cases where it is alleged that Mexico (or the United States or Canada) is gaining competitive advantages by not enforcing environmental laws. Investigation of these cases is followed by a resolution of the dispute through binding arbitration if both sides cannot otherwise agree.

The side agreement also established the North American Development Bank (NADBank) to either provide money or help to find money to pay for border cleanup costs. NADBank has several hundred million dollars of initial funds provided by the United States and Mexico, but the majority of funds are expected to come from either international agencies or private sources. Estimates of border cleanup costs vary widely, from $2 billion to $8 billion.

Like the labor side agreement, the environmental side agreement has not had much effect to date. This ineffectiveness, coupled with the fact that the NADBank has been slow in distributing funds for projects, has led many to complain that the positive institutional features of the side agreements are little more than window dressing and that—furthermore—they do not confront the real problems of trade between industrial United States and developing Mexico.

From the standpoint of trade economics, the question is not whether the institutions are effective or not, but whether labor and environmental issues should be linked to trade at all. While both the labor and environmental side agreements are mild in their requirements, the fear is that they are new forms of protectionism that seek to remove the comparative advantage of nations. For example, Mexico is abundantly endowed with low-skilled labor. Furthermore, it is reasonable to think that in some parts of the country, people would prefer to have more income even if it is at the cost of a dirtier environment. The imposition of higher labor standards removes some of the advantages of an abundant supply of unskilled labor. Similarly, stricter environmental standards negate some of the advantages that accrue to a nation when they prefer a different trade-off between income and environmental protection. While neither side agreement imposes external standards, there is fear that linking trade to labor and the environment begins a process that leads to such an imposition.

From the standpoint of many developing countries, not just Mexico, linking trade to nontrade issues is viewed with suspicion. Many intellectuals in developing countries see this not only as a new form of protectionism but also as hypocritical. The U.S. and most other industrialized nations freely used their natural resources to further their own industrial development. Until recently, and not until incomes had grown to relatively high levels, most industrial nations gave little thought to environmental issues. Furthermore, the disappearance of child labor and long work hours are relatively recent changes (and still ongoing).

Nevertheless, in most industrial countries there is a strong desire to manage these issues so that citizens do not feel threatened by trade and economic integration. NAFTA's tentative and weak linkage of trade to the important nontrade issues of labor and the environment was the beginning of a search for ways in which average citizens in the United States could begin to feel more comfortable with free trade. Since there is no clear resolution nor a politically dominant position, the debate over the linkage of these issues is certain to go on for some time.

Immigration

Probably the most contentious issue in U.S.-Mexico relations in the 1990s is illegal immigration. It is estimated that each year around 300,000 illegal immigrants from Mexico stay in the United States. Around 40 to 45 percent of these people settle in California; the remainder go to Illinois, New York, Texas, and a few other states. The total number of illegal border crossings is much higher because many people cross more than once, and most return to Mexico after a short visit or a few months' work.

Three factors are involved in the determination of the number of migrants. First, **demand pull factors** refer to the attraction of U.S. jobs. When the U.S. economy booms, it exerts a stronger pull on foreign labor. Jobs are more plentiful, and labor supply in the United States is relatively scarce. In some sectors, labor shortages may appear. The second set of factors are **supply push factors.** These are the forces inside Mexico that are pushing people to leave. They include recessions but also the structural changes taking place in the Mexican economy that have temporarily dislocated workers from jobs. For example, Mexico's agricultural policy has become more laissez faire with fewer subsidies for farmers. These and other changes are part of an effort to modernize agriculture and to attract more investment in agricultural capital. One effect of the policy changes is that Mexico hopes to reduce its agricultural labor force from 26 percent of the total labor force in the early 1990s to 16 percent by the turn of the century. Ten percent of the labor force represents around 9 million people if you include the families of those workers. Some, perhaps many, of these people may eventually try to find temporary employment in the United States. A third factor determining migration is the existence of **social networks**. California attracts a larger share of immigrants (both legal and illegal) than any other state because there are already a large number there, and the newcomers have contacts or even family on whom they can rely while they are establishing themselves.

> *Demand pull, supply push, and networks.* Demographers use these three concepts to categorize the factors that induce migration. Demand pull factors are economic conditions in the receiving country; supply push are economic, political, and social conditions in the sending country; and networks refer to the linkages of family, friends, and contact people in the receiving country.

Taken together, the impacts of demand pull, supply push, and social networks imply that illegal immigration from Mexico will continue to increase, all else equal. The increase may be averted if the United States puts more resources into controlling the border, but this is uncertain. In any case, Mexico's experience as a sender of migrants will probably continue to be typical because modernization and change within the economy will create more dislocated workers, and many of them will seek economic relief outside their home country. This is a typical pattern for countries that are in transformation to a more open economic environment.

For political reasons, many proponents of NAFTA chose to emphasize the claim that it would reduce immigration. President Salinas, for example, picked up this theme, and when addressing U.S. audiences, he often rallied support by stating, "Mexico wants to export goods, not people." His point was that NAFTA would give

Mexico greater access to the U.S. market and would create faster growth in Mexico. As a result, the nation would experience a greater capacity to absorb labor into the national economy. Most simulations of the effects of NAFTA found a similar effect: the faster the growth of the Mexican economy, the weaker the supply push factors will be. Nevertheless, the immigration-reducing supply push factors will be counter-balanced by numerous immigration-increasing supply push factors, such as agricultural reorganization and market openings that cause labor to be dislocated. The net effect is that NAFTA will probably cause immigration to be less than it would have been without the agreement, but the factors in Mexico's economy that are leading to modernization and structural change will cause immigration to increase.

The Impact of NAFTA

The most common issue in the internal U.S. debate over NAFTA was its effects on U.S. jobs. Many trade economists were discouraged by this because the key effect of any trade agreement is the increased productive efficiency that comes with a reallocation of resources, not job gains or job losses. Placing the focus of the debate on workers that might be dislocated was politically inevitable, but it ignored the real economic advantages of expanded trade.

Many people also lost sight of the fact that Mexico's economy is less than 5 percent as large as the United States'. This makes it roughly the same size as Illinois, Pennsylvania, or Florida in terms of gross output. Consequently, it is unlikely that expanded trade will have a large impact on the United States in the near future. This point is well illustrated by an examination of the predicted effects of NAFTA on the U.S. economy. Before its implementation, a number of forecasts were made by academic economists and various interest groups. In each category (employment effects, wage effects, impact on overall U.S. current account balance), a majority of forecasts predicted either no effect on the national economy or effects too small to be measured. Note that this does not imply that there are no local effects, particularly along the border or in states that have a relatively large share of their overall trade with Mexico—for example, Texas. In more general terms, however, U.S.-Mexico trade under NAFTA was predicted to grow but not in a way that had a significant impact on the overall U.S. trade balance.

U.S.-Mexico trade since 1989 is depicted in Table 12.3. Two features stand out. First, trade has been expanding since 1989, the first year of data in the table. Given the trend toward expanded trade prior to the implementation of NAFTA, it is difficult to know the independent effects of the trade agreement. Growth in U.S.-Mexico trade started with the reforms of the mid-1980s that began the opening of the Mexican economy, and NAFTA has been a part of the continued trend.

The second notable feature in Table 12.3 is the decrease in exports in 1995. The peso crisis began in late 1994, when Mexico nearly ran out of international reserves and was forced to devalue in order to shrink a trade deficit that was nearly 10 percent of its GDP. In late 1994 and early 1995, the peso fell in value by about 45 percent, leading to a nearly 7 percent decline in GDP during 1995. The peso's collapse and the recession that followed were caused by a combination of an overvalued

TABLE 12.3 U.S. Merchandise Trade with Mexico (Billions of Dollars)

Year	Exports	Percent Change	Imports	Percent Change	Balance
1989	24,984		27,162		−2,180
1990	28,279	13.2	30,157	11.0	−1,878
1991	33,277	17.1	31,130	3.2	2,147
1992	40,592	22.0	35,211	13.1	5,381
1993	41,636	2.6	39,930	13.4	1,706
1994	50,741	21.9	50,053	25.4	688
1995	46,300	−8.8	61,700	23.3	−15,400
1996	56,735	22.5	75,108	21.7	−18,373
1997	71,152	25.4	86,661	15.4	−15,509

Source: Bureau of Economic Analysis, *Survey of Current Business.* Washington, D.C.: Government Printing Office. Various issues.

exchange rate, political turmoil, and a weak banking sector that caused the government to hesitate to implement tighter monetary controls. (A more complete discussion can be found in Chapter 5.) In the early 1980s, when faced with a similar crisis, Mexico responded by imposing quotas and import duties of up to 100 percent. As a result, U.S. exports to Mexico in the early 1980s fell by 50 percent and did not return to their 1981 level for nearly seven years. This time, however, the Mexican economy and U.S.-Mexico trade resumed growing within one year.

Turning to analyses of the impact of NAFTA on U.S. jobs, recent careful analysis has concluded that most estimates have exaggerated both the number of job displacements due to imports and the number of jobs created due to exports. Measurement is difficult because Mexican imports usually do not displace U.S. goods one for one. Imported goods are often complementary to domestic goods, not substitutes. They may enter distinct market niches that complement the demand for domestically produced goods, or they may satisfy a part of the increase in overall domestic demand. As the U.S. and Mexican economies become more integrated, we should expect to see increased complementarities in production. For example, Detroit automakers may find it profitable to maintain within Mexico product lines that it would abandon if produced entirely in the United States and Canada. Maintenance of these product lines can easily increase the demand for related U.S. parts and components. In addition, imports from Mexico may in many cases displace imports from other Latin American or Asian nations. In that case, an increase in imports from Mexico is offset by a reduction in imports from another country. Similarly, job creation due to exports has probably been exaggerated by the pro-NAFTA side. A good deal of U.S. "export" business consists of intermediate inputs that are incorporated into final products that are shipped back to the United States. Consequently, as production of a final good moves to Mexico, shipments of intermediate inputs from the United States to Mexico are often misinterpreted as an increase in the number of jobs supported by exports.

Careful analysis has concluded that the impact of NAFTA on net job creation in the United States has been very small but positive, on the order of magnitude of a few tens of thousands of jobs. In order to put this into perspective, it should be noted that since the creation of NAFTA, the United States has generated about 2.25 million new jobs (net) a year. In other words, the jobs effect of three years' worth of NAFTA has been a small percentage of one month's worth of job creation.

The politics of trade make discussion of job impacts necessary; yet, economists are nearly unanimous that the ability of an economy to generate jobs is determined by labor market policies and fiscal and monetary policies, not by trade policies. Furthermore, there is widespread agreement that the real test of success or failure for a trade agreement is whether it leads to a more efficient allocation of resources. By this criterion, the growth in trade between all three NAFTA partners is a positive indicator of increasing specialization, economies of scale, and efficiency. It is interesting that this tendency predates NAFTA and has simply continued since its implementation.

Conclusion

With or without NAFTA, U.S.-Mexico economic integration is on the increase. As soon as Mexico began to open its economy to foreign trade and investment, U.S. firms were ready to explore their new opportunities. Mexico's market has 90 million people, and although they are not rich by U.S. standards, the sheer size of the market makes it significant for U.S. producers. In addition, the removal of many of the impediments to further growth and modernization creates the possibility that the country may become a fast-growing, superachiever, similar to the high-performance East Asian economies.

Whether Mexico will join the ranks of the rapidly industrializing, high-growth export economies of East Asia is anybody's guess. Whether it will prove a bonanza for large numbers of U.S. firms is equally uncertain. What seems increasingly certain, however, is that trade with Mexico and investment in Mexico will require minimal economic adjustment in the United States. Consequently, only a very small number of jobs will be lost, and those will be more than offset by gains elsewhere.

▲ Canada is the United States' closest ally. In addition, it is mostly English speaking, has a similar standard of living, and has a long democratic tradition. Mexico, on the other hand, is a vastly different society with historical reasons for wariness toward the United States. Furthermore, economic integration with Mexico is much more contentious than with Canada: labor and environmental standards, worker displacement, poorly developed infrastructure, corruption in the political and judicial systems, immigration, and the drug trade are areas of existing or potential conflict.

▲ The United States and Canada have had a free-trade agreement since 1989 (CUSTA). It was preceded by an agreement in 1965 (the Auto Pact) to allow free trade in autos and automobile parts between the two countries.

▲ U.S. benefits from NAFTA are political as well as economic. It offers the opportunity to develop institutions that provide formal mechanisms for discussion, consultation, and resolution of issues. An example is the NADBank, which has been created to deal with the long-festering problem of the border environment. Without these institutions, problems were addressed on an ad hoc basis, outside regularized, formal channels, and in political contexts where the discussants often had no power to take action. By creating new institutions such as the consultative bodies on trade, harmonization of standards, labor, and the environment, the two largest populations of North America have begun working toward greater cooperation and understanding.

▲ Mexico's long process of opening its economy began in the mid-1980s and was a result of the collapse of its traditional economic policy of import substitution industrialization (ISI). ISI stresses self-sufficiency and independence from world markets. The collapse of the Mexican economy in 1982 was due to its inability to repay its international loans; that episode began the Third-World debt crisis. The recessions that followed came to be known throughout Latin America as the Lost Decade.

▲ The most contentious issues in the United States related to the signing of the NAFTA agreement were issues of labor policy, environmental policy and enforcement, and migration.

▲ To date, the main impact of NAFTA has been to continue an ongoing trend toward increased trade. It is impossible to accurately measure the effects of NAFTA on jobs and wages, but most economists estimate a small, positive effect on job creation.

▲ Mexico's recession of 1995 was severe but short. It had nothing to do with NAFTA, but it was caused by macroeconomic mismanagement that let the trade deficit balloon under an overvalued peso. It is likely that NAFTA played a positive role in helping Mexico to escape from recession through increased exports. U.S. exports to Mexico fell in 1995 but rose above 1994 levels in 1996.

Vocabulary

Auto Pact	*maquiladora*
Brady Plan	North American Development Bank (NADBank)
Canada-U.S. Trade Agreement (CUSTA)	North American Agreement on Environmental Cooperation
debt crisis	North American Agreement on Labor Cooperation
demand pull factors	
export processing zone (EPZ)	North American Free Trade Agreement
import substitution industrialization	purchasing power parity
	social networks
Lost Decade	supply push factors

Study Questions

1. How does Mexico's GDP per person compare to that of the United States? Why does the answer vary?

2. Why is the openness indicator for Canada greater than that for the United States?

3. Explain how an increase in U.S. and Canadian intraindustry trade altered the level of productivity in the Canadian sector affected .

4. What were Canada's motives for proposing and signing the Canadian-United States Free Trade Agreement?

5. What were the forces at work in the Mexican economy that led to the market reforms and market opening of the mid-1980s?

6. What were Mexico's motives for proposing and signing the North American Free Trade Agreement?

7. In what areas are there NAFTA side agreements? Discuss the pros and cons of these agreements.

8. What are the three main categories of factors that determine the number of immigrants to the United States from Mexico? Give specific examples of each.

9. Explain why claims about job creation and job destruction due to NAFTA are likely to be misleading and inaccurate.

Suggested Reading

Freeman, Alan, and Patrick Grady. *Dividing the House: Planning for a Canada Without Quebec.* Toronto: Harper Collins, 1995.

Hinojosa, Ojeda, et al. "North American Integration Three Years after NAFTA: A Framework for Tracking, Modeling, and Internet Access in the National and Regional Labor Market Impacts." North American Integration and Development Center, UCLA, 1997.

Hufbauer, Gary Clyde, and Jeffrey J. Schott. *North American Free Trade: Issues and Recommendations.* Washington, DC: The Institute for International Economics, 1992.

———. *NAFTA: An Assessment.* Washington, DC: The Institute for International Economics, 1993.

Lustig, Nora. *Mexico: The Remaking of an Economy.* Washington, DC: The Brookings Institute, 1992.

———. Barry Bosworth, and Robert Lawrence, eds. *North American Free Trade: Assessing the Impact.* Washington, DC: The Brookings Institute, 1992.

Martin, Philip. *Trade and Migration: NAFTA and Agriculture.* Washington, DC: The Institute for International Economics, 1993.

Pastor, Robert. *Integration with Mexico: Options for U.S. Policy.* New York: Twentieth Century Fund Press, 1993.

U.S. Congress, Office of Technology Assessment. *U.S.-Mexico Trade: Pulling Together or Pulling Apart?* Washington, DC: U.S. Government Printing Office, 1992.

Wonnacott, Paul. *The United States and Canada: The Quest for Free Trade.* Washington, DC: The Institute for International Economics, 1987.

Appendix A: Important Provisions in Key Sectors and the Side Agreements

Key Sectors

Agriculture

▲ The provisions of the CUSTA are not changed.

▲ Mexico opens its field crops to foreign trade (including the all-important corn crop).

▲ The United States begins to phase out its restrictions on horticultural crops.

▲ National health and safety standards are not harmonized and continue to apply.

NAFTA has been described as having two policy regimes with respect to agriculture: one of them applies to the U.S.-Canada interface where supply management boards determine output levels in important Canadian crops; the other applies to the U.S.-Mexico interface where trade is moving in a more open and laissez faire direction.

Agricultural policy in Canada has focused on slowing the rate at which technological change causes labor to be shed from agriculture through the creation of supply management and marketing boards. NAFTA leaves these intact.

Agricultural policy in Mexico has recently shifted toward a more market-based system, as Mexico tries to modernize and improve the sector. Agriculture in Mexico in the early 1990s employed 26 percent of the labor force but produced only 9 percent of the GDP; rural incomes are one-third the national average; and 70 percent of all people below the poverty line live in rural areas. Market-based restructuring of the agricultural sector includes a cut in government subsidies for inputs and output prices, a reform of the system of semicommunal farms (*ejidos*), and a variety of policies designed to encourage people to leave the farming sector.

Autos

▲ The auto sector is already the most integrated of all sectors. Canadian-U.S. trade is virtually free of all restrictions since the implementation of the Auto Pact in 1965.

▲ Trade will be free from nearly all barriers within ten years.

▲ Mexico's domestic content requirements, trade balancing requirements, tariffs, and NTBs will be phased out over the ten-year period.

▲ Restrictions will be lifted on the auto financing subsidiaries of the car companies.

▲ Rules of origin are established at 62.5 percent for main components (engines, transmissions, etc.) and 60 percent for other parts.

NAFTA will lead to further integration of the North American auto market. Until the recession of 1995, Mexico had one of the fastest-growing major auto markets in the world.

Under CUSTA, the content requirement to qualify for free-trade status was 50 percent. The method of calculation led to conflicts between the United States and Canada. Parts were classified as 100 percent regional if 50 percent of their value was domestically produced. For example, suppose that two equally valued parts differed in their domestic value added: one had 50 percent domestic value added, and another had 0 percent domestic value added. These could be combined into a whole that would meet the 50 percent target: $(0.5 * 100) + (0.5 * 0) = 0.5$. In reality, only 25 percent was domestically produced. NAFTA changes the method for calculating domestic content and should avoid these problems.

Energy

▲ Mexico opens contracting by Pemex (Petroleos Mexicanos) and CFE (Comisión Federal de Electricidad). Contracts are expected to be worth around U.S. $8.5 billion per year. Foreign participation will be phased in from 50 percent in 1994 to 100 percent in 2004.
▲ Investment restrictions remain in the areas of exploration, production, refining, and gas retailing.
▲ Petrochemicals are liberalized for trade and investment, although some key products remain closed.
▲ Foreigners may operate their own electrical plants.
▲ Foreigners may supply natural gas, although delivery must go through Pemex and/or CFE.

CUSTA allowed restrictions in energy trade for reasons of (1) national security, (2) conservation, (3) shortages, and (4) price stabilization. It requires that any dislocation (cutoff in supplies) be shared equally between domestic and foreign consumers. This last clause did not extend to Mexico under NAFTA.

Financial Services

▲ Mexican banking will offer unlimited access after a period of phased-out controls on foreign ownership and foreign share of net assets.
▲ The same conditions apply to securities trading.
▲ U.S. restrictions will remain in place. (The Glass-Steagall Act of 1930 prohibits investment banking in the United States.)
▲ The insurance market opens, and nearly all restrictions are phased out by 2000.

Mexico's banking sector is extremely shaky and less efficient than its counterparts in Canada and the United States. Many observers expect there to be large and growing foreign investment as U.S. banks look for opportunities and Mexican banks look for financially stable investors.

Telecommunications

▲ Foreign firms are provided access to public networks in Mexico.
▲ Discussions are under way to harmonize standards.

▲ Existing ownership restrictions on TV and radio stations in all three countries remain in place.
▲ Most other trade and investment restrictions are dropped or phased out over five years. An exception is basic services (i.e., basic phone service).

As in the case of financial services, the goal is "national treatment." Restrictions remain on the ownership of television and radio stations.

Textiles and Apparel

▲ It imposes a "triple transformation" requirement for free trade: fiber-thread-cloth.
▲ This is the first attempt by Canada or the United States to open this sector to a developing country.
▲ Tariffs will be phased out over ten years; quotas on many Mexican goods are lifted or converted to the equivalent tariff.
▲ Trade diversion from the Caribbean is a possibility.

The "triple transformation" requirement gives this sector the toughest North American content requirements. In order to qualify for free trade, cloth must be woven in North America from thread spun in North America that, in turn, was made from fiber produced in North America.

Transport

▲ Foreign truck transport is permitted in border states by 1995, and all areas will be open by 2000.
▲ There will be mutual recognition of national (state/provincial) truck drivers' licenses.
▲ Significant differences continue in the area of allowable truck sizes and weights.
▲ Foreign investment in trucking will be completely open by 2004.

There is serious disagreement over trucking issues. This part of the agreement has not taken effect and is currently a subject of some tension between the United States and Mexico. The United States expresses concern about the safety of Mexican trucks on U.S. highways and asserts that the Mexican inspection and truck safety programs are inadequate. In addition, significant cabotage restrictions remain in place, and border facilities are inadequate.

Side Agreements and Other Issues

Safeguards, Dumping, and Subsidies

▲ All countries are permitted to use safeguards.
▲ Each country keeps its own national laws with respect to antidumping and countervailing duties.
▲ In disputed cases, binational panels will be formed to investigate. Their decision is binding, although there is an appeal process.

▲ There is a seven-year time period for reaching a common definition and methodology for measuring dumping.

Canada is quite interested in developing a common definition of dumping in order to limit U.S. unilateralism in the application of antidumping duties. (Antidumping duties have become a favored form for applying temporary protection in the United States.)

Investment Rules

▲ National treatment is the general standard for judging foreign investment.
▲ No new performance requirements are allowed.
▲ No expropriation is allowed except for public use and with compensation.

The main exceptions to free-investment flows are oil in Mexico; airlines, radio, and television in the United States; and cultural industries in Canada.

The North American Agreement on Labor Cooperation

▲ Ministerial-level (cabinet-level) labor officials will form a Committee on Labor Cooperation. The Committee's task is to ensure that each side lives up to its own labor laws.
▲ The Committee can impose fines and/or trade sanctions in cases relating to workplace health and safety, minimum wages, and child labor.
▲ Issues relating to workers' rights to organize and the treatment of labor organizations cannot lead to fines, expert reports, or sanctions.

Environmental Rules and Agreements

1. Within the NAFTA accord:

▲ Existing standards are maintained.
▲ National treatment with respect to environmental standards applies to inward FDI.
▲ International treaty obligations are preserved.
▲ Upward harmonization is favored.
▲ A North American Environmental Cooperation Commission is created.
▲ The border receives special consideration for cooperation and joint efforts at dealing with pollution.

2. The North American Agreement on Environmental Cooperation:

▲ The Commission for Environmental Cooperation is established. Its members include the environmental ministers (e.g., the head of the EPA) of each country.
▲ The Joint Public Advising Committee is created with five members from each country to investigate conditions and environmental disputes.
▲ Disputes may go to binding arbitration if the JPAC cannot resolve the issue. Fines and sanctions may be imposed.

▲ The North American Development Bank (NADBank) is created to raise funds for border cleanup.
▲ The Border Environmental Cooperation Commission (BECC) is created to investigate pollution and cleanup issues and to make funding recommendations to the NADBank.

Primary Source: Hufbauer and Schott, *NAFTA, An Assessment.* Washington, D.C.: Institute for International Economics.

Appendix B: Useful WWW Sites for Information About Mexico and Canada

The Canadian government has one of the easiest to access and best-organized information retrieval systems of any government with a Web site. One of its best features is that there is a single gateway to all federal agencies and provincial governments (*http://www.canada.gc.ca/main_e.html*). One of the most noteworthy links that can be found at this site is to the Canadian data collection agency, Statistics Canada, or Statcan (*http://www.statcan.ca/start.html*). Statcan is the Canadian equivalent of the U.S. Census Bureau. It provides data over the WWW on nearly every topic of Canadian society, economy, geography, and demography. The Ministry of Finance also provides links to a number of Canadian and international sites (*http://www.fin.gc.ca/links/itfe.html*).

The Mexican government also maintains a number of Web sites, but there is no single gateway. Consequently, Web users must either know the address of the agency or go through one of a number of commercial sites that provides links to Mexican sources. Most of the Mexican government sites are in Spanish, although most are also developing English versions. The Mexican census bureau is called Instituto Nacional de Estadística, Geografía, e Informática, or INEGI (*http://www.inegi.gob.mx/*). It provides access to a large volume of general statistical information. Official economic information about Mexico, including recently released data on the economy (GDP growth, private forecasts, inflation, etc.), can be found at the Web site sponsored by the Secretaría de Hacienda y Crédito Público (Mexico's IRS *http://www.shcp.gob.mx/*). An interesting American site that specializes in NAFTA is North American Integration and Development Center at UCLA (*http://www.naid.sppsr.ucla.edu/*).

CHAPTER 13

THE EUROPEAN UNION: MANY MARKETS INTO ONE

Introduction: The European Union

In 1987, the twelve members of the European Community (EC) embarked on an ambitious program to capture additional gains from trade. The members passed legislation amending the treaty that had originally brought them together after World War II. The 1987 legislation was named the Single European Act (SEA) because it sought to create a single European identity that would form an umbrella over the various national cultures, economies, and political systems.

The centerpiece of the Single European Act is the "four freedoms," which are defined as the free movement of goods, services, capital, and labor. Not only would Italian and other firms be able to sell their goods in France on the same basis as domestic French firms, but workers from Spain would be free to compete for jobs in Germany on an equal basis with German citizens. There was a great deal of excitement through the late 1980s and the early 1990s leading up to the implementation of the Single European Act in January 1993. In fact, the SEA enjoyed support from the citizens of the twelve countries, the national political parties, and the business community. In essence, there was no major opposition.

Despite this lack of opposition, it still required over five years of tough negotiations among the twelve, and at the end, not all the steps necessary for complete implementation had been taken. This raises an interesting question. If citizens, governments, and businesses are united in their desires to open their economies and to achieve greater gains from trade, then why is it so difficult to accomplish? If trade liberalization (the opening of markets to foreign competition) is contentious and uncertain even when everyone desires it, you can imagine how tough it is when constituencies are divided. The fight over the Single European Act is a graphic illustration of the fact that trade issues are rarely about trade only. In the rest of this chapter we will look at the process of economic integration in Western Europe (and in some of Central and Eastern Europe as well). One feature that will stand out is that the process under way in Western Europe has political, social, and cultural dimensions as well as economic ones.

Before moving on, it is useful to clarify the name European Union. European Union is the current name for a group of fifteen West European countries, formerly known as the European Community (EC) or as the European Economic Community (EEC). As the EEC took on more responsibilities of a social and political

European Union

Text Size Denotes

Members of the European Union
Leading Candidates for Membership in the European Union
Others

Scale

1: 26,423,000
1: 417.02 Inches to Miles

Lambert Equal Area Projection

SDSU Geography
Chris Lukinbeal

nature, the community began to consider itself as more than an economic community, and the use of the name European Community came into common usage. Then, with the ratification of the Maastricht Treaty on November 1, 1993, "Community" was replaced with "Union." Technically, the EC still exists within the expanded framework of the EU, and the term EC is still encountered when the discussion is focused on exclusively economic issues.

The Size of the Market in Western Europe

Before discussing the history or economics of economic integration in Western Europe, let us define the nations and groups that are important and get an idea of the size of the market. The European Union has the potential to become the largest integrated market in the world. By implication, the EU is likely to have a major role in determining future international political arrangements, trade patterns and rules, and international economic relations in general. Few countries will be able to grow and prosper without selling their goods in the European market, and this is a powerful incentive to accept European leadership on international issues.

Table 13.1 lists the members of the European Union (EU), their populations, and their gross domestic products. GDP is measured in current 1996 U.S. dollars, measured

TABLE 13.1 1996 Population and GDP in the EU

Original Members	Population (Millions)	Per Capita GDP (Market Exchange Rates)	Total GDP (Market Exchange Rates, in Billions)
Belgium	10.2	26,297	268.2
France	58.4	26,349	1,538.8
Germany	81.9	28,724	2,352.5
Italy	57.4	21,155	1,214.3
Luxembourg	0.4	42,891	17.2
Netherlands	15.5	25,326	392.5
New Members,* 1973–86			
Denmark (1973)	5.3	34,681	183.8
Greece (1981)	10.5	11,815	124.1
Ireland (1973)	3.5	19,254	67.4
Portugal (1986)	9.8	10,932	107.1
Spain (1986)	39.2	14,780	580.9
United Kingdom (1973)	58.8	19,709	1,158.9
Members in 1995			
Austria†	8.1	28,809	233.3
Finland	5.1	24,307	124.0
Sweden	8.8	28,607	251.7
Totals	372.1		8,614.7

*Year of membership in parentheses.
†1995
Source: International Monetary Fund, *International Financial Statistics*, Washington, D.C. July, 1998.

at market exchange rates. Comparisons at market exchange rates are a less accurate indicator of living standards than comparisons at purchasing power parity rates, but they are a more accurate indicator of the size of each market in terms of its ability to buy goods and services that are imported. Several features of Table 13.1 are worth highlighting. First, notice that not all West European nations are members. Despite the addition in 1995 of three new members, Norway (who voted not to join in 1970 and in 1995) and Switzerland are noticeably absent. In addition, a number of the supersmall nations, such as Iceland, Liechtenstein, San Marino, and Monaco, are not members, nor are any countries from the former East Bloc, such as Poland, Hungary, or the Czech Republic. Second, many non-Europeans are probably somewhat surprised at the small average population size of most West European nations. By most measures, only five nations are large: Germany, Italy, France, the United Kingdom, and Spain. The four largest (minus Spain) were each approximately the same size, just under sixty million, until West Germany merged with East Germany and became the single largest country. The fact that Germany is now over one-third larger than its nearest rival has implications that we will examine. Third, the nations of the EU form a combined market worth almost U.S. $9 trillion. In terms of external purchasing power and population, the EU is almost identical in size to the North American market created by NAFTA. In 1997, the NAFTA market had approximately 395 million people and around $9,100 billion in GDP at market exchange rates (see Chapter 12, Table 12.1).

Two additional facts about the size of the EU market are worth keeping in mind. The countries listed in Table 13.1 are not the full extent of the current free-trade area. The EU has formally included Iceland, Norway, and Liechtenstein in its common market area. This gives those countries many of the same rights as citizens of the EU to move, invest, and trade freely throughout the EU. Second, several former East Bloc countries in Central Europe have applied for membership in the EU and have an "associate member" status providing them with enhanced market access. Several nations are likely to join the EU over the next decade, including Poland, Hungary, The Czech Republic, Estonia, and Slovenia (and the Mediterranean island nation of Cyprus), and others are waiting in the wings. Membership depends on the ability of the countries to continue their political and economic reforms. The issue of widening the membership will be examined in greater detail toward the end of this chapter, but note that the EU is still under construction. In addition, the effective sizes of its free-trade area and common market are much larger than the list of official members.

The European Economic Community Before 1993

The European Economic Community was born on March 25, 1957, with the signing of the Treaty of Rome. The Treaty entered into force about nine months later, on January 1, 1958. The Treaty remains the fundamental agreement between the fifteen members, and more recent agreements such as the Single European Act and the Maastricht Agreement were passed as amendments to the original treaty. The six founding members were the Benelux countries (Belgium, Netherlands, and Luxembourg), along with France, West Germany, and Italy.

The Treaty of Rome

The European Economic Community grew out of the reconstruction of Europe at the end of World War II. The goals of the founders of the EEC were to rebuild their destroyed economies and to prevent the destruction from happening again. The original vision of the founders of the EEC was for a political union that they hoped to create through economic integration. The first step was a 1950 proposal by Robert Schuman, the foreign minister of France, to pool the European coal and steel industries. Coal and steel were chosen because they were large industrial activities that served as the backbone of military strength. Schuman's plan was to pool the industries of Germany and France, the two largest West European antagonists, but Luxembourg, Belgium, the Netherlands, and Italy signed on as well. The European Coal and Steel Community (ECSC) Treaty was signed in 1951 and included provision for the establishment of the ECSC High Authority, an international agency with regulatory powers. Coal and steel trade between the six members grew by 129 percent in the first five years of the treaty.

The success of the ECSC led to early attempts at integration in political and military areas (the European Defense Community and the European Political Community), but these efforts failed when they were rejected by the French Parliament in 1954. At that point, European leaders decided to focus their initial efforts on economic integration. In 1955, the six foreign ministers of the ECSC countries launched a round of talks in Messina, Italy, to discuss the creation of a European Economic Community and a European Atomic Energy Community (EAEC or Euratom). The goal of the former was to create a single, integrated market for goods, services, labor, and capital, and the latter sought to jointly develop nuclear energy for peaceful purposes. Two separate treaties were signed in 1957 in Rome, creating the EEC and Euratom.

Institutional Structure of the EEC

The founders of the EEC envisioned a federation in which local, regional, national, and European authorities cooperate and complement one another. The model was similar to the interaction between the cities, counties, states, and federal government in the United States, or local, provincial, and federal governments in Canada. An alternative view, called functionalism, favors a gradual transfer of national sovereignty to the European level. The functionalist approach is probably the more controversial of the two and has generated a great deal of resistance by those who fear a loss of national power and culture.

Both of these approaches can be seen today, however, and the actual performance of the European Union is a blend of both. In EU jargon, **subsidiarity** describes the relationship between national and EU areas of authority, and between national and EU institutions. Subsidiarity is defined as the principle that the Union will only have authority to tackle issues that are more effectively handled through international action than by individual nations acting alone. In some cases, these issues are easily defined, but in others they are not. Current thinking places under

EU control the responsibility for environmental and regional policy, research and technology development, and economic and monetary union.

> ***Subsidiarity.*** *Subsidiarity is the principle that the authority of the European Union to involve itself in individual national affairs is limited to those issues that are transnational in scope. In current practice, this includes environmental policies, regional policies, research and technology development, and economic and monetary union.*

Areas that are less clear cut and where there continues to be some degree of controversy include the issues of labor market policies, social policies, and competition policies. The presence of controversy, however, has not prevented the EU from agreeing to a common competition policy and a common set of labor market policies, called the Social Charter. Both of these areas continue to be sources of significant disagreement and political maneuvering. Recall from Chapter 10 that national policies reflect fundamental philosophical outlooks. National laws and institutions embody a set of national values that reflect different choices. Economic policies have implications far beyond economics, and consequently, these are precisely the issues on which many nations are extremely reluctant to transfer sovereignty to international organizations. The conflict between policies that reflect national values and the desire to obtain greater gains from trade through economic integration is a pervasive problem in every instance of economic integration. Given that nations rarely speak with a single voice but are themselves composed of factions and special interests, the struggle over the transfer of sovereignty is all the more contentious.

Decision making within the EU is split between four governmental bodies. These are the Commission, which is the executive branch; the Council of Ministers (or Council), which is equivalent to the legislative branch; the European Parliament, which is mostly an advisory body; and the Court of Justice, the judicial branch. Table 13.2 shows how votes are allotted in the first three branches.

The Commission.   The executive body of the EU is the Commission. Each of the five largest countries (France, Germany, Italy, Spain, and the United Kingdom) has two seats, and the remaining ten countries have one commissioner each for a total of twenty members. Commissioners serve five-year terms that are renewable, and they are appointed by national governments with the mutual approval of the member states. The Commission elects one of its own members to serve as the president of the European Commission. Work is divided in a way that gives each commissioner responsibility for one or more policy areas, but all decisions are a collective responsibility.

The Commission's primary responsibility is to act as the guardian of the Treaties, ensuring that they are faithfully and legally enforced. This role includes responsibility for creating the rules for implementing treaty articles and for EU budget appropriations. As the executive branch, the Commission has the sole right to initiate EU laws and the same right as the national governments to submit proposals.

The Council of Ministers.   The Council serves as the legislative branch of the EU and enacts laws based on proposals submitted by the Commission. It is composed

TABLE 13.2 Member Country Votes in the Main Institutions of the EU

	European Commission	Council of Ministers	Parliament
Germany	2	10	99
France	2	10	87
Italy	2	10	87
United Kingdom	2	10	87
Spain	2	8	64
Netherlands	1	5	31
Belgium	1	5	25
Greece	1	5	25
Portugal	1	5	25
Sweden	1	4	22
Austria	1	4	21
Denmark	1	3	16
Finland	1	3	16
Ireland	1	3	15
Luxembourg	1	2	6

of different ministers from each nation, depending on the subject under discussion. For example, farm issues are discussed by agricultural ministers from each nation, and any labor issues are handled by labor and economic affairs ministers. Representation is more or less proportional to national population. Eighty-seven total votes are split as follows: ten votes each for France, Germany, Italy, and the United Kingdom; eight for Spain; five each for Belgium, Greece, the Netherlands, and Portugal; four each for Austria and Sweden; three each for Ireland, Denmark, and Finland; and two for Luxembourg. The Council makes most decisions by majority voting (called a qualified majority), which requires sixty-two of the eighty-seven votes and at least ten of the fifteen states for a proposal to pass. A few issues that are sensitive—for example, tax law changes—require unanimity for passage.

The Council's leadership rotates among the member states in six-month terms. The chance to serve as president of the Council for six months is an important mechanism for individual member states to bring up their own legislative agendas and has been instrumental in the adoption of key EU regulations.

The European Parliament. The Parliament has 626 members, directly elected by the people for five-year terms and apportioned among the member states according to population. Members associate by political affiliation rather than national origin. To date, the primary function of the Parliament has been to act as the representative of popular interests with the power to question the Council and Commission and to issue nonbinding opinions. The lack of real legislative clout in the Parliament has raised concerns that there is a **democratic deficit** in EU governance. Proponents of the democratic deficit view have succeeded in the last few years in significantly increasing the real power of Parliament from the ability to amend some legislation to veto powers over new membership and "Associate Agreements" with nonmembers. The Maastricht Treaty, signed in 1991, will carry this evolution farther, and the direction of future change seems to be toward increasing the role of Parliament.

> ***Democratic deficit.*** *The EU is described as having a democratic deficit because its only popularly elected body, the European Parliament, is not a real parliament and lacks the authority to serve as a legislature. In addition, the least populated countries (e.g., Luxembourg) have more representatives on a per capita basis than the most populated countries (e.g., Germany).*

The Court of Justice.   The Court of Justice is the EU's Supreme Court. Each member state appoints one judge by mutual consent of the other members, plus there is a president of the Court. The Court interprets the treaties and ensures that they are applied correctly by other EU institutions. Their rulings are binding and take precedence over national courts. In addition to the Court of Justice, there is also the Court of First Instance, which hears cases brought by EU officials dealing with coal and steel cases, unfair competitive practices, and damage claims. The decisions of the Court of First Instance can only be appealed to the Court of Justice on the grounds of a point of law.

Other Institutions.   In addition to the Council, Commission, Parliament, and Court, several other institutions play central roles in the smooth functioning of the EU. The European Council is similar to the Council of Ministers, but it includes the heads of state of the members and the president of the European Commission. The European Council meets twice a year and serves as a forum for high-level contacts and policy setting. The Economic and Social Committee is a body of 189 members who represent the interests of labor, employers, agriculture, consumers, and professionals. They have an advisory role and serve as consultants to the Council and the Commission. The Court of Auditors consists of fifteen members appointed by the Council. They serve as supervisors of EU expenditures and attempt to ensure sound financial management.

Deepening and Widening the Community in the 1970s and 1980s

When Europeans speak of increasing the level of cooperation between member countries, they use the term *deepening*. Deepening refers to both economic and noneconomic activities that have the effect of increasing the integration of the national economies. For example, the movement from a free market to a customs union, or the harmonization of technical standards in industry, or agreements to develop a common security and defense policy are deepening activities that increase interactions between the member states. On the other hand, when Europeans speak about extending the boundaries of the EU to include new members, they use the term *widening*. Between the signing of the Treaty of Rome in 1957 and the Single European Act in 1987, six new members were admitted to the EC. These were Denmark, Ireland, and the United Kingdom in 1973, Greece in 1981, and Portugal and Spain in 1986. In addition, Austria, Finland, and Sweden joined more recently, in 1995. The issue of future widening remains very contentious throughout Europe, and we will look at it more closely later in this chapter. For now, however, we turn to the issue of deepening in the period before the Single European Act.

In 1979, the members of the European Economic Community began to link their currencies in an effort to prevent radical fluctuation in currency values. We saw the effect of changes in currency values in Chapter 9, where it was shown that a devaluation in a country's currency resulted in more exports, while a rise in the currency's value created more imports. The EC wanted to prevent member countries from devaluing their currencies as a means of capturing export markets at the expense of other members. This tactic, called **competitive devaluation,** inevitably generates conflict and leads to the breakdown of cooperation, since the devaluing country is viewed as gaining exports at the expense of others. Nations sometimes find it difficult to resist competitive devaluation, especially during recessions when the need to protect jobs is greater. The consequence is a shift in some of the effects of the recession from the devaluing country to the countries that lose their export markets and the jobs associated with exports. In general, this tactic is viewed as unfair, and in the medium to long run, it is usually ineffective since the nondevaluing countries are obliged to follow suit and retaliate by devaluing their currencies.

> ***Competitive devaluations.*** *Competitive devaluations occur when nations strive to reduce their currency's value in order to gain export markets.*

In addition to looking for a mechanism that might discourage competitive devaluations, the EC sought to remove some of the uncertainty and risk from trading and investing across national boundaries. Linking currencies so they fluctuate together is one way to do this. The problem of uncertainty and currency risk is one that pervades all international financial transactions. Chapter 9's discussion of forward markets showed that there are well-established ways to protect against these kinds of uncertainties, but they only work about six months into the future. The Europeans thought that by limiting the fluctuation of individual currencies they could obtain greater stability in their trade and investment relations.

The goal was to create an environment in which trade and investment throughout the EC was determined by considerations of comparative advantage and efficient resource allocation rather than by currency movements. Accordingly, in 1979, the EC created the European Monetary System (EMS) with its exchange rate mechanism (ERM). (Since the ERM is the central component of the EMS, the two terms are used interchangeably by most writers and commentators. Technically, however, a country can belong to the EMS and not participate in the ERM. The United Kingdom is one example.) The formation of the EMS in 1979 was probably the most significant deepening of the EC between the signing of the Treaty of Rome in 1957 and the signing of the Single European Act in 1987. It served to prepare the way for the eventual introduction of a single currency in the EU by linking the individual national currencies. It was designed to prevent extreme currency fluctuations by tying each currency's value to the weighted average of the others. The group average is known as the European currency unit (ECU). The ECU is used as a unit of account, but it is not used in actual day-to-day transactions. ECU-denominated financial instruments, such as bonds, trade on world currency markets, and their value floats up and down as the value of the ECU moves. Prior to the beginning of the single currency in January 1999, the ECU is worth around $1.10. After introduction of the single currency, called the euro, the ECU and the ERM will no longer function as components of the EU's exchange rate policy. However, as of mid-1998, there remains six months of uncertainty until the introduction of the ECU replacement.

The ERM fixes the value of each national currency to the ECU and permits fluctuations within a band around the ECU. The center point of the band is parity, which, in theory, should be the long-run equilibrium level of the currency. The original bandwidth was ±2.25 percent, but it was changed in 1993 to ±15 percent. In addition, some countries have wider bands at times than other EU members, and not all members of the EU participate in the ERM. By fixing each currency to the ECU, the EU currencies are tied to each other. For example, today's real value of the German mark is 1.89 marks per ECU and the French franc is 6.55 francs per ECU. Therefore, the exchange rate between Germany and France is (6.55 francs per ECU) / (1.89 marks per ECU), or 3.46 francs per mark.

When fluctuations in international exchange markets cause a currency to rise or fall by more than the bandwidth, then the member nations are required to intervene to prop up or hold down their currency. This can be done in a couple of ways, but the most direct method is for the central bank of the country to buy or sell the national currency. In September 1992, for example, the United Kingdom spent an estimated $30 billion in just a few days trying to protect the British pound from market speculators who had become convinced that it was going to fall in value. (The speculators were right, and the Bank of England lost a bundle of money trying to move against the market. Ultimately, they had to let the pound fall or else they would have run out of their reserves of foreign currency, which they were using to buy pounds.)

When markets are convinced about the direction a currency will move, central bank intervention is often ineffective. Given this helplessness in the face of a strong and determined market movement, most analysts predicted that the ERM would fail as a mechanism for maintaining stable European currency values. An ERM-type arrangement had actually been tried out in 1973, but it soon collapsed as a result of the first oil shortage and its effects on national inflation rates. When the EC proposed a similar arrangement in 1979, many were skeptical that it would survive for very long or that it would effectively stabilize currencies. To most economists' surprise, the ERM effectively linked EC exchange rates for two decades.

The ERM experienced several adjustments, but none of them threatened the functioning of the system until 1992. Oddly enough, it was the reunification of Germany that caused the system to nearly collapse, and that resulted in a much weaker linkage between exchange rates. Because German reunification had a profound effect on the ERM, and because it is an interesting lesson in the costs of tying currencies together, it is useful to look at this episode in more detail. (Recall the discussion in Chapter 9.)

Problems began in 1990 with Germany's decision to speed up its reunification with the German Democratic Republic (East Germany) after the fall of the Berlin Wall in November 1989. Economic conditions in East Germany were worse than many imagined, and it was soon apparent to everyone that the costs of building a productive economy would be enormous. The infrastructure (roads, bridges, ports, utilities, schools, hospitals, and so forth) was in much worse shape than most people realized, and environmental pollution was significant. In order to build a prosperous economy in its eastern region, Germany had to raise the productivity levels of the people living there, and this required huge investments in infrastructure, the environment, and in the factories and offices of the East. The unexpectedly large expenditures in raising the productivity of the East resulted in a very large fiscal stimulus to the German economy. Such large expenditures (both by the government and by the private sector) were also expected to have an inflationary impact, and the Bundesbank (Germany's central bank) acted to counteract the increased probability of future inflation by raising German interest rates. This is a normal policy move whenever it is thought that aggregate demand is rising too fast, as it was in the unified Germany. The increase in interest rates will slow the economy somewhat by increasing the costs of using borrowed capital. Germany, therefore, had an expansionary fiscal stimulus that was partially offset by a contractionary monetary policy.

In the rest of the EU, conditions were different, however. The rise in German interest rates put pressure on the monetary authorities in the rest of the EU to raise their rates, too. High German interest rates made German financial instruments more attractive and caused capital to flow into Germany from the other EU countries. This resulted in the selling of British pounds, French francs, and other currencies in order to buy German marks (and then German bonds) and caused the pound, the franc, and other currencies to fall in value. At first, the movement was within the 2.25 percent bandwidth, which was the official width at the time, and most of the EU hoped that they would somehow muddle through without making any drastic changes in the ERM or the EMS.

One solution would have been for the countries with falling currencies to raise their interest rates to match Germany's. This would have stemmed the outflow of financial capital looking for better rates of return in Germany. Some of the countries, the United Kingdom for example, were entering recessions in 1990 and 1991 and did not want to raise interest rates just as a recession was taking hold. The likely effect would have been to hasten and deepen the recession—something no policy maker wants to be accused of doing. Other countries, such as France, were not yet entering the recessionary phase of their business cycle, but they had very high unemployment rates, and contractionary monetary policy was not desirable.

In 1992, as the problem of downward pressure on their currencies grew, several EU members tried to convince the international currency market that they were willing to spend any amount necessary to buy up their currency and stabilize its value within the band. As mentioned earlier, the United Kingdom spent the equivalent of $30 billion in just a few days in this ultimately futile effort. The alternative to buying up currency was to raise interest rates, which was the technique adopted by France and a few other nations after an initial attempt at stabilization through currency purchases.

The horns of the dilemma faced by the EU countries is a good example of a recurring theme in the history of exchange rate systems. By tying their exchange rates to each other, the EU countries gave up a large measure of independence in their monetary policies. As the largest country and the one with the most influential central bank, Germany's monetary policy set the tone for the rest of the EU, and, at a time when many of the members wanted expansionary monetary policy, they were forced to adopt contractionary policies. The 1992 episode illustrates the recurrent dilemma that occurs between the appropriate external policies (exchange rate management) and the appropriate internal policies (full employment, reasonable growth, low inflation) when nations tie their exchange rates together. Since the "right" policy choice for meeting the exchange rate problem was diametrically the opposite for meeting the needs of the internal economy, EU members were left with a tough decision: honor their commitments to the ERM and make their unemployment and growth rates worse, or do the right thing for internal growth and watch the ERM fall apart. In the French case, the interest rate increase threw the country into recession, but France remained within the ERM. In the cases of Italy and the United Kingdom, the ERM was abandoned, and their currencies were allowed to freely float against other EU currencies. A third option was chosen by Spain, where the parity, or center of the band, was shifted. In order to lessen the possibility of future repeats of this problem, the bandwidth was widened in 1993 from ±2.25 percent to ±15 percent.

The ERM will cease to be meaningful for the countries that adopt the single currency in 1999, but for the countries that remain outside the monetary union, it will continue to be relevant. We will look at this issue later in the chapter.

The Second Wave of Deepening: The Single European Act

Other than the creation of the European Monetary System in 1979, the changes in the EC were minor through the 1970s and the first half of the 1980s. Indeed, by the early 1980s, the Community seemed moribund, like a good idea that lacked the will to become more than someone's dream about an unlikely and very distant future. In the early 1980s, most West European countries suffered through a recession that left their unemployment rates high even as they recovered their economic growth in 1984 and 1985. The United States had experienced a similar recession in 1981–1982, but strong growth in the years that followed brought down our rate of unemployment. The European economies seemed stale and incapable of new dynamism. The term that many in the United States used to refer to the European situation was "Eurosclerosis," signifying a permanent hardening of the arteries of commerce and industry.

By the late 1980s, people in North America and Europe had stopped using Eurosclerosis and begun to speak of "Europhoria." While both terms were exaggerations, dramatic events had reshaped the EC in the intervening years. What had been dismissed in the early 1980s as a hopeless case of bureaucratic inefficiency was now regarded as a dynamic, forward-looking, integrated regional economy. Europe seemed to be "on the move."

The Delors Report

Reshaping of the EC got under way with the selection of the former French finance minister, Jacques Delors, to serve a five-year term as president of the European Commission. Delors was a compromise candidate, and no one expected unusual or dramatic changes in the EC under his stewardship. Delors's vision of the EC, however, was of a fully integrated union, and as president of the EC's executive branch, he had a platform from which he could initiate significant change. In retrospect, it seems that his vision was shaped in part by the belief that the institutions of the EC could help to return the individual national economies to economic prosperity and in part by the desire to complete the task of building an economic and political union.

Delors's first step, and perhaps his most significant one, was to issue a report called "Completing the Internal Market," which detailed 300 specific changes necessary for the EC to move from a quasi-customs union to an economic union. It laid out a timetable for completing the changes and, importantly, removed the need for unanimous voting in the Council of Ministers. Most analysts agreed that the need for all measures to pass unanimously had created gridlock in the governing institutions; Delors proposed that many measures now be allowed to pass with a "qualified majority" (fifty-four out of the seventy-six votes in the Council of Ministers—the EC had twelve members and the Council was smaller) and that unanimity be reserved for only the most momentous issues, such as taxes. Although the qualified majority still allowed as few as three countries to block a measure (assuming that they include one large nation with ten votes), it prevented any single country from blocking a proposed change.

After some relatively minor changes in the Delors Report, it was adopted in its entirety in 1987. Its official title is the Single European Act (SEA), and legally it consists of a series of amendments to the Treaty of Rome. Of the 300 steps, or "directives," in Euro-jargon, 279 were included in the SEA. Many of the twenty-one not included were considered too difficult to accomplish in the time period the EC gave itself, but they have been taken up as goals of the next round of deepening. For example, monetary union under a single currency was moved forward to the next round of deepening.

The timetable for implementation of the SEA was January 1, 1993. By the end of 1992, it was expected that the "four freedoms" (freedom of movement for goods, services, capital, and labor) spelled out in the SEA would be instituted and, as a result, the EC would be at the common market level of economic integration. In order to accomplish these goals, it was necessary to determine the method of implementation of each of the 279 directives and for each of the twelve member nations to make the necessary changes in their internal laws, standards, and customary practices. While some areas remain incomplete, the vast majority of the directives were put into practice by the end of 1992, and the EC achieved common market status.

The steps taken to implement the SEA can be broadly divided into three areas: (1) the elimination of physical barriers, such as passport and customs controls at the borders between member countries; (2) the elimination of technical barriers, such as differences in product and safety standards; and (3) the elimination of fiscal barriers, such as differences in taxes, subsidies, and public procurement. Each of these poses its own benefits and challenges and will be discussed in more detail. First, we will consider the gains that the EC hoped to reap from the elimination of these barriers.

Forecasts of the Gains from the Single European Act

One of the central reasons for supporting the SEA was for the expected gains in economic efficiency. These gains had three main sources. First was the gain from removing customs and passport checks at internal national borders. Although tariffs and other customs-type inspections have been restricted or eliminated altogether, the gains from the elimination of border barriers have yet to be completely realized, since customs inspections have been replaced by "tax inspections" as a result of the failure of the EU to establish a uniform system of taxing goods. Still, substantial progress has been made in eliminating the long queues of trucks waiting to cross borders. The result is speedier, less costly distribution of goods throughout the EU.

The second and third sources of gains are the benefits from greater economies of scale and increased competitiveness. Economies of scale are possible because EU firms are able to produce at one site (or in a fewer number of sites) for the entire European market and will not have to duplicate production facilities across national boundaries. This enables some companies to consolidate their operations and to avoid duplication in their production and support services, such as accounting. The increase in competitiveness comes from several sources. For example, the increased pressure of competition will force some firms to make productive investments that they would not otherwise have made. In addition, the openness of the competitive environment will generate a larger, more mobile pool of labor that carries skills from one firm to another. Finally, the free flow of goods and services will generate a greater flow of information and ideas so that firms have easier access to the best new ideas.

In sum, internal EU analysis (the Cecchini Report) predicted increases in GDP in the range of 4 to 6.5 percent, with additional positive impacts on prices, employment, trade balances, and government budgets. There was no precise specification of the time frame over which these effects would be realized, but five to ten years seemed to be implied. As with all forecasts of future economic activity, the results are based on a great number of assumptions about the actual behavior of firms, industries, and nations. For example, the forecast assumes that each of the (then) twelve members of the EU would fully implement the changes negotiated in the Single European Act and that the adversely affected firms and industries could not stall or impede their implementation. In general, this has turned out to be the case in the years since January 1993; however, there remain a few sectors where goods and services are not freely traded, and many of the expected benefits have so far failed to materialize. This is probably not due so much to bad forecasts as it is to the recession that gripped most of Western Europe in 1993. Still, the often cited increase in GDP of 4 to 6.5 percent was viewed as overly optimistic by many analysts.

Problems in the Implementation of the SEA

One of the most interesting lessons of the Single European Act is that it is still diffi-cult to reduce barriers to trade and investment even when the citizens, businesses, and governments of the involved countries are united in their desire to do so. Ac-cording to all the polls, the SEA enjoyed very broad support throughout the EU. Still, from the time when it was first proposed in 1985 until its final implementation in 1993, there were very difficult negotiations among the member countries. In sev-eral cases, such as taxes and the harmonization of standards, the EU either set aside its attempts at reaching an accord or is still in the process of looking for agreement.

The Effects of Restructuring.   As we saw in Chapter 3, when a national economy goes from a relatively closed position to a relatively open one, economic restructur-ing takes place. The less efficient firms are squeezed out, and the more efficient ones grow; overall economic welfare expands as countries concentrate on what they do best, but that inevitably means abandoning some industries and expanding oth-ers. In the case of the EU after the implementation of the SEA, it was forecast that almost all manufacturing industries would see a shrinkage in the number of firms. The most extreme case was the footwear industry, which was predicted to lose 207 of its 739 firms. In some cases, the majority of the disappearing firms were concen-trated in one or two countries, such as the UK carpet industry, where it was pre-dicted that thirty-one of fifty-two manufacturers would go out of business.

The firms that go under are part of the economy-wide shift to a more efficient use of labor and capital resources; obviously, however, there are immediate human costs associated with this restructuring brought on by reducing trade barriers. In the long run, it is easy to show that the gains in efficiency and the improvement in liv-ing standards will outweigh the costs of the restructuring, but in the short run, indi-viduals and communities can feel acute pain. Because there are these inevitable costs from restructuring, many people predicted that adversely affected firms and labor unions, along with the communities and regions that depend on the firms, would fight to prevent the full implementation of the SEA. In some cases, they have been successful.

The auto industry is the best example of an economic interest that has fought to prevent the full realization of the goals of the SEA. Car prices vary throughout the EU by as much as 50 percent due to a lack of harmonization of national technical standards, documentation requirements, and rates of taxation. Ordinarily, such large price differences would present an opportunity for consumers and distribu-tors to move cars from the low-price countries to the high-price ones and, in the process, bring about a reduction in price differences. The auto industry is covered by a separate set of tax laws, however, that require buyers to pay the tax rate of the country where they register the car, not where they buy the car. This effectively dis-courages buyers from crossing national borders in order to search out the best deal on car prices and acts to maintain the status quo in automobile production. Fur-thermore, Japanese-brand cars produced inside the EU will continue to be treated as Japanese imports. Practices within the EU prior to the SEA varied a great deal with respect to the rules governing Japanese car imports. Some members permitted very few imports (e.g., Italy and Spain), and others had very open markets (e.g., the United Kingdom). The agreement reached in the SEA was to set EU-wide quotas that would be phased out gradually by the year 2000. There is significant pressure building to change the timetable and to continue the quotas indefinitely.

The automobile industry in the EU lags behind the United States and especially Japan in its switch to new, more flexible production systems that generate higher levels of productivity. As one of the largest industrial employers inside the EU, it has successfully argued that the complete elimination of all internal barriers would significantly reduce the overall size of the industry and create regional pockets of extreme distress. Because of its size, it is atypical in the political clout it can wield. Most industries have not been able to successfully make similar arguments, and the lowering of barriers throughout the EU has proceeded much more rapidly than the skeptics thought likely.

One significant reason why there have not been more exceptions to the dropping of trade barriers is that the EU has a broad array of programs to address the problems of structural change. Some of these programs are funded out of the EU budget, and others are national in origin. They include the EU's Regional Development Funds, which can be used to address problems of structural unemployment, and the member nation's income maintenance, education, and retraining funds. The latter vary across the member countries, but, in general, they reduce the costs to individuals and communities of unemployment and structural change by providing a generous social safety net for laid-off workers. They probably reduce political opposition to economic change as well, because workers in a factory that is shutting down may not fight the closing as strenuously if they know there is an economic support system for laid-off employees. At the same time, the society-wide perception that workers who have been hurt by restructuring will be taken care of may effectively reduce opposition to change from the rest of the society on the grounds of "fairness."

It should be noted that although the generosity of the social safety net in the EU may be politically instrumental in reducing opposition to economic restructuring, many economists and politicians are now arguing that the social safety net's generosity creates its own problems. In particular, many now see it as a primary reason for the high unemployment rates of the late 1980s and 1990s. By providing many benefits to the unemployed, the EU has reduced the cost to individuals of unemployment and removed some of the incentives to look for work. In addition, taxes for these social programs often fall on employers. As a consequence, many firms are reluctant to hire new employees during an economic expansion. This is an ongoing debate within the EU that has been taken up in the highest levels of the European Commission. The fact that the Commission is now debating what to do about unemployment illustrates the complex issues that shape policies designed to deal with economic restructuring. On the one hand, a high level of benefits in the social safety net is desirable in economic terms if it removes social and political opposition to getting rid of trade barriers and permits nations to realize the gains from trade. On the other hand, higher benefits imply a lower cost to remaining unemployed, fewer incentives to look for work or to seek out retraining, and fewer incentives for firms to hire new workers.

Harmonization of Technical Standards.   A second major obstacle to the creation of the four freedoms has been the difficulties involved in the harmonization of standards, including the types of certifications nations provide to skilled workers. These include everything from building codes, to industrial equipment, to consumer safety, to health standards, to university degrees and worker qualifications. The Cecchini Report estimated that there were more than 100,000 technical standards that required harmonization in order to realize the benefits of a completely integrated market. Some of these are somewhat trivial, such as the removal of Italy's Pasta Purity Law or Germany's regulations governing the ingredients in beer. Italy's law was designed to ensure that the worldwide reputation of Italian pasta was maintained. It required all pasta labeled as "Made in Italy" to be made out of a high-quality wheat that is best for pasta, but under the SEA, this was seen as a trade barrier since non-Italian companies could not set up factories in Italy to make pasta the same way they did in their home countries. Similarly, the German beer regulations prevented the use of beer-brewing techniques inside Germany that were common in the other EU countries. Other national foods were similarly questioned—for example, when French cheese came under attack for containing more bacteria than allowed by the health and safety standards and English sausages (known as "bangers") were in violation for containing too much oatmeal filler to meet the technical standards for sausage. Each of these cases illustrates the cultural issues involved in the harmonization of standards. Although they may seem rather trivial to outsiders, they directly touch the individual national identities of EU citizens and became far more contentious than a simple measurement of their economic importance would indicate.

Harmonization of industrial standards can have far greater economic impact than the cases of pasta or cheese imply. The process of harmonization is complicated, however, and requires a large number of boards and committees of experts in order to determine the best compromise between the existing national standards. Obviously, the closer the new standards are to those of a particular country, the greater the competitive advantage to the firms in that country. This makes the issue political and economic as well as technical.

It should be noted that standards do not have to be the same in order to create a single market, but the gains in economic efficiency that come from sharing the same standard can be significant. Shared standards permit manufacturers to produce to one standard, rather than fifteen, and to capture important economies of scale in the process. These economies also pass outside the EU, since U.S. or Japanese manufacturers share the benefits of being able to produce to one set of standards, and non-EU-based firms only have to get their product certified once in order to be able to sell in all fifteen countries. For this reason, the United States has had a keen interest in the standards-setting process and has looked to create joint U.S.-EU agreements on standards and the procedures by which they are set. The United States' preference has been to use the procedures of the International Standards Organization (ISO) to streamline the process of harmonization. (The ISO is an international organization that provides technical standards and whose ISO-9000 is a set of certifications applying to nearly all types of economic activity. ISO-9000 certifications and standards are gaining acceptance worldwide.)

It is also possible that shared standards can cause a loss of efficiency if the adopted standard is inferior. Harmonization, in other words, can be a means to locking in an inferior standard. Partly for this reason, but also because harmonization is so time consuming and labor intensive, the EU abandoned many of its efforts to harmonize standards under the SEA. In its place, it has agreed to a set of rules that vary according to the issue but that often offer an alternative to harmonization in the form of mutual recognition of each other's standards (see Chapter 10 for definitions of these two concepts). Mutual recognition permits nations to engage in a "competition of standards," and in the many cases in which there is no clear way to know that one standard is better than another, it avoids the problem of locking in on the inferior standard.

Value-Added Taxes.   A third difficulty standing in the way of completely realizing the four freedoms is the issue of value-added taxes (VAT). These taxes function essentially like sales taxes and are levied by each of the EU members but at a wide variety of rates and coverage. In addition, when the SEA was first proposed in 1987, there was a wide variation in the dependence of the member governments of the EU on value-added taxes, ranging from 19 to 35 percent of total government revenue. The European Commission studied the United States to determine the effects of different rates of sales taxation on the states sharing common borders and found that once the difference in sales taxes exceeded 5 percent, the higher-tax state lost revenues (and sales and jobs) to the adjoining lower-tax state. In other words, a 5 percent difference was sufficient to cause consumers to cross state boundaries to make purchases. The standard VAT rate in the EU before the SEA varied from 12 percent at the low end (Luxembourg and Spain) to 20 percent in the Netherlands, 22 percent in Denmark, and 25 percent in Ireland. In addition, there were special rates for sensitive goods, and these varied a great deal more than the standard rates.

VAT rates proved impossible to completely harmonize because they go to the heart of national political philosophy. High-tax countries tended to be the ones that expected the state to play a relatively greater role in national economic life. A number of EU states have socialist governments and are much more interventionist in their stance to the economy, while others have governments that are closer to the laissez-faire end of the political economy spectrum. The level of value-added taxes, and the degree to which the national government depends on them to fund its activities, is in large part determined by the political philosophy of the nation. In turn, these philosophical attitudes are shaped by complex historical, cultural, and social factors, as well as by economic ones.

The upshot of the attempt to harmonize value-added taxes was an inability to agree on a single rate. What was accomplished, however, was the creation of minimum and maximum rates that were set at 15 and 25 percent. Since this still exceeds the 5 percent differential that is the threshold at which high-tax countries lose revenue and sales, a number of controls have been established to prevent revenue loss. In effect, these controls prevent the complete realization of the four freedoms. Among the controls are the previously mentioned tax on autos that is levied at the rate of the country where the purchaser intends to register and use the car, rather than at the rate of the country where the car is sold. A similar rule applies in a few countries (e.g., Denmark) to many appliances and other costly consumer goods.

Despite these obstacles, however, there are still significant incentives for cross-border shopping. Although the SEA has not brought a 100 percent free flow of goods and services, it is important to keep the exceptions in perspective. For most goods and services, in most border regions, consumers are perfectly free to cross national boundaries to bring back unlimited quantities of goods, and they will not be stopped at a border inspection station.

Public Procurement.   Public procurement is the purchase of goods and services by governments or government-owned enterprises, such as state-run television companies, utilities, or hospitals. Most nations of the world tend to use procurement processes that discriminate in favor of nationally owned suppliers, although there are limits on their ability to do so if they belong to the General Agreement on Tariffs and Trade.

Since 1970, the EU has attempted to eliminate discrimination in public procurement but, as of 1990 only 2 percent was from nonnational firms. It is particularly a problem in the areas of telecommunications, pharmaceuticals, railway equipment, and electrical equipment. In many instances, national governments have attempted to create firms that would serve as "national champions" in world competition. One method was to favor those firms in the government procurement process so that they would have a guaranteed market for their output while they were still learning the most efficient methods of production. Firms and industries that receive favorable treatment often develop into effective lobbyists for the continuation of their special relationship with government. They are particularly effective as lobbyists for special treatment if there are a large number of jobs in the industry or if it shares the glamour of high technology and can raise concerns about national security if it is allowed to disappear.

Discrimination in public procurement, however, limits the benefits of restructuring and the gains from trade. If the EU countries are able to successfully develop a common security and foreign policy, the national security argument for discrimination in public procurement begins to lose a great deal of its justification.

The Third Wave of Deepening: The Maastricht Treaty

By 1989, planning for the implementation of the Single European Act in January 1993 was well under way. Europe had seen several years of economic expansion, and the excitement of the SEA seemed to signal that the time was ripe to consider some of the directives proposed in the Delors Report that had been set aside because they were too complex to accomplish by 1993. In 1990, the European Commission convened an Intergovernmental Conference on Economic and Monetary Union. The purpose of the conference was to bring together the leaders of the twelve nations to discuss the steps that would have to be taken to create a monetary union under a single currency. There were other issues on the agenda, but this was the one that attracted the most interest, both inside and outside the EU.

The Intergovernmental Conference continued through most of 1991. The final draft of the proposed agreement was completed in December in the Dutch town of Maastricht and, ever since, has been known as the Maastricht Treaty. Many of the provisions in the agreement are technical and cover such arcane issues as the tax treatment of holiday homes in Denmark or the status of the pope in trade disputes with the Vatican. Other issues are much more fundamental, dealing with basic EU social policy. For example, Maastricht calls for the creation of a "Social Charter" defining a uniform set of labor laws and worker rights; it defines the right of all residents in a community to vote and to stand for election in local contests, regardless of the resident's nationality; it puts more control over health, education, cultural, and consumer safety issues in the hands of the European Commission; it calls for a common defense and security policy along with a common military force; and it defines the steps necessary to achieving a common currency under the control of a European Central Bank by the year 1999 at the latest.

It is the last goal that has attracted the most attention, probably because it seems to imply the greatest surrender of national sovereignty to the supranational EU. Achieving a single currency requires each country to give up its ability to set its own monetary policy and to accept whatever contractionary or expansionary policy the European Central Bank chooses. This is the most controversial feature of Maastricht, both within and without the EU. The controversy stems from the fact that no group of countries has ever given up their national money to create a single currency, there is significant political opposition to its realization, and there are economic risks associated with voluntarily giving up one of the few tools that governments have to counteract recessions. If, for example, Germany is booming, but Spain is slumping, there is no common monetary policy that will be suitable to both countries. Germany would need a contractionary policy to cool off the economy and to prevent the ignition of inflation, while Spain needs an expansionary policy to create employment and growth.

These controversies have led to a very different public reception for the Maastricht Treaty than the Single European Act received. Whereas citizens, businesses, and governments were solidly behind the SEA, support for Maastricht has been much more tentative. It is interesting to speculate why it was proposed at all, given its controversial extension of EU powers at the expense of national sovereignties and given that implementation of the SEA was still two years into the future.

One explanation for the timing of Maastricht is that it is simply a consideration of all the directives that were dropped from Delors's original proposal of 1985. According to this view, Maastricht includes all the final steps necessary to create a single market, and the enthusiasm and momentum leading up to 1993 made it an opportune time to propose the controversial final steps. A second explanation for the timing of Maastricht is that it was in response to the rapid pace of German unification. According to this view, European fears of a united Germany, which would be about one-third larger in population than the next most populous state, pushed forward the timetable for a single currency. Furthermore, both Germany's close ties to Eastern Europe and the collapse of the Soviet Bloc threatened to focus German attention eastward rather than westward. The solution to a potentially dominant German economy was to bind it so tight into the European Union that its ability to act independently would be severely limited.

A third possibility for the timing of Maastricht is that the goal of a single currency became politically necessary as a result of the changes that occurred under the Single European Act. In this view, the lifting of controls on the free movement of financial capital in 1990 made it more likely that weak currency countries would experience speculative attacks, leading inevitably to currency devaluations. Ultimately, the impacts would be felt through the movement of industries and jobs, pitting nations against each other as they tried to keep or attract new industries and leading to serious strains on cooperation. In order to explain this point and to see its logic more clearly, however, it is necessary to examine the pros and cons of monetary union.

Monetary Union

The timetable for monetary union under a single currency is scheduled to occur in three separate stages. Stage one began in 1990 with the lifting of controls on the movement of financial capital within the EU. Stage two began in 1994 with the creation of the European Monetary Institute, based in Frankfurt, Germany. The Institute is charged with the responsibility of coordinating the move to monetary union and will gradually take on the role of a supranational central bank. If individual nations agree, it can begin to manage their foreign exchange and domestic money markets, both of which are roles currently performed by national central banks. Stage three is scheduled to begin no later than 1999 and may start with a minority of countries. Prior to the final stage, a European Central Bank is created and takes over some of the responsibilities of the EMI.

During the first and second phases, nations are expected to bring their monetary and fiscal policies into harmony. In order to judge when individual national policies are in agreement, the EU developed a set of **convergence criteria**. These are objective measures that signal whether the national policies are in conflict or in agreement and whether individual nations are ready for monetary union. They were developed under the assumption that the costs of monetary union would be far too high if it occurred under wildly different sets of fiscal and monetary policies. Table 13.3 lists the specific monetary and fiscal variables that are required to be coordinated and the target ranges for each.

> **Convergence criteria.** *The convergence criteria are the five indicators of readiness to begin the single currency in the EU. They are (1) stable exchange rates, (2) low inflation, (3) harmonization of long-term interest rates, (4) reduction of government deficits, and (5) reduction of government debt.*

Any nation meeting all five goals would be judged to be ready for monetary union. The experience of the first half of the 1990s, however, indicates that no nation (except perhaps Luxembourg) can consistently maintain each of these targets. The attempt to meet these targets has imposed strongly deflationary policies on most members of the EU and has exacerbated their high levels of unemployment. It also appears that some nations will be completely unable to meet all five criteria, no matter how hard they try. For example, Italian and Belgian central government debts are well over 100 percent of their annual GDP, and there is no way this can change in the span of a few years. Some economists have questioned why these

TABLE 13.3 Convergence Criteria for Monetary Union

Goals	*Targets*
1. Stabilize exchange rate	Maintain currency within the ERM band
2. Control inflation	Reduce it to less than 1.5% above the average of the three lowest rates
3. Harmonize long-term interest rates	Bring to within 2% of the average of the three lowest rates
4. Government deficits	Reduce to less than 3% of national GDP
5. Government debt	Reduce to less than 60% of national GDP

particular criteria were chosen in the first place, since a country that can maintain its interest rates, debts, deficits, inflation, and exchange rates in the target range is already doing what the EU hopes to achieve with monetary union. In other words, meeting the convergence criteria is an indicator that the nation can do what monetary union does but without actually giving up its currency. Why, then, should countries surrender control over monetary policy, and why should they give up their national currency, particularly since there are hidden costs?

Costs and Benefits of Monetary Union

There is no doubt that there are benefits to having one currency in a market as large as the EU's. For example, the average cost of currency conversion for travelers is 2.5 percent of the amount converted. A trip from Portugal to Sweden, with stops along the way, can quickly eat up a sizable portion of one's vacation money. Businesses fare much better, however, and if they buy in quantities greater than the equivalent of U.S. $5 million, then the costs are a much smaller 0.05 percent, or $5000 to convert $10 million. One estimate combining both tourists and businesses puts the total costs of currency conversion at 0.4 percent of the European Union's GDP. This is not a trivial sum, but it is not huge either. The 0.4 percent figure would certainly be higher, however, if we added to it the business costs of maintaining separate accounting systems and separate money management processes for the different currencies.

A second reason that people give for desiring monetary union is to reduce the effects of exchange-rate uncertainty on trade and investment. Since orders for goods are often placed long before delivery occurs, traders face a good deal of uncertainty about both their earnings (if they export) and their payments (if they import). Between the time orders are placed and goods are delivered, it is likely that there will have been at least some change in the value of their trading partner's currency. A single currency will eliminate this uncertainty, in the same way, for example, that California manufacturers can always be certain of the value of payments they will receive when they ship goods to Ohio. Recall from Chapter 9 that traders and investors can protect themselves from currency fluctuations with forward markets. Therefore, it should not be surprising that economists can offer little empirical evidence that increased variability in exchange rates has a significant impact on trade or investment flows. Traders simply need to sign a forward contract to buy the currency they need or to sell the currency they receive, and, for a small fee, they are protected against exchange rate fluctuations. This seems to imply that at least some of the expected benefits from a single currency may never materialize, since the problem the policy is designed to fix is not really a problem.

Given these considerations, the benefits of a single currency appear to be fairly mild. The same cannot be said for the potential costs. The theory of optimal currency areas (Chapter 9) is relevant on this issue. A single currency does not allow individual nations to pursue an independent monetary policy, in the same way as the state of New York cannot have a monetary policy that differs from New Jersey's or the rest of the United States. In other words, in a single-currency area, there is a "one size fits all" monetary policy. It is optimal to have a single currency, and to eliminate the costs of currency conversion and other transaction costs, as long as the regions in the single currency area have synchronized business cycles and mobile labor forces. Synchronization of business cycles means that there is a single monetary policy—expansionary, neutral, or contractionary—that is appropriate for everybody. A mobile labor force guarantees that if some regions are not well synchronized, labor will move from the shrinking region to the expanding one, making the business cycles move together. If, however, the business cycles are not synchronized and labor is relatively immobile, then the single monetary policy will be right for some areas but wrong for others.

Business cycles in Europe have never been synchronized, although the convergence criteria were partly designed with this goal in mind. In addition, the Single European Act's guarantee of freedom for labor mobility does not seem to have created significantly more continent-wide labor mobility. Europeans, for example, are far less mobile than Americans. Given that most conventional measures show that the EU fails both criteria for being an optimal currency area, it seems natural to ask why they are taking this momentous step.

The Political Economy of a Single Currency

Most policies that bring relatively small benefits at the cost of potentially large costs should be rejected. Why, then, is monetary union pushing ahead? This is the question that many economists have asked, and the answers are less than clear. The easiest answers are that there are hidden and intangible benefits of monetary union (but what?) or that the leaders of the EU are simply swept up in a euphoric rush to greater political and economic unity. The latter explanation suffers from the defect that the EU has been unable to forge a consensus around a common defense and security policy, as evidenced by the divisions over the conflict in the former Yugoslavia.

The best explanation for the push to monetary union seems to be that it is politically necessary in the wake of the capital market liberalization required under the Single European Act. Prior to 1990, many countries had controls on the movement of foreign exchange into their country. Regulatory measures were common, such as taxes on foreign currency holdings, or on assets denominated in foreign currencies, and limitations on the uses of foreign currencies. The removal of these controls made it easier to speculate in foreign currency markets. One outcome of the removal of capital controls was the turmoil of 1992, when speculators became convinced that a number of currencies in the ERM would ultimately have to be devalued, prompting them to sell off large quantities of the currencies. During the sell-off, Portugal, Ireland, and Spain all devalued; Italy temporarily suspended participation in the ERM; and the United Kingdom dropped out permanently. Ultimately, the British pound fell by 25 percent from its peak before the speculative attacks. Soon after it left the ERM, there were several cases of firms that announced their intentions to close plants inside EU countries and move to the United Kingdom. For example, Philips Electronics, the giant Dutch firm, closed plants in Holland, and S.C. Johnson and the Hoover Company closed French plants, all in order to open new plants in the United Kingdom. The countries that devalued their currencies became popular destinations for international investment because it is cheaper to produce in weak-currency countries where the foreign investor's own currency buys more land, labor, buildings, and machinery.

Needless to say, political friction increases and cooperation decreases when one country loses jobs to another as a result of currency fluctuations. The desire to reduce these types of frictions is the reason why the European Monetary System, with its Exchange Rate Mechanism, was created in 1979. Consequently, it is the reason why a flexible exchange rate system is not an option. Although floating exchange rates have the advantage of permitting the greatest amount of flexibility in a nation's monetary policies, the EU's economic integration plans have closed the door on the use of flexible exchange rate systems. Their reasons were based on the desire to prevent nations from devaluing their currencies in an attempt to draw industries from other EU members.

Given that flexible rates are ruled out, it seems logical to ask why the EU did not choose to institute a system of fixed exchange rates. In fact, the ERM acts somewhat like a fixed exchange rate system because it ties each country's currency to the other country's. Exchange rates are not completely fixed, however, and we saw that there are bands that the currencies try to stay within. The EU's problem with a fixed exchange rate system is that it lacks the ability to keep the currencies within their bands, let alone to completely fix them. International currency markets know that there are definite limits to the resolve and the resources of member countries trying to defend their currencies within the bands. The EU has partially solved this by changing the bandwidths from ±2.25 percent to ±15 percent, which removes the minor short-run speculative pressures against particular currencies by letting them float down more before intervention becomes required. This, however, does nothing about the kind of serious pressure against a currency that the United Kingdom and Italy experienced in 1992. Strong speculative movements against one or another currency will sooner or later result in devaluations. In other words, the EU is not willing to defend their fixed rates if the costs grow too high, which means that fixed rates are not really "fixed."

Implementation of the Single Currency

The inability of the EU to maintain a set of fixed rates, coupled with the political un-desirability of floating rates, makes the single-currency option an attractive choice. Membership in the monetary union will be a subset of the EU. The United Kingdom has left the ERM and, along with Denmark, Sweden, and Greece, will not join the move to a single currency. Few, if any, of the remaining eleven met the convergence criteria by the 1998 deadline for compliance. Nevertheless, in May of 1998, it was an-nounced that all eleven countries (the fifteen members of the EU, minus the U.K., Sweden, Denmark, and Greece) would adopt the single currency on January 1, 1999.

The new currency will be called the "euro." In the first stage of the implementa-tion process, countries keep their national currencies, but they fix their exchange rates to each other. During this period, there will be two forms of legal tender: the new euros and the old national money. Changing currencies is expensive for private firms, since they have to change everything from accounting systems and software to vending machines, so there is a period of several years to allow the changes to move forward. Similarly, there are questions about the speed at which public authorities will convert. Newly issued national bonds are expected to be denominated in euros from the start, but the speed of conversion for existing debt will take longer. The plan is that by the year 2001, the national currencies are replaced. The two-year period in which exchange rates are rigidly fixed is probably the most uncertain. In fact, many specialists in the economics of exchange rates are skeptical about the idea that any fixed rate is irrevocably fixed. A long period of fixed rates while the new currency is gradually phased into use could lead to periods in which the national currencies are vulnerable to speculative attack. Consequently, the locking in of rates in 1999 is not necessarily the final act before the disappearance of national currencies.

While the problems are real, it is also remarkable that there seems to be a strong determination to implement the program of monetary union. In fifty years, a short period in historical terms, the nations of Western Europe have moved from world war to a common market. Now, they stand at the beginning of an economic union that has elements that may eventually lead to a political union. The achievement is remarkable.

Widening the European Union

The struggle to achieve monetary union by no later than 1999 is one of the most pressing problems facing the EU. Another is the timetable and conditions under which new members will be added to the EU. Ten Central and East European coun-tries have applied, as well as Turkey and the small Mediterranean island nations of Malta and Cyprus.

Central and Eastern Europe

The ten applicants from Central Europe and Eastern Europe are "transitional economies." That is, they are in transition from state-controlled to market-based economies. In addition, they are in the process of reforming their political systems through the creation of democratic institutions. The ten include the three Baltic Republics (Estonia, Latvia, and Lithuania), the so-called Visegrad Four (Poland, Hungary, the Czech Republic, and the Slovak Republic), Slovenia (formerly a part of Yugoslavia), Romania, and Bulgaria. The EU has given a green light for membership to five of the ten (Poland, Hungary, the Czech Republic, Estonia, and Slovenia) and Cyprus. The others are not ruled out, but their rejection in the initial wave of Central Europeans signals that they have significantly more changes to make before they can be reconsidered.

The EU has three major criteria that it uses to judge applicants. First, they must be stable, functioning democracies in which respect for human rights and the protection of minorities is assured. Second, they must be market-based economies. Third, they must be willing to adopt EU rules and to put them into national legislation. In July 1997, the EU released a report entitled *Agenda 2000*, in which it named the five countries that it thought should be in the first wave of members from Central and Eastern Europe. Negotiations have begun with each of the five, and the expectation is that they will join in 2003, although the report left open the possibility that they might join as early as 2001.

The eastern movement of the EU began in 1991 when the Union signed free-trade agreements with each of the Visegrad Four. Similar agreements were negotiated with Romania and Bulgaria in 1993 and the Baltic Republics in 1994. The agreements provide for an "associate member" status in the EU and will phase in free trade in most, but not all, goods and services. These agreements are asymmetical in the sense that the EU lifts its barriers before the other countries. The idea is to give them time to complete their transitions to market-based economies. The short-run effect of the free-trade agreements has been positive, and most of the applicants have experienced strong growth in their trade with Western Europe (see Chapter 16).

The major problem with the planned expansion is agriculture and agricultural policies. Several of the prospective members in Central and Eastern Europe have large agricultural sectors. Poland, for example, is a large country (38 million) and has about 27 percent of its labor force in agriculture. Agriculture is important to several of the other applicants as well because it generates exports and earns badly needed foreign exchange, but large agricultural sectors are a problem for the EU. The problem is institutionalized in the EU's agricultural policies, known collectively as the Common Agricultural Program, or CAP. The CAP is the world's most extensive set of farm price supports and farm income maintenance programs. One indicator of the CAP's importance is that despite recent and ongoing reforms, it is still expected to soak up 45 percent of the entire EU budget in the year 2001.

The CAP sets farm prices and guarantees a market for farm produce. It also provides direct-income payment to EU farmers. Among its many effects are that it keeps the farm sector in the EU larger than market forces would make it, and it has created large stockpiles of excess products. It seems unlikely that the EU can absorb more agricultural products itself, but the political and economic realities in the EU make it difficult to reduce subsidies paid to farmers. Extension of the subsidies to Poland and the other applicants is even less feasible. Full membership in the CAP would entail an enormous flow of payments to Central European farmers and an output response that would significantly add to the unwanted stockpiles of agricultural commodities.

This situation has its own tensions, however. While it is politically difficult to permit Central Europeans to penetrate EU markets with their agricultural commodities, it is also in the political and economic interests of the EU to support the transition to a stable and prosperous Central Europe. If Eastern and Central European transitions to market economies fail, the consequences for Western Europe include an unstable eastern border, fewer markets for manufactured goods, and the possibility of significant East-West migratory flows.

It is impossible to measure accurately the pool of potential migrants from all of Central and Eastern Europe; some estimates place it as high as 40 million people, but other estimates place the number in the range of 5 to 15 million persons. At the two outer limits of the estimates, 5 to 40 million people, the yearly inflow for the next decade would be equivalent to 0.3 to 2.4 percent of 1990 EU population. For comparison purposes, the decade of largest relative inflow into the United States (1900–1910) saw an average annual inflow of migrants that equaled 1.16 percent of U.S. population. Many EU countries (Germany, France, Italy, Belgium, Netherlands, and Luxembourg) have experienced substantial immigration in the last decades and have national political systems that have become sensitive to the issue. A new round of large immigrant flows would undoubtedly strain the tolerance of these systems, as it has already begun to do in some countries, such as France.

There is no guarantee that the opening of EU markets to Central European agricultural products will create a smooth transition to greater prosperity and reduce migration, nor is it certain that prosperity will fail to materialize if the EU markets remain closed to agricultural imports. Given the importance of agriculture, however, it makes the hard task of economic transition even more difficult when agricultural exports cannot be used to finance economic development.

A Possible Direction for Institutional Evolution

As Western Europe contemplates the widening of its economic union, there are a number of institutional complications that it must consider. First, the Baltic Republics, the Visegrad Four, and a number of other states have special economic and cultural ties to individual EU countries and to each other. The Baltic states and the Visegrad Four, for example, have a free-trade area among themselves. The individual Baltic Republics have each signed free-trade agreements with both non-EU countries (Switzerland, Liechtenstein, and Norway) and with EU countries (Sweden and Finland). Swedish and Finnish memberships in the EU take precedence over their ties to the Baltic Republics, but it is unlikely that either Sweden or Finland will back away from the close relationship it has formed with the Baltic Republics. Furthermore, the Baltic Republics are likely to develop strong economic linkages to Russia and nearby states such as Belarus, partly for reasons of economic expediency and partly due to the residency inside their boundaries of large numbers of ethnic Russians.

From the EU's perspective, expansion becomes a more difficult task as all of the formal and informal ties are considered. Does inclusion of Sweden and Finland in

1995 mean, for example, that Russian goods in Lithuania will have a greater opportunity to enter the EU market through Lithuania's ties to Sweden and Finland? In most cases, the EU can probably prevent this sort of unwanted occurrence by tracking the location of production of the goods it imports, but the boundaries between EU and non-EU countries begin to blur.

Even within the formal boundaries of the EU, not all countries have equal participation. The United Kingdom, for example, does not participate in the Exchange Rate Mechanism, although it is technically a member of the European Monetary System, and its currency forms part of the value of the ECU. Greece belongs to neither the ERM nor the EMS. Denmark, Ireland, and the United Kingdom have chosen to continue their passport controls on intra-EU travel. Denmark has limitations on cross-border shopping for autos and major household appliances. The United Kingdom stressed that it will not accept EU standards for workers' rights or other labor legislation, a stand that it reversed with the election of a Labor party majority in 1997. And four countries will not move to the single currency when it is introduced in 1999.

As these examples indicate, the general rules of the EU permit countries to opt out of institutions in which they do not want to participate. This attribute led many to believe that the future will involve several layers of participation, ranging from core members that follow all or nearly all the institutional rules to peripheral members that have the loosest of institutional ties. At the core will be the countries that share the single currency as well as the four freedoms. The next tier of participation will include most of the rest of the EU, all of whom share the four freedoms. Outside this group will be the remainder of Western Europe, including Liechtenstein, Iceland, and Norway. These three share the four freedoms, but they have no voting rights in EU institutions, nor would they participate in the most important EU programs, such as the CAP and the Regional Development Fund. The next layer of participants includes the countries sharing free-trade agreements with the EU, including the Baltic Republics, Poland, the Czech Republic, Slovakia, Hungary, Bulgaria, Romania, and Turkey. The extent of their participation in EU institutions is yet to be determined.

An arrangement with a core group and then several layers of membership categories would solve many of the institutional issues facing the EU. In particular, it would create a series of stages that allow new members to progress from distant to full participants if their own political and economic institutions warrant greater inclusion. It would remove the risk to the EU of admitting potentially unstable members, while offering an incentive for new democracies to strengthen their democratic institutions. It also solves the problem within the EU of the differences in the willingness and ability of states to participate in the changes called for by the Maastricht Treaty, such as the single currency.

Conclusion

It is easy to overlook the accomplishments of the European Union. There is still indecision on foreign policy issues, many of the members appear hesitant to follow through on the Maastricht Treaty's call for a single currency, tax rates between countries vary significantly, and the call for harmonization of social policies has encountered strong opposition. In addition, there are nine official languages, and cultural differences show little sign of disappearing.

It would be a mistake, however, to view these differences of philosophy and culture as a sign of weakness. Most goods, services, labor, and capital are free to move throughout the EU, and a long queue of nations is waiting to get in. Europe is the site of a majority of U.S. foreign investment, and U.S. firms have a real stake in the changes occurring there. The EU has created the largest integrated market in the world; China and other Asian nations may have more people, but their lack of income makes their market much smaller than Western Europe's. Regardless of the outcome of the single currency project, the EU and its policies will be an expanding presence in world trade and politics.

▲ The EU has been created in several stages. The earliest stage involved agreements over open trade for coal and steel (ECSC) and cooperation over the peaceful development of nuclear energy (Euratom).

▲ The main institutions of the EU are the Commission (executive branch), the Council of Ministers (legislative), the Court of Justice (judicial), and the European Parliament (advisory). The role of the institutions has evolved, and the Parliament in particular is gaining greater power.

▲ The Treaty of Rome was signed in 1957 (it was put in force in 1958), creating a six-country free-trade area that was gradually phased in over the next ten years.

▲ The next wave of deepening was the creation of the European Monetary System in 1979, linking exchange rates.

▲ Following the EMS, the Single European Act was passed, creating a common market by 1993. While preparations were taking place for the implementation of the SEA, the Maastrict Treaty, or Treaty on European Union, was signed in 1991 and approved by the national governments in late 1993.

▲ The Maastricht Treaty's main item calls for a common currency no later than 1999. In preparation for the common currency, a set of convergence criteria was developed to determine which countries would be ready to change over. The criteria set targets for interest rates, inflation, government spending, and government debt.

▲ While the EU was undergoing its several rounds of deepening its integration, it was also widening its membership to nearly all of Western Europe. Between 1958 and 1995, it expanded from the original six members to fifteen.

▲ Several Central European nations have applied for membership, and at least five are expected to join by 2003.

Vocabulary

Baltic Republics	The Council of Ministers
competitive devaluation	The Court of Justice
convergence criteria	Delors Report

democratic deficit

European currency unit (ECU)

Euratom

European Coal and Steel Community (ECSC)

European Commision

European Community (EC)

European Monetary System (EMS)

European Parliament

European Union (EU)

exchange rate mechanism (ERM)

Maastricht Treaty

Single European Act (SEA)

subsidiarity

Treaty of Rome

Visegrad Four

Study Questions

1. What were the three main stages of deepening that occurred in the European Community after the passage of the Treaty of Rome?

2. What are the four main institutions of the EU, and what are their responsibilities?

3. The Single European Act was cited as a case in which it was difficult to create an agreement, despite the fact that there was near unanimity in support of an agreement. If everyone wanted the agreement, why was it hard to negotiate?

4. How did the EU expect to create gains from trade with the implementation of the Single European Act?

5. A sudden sharp increase in the demand for the mark almost destroyed the Exchange Rate Mechanism. Explain how a rise in the demand for a currency can jeopardize a target zone or exchange rate band.

6. Discuss the pros and cons of the single currency.

7. Why has the EU embarked on a policy of implementing the single currency?

8. What are the pressures on the EU to admit new members? What pressures are there if it goes ahead with its plan to let in five more countries?

Suggested Reading

Bakker, A. F. P. *International Financial Institutions*, Chapters 9–11. London: Longman, 1996.

Eichengreen, Barry. "Should the Maastricht Treaty Be Saved?" *Princeton Studies in International Finance.* Princeton, N.J.: Princeton University Press No. 74, 1992.

Henning, C. Randall, Eduard Hochreiter, and Gary Hufbauer, Editors. *Reviving the European Union.* Washington, D.C. Institute for International Economics, 1994.

Hirtis, T. *European Community Economics,* 2nd Edition. St. Martin's Press, 1991.

Hufbauer, Gary, Editor. *Europe 1992: An American Perspective.* Washington, D.C. Brookings Institution, 1990.

Wallace, William. *Regional Integration: The West European Experience.* Washington, D.C. Brookings Institution, 1994.

In addition to the above, the EU's Web site has a wealth of information about the history, organization, and policies of the EU, along with access to treaty documents, data, press releases, and individual country servers. Its URL is *http://www.europa.eu.int/*. A Web site that gives the European Union's views on trade barriers in the United States and elsewhere is *http://mkaccdb.eu.int/*. The Web site EuroData is searchable by topic and country and gives access to current economic data: *http://www.cerge.cuni.cz/infoknih/eurodata/eurofram.htm*. EuroData also provides some data on Central Europe.

CHAPTER 14

TRADE AND POLICY REFORM IN LATIN AMERICA

Defining a "Latin American" Economy

Latin America stretches from Tijuana on the U.S.-Mexico border all the way to Cape Horn at the southern tip of South America. Within this vast geographic area lies such a diversity of languages and cultures that any definition of Latin America must have exceptions and contradictions. For example, *Webster's Ninth New Collegiate Dictionary* defines the region as Spanish America and Brazil, a standard view that must leave out a few small countries in Central and South America (Belize, Suriname, Guyana, and French Guiana) and the island nations of the Caribbean that were outside the region of Spanish and Portuguese settlement. It is perhaps less important to give a precise definition than it is to recognize the variety of physical geography, cultures, and income levels that coexist within any definition. In fact, the variety is so great that it is worth asking if these nations can truly be said to constitute a single world region. In other words, what is the "Latin American" experience, and how does it allow us to group together nations as different as Argentina, with its European culture and relative prosperity, and Guatemala, with its indigenous culture and great poverty?

The diversity within Latin America should make us careful not to overgeneralize. Nevertheless, there are several common themes shared by all, or nearly all, the nations in the region. First, there are common historical threads, beginning with the fact that a great many nations share a heritage of Spanish and Portuguese colonization, giving them a common linguistic base. We should be aware, however, that in some countries the languages of indigenous people are important as well. A second part of their shared histories is that many Latin American countries gained their national independence from Spain and Portugal during the nationalist revolutions of the early and middle nineteenth century. This differentiates them from the other regions of European colonization, Africa and Asia, and implies that the national identities of Latin Americans are perhaps deeper than in many parts of the developing world.

During the twentieth century, the nations of Latin America shared most economic experiences. The Great Depression of the 1930s, for example, caused most nations to shift their policies away from an outward, export orientation toward an inward, targeted industrial strategy. The new strategy eventually developed its own theoreticians and came to be known as "import substitution industrialization."

More recently, most nations were borrowers in the 1970s, only to experience severe debt problems in the 1980s. Finally, beginning in the 1980s and continuing through the 1990s, the region has embarked on a wide-ranging set of economic policy reforms, equal in scope to the transformations that began in Central and Eastern Europe with the collapse of communism.

In this chapter, we examine the origins and extent of the crisis that hit Latin America in the 1980s and analyze the responses. Before we examine the crisis of the 1980s and the economic reforms of the late 1980s and 1990s, we must first step back and look at the long-run performance of the economies of Latin America. When seen in the light of history, it is understandable why the miserable economic growth record of the 1980s has given rise to a dramatic shift in policies.

Population, Income, and Economic Growth

Table 14.1 is a snapshot of the current levels of income and population. Taken as a whole, the nations of Latin America make up a region with approximately 458 million, or 100 million more people than the three nations of NAFTA, and almost 100 million more than the fifteen nations of the European Union. Population alone makes the region one of the largest markets in the world.

Table 14.2 classifies the nations of Table 14.1 according to the World Bank's definitions of low, middle, and high income. Latin America contains no high-income nations, although Argentina is close to breaking into their ranks. Most countries lie in either the lower- or upper-middle-income designations, while three are extremely poor.

Table 14.1 shows the extent to which five countries account for the bulk of the population and production in Latin America. These are, in order by size of population, Brazil, Mexico, Colombia, Argentina, and Peru. Taken together, they add up to about 74 percent of the population of Latin America and nearly 86 percent of the GNP. In fact, Brazil, Mexico, and Argentina by themselves account for more than three-fourths (78 percent) of the GNP and more than three-fifths (61 percent) of the population.

If we were to focus exclusively on the 1980s, Latin America's ability to create economic growth and rising living standards seems limited. The obvious and natural comparison with the high-growth nations of East Asia—South Korea, Singapore, Hong Kong, Taiwan, Malaysia, Thailand, Indonesia—paints a picture of persistent failure in Latin America. Fortunately, this picture would be wrong.

Table 14.3 shows the GDP per capita growth during the past three decades. For long stretches of the twentieth century, Latin America was one of the fastest-growing regions of the world. In particular, from 1900 to 1960, the region's real GDP per capita grew as fast or faster than Europe's, the United States', or Asia's. Individual experiences varied, but most countries saw adequate to excellent growth along with rising living standards. From 1960 to 1980, growth slowed somewhat, but the region continued to record solid growth and kept up with all but the fastest-growing Asian economies. As world economic growth slowed after 1973, the experiences of the main Latin American economies became more varied. Some grew faster or nearly as fast, while some experienced a dramatic slowdown.

TABLE 14.1 Population and GNP for Latin America and the Caribbean, 1995

Country	Population (Millions)	GNP per Capita (1995 $)	GNP per Capita, Purchasing Power Parity
Andean Community			
Bolivia	7.4	$800	$2540
Colombia	36.8	1910	6130
Ecuador	11.5	1390	4220
Peru	23.8	2310	3770
Venezuela	21.7	3020	7900
Central American Common Market			
Costa Rica	3.4	2610	5850
El Salvador	5.6	1610	2610
Guatemala	10.6	1340	3340
Honduras	5.9	600	1900
Nicaragua	4.4	380	2000
Mercosúr			
Argentina	34.7	8030	8310
Brazil	159.2	3640	5400
Paraguay	4.8	1690	3650
Uruguay	3.2	5170	6630
Other Latin America/Caribbean			
Chile	14.2	4160	9520
Cuba	11.1	*na*	*na*
Dominican Republic	7.8	1460	3870
Haiti	7.2	250	910
Mexico	91.8	3320	6400
Panama	2.6	2750	5980
Total Population and (Weighted) Average GNP per Capita	467.7	$3322	$5707

Source: World Bank, *World Development Report, 1997.* Tables 1, 1a. Author's calculations.

Then the crisis struck. The Lost Decade of the 1980s was a disaster, not only in Mexico but throughout Latin America. The entire region experienced negative per capita growth from 1980 to 1985. A few countries, notably Chile and Colombia, began to emerge from the crisis by the middle of the decade, but the largest economies continued to have negative growth over the entire decade. By the late 1980s, most were emerging from the crisis of the 1980s, with the notable exceptions of Brazil and Peru, which were late to begin reforms. (Mexico's negative growth from 1990–96 reflects the severity of the depression in 1995 when real GDP fell about 6 percent.) The effects of the crisis were profound. Nearly fifty years of economic strategy came to an end as each nation began to abandon the inward-oriented, closed, and

Latin America: Income Classification

INCOME CLASSIFICATIONS

- N.A.
- Low (less than $725)
- Low Middle ($725-2,895)
- Upper Middle ($2,896-$8,955)

Income Classification is based on GNP per Capita 1995 $. Source: World Bank, World Development Report 1997

1:46,578,000
1:735.14 Inches to Miles
Robinson Projection

Scale

SDSU Geography
Chris Lukinbeal

TABLE 14.2 Income Level Classification by World Bank Definitions	
Income Classification	*Country*
Low Income (≤ $725)	Haiti, Honduras, Nicaragua
Lower Middle Income ($726 to $2895)	Bolivia, Colombia, Costa Rica, Cuba, Dominican Republic, Ecuador, El Salvador, Guatemala, Panama, Paraguay, Peru, Venezuela
Upper Middle Income ($2896 to $8955)	Argentina, Brazil, Chile, Mexico, Uruguay
High Income (≥ $8956)	

interventionist policies. The degree and timing of these changes varied from country to country, and there are questions about their permanency, but there is no question that the crisis of the 1980s triggered a major shift in economic policies throughout Latin America.

General Characteristics of Growth in Latin America

Before we examine the changes that were made in response to the crisis of the 1980s, we must briefly consider the characteristics of economic growth in Latin America since World War II. While individual country experiences varied considerably, there are a handful of issues that apply to many of them. A general sense of these issues and the growth patterns of the region help to set the stage for understanding the profound changes beginning in the 1980s in the orientation of Latin America toward the world economy.

TABLE 14.3 Average Annual Growth in Real GDP, 1960–1996

	Annual Growth in Real GDP per Capita (Percent)		
Country	**1960–1980**	**1980–1990**	**1990–1996**
Argentina	1.9	–3.2	4.6
Brazil	4.5	–0.6	1.3
Chile	1.5	1.1	5.3
Colombia	2.8	1.1	2.4
Mexico	3.9	–0.3	–0.5
Peru	1.8	–2.7	3.1
Venezuela	0.7	–2.0	0.4

Source: Penn World Tables (Mark 5.6). Author's calculations. Inter-American Development Bank, *Latin America After a Decade of Reforms*. Washington D.C.: Johns Hopkins University Press. 1997.

Inward Orientation

The official name for the economic development strategy that predominated throughout Latin America from the 1940s to the 1980s is **import substitution industrialization**, or **ISI**. Recall from the description of Mexico's economic policy in Chapter 12 that the goal of ISI is to industrialize through focused development of industries producing goods that are substitutes for imports. These industries received a high level of protection from foreign competition and a disproportionate share of the nation's financial resources. In many cases, government involvement went all the way to direct participation in production through the creation of state-owned enterprises. One feature of ISI development was that it created disincentives to export. This effect varied by country, but it represented a general shift in the world orientation of Latin America. From the mid-1800s, economic growth has been closely tied to the export of primary commodities such as coffee, cotton, fishmeal, copper, tin, and petroleum. With the adoption of ISI strategies, primary commodities continued to be the main exports, but their role in the national economies of Latin America declined as exports in general were underemphasized.

The Problems of Inequality and Poverty

A second historical characteristic of economic growth in Latin America is the presence of a relatively high level of inequality. Not surprisingly, this characteristic is intimately connected to low levels of productivity in subsistence agriculture. Precise measures of inequality are difficult, but there is widespread agreement based on a variety of measurements that Latin American incomes are less equally distributed than in any other developing country region. In part, this reflects a failure of productivity growth in agriculture, but since many countries are relatively highly urbanized, it also reflects conditions in cities. In general, high levels of income inequality seem to be associated with slower growth and development, although the mechanisms are not well understood.

Poverty is sometimes associated with inequality, although the two concepts are not the same. In the Latin American case, a smaller share of the population lives in poverty than in Asia or Africa, despite the less equal distribution of income. Similarly, social indicators of health and education also are somewhat better than in other developing regions. Nevertheless, poverty is a major problem that has gotten much worse since the crisis of the 1980s.

Inflation and Macroeconomic Instability

A third historical characteristic of growth in most countries over the last twenty-five years has been the periodic reoccurrence of macroeconomic crises. Typically, a crisis entails high rates of inflation and large budget and trade deficits. Inflation is often the result of a central government that tries to stimulate the economy through large government expenditures. Many countries have very weak and unenforced tax laws, so that increases in government expenditures are not paid directly by tax revenues. Consequently, governments have paid for their current expenses by printing more money. Given an increase in the money supply without a corresponding increase in goods and services, inflation is the inevitable outcome.

Increased inflation often leads to an exchange rate that is overvalued in real terms. Recall from Chapter 9 that the real exchange rate is the nominal rate adjusted for inflation:

$$R_r = R_n(P^* / P)$$

where R_r and R_n are the real and nominal rates (home currency divided by foreign), P^* is the foreign price level, and P is the level at home. If prices at home rise faster than prices abroad ($P\uparrow > P^*\uparrow$), then R_r falls, which is an appreciation. Overvaluation soon leads to growing trade and current account deficits that, in turn, lead to a loss of foreign reserves and may culminate in a crisis if other capital inflows are insufficient. The Latin American pattern is that the crisis forces the adoption of expenditure switching (devaluation) and expenditure reducing policies (cuts in governmental budgets), often resulting in recessions and rising poverty.

The Debt Crisis of the 1980s

A fourth element of a shared economic experience is the debt crisis of the 1980s. In August of 1982, Mexico announced to the world that it could no longer make payments on the principal and interest it owed foreign lenders, mostly banks in the United States and Europe. Soon after, a number of other large and small borrowers revealed a similar state of affairs in their finances. Few countries had abstained from the borrowing binge of the 1970s when banks in the United States, Europe, and Japan offered easy access to the funds they had accumulated from deposits by rich oil-producing countries. The banks had to lend the deposits they took in or go broke paying interest to the oil producers. There was no memory in the banking community of the Latin American debt crisis of the 1930s, when many countries defaulted on their debts. Consequently, in the 1970s, it was thought that lending to a nation was not risky, since "nations never go broke."

The motivation to increase borrowings varied from country to country. Oil producers such as Mexico and Venezuela borrowed because they had valuable oil in the ground that future generations could use to pay the debt; oil importers such as Brazil and Chile borrowed to avoid cutting government expenditures; and some countries, such as Peru, borrowed because they had chronic trade deficits that they had to finance with capital inflows. There is no indication that the IMF, or the World Bank, or the world banking community realized that a crisis was brewing. When it broke in August of 1982, it caught everyone off guard. Lending to Latin America ceased, and the Lost Decade began.

> **The Lost Decade.** *The Lost Decade, or* Decade Perdida, *refers to the period of recession brought on by the regionwide debt crisis that began in August 1982. Growth rates for most countries in Latin America were low or negative from 1983 until the end of the decade. There is no official date ending the Lost Decade, but 1989 is a useful benchmark, since it coincides with a new strategy for handling the crisis.*

Reform Movements of the 1980s and 1990s

Throughout the region, the immediate effect of debt crisis was a severe depression. Capital flows from the industrial countries stopped, government programs and investment ceased, all expenditures were cut, imports dropped, and production shifted toward export sectors in order to earn the foreign revenue needed to make payments on the debt. As the decade of the 1980s wore on, Latin Americans began to refer to it as the Lost Decade because the depression stopped industrial development and all progress in improving the standard of living.

Out of the experience of the Lost Decade came a new consensus on economic strategy for industrial development. The consensus included three main elements: (1) a stronger role for market forces and a reduction in state-led economic growth; (2) more openness toward the world economy and a reduction in import barriers and export disincentives; and (3) institutional reform, including a reduced role for the military and a movement toward building stronger democracies. Throughout the experience of the 1980s, the high-performance economies of East Asia served as examples and an alternative development model. Policy makers throughout Latin America were very aware of the stunning growth rates and spectacular export performance of those nations during their own hard times in thc 1980s. In effect, the Asian economies reinforced the idea in the minds of many Latin Americans that there were alternative approaches to economic development.

Import Substitution Industrialization

Import substitution industrialization (ISI) was the dominant economic strategy of Latin America from the 1950s until the 1980s, although its origins go back to the 1930s. It was central both to the high growth rates of the region from 1950 to 1980 and to the creation of the Lost Decade of the 1980s. It is worth looking at in more detail.

Origins and Goals of ISI

From the second half of the nineteenth century until the middle of the twentieth, most of Latin America relied on exports of agricultural commodities (tropical fruits, coffee, cotton, grains) and minerals (petroleum, copper, tin) to earn foreign revenue. These export sectors were often developed or controlled by foreign capital and had few economic linkages to the domestic economy, functioning instead as foreign enclaves within the nation. In cases where the export sector was domestically owned, it usually brought wealth to a relatively small number of people and added greatly to the inequality of power and money that is pervasive in Latin American society. As a result of this history, powerful proindustrial interests have often viewed the traditional export sector with suspicion and hostility. Nevertheless, the exports produced in these sectors were important sources of foreign revenue. During the worldwide Great Depression of the 1930s, the countries that reestablished their exports first were also the first ones out of the Depression, and in the post–World War II period, the countries that grew fastest tended to be those that were able to export.

The disruption of world trade caused by World War I and the Great Depression was particularly hard on countries that depended on primary commodity exports as a major source of income. In particular, the Depression was harmful because it caused a large reduction in demand and falling prices for the agricultural and mineral commodities that Latin America exported. In the 1940s, however, primary commodity producers in Latin America found that many of the effects of the Depression were reversed by World War II. While it created new risks for shipping, many nations earned large reserves of foreign currency from the materials they sold during the war.

This trend ended after the war with a sudden decrease in the demand for primary commodities from Latin America. The United States no longer needed as many raw materials, and Europe was unable to buy. The problem of a loss of World War II export markets was put into a theoretical context by the Argentinean economist, Raul Prebisch. Prebisch argued that there was a long-run tendency for the **terms of trade** to decline for primary commodity producers such as Latin America. Prebisch's research predicted that exporters of raw materials would receive constantly falling prices for their goods while having to pay constantly increasing prices for their imports of manufactured goods. For obvious reasons, this view was referred to as **export pessimism**, and it formed the basis of the economic policy that was followed from roughly 1950 to the 1980s.

> **Terms of trade (TOT).** *The terms of trade is the average price of a country's exports divided by the average price of imports:*
>
> $$TOT = (index\ of\ export\ prices) / (index\ of\ import\ prices).$$
>
> *A decline in the terms of trade means that each unit of exports buys a smaller amount of imports. A decline in the terms of trade is equivalent to a fall in living standards, since exports earn fewer imports. The fall in living standards is proportional to the importance of trade in a nation's economy.*
>
> **Export pessimism.** *Export pessimism is the name given to the views of Prebisch and his followers. They believed that the real prices received by Latin American countries for their exports would fall over time. They adopted this view based on their studies that showed a long-run tendency for the terms of trade to fall for countries that relied on raw materials exports. In the 1960s, Prebisch partially reversed himself and began to favor a stronger effort at exporting.*

As the head of the United Nations' Economic Commission on Latin America (ECLA in English; CEPAL in Spanish), Prebisch guided economic policies throughout Latin America. These policies emphasized the decline in the terms of trade for raw material exports, industrialization as the means to greater prosperity, and the use of industrial policies, including extensive trade barriers, to develop the manufacturing sector. Prebisch's policy prescriptions reinforced a shift that had begun with the destruction of trade in the 1930s. The loss of markets during the Great Depression temporarily forced Latin America away from dependence on raw material exports and toward industrial development through the replacement of imported manufactured goods with domestically produced ones—hence the name "import substitution industrialization." Ironically, domestic production of manufactured import substitutes required the importation of large quantities of capital goods (factory machinery and parts), and, in order to earn the revenues needed to buy these imports, most nations continued to depend on raw material exports in the decades after World War II. Primary commodities still make up a significant share of today's exports from Latin America.

ISI is a form of industrial policy. Its answer to the question about which industries to target is that developing countries should focus on those industries that produce substitutes for imported goods. According to Prebisch, the inevitable decline in the terms of trade for primary commodities means that the biggest constraint on industrial development is the shortage of foreign exchange. Lower export prices mean that countries find it harder and harder to earn the foreign exchange they need in order to buy the machinery and other capital goods they cannot produce themselves. One of the most important roles of import substitution is to reduce the need for foreign exchange that is used to buy goods that could be made at home.

ISI theorists argued that a country should begin by producing inexpensive and relatively simple consumer items, such as toys, clothing, food products (e.g., beverages, canned goods, etc.), and furniture. Gradually, the focus of industrial targeting should move on to more complex consumer goods (appliances and autos) and intermediate industrial goods (pumps, generators, basic metals, etc.). In the third stage, complex industrial goods would be produced (chemicals, electronic equipment, machine tools, etc.).

Criticisms of ISI

The economic tools for implementing ISI are the same as those for industrial policies discussed in Chapter 7. These include a variety of different types of government support, from subsidies of all kinds to trade protection and monopoly power in the domestic market. In retrospect, import substitution industrialization generated a number of unintended consequences that caused inefficiencies and wasted resources. Among the many criticisms that have been leveled at ISI are the following: (1) governments misallocated resources when they became too involved in production decisions; (2) exchange rates were often overvalued; (3) policy was overly biased in favor of urban areas; (4) income inequality worsened; and (5) ISI fostered widespread rent seeking. These issues will be taken up in turn.

Foremost among the problems of ISI are those related to an overconfident and naive belief in the ability of the state to efficiently direct resources into their best uses. In the 1950s and 1960s, it was often assumed that **market failures** were far more common in developing nations than in industrial ones, and that one of the main goals of any state should be to correct these through selective and careful state intervention in the economy. In this context, ISI can be interpreted as a set of policies in which government uses its economic and political power to improve on the market. (Recall from Chapter 7 how difficult it is to measure market failures and to know the required corrective action.)

> ***Market failure****. Market failure is the name given to a situation in which markets do not produce the most beneficial outcome economically . This can happen for many reasons. In the case of Latin America and import substitution industrialization, it was assumed that industrial development would create benefits outside the industry or industries that were growing and that market forces would not lead to the development of industry.*

While this model is not altogether wrong, it does overestimate the technical ability of government officials to identify market failures and their solutions. It also assumes that government bureaucrats are selfless individuals who ignore political considerations and focus only on economic efficiency and what is best for the nation as a whole. This naive model of political reality caused an underemphasis on problems related to the implementation of economic policies, such as corruption and the lobbying power of economic elites. It also failed to take into account the slow accumulation of special provisions, favors, and economic inefficiencies that built up over time when policies were heavily influenced by politics. Naturally, this problem was magnified by the inequality in wealth and income throughout Latin America. Powerful interest groups were able to use ISI policies to their own ends rather than in the national interest.

A second problem of ISI was the development and persistence of overvalued exchange rates. Overvaluation was a deliberate policy in some countries, while in others it was a chronic problem stemming from the maintenance of a fixed exchange rate under conditions of higher rates of inflation. Overvaluation developed into a particularly serious obstacle to economic growth after world inflation picked up in the 1970s. As a deliberate policy, overvaluation of the exchange rate accomplished several goals. In particular, it made it easier for the targeted industries to obtain the imported capital goods they needed. It also helped to maintain political alliances between the urban working classes and the political parties in power. It did this by helping to maintain relatively higher living standards through providing access to relatively less expensive foreign goods. As evidence of the last point, when governments were forced to depreciate in the 1980s and 1990s, they often lost the political support of the urban classes.

Although overvalued exchange rates had some benefits, they also had costs. Most importantly, they made it difficult to export because they raised the foreign price of domestic goods. The effects were perhaps most harmful to agriculture and the traditional export sectors, but it hurt industry as well by making exports less attractive and reducing the pressures of international competition. Since agricultural exports were less profitable, capital investment was directed away from that sector which, in turn, held down the growth of agricultural productivity and caused incomes to be relatively stagnant in rural areas. Overvalued exchange rates also made foreign machinery cheaper and caused industrial investment to be too capital intensive and insufficiently labor intensive. Consequently, industry did not create enough new jobs to absorb the growing labor force and the labor that left agriculture for the cities. Furthermore, since most industry is located in urban areas, government investment in infrastructure improvements—such as transportation, communication, and water—were heavily targeted toward cities and their environs. The share of the population that lives in urban areas varies across countries, but in many nations the failure to develop rural infrastructure, from roads to schools to power

CASE STUDY

ISI in Mexico

The Mexican constitution of 1917 established the power and the responsibility of the federal government to intervene in the economy in order to act as the leading agent of economic growth and as the referee of social conflict. This role was not institutionalized inside the Mexican government until the Mexican revolution was consolidated in the 1930s under the presidency of Cárdenas (whose son has been a leading opponent of the dismantling of ISI during the reforms of the 1980s and 1990s).

In order to lead and direct economic growth, government could legitimately claim the need to be powerful—otherwise, powerful social classes could resist the government's directives and initiatives, particularly those with distributional goals or consequences. Therefore, economic policy served not only to meet the needs of the country for economic growth and a fairer distribution but also to increase the political power of government. Mexico nationalized its oil industries in 1938, and throughout the twentieth century, a number of sectors have been nationalized and turned into state-run monopolies (telephones, airlines, banks, railroads, mineral development companies). The use of the government budget in this manner guaranteed access to investment funds, while monopoly ensured that the favored firms would succeed, at least within the nation.

In addition, the government offered loans and loan guarantees to many firms in targeted industries. Loans and loan guarantees helped firms to obtain capital at interest rates that were below what they would have paid otherwise. Similarly, the government sold foreign exchange at artificially low prices to targeted firms who needed to buy imports. Mexican exporters were required to convert their foreign exchange earnings into pesos at an overvalued peso rate (too few pesos per dollar), which made exporting relatively less profitable; the government then sold the cheaply acquired foreign exchange to targeted industries. In effect, exporters were subsidizing the development of the targeted industries.

Unlike many ISI nations, Mexico limited foreign investment. Like most ISI nations, however, when investment was permitted (e.g., autos), performance requirements were placed on the foreign firms. A common requirement was that the foreign firm balance its foreign exchange requirements so that each peso of imports was matched by a peso of export earnings. Further interventions occurred in the area of commercial policy where import licenses limited many types of imports. Recall that import licenses are essentially quotas. About 60 percent of all imports were subject to licensing by the 1970s.

From 1950 to 1973, Mexican real GDP per capita grew at the rate of 3.1 percent per year. By comparison, the United States grew 2.2 percent per year; the fourteen largest OECD nations grew 3.5 percent per year; and growth in the six largest Latin American economies was 2.5 percent. At the same time that the economy was undergoing relatively rapid economic growth,

Case Study continues

Case Study continued

industrialization was changing the structure of the economy. Mexican manufacturing expanded from 21.5 percent of GDP to 29.4 percent. Growth began
to slow in the 1970s, as it did in many parts of the world. One widely shared
view is that Mexican growth began to stall because the country was running
out of easy targets for industrial development. Light manufacturing and simple consumer goods industries are relatively easy to start up, and the conversion of a part of the nation's economy from subsistence agriculture to apparel
manufacturing makes growth rates look good. The next stages require more
sophisticated manufacturing, however, and are relatively harder to start up.
According to this view, Mexico had run out of simple industries to start and
was inevitably having a harder time producing more sophisticated goods that
were further from its comparative advantage.

In spite of rapid economic growth during the 1950s and 1960s, poverty and
income inequality continued. Large numbers of Mexicans, many of them indigenous people living in rural areas, did not participate in the growth of the
economy. This is evidenced by the fact that in the 1980s, much of agriculture
was still at a subsistence level, using 26 percent of the nation's labor force to
produce just 9 percent of the nation's GDP. The urban bias in Mexico's development strategy turned Mexico City into one of the largest metropolises in
the world, with more than 15,000,000 people in the greater metropolitan area
by the late 1980s. The sensational growth and crowding of people and industry
into the basin that holds Mexico City resulted in serious pollution problems.

There is no consensus among economists as to the role played by ISI in the
Mexican debt crisis of the 1980s. Certainly, ISI policies expanded the role of
the federal government in economic activity and increased government expenditures and borrowing during the 1970s. Nevertheless, overall economic
growth remained fairly robust until the mid-1970s. One widespread view is
that the easy gains of ISI were gone by the 1970s, and in order to keep growth
on track, Mexican presidents used their power over public finances to dramatically increase expenditures. At first, the government argued that it could easily afford to borrow in foreign capital markets because the nation had recently
(1978) become a major oil exporter. Ultimately, the government's fiscal policies generated enormous public sector deficits, fears of devaluation, and capital flight. By 1982, a year after the price of oil fell, the nation had run out of
international reserves and could no longer service its international debt. If the
government had not resorted to unsustainable macroeconomic policies, would
it have fallen into the debt crisis and rejected ISI policies in the mid-1980s?
Were the faulty macroeconomic policies caused by the failure of ISI?

supply systems, meant that subsistence farmers and their families did not benefit
from (or contribute to) national economic development. The human costs are high,
since rural inhabitants are far more likely to live below poverty lines.

In addition to a persistent tendency toward overvalued exchange rates, ISI trade
and competition policies were heavily protectionist and often favored the creation
of domestic monopolies. The lack of foreign and domestic competition meant that

manufacturing remained inefficient and uncompetitive. With profits from a protected domestic market, many producers saw no reason to invest in modern equipment, further reinforcing the uncompetitiveness of their products. It is ironic that as a consequence many countries became more vulnerable to economic shocks that originated outside of Latin America, which was precisely the opposite effect from the one that motivated ISI in the first place.

A final problem of ISI behavior is the development of widespread rent seeking behavior. When governments intervene in the planning and directing of industrial development, they give government officials and bureaucrats a wide range of valuable commodities to distribute. These include the many subsidies and licenses that are a part of ISI policies. For example, in order to protect the domestic market and to ensure access to needed imports, governments often required import licenses and at the same time, provided foreign exchange at subsidized prices to the importer. When government policy creates something of value, such as the license to import or a subsidy to buy foreign exchange, the private sector will spend resources to obtain it. In the absence of strong institutions to ensure the independence of the bureaucracy (and, often, even when they are present), bribes and corruption become a part of the decision making. Ultimately, some decisions are made for the wrong reasons, and economic waste is the result.

Macroeconomic Instability and Economic Populism

Many economists are convinced that while ISI policies are suboptimal, they had less of a direct effect in creating the economic crisis of the 1980s than did misguided macroeconomic policies. The reasons are relatively straightforward. ISI policies involve trade barriers and government support for selected industries. Collectively, these policies may lower a nation's income by a few percentage points, but they rarely lead to a full-blown economic crisis. Faulty macroeconomic policies, on the other hand, often lead to hyperinflation, depression, and balance of payments crises. In addition, while most of Latin America used ISI policies from the 1950s through the 1980s, economic growth remained at fairly high levels for most countries until the early 1980s when growth turned negative in nearly all countries. While it is entirely possible that the 1980s crisis was the culmination of several decades of ISI policies, it is certain that the crisis was directly linked to the faulty macroeconomic policies of the late 1970s and early 1980s.

Populism in Latin America

Many Latin America specialists blame the faulty macroeconomic policies of the region on **"populist"** or **"economic populist"** political movements that use economic tools to reach specific goals, such as obtaining support from labor and domestically oriented business, or isolating rural elites and foreign interests. Examples of populist leaders abound: in Argentina, Juan Perón (1946–1955 and 1973–1976) and Raúl Alfonsín (early 1980s); in Brazil, Getúlio Vargas (1951–1954), Joaō Goulart (1961–1964), and José Sarney (1985–1990); in Chile, Carlos Ibáñez (1952–1958) and Salvador Allende (1970–1973); in Peru, Fernando Belaúnde Terry (1963–1968), Juan

Velasco Alvarado (1968–1975), and Alan García (1985–1990); in Mexico, Luis Echeverría (1970–1976) and José Lopez Portillo (1976–1982). Populist movements in Latin America share nationalistic ideologies and a focus on economic growth and income redistribution. The central economic problem generated by these movements is the use of expansionary fiscal and monetary policies without regard for the importance of inflation risks, budget deficits, and foreign exchange constraints.

Economic populism. Economic policies emphasizing growth and redistribution that simultaneously deemphasize (or deny the importance of) inflation risks, deficit finance, external constraints (i.e., trade and exchange rate issues), and the reactions of economic agents.

Economic populism is usually triggered by three initial conditions. First, there is a deep dissatisfaction with the status quo, usually as a result of slow growth or recession. Second, policy makers reject the traditional constraints on macro policy: budget deficits financed through printing money are justified by the existence of high unemployment and idle factories, which seem to promise room for expansion without inflation. Third, policy makers promise to raise wages while freezing prices and to restructure the economy by expanding the domestic production of imported goods, lessening the need for foreign exchange. In the words of one analyst, the policies call for "reactivating, redistributing, and restructuring" the economy.

Early in the populist regime, there is a vindication of the policies. The economic stimulus of government expenditures and newly created money leads to rising growth rates and rising wages. Soon, however, bottlenecks begin to set in. For example, construction firms run out of particular inputs, such as cement or specialized steel products, and manufacturing firms cannot find the parts they need to repair their machinery. Prices begin to rise, and the budget deficit grows. In the next stage, inflation begins an extreme acceleration, and shortages become pervasive throughout the economy. The budget falls into serious deficit as policies become unsustainable, and wage increases cease keeping up with inflation. In the final stage, countries experience massive capital flight as fears of a devaluation develop. The flight of capital out of the country depresses investment and further depresses real wages.

After all is over, real wages are often lower than before the cycle began, and there is an international intervention under the sponsorship of the IMF, which is designed to stop the high inflation and end a balance of payments crisis. Typically, the IMF oversees the implementation of stabilization and structural reform policies that call for serious budget cuts, a slowdown in the growth of the money supply, a reduction in trade barriers, and, in general, greater reliance on market mechanisms and less government intervention. In the short run, these policies often cause a recession. These stages of the populist cycle are an idealization. Reality, as always, is more complex. Nevertheless, the stages described capture the essence of the populist experience as it has occurred in many Latin nations.

The Debt Crisis of the 1980s

In August 1982, Mexico announced that it lacked the international reserves it needed to pay the interest and principal due on its foreign debt. Mexico was not the first country

CASE STUDY I

Peronism in Argentina

Juan Peron served as president of Argentina during two separate periods: 1946 to 1955 and then 1973 until his death in 1974. After his death, his second wife and vice president, Isabel Peron, took over the presidency and continued his policies until she was overthrown in 1977. Peron's two terms demonstrate the shift in populist economics from a more traditional or classical version to a cruder economic version. Classical populism was more aware of the limits imposed by budgets and the availability of foreign exchange, whereas the more recent versions of economic populism have largely ignored these constraints. Peron's presidency is also significant because it was a dramatic statement of the policies that led to much slower growth in Argentina and that caused the country to fall further behind the industrial nations of the world. Early in the century, Argentina was one of the ten or fifteen richest countries in the world, and although it continued to grow economically, its rate of growth was so slow by comparison to the rest of the world that by the end of Peron's first term, it had fallen into the ranks of developing nations.

Peron's early policies were built on two core ideas. First, the powers of the state should be used to ensure that growth did not lead to increased inequality. Second, the terms of trade for Argentina were going to deteriorate, so the nation should seek economic independence from world trade. Peron's rhetoric called for a "New Argentina" in which workers would receive their fair share, foreign influences would be eliminated, and industrialists would receive favorable credit policies. This required heavy state involvement, and the government asserted itself quickly by nationalizing foreign trade, communications, railroads, docks, and banking. A five-year economic plan was established, consisting of subsidized credit, wage increases, and an expansion of federal expenditures and the fiscal deficit.

The policies of the five-year economic plan were initially successful, with significant growth in GDP between 1946 and 1948, moderate inflation, and rising real wages. The data in Table 14.4 illustrate the typical populist pattern of rapid growth in 1946 through the first half of 1948, the early years of the policy. The fiscal deficit also rose steadily, along with real wages. The increase in wages caused inflation to begin rising, however, and the sizable trade surpluses of 1945 and 1946 deteriorated quickly, resulting in a serious decline in foreign reserves in 1949. In 1949, Peron was forced to name a new finance minister, who implemented an orthodox stabilization plan consisting of tight credit, reduced government expenditures, and wage and price controls. By 1952, the plan began to work, prompting a new five-year plan that froze wages for two years and focused on attracting foreign capital. At the end of 1952, wages were still higher than in 1945, despite the fact that many of the gains between 1945 and 1952 were given back.

The second Peron administration began in 1973 with the election of a caretaker president, Hector Campora. Campora was a stand-in until new elections

Case I continues

Case I continued

TABLE 14.4 Economic Indicators During the First Peron Administration

	1945	1946	1947	1948	1949	1950	1951	1952
GDP **growth**	–3.2%	8.9%	11.1%	5.5%	–1.4%	1.2%	3.1%	–6.6%
Real wage index	100	103	129	156	162	172	145	128
Deficit/ GDP	4.6	6.9	5.8	13.4	9.8	5.5	4.5	5.6
Inflation	8.6	15.7	3.6	15.3	23.2	20.4	49.0	31.2
Trade balance (millions of U.S. $)	$429	$568	$107	$90	–$160	$143	–$305	–$455

Source: Gerchunoff, "Peronist Economic Policies, 1946–1955," in *The Political Economy of Argentina, 1946–1983,* edited by di Tella and Dornbusch, 1983.

could be held to reelect Peron. Between his election and his resignation, Campora launched an economic plan that consisted of a one-time wage increase followed by a two-year wage freeze and a freeze on prices. Peron, with his wife, Isabel, as his vice presidential running mate, was easily elected in September 1973 with 62 percent of the vote. Meanwhile, Campora's economic program showed early success, as the GNP grew in 1973 and 1974, inflation fell, and real wages increased (see Table 14.5).

Peron died in July 1974, and Isabel assumed the presidency. Unions, which were an important component of the Peron constituency, negotiated 100 percent wage increases, and inflation increased to 335 percent. Exports declined significantly, and the government adopted a stringent stabilization plan in

TABLE 14.5 Economic Indicators During the Second Peron Administration

	1973	1974	1975	1976
GDP growth	5.8%	6.5%	–1.3%	–2.9%
Real wage index	100	109	106	63
Deficit/GDP	6.3	5.9	14.4	7.9
Inflation	44	40	335	364
Current account balance (Millions of U.S. $)	$731	$94	–$1,094	$125

Source: di Tella, Guido, "Argentina's Economy Under a Labour-Based Government, 1973–6," in *The Political Economy of Argentina, 1946–1983,* edited by di Tella and Dornbusch, 1983.

Case I continues

Case I continued

March 1976 in return for help from the IMF. By 1977, the inflation rate had declined from 364 to 160 percent, the fiscal deficit declined, and GNP began growing once again. The end result of the economic policies of the second Peron administration was a significant decline in real wages, and a reduction of labor's share of national income—the exact opposite of what was intended.

CASE STUDY II

Alan Garcia and Peru

Alan Garcia became president of Peru in July 1985. As part of the fallout from the debt crisis, the country had suffered through a serious recession in 1983, but it was on the mend. Garcia's policies were a textbook case of economic populism. He immediately began a program to raise real wages in order to stimulate demand and redistribute income. The economy responded to the stimulus of higher consumption with very robust increases in the GDP in 1986 and 1987. The presence of idle factory capacity along with unemployed workers enabled the GDP to expand without initially creating inflation. By mid-1987, however, some essential imported inputs became scarce and began to act as bottlenecks on further increases in production. Consequently, inflation rekindled. See Table 14.6.

Government policy for the exchange rate was based on a controlled rate that was periodically devalued. Inflationary price increases were greater than the exchange rate devaluations and thereby caused an appreciation in the real

TABLE 14.6 Economic Indicators During the Garcia Administration

	1984	1985	1986	1987	1988	1989	1990
GDP growth	4.8%	2.3%	9.2%	8.5%	−8.3%	−11.7%	−5.1%
Real wage	−8.0	−8.4	26.6	6.1	−23.1	−46.7	−14.4
Deficit/ GDP	6.7	3.4	5.7	7.9	8.1	8.5	5.9
Inflation	110	163	78	86	667	3339	7482
Current account balance (Millions of U.S. $)	−$221	−$137	−$1,077	−$1,481	−$1,091	$396	−$766

Source: Inter-American Development Bank, *Economic and Social Progress in Latin America,* various years.

Case II continues

Case II continued

exchange rate, which led to a significant increase in the current account deficit.

The rise in 1987's budget deficit, trade deficit, and rekindling of inflation late in the year would have been enough to cause a more cautious government to rein in expenditures. Garcia's administration responded to the deterioration in economic indicators by nationalizing the property of the financial services sector (banks, insurance companies, etc.) and expanding credit subsidies for favored groups in the agricultural and industrial sectors. In 1988, the government tried to tackle the problem of inflation through devaluations and price freezes, but in order to protect incomes and to bring relative prices into agreement, it simultaneously permitted selected price increases and compensating wage increases.

By 1990, the economy reached the deepest point in its recession. In July, a new government took office and implemented a relatively orthodox stabilization program of fiscal and monetary austerity in order to end inflation and curb the budget deficit. By then, however, real wages were well below the level they had attained when the previous government took power in 1985.

to declare its inability to service its debt, but it was the biggest up to that point. Its announcement soon led to the realization that a number of other countries, including most of Latin America, were in similar circumstances. Thus began the Lost Decade.

Proximate Causes of the Debt Crisis

In Mexico's case, the collapse of oil prices in 1981 undermined its ability to earn the revenue it needed to service its debt. The problem was compounded by the fact that a significant portion of its debt was owed in dollars at variable interest rates and that efforts to combat inflation in the United States and elsewhere had resulted in a higher level of world interest rates. Consequently, interest payments on Mexico's debt rose at the same time that the nation's ability to earn dollars shrank.

The collapse of oil prices in 1981 and the rise in world interest rates were not the only external shocks to the economies of Latin America. In 1981–1982, the world's industrial economies entered a deep recession that reduced world demand and prices for many of the raw materials produced in Latin America and elsewhere. In Mexico's case, oil was the critical commodity, but a number of other primary commodity exports experienced a similar decline in their world price.

The decline in the prices of Latin America's exports and the rise in interest rates were serious economic shocks and a significant part of the mix of events that led up to the debt crisis. These external economic shocks probably would not have caused a generalized debt crisis without some additional factors, however. Historically, debt crises require a set of external shocks to the indebted countries but also an acceleration of international lending; the rise in lending occurred between 1974 and 1982. Added to theses two factors was the complicating problem of mismanagement of national macroeconomic policies in the late 1970s and early 1980s.

During the 1970s, financial institutions throughout the developed world were awash in money that they were anxious to lend. The rise in oil prices in 1973 and 1974 (and again in 1979) led to an enormous expansion of bank deposits by the oil-rich nations of the world. Banks in New York, London, Paris, and Frankfurt were anxious to lend these deposits and aggressively sought out new borrowers beginning in 1974. For Latin America and the Caribbean, long-term, publicly guaranteed debt rose from slightly over $37 billion in 1973 to more than $261 billion in 1983. The sudden acceleration in commercial bank lending and the rise in the amount of debt made the economies vulnerable to a sudden and unforeseen economic shock.

Table 14.7 shows the size of the debt for some of the most heavily indebted countries after the first year of the crisis. The second column of numbers expresses the debt in net terms (gross debt minus debt owed by foreigners) as a percentage of GDP. The third column of Table 14.7 shows the net interest payments owed as a percentage of exports of goods and services. This is a useful indicator because ultimately nations have to pay the interest on their international debts out of the revenues they earn from their exports. What we see is that between 10 and 63 percent of the revenue earned by exports went to pay interest and, consequently, was unavailable for purchasing imports or for investing domestically.

Responses to the Debt Crisis

Initially, most analysts in the United States and in the international financial institutions such as the IMF perceived the debt crisis to be a temporary, short-run liquidity problem. Under this assumption, the reasonable response is to increase capital flows to Latin America and other indebted regions so that they would have the financial resources to service their debts. One of the biggest obstacles to increasing financial

TABLE 14.7 Debt Indicators at the Onset of the Debt Crisis, 1983

	Gross External Debt (Millions of U.S. $)	Net External Debt as a Percentage of GDP	Net Interest Payments as a Percentage of Exports
Argentina	43,634	75.3	62.8
Bolivia	3,328	141.9	38.5
Brazil	92,961	48.3	38.7
Chile	17,315	87.6	32.9
Colombia	10,306	25.1	18.8
Costa Rica	3,646	137.8	45.4
Mexico	86,081	63.8	32.1
Peru	10,712	52.4	20.1
Venezuela	32,158	38.8	9.6

Source: Cline, William, *International Debt Reexamined*, 1995; World Bank, *World Debt Tables*, 1987.

flows, however, was that commercial banks in the United States and Europe were no longer willing to lend after 1982, raising a question about the source of needed capital flows.

From the perspective of Latin governments, the choices were not attractive. Outright default and disavowal of the debt would cut off most of a nation's trade and investment linkages. The consequences for investment and growth would be risky and potentially disastrous, depending on the reaction of the United States and other governments. On the other hand, if they continued to make interest payments (and, potentially, principal repayment), it would require huge trade surpluses in order to earn the revenue they needed to pay for imports plus interest on the debt.

Recall from Chapter 8 the fundamental accounting balance of an open economy:

$$S_p + (T - G) = I + CA$$

where S_p is private savings, $(T - G)$ is government (public) savings, I is investment, and CA is the current account balance. Nations turn current account deficits into surpluses, or small surpluses into large ones, by following two kinds of policies: expenditure-switching policies and expenditure-reducing policies. Expenditure-switching polices, such as devaluations of the currency, turn the demand for foreign goods into a demand for domestic goods and raise CA directly. Expenditure-reducing policies, such as tax increases and cuts in government spending, raise $(T - G)$ and, indirectly, reduce consumption, investment, and imports. The net effect of expenditure-reducing policies is often a recession in which the demand for domestic and imported goods falls due to a fall in domestic income.

In other words, in order to accumulate the resources they needed for their interest payments, Latin governments were forced to follow contractionary policies that caused deep recessions throughout the region. Between 1982 and 1986, the average rate of growth of real per capita GDP was –1.8 percent per year in Latin America and the Caribbean.

From the standpoint of official U.S. policy, the solution was perceived to be more economic growth. Growth would give the indebted countries enough additional revenue to pay off their debt and to increase their own consumption and investment. Furthermore, the key to growth was thought to be increased investment, which was only possible if capital flows into the indebted regions were restored. The first policy proposal along these lines was the Baker Plan, which was put forward by the U.S. secretary of the treasury, James Baker, in 1985. The Baker Plan tried to formally organize a renewed lending program by the commercial banks. Needless to say, most banks that had Latin American loans in their portfolios were trying to reduce their exposure to the region, not increase it. Consequently, few resources were forthcoming under this plan.

By 1987, it was apparent to analysts throughout the world that restoring capital flows was not enough. There was a need for deep reform in the economies of Latin America. First, it was observed that the faulty macroeconomic policies of the region consistently left aggregate national expenditure above national income and that the likelihood of a return to growth was small as long as the gap between the two remained. Second, in their attempt to keep government expenditures higher than warranted, many countries had resorted to printing money, which resulted in high and increasing rates of inflation. Third, the burden of the debt itself was becoming apparent to everyone inside and outside Latin America. After the interest and principal payments were made, insufficient export earnings remained for domestic investment and consumption. Hence growth was stunted. By 1988–1989, both creditors and the multilateral lending agencies such as the IMF were in agreement that debt relief was in everyone's interest.

The growing consensus on the need for debt relief led to the Brady Plan (1989), named after the secretary of the treasury during the Bush Administration, Nicholas Brady. Essentially, the Brady Plan gave something to everyone. Creditors were required to restructure some of the old debt into longer-term debt with a lower interest rate and to make some additional new loans. The multilateral lending agencies, such as the IMF, were required to provide additional loans on concessional terms (i.e., below market interest rates), and borrowers were required to provide evidence of their willingness to begin serious economic reform before any new loans would be forthcoming. The Brady Plan did not end the debt crisis, but it was a significant step toward greater stability in the region. After 1989, capital flows began to return to Latin America but this time not in the form of bank loans. Rather, savers and investors in the United States, Europe, and Asia began to increase their direct investment in Latin America, as well as their holdings of various financial assets, such as stocks and bonds issued by private companies doing business there. While large inflows of capital can present problems (particularly if they reverse and flow out), they are the additional savings and investment that are needed if the region is to return to its historical levels of growth. To a large degree, the new capital that has been flowing into the region since 1989 is a vote of confidence by investors around the world.

From the vantage point of the late 1990s, the most lasting effects of the debt crisis, other than the foregone output due to the recessions of the 1980s, are the deep economic reforms that have taken place in country after country. The reforms of the late 1980s and 1990s are key to explaining the return of capital flows to Latin America. Reforms vary by country, both in kind and degree, but they mark a historical regional shift away from the protectionist and interventionist policies of ISI and economic populism toward more open and market-oriented policies.

Economic Policy Reform and the "Washington Consensus"

By the late 1980s, most countries in Latin America had started a series of economic policy reforms that began to alter the fundamental relationships between business and government and between their national economy and the world. After 1989, the reforms intensified and became more general. In most cases, the reforms consisted of three separate but interrelated features. First, and with varying degrees of success, governments implemented stabilization plans to stop inflation and to control their budget deficits. Second, most countries began privatizing the government-owned parts of their economies: manufacturing enterprises, financial and other services, mining operations, tourism, and utility companies. Third, trade policies shifted toward more openness and less discrimination against exports. Throughout Latin

America, this package of reforms has come to be known as the "**neoliberal model**" or **neoliberalism** because it represents a partial return to classic nineteenth-century European liberalism that favored free markets and minimal government intervention in the economy. By 1992, these reforms were beginning to pay off, as growth had returned to most countries.

In spite of the benefits of policy reform, however, many problems persist. Poverty and inequality continued to increase in many countries, since growth did not filter down into all the sectors. The problem of poverty was compounded by the lack of adequate infrastructure, which made it harder for all segments of society to benefit from economic growth. The absence of schools, health clinics, roads, clean water, and other infrastructure elements, particularly in rural areas where poverty is greatest, limits the reach of restored economic growth.

Stabilization Policies to Control Inflation

Many countries sought to avoid the recessionary consequences of the onset of the debt crisis by increasing government spending. The only way to finance government spending, however, was through the printing of more money, since tax systems were inadequate and government borrowing abilities were limited by the debt crisis. The reckless printing of money to finance government spending drove a number of nations into periods of hyperinflation, as detailed in Table 14.8.

The solution to the hyperinflation experienced by Argentina, Bolivia, Brazil, and Peru is simple to prescribe: cut government spending and stop printing money. The implementation of this prescription was difficult, however, mainly for political reasons. In the short run, if price increases outstrip wage increases (as is often the case in a period of disinflation), then the burden of bringing down the rate of inflation falls mainly on wage earners who experience a fall in their real wages. Consequently, anti-inflation policies alienate the political support of many wage earners

TABLE 14.8 Inflation Rates, 1982–1992

	Inflation (in Percents)		
Country	Average 1982–1987	Average 1987–1992	Highest 1982–1992
Argentina	316	447	4924 (1989)
Bolivia	776	16	8170 (1985)
Brazil	158	851	1862 (1989)
Chile	21	19	27 (1990)
Colombia	21	27	32 (1990)
Mexico	73	48	159 (1987)
Peru	103	733	7650 (1990)
Venezuela	10	40	81 (1989)

Source: Edwards, Sebastian, *Crisis and Reform in Latin America,* 1995.

and make governments unpopular with a large share of the population. In addition, it was argued that there was a great deal of inertia in the price increases: everyone expected future inflation to be high, and this caused producers to raise prices in anticipation of higher future input costs. The problem of inflation developing a momentum of its own and a lack of empirical information about the depth of this problem led to two different policy prescriptions for controlling inflation: the orthodox model and the heterodox model.

The **orthodox** model minimizes government involvement in the economy. Consequently, its anti-inflation prescription is straightforward: cut government spending, reform the tax system to make it effective, and limit the creation of new money. The **heterodox** model calls for the same actions plus the freezing of wages and prices. In the heterodox view, inflationary expectations are so embedded in economic decision making that price increases will continue even if government spending and new money creation cease.

Empirically, it is difficult to choose which model has performed best. Between 1986 and 1992, Brazil implemented five separate heterodox stabilization plans to end inflation, and not one of them worked. Similarly, heterodox plans in Argentina (1985) and Peru (1985) were successful for approximately a year but then failed, as inflation returned with a vengeance. Nevertheless, Brazil, Argentina, and Mexico each ultimately controlled inflation using heterodox methods.

> *Heterodox and orthodox stabilization plans. A heterodox stabilization plan is a policy designed to cure inflation by (1) cutting government spending, (2) limiting the creation of new money, (3) reforming the tax system, and (4) freezing wages and prices. Orthodox plans do (1) through (3) but omit (4).*

One issue that neither the heterodox nor orthodox models address directly is institutional reform. In Mexico's case, the freezing of wages and prices was an outcome of a formal agreement between labor interests, business interests, and the government, known as the Social Solidarity Pact (Pacto de Solidaridad Social, or "El Pacto"), which was passed in 1987. Brazil's successful plan under President Cardoso (the Real Plan, 1994) was widely discussed and commented on in Congress before it was implemented, and Argentina's plan (The Convertibility Plan, 1991) was part of a set of institutional reforms that limited the ability of the central bank to print new money. Bolivia was able to control its hyperinflation without the extensive use of price and wage freezes, but it depended on a series of financial reforms that significantly lessened direct government control over the financial services sector and reformed the tax system to make revenue collection more reliable.

One last issue that still confronts many nations is the problem of inconsistency between inflation stabilization and exchange rate policy. Mexico's experience is a good example of the problem and stems from the fact that the exchange rate is a powerful weapon in the fight against inflation. Mexico fixed its peso to the dollar in the mid-1980s as part of its anti-inflation strategy. (Argentina and Brazil did the same under their stabilization plans of 1991 and 1994, respectively.) Domestically produced goods that compete with U.S. goods were forced to avoid price increases so they would remain competitive. Furthermore, prices did not increase on imports of U.S.-made capital goods, which were essential to Mexican industry, thereby helping to hold down Mexican prices for finished manufactured goods. Since Mexican inflation was still slightly higher than U.S. inflation, the peso became overvalued over a period of time. Ultimately, this contributed to a serious trade imbalance and the collapse of the peso in December 1994, followed by a deep recession in 1995. Since 1994, Mexico has let the peso float against the dollar and has stopped trying to use the exchange rate as an anchor against the current of inflation.

Structural Reform and Open Trade

Stabilization policies to control inflation and curtail large budget deficits are usually one part of a package that also includes structural reform policies. One way to keep the two types of policies separate is to recognize that stabilization generally focuses on macroeconomic policies (e.g., inflation and government budgets), while structural reform tends to be more microeconomic, dealing with issues of resource allocation. For example, structural reform policies include the privatization of government-owned enterprises, deregulation and redesign of the regulatory environment of over-regulated industries such as financial services, and the reform of trade policy.

The many initiatives to privatize and reform the regulatory environments of the economies of Latin America are quite impressive, but this section will focus on the most impressive area of structural reform to date: the economic integration of the region with the world economy. Prior to the onset of the debt crisis, the economies of Latin America had the most restricted trade systems of all the nations in the noncommunist world. In many countries, the debt crisis reinforced the belief that isolation from the world economy was the only way to protect a nation from shocks that originated in the external environment.

A few countries broke with this tradition and began to reform their trade policies in the 1970s, most notably Chile. Mexico and Bolivia followed in 1985 and 1986, and by 1987–1988, it was apparent throughout Latin America that trade had to be more open if they were to succeed in restoring economic growth. In the late 1980s and early 1990s, nearly all the countries of Latin America began reducing both the level of tariffs and nontariff barriers (NTBs) and the variability of tariff rates across industries and goods. Table 14.9 shows the changes in tariffs and nontariff barriers that occurred between the mid-1980s, when the reforms began, and the early 1990s. Particularly in the removal and reduction of NTBs, the changes are dramatic.

Along with the removal of barriers to trade, many new regional integration initiatives were started. A number of these initiatives sought to revitalize existing trade blocs that had become little more than paper organizations by the early 1980s. For example, the Andean Pact, the Caribbean Community (CARICOM), and the Central American Common Market (CACM) each became the basis for new efforts toward regional integration and export promotion. In addition to the re-energizing of existing agreements, new trade blocs were created as well. The most important of these is the Common Market of the South (Mercado Común del Sur, or Mercosur), which combines two of the largest economies in Latin America plus two small economies. In addition to Mercosur, however, there is NAFTA; although it is not purely a Latin American trade bloc, it does include Mexico, the second largest economy in the region.

TABLE 14.9 Tariff and Nontariff Barriers in Latin America

	Average Tariff		*Percent of Imports Covered by Nontariff Barriers*	
	1985	**1991–1992**	**1985–1987**	**1991–1992**
Argentina	28.0	15.0	31.9	8.0
Bolivia	20.0	8.0	25.0	0.0
Brazil	80.0	21.1	35.3	10.0
Chile	36.0	11.0	10.1	0.0
Colombia	83.0	6.7	73.2	1.0
Costa Rica	92.0	16.0	0.8	0.0
Mexico	34.0	4.0	12.7	20.0
Peru	64.0	15.0	53.4	0.0
Uruguay	32.0	12.0	14.1	0.0
Venezuela	30.0	17.0	44.1	5.0

Source: Edwards, Sebastian, *Crisis and Reform in Latin America,* 1995.

A third set of regional integration initiatives developed out of the trade policies of a number of individual countries, most notably Chile and Mexico. These two countries began negotiating and signing a number of bilateral free-trade agreements with other countries, as well as agreements with other trade blocs. For example, Mexico has signed or is negotiating free-trade agreements with each of the Andean Pact nations, with Chile, with the CARICOM, and with the European Union. Chile has signed agreements with each of the Andean Pact nations, except Bolivia, and with Mercosur, and it is negotiating with the EU (see Table 14.10).

The three main goals of trade reform were to reduce the anti-export bias of national policy, to raise the growth rate of productivity, and to make consumers better off by lowering the real cost of importable goods. In response to the changes in trade policy, the growth rate of exports picked up in most countries, while nontraditional exports increased dramatically. Furthermore, productivity rose in a majority of countries for which there are data. The productivity increase is at least partly the result of trade opening due to the impact of technology transfers, the improved investment climate, and the pressures on local firms to remain competitive.

It is difficult to judge whether more open trade has, as yet, contributed to an increase in the standard of living of consumers throughout Latin America. As long as productivity is rising, living standards will follow, although often with a lag. It may also be the case that the benefits of rising productivity are limited to specific sectors, however, where productivity growth occurs or where unions have more bargaining power over wages. Overall, economic growth in the 1990s has far surpassed the experience of the 1980s, in spite of the setback caused by the collapse of the Mexican peso at the end of 1994. In many countries, however, growth has not reached into all sectors of society.

Latin America: Trade Blocks

Mexico

Cuba

Haiti

Dominican Republic

Honduras

Guatemala — Nicaragua

El Salvador

Costa Rica

Panama

Venezuela

Colombia

Guyana

Suriname

French Guiana

Equador

Peru

Brazil

Bolivia

Paraguay

Chile

Argentina

Uruguay

Atlantic

Ocean

Pacific

Ocean

TRADE BLOCKS

Mercosúr

Andean Community

Central American Common Market

Scale

1:46,578,000
1:735.14 Inches to Miles

Robinson Projection

SDSU Geography
Chris Lukinbeal

TABLE 14.10 Regional Trade Blocs

	Year	Members	Goals
Andean Community	1969	Bolivia, Colombia, Ecuador, Peru, Venezuela	Common market
Caribbean Community	1973	Antigua and Barbuda, Bahamas, Barbados, Belize, Dominica, Guyana, Grenada, Jamaica, Montserrat, St. Kitts and Nevis, St. Lucia, St. Vincent and the Grenadines, Suriname, Trinidad and Tobago	Common market
Central American Common Market	1961	Costa Rica, El Salvador, Guatemala, Honduras, Nicaragua	Customs union
Mercosur	1994	Argentina, Brazil, Paraguay, Uruguay	Common market
NAFTA	1994	Canada, Mexico, United States	Free-trade area

CASE STUDY

The Washington Consensus on Economic Policy Reform

The Washington Consensus is the name that has been given by the economist John Williamson to a set of economic policies that constitutes the specifics of the neoliberal model. The "Washington" part of the name refers not only to the site of the U.S. government but also the site of the leading institutions in the international financial community (IMF and World Bank) and the unofficial community of think-tanks that is centered there. The "Consensus" part of the name refers to the fact that these are fairly uncontroversial elements that a majority of economists in those institutions (U.S. government, IMF, World Bank, and Washington, DC think-tanks) believe to be good economic policy.

   The consensus has ten elements:

1.   Fiscal discipline: Primary surplus of several percent of GDP and an operational deficit of no more than approximately 2 percent of GDP.
2.   Public expenditure priorities: Favor efforts to improve income distribution via health, education, and infrastructure expenditures over administration, defense, indiscriminate subsidies, white elephants.
3.   Tax reform: Lower marginal rates, increase effectiveness of overall system, broaden the base.
4.   Financial liberalization: Ensure positive real rates; abolish preferential interest rates for favored borrowers.

Case Study continues

Case Study continued

5. Exchange rates: Set at a level to ensure competitiveness; make it credible.
6. Trade liberalization: Replace quantitative restrictions with tariffs, and progressively reduce them.
7. Foreign direct investment: Encourage it; allow foreign and domestic firms to compete on equal footing.
8. Privatization: State enterprises should be privatized.
9. Deregulation: Abolish barriers to entry or restrictions on competition; ensure an environmental, safety, or prudential rationale for remaining regulations.
10. Property rights: Make them secure for both the formal and informal sector.

Not surprisingly, some economists outside of Washington question the need for some of these policies—particularly those relating to numbers 6 through10, which might be considered more micro and less macro in scope. We will take up this issue in the next chapter when we look at the success stories of East Asia. It should also be noted that even within the Washington Consensus there is ample room for disagreement.

Disagreements include the following:

1. The use of capital controls
2. The need to target the current account
3. How fast, how far to reduce inflation
4. Whether to try to stabilize the business cycle
5. The use of incomes policies
6. The need to eliminate indexation
7. The best technique to try to correct market failures
8. The size of the tax burden and the size of government (as measured by GDP)
9. Whether to engage in deliberate income redistribution policies
10. Whether to use industrial policies
11. The correct model of the market economy (Anglo-Saxon versus social market economy or "Japanese style")
12. Priority of population control
13. Priority of environmental preservation

Source: John Williamson, "In Search of a Manual for Technopols," in *The Political Economy of Policy Reform.* Washington D.C.: Institute for International Economics. 1994

The effects of both stabilization and structural reform policies on the welfare of Latin Americans is crucial to the long-run sustainability of the reform programs. Ultimately, if economic policy reforms do not make a majority of the people better off, then there is no point in keeping to the reforms. Economic theory predicts that the reforms that have been set in place will eventually lead to more efficient allocations of resources, higher productivity, and higher living standards. Yet, many factors may stand in the way, not the least of which is the need for deep reform in the political systems of many nations.

Conclusion

In the last decade, the many nations of Latin America have undergone an enormous shift in policies as economic policy reform has been at the top of the agenda for nearly every nation. The reforms are fundamental and represent a historical shift away from the inward-oriented, relatively closed economies that have characterized the region since the 1940s. Both stabilization policies, to control inflation and end large budget deficits, and structural reform policies, to integrate and deregulate the economies, have significantly reduced the role of governments in economic production.

These changes should not be confused with the adoption of laissez-faire, or completely free, market economic policies. While governments have chosen to let market forces grow, there are a number of key economic issues that governments must address. Foremost are issues of poverty alleviation and infrastructure development. After the recessions and crises of the Lost Decade of the 1980s, most nations had far more people living in poverty, along with a badly neglected basic infrastructure of education, health care, potable water, and transportation systems. These are problems that market forces by themselves will not solve. By removing themselves from direct production of commercial goods and services, however, governments will have more resources to address issues of infrastructure and poverty.

▲ Latin America has been one of the fastest-growing regions of the world throughout most of the twentieth century. Growth came crashing to a halt in the 1980s, however, and only began to return in the late 1980s and early 1990s.

▲ Until the recent reforms, Latin American economic growth has tended to focus on inward development rather than outward orientation. Productivity in subsistence agriculture has lagged behind overall growth, leading to much higher rates of poverty in rural areas than in urban ones.

▲ The primary development strategy of Latin America was adopted in the 1930s, 1940s, and 1950s. It came to be called import substitution industrialization and focused on the inward-oriented development of industries that could produce goods that would substitute for imports. This model of development was favored because it was thought that Latin America would suffer ever-declining terms of trade for its primary commodity exports, and that ISI would reduce the need for foreign exchange and imports, thereby making the region less vulnerable to economic shocks from outside.

▲ Economic growth under ISI was adequate, but ultimately it led to an inefficient manufacturing sector, excessive rent seeking, a persistent tendency toward overvalued exchange rates, and too great a concentration of resources on the urban sector.

▲ ISI policies were often made worse by the tendencies of many countries to elect or support economic populists. Populists favored economic growth and redistribution while, in the extreme, they ignored economic constraints such as government budgets and foreign exchange shortages.

▲ Populist policies generated macroeconomic instability, which often led to hyperinflation and falling real wages.

▲ The debt crisis that began in 1982 affected every country of the region, even those without high levels of debt or debt problems. As a result of the crisis, it became extremely difficult to borrow internationally.

▲ The main causes of the debt crisis were the increases in lending during the 1970s and the external shocks of interest rate hikes and primary commodity price decreases, especially oil. The faulty macroeconomic policies of many Latin American governments during the late 1970s and early 1980s made them more vulnerable to the shocks.

▲ The debt crisis resulted in negative growth throughout the region for most of the period from 1982 through 1987. By 1987–1988, the need for significant reforms in economic policy was apparent to almost all governments.

▲ From the mid-1980s up to the present, the governments of Latin America have engaged in serious reforms of economic policy. The reforms have first tried to create macroeconomic stability through controlling inflation and reducing budget deficits. Stabilization policies have been followed by structural reforms that have opened trade, privatized, and reduced and redesigned the regulatory environment.

Vocabulary

Baker and Brady Plans

debt crisis of the 1980s

Economic Commission on Latin America (ECLA, or CEPAL in Spanish)

economic populism

export pessimism

import substitution industrialization (ISI)

Lost Decade

market failure

neoliberalism

orthodox and heterodox stabilization policies

structural reform

terms of trade (TOT)

Washington Consensus

Study Questions

1. What were the main characteristics of economic growth in Latin America from the end of World War II until the debt crisis of the 1980s?

2. What is import substitution industrialization? Explain its goals and methods.

3. What are the main criticisms of import substitution industrialization? Did ISI fail?

4. Describe a typical cycle of economic populism. Why does it often leave its supporters worse off than before the cycle begins?

5. Explain how economic populist policies usually lead to overvalued exchange rates and large trade deficits.

6. What were the proximate causes of the debt crisis? How did the U.S. and other industrial countries respond?

7. Why did the Latin American debt crisis of the 1980s cause recessions in each country?

8. What is the difference between stabilization policies and structural adjustment policies? Give examples of each.

9. What is neoliberalism? Why do some people consider it a negative term?

10. What was the content of Latin American trade reforms of the late 1980s and 1990s? How do the actions taken relate to the desired goals?

Suggested Reading

Cardoso, Eliana, and Helwege, Ann. *Latin America's Economy: Diversity, Trends and Conflicts.* Cambridge, MA: MIT Press, 1992.

Dornbusch, Rudiger, and Edwards, Sebastian, eds. *The Macroeconomics of Populism.* Chicago: University of Chicago Press, 1991.

Edwards, Sebastian. *Crisis and Reform in Latin America: From Despair to Hope.* New York: Oxford University Press, 1995.

Hirschman, Albert. "The Political Economy of Import Substituting Industrialization in Latin America," *Quarterly Journal of Economics.* Vol. 82, No. 1, February 1968.

Lustig, Nora, ed. *Coping with Austerity: Poverty and Inequality in Latin America.* Washington, DC: The Brookings Institution, 1995.

Lustig, Nora. *Mexico: The Remaking of an Economy.* Washington, DC: The Brookings Institution, 1992.

Rodrik, Dani. "Understanding Economic Policy Reform," *Journal of Economic Literature.* Vol. 34, No. 1, March 1996.

Thorp, Rosemary. "Reappraisal of the Origins of Import-Substituting Industrialization, 1930–1950," *Journal of Latin American Studies.* Vol. 24, Quincentenary Supplement, pp. 181–195, 1992.

Williamson, John. *The Political Economy of Policy Reform.* Washington, DC: Institute for International Economics, 1994.

In addition to these sources, the Organization of American States has an excellent Web site. The OAS is the main forum for political and economic dialogue in the Western Hemisphere: *http://www.oas.org/*. In particular, the OAS provides access to its Sistema de Información al Comercio Exterior (SICE), or the Foreign Trade Information System in English. SICE has the full text of Western Hemispheric trade agreements, summaries of agreements, quantitative data, information on the Free Trade Area of the Americas, and more: *http://www.sice.oas.org/*. The Library of Congress offers free access to an online version of the Handbook of Latin American Studies: *http://lcweb2.loc.gov/hlas/*, and the University of Texas Latin America Network Information Center (LANIC) is one of the most popular academic sites on the Web: *http://www.lanic.utexas.edu/*.

CHAPTER 15

INTERNATIONAL ASPECTS OF EAST ASIAN GROWTH

The High-Performance Asian Economies

One of the most remarkable events of the post–World War II period is the rise of the high-performance Asian economies, or HPAE. The term *high-performance Asian economies* was coined by the World Bank and refers to eight East Asian economies: Hong Kong, Japan, Indonesia, Korea, Malaysia, Singapore, Taiwan, and Thailand. In spite of the recent financial crisis that hit several of these nations in the summer and fall of 1997, their story is remarkable and worth studying. The fact that they have all experienced unusually high rates of growth in real GDP per capita for two or more decades means that they have laid the foundation for a return to robust rates of growth after the crisis of 1997 is resolved. The similarities in their economic policies and their differences from other developing regions such as Latin America point to important lessons for all developing regions.

> *HPAE, 4 Tigers, and NIE. HPAE is the acronym for the eight high-performance Asian economies of Hong Kong, Japan, Indonesia, Korea, Malaysia, Singapore, Taiwan, and Thailand. The 4 Tigers (also called the 4 Dragons or Little Dragons) are Hong Kong, Korea, Singapore, and Taiwan. Economic growth in the 4 Tigers began shortly after Japan's post–World War II development. They are all classified by the World Bank as either high-income or upper-middle-income economies. NIE is an acronym for Newly Industrializing Economy. There are a number of these economies in Latin America as well as East Asia (e.g., Argentina, Brazil, Chile, and Mexico). Indonesia, Malaysia, and Thailand fall into this category among the HPAEs. For the most part, their period of high growth began after the takeoff of the 4 Tigers.*

Economists agree on several of the keys to their growth. For example, unlike the experience of Latin America, and in spite of their own recent financial chaos, macroeconomic stability has been a high priority throughout the rapid-growth countries. A second fact that stands in contrast to other regions is that there is a strong and credible commitment to sharing economic growth with all layers of society, in part through access to education, health care, and land reform. This proved to have numerous benefits, including the rapid creation of a skilled workforce. A third difference is that the

High Performance Asian Economies (HPAEs)

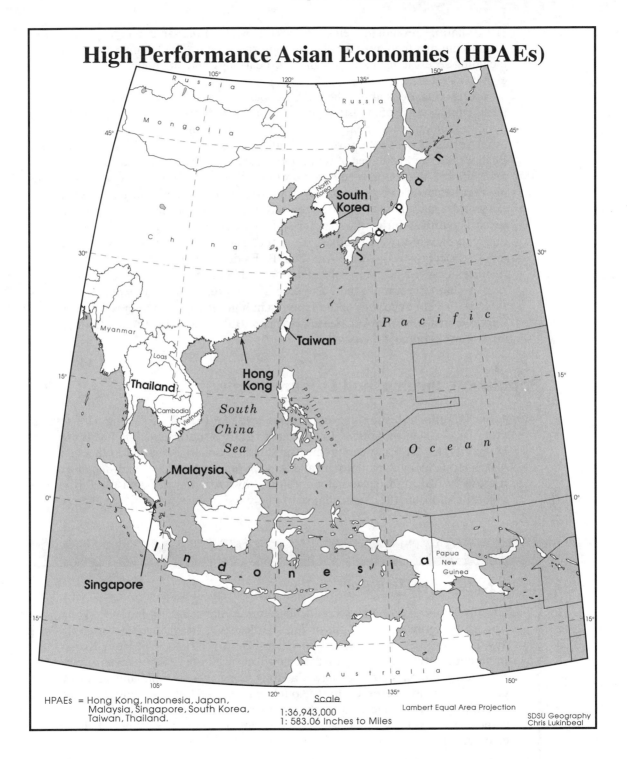

HPAEs = Hong Kong, Indonesia, Japan,
Malaysia, Singapore, South Korea,
Taiwan, Thailand.

Scale

1:36,943,000
1: 583.06 Inches to Miles

Lambert Equal Area Projection

SDSU Geography
Chris Lukinbeal

HPAE nations promoted their export sectors while at the same time they were more open to imports than most developing countries. This, too, had numerous advantages, including access to technology, high export earnings, and an implicit incentive to foreign investment.

Several questions about the HPAE experience remain unanswered. For example, the importance of industrial policies (industrial targeting) is unclear. Were these policies incidental and benign, or were they instrumental in creating growth? Another series of questions revolves around the use of interventionist government policies and the avoidance of rent seeking. Specifically, in the various government interventions in economic activity, how did nations avoid the problem of rent seeking that has been so costly to Latin America? On the other hand, perhaps they did not avoid it, and that is one of the reasons for the collapse of the financial sector in several countries during the summer and fall of 1997. This is a big unknown, particularly in light of the crisis. Finally, does the "East Asian Miracle" represent a new model for economic growth? Are the HPAEs doing fundamentally the same thing that the first wave of industrialized nations did in order to achieve high incomes?

This chapter examines these and several other questions as it explains the issues surrounding the successes of the East Asian high-growth economies. In particular, the contrast with Latin America is emphasized, along with East Asian trade and international economic relations.

Population, Income, and Economic Growth

Table 15.1 illustrates the size and income levels of the HPAEs along with several other large Asian economies. In contrast to Latin America, income levels are high in the HPAEs. GDP per capita (measured in U.S. dollars at market exchange rates) places Hong Kong, Japan, Korea, and Singapore in the ranks of high-income countries, while Taiwan is close behind. (Note, however, that the data for Taiwan are older. In addition, the 1997 collapse of many Asian currencies means that at 1998

A Note on Hong Kong

On July 1, 1997, Great Britain officially returned the colony of Hong Kong to China after more than 150 years of British rule. China has pledged itself to follow the policy of "one country, two systems" in its relations with Hong Kong. In practical terms, this means that China will allow Hong Kong to keep its own currency, will limit migration between Hong Kong and the mainland, and will generally try to preserve Hong Kong's current system. No one can say whether they will adhere to this policy or not. Insofar as this book is concerned, Hong Kong will be treated as a separate nation, as it was under British colonial rule.

TABLE 15.1 Population and GNP for the HPAEs and Selected Asian Economies, 1995

Country	Population (Millions)	GNP per Capita (1995 $)	GNP per Capita (PPP)
High-Performance Asian Economies			
Hong Kong	6.2	22,990	22,950[1]
Indonesia	193.3	980	3,800
Japan	125.2	39,640	22,110
Korea	44.9	9,700	11,450
Malaysia	20.1	3,890	9,020
Singapore	3.0	26,730	22,770
Taiwan	20.4[2]		8,063[2]
Thailand	58.2	2,740	7,540
Other Asian Economies			
Bangladesh	119.8	240	1,380
China	1,200.2	620	2,920
India	929.4	340	1,400
Pakistan	129.9	460	2,230
Philippines	68.6	1,050	2,850

[1]GDP instead of GNP.

[2]1990.

Sources: World Bank, *World Development Report, 1997* (Table 1).

exchange rates, GNP per person is considerably less. This would not greatly affect the purchasing power parity estimates, however.) Indonesia, Malaysia, and Thailand each began their periods of rapid growth somewhat later, and the other Asian economies are considerably behind in terms of their living standards.

Table 15.2 is arranged so that it is directly comparable to Table 14.3 in Chapter 14. Note that there is no growth slowdown in the 1980s and that, in fact, several of the HPAEs (as well as several other Asian economies) actually experienced growth speedups while the rest of the world was slowing down through the late 1970s and 1980s. This is one of the biggest contrasts between the recent experiences of East Asia and Latin America, and it is one of the primary reasons why East Asia has attracted the attention of economists and other scholars in Latin America. China's growth record might also qualify it as a member of the "high-performance" club, but the differences in its policies and institutions make it unlike any other Asian economy in Tables 15.1 and 15.2, so it is treated separately.

According to the "Rule of 72," if a variable (income, for example) grows at the rate X, then it doubles in approximately $72 / X$ years. In other words, Singapore's 7.5 percent growth rate for real GDP per capita between 1960 and 1980 implies that income doubled every $72 / 7.5 = 9.6$ years. Over the span of twenty years, income doubled and then doubled again; within the span of twenty years, average income rose more than four times. While Singapore, 1960–1980, is one of the most outstanding examples of rapid growth, each of the other HPAEs saw its income at least double between 1960

TABLE 15.2 Average Annual Growth in Real GDP, 1960–1996

Country	Annual Growth in Real GDP per Capita (Percent)		
	1960–1980	1980–1990	1990–1996
High-Performance Asian Economies			
Hong Kong	7.0	5.4	5.5
Indonesia	3.5	4.4	7.6
Japan	6.3	3.6	1.4
Korea	6.3	8.0	7.2
Malaysia	5.0	3.0	8.7
Singapore	7.5	5.2	8.4
Taiwan	6.5	6.1	
Thailand	4.3	5.1	7.9
Other Asian Economies			
Bangladesh	0.7	2.5	4.3
China	2.7	3.1	12.8*
India	0.7	3.7	5.1
Pakistan	2.8	2.3	4.5
Philippines	2.6	−0.6	2.9

*1990–1995

Source: Penn World Tables (Mark 5.6); Author's calculations; IMF, *International Financial Statistics.*

and 1980. Since 1980, growth has tapered off most notably in Japan, yet each of the HPAEs continues to enjoy rates of growth that are envied elsewhere in world.

General Characteristics of Growth in the HPAEs

Recall from Chapter 14 that from the end of World War II until the mid- to late 1980s, economic growth in Latin America was characterized by high levels of inequality, periods of macroeconomic instability, and an inward orientation. The contrast with the HPAEs could not be more striking: growth in those nations was built around falling inequality, generally sound macroeconomic fundamentals, and the promotion of exports. It is worth looking at each of the elements in more detail.

Shared Growth

One of the most remarkable features of growth in the HPAEs is that it was accompanied by rising economic equality. This feature is even more remarkable when it is realized that inequality in income and wealth was already relatively low at the start of the period of high growth. Since the 1950s pioneering work of the economist Simon Kuznets, it had been thought that growth in developing countries would result first in rising inequality, followed later by declining inequality. While Kuznets's work was based on measurements from a large number of countries, the East Asian experience has called into question the idea that economic growth in developing countries follows a "Kuznets's curve," in which equality first declines and then rises.

Table 15.3 compares income distribution in the HPAEs with Latin America. The last three columns show the percent of the nation's income received by the poorest 20 percent of households, the percent received by the richest 20 percent, and the ratio of the two. The poorest households in the five Latin American nations receive an average of 3.9 percent of society's income, while in the HPAEs, the poorest receive 6.5 percent. The richest 20 percent receive 55.6 percent in the Latin American sample and 45 percent of total income in the HPAEs. In other words, by comparison to Latin America, the rich receive a smaller share in the HPAEs, and the poor receive a larger share.

The conditions that led to greater income equality were rooted in the unique historical experiences of each country. Nevertheless, each nation had a similar set of highly visible wealth-sharing mechanisms. Specifically, these included land reform, free public education, free basic health care, and significant investments in rural in-

TABLE 15.3 Measures of Income Distribution, East Asia and Latin America

	Year[1]	Income Share of Bottom 20%	Income Share of Top 20%	Ratio of Top 20% to Bottom 20%
HPAEs				
Hong Kong	1980	5.4	47.0	8.7
Indonesia	1987	8.8	41.3	4.7
Japan	1979	7.9	37.5	4.3
Korea	1976	5.7	45.3	8.0
Malaysia	1987	4.6	51.2	11.1
Singapore	1982–83	5.1	48.9	9.6
Taiwan	1985	8.4	37.6	4.5
Thailand	1987	6.0	51.0	8.5
Average		6.5	45.0	7.4
Latin America				
Brazil	1983	2.4	66.6	33.3
Colombia	1988	4.0	53.0	13.3
Mexico	1984	4.1	55.9	13.6
Peru	1985–86	4.4	51.9	11.8
Venezuela	1987	4.7	50.6	10.8
Average		3.9	55.6	16.6

[1]Comparisons of income distribution must rely on country studies that are done in different years. No nation does annual surveys of income distribution.

Source: Campos and Root, *The Key to the East Asian Miracle*, p. 11.

frastructure, such as clean water systems and transportation and communication systems. These policies did not equalize incomes, but they provided people with the tools they needed to raise their individual incomes and gave hope for the future. This had several positive effects. For example, when purchasing power is spread more widely through a society, it increases the opportunities for small- and medium-scale entrepreneurs that produce for the local market. The experiences gained in meeting local demand may grow into larger enterprises and carry over into numerous other activities. In addition, rising incomes across a broad spectrum of socioeconomic groups raise everyone's hopes for future improvements and encourage cooperation among the different classes of society while conferring legitimacy on the ruling governments. Both factors contributed to political stability as well as the willingness by the business elites to commit to long-term investments.

Rapid Accumulation of Physical and Human Capital

Rising levels of equality were closely tied to very rapid rates of accumulation of physical and human capital. Rapid accumulation of physical capital is synonymous with high levels of investment. Investment, in turn, depended on high savings rates. The level of savings in the HPAEs is considerably higher than in many other parts of the world. The explanations behind the reasons for high savings are varied. In part, it is a result of the rapid **demographic transition** experienced by those nations after World War II. The demographic transition is the shift from high birth rates and high death rates to low birth and death rates. Countries that have completed a demographic transition have fewer children below working age and a larger percentage of the population engaged in economically productive work. Hence, they tend to have higher savings rates.

> ***Demographic transition.*** *The demographic transition is the term used to describe the shift from high birth rates and high death rates, which are characteristic of nearly all pre-industrial societies, to low birth and death rates, which are characteristic of high-income, industrial societies. Generally, death rates fall before birth rates, causing a "population explosion." As incomes rise, birth rates fall as well, and the overall rate of population growth slows. Within societies that have passed through the complete transition, children are a smaller percentage of the population.*

Another factor that increased both the level of savings and the level of investment was the absence of high inflation and the presence of stable financial institutions. The crisis of 1997 calls into question whether people will continue to have confidence in their financial institutions and whether this will affect savings rates. Nevertheless, until that crisis, most investors acted as if they believed that their financial savings were protected both against loss of value through high inflation and against a collapse in the banking system. If the crisis has lasting effects in undermining the confidence people have in their domestic savings outlets, it will perhaps prove to be far more costly than first anticipated.

While the rapid demographic transition, low inflation rates, and stable financial institutions appear to have caused savings rates to be high, probably the most important factor was simply the rapid rate of income growth. That is, savings and income growth are interdependent, and the HPAEs seemed to have created a "virtuous cycle" in which high-income growth caused high savings. Savings led to high rates of investment, which fed back into a second round of high income and high savings.

Investment in people was equally important to the accumulation of physical capital. One of the key features of the HPAEs' educational policy is that public investment in education was focused on the primary and secondary levels. Educational dollars go farther at this level, and the social impact is much greater per dollar spent than at the university level. These investments raised literacy rates dramatically and laid the foundation for a highly skilled workforce that was capable of tackling increasingly sophisticated forms of production. In effect, the continuous rise in human capital endowments of the HPAEs constituted an ongoing shift in the comparative advantages of those nations, so that new investments could continually push into new product lines.

Rapid Growth of Manufactured Exports

Each of the eight HPAEs actively and successfully promoted exports, although each began its development pushes with import substitution policies. ISI policies, however, were quickly replaced with an emphasis on export promotion. The timing of the switch from ISI to export promotion varied by country. Japan began promoting exports in the late 1950s and early 1960s, the 4 Tigers (Hong Kong, Korea, Singapore, Taiwan) started in the late 1960s, and the newly industrializing economies (NIEs—Indonesia, Malaysia, and Thailand) began in the early 1980s.

Table 15.4 shows the results of the export push. Between 1965 and 1990, the HPAEs made dramatic increases in their share of world exports and particularly in their share of world exports of manufactured goods. If we leave out Japan and only consider the seven HPAE developing economies, by 1990, the seven had over 56 percent of all exports from the world's developing countries and nearly 75 percent of manufactured exports.

In part, the success of the export promotion drives was the result of education policies that favored primary and secondary schooling. These policies created widespread literacy and an adaptable and easily trained labor force. In addition, each of

TABLE 15.4 The Share of HPAEs in World Exports, 1965–1990

	HPAE Share of World Exports (Percent)		
	1965	**1980**	**1990**
Total Exports	7.9	13.1	18.2
Exports of Manufactures	9.4	17.3	21.3

Source: World Bank, *The East Asian Miracle*, p. 38.

the HPAEs pursued various export promotion policies. For example, Japan and the 4 Tigers made export financing credit readily available; they required export targets for firms that wished to receive favorable credit terms or tax benefits; and they provided tariff-free access to imports of capital equipment used to manufacture exports. Policies in the NIEs were somewhat less interventionist and relied to a greater extent on attracting foreign direct investment in export activities.

The connection between export promotion and high rates of growth is an area of some controversy in economics. There are several possible connections that are explored in greater detail later in the chapter. A second controversy is the possibility of other nations using similar export promotion strategies. In many cases, these policies generate trade conflicts and may be at odds with the rules for fair trade agreed to by the signatories to the Uruguay Round agreement in the World Trade Organization.

Stable Macroeconomic Environments

A fourth and final characteristic of the HPAE economies is the maintenance of stable macroeconomic environments. Chapter 14 argued that one of the persistent problems of Latin America has been the frequent reoccurrence of macroeconomic crises. Even before the crisis of 1997, the high-performance economies of East Asia were not completely free of macroeconomic crises, but when they occurred, policy responses were usually quick and appropriate. Macroeconomic stability can have several components, and the factors that are usually emphasized in this context are a commitment to keeping inflation under control, good management of both internal government debt and externally owed foreign debt, and the quick resolution of crises when they occurred. In general, macroeconomic policy has been characterized as "pragmatic and flexible."

On average, budget deficits and foreign debt were not dramatically smaller than in other regions of the world. The difference in the HPAE, however, is that they were kept within the limits of the ability of the government to finance without having to print money or to borrow excessively. High growth rates helped ease the constraints imposed by a given level of debt, while foreign debts remained within acceptable limits, partly because of the high levels of exports that earned the foreign assets necessary for debt servicing. The crisis of 1997 is the exception that proves this rule, since one of the key triggers of the crisis was a significant reduction of export earnings in a couple of countries and the growth of large current account deficits. To many foreign investors, these deficits began to seem larger than was warranted, and this triggered significant capital flight.

The commitment to low inflation helped keep real interest rates stable and enabled firms to take a longer-run view of their investments. In addition, low inflation helped to avoid severe real appreciations in the exchange rate. Low inflation also meant that variations in the real exchange rate, the real interest rate, and the inflation rate were relatively low. In turn, this helped to foster a greater security in the minds of investors and probably encouraged them to take a long-run view of their activities.

The Crisis of 1997

The East Asian financial crisis began in Thailand during July 1997. From there, it spread to a number of other countries, including Malaysia, the Philippines, Indonesia, and South Korea. The outward symptoms of the crisis were fairly similar across countries: currency speculation and steep depreciations, capital flight, and financial and industrial sector bankruptcies. It is tempting to interpret these symptoms as signs of the region's weaknesses, but ironically, the causes are at least in part due to the region's great strengths.

A key element for the most severely affected countries was large trade deficits. Table 15.5 shows that current account deficits in 1996 averaged 5.4 percent of GDP for the five nations listed, while in the case of Thailand, it hit nearly 8 percent of GDP. The crisis was not limited to the countries in Table 15.5. Singapore, Taiwan, and Hong Kong felt the effects as well, but they each had trade surpluses and large stocks of foreign reserves, so their economies were far more capable of weathering the storm.

In addition to trade deficits, there were a number of other contributing factors. Foremost were the large capital flows to the region, brought on in part by the trade imbalances but also as a result of the widespread perception that East Asia was a good place to invest. The region averaged about 5 percent growth per year in real GDP over the last thirty years, and further growth seemed certain. In addition, slow growth in Japan and Europe caused many international investors to scour the globe looking for higher returns. The economies of southeast Asia each had histories of low inflation and small budget deficits (or consistent government surpluses, in several cases). In other words, the macroeconomic indicators looked good, and international lenders stood ready to make loans.

Most of the Asian economies pegged their currencies to the dollar. As the dollar appreciated in the mid-1990s, it caused the pegged exchange rates to appreciate

---

TABLE 15.5 Current Account Balances and Currency Depreciations

	Current Account Balance, 1996 as a Percent of GDP	*Currency Depreciation, July 1, 1997 to February 2, 1998 (Percents, relative to $ U.S.)*
Indonesia	–3.4	–76
Malaysia	–6.3	–39
Philippines	–4.5	–36
South Korea	–4.9	–43
Thailand	–7.9	–49

Source: Litan, Robert, "A Three-Step Remedy for Asia's Financial Flu," Brookings Policy Brief Series, no. 30. Available online: http://www.brookings.org/PA/PolicyBriefs/pb30.htm [March 28, 1998].

along with it, resulting in significant currency misalignments. The pegged exchange rates became harder and harder to sustain, in part due to the fact that it was more difficult for the pegged countries to export. According to some observers, this problem was exacerbated by a Chinese devaluation of its fixed exchange rate in 1994 and the significant depreciation of the Japanese yen throughout the period of dollar appreciation. The movements in these two currencies made the exports of Thailand and the others less competitive.

The downturn in export revenues exposed several other weaknesses, including those in regulatory systems, corporate structures, and financial systems. Many countries in East Asia rely on corporate structures that are built around family ties and personal networks. Business is often done on the basis of name rather than hard data. This can have significant advantages for small- and medium-sized enterprises, but as firms grow, the lack of disclosure and transparency makes it difficult for outside lenders to assess the microeconomic risks of lending. In addition, the lack of hard data and information makes it difficult to implement the kinds of regulatory controls that all economies need for the sake of stability, especially in the financial sector. For example, many banks were engaging in short-term borrowing in international capital markets and using their funds to finance real estate developments with long and risky payoffs.

Another major weakness in the financial sector stems from the politicization of the financial systems of many countries. Banks in these nations were forced to make loans to politically well-connected firms and favored industries. These loans were often at below-market interest rates and, in many cases, were a component of the industrial support policies of the national government. In other cases—for example, Indonesia—the favored industries were owned by the children of the nation's ruler or by individuals with personal political connections.

As long as growth remained robust, the weaknesses in the economy stemming from a lack of regulatory oversight and financial sector misallocations were covered up. Banks that were forced to make bad loans could make up for it by charging their other customers higher interest rates. Once export revenues slipped, however, the problems began to surface.

The IMF and a number of private economists warned of the building instabilities and advised Thailand (and others) to reduce their trade deficits. Still, the onset of the crisis in Thailand was a shock. The IMF is obliged to keep its warnings fairly quiet and behind the scenes in order to avoid setting off a crisis, so most people were unaware of its concerns. Many private investors, such as multinational banks, lack the kind of detailed inside information that a more transparent system provides. Predicting a financial meltdown is a bit like predicting earthquakes: everyone knows where the fault lines are, but no one can say when the earth will shift.

The actual trigger for a crisis is usually unimportant and can even be something relatively minor if all the conditions are in place. Some analysts blame the decline in Thailand's export earnings that stemmed from the downturn in prices for computer chips. In any case, the huge trade imbalance and the disappointment on export revenues undermined investor confidence in Thailand's ability to keep its exchange rate pegged to the dollar. People began to expect a devaluation, and they did not want to be holding the Thai baht (Thailand's currency) when it came.

How the Thai crisis spread internationally is one of the less certain components of the overall crisis. One hypothesis is that Thailand served as a wake-up call for investors to examine their holdings in other countries more closely. Another theory is that the Thai devaluation made exports from several neighboring countries less competitive and forced them to engage in competitive devaluations. Regardless, there was a contagion element in the Thai crisis that soon spread it to other countries.

It is difficult to see the rationality in some of the events that followed, as countries such as Taiwan and Singapore came under speculative attack in spite of the fact that they had trade surpluses and large stocks of foreign reserves. To outsiders, investor flight appears to have had elements of financial panic in which decisions were not based on the analysis of underlying macroeconomic fundamentals. Excessive fear and panic are certainly contagious, and when everyone heads for the exit, simultaneously trying to sell a country's currency, the hysteria pushes asset values below what is warranted by the underlying economy. In other words, the crisis left East Asia extremely cheap for foreign investors; it is too early to tell, however, if there will eventually be a stampede back into those economies.

In the short run, dealing with the crisis has required the IMF to step in and provide emergency loans to cover the mismatch between assets (long run) and liabilities (short run). For their part, the nations affected will have to export their way out of their problems, and it is hoped that in the process, they will restore investor confidence. How long this takes depends on a number of factors, for example, the extent of the collapse in the financial sector. If the collapse leads to a disappearance of credit, then short-run export financing may be unavailable, and exports could be difficult to expand. This is one possibility, although most observers are predicting growth in exports and a decline in imports.

The severe depreciations shown in Table 15.5 will make exports very cheap for foreigners and could seriously affect other regions. Assemblers of high-tech goods in Latin America, for example, may find it more difficult to compete. The U.S. trade deficit will probably grow significantly, with many estimates putting the effects at around a $50 billion net increase. Given the already large size of the U.S. deficit—and the growth of mercantilist ideology in Congress and the public—it is possible that there will be a political backlash.

In the long run, East Asia needs to reform its financial sector. This will involve more transparency and greater disclosure throughout the corporate sector. No one looks for these changes to happen quickly, however, because this requires deep sociological changes in the way business is done. Family units must give over to public shareholders and independent corporate boards. While the IMF and the World Bank can assist in these structural changes, neither is designed to carry out this kind of task. In addition, it is uncertain whether the outside pressures will be sufficient to create the degree of openness in business operations that foreign investors prefer.

It is too early to tell what the long-run effects, if any, will be or how soon countries will return to their long-run rates of growth. Certainly, the basic ingredients for growth are present: savings, human capital, physical infrastructure and capital equipment, and entrepreneurial spirits. Nevertheless, a couple of storm clouds loom over the horizon. The most serious is in Indonesia, where an authoritarian government delayed any action to deal with the crisis until it was thrown out of office. The failure to act decisively on IMF-imposed conditions for receiving emergency loans caused a postponement in the delivery of loan monies. This had the effect of prolonging the uncertainty and delaying the restoration of foreign confidence in the system. Furthermore, some observers fear that the depressions that are enveloping several economies will exacerbate underlying ethnic tensions and antiforeign xenophobia. Social and political instability related to ethnic and class conflict is a possibility, although at this point, it has been limited.

Three issues linger after the crisis: (1) Did the IMF make a mistake in advising that the borrowing countries raise their interest rates? (2) Was the crisis caused or made more likely by the bailout of the Mexican peso in 1995? (3) Should nations put some form of tax or regulatory control on short-run capital movements? Let's briefly examine each of these issues.

Some critics of the IMF's actions blame it for turning financial panics into full-blown depressions by counseling countries to raise their interest rates. The critics charge that the IMF treated the crisis as if it were the same as the Latin American debt crisis of the 1980s. The Latin America crisis, they point out, was caused by large government budget deficits and government-guaranteed private sector debts. In East Asia, governments were running surpluses or small deficits, so there was no need to temporarily contract the economy with interest rate increases. Defenders of the IMF, and the IMF itself, argue that the interest rate hikes were necessary as a means to stop the slide in currency values. The temporarily harmful effects on economic activity caused by interest rate hikes are much smaller than the harm that would be done if the fall in currency values was not stopped.

A second issue relates to the moral hazard of bailing out a bank or corporation. Moral hazard refers to an incentive that is created to do the wrong thing. For example, when you sell a used car or a house, there is a financial incentive not to disclose everything that may be wrong with it. That is why most states have laws that compel the seller to make full disclosure. In the East Asian case, if banks know they will be bailed out if they make bad lending decisions, then they have less reason to exercise prudence and caution and more reason to take greater risks that offer higher returns. Some critics allege that the IMF loans to Mexico set a precedent that taught lenders that their mistakes would be covered by loans from the IMF, and consequently, the East Asian crisis became more likely. The counterargument is that "bailouts" are not really bailouts in the full sense of the word because they do not protect investors from losses. Most investors in East Asia have seen sizable reductions in the values of their portfolios, so they have plenty of reason to exercise caution when lending.

A final unresolved issue is the problem of short-term capital flows. In general, it is recognized that capital flows are useful because they allow countries to invest more than they save. In East Asia, however, where savings rates are often over 30 percent of GDP, it is not at all certain that there are profitable investment outlets beyond those that absorb domestic savings. Much of the foreign investment was put into real estate that is of dubious value as a means to raising long-term growth. The problem with regulating foreign investment too severely is that it could easily choke off the valuable parts. At this point, there is a great deal of interest but very little certainty about the actual techniques that might be used to control investment flows. In addition, there is uncertainty whether any technique can be designed to do more good than harm.

The Institutional Environment

Economic success stems from an ability to mobilize and allocate resources. In the HPAEs, large flows of savings were generated, they were channeled into the financial system, and they were lent to business enterprises that used them productively. Simultaneously, the government built schools that drew in the vast majority of the population. Ultimately, an efficient mobilization and allocation of resources is based on the decisions of individuals and businesses that own resources. In order to ensure that individuals and businesses use their resources in the most productive manner, governments must create rules that foster efficient outcomes. In this regard, the institutional environments of the HPAEs are critical to their successes.

Several components of the institutional environment are critical insofar as they help to make government policy credible. In particular, property rights are relatively secure and free from the threat of nationalization. Bureaucracies are generally competent; individuals and businesses are free to make contracts that will be enforced; access to information is widespread; and regulations tend to be clear and well publicized. Of course, there are exceptions to each of the above, depending on the time and place, but, in general, these features characterize the institutional environments of the HPAEs.

These characteristics should not be confused with the characteristics of open, democratic societies. Measures of political rights and civil liberties (e.g., those of the Freedom House) place the HPAEs, other than Japan, in the middle of their rankings along with many African dictatorships. Japan is the only functioning democracy within the group, although Korea has moved a long way toward full democratic rights. The general lack of political and civil liberties raises a question about the relationship between authoritarian rule and economic growth. Specifically, do the lack of political and civil liberties and the concentration of power in the executive confer advantages for economic development?

The answer to this question is complex and beyond the scope of this book. Nevertheless, it should be noted that many dictatorships have failed in their bid to mobilize and allocate resources. Dictatorships or authoritarian regimes may be as likely to prey upon society as they are to foster its economic development. However authoritarian they are, the HPAEs fostered growth rather than the enrichment of a small elite at the expense of the majority.

A second issue that arises from the general lack of traditionally defined democratic rights is the relevancy of the HPAE experience to other regions of the world, such as Latin America. Some social scientists argue that the context of authoritarian rule makes the HPAE experience irrelevant to nations such as Bolivia and Argentina, where policy reform is taking place within an institutional setting that allows far more dissent.

Both issues, the relationship between authoritarian rule and economic growth and the applicability of the HPAE experience to the rest of the developing world, are contentious and lack consensus. Generally speaking, there does not seem to be a correlation between the type of government (democratic or authoritarian) and the ability to put good policies into place. Nevertheless, it is almost too much to believe that it was a coincidence that all the HPAEs lacked traditionally defined democratic liberties.

Fiscal Discipline

Whether democratic or not, governments must create a stable macroeconomic environment in order for economic growth to succeed. The characteristic of macroeconomic stability has already been discussed, but it is worth revisiting because of its central importance and because of its contrast with the experiences of other regions such as Latin America.

The maintenance of a stable macroeconomic environment requires fiscal discipline and an acceptance of the resource constraints that limit government actions. Budget deficits and foreign debt must be kept manageable, and the real exchange rate must be relatively stable. The benefits of accepting these limitations are that it increases the credibility of government policy and builds the private sector's confidence. The result is more investment and less capital flight.

Business-Government Relations

Stable macroeconomic policies are necessary for growth, but they are no guarantee. For example, macroeconomic stability does not address the very significant problem in all developing countries of the coordination of interdependent investment projects. The coordination problem results from the fact that many private sector investments are interdependent. That is, their profitability depends on the simultaneous or prior creation of a complementary investment. The same often holds true for private sector/public sector investments. For example, profitable investment in warehousing facilities at a seaport depends on the prior investment in sufficient port infrastructure to provide an adequate flow of goods through the warehouses. Yet, the port and related transportation linkages may not be worthwhile unless there is a simultaneous investment or a guarantee of future investment in the warehouses.

The coordination of interdependent investment activities is difficult in a purely free-market framework. The difficulty stems from the fact that the flow of information is not sufficient to let all investors know of the intentions of each other. Six of the eight HPAEs surmounted this problem through the creation of **deliberation councils**, a set of quasi-legislative bodies that bring together representatives from the private and the public sectors. In effect, deliberation councils coordinate the information flow between businesses and policy makers.

> ***Deliberation councils.*** *Deliberation councils are quasi-legislative bodies that combine representatives from industry with government for the purpose of discussing government policy and private sector investment. Japan, Korea, Malaysia, Singapore, and Thailand use deliberation councils. Their use in Hong Kong has been less well documented. Deliberation councils are instrumental in eliciting the cooperation of the business elite.*

CASE STUDY

Deliberation Councils in the Ministry of International Trade and Industry (MITI)

Japan's use of deliberation councils has been more extensive than any other country's. In Japan, the councils are attached to a particular ministry, or bureaucracy, such as the Ministry of International Trade and Industry (MITI). Since MITI is one of the largest bureaucracies in Japan, and because it has more control over Japanese economic policy than any other bureaucracy (with the exception of the Ministry of Finance), it has numerous deliberation councils. According to one account, in 1990, there were seventeen major regular deliberative councils attached to MITI.

Councils in MITI are of two basic types: they are either industry specific, such as the Textile Industry Council, or they are thematic, such as the Industrial Structure Council. Thematic councils deal with a broad range of issues and, consequently, are comprised of numerous committees. For example, the Industrial Structure Council had eighteen committees in 1990, ranging from the Industrial Finance Committee to the Industrial Labor Committee to the Industrial Location Committee.

The method for using deliberation councils involves a feedback process in which the first step is for MITI officials to call a hearing and invite comments from various interested parties. Based on the information it collects, MITI officials issue a draft report that is then forwarded for discussion to a deliberative council. The council may include affected industry representatives, academics, journalists, consumer and labor representatives, former bureaucrats, financial representatives, and politicians. Representation is not proportional in any sense, nor are representatives elected. Based on the feedback that MITI gets from the council, it makes changes in its draft plan and issues a final document that details the steps that will be taken, such as policy changes or new policy initiatives. The final action taken by MITI is essentially a public relations campaign to sell the plan to the wider public.

Source: Campos and Root, *The Key to the East Asian Miracle.*

Individual councils are usually created to deal with a limited set of issues involving one industry or a particular set of policy issues, such as the government budget. By bringing together government officials and affected business groups, the councils reduce the cost of acquiring information about new policies, they provide a forum for bargaining over policies, they instill greater investor confidence, and they raise the level of credibility of the government's policies. More than perhaps any other function, however, deliberation councils serve as a vehicle for the business elites to have a strong voice in the setting of government policy and thereby ensure their cooperation in the overall economic strategy.

Avoiding Rent Seeking

Economic policy in the HPAEs has been relatively interventionist. That is, the laissez-faire ideology of letting markets determine outcomes has not been followed. Hong Kong is somewhat of an exception, but even in Hong Kong, government has directed and actively participated in the creation of extensive public housing. In the next section, we examine some of the issues related to the effectiveness and extent of government intervention in the economy. Whether extensive or not, however, one of the biggest puzzles surrounding HPAE economic policy was the degree to which most countries were able to avoid the costs and inefficiencies associated with private sector rent seeking.

When governments intervene to help specific industries or to channel resources in a particular direction, they create benefits that are of value to someone. Generally speaking, when private interests perceive the possibility of obtaining something of value from government (e.g., credit subsidies, import protection, business licenses, etc.), they will devote scarce resources to obtaining those benefits. The result, as discussed in several earlier chapters, is wasteful rent seeking.

Government policies in the HPAEs created numerous benefits of value to specific industries, yet in spite of this, there was relatively little rent seeking by those interests. To be sure, rent seeking still occurs, and there is significant variation by HPAE nations. Nevertheless, there is less overall rent seeking, and it is less costly than in many other societies.

It is unlikely that there is a single, simple explanation for this lack of rent-seeking behavior, but the deliberation councils probably played a key role. By providing a policy forum in which various interests can make their views known and have a chance to argue in favor of policies that are particularly beneficial, the need to hire lobbyists is reduced. Furthermore, given that industrial and business interests meet with government officials as a group, rather than single interests by themselves, there is greater transparency and less worry about what competing interests may be doing behind the scenes.

In addition to the role played by deliberation councils, some analysts point to the fact that whenever governments offer something of value, they usually attach performance requirements. For example, firms receiving credit subsidies or import protection are usually required to meet specific targets—often export targets—or else the subsidies are taken away. What is remarkable, and not clearly understood, is how HPAE governments are able to enforce the performance requirements they lay down. Many nations outside East Asia, including many Latin American governments, have used performance requirements as incentive mechanisms, but often they have proven to be unenforceable. That is, when firms have not met their production or export targets, governments outside the HPAEs have often been unable to withdraw the special considerations they are providing to the noncompliant firms.

Two key elements that have played a role in enforceability are the presence of a well-educated bureaucracy along with its insulation from the political process. In most of the HPAEs, civil service careers are highly respected and well paid. Consequently, bureaucrats are well educated and competent. In addition to ability, their insulation from the political process gives them the room to make decisions based on merit rather than on the basis of special interests.

A final explanation for the relative lack of rent seeking is the commitment to shared growth that we saw at the beginning of the chapter. The fact that business elites are convinced that they will share the benefits of economic growth reduces the pressure for them to seek added benefits through the manipulation of the political process. In effect, greater equality in the HPAEs reduces the number of individuals and groups that feel left out of the growth process and eliminates the underlying cause of much rent seeking.

The Role of Industrial Policies

So far, the nature and purpose of government interventions have been kept relatively vague. It is time now to make their description more explicit and to tie them into the international economic environment. The most influential study to date of the high-performance Asian economies is the World Bank's policy research report entitled *The East Asian Miracle: Economic Growth and Public Policy*. The World Bank's large research team of distinguished economists concluded that government interventions were common in three areas: (1) targeting of specific industries, that is, industrial policies narrowly defined; (2) directed credit; and (3) export promotion. Two of the three, export promotion and industrial policies, have direct effects on the international economy and trade policy. In this section, we examine the debate over the effectiveness of industrial policies in the HPAEs, and then export promotion policies are examined.

Targeting Specific Industries in the HPAEs

Recall from Chapter 7 that industrial policies can be defined in broad or narrow terms. The broad definition is policies that alter a nation's endowment in a way that does not favor particular industries. For example, we have already seen that the East Asian success story involves high rates of primary and secondary schooling that altered the characteristics of the labor force and the high rates of savings and investment that created the infrastructure and capital goods necessary to enter more sophisticated lines of manufacturing.

The narrow definition of industrial policies is the targeted development of specific industries. In effect, targeted industrial policies attempt to change the comparative advantage of a nation through the alteration of its industrial structure. These policies channel resources to favored industries and are often criticized as "government bureaucrats picking winners and losers."

With the exception of Hong Kong, every HPAE has had or still has some form of targeted industrial policy. They were strongest in Japan, Korea, and Taiwan (the "northern tier" of HPAEs), but they were significant in the other countries as well. In Japan, the focus has been on steel, autos, textiles, shipbuilding, aluminum, electronics, and semiconductors, among others. The height of Korean policies was between 1973 and 1979 with the Heavy and Chemical Industries (HCI) program, which targeted steel, shipbuilding, petrochemicals, and other heavy industries. While lacking the same clear focus as Japan and Korea, Taiwan's programs have provided research institutes, science parks, and basic infrastructure for a variety of industries and seem to have targeted the development of import substitutes.

Malaysian policies took off in the early 1980s with the Look East policy, which emulated Korea's and Japan's industrial development. Malaysia created the Heavy Industries Corporation of Malaysia (HICOM) to develop steel, nonferrous metals, machinery, paper and paper products, and petrochemicals, but it ran into financial constraints in the late 1980s when a number of the firms under HICOM proved to be unprofitable and required government bailouts. Since then, Malaysia has privatized many firms and reduced the degree of state control in others. Indonesia and Thailand did not make systematic efforts such as Japan and Korea did, but the Thai Board of Investment has promoted industries that it deemed to have the potential for technological learning. Indonesia has attempted to use large state-run enterprises to leapfrog from labor-intensive to high-technology industries. Singapore's policies have focused largely on encouraging technology transfer from firms in industrial nations through the medium of promoting foreign direct investment.

The tools that nations use to promote specific industries are largely the instruments of trade policies. Restrictions on imports, either through licensing, quotas, or tariffs, and export subsidies were all used. In many cases, protection from foreign competition enabled firms to earn high profits in domestic markets, which compensated for the losses they suffered in foreign markets. In addition to trade policy, the HPAEs used numerous other mechanisms to channel resources to targeted industries. Directed credit was one of the most important tools, because even when it was small in size, it signaled the private sector that government policy favored the industry receiving the funds. This official stamp of approval was an important device for encouraging private lending to new and potentially risky industries. Other tools included subsidies, market information, especially with respect to foreign markets, infrastructure construction, and research and development funds.

There are two essential elements to these policies that make them different from most other national attempts to promote specific industries. First, resources were usually only provided as long as the companies receiving them met specific export targets. If the targets were not met, the resources (protection, credit, etc.) were withdrawn. Export targets are argued to be a better criterion than profits because many firms had monopolies or significant market power in their domestic markets; hence, profitability may be unrelated to efficiency. Second, governments placed macroeconomic stability above industrial policies. If they began to experience fiscal problems that were caused by the industrial promotion programs, they scaled back or abandoned them.

The World Bank view of these programs is that they were insulated from purely political influences so that industrial targeting decisions were based on technical analysis rather than politics. The collapse of the financial sectors in many countries has called this assumption into question. For example, government use of directed credit programs appears to be one of the main causes of the financial crisis. Government involvement in credit allocation forced financial institutions to make unsound loans. In turn, the failure to apply business criteria led to a mountain of bad debt, which ultimately sank many banks and whole financial sectors. In the future, conventional economic wisdom will undoubtedly be much more cautious about the benefits of directed credit programs to target industrial development.

Did Industrial Policies Work?

The role of industrial policies in the story of HPAE growth is controversial. Ideally, we would like to know the answers to two simple questions. First, did they work? A successful policy would be one that increases the overall rate of GDP growth or the rate of productivity growth. Second, if they worked, were they important? That is, was their contribution to economic growth significant enough to be considered one of the reasons for East Asian success?

With respect to the question of whether they made a positive contribution to growth, opinion ranges from "no effect" to "positive effect." The reason for the lack of consensus on this important issue is that, in general, it is difficult to measure the effects of policy interventions on growth rates. There are conceptual disagreements about the measurements that should be made, and few countries have data of sufficient quality. In the World Bank's view, "reasoned judgments" must be used to settle the issue. Unfortunately, the paucity of data together with disagreements over measurement techniques results in the use of qualitative judgments of the sort that inevitably lead researchers to confirm the opinions that they began with.

In spite of these obstacles to assessing industrial policies, the variety of opinions among researchers can be characterized as falling into two camps. One camp is represented by the World Bank's research. In their view, some government interventions fostered economic growth (export promotion and directed credit), but, in general, industrial policies did not. They assert that industrial policies usually targeted the same industries that market forces were developing and, therefore, were unnecessary. In the cases where the "wrong" industries were targeted, pragmatic and flexible policy makers of the HPAEs managed to quickly change policies before any damage was done to the rest of the economy.

The World Bank's analysis rests on two pieces of evidence. First, they compare the growth rates of productivity in the targeted and nontargeted sectors in the three countries with sufficient data (Japan, Korea, and Taiwan). In general, they find that productivity change in the promoted sectors was high but no higher than in the rest of the economy. Possible exceptions to their general finding are Japan's chemical and metalworking industries and Korea's chemical industry. One problem for the advocates of industrial policies is that the unpromoted textile sector did as well as any of the promoted sectors. Second, they examine the change over time in the industrial structure of the HPAEs. If industrial policies worked, they should have led to a different pattern of industrial growth than the pattern that is caused by a change in factor endowments. They conclude that industrial policies were at most marginally effective, since the sector by sector growth pattern is as expected, given the national endowments of labor and the high savings and investment rates.

Critiques of the World Bank's findings usually rest on two points. First, the fact that productivity growth was generally no faster in promoted sectors is irrelevant, according to the critics. The important issue is what the growth rates would have been without promotion. It is conceivable that without industrial policies, growth in the targeted industries would have been much slower than with the policies. Second, the critics point out that the World Bank analysis is overly general. In their view, it is based on industry groupings that are too broad to uncover the details of selective targeting. For example, some components of the textile industry were heavily promoted in both Japan and Korea in the early period of their industrial policies. Therefore, it is not surprising that textiles overall have experienced a rapid increase in productivity and that they remain a larger than expected component of Japanese and Korean industry.

At present, there is no way to resolve this debate. Consequently, there are a variety of opinions about the relevance of industrial policies for developing countries outside the HPAE group. To the extent that there is agreement, most analysts share the view that if industrial policies are used, there are three key elements. Countries must have (1) clear performance criteria such as export targets; (2) institutional mechanisms to monitor compliance and enforce compliance; and (3) low costs so that nontargeted sectors do not suffer.

CASE STUDY

HCI in Korea

Most observers agree that Korean industrial policies have at least partially succeeded. The most enthusiastic observers argue that they have accelerated the rate of overall growth without creating offsetting inefficiencies elsewhere in the economy. Less optimistic observers concede success in generating exports and in changing the industrial structure of the country, but they offset many of those gains with the huge financial costs of the Heavy and Chemical Industries (HCI) promotion in the 1970s.

Korea's industrial promotion drive began a few years after the Korean War in the early 1960s. Early efforts at industrial targeting focused on key industrial materials such as cement, fertilizer, and petroleum refining. The government typically supported large-scale conglomerates, called *chaebol*, which were given monopolies in the domestic market. Trade policy in the form of an aggressive promotion of exports along with high levels of protection was the main tool for targeting industries, but directed credit and tax breaks were important as well.

Industrial targeting evolved into the Heavy and Chemical Industries program, which was at its most active from 1973 to 1979. HCI targeted six specific industrial groups: steel, petrochemicals, and nonferrous metals for enhanced self-sufficiency, and shipbuilding, electronics, and machinery (especially earth-moving equipment and autos) for export. The tools used to promote these industries were the same as previously but with a different emphasis. By the mid-1970s, trade policy had become somewhat more liberal, although most industries still received significant protection. Greater emphasis was placed on subsidies, directed credit through loans at below-market interest rates, and special tax exemptions.

The cost of promotion during the HCI period was significant. Direct funds provided to targeted industries were around 5 percent of the overall budget, and tax exemptions amounted to about 3 percent of total tax revenues. In 1977, around 45 percent of the banking system's total provision of domestic credit went to the targeted industries. Gradually, bottlenecks and large debts began to accumulate.

By 1979, when the second oil crisis hit, inflation was high, the exchange rate had appreciated, causing exports to falter, and the targeted industries had significant idle capacity. In addition, the labor-intensive sectors (which had not been targeted) were starved for credits, and bad debts and financial insolvencies were growing in the HCI sector.

Policymakers quickly switched course. HCI promotion was curtailed, the currency was devalued, and financial market and import liberalization were hastened. One of the main efforts of policymakers in the 1980s was to restructure a number of the distressed industries that were overpromoted in the 1970s. The cost to the government budget has been significant, as it has been forced to bail out bankrupt firms and dispose of nonperforming loans.

Was HCI promotion worth it? It is impossible to answer this question definitively because we can never know what would have happened under an alternative set of policies. During the height of the HCI program and its immediate aftermath, Korea's growth rate dipped slightly (from the mid-1970s through the mid-1980s), but the change was slight, and growth overall remained extremely high, even by HPAE standards. Korea achieved classification as a high-income nation, a feat that only Japan and the city-states of Singapore and Hong Kong have accomplished in the twentieth century.

Source: World Bank, *The East Asian Miracle;* and Westphal, "Industrial Policy in an Export-Propelled Economy: Lessons from South Korea's Experience," in *The Journal of Economic Perspectives,* Summer 1990.

The Role of Manufactured Exports

The promotion of manufactured exports played a significant role in the industrial strategies of each of the HPAEs. These policies were largely successful, and the exports of each country grew even faster than their GDP. Given these facts, it is reasonable to assume that there might be a connection between the two. That is, a number of studies of the HPAEs and other regions have shown that higher rates of growth of exports are correlated with higher rates of growth of GDP. What is the mechanism that causes this?

The Connections Between Growth and Exports

It is true by definition that exports are part of the GDP, so it would seem that growth in exports is simply a part of overall GDP growth. Export growth may not add to GDP growth, however, if it crowds out growth in the output of goods for domestic consumption, such as consumer goods or investment. In effect, the idea that export growth causes faster GDP growth is an assertion that export growth causes the overall capacity of the economy to grow faster than it would have if production was focused on goods for the domestic market.

If production focused on exports results in greater overall growth, then there must be something in the production process or its links to the rest of the economy that is absent from domestically focused production. One possibility is that because exports are produced for the world market, economies of scale come into play in a way that is absent when firms produce for a small domestic market. Larger firms often have lower average costs because they can spread their fixed costs for capital and machinery over a larger volume of output. Production for the world market may also help ensure that the firms operate closer to full capacity. This also lowers average costs. Another possible reason why exports might foster growth is that as firms produce for a world market, there may be several added incentives to increase R&D. Economies of scale may make it more worthwhile, and the need to keep up with foreign competition may make it more necessary.

Other connections between export growth and GDP growth are possible as well. Exports may speed up the adoption and mastery of international best practices. Firms that operate in global markets are not protected from competition. In fact, they are going up against the world's best, and the competitive pressures may force firms to stay abreast of the latest developments in their product area and production process. Measurement of this possible effect is complicated by the presence of some form of export promotion in the HPAEs. An exporter does not have to be among the world's best if it receives subsidies (for example, direct payment or access to low-interest loans or tax breaks). Firms can be competitive due to subsidies received at home, which may reduce the pressures to compete based on efficiency or quality. Successful export promotion programs, such as those in Korea, are well aware of this problem, and since their goal is to develop firms that are capable of head-to-head international competition without special breaks, they put in place careful monitoring programs. Monitoring is done to ensure that the subsidies granted to the exporters, in whatever form, do not become the reason for competitive success abroad.

Production of exports has several other potential advantages. Exports make possible the purchase of imports. Developing countries are not usually on the technology frontier, and the creation of an efficient manufacturing enterprise is often dependent on imports of machinery and other capital goods. A scarcity of exports impairs a country's ability to purchase imports, with the result that firms are unable to obtain the imported inputs they need in order to raise their efficiency. A related advantage of exports is that the need to meet export targets tied the HPAEs to policies that openly encouraged inward foreign direct investment (FDI) and the acquisition of new technology. One way to overcome the backwardness of domestic manufacturing is to encourage foreign firms to invest. Most of the HPAEs welcomed FDI; Singapore went so far as to build its industrial policies around it. At the same time that FDI was encouraged, several countries also sought to provide incentives for the foreign firm to license its technology to potential domestic rivals. This was a particularly common strategy in Japan, where the incentive of access to the large Japanese market was sufficient to encourage many firms to sign technology licensing agreements.

The ability to import capital and modern technology is seen by some as the most critical ingredient in policies that successfully close the gap between developing and developed countries. Export promotion can encourage the acquisition of new technologies because in order to succeed, governments must allow access to whatever imports firms need to become efficient. Most of the HPAEs selectively protected their domestic markets, but they also adjusted their policies so that exporters were given access to needed imports. In general, they used less protection than other developing areas.

Is Export Promotion a Good Model for Other Regions?

The export promotion model has succeeded so well in East Asia that, inevitably, it is being prescribed for other developing areas. In Latin America, for example, the economic crisis of the 1980s, together with the very visible counterexample of East Asia, has propelled many nations into similar types of policies. The question in many people's minds is whether or not other areas can duplicate the export successes of the HPAEs.

The first issue is whether the world's industrial nations can absorb the exports of a series of newly industrializing countries. There are fears in some quarters that these exports will undermine industries in those industrial nations and lead to renewed trade conflicts and calls for protection. While trade conflict appears to be a permanent part of the international landscape, the fact of the matter is that developing countries currently account for only about 13 percent of the world's manufactured exports. Of this 13 percent of the world's manufactured exports, developing country HPAEs produce about 9.5 percent, meaning that the rest of the developing world produces only 3.5 percent of the world's export of manufactures. Clearly, the problem of saturating the markets of industrial economies does not appear to be close on the horizon, even if developing economies were to expand their exports at a furious rate.

Perhaps the greatest obstacle for countries that wish to replicate the export promotion policies of the HPAEs is the Uruguay Round of the GATT. Under the rules that went into effect in 1994, developing countries must eliminate any subsidies that are contingent on export performance. The phase-out period is eight years, and no new subsidies may be provided in the intervening years. Extremely poor countries with per capita GDP less than $1000 are exempted. Essentially, the new GATT rules eliminate the possibility that developing countries can use the same tools— credit subsidies, tax breaks, direct payments—that the HPAEs used. The only exceptions are the poorest of the poor, who do not export manufactured goods in any quantity. In all countries, subsidies for noncommercial R&D, regional development, and promoting compliance with environmental regulations are allowed.

CASE STUDY

East Asian Trade Blocs

Asia is the one region of the world without significant trade blocs. While there are numerous informal agreements, the only formal bloc is the Association of South East Asian Nations, or ASEAN. ASEAN was founded in 1967 as mainly a political cooperation and security agreement. Its current membership includes the nine nations of Brunei, Indonesia, Laos, Malaysia, Myanmar, Philippines, Singapore, Thailand, and Vietnam. Cambodia has observer status and is expected to join in the near future.

In 1977, ASEAN negotiated preferential trade among its members, but barriers did not begin to fall until 1987. In 1992, the nations negotiated a free-trade agreement, known as the ASEAN Free Trade Area, or AFTA, which has a fifteen-year time frame for the elimination of tariffs. As part of the process of reducing trade barriers, quantitative restrictions were converted to tariffs, and all countries were required to reduce tariffs on intra-ASEAN trade to 20 percent by the year 2001. In 1995, about 20 percent of total ASEAN trade was between member countries.

The ASEAN nations are one component of a far vaster trade region known as Asia Pacific Economic Cooperation, or APEC. In addition to ASEAN, APEC includes the HPAEs plus China, New Zealand, Australia, Canada, the United States, Mexico, and Chile. APEC was created in 1989. Its eighteen members have a combined GDP of more than $13 trillion (1995) and account for approximately 46 percent of world trade. The goal of APEC, as set forth in the 1994 Declaration of Common Resolve, is "free and open trade and investment in the region no later than 2010 for the industrialized economies and 2020 for the developing economies." APEC is not a trade bloc in the normal sense. Its goal, as just stated, does not commit the members to forming a free-trade area. Rather, it does something even more amazing: it commits members to implement free-trade and open-investment flows as part of their overall trade and investment policy, not just for other APEC countries but for all of the world's nations. No one can say if every member nation will honor its commitments to create free trade, but at annual meetings of each nation's finance ministers, along with the numerous working groups and committees, progress is slowly being made on a wide range of issues.

Another issue is the question of whether there is a trade bloc developing in East Asia that is centered around Japan. There seems to be a widespread popular belief that the world is forming into three blocs centered around the European Union, the United States, and Japan. In this view, Japan is using not only its foreign trade with East Asia, but also its foreign aid and extensive foreign investment ties to cement its role as the center of a developing Asian bloc. Empirical analysis of Japan's trade and investment, along with the growing role of the yen, argues against the idea. Europe, the Western Hemisphere, and East Asia each have trade patterns that are biased toward their own regions.

In the 1980s, the bias toward intraregional trade (i.e., trade within the region) increased in Europe and the Western Hemisphere. There was no increase in the East Asian intraregional bias. In fact, the most potent trade grouping for explaining the regional bias in East Asian trade seems to be APEC—a region that includes the NAFTA countries as well as Australia, New Zealand, and the leading economies of East Asia.

In terms of the use of the yen and the creation of a "yen bloc," the available evidence shows that yen usage, while growing, is not expanding as fast as Japan's economy and trade. As a leading industrial nation, it is reasonable to expect that the yen will inevitably play a greater role in world trade and finance. Indeed, the yen has grown as a percentage of official Asian reserves and as a percentage of Asian invoices for imports and exports. Nevertheless, neither the share of reserves nor the share of invoices has kept pace with the growth in Japan's trade.

Sources: Both ASEAN and APEC have Web sites: *http://www.aseansec.org.id* and *http://www.apec-sec.org.sg.* Empirical analysis of the role of Japan in Asian trade and the absence of a "yen bloc" can be found in Frankel, Jeffrey, "Is Japan Creating a Yen Bloc in East Asia and the Pacific," in *Regionalism and Rivalry: Japan and the United States in Pacific Asia*, edited by Frankel and Kahler.

Is There an Asian Model of Economic Growth?

The East Asian "Miracle" has given rise to a large number of studies that seek to explain rapid growth in the HPAEs and China. While the issue may superficially appear academic, it has become one of the more interesting and heated debates in recent popular economics. Proponents of laissez-faire economics have used the relative openness of the East Asian economies, their use of private markets, and their strong macroeconomic fundamentals to argue for government policies that are less activist. Proponents of a more activist government have pointed to selective interventions, such as export promotion, industrial policies, and deliberation councils, to argue in favor of a larger government role in the economy. Some Asian politicians have pointed to their restrictions on civil and political liberties as laying a foundation for order and the avoidance of chaos.

Is there an Asian model of the economy? That is, have the HPAEs managed to achieve their extraordinary growth rates through policies that are fundamentally different from the policy advice dispensed by proponents of the Washington Consensus (see Chapter 14)? At stake are the paths followed by today's developing economies and the future role of government policy in the industrial countries. Naturally, with a question so controversial, there are a variety of answers and opinions. Recent work, however, seems to be pointing toward a robust set of conclusions.

In order to describe some interesting recent studies, we must briefly review the idea of growth accounting. Recall that labor productivity is a measurement that is defined as output per worker. The growth in labor productivity is highly correlated with the growth in income (or output) per member of the population, but they are not the same thing. East Asian growth is remarkable for its growth in per capita income and its growth in labor productivity.

Any given rate of growth of labor productivity can be broken down into the share that is due to more capital and the share that is due to more skills or education. In the economics literature, such an exercise is called a growth accounting. When growth accounts are constructed for a country or a region, there is always some share of the growth in labor productivity that cannot be explained by the amount of additional capital or education. This share is a measure of the effects of using the available inputs more efficiently. That is, if more growth occurs than can be explained by the growth of capital or education, it must be due to a more productive use of the available inputs. For example, the organization of production may have changed so that people are working smarter, or the quality of technology may have changed so that each unit of capital and labor input produces more units of output.

Another name for the share of labor productivity that is not explained by capital or education is total factor productivity, or TFP. TFP growth reflects changes in output that are unrelated to changes in capital or labor inputs. According to most estimates, over the long run, the lion's share of per capita income growth in high-income countries has resulted from increases in total factor productivity.

> **Total factor productivity, or TFP**. *Total factor productivity is a measurement of the quantity of output per unit of input. Increases in TFP mean that overall productivity has improved and that a given level of inputs will create more output; hence, technology or enterprise organization must have improved.*

Growth accounting may seem a long way from the debate on East Asia, but it is actually very relevant. As it turns out, the vast bulk of Asian growth since 1960 can be accounted for by increases in capital and education, while TFP plays a much smaller role. Table 15.6 provides the details and some comparisons over the same period.

What we observe in Table 15.6 is that in the sample of six HPAEs, TFP growth accounts for between 24 and 36 percent of overall growth. In the slower-growing United States, it accounts for 27 percent, and in the other industrial nations, the figure is 37 percent. The fact that TFP growth accounts for about the same overall share of growth in the HPAEs was surprising to many observers for two reasons: First, the HPAEs are not on the frontier of new technologies as are the United States and the rest of the industrial world. Consequently, they should be able to more easily borrow techniques that increase their TFP. Second, the proponents of a new Asian model of economic growth have argued that the selective interventions such as industrial policies and export promotion have increased productivity. In fact, what they appear to have done, if anything, is to increase the quantity of capital per worker.

The last point is key to understanding this debate. When growth is decomposed into its various causes, what appears to account for the bulk of HPAE growth is capital accumulation and not increased total factor productivity. These results appear to be fairly strong, since several other researchers have done similar growth accounting exercises and have reached the same conclusions. The growth accounts for

TABLE 15.6 Sources of Growth, 1960–1994 (Percent)

Country	Growth of Output per Worker	Contribution of		
		Capital per Worker	Education per Worker	Total Factor Productivity
Indonesia	3.4	2.1	0.5	0.8
Korea	5.7	3.3	0.8	1.5
Malaysia	3.8	2.3	0.5	0.9
Singapore	5.4	3.4	0.4	1.5
Thailand	5.0	2.7	0.4	1.8
Taiwan	5.8	3.1	0.6	2.0
Latin America	1.5	0.9	0.4	0.2
United States	1.1	0.4	0.4	0.3
Industrial Nations[1]	2.9	1.5	0.4	1.1

[1]Including Japan, excluding the United States.

Source: Collins and Bosworth, "Economic Growth in East Asia: Accumulation Versus Assimilation," in *Brooking Papers on Economic Activity,* 2: 1996.

East Asia are important because they paint a consistent, if surprising, picture of the East Asian "Miracle." What they tell us is that there may be no miracle at all, just the hard work and sacrifice that comes from forgoing today's consumption in order to raise savings and investment rates. For example, between 1966 and 1985, Singapore raised investment from 11 percent of GDP to 40 percent. It is no surprise, then, that capital accumulation accounts for the bulk of its growth.

If these measures are accurate, then the argument for a distinct Asian model looks weak. Rather than selective interventions that target specific industries, the keys were high savings and high investment.

Conclusion

Cultural values have not been a prominent part of the story of East Asian growth as related in this chapter. A culture-based explanation for the spectacular growth rates of East Asia ignores the tremendous diversity that exists in the region, both contemporaneously and in the various historical traditions. Languages, religions, history, and intellectual thought are enormously varied, and, if it were not for the high growth rates in the countries singled out, their treatment as a single group would look suspiciously like a narrow, Western cultural bias. Indeed, some of the proponents of culture-based explanations for East Asian growth are Western chauvinists and their Eastern counterparts—authoritarian Eastern politicians who mistakenly view the denial of political and civil liberties as a blow against Western hegemony.

In addition to the diversity of cultures, the timing of the leap into high growth rates has varied, as have conditions at the start. Some countries were ethnically diverse, while others were nearly homogeneous; some had high percentages of their population in agriculture, while others were very urban; some had relatively high levels of schooling and income, while others had high rates of illiteracy and poverty.

The common elements in the stories of the HPAEs are that policy was flexible and adaptable and that policymakers used international markets to stimulate growth while maintaining macroeconomic stability. Along with growth came higher savings and investment rates, so that what began as low to moderate levels gradually developed into very high levels. In addition, growth brought greater income equality—quite the opposite of the early growth experience of other countries. These were not accidental spinoffs of the growth process, but they were intentional elements of policy.

Insofar as there is a key to the Asian Miracle, it is in the ability to accumulate savings and to put it to productive use through investment. Clearly, policies that reduce inequality and create a stake for all or nearly all elements of society are instrumental, as is the ability of policymakers to establish their credibility with the business elites and to adhere closely to policies that led to an efficient allocation of the accumulated savings.

▲   The major characteristics of economic growth in the high-performance Asian economies are (1) increasing equality, (2) rapid accumulation of savings and high rates of investment, (3) rapid increases in levels of schooling, (4) rapid growth of manufactured exports, and (5) stable macroeconomic environments.

▲   The institutional environment is instrumental in creating confidence in policymakers. The policymaking bureaucracy tends to be insulated from the push and pull of the political system. This leads some to decry the lack of representation of the population in policy decisions, but it allows decisions to be made on technical merit rather than political expediency. The voice of business and industry, and to a lesser extent other groups such as consumers, is often heard through consultative bodies known as deliberation councils. Deliberation councils are a mechanism for the private sector and government policymakers to exchange information and discuss policies.

▲   One of the key elements of policy is fiscal control over inflation, the budget, foreign debt, and exchange rates. While inflation, budgets, and foreign debt all vary country by country, inflation is kept under control, and budget deficits and foreign debt are kept within the boundaries defined by the government's and the economy's ability to finance them.

▲   With the exception of Hong Kong, each of the HPAEs followed industrial policies that targeted the development of particular industries. These policies were most focused in the "northern tier" of Japan, Korea, and Taiwan. The effects of these policies are difficult to measure, and there is a long and contentious debate about their efficacy.

▲   Each of the HPAEs promoted manufactured exports. These policies largely succeeded, although the mechanisms that link export growth to faster GDP growth are still uncertain.

▲ Recent empirical work shows that the main contributor to economic growth in the HPAEs is the extremely rapid accumulation of physical capital. Consequently, the argument that the HPAEs have pioneered a model that leads to more rapid total factor productivity growth appears false, and the keys to growth should be looked for in the policies that raise savings and investment.

Vocabulary

deliberation councils

demographic transition

4 Tigers

high-performance Asian economies (HPAEs)

newly industrializing economies (NIEs)

total factor productivity (TFP)

Study Questions

1. Contrast the characteristics of economic growth in the HPAEs with those characteristics in Latin America.

2. As long as economic growth remained robust, a number of weaknesses in East Asia were hidden from most observers. Once growth slowed, however, the weaknesses became apparent and were instrumental in the economic turmoil of 1997 and 1998. What were the weaknesses, and how did they contribute to the problems of 1997 and 1998?

3. How can passage through a demographic transition lead to high savings and investment rates?

4. What are the characteristics of East Asian institutional environments that contributed to rapid economic growth?

5. Economists are divided over the effectiveness of East Asian industrial policies. Provide a balanced assessment of the issues relevant to understanding the role of industrial policies in fostering growth. Do you think one point of view is better than another? Why?

6. How might manufactured exports contribute to economic growth?

7. Is there a uniquely Asian model of economic growth? What are the issues, and how might we go about answering that question?

Suggested Reading

Campos, Jose Edgardo, and Root, Hilton L. *The Key to the East Asian Miracle: Making Shared Growth Credible.* Washington, DC: The Brookings Institution, 1996.

Collins, Susan, and Bosworth, Barry. "Economic Growth in East Asia: Accumulation Versus Assimilation," in *Brooking Papers on Economic Activity,* 2: 1996.

Fishlow, Albert, Catherine Gwin, Stephan Haggard, Dani Rodrik, and Robert Wade. *Miracle or Design: Lessons from the East Asian Experience.* Washington, DC: Overseas Development Council, 1994.

Frankel, Jeffrey. "Is Japan Creating a Yen Bloc in East Asia and the Pacific," in *Regionalism and Rivalry: Japan and the United States in Pacific Asia,* edited by Jeffrey Frankel and Miles Kahler. Chicago: University of Chicago Press, 1993.

Stiglitz, Joseph. "Some Lessons from the East Asian Miracle," in *The World Bank Research Observer.* August 1996.

Westphal, Larry. "Industrial Policy in an Export-Propelled Economy: Lessons from South Korea's Experience," in *The Journal of Economic Perspectives,* Summer, 1990.

World Bank. *The East Asian Miracle: Economic Growth and Public Policy.* New York: Oxford University Press, 1993.

The library at Nanyang Technological University in Singapore has created a service called Statistical Data Locators, which is a compendium of Web sites all over the world. The section on Asia is excellent. They are located at *http://www.ntu.edu.sg/library/statdata.htm*. Both ASEAN and APEC have sites with a significant amount of information. In addition, they provide links to the official governmental sites of their members. ASEAN is located at *http://www.aseansec.org/* and APEC is *http://www.apecsec.org*. Another site with useful links and a variety of textual and statistical information is the Asia Society, located at *http://www.asiasociety.org/*.

CHAPTER 16

ECONOMIC INTEGRATION AND THE FORMERLY SOCIALIST COUNTRIES

Introduction: Economies in Transition

The Berlin Wall came down in the fall of 1989. It was impossible to mistake the historical symbolism: the Cold War was over. Two years later, in December 1991, the USSR divided itself into fifteen separate nations. These events catapulted those regions into an ocean of political and economic reforms. Unlike the Chinese opening that began in December 1978, in this case, political reform and democracy were on the agenda.

The transition from a centrally planned, bureaucratically controlled economy to one that relies on markets for all or nearly all its allocation decisions requires a common set of reforms, no matter how the histories and the cultures of nations vary. Macroeconomic policies must strive to create stability; domestic prices must be linked to world prices; labor markets and financial markets must be created; property rights have to be defined; and institutional structures to support markets must be developed. The transition may be fast or slow, macroeconomic policies may differ depending on initial conditions (debt or no debt, inflation or no inflation), and the privatization of state-owned assets may go forward or stall, but the major changes are qualitatively similar in each country.

At one time or another, every nation has gone through an economic reform process. What is different about these economic reforms is that they go far beyond anything in recent history. Even the deep Latin American reforms that began in the mid-1980s (Chapter 14) are small by comparison. A description of each of the steps that must be taken to complete the transition to market economies is far beyond the scope of this book. Instead, this chapter provides a general characterization of the transition process and focuses on trade issues. Along the way, it describes some of the similarities and differences between countries, especially the East Asian reformers (China and Vietnam), the nations of the former Soviet Union (FSU), and the Central and East European countries (CEEC).

Transition economies. The transition economies are the countries that are in the process of moving from bureaucratically controlled economies to market-based economies. They include most of the economies that adopted socialist or communist ideologies during the twentieth century. Among these countries, there is a wide range in the degree of reform and movement toward market-based economies.

Central and Eastern European Countries

Norway

Baltic

Sweden

Sea

Estonia

Latvia

Lithuania

North

Denmark

Sea

Kaliningrad
(Russia)

Belarus

Netherlands

P o l a n d

Belgium

Germany

Luxembourg

Czech

Republic

Slovakia

Ukraine

France

Switzerland

Austria

Hungary

Slovenia

Croatia

R o m a n i a

Adriatic

Bosnia &
Herzegovina

Yugoslavia

Italy

Sea

Bulgaria

Corsica

Montenegro

Macedonia

Albania

Tyrrhenian

Sardinia

Sea

Greece

Aegean

Sea

Ionian

M e d i t e r r a n e a n   S e a

Sea

Former Yugoslavia = Bosnia and Herzegovina, Croatia,
Macedonia, Montenegro, Yugoslavia
Baltic Republics = Estonia, Latvia, Lithuania
Visegrad Four = Poland, Czech Republic, Slovakia, Hungary

Scale

1: 9,512,000
1:150.12 Inches to Miles

Lambert Equal Area Projection

SDSU Geography
Chris Lukinbeal

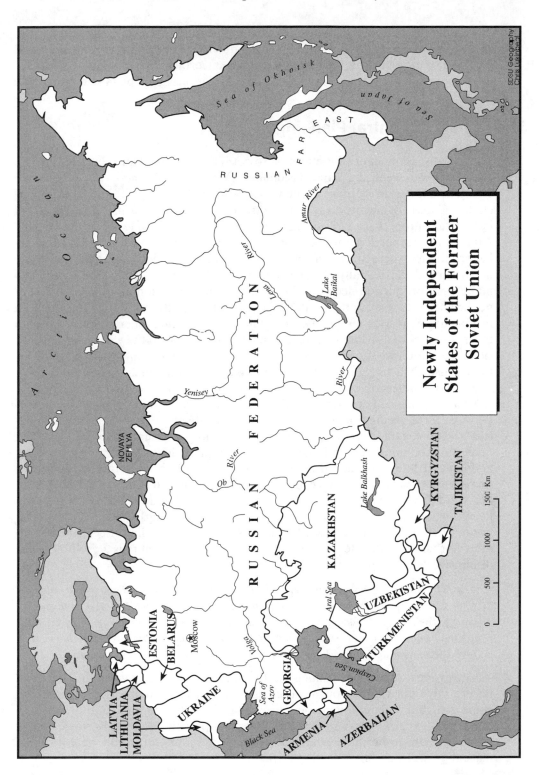

Newly Independent States of the Former Soviet Union

One world of caution is appropriate here: change is constant. Countries that seem to be making little or no progress can quickly turn into rapid reformers, and vice versa. Consequently, the path of reform is uncertain, and what may be true today about a country's trade regime or external relations could be false tomorrow.

The Legacy of Central Planning

The socialist economies of the former Soviet Union, Central and Eastern Europe, and China were **centrally planned economies**. Vietnam, Cuba, and a few other small countries shared this form of economic decision making as well. All countries (including Cuba) are moving away from central planning. Some, such as several nations in Central Europe, have become market-based economies, while others are lagging. All planned economies, however, have introduced significant reforms. Unlike market economies where individual entrepreneurs and firms decide what, how, and how much to produce, centrally planned economies rely on bureaucrats and planners to make basic production decisions. In a centrally planned economy, the central economic authority surveys the available inputs and production sites and formulates a production plan. Most enterprises are state owned, so implementation of the plan takes the form of distributing production targets (quotas) to the various production sites. Since enterprises have more specific information about their own capabilities, there is usually a bargaining process between the central state authority, the regions, and the local enterprises over the allotment of inputs and the output targets.

Centrally planned economies differ from market economies in some fundamental ways. First, production, prices, and external trade are all controlled by the central economic authority. In other words, there is no goods market in the sense that quantities and prices respond to demand and supply. Prices are administratively set and have little or no relationship to the scarcity or abundance of goods. Second, there are no asset markets, since most wealth is state owned (no need for stock markets) and financial flows to firms respond passively to the demands of the plan (no need for bond markets or other capital markets for lending). Third, there is no labor market in the normal sense. Wages are set along with other prices in the economy, workers are allocated to firms like other inputs, and there is a prohibition on dismissals.

> **Centrally planned economy**. *In a centrally planned economy, the fundamental decisions of what to produce, how to produce it, and who gets it are decided by a central planning authority. The central planning bureaucracy is usually staffed with production engineers who use mathematical models to set output targets for each industry. Prices reflect political as well as economic decisions. Markets have little or no role in allocative decisions.*

The promise of central planning was that it could free society from the chaos and uncertainty of markets through conscious control over economic development. Income distribution could be made more equal since the planning authority determines the level of economic rewards that each person receives. Basic economic necessities are to be made available to everyone: jobs, education, health care, a place to live, enough to eat, and so forth.

The reality of central planning is more complex. Unemployment is low, income distribution is more equal than in most market economies, and education and health care tend to be high relative to the levels of income. Furthermore, at least in its early years, massive investment in heavy industry, together with the powerful ideological commitment and willingness of people to make sacrifices, led to rates of economic growth that were very high. In effect, the coercive power of the state created forced savings that were invested in areas deemed important by the central planners and the political elite. Over time, economies became more and more distorted as the plan poured a vast amount of resources into heavy industry and neglected light industry, consumer goods, and especially service industries. Without prices to guide them, many manufacturing industries ended up creating negative value added. That is, the real value of the inputs (i.e., what they would command at world prices) was greater than the value of the output. As time went on, the cumulation of inefficiencies began to have a profound effect on overall economic growth, and the Soviet Union, Central Europe, and China fell further and further behind the West.

The core problems of central planning are that it does not provide incentives for efficiency or innovation and that it is impossible for planners to absorb enough information to coordinate all economic decisions as well as markets can. Firms have no hard bottom line, since inputs are allocated based on the set targets, and financial resources are forthcoming whenever necessary. As long as a firm meets its target, it never goes out of business. Consequently, there is no reason to consider quality, profits, customer service, or innovation. In order to ensure that they meet their targets, enterprise managers hoard excess labor and inputs, further eroding productivity growth.

External trade is limited and controlled through state trading monopolies. Under this system, a branch of the central economic authority controls the flow of all goods in and out of the country, with the exception of smuggled goods. Prices and currency values are irrelevant, since much of the trade is a form of barter in which government-to-government agreements designate the goods for export and import. Most foreign trade is limited to other centrally planned economies, thereby limiting the interaction of these economies with markets. When trade occurs with market economies, the state trading monopoly keeps the foreign currency earned on exports and uses it to purchase imports that are not bartered. Under central planning, countries do not have a trade policy. Quotas and tariffs are irrelevant because goods are exported and imported as specified by the plan. In fact, since prices are administratively set and in many cases have no relationship to the economic value of goods, a tariff that adds to a price is meaningless. Given the ability to set a price at any level, a tariff could always be offset by a change in the set price.

Economic Indicators

The transition economies of Tables 16.1 to 16.3 are divided into three groups: Central and Eastern European countries (CEEC) in Table 16.1; the newly independent states (NIS) of the former Soviet Union in Table 16.2; and the Asian transitional

TABLE 16.1 Transition Economies: Central and Eastern European Countries (CEEC), 1995

Country	Population (Millions)	GNP per Person (Dollars)	GDP per Person Purchasing Power Parity (Dollars)
Albania	3.3	670	*na*
Bulgaria	8.4	1,330	4,480
Romania	22.7	1,480	4,360
Baltic Republics			
Estonia	1.5	2,860	4,220
Latvia	2.5	2,270	3,370
Lithuania	3.7	1,900	4,120
Visegrad Four			
Czech Republic	10.3	3,870	9,770
Hungary	10.2	4,120	6,410
Poland	38.6	2,790	5,400
Slovak Republic	5.4	2,950	3,610
Former Yugoslavia*			
Croatia	4.8	3,250	*na*
Macedonia	2.1	860	*na*
Slovenia	2.0	8,200	*na*

*Data for Bosnia and Herzegovina and Serbia are unavailable.

na = not available.

Source: World Bank, *The State in a Changing World: World Development Report, 1997.*

economies in Table 16.3. Economic statistics for the transition economies should be treated with caution. Statistical agencies are grappling with the problem of measuring economic output in an entirely new system, often at a time of significant economic decline and scarce resources for data collection. The transition has also altered the structure of production and requires new statistical measures. For example, services, which are hard to measure in any economy, are a fast-growing share of total output and easy to miss, since they are often provided by small micro-enterprises. In addition, high inflation in some countries has made it difficult to disentangle price and output increases. A revision of Russia's national accounts, for example, showed that officials overestimated the 1990–1994 decline in the level of GDP by 12 percent.

While China has had longer to develop reliable economic statistics, there are still problems. Because of its size and strategic importance, its economic numbers have generated considerable interest and scrutiny. One result is that there is a wide range of opinions about the real purchasing power of Chinese income. One expert has estimated it to be about three times the official exchange rate estimate, or about $1600, considerably below the World Bank estimate in Table 16.3 ($2920).

Most of the countries in Tables 16.1–16.3 are developing countries classified as low income (GNP per person less than $725) or lower middle income ($725 to $2895) by the World Bank. The normal set of development issues are applicable, al-

TABLE 16.2 Transition Economies: Newly Independent States of the Former Soviet Union (NIS), 1995

Country	Population (Millions)	GNP per Person (Dollars)	GDP per Person Purchasing Power Parity (Dollars)
Russian Federation	148.2	2,240	4,480
Caucasus Region			
Armenia	3.8	730	2,260
Azerbaijan	7.5	480	1,460
Georgia	5.4	440	1,470
Central Asian Republics			
Kazakstan	16.6	1,330	3,010
Kyrgyz Republic	4.5	700	1,800
Tajikistan	5.8	340	920
Turkmenistan	4.5	920	*na*
Uzbekistan	22.8	970	2,370
Western Region			
Belarus	10.3	2,070	4,220
Moldova	4.3	920	*na*
Ukraine	51.6	1,630	2,400

na = not available.

Source: See Table 16.1.

though at times, it is difficult to disentangle the general problem of economic development from the issues of economic transition. Both development and transition aim at generating economic growth and raising living standards, and both call for policies to develop financial systems, build new infrastructure, and so forth. Nevertheless, in the discussion that follows, the focus is on the shift from central planning to a market orientation, and not on development. It would be a mistake, however, to interpret this as implying that development issues are unimportant.

The beginning date for the transition to market economies varies by country. China announced the beginning of its reforms in December 1978 and began to implement them gradually in 1979. Vietnam began gradual reforms in 1986, but after a period of few results, it switched to a faster pace in 1989. Most of the CEEC and NIS began their reforms between 1990 and 1994. Poland, for example, implemented a large number of deep reforms all at once in 1990. Several NIS initially resisted reforms and tried to hold on to central planning after the breakup of the Soviet Union. Uzbekistan, for example, has an abundance of natural resource exports that it tried to use to shield it from economic reform. By 1993, inflation was topping out at 13,000 percent, and in 1994, the government began a gradual transition toward a more market-based economy. Uzbekistan is an example of a country where political factors delayed the beginning of reform, but it is by no means the only country held back by politics. When the Soviet Union broke up, many analysts predicted that Ukraine had the best medium-term prospects of any NIS. It has a rich agricultural sector, seaports,

			GDP per Person
	Population	GNP per Person	Purchasing Power
Country	(Millions)	(Dollars)	Parity (Dollars)
China	1,200.2	620	2,920
Mongolia	2.5	310	1,950
Vietnam	73.5	240	na

TABLE 16.3 Transition Economies: Asia, 1995

na = not available.
Source: See Table 16.1.

an inland transportation network, shipbuilding, and machinery industries. Serious reform was delayed until 1994, however, and consequently, it lags behind several other countries. Political factors still hinder a number of nations—Belarus, for example. Belarus is in the center of Europe and relatively close to Western Europe. It has low costs, a skilled labor force, and low crime rates. Nevertheless, it has not fared as well as it should have because the inconsistent and arbitrary application of its policies and laws has scared away foreign investment and suppressed local business.

With the onset of economic reform, every country in the CEEC and the NIS went into a deep economic depression. In Asia, Mongolia shrank, but China and Vietnam both grew, and neither has experienced negative growth at any point in their transitions. (The causes of their positive responses to reform are explored later in the chapter.) Poland was a leader in the economic reform process, and consequently, in 1992, it returned to growth before most other countries. The remainder of the CEEC listed in Table 16.1 followed in 1993 and 1994 (except Macedonia). In general, the NIS have been slower to reform and, perhaps more importantly, have been less consistent in sticking to reforms. Possibly for this reason, the economic depressions in those countries have been deeper and longer.

In addition to variations in the starting dates of reform and the return to economic growth, there are variations in the degree of domestic peace and tranquillity. War delayed economic progress in several NIS as well as the headline-making states of the former Yugoslavia. Tajikistan suffered a Civil War from 1992 to 1993 and still feels the effects. Armenia and Georgia were also torn by war in the early 1990s. One additional cost of civil war beyond the human misery and suffering it brought was a delay in the implementation of economic reforms and, inevitably, a delay in returning to normal economic growth. See Table 16.4.

The Tasks of Reform

The transition to a market economy requires the central planning authority to relinquish its control over the economy while market forces become established. As less and less of the economy is directly controlled, there is greater scope for markets to grow, but unfortunately they do not magically appear when needed. Conse-

TABLE 16.4 Average Annual GDP Growth of the Transition Economies, by Region, 1990–1995		
	Average Annual GDP Growth (Percent)	
Region	**1990–1992**	**1993–1995**
CEEC	–10.1	1.0
Visegrad Four	–6.0	3.0
NIS	–10.0	–11.4
Asia	3.3	8.5

Source: Author's calculations based on data in World Bank, *From Plan to Market: World Development Report, 1996.* 1996.

quently, as the central plan's forced allocation of resources disappears, there is a period of uncertainty before clear market signals appear. The result is that many industries sit idle, especially those that are grossly inefficient or that produce goods no one wants. The machines and equipment may never be used, and the labor has no immediate place to go. In other words, there is a steep depression.

Negative growth lasts until enough of the transition process has been completed so that growth in the new economy outweighs the disappearance of the old. The time this takes depends on numerous factors, including the speed of reform, the degree of competency with which it is managed, and the ability of society to tolerate the uncertainty and change that result. The term "reform fatigue" has been coined to describe countries that have become exhausted from the loss of income and the associated uncertainty and that have slowed or partially reversed their transitions.

No matter what the culture or the history of a nation, there are several tasks it must accomplish to become a stable market economy. First, the government must implement macroeconomic policies that will stabilize the economy. Second, it must liberalize the domestic market, external trade, and the entry of new businesses. Third, it must clearly define property rights. Fourth, it must create the institutions it needs to support the market economy.

Economic Stabilization of the Economy

In Chapter 14, on economic policy reform in Latin America, economic stabilization was defined as controlling inflation, budget deficits, and the external debt. The same definition applies to the transitional economies. Chapter 14 also singled out stabilization as one of the first steps in the reform process. In addition, Chapter 15, on the high-performance Asian economies, showed the important role of stable macroeconomies in the extraordinary growth performance of those nations. The same reasoning applies to the CEEC, the NIS, and the other transitional economies.

In every transitional economy, the socialist legacy of overinvestment in heavy industry and state ownership placed a heavy burden on the central government's budget. The problem was compounded by the relative isolation of socialist economies from world trade and investment, as isolation severely limited competitive pressures and the incentive for efficiency improvements. One result is that a large part of the industrial sector in every country requires subsidies to stay afloat. An option is to let the enterprises collapse, but in some cases, this may cost more, since it leads to greater spending on social support programs for the people thrown out of work.

In most market economies, there are tax systems with fully developed legislative and administrative structures for levying, collecting, and enforcing the tax code. In addition, most countries have securities markets in which the government can borrow private savings to finance its expenditures. Initially, the transition economies had neither tax systems nor financial markets in which governments could borrow. There were essentially two options for financing their growing deficits: the transition economies could seek to borrow abroad, most likely from international agencies such as the IMF, or they could print money. Most countries did both, especially the printing of money. The predictable result was a rapid rise in inflation in the early years of the transition. In some economies, that was followed by restrictions on the issuance of new money, curbs on government expenditures, the development of effective systems of taxation, and ultimately, a market for government securities. In others, it has been politically difficult to limit subsidies to industry, and the government budget has continued to run up large deficits, with the corresponding inflationary effects.

Liberalization

In general, liberalization refers to the replacement of administrative controls with market-based allocative mechanisms. This is equivalent to saying that prices and outputs are left up to markets rather than the central plan. In practice, it means that domestic prices are free from bureaucratic control and that individuals and enterprises are free to buy and sell and to import and export. Liberalization also requires that the barriers to new firms entering a market must be lifted. As long as entry is controlled, prices and outputs will not reflect the value of goods and services.

Lifting the barriers to entry has an international dimension because firms may find it profitable to import foreign goods or to export domestic ones. In effect, this means an end to the state's total control of foreign trade and the replacement of the state monopoly with an explicit trade regime. The introduction of foreign goods in the domestic market also serves to link foreign and domestic prices. Their linkage has an important impact on inflation control, since the presence of foreign goods limits the amount of price increase that domestic producers can ask for.

Liberalization refers not just to markets for goods and services but to input markets as well. Labor markets and financial markets are more difficult to create but important nonetheless. Labor markets require provisions for unemployment, pension systems, and a social safety net separate from employment. Financial markets require a host of supporting measures, from tax and security laws to development of financial service firms. These issues are beyond the scope of this chapter.

Defining Property Rights

Property rights refer to the legal rights to use an asset, to exclude others from its use, to collect income from it, and to dispose of it. Market economies specify property rights in great detail, since they are a fundamental underpinning of market relations. Well-functioning markets require a clear definition of property rights. When property rights are ambiguous or subject to political whim, there is a built-in reluctance to exchange (labor, goods, or financial assets), as one's economic interest is uncertain. Property rights that are not clearly specified are major obstacles to generating new economic activity.

Property rights in transition economies are usually unclear and often not recognized. Most assets were owned by the state, so there was little need to specify them. In order for markets to play a greater role, this obstacle must be overcome. Obviously, it requires a large number of supporting actions, such as the development of contract and commercial law, privatization of state-owned assets, and explicit recognition of the commercial rights of individuals and enterprises. In many countries, there is a scarcity of people with the knowledge and skills necessary to create the needed legal systems.

Institutional Development

The transition to market economies has proven to be more difficult and to take longer than most people initially anticipated. Naively, many people thought that once input and output prices were freed, markets would magically begin to allocate inputs to their highest-valued uses. The reason for the disappointment is that most people who thought the transition would be quick—a couple of years at most—failed to recognize that there are a large number of market-supporting institutions that must be created if markets are to work as desired. In the industrial market economies, these institutions have evolved over decades or even centuries. In the transition economies, they were expected to spring fully formed from economic texts.

Recall that institutions are the "rules of the game" that limit human behavior. They include legal systems, the definitions of property rights and entitlements, social support programs, enforcement mechanisms, and information systems. Until regulatory and enforcement institutions are created, transition economies lack a large number of goods and services that are important to markets. Some examples may be useful. Credit reports, business directories, market research, and actuarial data are important pieces of information in market economies. Efficient provision of these services requires clearly specified rules with respect to personal privacy, business practices, and intellectual property. Once an enterprise or an individual has the required business information, it is important to also have a clear idea of the rules governing fair trade, foreign commerce, environmental impacts, taxation, and so forth. If a party to their economic enterprise fails to deliver, there must be a credible set of enforcement procedures within which to seek redress. Along the way, economic agents must rely on a significant number of institutions. In the advanced industrial economies, we tend to take these things for granted, but in the transition economies, the institutions must be created. As long as the rules are unspecified or ambiguous, or appear to be subject to somebody's whim, it raises the level of risk and discourages economic initiative.

ISSUE

Should the Transition Be Fast or Slow?

No issue is more controversial or has generated more debate than the question about the speed of the reforms. Two metaphors are often repeated. The proponents of a fast, "big bang" transition are fond of a saying that has been attributed both to a Russian proverb and to Václav Havel, former president of the Czech Republic: "You can't cross a chasm in two leaps." The gradualist preference is summed up in the quote from Deng Xiao-ping, the late Chinese leader and initiator of its reforms: Reforms are like "feeling the stones to cross the river."

The proponents of slow reforms point to China. Chinese reforms were first proposed in late 1978 and got under way in 1979. Until the mid-1980s, they mainly affected the agricultural sector, but since China had such a large share of its population in rural areas, the positive effects on food output and rural incomes were significant. Primarily, the agricultural reforms let families and villages take individual responsibility for meeting their production quotas and allowed them to keep for consumption or for sale whatever amount they produced above the quota. Villages and communes were allowed to disband the collectivist system of production, and individual incentives began to rule the efforts and decision making of producers.

In the mid-1980s, China extended its market-based reforms to a number of special economic zones (SEZs), economic and technology development zones (ETDZs), high-technology development zones (HTDZs), and other special developmental areas, mostly located along the coast. The rules of each type of zone varied, but in general, they allowed far more independent, profit-oriented, market-based decision making. The SEZs, in particular, were encouraged to experiment with new forms of economic organization and to develop joint ventures by attracting foreign investment. These areas began to account for the bulk of Chinese growth, exports, and foreign investment.

China's transition strategy is considered a gradualist strategy because it has not attempted to reform the entire economic structure in one fell swoop. Rather, it has used a "dual-track strategy," which localizes reforms to certain areas or sectors (e.g., agriculture) while maintaining traditional, central planning structures in the remainder of the economy. Slowly, subsidized prices were raised to the market level, and the mandatory production targets were reduced to a small share of the total output or zero. By the early to mid-1990s, more than 90 percent of retail prices and 80 to 90 percent of agricultural and intermediate goods prices were decontrolled. China has been much slower to privatize its state-owned sector, and state-owned enterprises continue to be a significant share of the economy.

Unlike the other transition economies, China's output never declined during its transition. (Vietnam's economy is the only other exception besides China.) Many proponents of the gradualist point of view argue that the phasing in of reforms relieves the pressure to instantaneously develop new institutions and economic relations. By adopting a dual-track approach, China has

Issue continues

allowed the market economy to develop alongside the centrally planned economy and to gradually take over more and more of its functions as it matured. Perhaps even more importantly than avoiding an economic downturn, it gave the Chinese people time to adjust their expectations to fit a market-based system, reducing the shock of change.

The proponents of rapid reform see China as a special case. First, central planning was less extensive in China, with the result that its economy was less distorted and less overconcentrated on heavy industry. Second, and most importantly, China's economy is much more agricultural. In 1978, when China began its reforms, 71 percent of the labor force was in agriculture. The figure for Russia in 1990, at the beginning of its transition, was 13 percent. Most of the CEEC are more like Russia than China. China's heavier concentration in agriculture gives it a large rural labor force that has very low productivity. If these workers leave the countryside, the resulting loss of output is very small, but the offsetting productivity gains from employment in urban and village industrial enterprises are significant. Hence, China can move labor from agriculture into the new enterprises, while the CEEC and most of the NIS must take labor out of heavy industry to staff the new enterprises.

Proponents of the "big bang" approach to the transition also cite Vietnam. Vietnam began its reforms gradually in 1986, then suddenly switched to an "all-at-once" strategy in 1989 when the gradualism failed to produce results. Agriculture and trade were liberalized; prices throughout the economy were decontrolled; foreign investment was encouraged; the fiscal deficit was cut along with subsidies to state enterprises; and new business enterprises were encouraged. The result was a jump in the growth rate. Like China, low-productivity agriculture employs the bulk of Vietnam's labor force.

Gradualists counter with the argument that rapid transitions lead to "reform fatigue." The psychological and social costs of the transition can be high: workers are confronted with the possibility of getting laid off for the first time in their lives; fundamental necessities such as shelter, health care, and bread are suddenly expensive and unobtainable for some; and crime, alcoholism, and other social ills increase. The uncertainty of it all produces enormous stress and a high social cost. It is at least conceivable that the reforms might actually be undone in some cases.

Empirical measures seem to support the proponents of a fast transition. Although there is no final word as yet, there seems to be an emerging consensus that the more consistent and rapid the reform policies, the quicker the return to growth. Data from the World Bank (remember that data on the transition economies are suspect) show on average a smaller decline in GDP and a quicker return to growth for the rapid reformers. For example, the Visegrad Four (Poland, Hungary, Czech Republic, Slovakia) in Table 16.4 have a shallower decline and a quicker return to growth than the other CEEC and the NIS. They are among the most rapid and consistent reformers. Countries that reversed or partially reversed their reforms, or that applied them in a stop-and-go fashion (e.g., Russia), have had a harder time restoring growth.

Issue continues

Issue continued

During the first half of the 1990s, several studies seemed to show that radical stabilization policies (inflation control and reductions in government spending) were the causes of the depressions. More recent analysis points to three factors as having caused the depressions: (1) the disruption of traditional trading patterns; (2) the shift in internal demand away from the state-produced goods toward the as-yet-small consumer goods sector; and (3) disruptions in the supply of inputs that were brought on by the collapse of central planning and the absence of its replacement with market institutions. The debate continues.

It is increasingly clear, however, that whether governments adopt a "big bang" or a "go slow" approach, different tasks of transition require different time dimensions, and not all reforms can be done quickly. For example, while prices can be liberalized quickly, the building of new institutions such as legal structures or securities markets requires more time. In part, this stems from the fact that there are scarcities of people with the relevant skills and experience, and training takes time. Privatization of state-owned enterprises can be accomplished relatively fast when the assets are small, such as houses and retail shops. Large industrial enterprises have been more complex, however, and have taken longer to privatize.

Old and New Trade Patterns

One of the most remarkable features of the transition has been the shift in trading patterns. The most dramatic changes have come in the CEEC and in China. Throughout the NIS, traditional trade patterns have collapsed, but with the exception of Russia, new ones have not grown in their place. The shift in the CEEC trading pattern has affected both the direction of trade and, to a lesser degree, the composition of trade. When Soviet domination ended, the trade it had created disappeared, and new trade relations quickly developed. The shift in the commodity composition of CEEC trade illustrates the difficulties many countries have in trying to make their manufacturing sectors competitive in the world market.

The Council for Mutual Economic Assistance (CMEA)

After World War II, as relations between the Allies deteriorated and the Cold War began to heat up, the Soviet Union tried to create organizations of economic cooperation within its sphere of power. In trade, the result was the Council for Mutual Economic Assistance (CMEA). In the West, it has also been known by the acronym COMECON. Originally, the CMEA included the CEEC and the Soviet Union. The former Yugoslavia was never a member, nor was China. Vietnam and Cuba joined later.

The CMEA was a trade bloc much like any other; the main difference was that none of the countries had currencies that were freely convertible. Partly for this reason, trade between the CMEA countries was a form of barter, known as **counter-trade**. Counter-trade has several forms, including pure barter. A more common form, known as **counter-purchase trade**, occurs when an exporting country is required to spend its earnings on imports of equal value from the country receiving its exports. In this way, trade is always balanced.

> **Counter-trade**. *Counter-trade includes pure barter (goods exchanged directly for goods) and counter-purchase trade, in which exports are sold, but the proceeds must be spent on imports from the country receiving the exports. A third, less common form is buy-back trade, in which the sale of exports is tied directly to the purchase of imports. For example, an exporter of manufacturing equipment agrees to buy the output of the manufacturing firm. Most trade within the CMEA was counter-trade, as was most East-West trade before the collapse of communism.*

The pattern of commodity trade within the CMEA was for the CEEC to export machinery and equipment to the Soviet Union in exchange for raw materials and oil. The goal of the CMEA was to organize the coordination of national economic plans. Trade flows were built into the plan and different countries and regions specialized in products for the whole bloc. The CMEA was only partially successful in coordinating economic plans. One major problem was the determination of prices for trade. Domestic prices were entirely artificial and conveyed no information about scarcity. Beginning in the mid-1970s, the CMEA attempted to set trade prices at world levels, but the application of an "adjustment factor" led to the valuation of most goods at levels far below world prices. Undervaluation became an especially acute problem for oil as world energy prices rose.

In 1991, the rules were changed to reflect the reform processes that had begun in many countries. Beginning in January of 1991, all countries were required to pay hard currency for imports, and prices were set at prevailing world market prices. Trade shrank dramatically, and the CMEA was formally ended later in 1991.

The collapse of trade had a negative impact on the CEEC and the NIS. There are differing estimates of the decline in trade among the NIS (intra-NIS trade), but they all show a dramatic fall. Unlike the NIS, and after a few years of falling trade, most of the CEEC was able to offset the loss of CMEA trade with new markets in the high-income, industrial economies. Figures 16.1 and 16.2 illustrate the decline of trade with the CMEA and the rise of trade with the advanced market economies. The patterns for the other CEEC are essentially similar. (Note that East Germany was a member of the CMEA until 1989, and after that, its trade statistics are included in those for Germany. This causes the graphs in Figures 16.1 and 16.2 to overstate both the rise in trade with the industrial market economies and the decline in trade with the CMEA. Nevertheless, the point is still valid, and if Germany were taken out of the data, the pattern would remain.)

Figure 16.2 shows a rise in CMEA trade after 1992. It is too early to know if this is a long-run trend, but it is an encouraging sign. The CEEC countries have signed a number of regional trade agreements, and it is possible that they can explain the reemergence of trade. These agreements are discussed later in the chapter.

FIGURE 16.1 Exports to Industrial Nations

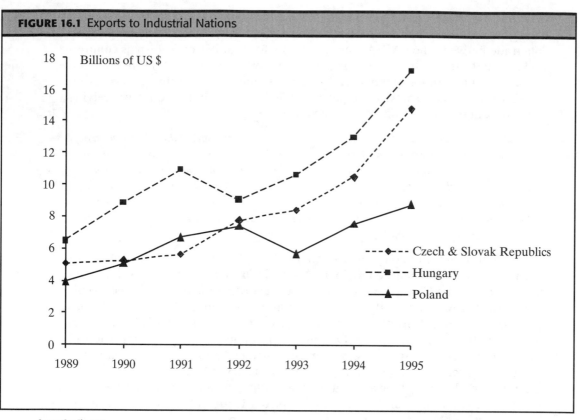

Source: See Fig. 16.2.

Figures 16.1 and 16.2 are for exports alone, but imports show a similar pattern: a breakoff in trade with the former CMEA countries and a rise in imports from the industrial market economies. Import flows tend to be greater than the increase in exports, and many of the CEEC have begun to run sizable trade deficits. Nevertheless, the remarkable increase in overall trade, both imports and exports, has raised living standards and is an encouraging sign that the economies are becoming integrated into the world trading system.

In addition to worries over deficits, the growth of trade has presented several additional challenges. Under the old system of CMEA trade, the CEEC exported machinery and equipment to the Soviet Union in exchange for Soviet fuel and raw materials. This was particularly true for the Visegrad Four. Trade with Western Europe and North America was more balanced and included a larger share of basic metals, food and other agricultural products, chemicals, and apparel and textiles. The expansion of trade with the West required the CEEC to expand their exports of these items; equipment and machinery could not be as easily redirected from the old Soviet Union to Western Europe because CEEC industrial plants were significantly less competitive, and there were serious questions about the quality of machinery they produced.

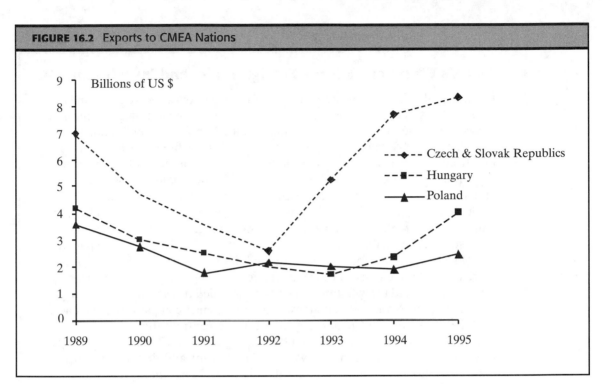

FIGURE 16.2 Exports to CMEA Nations

Source: International Monetary Fund, *Direction of Trade Statistics.* Washington, DC: IMF, 1996.

One problem with this composition of trade is that basic metals, food and agricultural products, chemicals, and textiles and apparel are in abundant supply around the world. They tend to be labor intensive (except chemicals), and they are relatively highly protected. For example, Western Europe's system of agricultural subsidies limits their market to outsiders (Chapter 13), and protection in the United States is highest in the textile and apparel industry (Chapter 6). Furthermore, steel and iron have had off-and-on quantitative restrictions in the United States and Europe over the last few decades. Nevertheless, most industrial economies have dropped the trade barriers they had that were aimed at centrally planned economies.

Recent surveys of exporters in the CEEC have shown that the greatest barriers to export are domestic problems inside the CEEC. Undoubtedly, the same is true of the NIS economies as well. The main obstacles according to exporters are the lack of domestic infrastructure, particularly the poor condition of telecommunications and the inefficiency in border crossings. In addition, exporters cite their lack of information about Western markets and their own government's policies, particularly changes in domestic regulations that affect exports.

Trade Policy and the Transition

Centrally planned economies generally lack anything resembling a trade policy. Imports fill gaps in central plans, and exports are above-target outputs that are

CASE STUDY

China's Economic Reform, Foreign Trade, and Investment

China's gradualist reforms began in late 1978. Its go-slow approach, "feeling the stones to cross the river," was not the result of an overarching strategy as much as it was a response to the political constraints of the Chinese system. Proponents of reform were not certain how to proceed, and at the same time, they feared a reaction from the hard-line, conservative antireformers. Under the old system of foreign trade, there were twelve Foreign Trading Corporations (FTCs) that were attached to the various branches of government. All exports and imports went through these twelve FTCs. As in other centrally planned economies, trade was a balancing item in the central plan. Imports were sought only when domestic enterprises were incapable of filling the targets set by the plan. They were paid for out of surplus production that was also built into the plan. The FTCs were required to sell to the Bank of China the foreign exchange they earned on exports. Imports were paid for with foreign currency provided by the Bank according to the central plan. No considerations were given to China's comparative advantage.

A critical feature of China's reforms was the decentralization of this system, leading to the opening of trade and the reintegration of China into the world trading system. First, China allowed the creation of additional FTCs in the hands of national, provincial, and local authorities. In addition, large state-run enterprises were given the right to trade. Second, price reforms were implemented. Under the old system, the domestic price of imports was arbitrarily set equal to the price charged for similar goods produced domestically. Consequently, Chinese manufacturers were completely isolated from fluctuations in world prices. Gradually, larger and larger shares of import prices have been set equal to the world price (i.e., the dollar price converted to yuan at the official exchange rate). Tariffs and other barriers keep domestic prices from equaling the world price, but there is no longer a complete separation of the two. A third element of trade reform was the curtailment of mandatory targets for exports. These have been reduced in stages so that required exports were a decreasing share of total exports and then disappeared altogether. At the same time, subsidies for exports have fallen as China has tried to bring its trade policy into alignment with the requirements for membership in the World Trade Organization.

In order to limit the initial impact of reforms on the domestic economy and to prevent a political backlash, China turned to an innovative concept that they labeled special economic zones (SEZs). SEZs were modeled on the export-processing zones of some East Asian economies, but they went far beyond in scope. Export-processing zones are special regions in which manufacturers are given rebates on tariffs they pay for imported goods if the imports are incorporated into an export. SEZs go beyond this by giving provincial and local authorities a wide latitude to experiment with economic and trade policies that are radically different from national policies. In China's view, SEZs are "windows and bridges" to the outside world. Foreign enterprises "looking in" can see the Chinese market through the SEZ and are given incentives to build production fa-

Case continues

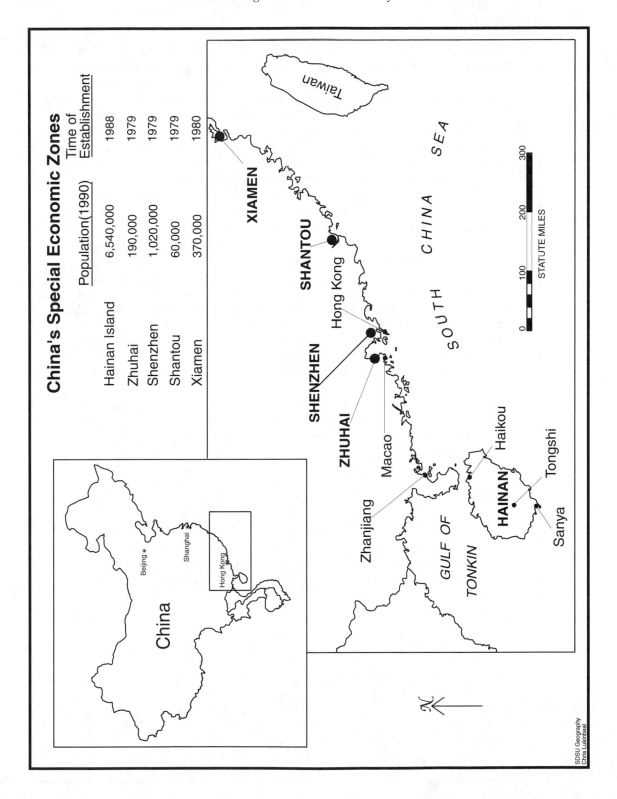

China's Special Economic Zones

	Population(1990)	Time of Establishment
Hainan Island	6,540,000	1988
Zhuhai	190,000	1979
Shenzhen	1,020,000	1979
Shantou	60,000	1979
Xiamen	370,000	1980

SDSU Geography
Chris Lukinbeal

Case continued

cilities. Chinese firms "looking out" can learn about technology and world markets. Special incentives to form joint ventures and set up production facilities (tax breaks, relaxed rules on tariffs, licensing, foreign exchange conversion, and so forth) create a "bridge" between China and the rest of the world.

China created its first SEZ in 1979 and its fifth and final one in 1988. The enormous success of these regions in attracting foreign investment (particularly from Taiwan, Hong Kong, and the overseas Chinese business communities) and in generating exports and economic growth created a demonstration effect for the rest of China. Additional regions began to push for similar treatment, and the central government has responded with a number of new designations (eg., ETDZs, HTDZs). These areas are more restricted than the SEZs but still more open than the rest of the country. The special regions have been so successful that many now fear that China's next big problem is its growing regional inequality. Most of the regions that have received favorable treatment are coastal, so there is a clear bifurcation in overall Chinese economic development. For example, in 1992, over 88 percent of all foreign direct investment in China was directed to coastal provinces and cities. Guangdong province, adjacent to Hong Kong, accounted for one-third of total inward FDI by itself.

Another key question for China is whether its reforms continue to move forward outside the special regions and whether they extend to the numerous state-run enterprises that still largely function outside of hard budget constraints. State-run enterprises employed about the same share of the labor force in 1992 that they did in 1980 (18 to 19 percent), even though most of the growth in China's economy has occurred in the nonstate sector. State ownership gives firms political clout that other firms lack, and as a result, they are still largely outside of a market-based economy. For example, large numbers operate at a loss, even in good years. Their ability to obtain subsidies raises the central government's budget deficit and makes the macroeconomy less stable. As of 1997, reform of these state-run enterprises has become a priority of the Chinese government, but there is widespread uncertainty among outside observers as to the political feasibility of reform.

China's technique for economic opening has, so far, been unable to reform loss-making state-owned enterprises and has led to the creation of growing regional inequality. Nevertheless, at the national level, its policies must be seen as a major success. Over the last decade, growth in the national economy has been in the neighborhood of 10 percent per year, while exports have grown an even faster 15 percent. By 1996, China was the fifth largest exporter in the world and the second largest recipient of foreign investment. One of the main reasons for the phenomenal growth of China's exports is that the reforms have shifted production toward its comparative advantage: labor-intensive products and assembling and processing firms. In the past, comparative advantage was never considered. In the current system, firms must be more responsive to world prices and profitability. While barriers to imports remain a concern to industrial economies, China's "open door" policy for trade, investment, and technology transfers has successfully linked the economy to the world trading system.

exchanged for imports. Furthermore, both inward and outward foreign investments are highly controlled and, consequently, there is a limited need for foreign currencies. In most cases, domestic currencies were not convertible, meaning that they could not be freely exchanged for foreign money. Hence, balance of payments problems, such as capital flight or prolonged periods of trade deficits, were not possible. The goal of trade and exchange rate policies is to help manage the transition through greater interaction between the domestic economy and the rest of the world. Greater integration with the world trading system is expected to bring the benefits of foreign trade and investment: larger markets and the opportunity to specialize, technology transfer, foreign investment, and a wider variety of consumer goods. It can also bring currency instability and balance of payments crises if the policies are inappropriate or lack credibility.

Steps to Trade Liberalization

The earlier discussion of China's case illustrates most of the steps involved in the opening up of trade. One of the first is to end the state monopoly on trade. Centrally planned economies allow only a handful of designated state-owned enterprises to engage in trade. Rather than acting independently, these firms are required to be purchasing agents of the central plan. With the removal of the barriers to entry in the trade sector, private firms can enter and become trading firms. This is only the beginning, however, and market economies require several additional steps.

In order for firms to know which goods to trade, domestic prices must convey information about relative scarcities. Under central planning, prices are artificial and do not convey real information. Therefore, a key component of trade liberalization is the linking of domestic prices to world prices. That is, fluctuations in world prices that convey information of either greater scarcity or greater abundance should be felt inside the economy. In China's case, prices were liberalized on a gradual "dual-track" plan. Over time, the artificial prices set by the central plan and used for internal transactions were limited to a smaller and smaller share of the economy, while they were simultaneously raised gradually to world levels. In Poland's case, price controls were abolished on January 1, 1990, along with many other controls over the economy.

A third step is to formulate an explicit trade policy. Decisions must be made about import substitution strategies, export promotion strategies, and key industries that might need protection. If protection is adopted, governments must decide which form of protection to use: tariffs, quotas, licensing, or some other nontariff barrier. Additional considerations are membership in the WTO and the constraints it imposes on trade policy. Fourth, nations must adopt rules governing foreign investment. For many countries—China, for example—foreign investment is an important supplement to domestic savings. Key considerations are how it will be encouraged, how it is affected by the other parts of the trade regime, and whether capital controls should be used to limit financial flows into and out of the country. Fifth, nations must formulate an exchange rate policy, including decisions about convertibility, both in timing and degree. Exchange rate policy has direct links to trade balances, foreign investment, domestic inflation, and macroeconomic stability. Consequently, it is one of the most important policy decisions.

Commercial policy and the exchange rate play such central roles in the transition process that each are discussed in greater detail in the following two sections.

Transitional Protection and Balance of Payments Problems

Trade policy reform in the CEEC has been fast and deep. Quantitative restrictions have disappeared along with most other nontariff barriers. Furthermore, overall tariffs are relatively low. The exceptions to these generalizations have mostly occurred in cases where there is a need to protect the balance of payments from large trade deficits. Six of the CEEC are members of the GATT and WTO. In most instances, GATT rules require nontariff barriers to be converted to tariffs or to be eliminated altogether. Furthermore, membership in GATT limits the ability of countries to raise tariffs.

The NIS countries have lagged in their opening, and many still have extensive quantitative restrictions. Since they are outside the GATT, the NIS are less bound by international rules. In addition, the fact that large parts of many national economies remain in state hands makes it politically difficult to open to international competition. It is common in these cases to hear a type of infant-industry argument along the lines that certain enterprises will ultimately become competitive, but in the short run, they need protection from outside competition. Exposing them to competition without a transitional period to prepare would result in the needless loss of their productive capacity. As always, in the short run, it is difficult to separate legitimate claims for protection from rent seeking.

In the early stages of the reform process, import surges are common. There are two reasons. First, consumers in centrally planned economies lived under regimes that channeled too many resources into heavy industry and capital goods production. Consequently, there is an excess demand for consumer goods that can be met only through imports. Second, the modernization of infrastructure and industry requires imported technology and capital goods. Increased imports raise social welfare because they provide consumers with access to the goods they desire and producers with the tools they need to become competitive. Nevertheless, import surges can also lead to large trade deficits and balance of payments problems that undermine the economy's overall macroeconomic stability.

Recall that trade deficits must be financed through capital inflows—borrowing, foreign investment, or aid. When capital inflows are insufficient to sustain the trade deficit (or, more accurately, the current account deficit), the economy enters a crisis. Mexico at the end of 1994 and Thailand in July of 1997 are examples. The usual solution to the crisis is an emergency loan from the IMF and a steep devaluation of the currency (expenditure switching).

The problem of trade balances in the early stages of the transition is compounded by three interrelated factors. One, most countries implemented stabilization policies to control inflation and reduce budget deficits. Stabilization policies often entailed a squeeze on bank credit that made it difficult for firms to gain the financing they needed to export. This fed into the second factor: the collapse of trade within the former CMEA countries. Stabilization reduced overall aggregate demand, including the demand for foreign goods, so that stabilization in, say, Poland, reduced the demand for goods produced in the Czech Republic. Third, the time lag in institutional development, especially regulatory and legal institutions, created a climate of uncertainty and made it difficult to export. As mentioned earlier, surveys of exporters have shown that the biggest obstacles to exports included the lack of information about regulatory and legal changes. Stabilization policies, the collapse of traditional export markets, and the institutional lag each limited the supply response of exporters and contributed to export growth that was weaker than the growth in imports. This was not true in every case, but even in cases such as Poland, the trade surpluses during the first year of radical reform (1991) proved to be fragile, and large deficits opened thereafter. One bright spot, however, was the rapid growth in trade with high-income industrial market economies, as illustrated in Fig. 16.1.

Exchange Rate Regimes and Convertibility

Most transitional economies began their stabilization and transition programs with large devaluations. Devaluation was usually done to protect the balance of payments during the transition and is preferred to tariffs or quotas because it is neutral in its effects on specific industries while providing incentives to export. Furthermore, tariffs, quotas, and other quantitative restrictions, if used selectively, provide a protective wall around domestic producers that delays their adjustment to world prices and perpetuates the misallocation of resources that has plagued those economies.

For most countries, it has proven hard to maintain a devalued exchange rate in real terms. Higher rates of inflation have led to real appreciation and have undone the initial effects of the nominal devaluation. Consequently, there has been increased pressure to use tariffs and nontariff barriers to address the macroeconomic problem of trade balances and the microeconomic problems of competitiveness in specific sectors. For example, Czechoslovakia (prior to its breakup in 1993) and Hungary supplemented their devaluations with import surcharges, which are a uniform tax on all imports, and import quotas on consumer goods. These types of protection are generally viewed as temporary. Within the NIS and China, liberalization of imports has not progressed as far, and various quantitative restrictions are in place, including the very common requirement that importers obtain a government-issued license.

Along with devaluation of the official exchange rate, transitional economies were required to unify their exchange rates, choose an exchange rate regime, and agree on a timetable for convertibility. Most countries operated with multiple exchange rates prior to the transition. Official exchange rates generally overvalued the domestic currency. Under normal conditions, overvalued currencies lead to large trade deficits and balance of payments problems, but since trade and the purchase of foreign exchange was strictly controlled, this was not as great a problem under central planning.

> *The swap rate.* The rate of exchange used when the monetary authorities of two countries exchange the assets they have acquired against each other is called the swap rate. In centrally planned economies, the swap rate was different from the official exchange rate.

In addition to the official exchange rate, the monetary authority usually set a rate for so-called swaps. The **swap rate** was the rate at which two monetary authorities settled claims on each other. For example, suppose that countertrade between Romania and Bulgaria resulted in each country's monetary authority acquiring the currency of the other country. The rate of exchange between the two currencies is the swap rate, and it usually differed from the official exchange rate. Multiple exchange rates imply that there are potential differences in the domestic price of foreign goods, depending on which exchange rate is used. Consequently, unification of the official rate and the swap rate into one exchange rate is a necessary step in the elimination of resource misallocations caused by arbitrary and inaccurate prices.

There is considerable debate about the type of exchange rate regime appropriate for the transition process. Both flexible and fixed rates have been successful. Fixed rates require consistent fiscal and monetary policies in order to maintain the credibility of the exchange rate and to avoid inflation and real appreciation. Overly loose macroeconomic policy can feed the self-fulfilling perception of speculators that a devaluation is unavoidable. Floating rates, on the other hand, while appropriate in the long run, are less powerful than pegged rates or fixed rates as signals of the monetary authority's determination to end the period of inflation that is common in the initial stages of the transition. Given the liabilities of completely fixed and freely floating rates, pegged exchange rates have been adopted in a number of countries.

In addition to unifying the exchange rate and choosing an exchange rate regime, individuals and enterprises must be granted the right to freely purchase foreign currencies at the official, unified exchange rate. Generally, convertibility has been limited to transactions within the current account. Either unrestricted convertibility or current account convertibility is necessary for trade liberalization, and each is complementary to it. Importing is impossible if individuals and enterprises are not permitted to purchase foreign exchange, and, conversely, convertibility is meaningless if they are not allowed to import.

> *Currency convertibility. A currency is convertible if it is freely exchangeable for another currency. It implies the right to convert at the legal exchange rate. Convertibility may be unrestricted—that is, it can occur for any type of transaction. More commonly in the transition economies, it may be "current account convertibility"—limited to transactions that fall into the current account.*

One complication that delayed the introduction of convertibility in many of the NIS and CEEC was the presence of a **monetary overhang,** also called a liquidity overhang. Monetary overhang is another of the legacies of central planning and is simply the accumulation of a large amount of unspent domestic currency. It exists because consumers cannot find the goods and services they want to buy while the government has resorted to excess money creation to finance its deficits. Movement to a convertible exchange rate usually fails if the monetary overhang has not been disposed of or if government spending is excessive. The reasons are that convertibility requires a sufficient inflow of capital to finance the current account deficit, if there is one, and that there is a sufficient stock of foreign exchange reserves to meet the expected day-to-day variation in demand. Either a large monetary overhang or excessive government spending can unravel the implementation of convertibility by raising the level of domestic demand for imports above the level that can be sustained out of existing reserves and inflows of new reserves.

> ***Monetary overhang***. *Monetary overhang refers to the large stock of unspent domestic money that was present in most transitional economies. (China is a major exception to this generalization.) Monetary overhang existed because consumers could not find the goods and services they wanted to buy, because consumer goods prices were kept below equilibrium levels, and because too much money was created.*

Under the policy of current account convertibility, the purchase of foreign currencies is limited to transactions that fall into the current account, for example, exporting and importing, tourism, and remittances of investment and labor income. The point of limiting convertibility to this level is to avoid large and sudden flows of capital out of the country (capital flight) and the resulting macroeconomic instability. Current account convertibility does not necessarily discourage inward foreign investment as long as there are assurances of the right to repatriate profits.

The Links Between Trade Policy and Other Areas of Reform

International trade and the exchange rate have numerous effects on each of the areas of reform discussed in this chapter. Probably the most important effect is to act as an accurate source of information about prices and scarcities. The resource misallocations of centrally planned economies cannot be corrected without price signals that accurately convey information to producers and consumers. Accurate prices allow producers to correctly decide what to produce, as well as how to produce it, and help consumers decide how to allocate their income. Trade, therefore, helps in the task of industrial restructuring and furthers the process of modernization. Even in sectors where trade is relatively inconsequential or nonexistent, the potential to trade ensures that domestic prices are more or less equivalent to world prices after adjustments for transportation, tariffs, and so forth. More importantly, the potential to trade ensures that changes in the world economy that result in price changes are also felt in the domestic economy. Trade is the vehicle by which the isolation of national economies is broken.

While international trade's strongest effect may be to help with the process of liberalization, it also has important effects on institutional reform, such as privatization, legal reform, and regulatory changes. The freeing of trade from the government's monopoly is a first step in the creation of new businesses. The freedom to export and import encourages new entrepreneurs, and the competitive pressures of imports can be an added incentive for governments to sell off enterprises that demand large subsidies to stay afloat. In addition, trade puts pressure on the authorities to move forward with regulatory and legal reforms. Exporters and importers need to know the rules of the game in order for them to be willing to take risks. When trade opportunities exist, businesses lobby for more transparency and less arbitrariness in regulatory structures, putting pressure on governments to design new institutions.

Integration into the World Trading System

Many of the trade reforms of the NIS, CEEC, and the Asian transitional economies are motivated by their desire to become full members of the world trading system. Access to foreign goods, foreign technology, and foreign investment are essential to raising their living standards. The most direct route to becoming fully integrated in the world economy is through full membership in the multilateral organizations, such as the GATT, the WTO, the IMF, and the World Bank. In addition, several countries have sought closer ties with their most important trading partners, for example Western Europe and the former members of the CMEA.

The WTO and the Transitional Economies

As of mid-1997, six transitional economies (Poland, Hungary, the Czech and Slovak Republics, Romania, and Slovenia) are members of the WTO. Czechoslovakia (the dissolved union of the present-day Czech and Slovak Republics) was one of the original twenty-three members, while Poland, Romania, and Hungary joined between 1967 and 1973. Most of the other transitional economies, including China and Russia, have applied for membership and currently have "observer" status. Most likely, a number of them will become full members over the next few years.

Membership is granted on a case-by-case basis after a period of consultations to determine the **accession protocol**. The accession protocol is a set of steps that new members must take in order to put their economic policies in compliance with the rules of the WTO. These are negotiated on a case-by-case basis because each applicant has unique features in its economy that must be considered. During the period of negotiation, the applicants have observer status that allows them to participate in most functions without having a voice in any decisions. It is a period of observation, in which the applicants learn the rules and procedures of the WTO.

In the past, it was possible for a country to join even if its economy was radically at odds with the spirit of GATT. For example, Poland, Romania, and Hungary joined while their economies were centrally planned. They were so far from market-based economies that many of the rules and privileges of GATT membership made no sense. For example, exports and imports discriminated heavily in favor of the CMEA area and were completely controlled by the central plan. Consequently, key values of the GATT, such as MFN status and national treatment, were impossible. In compensation, their accession protocols required them to make commitments to import from outside the CMEA and to submit to periodic reviews of their compliance. Furthermore, other members were permitted to discriminate against them on a selective basis. The experiment of admitting centrally planned economies under restrictive conditions is generally considered a failure, and it is unlikely that countries will be admitted in the future unless their trading systems are substantially market driven.

One of the key requirements for membership is transparency in the trade regime. Recall that transparency means that all the rules and regulations relating to importing and exporting are readily available and clearly stated. In economies with large state-owned sectors or state-owned trading corporations, the lack of transparency can lead to favorable treatment for state-owned enterprises and discrimination against foreign and domestic firms that are privately owned. Another membership requirement is that countries adjust their economic policies to eliminate all export subsidies and most direct production subsidies. In some cases—China, for example—this is a complex issue, since accounting procedures and ownership structures differ greatly from the norms in industrial market economies. Consequently, determining if a state-owned enterprise is subsidized is complex and has various answers, depending on the procedure used to measure subsidies.

Compliance with GATT and WTO rules is more easily accomplished in the areas of tariffs and quotas. Nations must adopt an acceptable timetable for converting quantitative restriction to tariffs and "bind" their tariffs. Tariff binding refers to the fact that once the tariffs are set, they may be lowered, but they cannot be raised without first seeking an exception through the WTO.

The advantages of membership in the WTO are significant, which is why all but two (Tajikistan and Turkmenistan) transitional economies are in the WTO or have observer status. With membership comes the guarantee of MFN status and low tariff rates for exported products. (By 1995, most transitional economies had been granted MFN status by the industrial market economies. Membership in the WTO would guarantee that this will not be revoked.) Other benefits include the binding of tariffs, which reduces rent seeking by domestic producers, and access to the dispute settlement body of the WTO. In addition, it is a strong positive signal to the rest of the world that a country's trade policies are acceptable. In the long run, membership is valuable because it gives a nation a voice in the creation of future rules.

Integration with Western Europe

The natural trading partner for the CEEC and the westernmost NIS is Western Europe. Proximity, culture, and history all point in this direction, and the rapid growth of trade with the industrial nations has already begun to take place. Formal integration is moving forward on several tracks. In 1992, the EU signed free-trade agreements with each of the Visegrad Four; in 1993, agreements were concluded with Romania and Bulgaria; and in 1994, with each of the Baltic Republics. The terms varied somewhat, but each called for an asymmetrical opening in which EU barriers to CEEC goods were lifted more quickly than CEEC barriers to EU goods. These agreements, sometimes referred to as the **Europe Agreements**, opened the door to eventual EU membership for the CEEC participants.

Membership requirements for the transition economies are spelled out in a number of EU documents, and most of the CEEC have applied. Albania and the war-torn areas of the former Yugoslavia are the exceptions. The EU has laid down three basic criteria. Transitional economies must be stable democracies that protect minorities and respect human rights. They must have functioning market economies and be willing and able to implement EU policies. Following these criteria, in July 1997, the EU released a list of applicants that it expected to meet these criteria in the next few years. The list included Estonia, Poland, the Czech Republic, Hungary, and Slovenia. This group may enter as early as 2001, but 2003 is set as a more likely date for membership.

Several difficult problems stand in the way, however, some of which are in the EU and some of which are in the CEEC. For the CEEC, the greatest problems are the need to continue creating the institutions they must have in order to move forward on their market reforms. Specifically mentioned is the need to move forward in the development of banking, financial, and social security systems. Furthermore, EU legislation must be embodied in the national laws of the prospective members. In particular, there are concerns about the administrative and judicial capacity to apply and enforce the laws. On the EU's side, there are the budgetary problems of agricultural supports and internal EU development funds. EU enlargement requires a redirection of current spending, as well as changes in the formulae that determine spending, both of which are contentious. In addition, the EU is currently engaged in internal negotiations to change the number of votes each member state has in the various EU institutions. Small countries have relatively more votes than their populations warrant, and large countries would like to see this changed, but, naturally, the small countries do not want to give up some of their power.

The message from the EU is that applicants who were not selected to be in the first wave of enlargement to the East will get in eventually. Over the next two decades, it is not unreasonable to expect that the EU will take in more of the CEEC and the western states of the NIS, if they care to join. The speed of membership will most likely be determined by the consistency and progress of reforms, both economic and political, in the countries seeking membership.

In addition to the Europe Agreements with individual CEEC, the EU has signed a number of **Partnership and Cooperation Agreements (PCAs)** with individual NIS. These agreements have given the NIS access to the EU market within a GATT/WTO framework. The PCAs usually begin with the granting of MFN status to the NIS. By adhering to the GATT/WTO framework, discrimination against third-party countries is avoided, and no obstacles are placed in the way of membership in the WTO.

Other Regional Agreements

Several other regional agreements have been concluded both within the group of transitional economies and between transitional economies and "outsiders." The CEEC, for example, wanted to revive trade within the region, but it also found it necessary to strike deals among its own members in order to compensate for the preferential opening it made to the EU. In 1992, the agreement creating the Central European Free Trade Area (CEFTA) was signed. CEFTA is limited to the Visegrad Four, but the growth in trade among those countries indicates that it may be one factor in the economic recovery of Central Europe. A large number of additional agreements have been signed between pairs of CEEC. Finally, Western European nations not in the EU (Switzerland and Norway) have signed free-trade agreements with most of the individual CEEC.

Outside of the CEEC, there have been two strands of negotiations to revive trade through preferential trade agreements. One strand has focused on the revival of trade within the NIS, while the other has looked to develop new trade patterns, particularly between the Central Asian Republics and the Middle East. In 1992, Russia,

Ukraine, and several other NIS signed bilateral agreements with each of the other NIS to continue state-to-state trade. The success of these agreements depended on the ability of governments to compel enterprises to deliver the goods that governments contracted to sell, which no state could do any longer. In essence, these agreements were an attempt to hold onto central planning in the area of international trade, while the rest of the economy was changing into a market economy.

All of these agreements failed, and trade within the NIS continued to collapse. Russia, which dominates the exports and imports of every NIS except Turkmenistan, turned to another strategy to revive trade. The strategy was patterned after the EU; its main institutional form was the Treaty on Economic Union, signed in 1993 by eleven of the twelve NIS (Ukraine did not sign). There was no timetable and no implementation procedure, and there appears to be no practical effect on trade. The third strategy tried by Russia was a customs union to include Russia, Belarus, and Kazakstan, signed in 1995. This agreement appears to have had no practical effect either. The problem for each of these agreements is that they try to reestablish trade when the reforms are very incomplete. In particular, prices are still set at artificially low levels in many countries, and this necessitates controls on exports. If there were no controls, entrepreneurs could buy up subsidized goods at the artificially low prices and then sell them outside the country at world prices, draining the government's budget and contributing to macroeconomic instability. The solution is to press forward with reforms, particularly the decontrol of prices. Furthermore, trade between republics in the former Soviet Union was overintegrated. It is unclear at this point in time what the right level of integration might be. The desire to break out of the overintegrated NIS manifested itself in the second strand of negotiations outside the CEEC. Rather than reestablish trade within the NIS, it has focused on creating new trade patterns by exploiting the proximity and cultural similarities of the Central Asian Republics to Middle Eastern nations such as Iran, Pakistan, and Turkey. The most important agreement formed the Organization for Economic Cooperation (1991), including all five Central Asian Republics and Iran, Pakistan, and Turkey. It does not appear to have had a practical effect as yet, but geography and a shared Islamic heritage will most likely lead to growth in trade between these two groups.

The Impact of the Transition Economies on the World Economy

China is so large—1.2 billion people—that it is difficult to imagine a scenario in which it does not have a significant impact on the world trading system and world economy. When its rapid rate of economic growth over the last two decades is added to the mix, it seems certain that its impact is likely to be profound. Even if the rate of real GDP growth slows from its current level above 10 percent per year, as most analysts expect, the economy is still likely to become the largest in the world sometime in the middle of the twenty-first century. (If China grows twice as fast as the United States, its GDP surpasses the United States' sometime around 2040. It does not approach U.S. living standards, however, until around the year 2200—a long way into the future.)

CASE STUDY

The U.S.-China Trade Balances and Conflict Over MFN Status

China applied to join GATT in 1986. It has been negotiating the terms of its accession since 1988, but as of mid-1998 it is still not a member. Since China is not in GATT or the WTO, the United States and other countries have no formal obligations to treat it the same way they treat GATT members. In the United States, the Jackson-Vanik Amendment to the U.S. Trade Act of 1974 applies special trade rules to communist countries.

Normally, the United States grants Most Favored Nation trade status to non-WTO nations. The Jackson-Vanik Amendment forbids the granting of MFN status to communist countries unless the president asks congress for a waiver of the Amendment. The legal basis for congressional approval of a waiver is a presidential certification that the nation in question does not prevent emigration. In the 1970s, when the Amendment was passed, many communist countries prevented political dissidents from leaving. Obviously, with the collapse of communism in Central and Eastern Europe, this is no longer an issue, except in the case of China and a handful of other nations.

China has clearly demonstrated a great willingness to let people emigrate, except for a few high-profile political dissidents who are in jails. Therefore, the reason that there are not large flows of people out of China and into the United States is due to U.S. immigration policy and not Chinese prohibitions on emigration. Consequently, waiving the Jackson-Vanik Amendment and giving China MFN status in its trade relations with the United States should be more or less automatic. In practice, however, relatively few things are automatic in U.S.-China relations. When Congress votes each year on whether to waive the Jackson-Vanik Amendment and to grant MFN status to China, three sets of issues arise: trade issues, national security issues, and human rights issues. In effect, the U.S. debate over MFN has nothing to do with Chinese emigration policy, but it is a device to try to move China on each of these three issues. For example, one school of thought in the United States argues that if the United States withholds MFN trading status, then it will provide an incentive for China to improve its human rights record by acknowledging greater respect for civil liberties. The counterargument is that meddling in internal Chinese affairs is more likely to harden Chinese policies and that the authorities would interpret this as a challenge to national sovereignty that cannot be accommodated.

Security issues revolve around Chinese sales of missile technology and other strategic military hardware. Some U.S. politicians would prefer not to trade with China whatsoever since it has the world's largest army and, in their view, poses a threat to security and stability in East Asia. Again, the counterargument is that "constructive economic engagement," that is, trade and investment, is the best way to encourage a more cooperative and less aggressive China.

Case Study continues

On the trade side, China's export growth has intensified the scrutiny it gets from the U.S. Congress. Over the last decade, Chinese exports have grown about 17 percent per year, and manufactured exports have grown an even faster 22 percent per year. The United States' trade deficit in merchandise goods has expanded from $10.5 billion in 1990 to just under $50 billion in 1997. Meanwhile, China has become the eleventh largest exporter in the world, and as Hong Kong (now part of China but a separate customs district), Taiwan, and other East Asian nations move their labor-intensive production into China, the U.S. trade deficit with China is likely to grow. Some analysts have pointed out that the U.S.-China trade figures overemphasize the U.S. deficit because U.S. goods that are exported to Hong Kong and then re-exported to China are not counted as exports to China. In addition, U.S. trade figures count as imports from China those goods that are sent through Hong Kong, but they make no correction for the value that is added there. If these two corrections were made to official U.S. figures, then the deficit would be about one-third less, or about $33 billion in 1997. China would still be the second largest U.S. bilateral deficit, behind Japan's $56 billion in 1997.

Imports from China are of two types. There are labor-intensive, low-tech goods, such as textiles, apparel, sporting goods, and toys. The second types of goods are also labor intensive but require larger capital investment. These include radios, telephones, and large household appliances, all of which are standardized goods that have moved through the product cycle (see Chapter 4). Most of these goods are assembled in China from imported components, usually in factories that are partly foreign owned.

The United States and the European Union have both noted the lack of clarity in China's import rules. Virtually all areas of Chinese economic administration are cited as inconsistent, nontransparent, and subject to arbitrary decision making. For example, tariffs are levied in an unpredictable way so that some goods pay the published rate, others pay less than the published rate, and some pay a zero rate. Similarly, nontariff barriers are extremely arbitrary and nontransparent. There are, for example, complaints in both the EU and the United States of secret provisions that limit imports but are never published.

One of the most important issues for the United States is the protection of intellectual property rights in China. In the early 1990s, China signed many of the international agreements governing intellectual property rights, such as the Paris Convention on Patent Protection and the Berne Copyright Convention. In 1992, the United States and China reached an agreement after several rounds of negotiations that committed China to protect U.S. intellectual property in return for U.S. support for China's accession to the WTO. Subsequent events convinced the United States that China was not enforcing its side of the agreement. Plants inside China, some of them owned by highly placed government officials, continued to turn out pirated videos, music CDs, and software. Several more rounds of negotiations led to more specific Chinese commitments to increase their enforcement of the earlier agreements.

Case Study continues

Case Study continued

China badly wants into the WTO. Membership not only guarantees it MFN status and reduces trade barriers for its products, but it will also enable China to use the dispute settlement body of the WTO. Disputes between the United States and China over intellectual property, for example, will have an international forum for settlement, while bilateral U.S.-China negotiations will take a back seat. Perhaps most importantly, membership symbolizes international acceptance and recognition of China's economy.

Negotiations over China's accession protocol have dragged on for both political and economic reasons (for example, they were suspended for a while after the Tiananmen Square massacre in 1989). The biggest obstacles in China's economic system are the lack of transparency in its trade rules, the requirement that all imports for sale in China's domestic market must go through state-owned foreign trading companies, and subsidies to various enterprises. China has opened its trading system dramatically, and thousands of firms may now engage in international trade. Imports, however, all go through state-owned firms except enterprises that receive permission to import the capital and intermediate goods they need for their own production. Direct subsidies to firms have been cut dramatically and are now a small share of China's GDP. However, questions remain due to the lack of transparency in the financial system and the appearance of special treatment for state-owned firms.

Reform of the state-owned trading sector and the state-owned production firms (e.g., privatization or the ending of special treatment) is difficult because of their political connections. Nevertheless, the need for reform is greatest in this sector. Politically, there is a strong desire in China to become a member of the WTO, and, ultimately, this adds to the pressure for the reform of state-owned enterprises.

In the short to medium run, the economic impacts of Chinese economic growth show up in two areas. First, China now attracts more foreign investment than any other developing nation. In fact, it is safe to say that while its own savings rate compares favorably with the high rates of the other rapidly growing Asian economies, China depends more on foreign savings. Foreign investment has been particularly central to the development of export goods and the introduction of modern technology. In addition to direct investment, however, China is a major borrower from the World Bank and the IMF, which it joined in 1980, and the Asian Development Bank. The fact that China has become a large consumer of foreign capital in all forms means that other developing countries are forced to settle for smaller shares of foreign savings.

The second area of international economic impacts stems from its development into a major trading nation. For example, China's successful export drive has emphasized goods for which it has a comparative advantage. These are labor-intensive goods and are similar to the ones produced in other developing economies, particularly in other parts of East Asia. In other words, China's rising share of world markets for labor-intensive products has come at the expense of Taiwan and Hong Kong. These countries rightly recognized that they would be challenged by China and other low-wage producers and have successfully moved into more complex forms of manufacturing. In future years, it is likely that there will be greater competition between China and other East Asian producers of labor-intensive goods, for example, Thailand, the Philippines, Indonesia, and so on. Ultimately, this is one reason why it is important that China's internal market be opened further. If China promotes exports but limits imports, trade conflicts will inevitably get worse. Given its size and its capacity to both produce and consume, it is difficult to imagine that the world's nations will grant market access without a reciprocal opening in China.

The CEEC and NIS transitional economies, while smaller than China, could still have a significant impact on the world trading system. First, several of them are quite large in their own right. Poland, Romania, Russia, Ukraine, and Uzbekistan are each over 20 million people. Their markets are significantly large already, and their demand for capital and production of tradeable goods will undoubtedly grow over time. Several of the NIS are well endowed with natural resources, including minerals and petroleum. Several countries, both in the NIS and CEEC, are rich agricultural regions, and incorporation of some of the production in those states into Western Europe through inclusion in the EU (Poland, for example) will require a significant alteration in European agricultural policies to deal with the potential surplus. While trade and petroleum reserves are important, probably the most significant impacts of the end to the relative isolation of the CEEC and NIS are the possibilities for those economies to develop along peaceful lines without the cloud of potential military conflict. While peace is still an elusive goal in countries such as Bosnia, the ending of the Cold War, the reduction in East-West tensions, and the development of market economies have made it possible to address economic issues without filtering them through the lens of East-West relations and Cold War strategy.

Conclusion

No series of events in the second half of the twentieth century can claim to be more important than the collapse of communism and the end of the Cold War. The lifting of the Iron Curtain in 1989 and the dissolution of the Soviet Union in 1991 will undoubtedly appear to future historians as defining moments in the late twentieth century. Similarly, the gradual emergence of China, while less sudden, is also likely to be seen as a major force that shaped the start of the twenty-first century.

The transition from central planning to markets is one of the most difficult, uncertain, and stressful tasks imaginable for a nation to undertake, so it is not surprising that the degree of accomplishment of the transition is highly varied. Several countries are so far along in their transitions to liberal democracies and market-based economies that their reforms are essentially locked in. Others are much less further along, and the outcome is uncertain. Nevertheless, in every country, the collapse of central planning has forced even the most reluctant reformers to make significant progress toward creating market-based economies.

▲ Economic reform of the formerly socialist economies of Central and Eastern Europe (CEEC) and the Newly Independent States (NIS) of the former Soviet Union requires four sets of actions. First, nations must stabilize their economies by reducing the rate of inflation and cutting the budget deficit. Second, they must liberalize markets by freeing prices to create a market for goods and services, create labor and financial markets, and end barriers to the entry of new businesses. Third, they must clearly define property rights. Fourth, they must develop the institutions, such as legal and regulatory rules, which support markets and without which they cannot function.

▲ There is a lack of consensus about the speed of the overall transition. Go-slow proponents point to China's gradualist reforms and argue that reforms must allow people time to adjust their ways of thinking and allow institutions time to develop. Go-fast proponents argue that speed is necessary to prevent back-sliding and that once central planning ceases to work, a quick transition to markets is the only alternative. Empirical studies indicate that fast reformers had shorter and shallower recessions, but it is too early to draw definitive conclusions.

▲ Before 1989, trade in the CEEC and the NIS was regulated by the Council for Mutual Economic Assistance (CMEA), which coordinated the individual central plans of nations in the trade area. During the transition, trade between the CMEA countries broke down. The CEEC nations were largely successful in creating new trade with Western Europe and other industrial areas, but the NIS remained much more isolated.

▲ China was not part of the CMEA, and it began its reforms a decade earlier, in 1978. China adopted a dual-track strategy of trying to develop a market-based economy alongside the traditional state-controlled economy. It relied heavily on Special Economic Zones it created in five coastal areas, along with a number of other targeted development areas, to act as "windows and bridges" to the outside world. One key reason for the success of China's gradualist approach is that it has a large supply of low-productivity agricultural labor that can be redirected to new enterprises in the special zones without losing output in the countryside.

▲ The steps that every country must take to liberalize its trade are (1) end the government monopoly on trade by permitting new enterprises to enter; (2) link domestic prices to world prices; (3) adopt an explicit trade policy concerning tariffs, quantitative restrictions, and so forth; (4) develop polices toward foreign investment; and (5) unify the exchange rate while choosing an exchange rate system.

▲ Many countries experience balance of payments problems when they open their economies. Usually, they devalue the exchange rate to keep the trade deficit from soaring. However, if inflation is high or if residual barriers to imports remain, the effect of a nominal devaluation can quickly disappear with real appreciation. Hence, some countries prefer to impose import controls even though it potentially puts them at odds with the requirements for WTO membership.

▲ Nearly every transition economy has applied to join the WTO. Six CEEC are already in, and several more will soon become full members. In addition, most of the individual CEEC have signed free-trade agreements with the EU, and several are slated to join by 2003. Trade agreements in the NIS have been much less effective at restoring trade.

Vocabulary

accession protocol	Europe Agreements
Baltic Republics	Jackson-Vanik Amendment
buy-back trade	monetary overhang
central planning	newly independent states
Central and East European	of the former Soviet Union (NIS)
countries (CEEC)	Partnership and Cooperation
Council for Mutual Economic	Agreements (PCAs)
Assistance (CMEA or COMECON)	special economic zones (SEZs)
counter-trade	swap rate
counter-purchase trade	transition economies
currency convertibility	Visegrad Four

Study Questions

1. What is a centrally planned economy? What are the main ways in which it differs from a market-based economy?

2. What are the main tasks in the transition from central planning to a market-based economy?

3. Should countries go fast or slow in the transition? Describe the pros and cons of each.

4. How did the end of communism in Central and Eastern Europe, and in the Former Soviet Union, alter the trade patterns of the countries in those regions?

5. What steps must be taken by the formerly centrally planned economies in order to liberalize their trade?

6. Why does trade liberalization in the transition economies usually lead to import surges? What can countries do to avoid the balance of payments problems that these surges create?

7. How does trade reform in the transitional economies impact reforms in other parts of the economy?

8. What is currency convertibility? Why is it desirable?

9. What steps are being taken by the transitional economies to join the world trading system?

Suggested Reading

Lardy, Nicholas. *China in the World Economy*. Washington, DC: Institute for International Economics, 1994.

Naughton, Barry. "China's Emergence and Prospects as a Trading Nation," *Brookings Papers on Economic Activity,* 2, 1996.

OECD, Centre for Co-operation with the Economies in Transition, *Integrating Emerging Market Economies into the International Trading System*. Paris: OECD, 1996.

OECD, Centre for Co-operation with the Economies in Transition, *Trade Policy and the Transition Process*. Paris: OECD, 1996.

Woo, Wing Thye, Stephen Parker, and Jeffrey Sachs. *Economies in Transition: Comparing Asia and Eastern Europe*. Cambridge, MA: MIT Press, 1997.

World Bank. *From Plan to Market: World Development Report, 1996*. New York: Oxford University Press, 1996.

In addition to the above sources, there is a growing amount of information on the World Wide Web. An excellent source for an overview of conditions in individual countries is the World Bank (*http://www.worldbank.org/*). Once there, select countries and regions, and click on Eastern Europe and Central Asia on the map. Or, go directly to *http://www.worldbank.org/html/extdr/eca.htm*. The University of Pittsburgh has created a Web site called the Russian and East European Studies Internet Resources, at *http://www.pitt.edu/~cip/rees.html*. Some data are available in both of these places and in the EuroData Web site at *http://www.cerge.cuni.cz/infoknih/eurodata/eurofram.htm*.

Absolute productivity advantage. A country has an absolute productivity advantage in a good if its labor productivity is higher; that is, it is able to produce more output with an hour of labor than its trading partner can.

Adjustable peg exchange rate. An exchange rate that is fixed in value to a foreign currency, but that is periodically devalued or revalued as conditions warrant.

Antidumping duty. A tariff levied on imports in retaliation for selling below fair value. *See also* Fair value.

Appreciation. An increase in a currency's value under a floating exchange rate system. *See also* Revaluation.

Asia Pacific Economic Cooperation (APEC). A grouping of fifteen Pacific-region nations founded in 1989 with the purpose of creating free trade among all its members by 2020. APEC includes the U.S., Japan, and China, among others. APEC's goal is not a free trade area; instead, it is to get all members to commit to free trade and open investment flows as a part of their trade policies towards all nations.

Association of Southeast Asian Nations (ASEAN). Mainly a political and security grouping of seven nations in Southeast Asia. ASEAN was founded in 1967 and has recently begun a slow movement towards creating a free trade zone.

Autarky. The complete absence of foreign trade; total self sufficiency of a national economy.

Bretton Woods. A small town in New Hampshire that was, in July 1944, the site of talks establishing the international financial and economic order after World War II. The International Monetary Fund and the World Bank came out of the Bretton Woods conference.

Capital account. A record of the transactions in financial assets and liabilities between the residents of a nation and the rest of the world.

Capital controls. National controls on the inflow and/or outflow of funds.

Centrally planned economy. An economy in which the fundamental decisions of what to produce, how to produce it, and who gets it are decided by a central planning authority. The central planning bureaucracy is usually staffed with production engineers who use mathematical models to set output targets for each industry. Prices reflect political, as well as economic, decisions. Markets have little or no role in allocative decisions.

Common market. A regional trade agreement whose member nations allow the free movement of inputs as well as outputs, and who share a common external tariff towards non-members.

Comparative productivity advantage. A country has a comparative productivity advantage in a good, or simply a comparative advantage, if its opportunity costs of producing a good are lower than those of its trading partners.

Competition policy. A rule within a nation that governs economic competition. Competition policies are primarily concerned with the limits to cooperation between firms, especially mergers, acquisitions, collusion, and joint ventures.

Competitive advantage. The ability to sell a good at the lowest price. Competitive advantage may be the result of high productivity and a comparative advantage. Alternatively, it may be the result of government subsidies for inefficient industries.

Competitive devaluation. A devaluation or depreciation in a currency with the intent to gain export markets.

Consumer surplus. The difference between the value of a good to consumers and the price they have to pay. Graphically it is the area under the demand curve and above the price line. *See also* Producer surplus.

Convergence criteria. The five indicators of readiness to begin the single currency in the European Union. They are (1) stable exchange rates, (2) low inflation, (3) harmonization of long-term interest rates, (4) reduction of government deficits, and (5) reduction of government debt.

Council for Mutual Economic Assistance (CMEA). The economic assistance and trade agreement between the former Soviet Union and allied nations, primarily in Central and Eastern Europe.

Counter-trade. Counter-trade includes pure barter (goods exchanged directly for goods) and counter-purchase trade, in which the proceeds from sold exports must be spent on imports from the country receiving the exports. A third, less common, form is buy-back trade, in which the sale of exports is tied directly to the purchase of imports. For example, an exporter of manufacturing equipment agrees to buy the output of the manufacturing firm. Most trade within the CMEA was counter-trade, as was most East–West trade before the collapse of communism.

Countervailing duty. A tariff on imports that is levied in retaliation against foreign subsidies. *See also* Subsidy.

Covered interest arbitrage. Interest rate arbitrage that includes the signing of a forward currency contract to sell its earnings when its foreign assets mature. By signing such a contract the firm protects itself against unforeseen fluctuations in currency values. *See* Interest rate arbitrage.

Currency convertibility. A currency is convertible if it is freely exchangeable for another currency. It implies the right to convert at the legal exchange rate. Convertibility may be unrestricted—occuring for any type of transaction. More commonly in the transition economies, it may be "current account convertibility"—limited to transactions that fall into the current account.

Current account. A record of transactions in goods, services, investment income, and unilateral transfers between the residents of a country and the rest of the world.

Customs union. An agreement among two or more member countries to engage in free trade with each other and to share a common external tariff towards nonmembers.

Deadweight loss. A pure economic loss with no corresponding gains elsewhere in the economy. *See also* efficiency loss.

Deep integration. The elimination or alteration of domestic policies when they have the unintended consequence of acting as trade barriers. Major examples include labor and environmental standards, investment regulations, the rules of fair competition between firms, and allowable forms of government support for private industry.

Deliberation councils. Quasi-legislative bodies that combine representatives from industry with government and that have the purpose of discussing government policy and private sector investment. Japan, Korea, Malaysia, Singapore, and Thailand use deliberation councils. Their use in Hong Kong has been less well documented. Deliberation councils are instrumental in eliciting cooperation in the business elite.

Demand pull factors in migration. Economic conditions in the receiving country that "pull" in migrants. *See also* Supply push and Network factors in migration.

Democratic deficit. The EU is described as having a democratic deficit because its only popularly elected body, the European Parliament, is not a real parliament and therefore lacks the authority to serve as a legislature. In addition, the least populated countries (e.g., Luxembourg) have more representatives on a per capita basis than the most populated countries (e.g., Germany).

Demographic transition. The shift from high birth rates and high death rates (characteristic of nearly all pre-industrial societies) to low birth and death rates, characteristic of high-income, industrial societies. Generally, death rates fall before birth rates, causing a "population explosion." As incomes rise, birth rates fall as well, and the overall rate of population growth slows. Within societies that have passed through the complete transition, children are a smaller percentage of the population.

Depreciation. A decrease in a currency's value under a floating exchange rate system. *See also* Devaluation.

Devaluation. Equivalent to a depreciation, except that it refers to a decline in a currency's value under a fixed exchange rate system. *See also* Depreciation.

Dumping. Selling in a foreign market at less than fair value. *See also* Fair value.

Ecodumping. The pricing of a product below the competition's price, when the lower price is partly or wholly possible as a result of production in a country with weak environmental standards. *See also* Social dumping.

Economic nationalism. The modern form of mercantilism. Nationalists discount the benefits of trade. They share the fallacious belief that national welfare can be improved by limiting imports and curtailing foreign investment.

Economic populism. Economic policies emphasizing growth and redistribution that simultaneously de-emphasize (or deny the importance of) inflation risks, deficit finance, external constraints (i.e., trade and exchange rate issues), and the reactions of economic agents.

Economic restructuring. A movement from one point to another along a country's production possibilty curve.

Effective rates of protection. Effective rates of protection take into account levels of protection on intermediate inputs as well as the nominal tariff levied on the protected good. Effective rates are measured as the percentage change in the domestic value added after tariffs on the intermediate and final goods are levied. *See also* Nominal rates of protection.

Economic union. The most complete form of economic integration, these unions are common markets that also harmonize many standards while having the same or substantially similar fiscal and monetary policies. Economic unions may include a common currency.

Economies of scale. A decline in average cost while the number of units produced increases.

Efficiency loss. A form of deadweight loss that refers to the loss of income or output occuring when a nation produces a good at a cost higher than the world price.

Escape clause relief. Temporary tariff protection granted to an industry that experiences a sudden and harmful surge in imports.

European Union. Fifteen Western European nations that are in the process of forming an economic union. The EU began as a free trade area in 1958 with the gradual phasing in of the Treaty of Rome.

Exchange rate. The price of one currency expressed in terms of a second currency. Exchange rates may be measured in real or nominal terms.

Exchange rate risk. Risk occuring when an individual or firm holds assets that are denominated in a foreign currency. The risk is the potential for unexpected losses (or gains) due to unforeseen fluctuations in the value of the foreign currency.

Expenditure reducing policies. Policies that reduce the overall level of domestic expenditure. These are appropriate for addressing the problem of a trade deficit, and they include cuts in government expenditures and/or increases in taxes.

Expenditure switching policies. Policies designed to shift the expenditures of domestic residents. If the problem is a trade deficit, they should shift towards domestically produced goods; if the problem is a trade surplus, they should shift towards foreign goods. Examples of these policies are changes in the exchange rate and changes in tariffs and quotas.

Export pessimism. The views of Argentine economist Raul Prebisch and his followers, who believed that the real prices received by Latin American countries for their exports would fall over time. They adopted this view based on their studies that showed a long-run tendency for the terms of trade to fall for countries that relied on raw materials exports. In the 1960s, Prebisch partially reversed himself and began to favor a stronger effort at exporting.

Export processing zone (EPZ). A geographical region in which firms are free from tariffs so long as the export the goods that are made from imports. Rules and regulations governing EPZs vary by country but all are aimed at encouraging exports, often through encouragement given to investment.

Externality. A divergence between social and private returns.

Fair value. A standard for determining whether dumping is occurring or not. Generally, in the U.S., fair value is the average price in the exporters home market or the average price in third country markets. Definitions vary by country, making fair value a source of disagreement.

Foreign direct investment (FDI). The purchase of physical assets such as real estate or businesses by a foreign company or individual. It can be outward (citizens or businesses in the home country purchase assets in a foreign country) or inward (foreigners purchase assets in the home country). *See also* Foreign portfolio investment.

Foreign portfolio investment. The purchase of financial assets such as stocks, bonds, bank accounts, or related financial instruments. As with FDI, it can be inward or outward.

Forward markets. Markets in which buyers and sellers agree on a quantity and a price for a foreign exchange transaction that takes place in (usually) 30, 90, or 180 days from the time the contract is signed. *See also* Spot markets.

Four Tigers. Hong Kong, Korea, Singapore, and Taiwan. Their economic growth began shortly after Japan's post-World War II development. They are all classified by the World Bank as either high-income or upper-middle-income econ-omies. (The Four Tigers are sometimes called the Four Dragons or the Little Dragons.) *See also* High performance Asian economies and Newly industrializing economies.

Free riding. Occurs when a person lets others pay for a good or service, or lets them do the work when they know they cannot be excluded from consumption of the good or from the benefits of the work.

Free trade area. A preferential trade agreement in which countries permit the free movement of outputs (goods and services) across their borders as long as they originate in one of the member countries.

General Agreement on Tariffs and Trade (GATT). The main international agreement covering the rules of trade in most, but not all, goods. The GATT's origins can be traced back to the original negotiations that took place in 1946, after World War II.

General Agreement on Trade in Services (GATS). An attempt to extend the rules and principles of the GATT to trade in services. GATS was one of the outcomes of the Uruguay Round.

Gains from trade. The increase in consumption made possible by specialization and trade.

Gross domestic product (GDP). The market value of all final goods and services produced in a year inside a nation.

Gross national product (GNP). The market value of all final goods and services produced by the residents of a nation, regardless of where the production takes place. GNP equals GDP minus income paid to foreigners plus income received from abroad.

Harmonization of standards. Occuring when two or more countries negotiate a common standard or policy. Harmonization can occur with respect to safety standards, technical standards, environmental standards, legal standards, certification, or with respect to any requirement set forth by national policies. *See also* Mutual recognition of standards.

Heterodox stabilization policies. A heterodox stabilization policy is designed to cure inflation by (1) cutting government spending, (2) limiting the creation of new money, (3) reforming the tax system, and (4) freezing wages and prices. *See also* Orthodox stabilization policies.

High performance Asian economies (HPAE). The eight high-performance Asian economies of Hong Kong, Japan, Indonesia, Korea, Malaysia, Singapore, Taiwan, and Thailand. *See also* Four Tigers and Newly industrializing economies.

IMF conditionality. The changes in economic policy that borrowing nations are required to make in order to receive International Monetary Fund loans. The changes usually involve policies that will reduce or eliminate a severe trade deficit and/or a central government budget deficit. In practical terms, they involve reduced expenditures by the government and by the private sector (to reduce imports) and increased taxes. *See also* IMF.

Import substitution industrialization (ISI). An economic development strategy that emphasizes the domestic production of goods that substitute for imports. ISI policies decrease both imports and exports.

Industrial policy. A policy designed to create new industries or to provide support for existing ones.

Infant industry argument. An argument for tariff protection based on the belief that a particular industry is incapable of competing at present but that it will soon grow into a mature and competitive industry that no longer needs protection.

Institution. A set of rules of behavior. The institution sets limits, or constraints, on social, political, and economic interaction; and in so doing, it plays a determining role. An institution may be informal (e.g., a manner, taboo, custom) or formal (e.g., a constitution or law).

Interest rate arbitrage. Interest rate arbitrage is the transfer of funds from one financial asset and currency to another to take advantage of higher interest rates. *See also* Covered interest arbitrage.

International investment position. The value of all foreign assets owned by a nation's residents, businesses, and government, minus the value of all domestic assets owned by foreigners.

International Monetary Fund (IMF). One of the original Bretton Woods institutions, IMF responsibilities include helping member countries that suffer from instability or problems in their balance of payments. It also provides technical expertise in international financial relations.

J-curve. A currency depreciation often results in a worsening of the trade deficit in the short run and an improvement in the long run. The J-curve is the hypothetical shape of the path traced out by the trade deficit after a depreciation and over a period of one to two years.

Keiretsu. Keiretsu are groups of Japanese firms tied together into family-like relationships through cross-ownership, business relations, and interlocking directorates. Keiretsu members usually seek another member to do business with before going outside the group.

Labor productivity. The amount of output per unit of labor input.

Lender of last resort. In international economics, a place where nations can borrow after all sources of commercial lending have dried up. Today, the IMF (International Monetary Fund) fills this role.

Lost Decade. The period of recession brought on by the region-wide debt crisis beginning in August 1982. Growth rates for most countries in Latin America were low or negative from 1983 until the end of the decade. There is no official date ending the Lost Decade, but 1989 is a useful benchmark, since it coincides with a new strategy for handling the crisis.

Maastricht Treaty. Also sometimes called the Treaty on Economic and Monetary Union. Ratified in 1991 by the members of the European Union, its most visible provision includes the single currency program that will begin in 1999. It has several other important provisions, however, and will create an economic union among the members of the European Union.

Managed trade. An attempt to reduce trade friction by either (1) specifying a set of rules of fair practices in sectors where there has been conflict or (2) specifying an outcome, such as the percent of a country's market that should be held by foreigners. The first type is generally more consistent with the goal of using markets to allocate inputs and outputs. Managed trade can be bilateral or multilateral.

Maquiladora. Mexican manufacturing firms, mostly along the U.S.–Mexico border that are not required to pay tariffs on inputs so long as they export the goods they produce. Under the terms of North American Free Trade Agreement (NAFTA), the tariff preference is scheduled to be phased out by 2001.

Market failure. A situation in which markets do not produce the most beneficial outcome economically. Market failure has numerous causes, including externalities and monopolistic or oligopolistic market structures.

Mercantilism. The economic system that arose in Western Europe in the 1500s, during the period in which modern nation states were emerging from feudal monarchies. Mercantilism has been called the politics and economics of nation building because it stressed the need for nations to run trade surpluses to obtain revenues for armies and national construction projects. Mercantilists favored granting monopoly rights to individuals and companies, they shunned competition, and they viewed exports as positive and imports as negative. Today, the term mercantilism is sometimes used to describe the policies of nations that promote their exports while keeping their markets relatively closed to imports.

Mercosúr. The Mercado Común del Sur, or Common Market of the South, is the largest regional trade grouping in South America. It includes four countries: Brazil, Argentina, Uruguay, and Paraguay.

Monetary overhang. The large stock of unspent domestic money that was present in most transitional economies. (China is a major exception to this generalization.) Monetary overhang existed because consumers could not find the goods and services they wanted to buy, because consumer goods prices were kept below equilibrium levels, and because too much money was created.

Most favored nation (MFN). The idea that every member of WTO (World Trade Organization) is required to treat each of its trading partners as well as it treats its most favored trading partner. In effect, MFN prohibits one country from discriminating against another. The main exception to MFN is that it permits trade agreements such as NAFTA (North American Free Trade Agreement) and does not require a country to extend the same treatment to countries outside the agreement.

Multilateralism. An approach to trade and investment issues which involves large numbers of countries. Multilateralism stands for the belief that market openings should benefit all nations. Multilateral institutions include the World Trade Organization, the World Bank, and the International Monetary Fund.

Mutual recognition. An alternative to the harmonization of standards. Under a mutual recognition system, countries keep different standards while agreeing to recognize and accept each other's standards within their national jurisdictions. Under these circumstances, competition between standards will ensue. Individuals and businesses will prefer to adopt the standard that most closely meets their needs or that gives them an economic advantage. It is argued by some that over time the best standard will emerge as the one in greatest use.

National treatment. The idea that foreign firms operating inside a nation should not be treated any differently than domestic firms.

Neoliberalism. Market oriented reforms that became common throughout Latin America in the late 1980s and 1990s. *See also* Washington consensus.

Network factors in migration. The networks or webs of family, community, and social relationships that migrants use to support themselves when they arrive in a new country. *See also* Demand pull and Supply push factors in migration.

Newly industrializing economies (NIE). The most recent wave of rapidly growing and industrializing developing nations. There are a number of these economies in Latin America (e.g., Argentina, Brazil, Chile, and Mexico) as well as in East Asia (among the HPAE, Indonesia, Malaysia, and Thailand fall into this category). For the most part, their period of high growth began after the takeoff of the Four Tigers.

Nominal exchange rate. The price of a unit of foreign exchange. *See also* Real exchange rate.

Nominal rates of protection. Nominal rates are measured as the amount of a tariff (or the tariff equivalent of a quota) expressed as a percentage of the good's price. *See also* Effective rates of protection.

Nontariff barriers (NTBs). Any trade barrier that is not a tariff. Most important are quotas, which are physical limits on the quantity of permitted imports. Nontariff barriers include red tape and regulations, rules requiring governments to purchase from domestic producers, and a large number of other practices that indirectly limit imports.

North American Free Trade Agreement (NAFTA). The free trade area formed by Canada, Mexico, and the United States. NAFTA began in 1994.

Official reserve assets. Assets held by governments for use in settling international debts. Primarily official resource assets consist of key foreign currencies, such as the dollar, the yen, the mark, the Swiss and French francs, and the British pound. In addition, they include gold and SDRs (special drawing rights), which are the unit of account used by the IMF (International Monetary Fund).

Opportunity cost. The value of the best forgone alternative to the activity actually chosen. For example, if the United States chooses to produce another loaf of bread, the best forgone alternative is steel production; and the amount or value of steel given up in order to produce another loaf of bread is 1.5 tons.

Optimal currency area. A region of fixed exchange rates or a single currency. A currency area is optimal in the sense that it is precisely the right geographical size to capture the benefits of fixed rates without incurring the costs.

Orthodox stabilization policies. A orthodox stabilization policy is designed to cure inflation by (1) cutting government spending, (2) limiting the creation of new money, and (3) reforming the tax system. *See also* Heterodox stabilization policies.

Pauper labor argument. The argument for trade protection based on the false belief that high-wage countries will be "pauperized" by imports from low-wage countries.

Private returns. The value of all private benefits minus all private costs, properly adjusted to take into account that some costs and benefits are in the future and must be discounted to arrive at their value in today's dollars. *See also* Social returns.

Producer surplus. The difference between the minimum price a producer would accept to produce a given quantity and the price they actually receive. Graphically it is the area under the price line and above the supply curve. *See also* Consumer surplus.

Production possibilities curve (PPC). This curve shows the maximum amount of output possible, given the available supply of inputs. It also shows the tradeoff that a country must make if it wishes to increase the output of one of its goods. In other words, the PPC shows how much of one good must be given up in order to increase output of the alternative good.

Public goods. Goods that share two characteristics: nonexcludability and nonrivalry or nondiminishability. If they are excludable but nondiminishable goods, they are sometimes called collective goods.

Quota. A numerical limit on the volume of imports.

Quota rents. The excess profits earned by foreign producers (and sometimes domestic distributors of foreign products) in an export market. Quota rents occur whenever a quota causes a price increase in the market receiving the exports.

Real exchange rate. The inflation-adjusted nominal rate. The real rate is useful for examining changes in the relative purchasing power of foreign currencies over time.

Regional trade alliance (RTA). Agreements between two or more countries, each offering the others preferential access to their markets. RTAs provide varying degrees of access and variable amounts of deep integration. Examples include the European Union (EU), which is a highly integrated bloc, and the North American Free Trade Agreement (NAFTA) where the countries are not deeply integrated. RTAs are synonymous with trade blocs.

Relative price. The price of one good in terms of another good. It is similar to a money price, which expresses the price in terms of dollars and cents; but relative price is in terms of the quantity of the first good that must be given up in order to buy a second good.

Rent seeking. Any activity by firms, individuals, or special interests that is designed to alter the distribution of income to their favor. Political lobbying, legal challenges, and bribery are common forms of rent-seeking behaviors, which use resources (labor and capital) but do not add to national output. For this reason, rent seeking is a net loss to the nation. Rent seekers are successful only to the extent that they are able to take income from some other group, usually consumers or the losers in a legal battle. The more a society rewards rent seeking, the greater the quantity of resources that will be devoted to it, and the less efficient the nation's economic system will become.

Revaluation. An increase in the value of a currency under a fixed exchange rate system. *See also* Appreciation.

Section 301. A clause in U.S. trade legislation that requires the United States Trade Representative to take action against any nation that persistently engages in what the U.S. considers unfair trade practices. *See also* Super 301.

Shallow integration. The elimination or reduction of tariffs, quotas, and other border-related barriers (such as customs procedures) that restrict the flow of goods across borders. *See also* Deep integration.

Single European Act (SEA). The act that created a common market among the members of the European Community. The SEA was implemented in 1993.

Social dumping. Pricing a product below the competition's price when the lower price is partly or wholly possible as a result of production in a country with weak labor standards. *See also* Ecodumping.

Social returns. Social returns include private returns, but they add costs and benefits to the elements of society that are not taken into consideration in the private returns. For example, a firm that generates pollution that it does not have to clean up imposes costs on society, which causes social returns to be lower than private returns. Similarly, a firm that creates labor-force skills that can be transferred to other activities creates benefits that raise social returns relative to private ones.

Special drawing right (SDR). The unit of account and artificial currency used by the International Monetary Fund (IMF). The SDR is a weighted average of several currencies and serves an a official reserve asset.

Special economic zone (SEZ). A special region in China, in which local officials are encouraged to experiment with new economic policies. SEZs are designed to encourage foreign investment and exports.

Spot markets. Market transactions that are concluded at the same time the price is agreed upon, although there is usually a day's lag before the currency is actually delivered. *See also* Forward markets.

Stabilization polices. National macroeconomic policies designed to cure inflation and reduce a government deficit. Stabilization policies are usually a first step in compliance with IMF conditionality during a macroeconomic crisis. *See also* Structural adjustment policies, Orthodox stabilization, and Heterodox stabilization.

Strategic trade policy. The use of trade barriers, subsidies, or other industrial support policies designed to capture the profits of foreign firms for domestic firms.

Structural adjustment policies. Policies that are designed to increase the role of market forces in a national economy. Structural adjustment policies are mainly microeconomic in nature and include privatization, deregulation, and trade reform. *See also* Stabilization policies.

Subsidiarity. The principle that the authority of the European Union (EU) to involve itself in individual national affairs is limited to those issues that are transnational in scope. In current practice, this includes environmental policies, regional policies, research and technology development, and economic and monetary union.

Subsidy. Government assistance for industry. The Uruguay Round of the GATT defined subsidies as direct loans or transfers, preferential tax treatments, a direct supply of goods, or income and price supports.

Super 301. A 1988 addition to U.S. trade law requiring the United States Trade Representative (USTR) to publicly name countries that, in the opinion of the U.S., systematically engage in unfair trade practices. Super 301 requires the USTR to open negotiations with the targeted country and to recommend retaliation if the negotiations are unsuccessful. *See also* Section 301.

Supply push factors in migration. The factors that "push" migrants out of their home country. *See also* Demand pull and Network factors in migration.

Swap rate. The rate of exchange used when the monetary authorities of two countries exchange the assets they have acquired against each other. In centrally planned economies, the swap rate is different from the official exchange rate.

Target zone exchange rate. An exchange rate system in which currencies are allowed to float against another currency or group of currencies, so long as it stays within a predefined band. Once the currency begins to move out of the band, the nation must intervene to pull it back.

Tariffs. Taxes imposed on imports. Tarrifs raise the price to the domestic consumer and reduce the quantity demanded.

Terms of trade (TOT). The average price of a country's exports divided by the average price of imports: TOT = (index of export prices)/(index of import prices). A decline in the terms of trade means that each unit of exports buys a smaller amount of imports—equivalent to a fall in living standards, since exports earn fewer imports. The fall in living standards is proportional to the importance of trade in a nation's economy.

Total factor productivity (TFP). A measurement of the quantity of output per unit of input. Increases in TFP mean that overall productivity has improved and that a given level of inputs will create more output; hence, technology or enterprise organization must have improved.

Trade adjustment assistance. Government programs that offer temporary assistance to workers who lose jobs because of foreign trade or their firms moving abroad.

Trade creation. The opposite of trade diversion, trade creation occurs when trade policies cause a shift in production from a higher cost producer (often a domestic one) to a lower cost producer.

Trade diversion. The opposite of trade creation, trade diversion occurs when trade policies cause a shift in production and imports from a lower cost producer to a higher cost producer.

Transaction costs. The costs of gathering market information, arranging a market agreement, and enforcing the agreement. Transaction costs include legal, marketing, and insurance costs, as well as quality checks, advertising, distribution, and after-sales service costs.

Transition economies. Countries that are in the process of moving from bureaucratically controlled economies to market-based economies. Transition economies include most of those that adopted socialist or communist ideologies during the twentieth century. Among these countries, there is a wide range in the degree of reform and movement toward market-based economies.

Transparency. Any trade barrier that is clearly defined as a barrier. Tariffs have the most transparency—are the most transparent—because they are usually clearly specified and published in each country's tariff code. Any disguised or hidden trade barriers cause a country's trade policy to be nontransparent. An example of a nontransparent trade policy is a government regulation that requires foreign imports to meet a poorly defined safety requirement, or that requires testing imports in special laboratories that have a limited capacity and that charge extremely high prices for testing. The net result is the same as a tariff—a reduction in imports—but producers of the foreign imports are never quite certain what the added costs will be or how many units they will ultimately be able to get into a country.

Treaty of Rome. The funding document of the European Economic Community (EEC), the Treaty of Rome was signed by six nations in 1957 and went into force in 1958. The EEC has since become the European Union (EU) and includes fifteen members, but the Treaty of Rome remains its core legal document.

Uruguay Round. The latest round of tariff negotiations within the GATT framework, the Uruguay Round began in 1986 in Punta del Este, Uruguay, concluded in 1993, and was ratified in 1994. Among other things, it created the World Trade Organization.

Value added. The price of a good minus the value of intermediate inputs used to produce it. Value added measures the contribution of capital and labor at a given stage of production.

Voluntary export restraint (VER). An agreement between nations in which the exporting nation voluntarily agrees to limit its exports in order to reduce competition in the importing country. In practice, there is often an element of coercion through threat of tougher protective measures if the exporting nation does not comply. VERs have been forbidden by the Uruguay Round.

Washington Consensus. A set of policies prescribed for developing countries by the U.S. government, the International Monetary Fund and World Bank, and the unofficial community of think-tanks centered in Washington D.C. In Latin America, these policies are more or less synonymous with neoliberalism. In general, they favor the use of market forces over government direction as allocative mechanism.

World Bank. A Bretton Woods institution, originally charged with the responsibility for providing financial and technical assistance to the war-torn economies of Europe. In the 1950s, the World Bank began to shift its focus to developing countries.

World Trade Organization. An umbrella organization created by the Uruguay Round of the GATT talks, the WTO houses the GATT and many other agreements. The WTO is the main international body through which multilateral trade talks take place.

Zero sum. The costs and benefits of an activity cancel each other (equal zero). The outcomes of competitive games are usually zero sum because in football, baseball, and other sports one side wins and the other loses. Aerobics and dance are physical activities that are positive sum—all participants win. In the economic realm, voluntary exchange (domestic and foreign trade) are positive sum. It is true that individual businesses may engage in fierce competition; but, from the perspective of national economies, trade is more like dance than football.

Pages in boldface indicate the location of a definition.